The Bodley Head
Bernard Shaw

SHAW'S MUSIC

VOLUME II

The Bodley Head
Bernard Shaw

SHAW'S MUSIC

*The complete musical criticism
in three volumes*

Second Revised Edition

Edited by

Dan H. Laurence

VOLUME II
1890–1893

THE BODLEY HEAD

LONDON

A CIP catalogue record of this book is
available from the British Library.

ISBN: 0-370-30249-4
       0-370-30333-4 Set of 3 vols
       0-370-31271-6 Pbk

Printed and bound in Great Britain for
The Bodley Head Ltd,
31 Bedford Square, London WC1B 3SG
by Mackays of Chatham PLC
Set in Clowes Plantin Light by CCC.
This edition first published 1981
Second revised edition 1989

Shaw's Music

is published in three volumes
Volume I: 1876–1890
Volume II: 1890–1893
Volume III: 1893–1950 with appendix and
biographical and general indexes
to the entire edition

STUFFING A SONATA

The Star, 21 March 1890

The Star printers are getting so musical that I can no longer depend on having my plain and studiously untechnical language set up faithfully. The other day I wrote about "a couple of moments" during a performance; and it came out "a couple of movements." What I wanted to say about the Popular Concert was, that it introduced to us a pianoforte quintet by Giovanni Sgambati, a Roman composer who is pretty well known here. My objection to him is that though he is at Rome he does not do as the Romans do, but writes academic music in sonata form, as the Germans and the English, in spite of my remonstrances, persist in doing.

The fact is, that musicians fail to see the real difficulties of the sonata form through allowing their teachers to engross their attention with a horrible conceit of its technical difficulties, which any fool can master. There is no more to prevent you or me from turning out a string of bars in the form of a sonata than to prevent us from turning out a string of lines in the form of a sonnet or a tragedy in five acts and in blank verse. It is not the form that baulks us of a Shakespearean immortality, but the inordinate quantity of first-class stuffing that is required to make these forms, long, severe, and tedious as they are in themselves, interesting, or even endurable, to any but the performers or the author. You really must have something very important to say to a man, if you expect him to allow you to buttonhole him and claim his undivided attention for even twenty minutes at a stretch, much more (as in the case of a tragedy) for a whole evening.

Sgambati had matter enough in hand to amuse an audience for eight or nine minutes. But in trying to make a whole quintet with it, he had so to wire-draw it and to pad it with desperate commonplaces, culminating in that last resource of musical bankruptcy, a *fugato,* that he failed to amuse us at all. Madame Backer-Gröndahl managed to scatter a handful of pearls here and there over the dull fabric; but the general feeling (I always speak of my own private sensations as the general feeling) was that of Christopher Sly at The Taming of the Shrew: "Would 'twere done!"* The Schubert quintet (C major) went beautifully, Joachim being in excellent form.

And here a question occurs to me. Joachim is famous for the austerity of his repertoire. He will play nothing meretricious: he stands inflexibly by the classics; and will none of your Sarasate dance tunes and national airs. A pupil of his once flatly refused to believe me when I mentioned that I had heard him play in public an air by Félicien David. But I cannot, for the life of me, see that Joachim has any valid standard of criticism. It seems to me that if he is prepared to tolerate second-hand Mozart, faked by Spohr, and mechanical padding by Sgambati, he is hardly in a position to turn up his nose at the free and original compositions of Sarasate and Wieniawski. Joachim cannot be sufficiently applauded for teaching his pupils to refuse to play unworthy music. He might with equal righteousness urge them not to keep the company of unworthy persons. But as, in the latter instance, the adoption of a tall hat and an income of not less than £1000 a year as the criterion of worth would at once reduce the wise counselor to the level of a most malignant snob, I suggest that the acceptance of conformity to any special form as the criterion of worth

* Act I, Scene I.

in a musical composition is the snobbery of art. Imagine the state of soul of a neophyte who should interpret Joachim's precept and example as meaning that any fiddler who considered folk music beneath his notice would be entitled to consider himself as superior in artistic rank to Ole Bull or Sarasate!

I have nothing more to say about the concert except to chronicle the three recalls, culminating in an *encore,* which formally stamped Madame Backer-Gröndahl as an indispensable addition to Mr Chappell's list of artists without whom no Monday Popular spring season is complete. I should like to remonstrate with Miss Liza Lehmann for singing some unsuitable triviality about Robin: come and kiss me, in response to an invitation to repeat a song of Stopford Brooke's, set by Mr Somervell; but I had perhaps better let my indignation cool first.

The other day I met Mr William Archer, fresh from a study of the theatre at Copenhagen. I am specially interested in the publication of his observations, because my sanity was seriously called in question a year ago when I suggested that Mr Harris should offer Coquelin an engagement to play Leporello in Don Giovanni. However, I am but mad nor'-nor'-west: when the wind is in the south I do not know a hawk from a hernshaw, for I am no ornithologist; but I know what I am talking about. In Denmark the most famous actors belong to the operatic as well as the dramatic staff of their theatre; and the same man will play Shylock in Shakespear's Merchant of Venice and Mephistopheles in Gounod's Faust.

BASSETTO GOES TO CHURCH

The Star, 28 March 1890

On reaching St James's Hall on Saturday afternoon, I found that the room was full. This seemed a very extraordinary success for Mr Arthur de Greef, whom I had come specially to hear. But I presently noticed that the program included Bach's concerto in D minor for two violins. "There!" I said, as I turned away from the ticket office and made for Prince's Hall: "that is the true attraction." Now a foreigner might suppose from this that we are so far advanced in music in this city that Bach is our first favorite. Would it were so! The truth is that Bach had nothing to do with the crowd. When Boswell disparaged Vauxhall, and said it was not worth half a guinea, Johnson pointed out that the real consideration for the money was relief from the stigma of not having been to Vauxhall. In London no person can pretend to musical culture unless he or she has heard Joachim and Norman-Neruda. As they do not usually play at the same concert, this costs, as a rule, two shillings. But when they play together in Bach's concerto, then you can kill two birds with one stone, getting your diploma as one who has heard both Joachim and Neruda, at half-price. When Lady Hallé played the same work with Mr Willy Hess, and when Joachim played it with Mr Gompertz, I got a seat easily enough.

At Prince's Hall I found Miss Frederika Taylor and Miss Teresa Aungier giving a concert. Señor Guetary, of whose singing particular mention has been made here and there of late, gave us *Com' è gentil!* He reminded me of Gayarré. This unfortunately means that his singing is not to my taste. The actor who moved Hamlet so deeply had "a broken voice, and his whole function suiting with forms to his conceit." I confess I bar the broken voice in a lyric artist, even when he sings dramatic music. Not, of course, that Gayarré's voice was actually broken, any more than Señor Guetary's is. But it was harsh, acute, piercing, disquieting: its finish and polish were like those of a circular saw. This did not prevent so great a critic as Wagner from placing Gayarré in the front rank of Lohengrins; and Señor Guetary may, for all that his voice does not happen to please me, achieve a reputation as great as De Reszke's; but it will not be a reputation for beauty of tone or for realizing the summer night charm of the irresistible Don Pasquale serenade. Were I Saul, and De Reszke David, his singing would do me good. But if Gayarré or Guetary were David I should get mad and shy javelins.

On trying the Popular Concerts again on Saturday, I found Mr de Greef still there, but the crowd gone. Yet I will swear that Joachim was better worth hearing in the Beethoven quartet (Rasoumowski in E minor) than in the Bach concerto. It was as fine a piece of playing as any mortal has a right to expect. It is all very well for me to protest against Joachim's abortive struggles with Bach fugues, and to point out that his intonation is no longer to be depended on in prolonged quick movements; but every quartet I have heard him lead this season has renewed and increased my admiration for him. Mr de Greef is a true Belgian, spirited, brilliant, neat, confident, clever, and intensely happy in the consciousness of being all that. His execution is extremely ambidexterous; and he has a prodigious musical gift, besides having a fair share of sense and taste. Señor Albéniz will find in him a formidable rival; but I do not think that Stavenhagen or Madame Gröndahl need fear the strength of his youth. I base upon his reading of the Chopin scherzo the opinion that he is not a very deep player. However, this must not be taken as final: if he gives a recital, I shall be open to further light on the subject.

It is one of the inevitable evils of my profession that I am asked to go to all manner of places; but hitherto I have drawn the line at going to church. Among the pious I am a scoffer: among the musical I am religious. What has a man who knows Die Zauberflöte, the Schiller Ode to Joy as set in the Ninth Symphony, and Parsifal to do with your collects and rubrics and Jackson in F and all the rest of it? I do not believe that many of the people who compound for their essential irreligiousness by putting in a couple of penitential hours in church once or twice every Sunday have any better motive than escaping damnation, in which case they are plainly damned up to the neck already, though they do not know it. However, since I know it, I am bound to look on the poor devils in a friendly and forbearing spirit, as becomes a happier and more fortunate soul. Anyhow I went to church on Tuesday last, to St Nicholas Cole-Abbey.

I had some difficulty in finding St Nicholas. He has an old Tower in Thames-street, among the warehouses; but a glance at it convinced me that if there was an organ inside, there would be no room for me. Besides, there was no sign of its having been opened since the great fire of London; so I made for a red brick mansion which I took to be the Saint's private house, and was there directed by a young lady to go back to Queen Victoria-street and look about me, which I had no sooner done than I perceived St Nicholas staring me in the face on the other side of that spacious thoroughfare. Inside I found some sixty people listening to Mr John Runciman,* who was compelling a loud-mouthed

* John F. Runciman abandoned the church organ in 1894 for a new career as musical critic for the Saturday Review and

intractable organ to discourse to the following effect: 1. *Andante con moto* from Beethoven's C minor symphony. 2. The Parsifal prelude. 3. Bach's organ fugue in A minor. 4. The Death March from the Götterdämmerung. 5. Mr Marshall-Hall's Witenagemot music. 6. The prelude to the third act of Lohengrin.

This is exactly the right sort of program for an organ recital in a church. An organist who plays Guilmant and Lemmens, finishing up with a transcription of the Hallelujah chorus, and perhaps throwing in the fugue which he wrote for his Doctor's degree, would be much better employed outside with a mechanical piano, to which the girls could at least dance. But he who sticks to Wagner and Bach, and can play them, as Mr Runciman did, in an imaginative way, will eventually get the choicest spirits in the parish into the way of coming to the church and learning something there. In some churches it might even end in the organist educating the parson; though that is not necessary at Cole-Abbey, where, I blush to say it, the parson (Canon Shuttleworth, a muscular Christian Socialist) sometimes finds it hard enough to educate the organists.

It is a curious sort of church, architecturally, this of St Nicholas. I cannot help suspecting that it was designed in the days of St Nicholas Without and St Walker Within, alluded to by Anthony Weller.* The altar reminds me feebly of that church of St Carlo Borromeo at Antwerp, from which, after one glance, I fled with yells of agony and disgust. The platitudinous ceiling suggests Cannon-street Hotel. The rack in which the Rev. George Allen hoists the program number of

---

as correspondent for Boston and New York musical papers. He also wrote biographical studies of Wagner and Purcell.

* Character in Dickens's Pickwick Papers, father of Sam Weller.

each piece has a touch—quite welcome and congruous in view of the labors of the Church and Stage Guild—of the music hall. The stained glass is not so bad as I naturally expected it to be—always excepting the rose window, with its plausible, empty, conventional representation of the figure that ought to be more real and deeply felt than any other in the place. But the mother and child over the south door, by Mr Heaton, is all sunshine; and the two large windows behind the altar, though they are hopelessly off the lines of the great glass painters, are dignified, rich in local color and in design, and contain a couple of expressively drawn figures.

The organ recitals, let me add, take place every Tuesday at one o'clock.

POOR OLD PHILHARMONIC
The Star, 5 April 1890

The Philharmonic Society is, I fear, hardly to be held responsible for its actions. It is very old; and it never even in its best days had much sense. Some years ago it brought itself to the verge of extinction by its conservatism. Since then it has been desperately spurting to get abreast of the times—trying new composers, new conductors, new virtuosos, new everything. Now if the Philharmonic had any musical intelligence it would stick to its old line by bringing forward only what is new in that line. It should concern itself mainly with abstract music and the very highest class of dramatic music: that class of dramatic music which may be called secularly religious music. But whatever else it may see fit to do— and Providence only knows what it will be up to next— it had better avoid such senseless vagaries as its last effort at a concert program.

[14]

First, by way of shewing that it has learnt nothing and forgotten nothing, it put down the Naïads overture, a genteel musical mongrel which would be a musical description of the Rhine if it were not meant to be a formal concert overture, and which would be a formal concert overture if it were not meant to be a musical description of the Rhine, the net result being, of course, that it is neither the one nor the other. At this time of day, wasting the Philharmonic orchestral forces on it is about as sensible as engaging Rubinstein to play pieces by Stephen Heller would be. Mr Joseph Bennett helps out the society by bravely eulogizing the work in his analytical program as "enjoying universal recognition as among the most beautiful of its kind" (observe that the mischief is just that it is of no kind at all), and by peppering in such adjectives as "divine" and the like; but who is taken in thereby? We all know that Mr Bennett loves Mendelssohn with a love that overflows upon Mendelssohn's most slavish imitator; and how firmly persuaded he is that Wagner wrote music only to revenge himself by its ugliness on the Parisians for not producing Rienzi at the Grand Opéra in 1840; but the value of these opinions is a purely historical one, like that of the fossils in the Jermyn-street museum. When I want to impress a young man with the vastness of my musical experience, I hand him the criticisms of Mr Bennett on Wagner and Mendelssohn, and say "Young man: I can remember the days when everybody talked like that." To which the neophyte always reverently responds "Indeed, sir?" meaning "Poor old buffer!"

Therefore I would counsel the Philharmonic to drop Sterndale Bennett until they begin to find their audiences falling off for lack of his attraction, when they can easily recover the lost ground by devoting an entire concert to his works, with a few antiques by Smart or Bishop, a novelty by Sir Arthur Sullivan, and a song from Costa's Eli, thrown in for the sake of variety. Such a concert would be crowded with old associations; but otherwise there would be plenty of room at it.

The selection of Haydn's symphony in B flat (The Queen of France) was dictated by all that is good in the conservatism of the Philharmonic. Haydn would have been among the greatest had he been driven to that terrible eminence; but we are fortunate in having had at least one man of genius who was happy enough in the Valley of Humiliation to feel no compulsion to struggle on through the Valley of the Shadow of Death to attain only a moment's glimpse of the Celestial City from the summit of the Delectable Mountains. However, that is not the question just now. We are justified in expecting a very fine performance of a Haydn symphony from an orchestra like that of the Philharmonic Society. That it should be perfectly smooth and neat is nothing: technically a Haydn score is child's play to men accustomed to tackle Berlioz and Wagner. Yet there was nothing more than that in the performance last week. The charming, tender Romance in E flat went as mechanically as upon a musical box; and, what was worse, there was a touch of that traditional haste to get the slow movement over before there was time to go asleep which is quite the most ignoble of all the Philharmonic traditions. I do not allude to the omission of the repeats; though why they should be omitted in the Romance, where they are not unwelcome, and observed piously in the *allegro,* where they are tedious and obsolete, passes my understanding.

When Haydn and Sterndale Bennett were solemnly disposed of, a wild rush to the opposite extreme followed. What has the Philharmonic Society to do with Peter Benoît, of all composers? His Lucifer conclusively shewed that he was an excitable and imaginative musician, without the slightest originality as a composer

[16]

or depth as a poet. The essential poverty of his scores was only emphasized by their bigness, their ferocity, their grandiosity, their mechanical extravagance. Anyone with two pennorth of critical faculty and experience could have seen that the sort of overture and *entr'actes* he would be likely to compose for a drama on the subject of Charlotte Corday would attain the maximum of unsuitability for a Philharmonic concert. And so, of course, it proved. The music was very strenuous: the Marseillaise was duly intoned and the *Ça ira* madly whistled on "red fool-fury of the Seine"* lines; the wood wind went into the greenroom and played a waltz, of which I only heard the flute part (which did not happen to be the theme); but we thought of Egmont—indeed, it would have been sufficient almost to think of Struensee†—and felt that the Philharmonic was making an idiot of itself.

Yet it was not Mr Benoît who suffered in person for the stupidity of the program. There was another composer in the bill, a Mr Huberti, who followed with a couple of unconscionably spun-out songs in the sentimental manner of Gounod, one of which he accompanied very prettily on the organ. But they took so long, and the hour was so late, and the listeners were so afraid that they would not be able to wait for Ysaÿe's second piece, that they fell on the unfortunate stranger with hisses: actually with hisses! so mortally alarmed were they lest Mr Blauwaert, the singer, should take the slightest applause for an *encore*. So poor Mr Blauwaert retired, an astonished man; and Ysaÿe came on at last. Ysaÿe was on his mettle: he had probably heard that London is under the impression that Joachim can play

* Alfred Lord Tennyson, In Memoriam (1850), CXXVII.
 † Meyerbeer wrote incidental music in 1846 for this drama by his brother Michael Beer.

[17]

Bach; and he accordingly gave us the prelude and gavotte in E, just to shew us what real Bach playing meant. He had already astonished the audience to the extent of three furorious recalls by his playing of Vieux-temps' fourth concerto; and in both works his performance must have opened the eyes of those who have accepted the concerto playing of Joachim and Lady Hallé today as examples of what a great executant can do in his prime. Even Sarasate is five or six years past attacking a concerto—a true violinist's concerto—with the superb, prodigious, transcendent impetus of Ysaÿe. Of course he overdid it. Instead of being content with a speed which would have been impossible to any other violinist, he dashed into a speed impossible to himself; but what he succeeded in doing without sacrificing the accuracy of his intonation or the quality of his tone, was astonishing. And he knew it, and revelled in it. As I said the other day, Ysaÿe is bumptious. But then he has a good deal to bounce about, and must have paid a heavy price in labor for his dexterity.

I am full of admiration for the vigor and enterprise of Miss Caroline Holland, who has just introduced Tinel's oratorio Franciscus to us with the aid of her own choir, her own piano, a harp, and a triangle. Under these restricted conditions, the thing could hardly have been better done; and I only wish that those who have larger opportunities would make half as good use of them. But I cannot agree with her that Franciscus is a "magnificent work." Musically it is as barren as Benoît's Lucifer, though its poem is much superior to the vaporing nonsense of that huge ado about nothing. I do not at all doubt that it created a great sensation in Brussels. The city which municipalized Wiertz's show* as a temple of

* Antoine-Joseph Wiertz (1806–65) was a Belgian painter of historical pictures of gigantic size. His studio in Brussels became the Musée Wiertz.

[18]

Miltonic genius, and regards Léon Gallait as a great painter, is capable of admiring anything that has nothing in it; but for my part, I must beg to be excused. I give much more credit to Miss Holland for the performance than to Tinel for the composition.

The following letter, signed with an Italian name, has reached me. "Let me correct your paralytic version of a favorite old wheeze *re* the fiddler in The Star of a day or two ago. You say he replied 'I daresay I could play the fiddle if I tried,' or words to that effect. That is leprous nonsense. The only true version is thus. Being asked if he could play the fiddle he answered 'I dont know: I have never tried.' There is some humor, some point in this. But in your version—?"

I do not deny that there is more humor and more point in the above way of describing the incident. But my business in this column is not to be funny, but to be accurate. My version, whatever its artistic shortcomings may be, is the true one; for *I was present on the occasion,* and can positively answer for it that the gentleman replied in the exact terms I attributed to him. I hope this will teach my correspondent to be a little more careful henceforth in dogmatizing on subjects of which his knowledge is but secondhand. As to the pamphlet which he enclosed, proving vegetarianism to be an enfeebling and ultimately fatal practice, I confute it by the simple statement that I—Corno di Bassetto—have been a vegetarian these ten years. Pamphlet or no pamphlet, a mind of the calibre of mine cannot derive its nutriment from cows.

PARIS: A PEDANT-RIDDEN FAILURE

The Star, 11 April 1890

I am strongly of opinion that the Channel Tunnel should be proceeded with at once. There are worse things than foreign invasions, worse things even than foreign conquest, worse things than the extinction of England as a nation, if you come to that. I came over yesterday morning from Calais; and—but enough! The subject is not dignified; and it is hackneyed. All I will say is, that never again whilst I live—and yet I have made the same vow before, and broken it. Still, do not suppose that that silver streak of which you are so proud does not cost you something in the way of Continental musical news in the course of the year. But for it, The Star would be as great a musical power in Europe as it is in England.

Paris is, as usual, imposing on American greenhorns and British Philistines as a city artistic before everything, with specialities in cookery and welldressed women. I am not an artistic novice, English or American; and I am not to be taken in. Paris is what it has always been: a pedant-ridden failure in everything that it pretends to lead. Mozart found it so more than a hundred years ago: Wagner found it so half a century ago: Corno di Bassetto regrets to say that he finds it so today. In music, it prides itself on its Opéra, which is about twenty years behind Covent Garden; and Covent Garden, as everybody knows, is thirty years behind time: even New York leaving it nowhere. I went to the Paris Opéra on Monday to fulfil my mission of hearing Saint-Saëns' new opera Ascanio. I need not waste many words on the music of it. There is not an original phrase in it from beginning to end. The tragic scenes are secondhand Verdi; the love scenes are secondhand Gounod; the "historic" scenes are secondhand Meyerbeer. A duller potboiler I would not desire to hear anywhere. The orchestra is hardly better than the Covent Garden orchestra was in the 'seventies, before we got tired of the Gye-Mapleson managements that learned nothing and forgot nothing, and passed Vianesi, the conductor, on to Paris, where his immense industry, his cleverness, his ostentation, and his thorough superficiality enabled him to take root at once. Vianesi looks younger than ever, and is still on the alert for opportunities of turning conspicuously to the woodwind and brass, and offering them superfluous leads to shew how completely he has the score at his finger-ends; whilst the men have cultivated his slapdash, noisy style—or want of style—to the highest imperfection.

As to the singers, there is Lassalle, who brings down the house in a roaring duet with the tenor in the second act, and moves it to sentimental admiration in a mock pathetic passage in the fourth, beginning, *Enfants: je ne vous en veux pas.* Lassalle can hardly believe in the part of Benvenuto Cellini; but he believes immensely in Lassalle, and so manages to make things go with an effective air of conviction. Madame Adiny is undeniably what we call a fine figure of a woman; but her *tremolo* and her superb screaming power leave in the shade even the lady who played Desdemona here in Verdi's Otello at the Lyceum last year. Plançon, as Francis I., and Madame Eames, as Colombe, sang pleasantly enough; and I have no right to find fault with Madame Bosman as a capable if not highly distinguished representative of the old-fashioned type of "dramatic" singer, merely because I object to the entire species. The acting was the old impossible Richardson's Show strutting and swaggering, pitiful to see; and the libretto, like the music, was a string of commonplaces, culminating in Madame Adiny keeping Madame Bosman in a golden shrine in a public room for three days, at the expiry of which Madame Bosman was found dead "for Benvenuto's sake," which was the more affecting inasmuch as there was not the smallest reason why she should have got into the shrine in the first place or forborne to call on somebody to let her out in the second.

On the whole, I am afraid I must dismiss Ascanio as an elaborate and expensive tomfoolery, and applaud the wisdom of those frequenters who came only for the ballet, which, though artificial as it well could be—classical, in short—was good of its kind. Yet Ascanio bored me less than Barbier's Joan of Arc at the Porte St Martin, with Gounod's music, and Sarah Bernhardt in the title part. Barbier, as everybody knows, is the man to go to if you want a great subject debased for operatic purposes. He can turn a masterpiece by Shakespear or Goethe into a trashy melodrama in the twinkling of an eye. He fell on Joan of Arc years ago and fixed her up (no other expression conveys the process) for the Gaieté. Now she is dragged to light again with considerable excisions—all heartily welcome—for Madame Bern-hardt. In the music, Gounod imitates himself almost as mechanically as Saint-Saëns, and more exclusively. The best number is the vision of St Margaret and St Catherine. Even now, when his fount runs drier than in the last decade, Gounod can always write heavenly music. But Sarah is really too bad. We all know her way of pretending to act when there is no part for her—how sweetly she intones her lines and poses like a saint. This is what she does in Joan. There is no acting because there is no play; but she sends the lines out in a plaintive stream of melody throughout [of] which only a fine ear can catch the false ring. You would almost swear that they meant something and that she was in earnest. Not until the final scene at the stake does the affair become thin enough for even the American and British tripper to see through it. Sarah did not wink once: perhaps because she did not catch my eye, perhaps because she was in no humor for making fun of herself. It must be wearisome to keep up that make-believe night after night, knowing all the time that her serious work is going on without her at the Français.

Of course, I went to the Français for the sake of the traditions of the house of Molière, and found them to consist of equal parts of gag and horseplay, in no way superior—distinctly the contrary, in fact—to those established only the other day in Mr Benson's company for Hamlet and The Taming of the Shrew. But if the traditions are feeble, the acting is not; and not many things are more enjoyable than an Easter Monday afternoon performance of Le Bourgeois Gentilhomme by the Comédie Française. Monsieur Jourdain can only be enjoyed in Paris, because he is himself bourgeois Paris incarnate. When the play is over you can continue your study of his flunkeyism in his petrified Lord-Mayor's-coach of an opera house; his helpless incapacity for art, and consequent subjection to any pedant who will talk to him about something that he can understand (something quite beside the purpose of art, necessarily) in the Louvre; and his petty rationalism and delight in unreasonable scraps of logic anywhere you please. If I ever take to playwriting (one never knows how low one may fall) I shall do a London Bourgeois Gentilhomme— quite as curious a creature in his way.

However, my main business here is not with the Comédie Française, but with a certain "Soirée Musicale et Littéraire du Vendredi Saint" at the Winter Circus. The sensation here was the appearance of the divine Sarah in a divine character—that of the Virgin Mary, no less. She did more than this, however: she doubled her part with that of Mary Magdalen. Philippe Garnier confined himself to the leading character of Jesus; and Brémont compendiously undertook Pilate, Annas, Caiaphas, Peter, and Judas Iscariot. The work was described as "a mystery in five parts" by Edmond Haraucourt, and was entitled The Passion. A large dose of Berlioz, Beethoven, and Wagner was administered first to get us into the proper frame of mind; and then the mystery began. Sarah, in a dress of the purest, softest white, and with her complexion made up with really exquisite delicacy into a faint blush that could hardly have been more virginal, was well received. The Passion began amid a hush of expectation, and soon proved to be fully equal in depth of thought and novelty of illustration to our finest specimens of modern oratorio libretti. Sarah sang—sung as usual, holding the book in her right hand and waving her left in the air with a rhythmic persuasiveness that did wonders in soothing the distressing cough that soon became epidemic. On the whole the audience bore up bravely until Garnier rose to deliver a sort of Sermon on the Mount some forty minutes long. In quarter of an hour or so the coughing took a new tone: it became evident that the more impatient spirits were beginning to cough on purpose, though their lungs were as sound as Garnier's own. Then came a voice crying "Music, music," followed by applause, laughter, and some faint protest. Garnier went on, as if deaf. Presently another voice, in heartfelt appeal, cried, "Enough, enough." The reception of this was unmistakably sympathetic; and Sarah's shoulders gathered themselves expressively; but Garnier held on like grim death; and again the audience held their hand for a moment on the chance of his presently stopping; for it seemed impossible that he could go on much longer. But he did; and the storm broke at last all the more furiously because it had been so long pent up. In the midst of it a gentleman rushed down the grades of the amphitheatre; crossed the arena; and shook hands demonstratively with Sarah, then Garnier, then with Brémont. This was Haraucourt himself; and he capped his protest by shaking his fist at the audience, who reiterated their fundamental disagreement with him on the merits of his poem by yells of disapproval. Hereupon, exasperated beyond endurance, he took the extreme step of informing them that if they persisted in their behavior he would there and then leave the room. The threat prevailed. An awestruck silence fell upon the multitude: and the poet was moving loftily towards his seat when a lady, presumably his wife, threw herself on his neck and rained kisses on him. This affecting spectacle moved the gentlemen in the neighborhood to offer him their hands, which he took in an impressive attitude. Then he sat down; and the imperturbable Garnier started again. But soon the conviction spread that even at the risk of Haraucourt fulfilling his terrible threat, the speech must be stopped. Garnier, whose demeanor throughout was a model of perfect taste, at last exchanged glances with his colleagues, and then with the politest deprecation began: "Ladies and gentlemen: if you dont wish it"— whereupon the people in the arena expressed their opinion that the conduct of the five franc snobs was disgraceful, and the snobs in question vehemently gave Garnier to understand that there was no "if" at all in the question—that they didnt wish it and wouldnt have it. Sarah, in lively pantomime, conveyed her thanks to the arena; but I could not help suspecting that she was privately of the gallery's opinion. At last the three artists held a consultation, at the end of which Garnier sat down, and Sarah started at a scene only a few pages from the end. The audience accepted the compromise; Haraucourt made no further protest except by applauding occasionally; and the remainder of The Passion was dispatched without further interruption.

The anti-Wagner party was present in full force. It consists of six old gentlemen, more or less like the Duke of Cambridge in personal appearance, who make faces and stop their ears whenever an unprepared major ninth occurs in the harmony. As the audience was some thousands strong, and enthusiastically opposed to the veterans, they did not make much headway. Wagner always maintained that the great Tannhäuser fiasco was a success with the gallery; and there is no serious reason to doubt that he was right. Lamoureux's orchestra played with refinement and precision; but the first movement of the C minor symphony was taken in the old empty, hurried, vapidly elegant way; and in the overture to Tannhäuser the brass, reinforced by two extra cornets and a fourth trombone (a monstrous license), played like a coarse cavalry band, and blared out the Pilgrims' March in a most detestable manner, making the famous violin figure quite inaudible. One moral of which is that London, which declined to accept Lamoureux as a great conductor, and took Richter to its bosom, is as far ahead of Paris in musical judgment as in most other things.

I have only had one peep at the Carl Rosa company. That was last night at Mignon. For the present, I shall say no more than that the performance was a very creditable one—much more enjoyable than that at the Paris Opéra, for instance.

I have returned to Mr F. R. Benson a couple of stalls which he has been kind enough to send me for his Hamlet at the Globe Theatre; and I shall make my reason public. The tickets were inscribed "Evening dress indispensable for stalls, dress circle, and private boxes." Now, I object to be forced into the uniform of any class—most of all that of the class of gentlemen to which

I do not belong, and should be ashamed to belong. I need not here repeat the refutation of the stale pretence that the evening dress regulation ensures decency and cleanliness. A man can be just as offensively unclean in evening dress as in any other costume. It is, as I have said, a class uniform and nothing else. Now I submit to it at the opera (in London) because I cannot effectively challenge Mr Harris's right to place his theatre on the footing of a West End drawing room as long as the West End people pay up the subvention which in France comes from the nation. But I submit reluctantly, and take a distinct pleasure in the fact that my evening suit is by far the seediest article of clothing I possess. When Mr Benson tries on the same tyranny without the same excuse, I object. I prefer to pay two shillings and go into the pit, where I can wear what I like. That is what I did some weeks ago, when I went to see Mr Benson as Hamlet on my own initiative, and remarked that he keeps up the pleasant old tradition by which the Danish court enters to the strains of the march from Judas Maccabeus. The performance is an interesting and enjoyable one; and Mr Benson is better as Hamlet than in any other of the parts he has played here this season. But he is not going to force his inky cloak and customary suits of solemn black on me, for all that. And his attempt to do so makes me half suspect him of being a relative of the archbishop after all.*

* F.R. Benson was appearing in London for his first season following six years of touring the provinces with his own company. He was, in fact, a nephew of Edward White Benson, archbishop of Canterbury.

LURLINE

The Star, 14 April 1890

Saturday was an eventful day in my musical life. After two hours of Wagner at the Crystal Palace, I heard Lurline for the first time. Evidently indeed for the first time; since if I pretended that, having ever before heard Wallace's masterpiece, anything short of being in love with one of the performers could have induced me to go a second time, I should not be believed by any expert. No: once is enough, if not once too much. And yet there are several moments in the opera in which the string of hackneyed and trivial shop ballad stuff rises into melody that surges with genuine emotion. During the first half of the overture you say to yourself "Now, if he can only keep this up, Lurline will come out at the head of modern English operas." But he does not keep it up; and presently you are wallowing in banalities that are fully worthy of the desperate trash—the naked and unashamed nonsense—of Fitzball's libretto. If Wallace had taken his art seriously, he would no more, in his mature age, have set a line of such fustian to music than Wagner would have turned aside from the score of Parsifal, to set Scribe's Robert the Devil. And the poor silly public forgave Wallace for the sake of Sweet Spirit, hear my prayer, just as they make much of that other absurdity The Bohemian Girl for the sake of When other lips, and I dreamt that I dwelt.

I cannot say that the performance was much less ridiculous than the piece itself. Obviously a good deal might be done with the Rhine scenery, and the changes from the depths of the river to its surface. The problem of making Lurline look like a water spirit without exposing her to an undue risk of catching cold is also one for a costumier of genius. But Mr Harris knows the value of Lurline too well to spend an extra five shillings on it. As for the costumes, Madame Georgina Burns boldly followed the example of Mrs Leo Hunter* at the fancy ball, and put on a silk gown with spangles—a thing not to be contemplated without amazement and laughter. Mr Crotty, as the Rhine King, fell back on the habiliment of a pantomime demon, and left to the monster the distinction of being the sole representative of rational dress.

Madame Burns secured a great success as Lurline. I hinted the other day that Madame Adiny, of the Paris Opéra, had considerable power of making herself audible; but I had not then heard Madame Burns in her latest phase. In the concerted piece in the last scene of the second act, she had much to contend against. The brass blared; Mr Lely roared; Mr Crotty shouted; Mr Eugene bellowed; and the chorus lent a willing hand; but Madame Burns was able for them all. She sent her voice ripping, tearing, piercing through the hurly burly until the gallery, astounded and almost hysterical, madly demanded a repetition of the unparalleled sensation. It was magnificent; but it was not singing. However, it brought down the house; and if that is all Madame Burns cares for, I have only to congratulate her on her entire success. Her other efforts were comparatively lustreless. The first lines of Sweet Spirit were not ill sung; but Take this cup of sparkling wine was given in a fashion which in London is generally confined to the music hall; and the shakes which she introduced were made up of wrong notes—not even the right notes sung flat, but actually of notes far remote from those which she intended to sing. Mr Crotty sang his ballad in the

* Character in Dickens's Pickwick Papers.

second act very well; and the hearty *encore* he got was the heartiest of the evening. I have only to beg him to reconsider the advisability of treating London to such an unheard-of provincialism as beginning a high note with a double attack. Mr Lely got on fairly as Rudolph the Ridiculous; but Mr Eugene, whether his cramped attitude disabled him, or whether his Neptune-like beard got into his mouth, could do nothing with the florid passages in the drinking song. Not that it mattered: the song is not worth singing well, because it is not worth singing at all. The work will be repeated on Tuesday, on which occasion I shall make a point of being elsewhere.

OPERA, APPLAUSE, AND MRS LANGTRY
The Star, 18 April 1890

I hope the Carl Rosa Company will get severe criticism and plenty of it during their stay in London. "The Italian Opera" is a class affair at best; and its influence in the country generally is small. But these Carl Rosa people play everywhere. They are at it practically all the year round; and the rising generation in the provinces—from which, be it remembered, the future critics and connoisseurs of London will be largely recruited—will have its ideas formed by witnessing the sort of thing now proceeding at Drury Lane. Consequently I regard every member of the company as saddled with a heavy national responsibility. I wonder how many of them have any adequate sense of this!

The company has yet to recover from the effects of what was in many respects a bad start. Carl Rosa was a sensible, pertinacious, shrewd man of business, with a turn for music, but without that quick keen sympathy with the artistic instinct in its human vehicles—that confidence, power, and tact in developing it and stimulating it to courageous action, which make the really able *impresario*. For if anybody supposes that operatic companies, or dramatic companies, or, for the matter of that, political parties can be made by simply enrolling a number of more or less clever individuals, and then expecting them to do spontaneously what they have undertaken to do, such a one knows little of the incapacity of his species for concerted action. In the old times I never saw in the Carl Rosa Company much more than a fortuitous assemblage of middle-class amateurs competing with one another for applause under a certain factory discipline. Of artistic discipline there was very little. The singers were allowed to play to the gallery by introducing such alterations and interpolations as their vanity and ignorance suggested. They were allowed to take sham Italian names, and to sing broken English that would not have imposed on a moderately intelligent cockney poodle. How vulgar and offensive the follies of the Italian stage become when they are aped by young people of the Irish and American middle classes need not be described. Carl Rosa could have checked it if he had cared to: there is never any difficulty in checking practices that do not pay. As they were not checked, I think it is fair to conclude that he had no adequate sense of the mischief they did in his company; and I would earnestly impress on the surviving members thereof that instead of having a great past to live up to, they have an inglorious and third-rate record to retrieve by renouncing all the lusts of operatic vanity and making it their sole aim every evening, not that this song shall be encored, or that popular favorite called before the curtain, but that they shall collectively achieve a representation of the work in hand as nearly perfect as their individual shortcomings will allow.

The operatic stage is improving, like other things. But it is still possible for a *prima donna* to bounce on the stage and throw her voice at the heads of the audience with an insolent insistence on her position as a public favorite, and hardly the ghost of a reference to the character she is supposed to impersonate. An ambitious young artist may easily be misled by illustrious examples of stage misconduct. To tell an average young opera singer that she is a Patti or a Nilsson is to pay her the highest compliment she desires. Yet Madame Patti's offences against artistic propriety are mighty ones and millions. She seldom even pretends to play any other part than that of Adelina, the spoiled child with the adorable voice; and I believe she would be rather hurt than otherwise if you for a moment lost sight of Patti in your preoccupation with Zerlina, or Aïda, or Caterina. Nilsson, a far greater dramatic artist, so far stood on her dignity that she never came before the curtain to bow until there had been applause enough to bring out her rival at least six times (Patti will get up and bow to you in the very agony of stage death if you only drop your stick accidentally); and yet it is not sixteen years since I saw Madame Nilsson, in the wedding scene in Il Trovatore, turn to the tenor at the end of *Ah, si ben mio,* and slap him on the back with a loud "Bravo" that was audible—and meant to be audible—all over the house. Try to imagine Miss Ellen Terry doing that to Mr Irving after the "palace lifting to eternal summer" speech in The Lady of Lyons; and you will begin to realize how far the opera house is behind the theatre in England, and how any young lady, by the exercise of the simplest good sense and taste, may attain a higher normal level of dramatic sincerity than the two most famous of her predecessors.

And this reminds me of a writer in The Musical World who last week advocated the abolition of applause.

I wish there were any chance of his suggestion being carried out. The writer supposes that it has been abolished at Bayreuth; but he is wrong: it has only been reduced to the comparative innocence of a burst at the end of the representation, acknowledged by raising the curtain for a moment on the last tableau; and I am by no means sure that when they come to perform Mozart's masterpieces there it will be possible to avert an *encore* of *Là ci darem* or *Voi, che sapete*. I am against applause on the balance of its advantages (to which I am keenly sensible) and disadvantages. The latter are enormous, especially at dramatic representations, where the interruption of the illusion is an obvious and conclusive objection. Further, it enables a noisy minority to tyrannize over a silent and disgusted majority; it gives a false importance to claptrap which does nothing to attract audiences to the theatre, however much it may excite them when they are once inside; and its quantity and frequency are necessarily in inverse ratio to the preoccupation of the audience with the drama. The worst offenders are the people who clap because they are constitutionally ready to be good-natured when it costs them nothing, and those who clap because the others do. For my own part, I always regard the money I pay at the doors as sufficient evidence of my appreciation of the performers; and in the normal course of things I hardly ever applaud. When I do, it is usually to join in some personal demonstration apart from the merit of any particular performance.

For instance, at the Crystal Palace last Saturday Mr Manns marked his appreciation of the occasion (the afternoon was devoted entirely to Wagner) by discarding his velvet jacket and appearing in a frock coat, as if he had been marrying or burying somebody. At the end, the audience, instead of rushing off to the tea room to snatch a refresher before the half-past five train, felt a common impulse to give Mr Manns a spontaneous assurance of their unaltered affection for him. So they waited long enough to disconnect their projected ovation from the effect produced by the performance of the Kaisermarsch which had just ended the concert, and then gave a great salvo of clapping, which soon brought the frock coat back from the depths. Thus was a pestiferous custom for once turned to account conveniently, appropriately, sensibly, and feelingly; and I joined in the applause with much satisfaction to myself and no harm to anyone else.

I have been for some time waiting for an opportunity of saying a word about Mrs Langtry's revival of As You Like It at the St James's Theatre. I submit that the play is spoiled by the ruthless cutting to bits of the last half of it. This has been forced on the management by want of skill and want of thought on the part of the actors. The problem is to get through a play of so many lines between eight o'clock and eleven. Any fool can solve this in the fashion of Alexander (I allude to the man who stopped a hole to keep the wind away, and not to the lessee of the Avenue Theatre) by cutting out a chunk here and a scrap there until the lines are few enough to fit. But, somehow, the shorter you make your play in this fashion, the more tedious it becomes. The proper way is to divide your play into movements like those of a symphony. You will find that there are several sections which can be safely taken at a brisk *allegro,* and a few that may be taken *prestissimo*: those, for instance, which serve only to explain the mere mechanism of the plot. Each *allegro* will improve the representation if it is judiciously chosen and managed. Mr Benson has introduced one or two in Hamlet with the happiest effect. Of course the thing must be honestly done: the familiar star system trick of making the minor characters slur their work in order to leave plenty of time for the mock pregnant pauses, head waggings, and elaborate business of the leading actor, is vile, and shows a pitiful ambition in the fool that uses it. The star must not take a minute more than his lines are worth, or put off the third murderer with a minute less. Under these conditions, I believe it would be quite feasible to play As You Like It right through in a little over three hours without sacrificing a point.

However, it would be necessary to get another Jaques than Mr Bourchier, or else to rudely shake his conviction that the secret of effective elocution is to pause at every third word and look significantly out of the corners of his eyes at anybody who happens to be in that direction before letting out the fourth. Mr Bourchier can easily make himself a competent Jaques; but he may take it from me that he is at present as bad a one as London has seen for some years. Mrs Langtry makes a very womanly Rosalind, and succeeds better than any other actress within my recollection in making her love for Orlando the keynote of the part. I may remark that in spite of the beauty of the verse and the deep feeling for sylvan and pastoral scenery which pervades the play, the human part of it is excessively conventional, and might almost have been planned by Tom Taylor. Like Henry V., it belongs to that moment of sympathy with the common morality and thought of his time which came between the romanticism of Shakespear's early plays and the independent thought of his later one; and this is why it is so easily played by any company with a fair share of sense and skill. There is no confounded insight required in the business.

One member of the cast, dressed as a young god (Hymen, in fact), seemed to me to be no other than Karl Armbruster fresh from a rejuvenating dose of the elixir of life. The playbill explained that Hymen is Karl's daughter. I have been so accustomed to regard him as

[35]

one in whom the energy and vehement enthusiasms of early manhood will achieve a perfect balance and mellowness on his attaining middle age, that I cannot quite believe that this young lady of eighteen is his daughter. When she was at school with the Moravians at Neuwied, and subsequently went to Miss Geneviève Ward to study for the stage, it was hard to give her father credit for a daughter of more than ten at the outside; but it appears that Time was, as usual, hurrying faster than I thought. I shall be a grand old man myself presently.

THE STAR OF THE NORTH
The Star, 19 April 1890

I am not disposed to quarrel with the Carl Rosa Opera Company over L'Étoile du Nord on no better ground than that the principal parts are entirely beyond the means of their principal singers. *Le mieux est l'ennemi du bien*; and it is perhaps better to play Meyerbeer's operas with half the *bravura* left out and the other half more or less botched than not to play them at all. Besides, the inadequacy is not really greater in L'Étoile du Nord than in many other works which are regarded as the natural prey of English opera companies. It only appears so because Meyerbeer's music leaves no latitude for that unaffected slovenliness which makes life comparatively easy for the Carl Rosaists, in spite of their hard work in the provinces. A Meyerbeer opera requires extreme mechanical precision of execution and unflagging energy and attention. Everybody must be smart, polished, alert; there must be no hitch, no delay, no fluking or trusting to *laisser-aller*. It follows that the company must be clever and in good condition, fresh as paint every time. Now I do not say that the Carl Rosa Company is not clever, nor do I deny that it is always ready to do rough and ready work with a will. But if it is jolly it is also a little jaded, and has come to think itself lucky if it gets through its seven operas a week without an actual breakdown; so that though it never gets quite down to the level of a subscription night during the regular Italian season, yet it certainly does fall considerably short of the Meyerbeer standard of finish.

It must not be supposed that completeness has been aimed at in adapting The Star of the North to the requirements of the Carl Rosa Company. The camp scene is given in full, except for an ugly cut in the quintet in the tent scene (which should, by the bye, have been taken more swiftly and delicately), and the necessary excision for Madame Burns's sake of the brilliant *coda* to the *trio* in which Peter drinks Catherine's health. But the first act was vigorously scissored. Danilowitz's polonaise, the *trio* in which Catherine describes her visit to Prascovia's father, and even the great duet in which Catherine fires Peter's ambition, were all sacrificed, whilst the third act was simply gutted, nothing being left but a verse of Peter's song, an air for Prascovia, and Catherine's *scena* cut all to ribbons. The act would bear with advantage the restoration of Danilowitz's charming air in E flat, and the concerted piece for Peter, Danilowitz and Gritsenko, which is given in dialogue.

I am not going to shoot at the performers, though I am by no means prepared to admit that they all did their best. Mr Celli might have sung By thy side, oh beauty cruel, a little more carefully, even if he had substituted mere vocalizing for the impossibly ridiculous words of Chorley. Mr Aynsley Cook can scarcely be quite incapable of giving at least some suggestion of Gritsenko's eccentric devotion to discipline, which eventually leads the monomaniacal Cossack to approve of the Tsar's proposal to shoot him. That very rough diamond, Mr Child, may rest assured that a spell of patient practice would open his ears to some of the refinements of Meyerbeer; but unfortunately I cannot believe that practice is encouraged in the company: it would give the artist who tried it a mean advantage over the others. At least it seems to me that the average Carl Rosa execution is that of singers who have not worked at their scales for years. The minor parts were well done; the chorus, which is ordinarily too much addicted to shouting, acquitted itself capitally; and the military bands covered themselves with well-earned glory. The orchestra was not so good: it was sluggish and blurred in many passages where neatness and delicacy were needed: for instance, the excellently imagined accompaniment to Catherine's scene on her entry in the third act. Mr Goossens seemed to me to be imperfectly in sympathy with the electrical Meyerbeerian atmosphere. On the whole, however, I think the audience felt that they had had their money's worth. The immense adroitness and genuine fire of the camp scene were sufficiently brought out to interest and please the house in an exceptional degree.

P.S. Is it an established English custom to speak of the Ukraine as the You-Crane? I do not know whether it is good Russian to call it the Ooookra-eena; but it is much prettier.

THORGRIM

I

The Star, 23 April 1890

There are two possible reasons for Mr Cowen's consenting to set Mr Joseph Bennett's Thorgrim to music. 1. Because its poesy and dramatic force inspired him. 2. Because he was afraid to offend the critic of the Daily Telegraph by refusing. In order to help the reader to an unprejudiced choice of these alternatives, I give the following samples of the verse:

> Dear lady, what sorrow
> Thy young heart oppresseth?
> May we not cheer thee
> With music's diversion?

The following rises involuntarily to the lips of the heroine when she beholds the hero. It is in rhyme.

> With noble mien and moving words he pleads,
>   His form is grace, his voice makes music sweet,
> And I would follow wheresoe'er he leads—
>   This must be love, since joy and anguish meet!

The punctuation is copied from the libretto. Another sample, one of the best I can find. It is from the love duet:

> This moment fades the world away,
>   Far, far from thee and me,
> And lost the thought of yesterday
>   In love's immensity.
> The cruel morrow may us part—
>   To Fate's decree we bow.
> There is no time but Now, dear heart;
>   There is no time but Now.

[39]

One more specimen, again a specially favorable one:

Thine through all the future years,
Thine in gladness, thine in tears,
Thine amid the summer flowers,
Thine in winter's dreary hours,
Thine on land and thine on the sea,
Thine wherever thou shalt be.
Love till I this life resign,
Everywhere and always thine.

The story, the drama, the interest, the characterization, the subject even need not detain us. There are none. Mr Cowen conducted the performance himself. I was sorry for him; I would as soon have sat in the pillory, in spite of the applause. I did not wait for the fourth act.

I was agreeably surprised to find that Miss de Lussan, whom I had not heard since her solitary appearance as Carmen at Drury Lane two years ago, has added to the cleverness and self-possession she then exhibited, an artistic feeling and a degree of vocal skill and tact that must make her a valuable acquisition to the Carl Rosa company. Her voice has gathered color and individuality; and she knows how to use it, a refreshing thing in a company where every *prima donna* screams more or less. I look forward with interest to seeing her in some part which has dramatic importance, and which has vitality enough to keep the stage long enough to give her time to mature her conception of it. If Thorgrim is done again, Mr Harris would do well to withdraw the girls who dance with the swords in the first act. They should be replaced by men. If Mr Crotty and Mr McGuckin were engaged at an ordinary theatre to play Charles and Orlando in As You Like It, they would be expected to study their wrestling match as Mr Irving and Mr Bancroft studied the duel in The Dead Heart. Being operatic artists, they gave themselves no such trouble, and simply shoved each other back and forward as drunk and disorderly persons do when they quarrel and do not know how to fight. They evidently have made a shrewd guess at the number of times they are likely to have to play in Mr Cowen's opera.

II

The Hawk, 6 May 1890; unsigned

The criticizing of Thorgrim is really not so easy a matter as might be supposed. The librettist is a brother critic; and there is fellow-feeling and *esprit de corps*, not to mention the terror spread by Mr Sala's onslaught on Mr Furniss,* all prompting one to do the safe and the genial thing—to swear, in fact, that there never was such a libretto and such a score produced since English opera was born as this joint effort of the most widely circulated of our critics and the most popular of our song purveyors. But then the fact is so very obvious that Thorgrim is not good. It is worse than that: it is bad—desperately bad, confoundedly bad, unbearably bad, infernally bad; and everybody knows it. How is this to be put delicately, printably, unlibelously? It is easy for the irresponsible pittite to lean across to his neighbor and dismiss the work as "tommy rot"; but you cant use such expressions in a public paper: it is bad form—vulgar; English

* George Augustus Sala, a journalist, had brought an action for libel against the Punch caricaturist Harry Furniss for an indiscreet and indelicate statement, in a lecture, that Sala had once been rejected by the Art School of the Royal Academy. It was a silly affair, largely concerned with Furniss's disparagement of Sala as a would-be artist, and Sala eventually lost the case, but not before the press had joyously played up the action, for the delectation of its readers, as "The Great Six Toes Trial."

[41]

criticism, being untempered by duelling, could not be carried on if the rough edge of the truth were not taken off better than that. Rather let it be led up to gently by a reference to one of the sister arts.

Nobody can complain of an art critic admiring his favorite old or new master. Nobody can complain of his buying a picture by that master. Nobody can take exception to his praising that master more than ever when he has had a piece of his work for a year over the sideboard. Nobody can be injured if the American millionaire, educated by the English critic, and yearning consequently to possess a masterpiece by the favored limner, should make golden offers for the picture over the sideboard—offers which the critic has obviously a perfect right to accept. A set of circumstances involving less blame to everybody concerned could not possibly be imagined. And yet, when that critic next goes enthusing, the thought that he may possibly have another deal in view enters the mind unbidden, and discounts his raptures in spite of the utmost resolution to think no evil. And so people get [to] saying that a critic should never be a dealer, even in an amateur way—as if he had not as good a right to buy in the cheapest market and sell in the dearest as any other Briton.

Mr Joseph Bennett, the author of Thorgrim, is the victim of a somewhat cognate prejudice. He is credited with enormous power as musical critic to the Daily Telegraph and editor of the Musical Times. We are all familiar with his demonstrations of the objectionable character of Wagner's music. He provides "books of words" for oratorios; and these are performed at the great provincial English festivals and published by Messrs Novello. He writes analytic programs for the concerts of the Philharmonic Society. And he composes opera librettos. Now his position as critic gives him such power and independence that it is idle to pretend to believe that the Philharmonic gets off any the more easily in the D.T. because the writer of the notices is in the employment of the Society as a programist. And his connection with the Novello firm as editor of their paper and poet of their oratorios probably only makes him more scrupulous in dealing with their publications and with Festival performances than he would otherwise be. And it would be unreasonable jealously to expect a man so variously gifted to confine himself to a single department of literary activity—and that none too well paid a one—for the sole purpose of narrowing his own influence. Surely that influence should rather be accepted as the inevitable concomitant—nay, the just reward—of many-sided talent.

But look at it from the point of view of the *impresario* or the composer. When Mr Harris makes up his mind to commission Mr Cowen to compose an opera, the advantages of enlisting Mr Bennett as author of the libretto are, through Mr Bennett's merit and not through his fault, too obvious to be disregarded. The libretto is accordingly ordered, executed, and handed to Mr Cowen. Perhaps Mr Cowen is delighted, inspired, fitted to a hair. If so nothing need follow save general rejoicing. But what if on the other hand he is disappointed, and is fain to protest that there is no plot; that the incidents have no organic *raison d'être*; that the verse is doggerel; that Mr Bennett is Fitzball* without even Fitzball's folly. Will not the startled *impresario* reply that it would be madness to make an enemy of the Daily Telegraph; that the book is really a very good one when you get used to it; that the Daily News will declare that "some of Mr Bennett's lines fairly yearn for musical expression"; that the musical papers will vouch for it

* Edward Fitzball (1792–1873), hack playwright, and librettist of W. Vincent Wallace's Maritana and Lurline.

that he is "a man of undoubted literary ability"; that, in short, to secure his cooperation is to secure such a backing of press bluff and press butter as would push and slide anything into good repute for a season at least. It is easy to imagine Mr Bennett's pain and indignation at the assumption that his impartiality as a critic would be affected by the verdict of the composer on his attempt at poetry; but it is not easy to imagine the composer himself feeling quite so sure of that. The tempted musician would certainly try hard to persuade himself that the libretto might have been worse, before he would face the crushing responsibility of rejecting it, especially if he had contracted beforehand to supply the score without reserving any right to a voice in the matter.

Enough! Let us not blame Mr Bennett for failing to see that he was not born a poet or dramatist; and let us forgive Mr Cowen for not having had the courage to tell him so.

THE ATHLETIC MADAME MENTER
The Star, 25 April 1890

I confess to a weakness, not altogether musical, for Madame Sophie Menter. There is an enormous exhilaration and sense of enlarged life and freedom communicated to me by her superlative and victorious power and adroitness. I worship her magnetic muscle: I admire her puissant hands: I expand in the reflection of her magnificent strength, her suppleness, her swiftness, her inexhaustible, indefatigable energy. I grant that this may be the rebellion of the old Adam in me—a diabolic turbulence of the unchastened will-to-live, inherited from my beefsteak-eating ancestors: I even insist on the superiority of the plane upon which I am raised by the spiritual intensity and purely musical instinct of a player like Madame Backer-Gröndahl, whose right arm seems

[44]

frailer than Madame Menter's little finger. All the same, I have no intention of restraining my enjoyment of her immense execution, which places her beside the violinist Ysaÿe at the head of the musical athletes of the world.

No doubt the admirers of Schumann were disappointed with the performance of his concerto by Madame Menter at the Crystal Palace on Saturday. But what could they expect? To the superb Sophie, solid, robust, healthy, with her mere self-consciousness an example and sufficient delight to her, playing Schumann was like bringing a sensitive invalid into the fields on a sunshiny day and making him play football for the good of his liver. You could hear Schumann plaintively remonstrating in the orchestra, and the piano coming down on him irresistibly, echoing his words with goodnatured mockery, and whirling him off in an endless race that took him clean out of himself and left him panting. Never were the quick movements finished with less regard for poor Schumann's lungs.

The intermezzo delighted me beyond measure. Ordinarily, no man can put into words those hushed confidences that pass in it between pianos and orchestra, as between a poet and a mistress. But I can give you what passed on Saturday, word for word. Here it is:

SOPHIE: Now, then, Bob, are you ready for another turn?

SCHUMANN: Yes. Just half a moment, if you dont mind. I havnt quite got my wind yet.

SOPHIE: Come! you feel all the better for it, dont you?

SCHUMANN: No doubt, no doubt. The weather is certainly very fine.

SOPHIE: I should think so. Better than sticking indoors at that old piano of yours and sentimentalizing, anyhow.

SCHUMANN: Yes: I know I should take more exercise.

SOPHIE: Well, you have got wind enough by this time. Come along, old man: hurry up.

SCHUMANN: If you wouldnt mind going a bit slower——

SOPHIE: Oh, bother going slow. You just stick to me and I'll pull you through. Youll be all right in a brace of shakes. Now: one, two, three, and——

(*attacca subito l'allegro*).

And it really did Schumann good.

Pray do not suppose that Madame Menter is a hard, bloodless, unsympathetic: in a word, an unkind player. Not a bit of it. When, after an indescribable performance of a piece by Scarlatti and a Hungarian rhapsody by Liszt, she was recalled once, twice, thrice, four times, and eventually seized bodily by the intrepid Mr Manns and led in custody back to the piano, she played Liszt's transcription of Beethoven's Wonne der Wehmut,* and by that selection, as well as by the strong tenderness with which she played, completed the conquest of the already heavily-smitten Bassetto.

The orchestra was in fine form; and I cannot recall a performance of the Pastoral Symphony which has afforded me more pleasure. But the vocalist, Mr Charles Manners, who, if I recollect aright, first burst on London as the meditative sentinel in Iolanthe, threw away a chance of distinguishing himself by finishing The Two Grenadiers with an interpolation which he honestly meant to be decorative, and to give the song a rounding-off which Schumann had not been equal to. I hope that Mr Manners is under no illusion as to the effect he produced. The minority who applauded him

* A pianoforte transcription (1849) of No. 5 of Beethoven's Lieder von Goethe.

[46]

may have distracted his attention from the eloquently grim expression of the majority who did not. If so, let him take my word for it that his *cadenzas* had better be reserved for his next tour to Juan Fernandez. As it is the custom to sing *Qui sdegno* sharp, and to spoil the end by going down to the low E, I do not greatly blame him for that. But as he seems to have a genuine love of his profession, and considerable qualifications for success in it, I can do no less than warn him against those failings in taste and good sense which, more than any deficiency in voice or musical aptitude, keep so many of our singers in the second or third rank as artists.

[U] I am told that my account of the organ recitals on Tuesdays at St Nicholas Cole-Abbey, in Queen Victoria-street, has created a yearning among City men to retire from the struggle of business for an hour into the quiet of a church, there to drink in Wagner and recuperate for another Capel Court foray. I dont believe it; but I have no objection to announce that Mr John Runciman will at one o'clock next Tuesday give an organ recital of works by Wagner, Bach, Handel, and Beethoven. There will be no service and no collection—nothing, in short, that could offend the most sensitive atheist or the most economical stockbroker. [U]

Miss Dell Thompson made me laugh so exceedingly at the soirée given by the Norwegian Club some time ago that there was no difficulty in inducing me to go to her recital at Prince's Hall this day week. I will not attempt to describe her personally, because I do not know which is the real Miss Thompson: the small girl of three feet high, with staring eyes, infantile mouth, elbowless little sticks of arms, and absurdly laughably childlike squeak of a voice, or the young woman who is like any other well-favored and graceful young woman, except in respect of being clever and able to do something. Anyhow, she is gifted in a remarkable degree

[47]

with the qualities needed for distinguished success in naturalist comedy. As a reciter, what she wants at present is a little criticism from the London point of view; and that is what I now propose respectfully to offer her.

First, then, as to her selection of pieces for recitation. She laid a good deal of stress on The Chariot Race from Ben Hur,* which I took to be a novel in the manner of Mr Rider Haggard. It is without literary grace, being as businesslike a piece of three-volume prose as ever was penned; and the chariot race is imagined in a perfectly commonplace way. There is nothing in it that specially suits Miss Thompson's style; and she adds nothing to it; indeed, she finds the incidental specifications of the arena so hopelessly insusceptible of artistic treatment that her air of intelligent explanation verges harder upon the ridiculous than I quite like to say. And when, in a hopeless effort to churn the literary skim milk into some presentable sort of oleomargarine, she lavishes all the vigor of her young lungs on it, the strain on the patience of the audience becomes severe. There were people who hissed on Friday, as well as people who applauded. Both were fools for their pains: they should have let Ben Hur fall with his own unaided flatness. Miss Dell Thompson is clever enough to see, on reflection, that it would serve him right. I certainly think she has formed either an over-estimate of Ben, or an under-estimate of the taste of London.

Another point. Miss Thompson has an irresistible American accent: merely to hear her say "Tom" sets me wondering whether, if she whispered the more euphonious "Corno di Bassetto," it would be possible to refuse her anything. But when she passes from impersonation

* A novel (1880) by the American writer General Lew Wallace.

to description—from the first person to the third—from dramatic utterance to abstract recitation, then I confess that the need for classical diction asserts itself imperatively, and I voluntarily make notes of such words as bawlcony, fahllowed, invahlved, invahlunterry, necesserrily (with a stress on the third syllable worthy of Mr Henry George himself), sympithy, equil, tern for turn, dew for do, and a ringing nasal ah-oo which is sometimes charming, but which does not seem at its best in words like bound, round, &c. Then Miss Thompson has deliberately cultivated an R which is neither the no R at all of Middlesex nor the clean trilled R which is the only pleasant alternative to it. She just rolls her tongue up and treats us to a thick gutteral R which makes such a word as "neared" (for example) an ugly obstruction in the middle of the silver stream of her speech.

London is full not only of cockneys who have too many and horrible defects of their own to leave them any excuse for fastidiousness, but with provincials and Americans who have got the better of the ugly features of their native dialects, and who are therefore rather intolerant of professional speakers who shew any indisposition to take the same trouble. I am myself disposed to insist on the right of the individual to the widest latitude; but obviously a line must be drawn somewhere; and it should be drawn higher for one who professes speaking as an art than for a private person or a propagandist lecturer. My own diction when I speak in public is perhaps slightly less artistic than that of Coquelin; and Mrs Victoria Claflin Woodhull* falls considerably short of Miss Ada Rehan as an American exponent of the art of diction. Nevertheless, the critic who should object to our lectures on that ground would

* American suffragist, resident in London, who advocated a single standard of morality and equal rights for women.

be justly contenmed as an unmitigated prig. Not so in the case of Miss Dell Thompson. It is her business to be word-perfect; and nobody who heard her recite What my lover said can doubt her capacity for the most delicate degree of excellence, if she chooses to set about attaining it. Nobody can even doubt that her artistic insight will compel her to insist on attaining it the moment she becomes conscious of the smallest refinement not yet mastered by her.

As I do not wish to confine myself exclusively to destructive criticism, I may as well point out to Miss Thompson that she has a substitute for Ben Hur of the highest order ready to her hand in William Morris's Atalanta's Race, which she will find in The Earthly Paradise. Further, it may interest her to know that The Owl Critic is played out here, and that our very souls loathe Poor Little Jo and the quagmire of sloshy false sentiment to which he belongs. Besides, only artists who are born third-rate ever really succeed with third-rate stuff. I suspect that Miss Dell Thompson's future will be chiefly devoted to the stage; but in the meantime I hope she will not mistrust herself and us so far as to play low down in her selections. If I were a reciter I should get up a single program and stump the country with it. Here it is:

PART I

The Ancient Mariner—S. T. Coleridge.

PART II

John Gilpin—Cowper.

CARL ROSA OPERA COMPANY: LOHENGRIN

The Star, 28 April 1890

Lohengrin is so much the best thing the Carl Rosa company has done this season—unless Romeo and Juliet, which I did not see, was better—that the more they give us of it, and the less of Maritana, Lurline, and so on, the better their position will be at the end of their season in London. The choral parts and the stage business have had something approaching a due proportion of the total available Drury Lane energy put into their preparation; and the result is that all the great situations in the first and second acts produce an immense effect. The work is, of course, mutilated; one particularly exasperating aggravation of the atrocious cut in the prelude to the second act has been perpetrated by cutting out the whole of the dawn music with the exception of two beggarly trumpet calls and their echoes. I hope the next world may see a great gulf fixed between me and the man that made that cut. But what is done is done very well, considering the possibilities of the case— well enough, at any rate, to convey much of the force and feeling of Wagner's conception of his work.

The excellence of Miss Amanda Fabris's Elsa was a surprise to the house. I am not sure that they all quite saw where the unwonted charm of it lay. It was not altogether in her singing, though that was pleasant at its weakest, and intelligent and full of appropriate expression at its best. Nor was it in her acting, in the deeper sense of acting, though in that she was successful, as a matter of course. I say a matter of course because no woman ever fails as Elsa, just as no man ever fails as

Hamlet, even when they are unable to play much simpler parts. The novel and characteristic element in her impersonation is her admirable pantomime. If I might hazard a guess, I should say that Miss Fabris was either trained in the first instance as a dancer, or has had the good sense and artistic conscience to voluntarily go through that part of a dancer's education which deals with dramatic pantomime. She filled up all the long intervals of orchestral illustration without turning them into something dangerously like stage waits, as so many Elsas have done through sheer pantomimic incompetence. And she was never for a moment out of her part. Altogether, with her long eyes, her slim figure, Tuscan school profile, and Botticellian grace, she made a very marked impression which the audience gave vehement emphasis to after each descent of the act-drop. The other notable success of the evening was that of Ffrangcon Davies, who sang up to the promise of his stupendous Christian name in a fresh, unspoiled baritone voice which pleased the audience immensely. Mr Barton McGuckin, who is, on the whole, second only to Jean de Reszke (a less indisputably pure tenor) among the singers familiar to Londoners, bore himself with dignity as Lohengrin, and sang well. But cannot Mr McGuckin, who has learnt so much, and who has never fallen into the error, common among tenors, of mistaking the beginning of his reputation for the completion of his education—cannot he get the better of his native tendency to maltreat the first letter of the alphabet? His delivery of Lohengrin's declaration in the last act is not improved by such locutions as "In distant londs ... a costle stonds ... Montsolvot," &c.

Miss Tremelli must bear with my old and rooted prejudices against the substitution of attitudinizing for acting, and against a method of singing that involves a gasp for breath between every note almost. I do not like it; and I do not feel called upon to disguise my sentiments on the subject. Mr Max Eugene has done worse things than his Telramond. Mr Goossens conducted, and made an original point or two. The audience waxed impatient at last with the length of the waits, and went so far as to whistle We wont go home til morning, a performance which was interrupted by the now well-known Drury Lane cat, which turned over on its back in the stalls, and rolled about in mockery, amid hearty Wagnerian applause. It was extinguished by the passing skirt of Madame Marie Roze, whom it followed out with some show of indignation. I am not in a position to chronicle its subsequent proceedings. I must add, for Mr Harris's information, that there was a good deal of noise made on the stage during some of the preludes. A hint from him on the subject would probably have some weight with the carpenters.

AN ENGLISH MEISTERSINGER?
The Star, 2 May 1890

Although Mr Manns was inconsiderate enough to select the very wettest day he could find for his benefit, the audience was of the largest; and as they all had umbrellas to thump with, the applause was exceptionally effective. Not so the program. The Freischütz overture, played without the Wagnerian interpretation of the *decrescendo* mark over the chord preceding the entry of the "feminine theme" in the *coda*, was as fresh as ever; though, with all respect to Mr Manns, Wagner was assuredly right. The Tannhäuser overture was equally welcome. But then the Freischütz was played at three and the Tannhäuser at five; and between the two were two mortal hours of music which did nothing to restore that alacrity of spirit which the rain had washed out of me.

[U] First there was a serenade by Miss Smyth, who wrote the analytic program in such terms as to conceal her sex, until she came forward to acknowledge the applause at the end. No doubt Miss Smyth would scorn to claim any indulgence as a woman; and far from me be it to discourage her righteous pride; but that does not alter the fact that when it became apparent that the serenade, though fancifully carpentered and pretty, was a plain case of *parler pour ne dire rien*, as an intelligent foreigner near me remarked, I am convinced that we should have resented the disappointment less had we known that our patience was being drawn on by a young lady instead of some male Smyth. It is very neat and dainty, this orchestral filigree work; but it is not in its right place on great occasions at Sydenham.*[U]

Then there was Dr Sapellnikoff's playing of Tchaikovsky's pianoforte concerto in G (No. 2) for the first time in England. The apology made by Sir George Grove in the program for the absence of an analysis was the less needed because the work contains nothing new. It is impulsive, copious, difficult, and pretentious; but it has no distinction, no originality, no feeling for the solo instrument, nothing to rouse the attention or to occupy the memory. It left me without any notion of Sapellnikoff's rank as a player: he is, of course, swift and powerful with his fingers; but six bars of a Mozart sonata would have told me more about his artistic gift than twenty whole concertos of the Tchaikovsky sort.

And here let me remark that whenever you hear of a great composer from Russia, or from Hungary, or from any other country which is far behind us in social development, the safest plan is not to believe in him. You cannot be too intensely insular on the art question

* At Charlotte Shaw's suggestion this early criticism of a composition by Dame Ethel Smyth was not reprinted in London Music (1937).

in England. If England wants music to reach her own highest standard, she must make it for herself. The adolescent enthusiasms, the revolutionary ardors, the belated romanticism of Slav and Czech can produce nothing for England except toys for her young people. Wagner himself is, on some points, too sentimental for us: we must have an English Wagner: perhaps he is starving somewhere whilst I write. If we would only give a chance to every potential Wagner among our millions—that is, secure him adequate schooling and adequate grub—we should have an actual one in two generations at latest.

Perhaps you doubt the national capacity for music of Wagnerian depth and strength. No Englishman, you think, has a Meistersinger in him. Pinchbeck Handel and secondhand Mendelssohn, with words by Mr Joseph Bennett: that, according to your experience, is English music. But every nation has its plague of "kapellmeister's music"; and if the critics are fools enough to mistake such academic trifling for genuine art, so much the worse for them and not much the better for the kapellmeisters and Mr Joseph Bennett. Not all the goodnatured puffing of Mr Bennett's colleagues will get as much wear out of Mr Cowen's Thorgrim or Mr Parry's Judith as I shall get out of my second best pair of boots before they descend into the blind cave of eternal night. As to where an English Meistersinger is to come from, all I know is that long before Wagner was born England produced Henry Purcell's Yorkshire Feast, a work cognate with the Meistersinger in its most characteristic feature. We cannot count on another Purcell; but in my opinion England's turn in art is coming, especially since there is a growing disposition among us to carry our social aims further than providing every middle-class dog with his own manger as soon as he is able to pay for it.

Some time ago I suggested that Mr Manns should give us some medieval trombone and organ music at the Saturday concerts. Consequently I should be praising myself if I were to applaud the selection of Heinrich Schütz's Lamentatio Davidis for performance on Saturday. Besides, the chief credit on this score must surely be due to Mr George Case, who probably induced the Wind Instrument Society to bring it forward at a concert last month. I guess this because I first heard the work in 1885 at South Kensington, where he played it with Mr Geard and Messrs J. and Antoine Matt, the voice part (taken by Mr Henschel on Saturday) being sung by Mr Stanley Smith. On that occasion they also played Luther's Eine feste Burg, which I can recommend to Mr Manns if he feels disposed for more trombone music. We all know the trombone in its melodramatic moods; but its noblest qualities never come out so impressively as when it is treated in what I may call a spirit of pure counterpoint.

I have to apologize to Mr Harold and Miss Ethel Bauer for missing their concert on Monday. I allowed myself to be seduced by the management of the Prince of Wales's Theatre into attending the 100th night of Marjorie, intending to leave after an act or two and go on to the concert. But my Herculean frame suddenly yielded to the strain which the present stress of pictures, politics, and music put on a critic who is engaged in all three departments simultaneously. I settled down lazily in my stall and never budged until the curtain fell. Not that the performance, though it amused me, can be said to have enthralled me. I can tell you very little about it—not even how often Mr Coffin kissed Miss Broughton. He seemed to me to be kissing everybody with a reckless disregard of propriety. I must say that Mr Coffin, being a handsome young man, and considerably under-parted to boot, had an easy time of it. Had he been trying his prentice hand at Iago or Don Juan I should have set my brains seriously to the task of criticism; but Marjorie is child's play for him. As a singer he has been better, and he will some day again be better, than he is today. He insists too much on the manly roughness of his voice, and is, it seems to me, actually impatient of the delicate color and the rich, light, smooth tone with which he started, and which was the cause of his success; for anybody can produce the rough, loud article if he sets himself at it. Mr Coffin has only to cast back after his old charm to get two stops to his organ. Then skill and taste in their employment, with the dramatic intelligence of which, even in this Marjorie nonsense, he shews plenty, will keep him in the front rank when he becomes a middle-aged operatic villain, and takes to serious business.

Mr Slaughter has not allowed the better to become the enemy of the good in composing Marjorie. The score is sufficient for its purpose; but I think he really might have devized some worthier climax for Mr Coffin's song in the third act than a hackneyed waltz refrain. Marjorie compares favorably with Dorothy as to the book: unfavorably as to the music. The book of Dorothy was not only silly, but stupid. The book of Marjorie is also silly, but it is amusing. On the other hand, the music of Dorothy was pretty, and had a certain elegance and technical finish, which belonged to the Mendelssohn-Sterndale Bennett traditions in which Mr Cellier, like Sir Arthur Sullivan, was trained. Mr Slaughter has been less fastidious; and his share in the success of Marjorie is proportionately less than that of Mr Cellier in the success of Dorothy, which, by the way, is still ravaging the provinces.

I must bring these disjointed remarks to a close. The fact is, I have been at the Royal Academy all day, "Press-viewing" it; and my mind is unhinged by the contemplation of so much emptiness and so much bungling. My wits were in a sufficiently unsettled condition before I went there: for last week I described how Madame Sophie Menter played Liszt's transcription of Beethoven's *Wonne der Wehmut*, wheras what she did play was—as I heard with my own ears and knew perfectly well—his transcription of Mendelssohn's *Auf Flugeln des Gesanges*. I have before this gone to a performance of Don Giovanni, and begun my notice thereof with half a column about Fidelio before, in trying to remember how the statue came into the prison scene, the truth flashed on me. I therefore give warning that I will not be answerable for the accuracy of any statement that may appear in this column—or out of it, for that matter.

P.S. I forgot to say that the omission of any reference to Dvořák's new symphony is due to that idiotic body the Executive Committee of the London Liberal and Radical Union, which selected for a council meeting the night fixed long beforehand for the Philharmonic concert. These Goths think that a concert is a thing of no importance. If it were a horserace now——!

A CRITICS' TRADE UNION

The Star, 9 May 1890

I occasionally get letters from artists whom I have criticized, explaining away their misdeeds, or thanking me for my valuable suggestions, or arguing the point with me, or threatening me with personal violence, either to relieve their feelings or to follow up a small opening. Some of them mean nothing more than to nobble me with a little flattery; and these are the wise ones; for I need not say that I delight in flattery. Even when there is no mistaking it for sincere admiration, I am pleased to find that anybody attaches sufficient importance to my opinion to spend a postage stamp on an attempt to humbug me. Therefore let no diplomatic young singer be deterred from paying me compliments by the certainty of my seeing through them. Flatter by all means; and remember that you cannot lay it on too thick. The net pleases the bird no less than the bait. But be particularly careful not to discuss artistic points with me; for nothing is easier than to drop some remark that will make me your enemy for life.

For instance, I have before me a letter from a singer who wrote to me to ask whether a certain song should not be sung with a high note interpolated at the end for the sake of effect. As the song was by Mozart, my reply may be imagined. The following is the astonishing rejoinder of my correspondent: "I see plainly that you are quite right; and when I sing at another *classical* concert I shall act on your view. But you will, of course, agree with me that a singer must try to be popular; and therefore at ballad concerts, &c., if he finds a high note brings him success and secures him the applause of the public, it is only common sense for him to do it. I confess it is inartistic; but what is one to do? To earn my living I must please my audience."

Imagine my feelings on being calmly told that "of course I will agree" with the assumption that it is "only common sense" to act against your conscience whenever there is money to be made by doing so. However, this is not really the position taken by my correspondent. He does not feel that the high note is inartistic at all: he only knows that certain cranks like myself, who are supposed to be authorities on the subject, say that it is inartistic; and he agrees as a pure matter of convention. Consequently, the high note is not against his conscience: it is only against mine, which is not morally binding on him, though he supposes himself let in for admitting that I know better than he. Therefore I now say to my correspondent, Go on singing the high note. If you like it better than Mozart's ending, or if the repugnance you feel to the alteration is so slight as to be profitably compensated by the applause which the note brings you from people who have not even that slight repugnance, then fire away. Your artistic sense will be satisfied: mine will be outraged. You guarantee the applause from the audience: I guarantee the slating from at least one critic. The fact is, that if the singers felt about these interpolations as a cultivated musician does, they could not sing them without an intolerable sense of discomfort and humiliation. And until a singer has that sense it is idle for him to suppose that the word "inartistic" has any genuine significance for him.

As to the distinction between classical and popular concerts, it conveniently describes the difference between a Crystal Palace Saturday concert and one of Messrs Boosey's ballad concerts. But it does not mean that the right way to sing a song by Mozart at one concert is the wrong way at another. At a ballad concert you may substitute the music of Milton Wellings for the music of Mozart; but you most certainly may not substitute the wrong way of singing Mozart for the right way.

Here is an affectionate comment of The Musical World on the unmusical World:

"We have more than once pointed out, with friendly amusement, the harmless mistakes which have been made in speaking of English art by our excellent contemporary 'Le Menestrel.' But there is a limit to our toleration. When it asserts, as in its last issue, that Mr Louis Engel is a member of our staff, we are bound to protest.* We do not pretend to know what evil days may

* Engel was music critic of The World, a post to which Shaw succeeded a fortnight later, after Engel had suddenly defected.

be in store for The Musical World; but our readers may be assured that these days are not yet."

Now, in the name of all that is easygoing, why this unprovoked onslaught? Ordinarily, I have only one fault to find with Mr Jacques (that is the M. W.'s name). It is that he is scandalously goodnatured: so much so that he wrapped up the nakedness of the bitter truth about Thorgrim in an article 500,000 words long, in order to spare the feelings of Mr Cowen and Mr Bennett. I believe that the indignation unnaturally pent up by this effort demanded an outlet; and so feeling that he must have somebody's blood, he flew at the unfortunate L. E., and wreaked on him the rage that ought to have laid Thorgrim low. This sort of Berserkerism must not be encouraged; for how do I know who may be the next victim? myself, perhaps!

Some time ago a weekly paper, criticizing a performance of Gounod's Ave Maria by Madame Patti, took occasion to observe that the harmonium *obbligato* was vilely played. It was L. E. who played it; and he played it with admirable discretion; but the critic evidently despised The World's musical column, and felt that he must assassinate its author. Now the reason L. E. is thus pursued is that he is beyond all comparison the best musical critic of his school in London, as far as my knowledge goes. His school (mid-century Parisian) is not mine: I was brought up in it, and soon had enough of it, finding its arch enemy Wagner more to my taste; but that does not prevent me from seeing that he knows his business, and that he has the force to write individually, originally, making his mark with every opinion he delivers. Of how many critics in London is it possible to say as much? When one thinks of the average critic, with his feeble infusion of musical dictionary and analytical program, the man who has no opinion, and dare not express it if he had, who is afraid of his friends, of his enemies, of his editor, of his own ignorance, of committing an injustice (as if there were any question of abstract justice involved in the expression of a critic's tastes and distastes), it is impossible not to admire L. E., who, at an age at which all ordinary journalists are hopelessly muzzled by the mere mass of their personal acquaintance, can still excite these wild animosities in the breasts of his colleagues.

Another critic, Mr Clement Scott, has been describing how he was boycotted in the early days of his warfare against the managers. But my advice to managers and concert givers is Boycott all good critics. I am myself vigorously boycotted; and I take it as a sincere compliment. Concert givers are perfectly well aware that my criticism will be exactly the same whether I pay for my seat or not; and they naturally think they may as well have my money as well as my notice. In my opinion the whole system of complimentary tickets for the Press should be discontinued. The managers have only to combine against the free list, and the thing is done. The papers must have criticisms; the critics must see the plays; and the proportion between praise and blame must remain practically the same, however freely and sincerely expressed. Unfortunately, the initiative in the matter ought to come from the critics and not from the managers. Just as waiters will have their wages made precarious by the tipping system until they have the sense to refuse tips; so managers will send tickets as long as the critics will accept them. We should form a Critics' Trade Union, and pledge ourselves never to enter a place of public entertainment without paying (and charging the price to our paper). If we are anything like so highly skilled as we ought to be, there could be no danger of blacklegs taking our places on papers of any pretension to highclass literary matters. Who will join? There would be no gain or loss to speak of, except to ourselves in independence. The managers would make the papers pay for the stalls; but then the papers would make the managers pay for advertisements to replace the purely complimentary puffs which are a feature of the present system.

Miss Elsie Hall is an infant phenomenon of the latest fashion, that is, a twelve-year-old pianist. She played last Monday at Steinway Hall with all the vigor and enjoyment of her age, and as dexterously as you please, being a hardy wiry girl, with great readiness and swiftness of execution, and unbounded alacrity of spirit. At the same time, there is not the slightest artistic excuse for exploiting her cleverness at concerts; I hope we may not hear of her again in public until she is of an age at which she may fairly be asked to earn her living for herself. And this reminds me of a matter I omitted to mention in connection with Marjorie last week. It is that the stage is "dressed" with children in the first set, quite unnecessarily. I again urge on the notice of our legislators the cynical unscrupulousness with which the loophole made in the Act for the purpose of enabling Richard III. to have his little Duke of York on the stage has been abused to the extent of making the Act, so far as the stage is concerned, almost a dead letter.

I deserted Miss Meredyth Elliott's concert on Wednesday to hear Dr John Todhunter's pastoral entitled A Sicilian Idyll at the little theatre of the club in Bedford Park. It is not every poet who could reconcile me to an hour's transparent Arcadian make-believe in the classic Sicily of Theocritus; but Dr Todhunter did it. There is nothing in music more beautiful in its way than blank verse in its early simplicity of line by line, each beautiful and complete in itself. Marlowe's line was not "mighty": blank verse did not become mighty until the lines had grown together into the great symphonic movements of Shakespear's final manner; but it was

[63]

tuneful, exquisitely emphasized, and sometimes gorgeous in its sound color. Sometimes, on the other hand, it was vulgar and swaggering. Now Dr Todhunter writes a line that is guiltless of swagger. It is melodious, tender, delicately colored, and with that convincing cadence that only comes from perfect fitness of emphasis. It was quite enchanting to sit listening to it, and to escape from the realistic drama of modern life for a whole hour. The performance was very creditable. Music, dancing, costumes, scenery were all excellent. Mr Paget (Alcander) seemed to me to have no experience of using his voice except for private conversation: there was not enough tone and weight in his lines; but I have no other fault to find with him. Florence Farr's* striking and appropriate good looks no doubt helped her to a success that would have cost a plainer woman more to achieve; but her intelligence and her instinct for the right fall of the line was never at fault. Miss Linfield's ear is perhaps not quite so sure as that of her lover Daphnis, enacted by "Mr John Smith." I may mention that Dr Todhunter has evidently never experienced the vicissitudes known as "having the brokers in." He has therefore never heard the terrible word "inventory" pronounced. If he ever does (*absit omen!*) he will discover that the accent is on the first syllable instead of, as he supposes, on the second.

* Young actress who became Shaw's lover. She appeared in the first productions of his Widowers' Houses (1892) and Arms and the Man (1894).

GAS AND GAITERS

The Star 16 May 1890

I cannot quite account for the crowded state of the
concert room at the Philharmonic last week. And they
were so enthusiastic, too. Young Mr Borwick is hardly
an established favorite as yet (it was his first appearance
in England); and Signor Mancinelli, though he has
conducted for a few seasons at Covent Garden, is not
absolutely the idol of London. I could not help thinking
that both these gentlemen must have been treated very
liberally by the Society in the matter of complimentary
tickets. Nothing could be more natural under the
circumstances; but the effect, as far as the public is
concerned, is much the same as if the *claque* system had
been introduced for the evening. For instance, I do not
believe that the desire to hear the third movement of
Signor Mancinelli's Venetian Suite was as general
among those who had paid for their tickets as among
those who had not. The orchestration is after the pattern
of that glittering sample which Signor Mancinelli
shewed us in his *finale* to Bizet's Pêcheurs de Perles at
Covent Garden. The success of its execution by "the
famous Philharmonic orchestra" was a melancholy proof
of the sort of work which that kid-gloved body is now fit
for. It is an unapproachably noiseless, delicate, well-
bred band, too superfine for the vulgarities of Beethoven
or the democratically unreticent Wagner, but incomparable for a Venetian suite or a quadrille at a Court
ball.

Mr Leonard Borwick would have made a greater
success if he had not been a little over-newspapered
beforehand. I have no fault to find with his playing: it is

well studied, accurate, and earnestly and enthusiastically set about, as it should be; but he is still a pupil and not a master. Whether Mr Borwick will be spoken of hereafter only once a year (after his benefit concert) as "that excellent pianist and wellknown professor," or whether he will be current throughout Europe as "Borwick" *sans phrase*, is a question which the Philharmonic concert has left unsettled. It is sufficiently high praise for the present to say that it was not settled adversely.

Mr Cowen's conducting reminded me rudely of the flight of time. We have been so long accustomed to regard Mr Cowen as a young man that the sudden discovery of such signs of age as slowness, timidity, exhaustion of musical eagerness, come upon us with a shock: at least, they do on me. I forget Mr Cowen's exact age; but if I were to judge of the funereal way in which he led the Frischka of Liszt's Fourth Hungarian Rhapsody—one of the maddest of them—I should put him not far from eighty. The allegro of *Dove sono* was also far too tame. Miss Macintyre, whose popularity increases each time she sings, got through it very creditably; but if I were to say that she sang it quite satisfactorily, I should imply that she is a singer of the very highest rank, which she can hardly yet claim to be.

It seems to me that there are more champion pianists in the world at present than any previous age has seen. Possibly the introduction and general use of the street piano has raised the standard of swiftness and certainty in execution. However that may be, mere technique, which used to suffice to stamp as a "great player" any dullard who had perseverance enough to become a finger acrobat, is now a drug in the market; and the seat of the higher faculties of the pianist is no longer supposed to be the left wrist. Consequently I went to hear the famous Paderewski without the slightest doubt that his execution would be quite as astonishing as everybody else's; and I was not disappointed. He plays as clearly as Von Bülow—or as nearly so as is desirable, and he is much more accurate. He has not enough consideration for the frailty of his instrument; his *fortissimo,* instead of being serious and formidable like that of Stavenhagen, is rather violent and elate. He goes to the point at which a piano huddles itself up and lets itself be beaten instead of unfolding the richness and color of its tone. His charm lies in his pleasant spirit and his dash of humor: he carries his genius and his mission almost jauntily, which is more than can be said for Stavenhagen, whose seriousness, however, is equally admirable in its way. He began with Mendelssohn, and knocked him about rather unceremoniously; then he took the Harmonious Blacksmith and spoiled it by making it a stalking-horse for his sleight-of-hand—playing it too fast, in fact; then he went on to Schumann's Fantasia, which seems so hard to fathom because there is next to nothing in it; and then the way was cleared for Chopin. His playing of that great composer's studies—three of them—was by far the best thing he did. The other Chopin pieces were not specially well played; and his execution of the Liszt rhapsody at the end was by no means equal to Sophie Menter's. Still his Parisian vogue is not to be wondered at: he makes a recital as little oppressive as it is the nature of such a thing to be.

I desire to thank Mr William Stead publicly for getting out the Review of Reviews in time for the Bach Choir concert on Saturday afternoon, and so lightening for me the intolerable tedium of sitting unoccupied whilst the Bachists conscientiously maundered through Brahms's Requiem. Mind, I do not deny that the Requiem is a solid piece of music manufacture. You feel at once that it could only have come from the establishment of a first-class undertaker. But I object to requiems altogether. The Dead March in Saul is just as long as a soul in perfect health ought to meditate on the grave before turning lifewards again to a gay quickstep, as the soldiers do. A requiem overdoes it, even when there is an actual bereavement to be sympathized with; but in a concert room when there is nobody dead, it is the very wantonness of make-believe. On such occasions the earnest musician reads the Review of Reviews; and the Culture Humbug sits with his longest face, pretending to drink in that "solemn joy at the commencement of a higher life" which Mr Bennett, in the analytical program, assures him is the correct emotion for the occasion. By the bye, I must quote Mr Bennett's opening remark, as it put me into high spirits for the whole afternoon. "This Requiem" he writes "was composed in 1867 as a tribute by the composer to the memory of his mother, a sentiment which lends especial interest to the soprano solo." For boldness of syntactical ellipsis, and farfetched subtlety of psychologic association, Mr Bennett must be admitted the master of us all.

Somebody is sure to write to me now demanding "Do you mean Mozart's Requiem?" I reply, that in the few numbers—or parts of numbers—in that work which are pure Mozart, the corpse is left out. There is no shadow of death anywhere on Mozart's music. Even his own funeral was a failure. It was dispersed by a shower of rain; and to this day nobody knows where he was buried or whether he was buried at all or not. My own belief is that he was not. Depend on it, they had no sooner put up their umbrellas and bolted for the nearest shelter than he got up, shook off his bones into the common grave of the people, and soared off into universality. It is characteristic of the British middle class that whenever they write a book about Mozart, the crowning tragedy is always the dreadful thought that instead of having a respectable vault all to himself to moulder in for the edification of the British tourist, he should have been interred cheaply among the bodies of the lower classes. Was it not the Rev. H. R. Haweis who waxed quite pathetic over this lamentable miscarriage of propriety, and then called his book Music and Morals!?

However, I am not yet done with the Bach concert. It turned out that the Requiem was only a clever device of Mr Stanford's to make his setting of Tennyson's Revenge seem lively by force of contrast. But it would have needed half a dozen actual funerals to do that. I do not say that Mr Stanford could not set Tennyson's ballad as well as he set Browning's Cavalier songs, if only he did not feel that, as a professional man with a certain social position to keep up, it would be bad form to make a public display of the savage emotions called up by the poem. But as it is, Mr Stanford is far too much the gentleman to compose anything but drawing-room or classroom music. There are moments here and there in The Revenge during which one feels that a conductor of the lower orders, capable of swearing at the choir, might have got a brief rise out of them; and I will even admit that the alternating chords for the trombones which depict the sullen rocking of the huge Spanish ship do for an instant bring the scene before you; but the rest, as the mad gentleman said to Mrs Nickleby,* is gas and gaiters. It is a pity; for Mr Stanford is one of the few professors who ever had any talent to lose.

* Characters in Dickens's Nicholas Nickleby.

BASSETTO'S VALEDICTION

The Star, 16 May 1890

"We are losing, we are sorry to say, Corno di Bassetto. The larger salary of a weekly organ of the classes has proved too much for the virtue even of a Fabian, and he has abandoned us. We wish him well, and twice even the big salary that is coming to him from the bloated coffers of the organ of the aristocracy. Let us give his adieu to The Star readers, with whom he has been on terms of such pleasant intercourse, in his own words."—T.P. [O'Connor]

After the malediction, the valediction. I have now to make a ruinous, a desolating, an incredible announcement. This is the last column from the hand of Corno di Bassetto which will appear in The Star. Friday will no longer be looked forward to in a hundred thousand households as the day of the Feast of Light. The fault is not mine. I proposed long ago that not only this column, but the entire paper, political leaders and all, should be conducted on Bassettian lines, and practically dictated by me. This perfectly reasonable proposition, which would have spared the editor much thought and responsibility, he refused with such an entire blindness to its obvious advantages that I could do no less than inform him that he knew nothing about politics. It will hardly be believed that he retorted by aspersing my capacity as a musical critic. One memorable Friday, when the machines failed to keep pace with the demand for the paper, he declared that the newly-issued report of the Parnell Commission, and not my column, was the attraction. He even said that nobody ever read my articles; and I then felt that I owed it to myself to affirm that nobody ever read anything else in the paper.

At last our relations became so strained that we came to the very grave point of having to exchange assurances that we esteemed oneanother beyond all created mortals, and that no vicissitude should ever alter those feelings of devotion. Upon this brotherly basis I had no hesitation in magnanimously admitting that a daily paper requires, in the season at least, a daily and not a weekly chronicle and criticism of musical events. Such a chronicle I am unable to undertake. A man who, like myself, has to rise regularly at eleven o'clock every morning cannot sit up night after night writing opera notices piping hot from the performance. My habits, my health, and my other activities forbid it. Therefore I felt that my wisest course would be to transfer myself to a weekly paper, which I have accordingly done. I ask some indulgence for my successor, handicapped as he will be for a time by the inevitable comparison with one whom he can hardly hope to equal, much less to surpass. I say this on my own responsibility, as he has not invited me to make any such appeal on his behalf, perhaps because it is not yet settled who he is to be. Whoever he is, I hope he will never suffer the musical department of The Star to lose that pre-eminence which has distinguished it throughout the administration of Corno di Bassetto.

FAUST AND ANCIENT INSTRUMENTS

The World, 28 May 1890. This was the first of Shaw's weekly musical criticisms, contributed to The World until 4 August 1894, signed with the initials "G.B.S."

Something had better be done about this Royal Italian Opera. I have heard Gounod's Faust not less than ninety times within the last ten or fifteen years; and I have had enough of it. Here is Tristan und Isolde, which we can no longer afford to do without, now that all the errand boys in New York can whistle it from end to end: yet to hear it I have to go to Germany—to cross that unquiet North Sea, the very thought of which sets my entrails aquake. Tristan is more than thirty years old; and as the composer died in 1883, at the age of seventy, I am sanguine as to the possibility of driving Mr Harris to produce it presently as "Wagner's new opera." It pays to pitch into a man like Mr Harris: the stirrings of the new time have got into him: there is enterprise in his profile: only hit him hard enough, and you will fetch him out of the Donizettian dark ages as you never could have fetched Gye or Mapleson, whose benightedness left him with half a century of leeway to make up. (I know that this metaphor is mixed, and I dont care: it is as well to come to an early understanding on these points.) Mind, I do not say that Gounod's Faust, &c., is not to be kept on the stage. The rights of the younger generation include access, and frequent access, to Faust; but I protest against the inhumanity of selecting it to introduce new *prima donnas*, since on such occasions the critics have to attend; and what critic has not long ago exhausted the interest of Jean de Reszke's Faust, Madame Scalchi's Siebel, Brother Edouard's Mephistopheles, and the soldiers' chorus as performed by the Augustan Household troops, horse and foot, from Drury Lane? However, the thing is done now; and I have sat Faust out again. The house was in a bad temper, Brother Edouard having cried off on account of sudden indisposition, and his place being taken by M. Orme Darvall. If this unfortunate gentleman had sung like an angel, the gallery would have borne him a grudge for supplanting their beloved *basso cantante*; but as he entered into his part to the extent of singing quite in the contrary manner, pressing every note hard on the grindstone, and trying to make *Dio dell' or* go by sheer violence, with the natural result that he was inhumanly hissed, and did not recover his voice for an act and a half afterwards; as, furthermore, he went out by the wrong doors, and got into difficulties with his sword, which came off just before he wanted it in the Kermesse scene; as, by way of climax, he finished the church scene in an attitude under the curtain, to an improvized choral episode of "Look out, there!" "Mind your head, sir!" &c., from the flies, I am afraid it would be useless to pretend that M. Darvall was not a failure.

Before reproaching him for having thus thrown away an enviable chance, mainly by subordinating his commonsense to his artistic ambition, I must confess with a blush that the critics are much to blame in the matter. If we had not set a silly fashion years ago—in Faure's day—of writing up Barbier and Carré's stage fiend as an acting part of all but unfathomable profundity, we should not now be plagued with the puerile inanities of baritones with impossible eyebrows, who spend the evening in a red limelight and an ecstasy of sardonic smiling.

Mlle Nuovina, the newest Margaret, did not promise well at first. To begin with, she wore her own black hair. There was no suggestion of *naïveté* in her manner: her very self-possession jarred with our notions of Gretchen. Besides, her voice, for Covent Garden, lacks amplitude: in the broader concerted passages she was shrill and unsteady. Nevertheless, she ended by conquering a safe position for herself. Artists are always indignant if you call them useful; otherwise I should congratulate her on having established herself in the front rank of thoroughly useful dramatic sopranos. Her voice, instead of having, as usual, no middle and a few screams at the top, is sound and pure, if a little thin, all over; whilst her vocal touch is light, and managed with intelligence and discretion. She has dramatic intelligence, too, and is

[73]

never for a moment out of her part, or at a loss for appropriate business. For love of a heavenly piece of music she sang the last *trio* right through without sparing herself according to custom by shirking the full repetition in B natural. Finally, she shews none of the operatic bumptiousness of our modern American and cornstalk *prima donnas*.

Brother Jean's voice is better than it was last year. He sang *Salve dimora* very finely indeed; and when the audience, foolishly disappointed at his not taking the high C from his chest, hesitated a moment at the end, he gave them to understand, gracefully but firmly, that he had done his duty, and now expected them to do theirs. Whereupon, abashed, they gave him a salvo of prolonged and reverent applause. Brother Jean is still vaguely romantic rather than intelligent in his acting. The only part in Faust I ever saw him act reasonably was Valentin; but that, of course, was in his baritone days. D'Andrade falls very short of him in the part. In an opera company, d'Andrade passes for a good actor because he always makes it plain that he knows what the opera is about; but when this intellectual triumph becomes a little more common, he will find his place hard to hold. Would any really fine actor sing *Dio possente*—that tremblingly earnest prayer of a simple-minded young soldier—with the air of a man obstreperously confident that no difficulty could be made over any application from a baritone hallmarked with the unreticent throatiness familiar to the patrons of the Paris Opéra?

Valero, the new tenor from Madrid, made his first appearance on Tuesday in Carmen with Miss de Lussan. As he is a finished exponent of the Gayarré style of singing, which I maintain to be nothing but bleating invested with artistic merit (though I admit the right of anybody to prefer it to the round pure tone and unforced production without which no singing is beautiful to my ears), I should probably have had nothing good to say of him had he not disarmed me by acting throughout with unexpected willingness, vivacity, and actually with a sense of humor. My heart retained the hardness set up by his vocal method until Carmen began singing the *seguidilla* at him, when he licked the finger and thumb with which he was putting on his glove (to shew his indifference to the siren, poor wretch!), and gave a little toss of his head and knock of his knee that there was no resisting. A man who makes me laugh by a legitimate stroke of art charms all the criticism out of me; and I confess to having enjoyed Valero's Don José as well as any that I have seen, although he is too transparently amiable and social to seriously impersonate Mérimée's morbidly jealous and diffident dragoon.

Miss de Lussan shews remarkable cleverness as Carmen; but Carmen is degenerating into a male Mephistopheles. Every respectable young American lady longs to put on the Spanish jacket and play at being an abandoned person, just as the harmless basso craves to mount the scarlet cock's feather and say to himself, like Barnaby Rudge's raven "I'm a devil, I'm a devil, I'm a devil!" Miss de Lussan is no more like Carmen than her natty stockings are like those "with more than one hole in them" described by Mérimée. Perhaps, as Charles Lamb's ghost may think,★ stage Carmens are only delightful when and because everybody can see that they are pure make-believe. But I am not a Lambite in this matter. I miss the tragic background of ungovernable passion and superstitious fatalism to the levity and insolent waywardness which Miss de Lussan makes so much of. The truth is, she cannot act the tavern scene, nor sing the prophetic episode in the fortune-telling *trio*, to anything near conviction point.

★ In Lamb's essay My First Play (Essays of Elia, 1823).

The loan collection of portable wind instruments at the Military exhibition is worth a visit, though it is exasperating to have to study them as a professor of harmony studies classical music—with one's eyes. It is all very well to hang a facsimile of a veritable buccina (found in Pompeii) on the wall for my inspection; but I had as soon inspect a gaspipe—what I want is to hear it. Richter, for whose entertainment the original was blown at Brussels, declares that it sounds like four trombones rolled into one. Such a description makes my ears water; for I love an apocalyptic trumpet blast.* From the buccina up to the sarrussophone and the latest brass counterbassoon of Mahillon,† nothing, as far as I can recollect, is wanting. Those who have pestered me of late with the question "What on earth is a corno di bassetto?" I can now refer to this loan collection, where there are plenty to be seen. The giant bassoon made for Handel is only one of several curious monsters in the collection. Distin's‡ amazing tenor saxhorn would make a capital electrolier if an incandescent light were placed in each of its seven bells.

The old *flauti d' amore* and *oboi di caccia* will interest Bach students; but I do not want to hear the big *flûtes-à-bec*. I have heard them already, and can certify that their tone, though quaint, is abjectly feeble, whilst their intonation I must really be allowed to describe as damnable. The new instruments are wonderful; but where are the performers to come from? At the concerts of the Royal College of Music, the wind instruments

* Shaw subsequently employed the instrument in his play Cæsar and Cleopatra, written in 1898.

† Charles Victor Mahillon was an author, editor and wind-instrument manufacturer.

‡ Firm of musical-instrument sellers, which commissioned instruments from the French firm of Antoine Sax. It later was absorbed by Boosey and Company.

have to be taken for the most part by professional players; and even in the profession the state of things is such that, by simply assassinating less than a dozen men, I could leave London without a single orchestral wind instrument player of the first rank. I was studying the woodwind during those delicate *entr'actes* in Carmen the other night; and with the exception of an occasional touch from Mr John Radcliffe, I did not hear a single phrase that surpassed in elegance or individuality the playing that Mr Maskelyne★ gets from his automata. Imagine a city with five million inhabitants and only one satisfactory bassoon player!

I was not able to get to the Grosvenor Club on the ladies' night in time to hear Sapellnikoff play; and there is nothing fresh to be said about the *salon* performances of Johannes Wolff and Hollmann. The worst of it is that the extreme smartness of these functions leaves the audience entirely preoccupied with their consciousness of being immensely in it; so that the artists, hampered and distraught by the incessant chattering and rustling, do not settle down to any sort of serious work. One irascible *virtuoso* was driven to astonish an incorrigible group of talkers by a fierce "Sh-sh-sh-h-h-h-h!" in the middle of his piece and of their conversation.

Paderewski, like the Philharmonic, must excuse me until next week, when I shall have a legion of pianists to deal with.

★ John N. Maskelyne was a flamboyant English illusionist, whose Home of Magic had since 1873 been a fixture in the Egyptian Hall.

TROVATORE AND THE HUGUENOTS

The World, 4 June 1890

Last week I mildly suggested that the usual combination of a new *prima donna* with an old opera was a little hard on the critics. The words were still wet from the pen when I received a stall for Madame Tetrazzini's first appearance as Leonora in Il Trovatore. Now a subscription night Trovatore is a dreadful thing. This is not an explosion of Wagnerian prejudice. I know my Trovatore thoroughly, from the first drum-roll to the final chord of E flat minor, and can assert that it is a heroic work, capable of producing a tremendous effect if heroically performed. But anything short of this means vulgarity, triviality, tediousness, and failure; for there is nothing unheroic to fall back on—no comedy, no spectacle, no symphonic instrumental commentary, no relief to the painful flood of feeling surging up repeatedly to the most furious intensity of passion; nothing but love—elemental love of cub for dam and male for female—with hate, jealousy, terror, and the shadow of death throughout. The artists must have immense vital energy, and a good deal of Salvini's skill in leading up to and producing a convincing illusion of terrible violence and impetuosity, without wrecking themselves or becoming ridiculous. At no point can the stage manager come to the rescue if the artists fail. Mr Harris has secured the success of Les Huguenots, Faust, Die Meistersinger, and William Tell by drill and equipment, costume and scenery; but for Il Trovatore he can do nothing but pay band, conductor, and principals, let them loose on the work in his theatre, and sit looking at them, helpless. Unless, indeed, he were to go down next day and read out the unfavorable press notices to them, emphasizing the criticism with the homely eloquence of which he is a master.

On Saturday week Trovatore was bâtoned by Bevignani, concerning whom some of my fresher colleagues came out last winter (in dealing with the Promenade Concerts at Her Majesty's) with the goodnatured and entirely novel idea that he is a superb conductor—rather an important secret to have kept itself for twenty years if there is really anything very serious in it. The conductor at Covent Garden ought to be nothing less than the greatest in the world; and the truth is that Mr Harris's three conductors, with all their considerable merits, would not, if rolled into one, make a Richter or a Faccio. Therefore I am not going to trifle with an old and sincerely respected public acquaintance by joining in the latest chorus of "Good old Bevignani." I shall even venture to ask him why he takes an impulsive *allegro* like *Mal reggendo* at an easy *andante*, and whether he really thinks Verdi meant *Perigliarti ancor* as an *allegretto* when he marked it *velocissimo?* But worse things than these befell Verdi. The young bloods of the string band, nursed on the polyphony of Wagner and Brahms, treated the unfortunate Trovatore as mere banjo work. They relieved the tedium of their task by occasional harmless bursts of mock enthusiasm, usually ending in a smothered laugh and a relapse into weariness, until they came to the hundred and forty bars, or thereabouts, of slow and sentimental *pizzicato* to the tune of *Si la stanchezza* in the prison scene. This proved too much for their sense of duty. Languishing over their fiddles, they infused a subtle ridicule into their toneless "pluck-pluck, pluck-pluck" that got the better of my indignation. It was impossible to help laughing. But why had not Bevignani shewed these young gentlemen that there is room for their finest touch and most artistic phrasing in Verdi's apparently simple figures of accompaniment, and that a band which cannot play a simple prelude of nine common chords with even the prosaic virtue of simultaneous attack, much less with the depth and richness of tone upon which the whole effect depends, is not in a position to turn up its nose at Italian opera, or any other style of instrumental composition? As for the poor silly public, it yawned and looked at its watch, quite ready to vote Verdi empty, stale, and played out, but incapable of suspecting perfunctoriness and tomfoolery in a precinct where evening dress is indispensable.

As to the singing, there was a tenor who was compendiously announced as "Signor Rawner, who has created so great a sensation in Italy," and who is undoubtedly capable of making an indelible mark anywhere. I listened expectantly for *Deserto sulla terra*, knowing that if the sensationist were a fine artist, his interpretation of its musical character would surround it with illusion, making it come from among the trees in the moonlight, soft, distant, melancholy, haunting; wheras, if he were the common or Saffron Hill Manrico, he would at once display his quality by a stentorian performance in the wing, putting all his muscle and wind into a final B flat (substituted for G), and storming London with that one wrong note alone. My suspense was short. Signor Rawner, knowing nothing about the musical character of the serenade, but feeling quite sure about the B flat, staked his all on it; and a stupendous yell it was. It is said that he can sing D; and though he mercifully refrained from actually doing so, I have not myself the smallest doubt that he could sing high F in the same fashion if he only tried hard enough. As may be inferred, I do not like Signor Rawner, in spite of the sensation he has created in Italy: therefore let me not do him the injustice of pushing my criticism into further detail. Madame Tetrazzini, with her tip-tilted nose, her pretty mouth, her ecstatic eyes, her delicately gushing style, and the intense gratitude of her curtsy whenever she brought down the house, did very well as Leonora, though I would suggest to her that *D'amor sull' ali rosee* might have been encored had she chosen her breathing places with some regard for the phrasing, and either restored Verdi's *cadenza*, or at least omitted that flagrant pianoforte sequence (G, B, A, G, &c.) from the one she substituted.

As Valentine in The Huguenots she did not improve on her first attempt. Her Italian *tremolo* and stage hysteria were so intensified that but few of her notes had any definite pitch; whilst her playing was monotonously lachrymose from end to end. When she sings in the manner of a light soprano, and so steadies her voice for a moment, everybody is pleased; but when she becomes "dramatic" the charm vanishes. And yet you cannot get these Italian ladies to believe this. The more we shew by our encouragement of Miss Nordica, Miss Russell, and Miss Macintyre, and by our idolatry of Madame Patti with her eternal Home, Sweet Home, that our whole craving is for purity of tone and unwavering accuracy of pitch, the more our operatic visitors insist on desperately trying to captivate us by paroxysms of wobbling. Remonstrance, in English at least, is thrown away on them. For example, although Ravelli, who appeared as Elvino on Thursday, is no Rubini, yet the delight of the house at escaping from the detested *tremolo*, and hearing some straightforward, manly singing, was so extravagant, that he was recalled uproariously three times.

Miss Russell's Violetta, a part in which the *tremolo* rages throughout Europe worse than the influenza, is a triumph of good singing. Hard as it is to drag me to Covent Garden oftener than my bare duty requires, I would go again to hear her sing *Parigi, o cara* as she sang it on Saturday last. Madame Fursch-Madi has not Miss Russell's youth and beauty, but she never wobbles and never fails. The idolized De Reszkes sing like dignified men, not like male viragos. But do you suppose that Madame Tetrazzini or Signor Rawner will take the hint, or that Dufriche, the St Bris of Tuesday week, will cease to discount the beautiful quality of his voice by a laborious *vibrato*? Not a bit of it: they will only wonder at the simplicity of our insular taste, and modestly persist in trying to teach us better.

The Huguenots, admirably rehearsed, goes without a hitch. Ybos, another new tenor, with a much better forehead and brow (to put the point as delicately as possible) than the usual successor to Mario, appeared as Raoul; and though he did not attempt the C sharp in the duel septet, any more than Madame Tetrazzini ventured on the chromatic run through two octaves in the fourth act, he came off with honor, in spite of the shyness which hampered his acting. In the absence of a first-rate *basso profundo*, Edouard de Reszke was forced to repeat the double mistake of relinquishing the part of St Bris, which fits him to a semitone, and taking that of Marcel, which lies too low for him. He has to alter the end of the chorale, and to produce the effect of rugged strength by an open brawling tone which quite fails to contrast with the other bass and baritone voices as Meyerbeer intended. D'Andrade, too, whose voice is only effective (I had almost said only tolerable) when he is singing energetically between his upper B flat and G, repeatedly transposes passages an octave up, quite ruining the variety and eloquence of Never's declamation in the conspiracy scene. It is hardly necessary to add that every artist brought his or her own *cadenza*; but as none of them were quite so accomplished as Meyerbeer in this sort of composition, they only spoiled the effect they might have produced by sticking to the text. All these drawbacks notwithstanding, the performance reached a high degree of excellence; and the instrumental score was played (under Bevignani) with great spirit and accuracy.

Madame Gerster has grown mightily since June 1877. Her columnar neck and massive arms are now those of Brynhild rather than Amina; and I am afraid that her acting, though it was touchingly good, did not reconcile the Philistines to the incongruity. I see, too, that the comparative ineffectiveness of her *Ah! non giunge*, and a certain want of ringing quality in her extreme upper notes, are being cited as results of the loss of voice which placed her for awhile in the position of George Eliot's Armgart.★ But the *Ah! non giunge* fell equally flat in 1877; and her Astrifiammante in that year shewed exactly the same want of the delicate tintinnabulation which was so enchanting in Di Murska's singing of *Gli angui d' inferno*. I could detect no falling off that the lapse of fourteen years does not account for; and the old artistic feeling remained so unspoiled and vivid, that if here and there a doubt crossed me whether the notes were all reaching the furthest half-crown seat as tellingly as they came to my front stall, I ignored it for the sake of the charm which neither singer nor opera has lost for me.

The pre-eminent claims of Covent Garden again compel me to leave the concerts aside for the moment; but next week St James's Hall and its legion pianists shall have their due without fail.

P.S. [1932] Eva Tetrazzini, criticized above, must not be confused with her more famous sister Luisa.

★ *Prima donna* in a poem entitled Armgart (1871); in The Legend of Jubal, and Other Poems (1874).

A MOZART CONTROVERSY

The World, 11 June 1890

I see that the Bishop of Ripon's description of Mozart as "first in music" has been too much for Mr Labouchère,* who intimates that it is quite enough to have to admit the pre-eminence of Shakespear in drama, and to leave uncontradicted the compliment paid by the Bishop in the department of morals. I do not blame Mr Labouchère for rushing to the conclusion that the Bishop was wrong; for Bishops generally are wrong, just as Judges are always wrong. Such is the violence of anti-prelatic prejudice in me (for the Bishop never harmed me, and may be, for what I know, a most earnest and accomplished musician), that though I happen to agree with him in the present instance, yet I take his declaration rather as a belated conventional remark surviving from the Mozart mania of the first quarter of the century, than as expressing an original conviction. The mania was followed, like other manias, by a reaction, through which we have been living, and which will be succeeded next century by a reaction against Wagner. This sort of thing happens to all great men.

I once possessed an edition of Shakespear with a preface by that portentous dullard Rowe, wherein Nicholas apologized for William as for a *naïve* ignoramus who, "by a mere light of nature," had hit out a few accidental samples of what he might have done had he enjoyed the educational advantages of the author of Jane Shore. I kept Rowe for a long time as a curiosity; but

* Henry Labouchère, Liberal M.P. and political leader, was the founder and editor of the journal Truth.

when I found a fashion setting in of talking about Mozart as a vapidly tuneful infant phenomenon, I felt that Rowe was outdone, and so let him drop into the dustbin. Of course all the men of Rowe's time who knew chalk from cheese in dramatic poetry understood Shakespear's true position well enough, just as Wagner understood Mozart's, and laughed at the small fry who quite believed that Schumann and Brahms—not to mention Beethoven—had left Mozart far behind. For my part, I should not like to call Schumann a sentimental trifler and Brahms a pretentious blockhead; but if the average man was a Mozart, that is how they would be generally described.

Unfortunately, Mozart's music is not everybody's affair when it comes to conducting it. His scores do not play themselves by their own physical weight, as many heavy modern scores do. When a sense of duty occasionally urges Mr Manns or the Philharmonic to put the G minor or the E flat or the Jupiter Symphony in the bill, the band, seeing nothing before them but easy diatonic scale passages and cadences smoothly turned on dominant discords, races through with the general effect of a couple of Brixton schoolgirls playing one of Diabelli's pianoforte duets. The audience fidgets during the *allegro*; yawns desperately through the *andante*; wakes up for a moment at the minuet, finding the trio rather pretty; sustains itself during the *finale* by looking forward to the end; and finishes by taking Mr Labouchère's side against the Bishop of Ripon, and voting me stark mad when I speak of Mozart as the peer of Bach and Wagner, and, in his highest achievements, the manifest superior of Beethoven.

I remember going one night to a Richter concert, at which an overture or prelude to nothing in particular, composed in a moment of jejune Wagner-worship by Mr Eugene d'Albert, was supposed to be the special

[85]

event. But it was preceded, to its utter ruin, by the E flat Symphony; and that was the first time, as far as I know, that any living Londoner of reasonable age was reached by the true Mozart enchantment. It was an exploit that shewed Richter to be a master of his art as no Valkyrie ride or fire charm could have done. And yet he has been kept mainly at the exciting obviousnesses of the Valkyrie ride and the fire charm ever since, with Beethoven's seventh symphony for the hundredth time by special request for a wind-up to them.

Last week, however, came the announcement that the Richter concert would end with Mozart's Symphony in C—not the Jupiter, but that known as No. 6. I left the Opera to hear it, and was fortunate enough to arrive just in time to catch the symphony, and to miss an attempt to give the thundering Gibichung chorus from the Götterdämmerung with a handful of feeble gentlemen, whose native woodnotes wild must have been cut to ribbons by the orchestra. The performance of the symphony was a repetition of Richter's old triumph. The slow movement and the *finale* were magnificent: the middle section of the latter, which I confess had quite taken me in by its innocent look on paper, astonished me by its majesty, and by a combination of vivacity with grandeur.

I must add, by the bye, that the opera I left for the Symphony was Don Giovanni, as conducted by Signor Randegger. My compliments to that gentleman, with my heartfelt assurance that a more scandalously slovenly, slapdash, and unintelligent performance of the orchestral part of a great work was probably never heard in a leading—it should be, and shall yet be, *the* leading—European opera house. I hope the recording angel has put down to Signor Randegger, and not to me, the imprecations which the murder of that incomparable overture wrung from me. The other masterpiece of the

Covent Garden repertory, Die Meistersinger, is the triumph of the season. Although dozens of details are neglected—although Lassalle still plays Sachs with the gestures of Benvenuto Cellini—although the cuts necessary to fit the performance in between half-past seven and half-past twelve are mighty ones and millions, yet the work is such a wonder and a treasure of everything lovely and happy in music that it is impossible to grumble. The chance of hearing such a Walther as Jean de Reszke with such a Sachs as Lassalle (they both surpass themselves in singing the two parts) ought to set on foot a Wagnerian pilgrimage to London from the ends of Europe. Tavary, the new *prima donna*, is a hardworking and very capable German lady, a second-rate Donna Anna, but a satisfactory Eva, as far as singing and acting go.

Mr Kuhe's concert at the Albert Hall proved that Madame Albani cannot fill the Albert Hall as Patti can. The reason, I take it, is that the public only care for Madame Albani's voice as an instrument to make their favorite music for them; wheras Madame Albani, apparently, is only interested in music insomuch as it happens to be a means of displaying her voice. Certainly it is a very remarkable voice: the soaring of the upper notes is as wonderful as ever; the once faulty middle has been rounded and brought under control; the art of the singer has reached the limit of her capacity for art. But all this, instructive as it is to the singing master, does not concern the public. If the net result for them is that *Ah, fors' è lui*, as sung by Madame Albani, is a bore—and a bore it certainly was at the Albert Hall—then no mere vocal virtuosity, however seconded by the thousand little raptures, the wafted kisses, the effusions and unbosomings of the popular favorite, will avail one single *encore*.

Madame Trebelli's reappearance in so huge a hall was

ill-advised. Those who try to persuade her that she is as good as ever shew how little they understood or appreciated her former excellence. She herself is misled, possibly, by her consciousness that the voice is there still, as well as the artistic subtlety that enabled her to use it to such good purpose. But the muscular control of the vocal machinery is impaired, and the days of *C'est l'Espagne* and *Il Segreto* are past. Even in her prime, Handel and Mozart were better friends to her than Donizetti and Offenbach.

Mr Sims Reeves appeared, and attacked The Message with mingled guile and gallantry, though it was rather the guile that got him safely to the end. In spite of all his husbandry, he has but few notes left now; yet the wonderfully telling effect and unique quality of these few still justify him as the one English singer who has worked in his own way, and at all costs, to attain and preserve ideal perfection of tone.

The fact that Stavenhagen played a concerto of Liszt's at this concert reminds me of all the pianists I have neglected. There is Paderewski, a man of various moods, who was alert, humorous, delightful at his first recital; sensational, empty, vulgar, and violent at his second; and dignified, intelligent, almost sympathetic, at his third. He is always sure of his notes; but the license of his *tempo rubato* goes beyond all reasonable limits. Sapellnikoff is never at fault in this or any other way in the domain of absolute music; but when the music begins to speak, his lack of eloquence is all the more startling. In such phrases as that which opens Chopin's Fantasia in F minor, or the first subject of the Appassionata, or the Pilgrims' Chorus in the Tannhäuser overture, he demonstrated how completely musical faculty may be divorced from dramatic sense. But his playing of the Polonaise in A flat was stupendous: the room woke up amazed, and recalled him again and again. Stavenhagen, on the whole, is the finest, most serious artist of them all: there is much less curiosity and more esteem and affection in the attachment of his audiences (not to mention that they are larger) than the others have attained or deserved. Of course there is the inimitable Sophie Menter, with the airs of an invalid and the vigor of a Valkyrie, knocking the breath out of poor Schumann at the Crystal Palace, laughing Weber's delicate romance out of countenance at the Philharmonic, playing everything like lightning, and finishing always with a fabulously executed Liszt rhapsody for which all her sins are at once forgiven her. Madame Teresa Carreño is a second Arabella Goddard: she can play anything for you; but she has nothing of her own to tell you about it. Playing is her superb accomplishment, not her mission. A newcomer, Pierre-René Hirsch, is clever and skilful; but he is not in the front rank, and will probably be better known in the *salons* than by the public if he settles in London. Clotilde Kleeberg, now recitalling at Prince's Hall, and Bertha Marx, again in her old place at Sarasate's Saturday afternoon concerts in St James's Hall, are as dexterous as ever. Buonamici, who played Beethoven's E flat concerto at the last Philharmonic, is a neat and finished executant, hardly as interesting, perhaps, as Albéniz, at whose recital on Saturday I was much scandalized on hearing the original version of Weber's Invitation replaced by that impertinent paraphrase of Tausig's, which I thought London had outgrown these many years. The Philharmonic directors, by the bye, have again attempted to float Moszkowski here as a serious composer. He landed them this time by a monstrous orchestral fugue—a sort of composite phonograph of all the fugues that ever were written, with the *point d'orgue* literally given to that instrument. The concert was otherwise worthy of the Society.

A LEGION OF PIANISTS
The World, 18 June 1890

By the time I reached Paderewski's concert on Tuesday last week, his concerto was over, the audience in wild enthusiasm, and the pianoforte a wreck. Regarded as an immensely spirited young harmonious blacksmith, who puts a concerto on the piano as upon an anvil, and hammers it out with an exuberant enjoyment of the swing and strength of the proceeding, Paderewski is at least exhilarating; and his hammer-play is not without variety, some of it being feathery, if not delicate. But his touch, light or heavy, is the touch that hurts; and the glory of his playing is the glory that attends murder on a large scale when impetuously done. Besides, the piano is not an instrument upon which you can safely let yourself go in this fashion.

Sophie Menter produces an effect of magnificence which leaves Paderewski far behind; but she balances the powerful bass of the instrument against the comparatively weak treble so as to produce a perfectly rich, full, and even body of sound, whilst with Paderewski the bass and middle elbow the treble into the corner in a brutal fantasia on the theme of the survival of the fittest. Again, Madame Menter seems to play with splendid swiftness, yet she never plays faster than the ear can follow, as many players can and do: it is the distinctness of attack and intention given to each note that makes her execution so irresistibly impetuous. At her recital she pleaded a broken fingernail, from which inflammation had set in. But had it been possible to believe that those *glissandos* in the Strauss-Tausig waltz were played with a really bad nail, I should have flinched and fled. As usual, the Soirées de Vienne* were superb, and the Beethoven sonata hardly recognizable. Beethoven defies her Austrian temperament.

At the Richter concert Berlioz's Carnaval Romain overture really came off. I am afraid the public is under the impression that performances of this sort come off every time they are put in the bill; but an expert can usually count on the fingers of one hand the number of performances at which he has felt that the composer would not have been more or less baulked and disappointed. At this very concert, for instance, the Egmont overture was heavy and forced, as it often is when placed first on the program. It was followed by the two great successes of the evening—the Good Friday music from Parsifal, the enchantments of which pass all sane word-painting, and the Carnaval, which slipped into the right vein after the first hundred bars or so, and finished to a miracle.

The Valkyrie Ride, which came next, excited the audience furiously; but it also made a lady on the orchestra put her fingers into her ears. The lady was quite right. The Valkyrie Ride requires above all things fine trombone-playing—such playing, for instance, as Mr Manns seldom fails to get at the Crystal Palace from Messrs Hadfield, Geard, and Phasey, who generally contrive to stop short of that brain-splitting bark which detaches itself from the rest of the orchestra, asserting itself rowdily and intrusively in your ear, preventing you from hearing the music, and making you wonder, if you accept the hideous din as inevitable, how Berlioz could ever call such an ignobly noisy instrument "Olympian." No matter how many *fortissimo* marks the composer writes, there is no use in forcing the tone of the trombone, unless, indeed, you are to be intentionally

* Liszt's Valses-caprices d'après Schubert, Op. 72.

hellish, as in Liszt's Inferno. But if you want to be majestic, as in the Valkyrie Ride and the Francs-Juges overture, then it is not to be done by bawling like a mob orator who does not know his business. Why Richter permits forcing, and even encourages it, not only in the Valkyrie Ride but in the first movement of the Tannhäuser overture, can only be explained as the result of his share of original sin. It is not that his players cannot do better: they are always dignified in the Valhalla motif in the Nibelungen music.

I once heard Herr Müller, Richter's first trombone, play the *"oraison"* in Berlioz's Sinfonie Funèbre et Triomphale very finely. But on Monday week the only tolerable brazen sound in the piece came from the other side of the orchestra, where Mr Geard was playing the bass trumpet part on an alto trombone. During the few bars in which the theme was left to him the lady did not keep her fingers in her ears; and the volume of sound from the orchestra was greater instead of less than when his colleagues were blaring away, because the accompaniment could be heard through his transparent and musical tone, wheras the others drowned everything else with their distracting rattle. I am not squeamish about the quantity of sound that comes from an orchestra: the more thundering its *fortissimo*, the better I like it. I delight, for example, in Richter's tremendous handling of the Rienzi overture. But I am fastidious as to the quality of the tone, however voluminous it may be; and, frankly, the Valkyrie Ride might as well be conducted by Buffalo Bill as by Richter, if some regard is not paid to the artistic spirit, if not to the snobbish expression, of Sterndale Bennett's remark about treating trombone players as gentlemen. I am aware of the full horror of recommending to Richter a precept by the Mendelssohnian Sterndale Bennett; but I cannot help that: much as I respect Richter, and appreciate the relief he brought us thirteen years ago in the midst of a dire music famine, I am not going to be tromboned out of my senses for him or any conductor alive when the remedy is so easy.

My temper was not improved by Brahms's Symphony in E minor, though I have no fault to find with the execution of it. Euphuism, which is the beginning and end of Brahms's big works, is no more to my taste in music than in literature. Brahms takes an essentially commonplace theme; gives it a strange air by dressing it in the most elaborate and farfetched harmonies; keeps his countenance severely (which at once convinces an English audience that he must have a great deal in him); and finds that a good many wiseacres are ready to guarantee him as deep as Wagner, and the true heir of Beethoven. The spectacle of the British public listening with its in-churchiest expression to one of the long and heavy fantasias which he calls his symphonies always reminds me of the yokel in As You Like It quailing before the big words of the fool. Strip off the euphuism from these symphonies, and you will find a string of incomplete dance and ballad tunes, following one another with no more organic coherence than the succession of passing images reflected in a shop window in Piccadilly during any twenty minutes in the day. That is why Brahms is so enjoyable when he merely tries to be pleasant or naïvely sentimental, and so insufferably tedious when he tries to be profound. His symphonies are endured at the Richter concerts as sermons are endured, and his Requiem is patiently borne only by the corpse; but Mr Orton Bradley, who gave a Brahms concert the other day at Steinway Hall, "his custom always of an afternoon" in the season, was able to entertain us happily enough by reverently letting alone the more ponderous nothings of his favorite composer.

Pianoforte-playing is becoming an accomplishment

most hateful to me. Death is better than eighteen recitals per week. I got only a glimpse of Madame Roger-Miclos, playing in her cold, hard, swift style on one of those wonderful steel dulcimers made by Pleyel. Then off to Steinway Hall to hear the opposite pole of the Pleyel instrument under the fingers of Mr Friedheim (now transformed from a wild-looking German student to a staid professor) and Mrs Friedheim. Also a young Polander named Leopold Godowsky, pupil of Saint-Saëns, who amazed us by substituting Beethoven's theme with the thirty-two variations for the first movement of the Appassionata, in which he proved a brilliant and all too rapid executant, but a frankly twenty-year-old interpreter of Beethoven, about whom, as might be expected, he has not learnt much from the composer of Ascanio. He next tried Schumann; and though the difficulties of the Etudes Symphoniques seemed to give him no trouble, a certain shyness, rather engaging than otherwise, prevented him from standing on his merits emphatically enough to get full credit for his performance. By this time, however, the audience had come decidedly to like him; and when he got on to Chopin, with whom his musical instinct and natural grace of expression had their way unembarrassed, his battle was won. I left him playing some excellent little *salon* pieces of his own in triumph, he and his audience on the best of terms.

The violinists are gathering to share the spoils of us with the pianists. Sarasate, less high-spirited than he was at that golden age which his only competitor, Ysaÿe, has just reached, but perfect as ever, is playing at St James's Hall on Saturdays. Ysaÿe is announced for the next Philharmonic (on the 28th); and as these two are now the greatest fiddlers in the world, as far as we know, it will be well for novices to hear them at once, instead of waiting for ten or twenty years, and supposing that because the men are still there and their reputations undiminished, their powers must be in equally satisfactory preservation. And this reminds me, by an association of ideas which experts will find no difficulty in tracing, of a young pupil of Joachim's, named Felix Berber, who gave a concert on Thursday at which Sapellnikoff repeated his amazing performance of Chopin's Poloniaise in A flat, the middle episode in which comes from his puissant hands like an avalanche. Felix Berber is a very remarkable executant; but he has succumbed so completely to Joachim as to have actually caught his intonation, which unfortunately means that in *bravura* passages every note is out of tune except the keynote. My advice to Herr Berber is: "Get another fiddle; and call no man master." I know the gratitude and devotion with which Joachim inspires his pupils; but gratitude never made anybody an artist yet; and a violinist needs all the artistic devotion of which he is capable for himself. Johannes Wolff is now to be heard in all directions, playing difficult pieces as if they were easy, and easy pieces (Raff's cavatina and the like) as if they were immensely important and difficult; but always coming off with distinction.

At the Opera, Madame Melba has appeared as Elsa, singing with great skill, but playing artificially and without the sensibility that the part requires. De Reszke's Lohengrin ought not to be missed, as the chances are heavily against any of us hearing a better if we put the matter off. The Favorita on Friday was terribly dreary. Mlle Richard sings perfectly in tune, avoids the *tremolo*, and has a mezzo-soprano voice of fair power and quality; but her old-fashioned operatic stage business is not acting, and her personal likeness to Titiens involves a quite conclusive unlikeness to La Favorita as fancy paints her.

ORATORIOS AND SHAMS

The World, 25 June 1890

I have been getting my mind improved at the Crystal Palace. Naturally that was not what I went for. My sole object in submitting to the unspeakable boredom of listening to St Paul on Saturday afternoon was to gain an opening for an assault on the waste of our artistic resources—slender enough, in all conscience, even with the strictest economy—caused in England every year by the performance and publication of sham religious works called oratorios. Insofar as these are not dull imitations of Handel, they are unstaged operettas on scriptural themes, written in a style in which solemnity and triviality are blended in the right proportions for boring an atheist out of his senses or shocking a sincerely religious person into utter repudiation of any possible union between art and religion. However, there is an intermediate class in England which keeps up the demand in the oratorio market. This class holds that the devil is not respectable (a most unsophisticated idea); but it deals with him in a spirit of extraordinary liberality in dividing with him the kingdom of the fine arts. Thus in literature it gives him all the novels, and is content to keep nothing but the tracts. In music it gives him everything that is played in a theatre, reserving the vapidities of the drawing room and the solemnities of the cathedral for itself. It asks no more in graphic art than a set of illustrations to its family Bible, cheerfully devoting all other subjects to the fiend. But people who make a bad bargain never stick to it. These ascetics smuggle fiction under the covers of the Society for the dissemination of their own particular sort of knowledge;

drama in the guise of "entertainments"; opera in scores labelled "cantata" or "oratorio"; and Venus and Apollo catalogued as Eve and Adam. They will not open a novel of Boisgobey's,* because novels are sinful; but they will read with zest and gloating how The Converted Collier used to beat his mother in the days when he was an unregenerate limb of Satan. They console themselves for Coquelin by Corney Grain; and, since they may not go to Macbeth at the Lyceum, they induce Mr Irving to dress the Thane in a frock-coat and trousers, and transport him, Sullivan, Miss Terry, and all, to St James's Hall. It is just the same with music. It is wrong to hear the Covent Garden orchestra play Le Sommeil de Juliette; but if Gounod writes just such another interlude, and calls it The Sleep of the Saints before the Last Judgment, then nothing can be more proper than to listen to it in the Albert Hall. Not that Gounod is first favorite with the Puritans. If they went to the theatre they would prefer a melodramatic opera with plenty of blood in it. That being out of the question, they substitute an oratorio with plenty of damnation. The Count di Luna, grinding his teeth and longing to *centuplicar la morte* of his rival with *mille atroci spasimi*, is a comparatively tame creature until he takes off his tunic and tights, hies to a "festival," and, in respectable evening dress, shouts that "the Lord is angry with the wicked every day," and that "if the wicked [meaning the people who go to the Opera] turn not, the Lord will whet His sword and bend His bow." What a day Sunday must be for the children of the oratorio public! It was prime, no doubt, at the Crystal Palace on Saturday, to hear the three thousand young ladies and gentlemen of the choir, in their Sunday best, all shouting "Stone him

* Fortuné du Boisgobey (1824–91) was a prolific French writer of detective fiction.

[97]

to death: stone him to death"; and one could almost hear the satisfied sigh of Mr Chadband* as St Paul's God shall surely destroy them was followed in due time by the piously fugal See what love hath the Father bestowed on us. But to me, constitutional scoffer that I am, the prostitution of Mendelssohn's great genius to this lust for threatening and vengeance, doom and wrath, upon which he should have turned his back with detestation, is the most painful incident in the art-history of the century. When he saw Fra Diavolo, he was deeply scandalized at the spectacle of Zerlina undressing herself before the looking-glass on her wedding eve, singing "Oui, c'est demain," with the three brigands peeping at her through the curtains. "I could not set such things to music" he said; and undoubtedly the theme was none too dignified. But was it half so ignoble and mischievous as the grovelling and snivelling of Stiggins,† or the raging and threatening of Mrs Clennam,‡ which he glorified in St Paul and Elijah? I do not know how it is possible to listen to these works without indignation, especially under circumstances implying a parallel between them and the genuine epic stuff of Handel, from which, in spite of their elegance, they differ as much as Booth# does from Bunyan. The worst of it is that Mendelssohn's business is still a going concern, though his genius has been withdrawn from it. Every year at the provincial festivals some dreary doctor of music wreaks his counterpoint on a string of execrable balderdash with Mesopotamia or some other blessed

* Character in Dickens's Bleak House.
† Character in Dickens's Pickwick Papers.
‡ Character in Dickens's Little Dorrit.
# George Booth (1622–84), 1st Baron Delamere, was a politician and military leader of the so-called New Royalists, who abetted the Cavaliers in an attempt to restore the English monarchy.

word for a title. The author is usually a critic, who rolls his own log in his paper whilst his friendly colleagues roll it elsewhere. His oratorio, thus recommended, is published in the familiar buff cover, and played off on small choral societies throughout the country by simple-minded organists, who display their knowledge by analyzing the fugues and pointing out the little bits of chorus in six real parts. In spite of the flagrant pedantry, imposture, corruption, boredom, and waste of musical funds which the oratorio system involves, I should not let the cat out of the bag in this fashion if I thought it could be kept in much longer; for who knows but that some day I might get into business myself as a librettist, and go down to posterity as the author of St Nicholas Without and St Walker Within, a sacred oratorio, founded on a legend alluded to by Charles Dickens, and favorably noticed in the columns of The World and other organs of metropolitan opinion? But I fear I was born too late for this. The game is up; and I may as well turn Queen's evidence whilst there is some credit to be got by it.

As for the performance at the Crystal Palace, it was, with the three thousand executants, a rare debauch of its kind; and except that it was dragged out to twice its normal length by the slow *tempi* taken by Mr Manns—unnecessarily slow, I think—the effect was not so inferior to that of a performance on the proper scale as might have been expected from so monstrous a piece of overdoing. Edward Lloyd sang without a fault, and Mr Watkin Mills's vocal style was excellent. Madame Albani pulled the music about in her accustomed fashion by hanging on to every note that shewed off her voice, and her intonation, compared with that of her three colleagues, was fallible, but she was otherwise equal to the occasion. Madame Patey was at her best, as she generally is at such functions.

In the ordinary course of music, nothing more paradoxical could be imagined than Richter conducting a composition of Wagner's worse than Hallé, and at the same concert surpassing Hallé at a work by Mendelssohn. An adept will at once see that the Wagner piece must have been the Siegfried Idyll, which is music and nothing else, and the Mendelssohn one an overture (it was in fact Ruy Blas), which is music and dramatic poetry too. Ruy Blas has always hitherto appeared a weaker, if more refined, overture than that to Euryanthe; but at his last concert but one, Richter drew out Mendelssohn with a force that enabled him to sustain the comparison with Weber triumphantly. The performance was a remarkable example of the power of the sustained tone which Richter insists on from the orchestra, in contrast to the shortwinded puffs and scrapes with which our own kid-gloved conductors are satisfied. Unfortunately, this splendid beginning was followed by a pianoforte concerto by Brahms, a desperate hash of bits and scraps, with plenty of thickening in the pianoforte part, which Mr Leonard Borwick played with the enthusiasm of youth in a style technically admirable. The Siegfried Idyll followed, and was not a patch on the Manchester band's recent performance of it in London—was, in short, a downright blank failure, numbed by the Brahms boredom. Mr Borwick, by the bye, might be forgiven for venturing on a recital; for performances of concertos by Schumann and Brahms do not afford a sufficient basis for a critical verdict upon a player of his pretensions. This reminds me that Madame Teresa Carreño gave a third recital on Tuesday, treating us impartially to her Beethoven-Chopin repertory and to such arrant schoolgirl trash as I thought never to have heard again save in dreams of my sisters' infancy. It would not be strictly true to say that she went back to Prudent's fantasia on Lucia; but it is a positive fact that she substituted for Mendelssohn's Prelude and Fugue in E minor nothing less than a thumping scamper through Gottschalk's Tremolo. Certainly she is a superb executant, and her bow is Junonian; but Gottschalk!—good gracious! On Wednesday I went to hear Madame Haas play at Steinway Hall, and was glad to find in the program that most beautiful Beethoven sonata (Op. 110) which she has made so thoroughly her own. Paderewski should have been there to take a lesson in it from her.

At the Opera last week they put on the Figaro on an offnight; but the performance was a mere run through the voice parts and accompaniments: there was no attempt to bring the subtle and elaborate comedy to a serious representation. Dufriche, who appeared for the first time as the Count, at least stuck to the text; and since he did his best to keep his *tremolo* out of action, the disapproval manifested by the gallery and acknowledged by him in several ironic obeisances after *Vedrò mentr' io sospiro*, was undeserved at that particular moment; but his notions of what he was on the stage for were evidently of the vaguest: he repeatedly bungled the business of the scene. Madame Scalchi slipped through the part of Cherubino with wonderful adroitness, and with a feeling for the music which was hardly sufficiently acknowledged. Miss Russell made a shocking interpolation in *Perchè crudel* (high note, of course), and the *Deh vieni*, lying unfavorably for her voice, did not make its due effect; but, except for an occasional hardness of tone, her Susanna, vocally at least, was satisfactory, and her acting, as far as it went, was intelligent. Madame Tavary sang well as the Countess; indeed, the singing was good all round except in the case of d'Andrade, who took the greatest pains to be a failure as Figaro, and succeeded. The orchestra was not quite so bad as in Don Giovanni; but Signor Randegger did not induce them to take very much trouble with the score. On the whole, the critic who found Le Nozze "trite" was not far wrong; only he was mistaken in supposing that the triteness was Mozart's fault.

MODERN MEN: HANS RICHTER

The Scots Observer, 28 June 1890; unsigned. Reprinted in Twenty Modern Men from the National Observer (2nd series), London, 1891

Dr Richter came to London in 1877, with Wagner. Well, London had plenty of conductors in 1877. There was Mr Cusins at the Philharmonic; and the Philharmonic was on the verge of extinction. Then there was Costa—Sir Michael Costa—the autocrat of Her Majesty's, whose band—brazen, cold, correct—never presumed to play anything as if it enjoyed it, except perhaps a score of Rossini's. At Covent Garden there was Vianesi; and inasmuch as a Parisian has an exquisitely tasty way of being vulgar and childish—that being, in effect, what he supposes art to mean—while a stolid Brixton band can only respond to the call of the Parisian ideal by bumptiousness and blaring, Vianesi who does well enough for Paris is an artistic failure here. Arditi was an operatic conductor pure and simple: he was content to compose Il Bacio and to pull through scratch performances of the old Italian repertory, leaving Costa to conduct the Handel Festival and compose Eli and other sacred contributions to that school of oratorio in which inspiration is a sin. Arthur Sullivan was very neat, tolerated no want of refinement, and got over the ground as fast as possible lest Beethoven should sound tedious and Mozart vapid, yet never made an orchestra go fast enough for that, though every *allegro* was what Mozart would have called a *prestissimo*. Leaving Mr Barnby, with his hopelessly expressionless horde of middle-class oratorio choristers aside as lost to living music, there remained only two conductors of any pretensions; and they were much the best of the set. One was the enthusiast August Manns, who was absorbed by the Crystal Palace concerts, and the other Mr Weist Hill, who was presently drawn off into the Guildhall School of Music founded by the City of London. And none of these could draw the town to orchestral concerts except Manns and Weist Hill, who would certainly have established the Viard-Louis concerts permanently if capital had been forthcoming to tide over the initial wait for remunerative success.

At that time nobody in London except a few readers of Wagner's hard and clotted, desperately German prose saw any point in the term "Mendelssohnian Conductor." As to its being reproach, that would have seemed a paradox. When Wagner came over here in 1877 to try and retrieve the pecuniary losses of his triumph at Bayreuth in 1876, many admirers, professed disciples of his, were not behindhand in misrepresenting him. They talked and wrote as if it were eminently Wagnerian to decry Mozart and to find deep meanings in Brahms and Schumann. "The Meister" himself, as might have been expected, was bored by Brahms, indifferent to Schumann's "deeper" meanings, fond of Don Giovanni like the rest of us, given to ask pianists to play him the Hebrides overture on the piano, as pleased with Masaniello as the greenest, slow to outgrow the childish delight with which he used to conduct the pleasant operas of Boïeldieu, and with a passion for Beethoven far surpassing that of the late Edmund Gurney:* in

* Edmund Gurney was a musicologist, man of letters, and psychical researcher, who died in 1888 of an accidental drug overdose, at the age of 41.

short, a man of strong commonsense, whose tastes were the most simple and obvious to be found on his plane. As his music made extraordinary and continuous demands on the orchestra for expression and "vocality," he was always at war with incompetent conductors, whom he named without the slightest fear of consequences whenever it was necessary to give a practical illustration of what he complained of; and naturally they urged that, as he had also denounced Mendelssohn and Meyerbeer with the envy of an unsuccessful inferior, his spleen should not be a hurt to them. The unsuccessful inferior theory is perhaps a little *passé*;* but Wagner is still unappreciated as a critic; for the musical critics, though they see that Richter produces noble results with poor materials, are able to give no intelligible account of the process, but seem to suppose the man to have some natural magic which eludes analysis. Sometimes they try to explain that the charm consists in his ability to play the horn and trumpet, his remarkable memory, and his address in giving cues to his band, on all which irrelevant points he is equaled not only by several distinguished musicians who are hopelessly weak conductors but by dozens of military bandmasters. Wagner had the advantage of knowing what he was talking about when he said "The whole business of a conductor is to give the right time to the band."

* W. E. Henley, editor of The Scots Observer, audaciously injected into the article a few anti-Wagnerisms, drawing from Shaw the retort: "I had heard of [your] deplorable darkness as to Wagner, and so had to overcharge my article to receive your misguided watering down. On the whole you have done your spi—I mean your watering most artistically, and without lacerating my feelings; for though your 'perhaps a little *passé*' was maliciously intended, it reads like a keen Wagnerian sarcasm." 1 July 1890, in Shaw, Collected Letters 1874–97 (1965).

This seems simple; but as nothing short of a complete and original comprehension of the composer's intention, and above all of the melody with which modern symphonic movements, the fast as well as the slow, are saturated, can guide anyone to the right time, it is evident that a man may know that *adagio* means slow and *allegro* fast; his *coup d'œil* over a score may be swift and unerring as far as the notes and entries are concerned; he may be able to play The Last Rose of Summer with variations on every several instrument in his orchestra; and yet he may conduct Beethoven's Coriolanus overture in such a fashion that every honest novice will vote it as meaningless as Zampa, and not half as pretty. A conductor who takes the time from the metronome and gives it to the music is, for all conducting purposes, a public nuisance: a conductor who takes the time from the music and gives it to the band is, if he take and give it rightly, a good conductor. This is what Richter does and would do if he were as incapable of playing the horn as Beethoven himself. And this enables him also to understand what is wrong with the ordinary pseudo-classical orchestra. The Philharmonic band, with all its "refinement," never produces sustained tone: the players attack a note and then let it go without feeling or gripping it; there is no heart in their *forte*, no sensibility in their *piano*; and their conductors find that the only way to avoid an intolerable insipidity is to take Mendelssohn's famous advice, and scamper along as fast as possible. This is all very well in a Bach *allegro* with not a sustained note in it, or in a piece of rattling Margate Pier music like Signor Mancinelli's Venetian Suite; but imagine the effect of it in Beethoven, with his pregnant and terrible pauses on held notes and his restless ground-swell of melody! In all Beethoven's symphonies there is one movement, and only one, that the Philharmonic band can play, and that is the *finale* of the Fourth, which consists almost entirely of semi-quavers. Yet this vapid and useless orchestra needs but a good conductor—a conductor who at rehearsal would do something more than race it through a symphony with an occasional wry face, and a superior "O, coarse, gentlemen! *so* coarse!" or "Cant you bring that out a little more?" or some other equally futile expression of helpless dissatisfaction—to be the best in the world. But for Richter, it would be as true now as in 1869 that, as Wagner declared, "the real reason of the success of Beethoven's music is that people study it not in concert rooms but at their own pianos; and its irresistible power is thus fully learnt, though in a roundabout way. If our noblest music depended solely on our conductors, it would have perished long ago."

Richter is the man who felt what Wagner wanted, as indeed we all felt it—as even Mr Cowen, Villiers Stanford, Dr Mackenzie, Mr Cusins, and all the other captains of the *bâton* feel it more or less acutely, if they had but the courage, the energy, the belief in themselves, and the power over their orchestras that these carry with them, to insist on bringing their want to its fulfilment. Richter has these qualities; and in addition he has the teaching and the confirmation of Richard Wagner. But that teaching is still open to everyone who is capable of appreciating it. There is no celestial arcanum about the Richter orchestra. The tremendous *fortes* of the Rienzi overture, the delicate *piano* of the Meistersinger prelude (that to the third act), the insistence on the melodic character of the Beethoven *allegro*, the smoothing-out of all the old jerks and jigs and *sforzandos* from the surface of the stream of melody, the substitution of the natural movement of the music for the detestable *presto*—all these reforms are obvious enough now that Richter has carried them through. It is time for younger men to make these qualities a matter of course; but whilst music in London is dominated to the extent it is by musicians to whom music is a mere phase of gentility—or "culture," as they call it—the capital for musical enterprise will not easily find its way into the right hands. Still, the thing will be done. Richter has his post (with its pension) at Vienna to attend to; the Crystal Palace concerts are far off and expensive; the opening for a new man is plain. He may lack Richter's genius; but if he also lack some of his fortyseven years, some of his growing tendency to trust for victory to the excitement of the evening, he may be—(should he prefer his work to society and royal patronage)—at least as great a man as Habeneck, of whom you are told that although he had not a scrap of genius he achieved *the* classic performance of the Ninth Symphony at the Paris Conservatoire.

MUNICIPAL BANDS AND OPERA TRICKS

The World, 2 July 1890

The concert last week in aid of the project for establishing a municipal band in London reminded me of the late Edmund Gurney's demand for an orchestra for the East End. If I had my way in the matter the money should not be raised by a concert and a subscription list, as if the London County Council were a distressed widow: a fitter course would be to levy the cost by the strong hand of the tax collector on the thousands of well-to-do people who never go to a concert because they are "not musical," but who enjoy, all the same, the health-giving atmosphere which music creates. Just as the river is useful to men who do not row, the bridges to West Enders who never cross them, and the railways to the bedridden, so the provision of good music and plenty of it smooths life as much for those who do not know the National Anthem from Rule Britannia, as for those who can whistle all the themes in the Ninth Symphony. Now that we have renounced the hideous absurdity of keeping up Waterloo Bridge out of the halfpence of the people who actually go over it, it is pitiable to have to go back to that ridiculous system for a town band. We certainly want such a band, though not because private enterprise has been behindhand in the matter. On the contrary, it is because private enterprise every Sunday sends a procession, religious or Radical, past my windows every five minutes or so, each headed by a band, that I feel the need for some model of excellence to hold up to these enthusiastic instrumentalists. In Lancashire and Yorkshire there are, it is computed, twenty thousand bandsmen.

When I was in Bristol some time ago, a fifteen minutes' walk through the working-class quarter on Sunday morning brought me across three bands, two of them by no means bad ones. In London you can, on the occasion of a big "demonstration," pass down a procession miles long without ever being out of earshot of at least two bands. The cultured class sometimes, when suffering from an attack of nerves, wants the band-playing class to be dispersed and silenced; but this cannot now be effectively done, for the band-playing outnumber the cultured five to one, and two-thirds of them have votes.

Whether we like the bands or not, we must put up with them: let us therefore, in self-defence, help them to make themselves fairly efficient. It is certain that they are not so good as they might be at present, and that as long as they never hear anything better than their own music they will remain much as they are. Their instruments are not so bad as might be supposed. They may not come from the first-class stocks of Mahillon,

Courtois, or Boosey; but the competition between instrument-makers has resulted in the production of fairly good brass instruments of the simpler types (cornets, saxhorns, &c.) at reasonable prices payable by instalments. Hence the fortuitous German bombardon with cylinders, bought at a pawnshop, and pitched nearly half-a-tone lower than its British companions in the band, is now scarcer than it used to be, though unhappily it is not yet extinct.

But even in bands in which the instruments are all manufactured to English military pitch and of endurable quality, with players whose ears are not satisfied until they have adjusted their tuning-slides and their blowing so as to get the notes made with the pistons tolerably in tune, chaos sets in the moment the music goes beyond the simplest diatonic harmonies. At the occurrence of one of the series of tonic discords which are so freely used in modern music, and which make the six old gentlemen who form the anti-Wagner party in Paris put their fingers to their ears, the working-class bandsman not only does not know whether he is in tune or out, but he actually does not know whether he is playing the right note, so strange is the chord to his ear. Consequently he is limited to the banal quicksteps and tiresome Boulanger marches which confirm him in his vulgar and obvious style of execution. Even a Schubert march is beyond him, because the modulations, simple and brilliantly effective as they are, are not solely from tonic to dominant and back again. The only way to rescue him from his groove is to familiarize him with the sound of modern polyphony in all its developments. A gentleman can do this for himself at his pianoforte; but a wage-earner who has to buy a modest two-guinea cornet by laborious instalments is as likely to learn driving on his own four-in-hand as modern music at his own Steinway.

[109]

You must send round to Victoria Park, Finsbury Park, Battersea Park, Peckham Rye, Hampstead Heath, and Blackheath a numerous, well paid, honorably esteemed, highly skilled, and splendidly equipped band, with a conductor who puts music before applause, the chance of a knighthood, loyalty, morals, religion, and every other earthly or unearthly consideration—a municipal August Manns, in short. This is the only way to teach the bandsman of the street and his patrons how his quicksteps with their three chords and one modulation have been improved on by Schubert, Offenbach, Auber, and Rossini, by Weber, Mendelssohn, and Goetz, and finally by Beethoven and Wagner. Let him pick all this up through his ears, and he will come out with a much sounder knowledge than that of the literate person who knows that Wagner is "marvelous" by reading statements to that effect in the critical scriptures of the day. In the end he will pay back the outlay; for when he is qualified as a consumer and producer of good music, the resultant cheapness and plenty will bring down the exorbitant cost of even the Opera. Think of that, ye golden ones whose Oriental names I read on the box doors as I stroll about Mr Harris's corridors of an evening during the *entr'actes*; and do not let the Municipal Band Fund fall through for lack of subscriptions.

I cannot congratulate Lassalle on his Rigoletto last Thursday at Covent Garden. A massive gentleman with all the empty pomposity of the Paris Opéra hampering him like an invisible chain and bullet tied to his ankle, and whose stock-in-trade as an actor consists of one mock-heroic attitude, cannot throw himself into a part which requires the activity of a leopard; nor, by merely screwing up his eyes in an ecstasy of self-approbation, convey the raging self-contempt, the superstitious terror, the impotent fury, the savage vindictiveness, the heartbroken grovelling of the crippled jester wounded in his one vulnerable point—his fierce love of his child, the only creature who does not either hate or despise him. In such a character, burnt into music as it has been by Verdi, Lassalle's bag of hackneyed Parisian tricks makes him egotistical and ridiculous.

Further, he spoils the effect of the great scene with the courtiers, and makes a most unreasonable demand on the orchestra, by transposing his music a whole tone down, a monstrous liberty to take. No one can blame a singer for requiring a transposition of half-a-tone from our Philharmonic pitch; but where, as at Covent Garden, the French pitch is adopted, a demand for "a tone down" could only be justified in the case of a singer of very limited range, but with sufficiently remarkable acting power to compensate for the injury to the musical effect. As Lassalle has neither excuse, it seems to me that we are entitled to expect that he shall in future either sing the part as Verdi wrote it, or else let it alone. At the same time, it is but fair to add that when an unfortunate baritone has to sing fifty bars in what is practically twelve-eight time, *andante,* on the four or five highest notes in his compass, without a rest except for two bars, during which he is getting out of breath in a violent stage struggle, the composer has only himself to thank when the same artist, who sings the much longer part of Wagner's Hans Sachs without turning a hair, flatly declines to submit to the strain of Rigoletto.

As it was, the honors of the occasion were carried off by Madame Melba, who ended the famous quartet on a high D flat of the most beautiful quality, the license in this instance justifying itself by its effect. Valero, if he did not realize the masterful egotist, full of *la joie de vivre,* as conceived by Victor Hugo and Verdi, yet played with such spirit and humor that he may put down the Duke as one of his London successes. His singing, to be sure, was only a tasty sort of yelling, without spontaneity or purity of tone; but it was pretty enough to bring down the house in *La donna è mobile.*

At the revival of Meyerbeer's Prophète many critics, including myself, were reduced to the humiliating necessity of buying books of the play, containing a French and an English version, both different in arrangement from the one used on the stage. I had never seen the opera except on paper. The three Anabaptists rather interested me when they started an open-air revolutionary agitation, as I am a bit of an amateur in that line myself; but when they turned out badly in the end I felt much as the mottle-faced man in Pickwick did when Sam Weller sang of the Bishop's coachman running away from Dick Turpin. "I say" said the mottle-faced man on that occasion "that the coachman did not run away, but that he died game—game as pheasants; and I wont hear nothing said to the contrary." In a similar spirit I affirm that the Anabaptists died "game as pheasants," and that Scribe's history is trash.

But, indeed, Scribe never shewed his radical incapacity for anything deeper than his deadly "well-made plays" more conclusively than when he mistook for a great musical delineator of the passions of the multitude the composer who, in Les Huguenots, set forth the Reformation as a strife between a Rataplan chorus and an Ave Maria, the two factions subsequently having it out in alternate strains of a waltz. The Prophet, meant to be luridly historical, is in fact the oddest medley of drinking songs, tinder-box *trios*, sleigh rides, and skating quadrilles imaginable; and even John of Leyden, whose part detaches itself from the dead mass of machinery as something alive and romantic, if not exactly human, is at the disadvantage of being a hero without having anything heroic to do, and of having finally to degrade himself by shouting a vile drinking song amid a pack of absurd nautch-girls. The orchestra seemed to feel this on Monday; for they brought the scene to an end in ruin and confusion by differing on the subject of the last cut in the score. Jean de Reszke, though a little hoarse, made as much as was possible of the part under the circumstances; and Mlle Richard's Fidès was at least more credible than her Favorita. Madame Nuovina, on the other hand, seems to have gone completely to pieces. The shrillness of her highest notes is worse than ever; and she has developed a *tremolo* which sounds like a burlesque of Madame Tetrazzini's. It is a pity; for her first appearance as Margaret in Faust promised better things.

CONCERTS BEYOND COUNT
The World, 9 July 1890

I am inclined to think that the most important event of the past week is the revolt of the Private Man against the Philharmonic Society and the critics. As a rule the Private Man, conscious of the guilt of ignorance, submits to musical imposture without a murmur, and even pretends to like it. He writes to the papers if he is overcharged by an hotel proprietor, or if a lady is rude to him, or if the sandwiches at a railway refreshment room are stale; but when he pays to hear the Ninth Symphony at a Philharmonic Concert, and has that work served up in such a fashion that a whole meal of stale sandwiches would be ambrosial in comparison, he dissembles his loathing, and secretly deplores his own want of taste for the classics. And the critics chime in with a conventional compliment or two about "the celebrated Philharmonic orchestra," as if they did not know as well as I do that this band, potentially the best in the world, is actually as vapid and perfunctory an institution as ever drove a musician wild with disappointment by heartless trifling with great works.

But its last performance of the Ninth Symphony seems to have aroused the British lion. The critics said the usual thing; but one Edward Carpenter,* an unattached essayist of credit and renown, declares, on the contrary, that the symphony was miserably unsatisfying. I was not at the concert myself, because, though I forewent Patti and the Albert Hall to attend, yet when I reached St James's Hall it was so full that I could only get one of those acutely uncomfortable stalls in the niches of the wall for my seven-and-sixpence. Now, for a good performance of the Ninth Symphony I would cheerfully sit the whole time on a sack of nails. For an average Philharmonic performance no seat, I regret to say, could be too comfortable—a fourposter would be best of all; so I looked askance at that ticket, with its discouraging "Row FF"; hesitated a moment; and—got my money back.

Therefore I cannot say from my own observation whether Mr Carpenter or the critics were right; but I implicitly believe Mr Carpenter. I have too often suffered from what he complains of to doubt him. Perhaps the society's directors will now wake up to the necessity of providing their band with a conductor capable of making it actually what I have said it is potentially. They once hit on a great conductor, no less a one than Richard Wagner; but instead of having the sense to hold on to him like grim death, as they should have done, they dropped him like a hot potato after one year, and clung to Mr Cusins (after eleven years of Sterndale Bennett) from 1867 until it became evident, a few years ago, that decomposition had set in;

* Cambridge-educated Anglican minister, who became a Socialist writer and artisan.

whereupon they tried Sir Arthur Sullivan, Dr Mackenzie, and Mr Cowen, only to find that these talented, polite, and estimable musicians take much the same view of Beethoven as Mr Andrew Lang* (for instance) takes of Dickens or William Morris, and are about as competent to regenerate the British orchestra as he is to regenerate the British drama.

If they cannot find a true Beethovenian conductor, why can they not leave that much-abused genius in peace, and stick to the Moszkowski trivialities and the ballroom and jetty music which they play so prettily? An occasional old-fashioned Handelian allegro, consisting of rapid figurations, which only need to be played in strict time as fast as possible, could be thrown in to keep up the classical tradition; and Wagner and Beethoven could be left out on the ground that they were demonstrative and given to striving after effect (not to mention generally getting it)—in short, that they were no gentlemen.

Meanwhile the Richter concerts flourish by doing what the Philharmonic ought to do, and professes to do, and does not do, and probably never will do. There, if one cannot always avoid Wagner's *bête noire*, "the blessed Johannes," known to a long-suffering British public as Brahms, one can at least hear a Beethoven symphony or a Wagner prelude played with sympathy and understanding. That absurd body, the London branch of the Wagner Society, having nothing better to do with its superfluous funds than to endow Richter concerts which can get on perfectly well without it, was in St James's Hall in force last week, when Miss Pauline Cramer sang the closing scene from the Götterdämmerung. Over most German singers of her heroic build she has the advantage of a voice of very bright quality. She is

* Scottish classical scholar, folklorist, poet, and journalist.

evidently highly sensitive to the Wagnerian emotions—
an enthusiast, in fact; but enthusiasm is dangerous in
such mad bits as that when Brynhild springs on her
horse and rides into the fire. Abandonment to a suicidal
situation is impossible: the effect must be an illusion
produced by skilful husbandry of force; and for this
husbandry Miss Cramer has hardly sufficient *sang-froid*.
She also falls occasionally into the common fault of her
school: she emphasizes the high notes too much,
somewhat in the fashion of the early Wagner singers,
who made his vocal music sound like a succession of
screams. If Miss Cramer would only pass from her
middle to her highest register without a *sforzando* every
time, I should have as much praise for her singing as for
her admirable earnestness.

Of recent concerts I have lost count. Miss Zoe Caryll,
whose position as a pianist cannot be ascertained from
a performance of Liszt's Hungarian Fantasia under
rather nervous conditions, promised to produce both
the De Reszkes on the platform of St James's Hall; but
Jean sent an apology; and as Edouard brought only one
song (*O lieti di* from L'Etoile du Nord), a stupendous
encore elicited nothing fresher than a repetition. Sarah
Bernhardt was so hoarse that she barely contrived to
read a dozen lines which no one could hear; Lassalle and
Madame Fursch-Madi sang French routine music
(Massenet and so on) which nobody cared a straw about;
the celebrated orchestra did its worst; and if it had not
been for Madame Melba's *Caro nome*, Brother Edouard's
essay aforesaid, and a skilful and artistic recitation by
Paul Plan of the Gymnase, the concert would have been
nearly as great a disappointment as all miscellaneous
concerts deserve to be. The pianists are still active every
afternoon and evening. I have, in spite of all my
evasions, heard a young Dutchman named Zeldenrust,
a neat player, with a certain individuality which is not

[116]

exactly musical individuality; a Mr Ernest Denhoff, an expert who shewed little feeling for his business; Mr Schönberger, a born player, if not a very deep one; and Albéniz, who let an orchestra loose on his own compositions in the little Steinway Hall, where we all wished it outside, though we could not very well get up and say so. Albéniz will find the professors inclined to dispute his right to call his spontaneous effusions "sonatas" and "concertos"; but if he sits tight and does as he pleases in this respect, he will find himself none the worse. He is, so far this season, the most distinguished and original of the pianists who confine themselves to the rose-gathering department of music. There was also a Mr Leon de Silka, a young Spanish amateur, who invited the Spanish Ambassador and some other people to hear him play. Mr de Silka must not let his friends mislead him as to his present position as a player. Just now young Mr Leonard Borwick, for example, could play his head off. He can hit the right notes dexterously enough; but he has all the faults of an amateur— unevenness of finger, bad habits of pouncing on every time accent in the bar, moments of irresolute artistic feeling scattered here and there between *longueurs* of diffident prose, and a tendency to repress himself in the manner of a gentleman rather than to realize his conception in the manner of an artist. If Mr de Silka asks me whether he is a consummate pianist, I answer No. If he asks whether it is worth his while to undertake the two or three years' more hard study needed to make him one, I answer Yes. My tale of pianoforte recitals ends with Miss Else Sonntag, who has been carefully instructed in the school of Liszt. In that school the race is to the swift and the battle to the strong; and Miss Sonntag is neither the one nor the other; but she does all the more credit to her school by the measure of success she attains.

I did not know that there were twenty students of the harp in England until I went to Mr John Thomas's concert the other day and saw two score young ladies in white twanging away at Rossini's Carita. In my childhood this would have exactly embodied my notion of heaven, and would consequently have terrified me out of my wits. Even now that I am a grown-up critic I cannot pretend that I faced them without misgiving; for beautiful as the notes of the harp are when a cunning hand sprinkles them over the orchestra, they are apt to get on the nerves when taken neat in large doses. Miss Edith Wynne, still an admirable ballad singer, helped; and so did Mr Ben Davies. All went well until a sacrifice to pseudo-classicism was offered up in a tepid trio by Spohr—Mozart-and-water, as usual. Miss Marianne Eissler did not succeed in catching the pitch of the harp, nor Mr Thomas the pitch of her violin; and Hollmann, with his ears on edge, steered a middle course. Hollmann is a connecting link between Mr Thomas's concert and Mr Isidore de Lara's, at which he played an aria of Bach's as only a great artist can play that great composer's music. I am not fond of the violoncello: ordinarily I had as soon hear a bee buzzing in a stone jug; but if all cellists played like Hollmann, I should probably have taken more kindly to it. De Lara made his *début* as a dramatic singer and epic composer. Nothing is easier to write than a cantata, except, perhaps, a tragedy in blank verse; and I suppose people must go through the stage of thinking that all cantatas are music, just as they had to go through the stage of thinking that Hoole's translation of Tasso was poetry. When I was at Mr Grossmith's recital* the other day, I could not help

* George Grossmith, who created many of the chief parts in the Gilbert and Sullivan comic operas, frequently entertained with "humorous and musical recitals."

feeling thankful that he was born with a sense of the ridiculous. Lacking it, he would have strung his tunes into first subjects and second subjects, connected by a modulation to the dominant shewing the hand of the accomplished musician; hashed them up into a free fantasia to an accompaniment of their own fragments; and put them together again and recapitulated them (after a masterly return to the tonic) with a *coda* or tail consisting of inversions of the common chord on the keynote. Then the whole would have been produced at a Philharmonic Concert as a Symphony in C, by George Grossmith, Mus. Doc. Oxon.; and when the British public had been duly impressed by the description as above in a shilling analytical program, and had read the criticism in the morning paper (by the same gentleman who wrote the program), no eloquence of mine would ever have persuaded them that all this technical stuff bears no more vital relation to music than parsing does to poetry. However, this excursus is not meant for Mr de Lara, who avoids academics and simply gratifies his turn for writing voluptuous lyrics, which are none the worse for a little opium-eating orchestration, heightened by an occasional jingle of the *pavillon chinois*. I did not care much for that part of the cantata where Miss Russell told the composer that the pity in his look was awful, and his visage like a god's; but the audience were encoring it very heartily as I withdrew. Mancinelli looked after the orchestra and gave us some bits of an oratorio of his own (an amiable weakness in an Italian, although it would be a deliberate fraud on the part of an Englishman); and Tivadar Nachéz played Bruch's First Concerto. Nachéz is one of the most musically intelligent violinists we have; but his technique fails him in rapid and difficult movements. Talking of the violin, why on earth does not Ysaÿe give a concert? At Collard's rooms, on Friday, two ladies, who announced themselves as "the sisters the countesses Augusta and Ernesta Ferrari d'Occhieppo," sang several songs and duets in the popular outdoor Italian manner, which came rather as a surprise to those who were not familiar with our own music hall school of vocalism. I never heard Miss Bessie Bellwood* sing Beethoven's *In questa tomba*; but I think she could more than hold her own with the Countess Ernesta Ferrari.

BALDERDASH AND ESMERALDA
The World, 16 July 1890

[U] In view of the late alarums and excursions at the Opera, I am not disposed to complain of the postponement of Esmeralda for a few nights. I have an unconstitutional objection to being ridden over by the mounted police; and flour bags and market refuse, not to mention spittoons and sections of metal shutters, make no distinction of persons when they get into full circulation. On Saturday night, however, order reigned in Bow-street. Even the vendors of last year's libretti were absent—no doubt slain to a man in the fray; for nothing short of that could have effectually suppressed them. And yet, as the *genre* to which Esmeralda belongs, Paris Grand to wit, is tedious, one could not help regretting that it was no longer possible to refresh oneself by slipping out for a moment for a spirited rally against the Guards, and then coming back to sink luxuriously into a stall and recover breath to the soothing strains of *Daignez reparaître, o lumière*. Esmeralda is not a fair specimen of what Mr Goring Thomas can accomplish now; but it proves up to the hilt that the same sort of thing that is done by Gounod, Saint-Saëns, and

* Music hall comedienne, who died in 1896, at 39.

Massenet for the Opéra in Paris can be done with more vigor and variety by English composers. People call Esmeralda Gounod-and-water, but I do not agree: Gounod is the basis, no doubt; but Mr Goring Thomas has fortified instead of diluting it. Without placing the follower before the leader, or denying that Gounod fortified with Goring Thomas is sometimes suggestive of hock fortified with whisky, it is still due to English opera to insist on the fact that a performance of Esmeralda is much less monotonous than a performance of Roméo et Juliette.

The translation of an English opera into French for performance at the leading English opera house is, of course, only defensible on the ground that there is not a line in the book that any intelligent person could possibly want to understand when he has once picked up the story from Victor Hugo—though even that story has been spoiled by an ending so outrageously idiotic that its toleration proves how little the public have yet learnt to take opera seriously. Some day Mr Harris will have a great inspiration. It will flash on him that perhaps, after all, a dramatic poet, or even a dramatic proser, might be a more suitable person to order a libretto from than either a musical critic or a singing master. Suppose he were to ask Mr D'Oyly Carte whether the Savoy operas would have been equally successful if Sir Arthur Sullivan's genius had been wreaked on books by Mr Joseph Bennett or Signor Alberto Randegger? If Mozart and Weber could not save bad opera books from failure, how can Mr Goring Thomas and Mr Cowen be expected to do it? We are growing out of the notion that only a very stout and elderly woman can look the parts of Valentine in Les Huguenots and Leonore in Fidelio. In the course of time we shall discover that balderdash is not so specially appropriate to English opera as we have hitherto supposed.

[121]

I did not go to the students' concert at Trinity College because the conditions were so onerous, being (1) that I should be properly dressed, (2) that I should not attempt to take a seat in the five front rows, and (3) that I should countenance the performance in an educational establishment of that monstrous impertinence of Grieg's—his addition of a part for a second piano to Mozart's perfect and unalterable Fantasia in C for piano solo. My unassuming and submissive attitude towards concert givers is well known, but even I have to be managed with more tact than this.

I am inclined to remonstrate with the Royal College of Music for sending me a ticket which only mentioned that if I went to Kensington Gore on Tuesday last week I should see the foundation stone of the new fortyfive-thousand-pound building laid. What do I care about foundation stones? To draw me to the spot, the ticket should have stated that the Leeds Forge Band, consisting of twentyseven workmen provided with £300 worth of instruments, was to play. Mr Samson Fox (the donor of the fortyfive thousand) put down this £300 eight years ago, his brother William standing in. As the band has made nearly a thousand pounds since in prizes at band competitions, which are popular sports in the north, it keeps itself going without further expense. Perhaps this success is not quite relished by the unfortunate competitors who have to provide their own instruments; but I am not here concerned with abstract ideals of justice: anything that raises the standard of equipment and execution in an art which grows spontaneously in England is to be rejoiced in. I therefore suggest to those large employers that though £45,000 is undoubtedly a heap of money to devote to music in a public way, yet Mr Samson Fox has shewn how to help on a reasonably handsome scale as well as on a gigantic one. The musical return from the Leeds Forge Band may very possibly prove more valuable than that from the Royal College of Music. There are dozens of people in London who would not feel the loss of £300, and who would rather enjoy cutting out Mr Samson Fox if it could be done splendidly. It can be done very splendidly by establishing a municipal band in London. By the bye, can anybody who has gone into the figures let me know what that band would cost?

A matter of more immediate importance in connexion with the Royal College is the performance by its pupils in the Savoy Theatre tomorrow (Wednesday), at the inconvenient hour of two, of no less a work than Mozart's Così fan tutte. The chance of hearing this unlucky classic is not to be missed lightly; for such chances will not come often, as may be judged from the fact that the opera, composed a century ago, has never before been performed here in its original form, and only once or twice in hopeless attempts to fit the music to a new libretto. Imagine *La donna e mobile* spun out into two long acts; and you have the book that seems to have struck Da Ponte as Molièresque in its fun and Ibsenic in its insight. Mozart did what he could for it: that is to say, more than anybody else, before or since (except Goetz, perhaps), could have done; but it was no use. He saturated it with music, tender or playful, as the case seemed to demand—he supplied imaginary drama and characterization sooner than leave the play utterly barren; but until we have artists who can sing with such rare charm of voice and delicacy of expression as to raise the lost Mozartian enchantment and keep its spell unbroken for three hours at a stretch, Così fan tutte will never conquer a place on the stage. I suppose the best known concerted number in it is the quintet *Di scrivermi*, a ravishing piece of music and comedy, which was ingeniously plagiarized by Rossini in the trio *L'usato ardir* at the end of Semiramide.

I am rather at a loss as to little Max Hambourg, a ten-year-old Russian boy, who gave a recital at Prince's Hall on Saturday afternoon. If I say that he plays like an angel, the result will possibly be to send him whirling through Europe and America until he collapses from nervous exhaustion. It appears to me to be an infamous thing to exploit a child commercially, whether in the factory or on the stage or concert platform; and I refused to go to the Hegner and Hofmann concerts on that ground. My abstention, unfortunately, did not prevent the sweating of Hofmann to a point at which a public outcry rescued him; so I used the ticket sent me for young Hambourg's recital, and found him playing Bach's chromatic fantasia much better than Sapellnikoff. The right comprehension of the Bach fugue subject as a true melody came to him naturally; and he played the theme from Beethoven's Sonata in A flat (that with the funeral march) with an instinctive knowledge of how to do it that not one great pianist in twelve can claim. His blunders, his boyishnesses, his occasional imitation of some antic that he has seen Mr de Pachmann or some one like him perform: all these are compensated by his innocent rightness when he touches a beautiful and expressive melody.

Nature, in short, has fully qualified him to be led like a lamb to the slaughter. We shall be told that he likes it, that it is good for him, that medical certificates shew that he gains a stone weight every time he plays a Beethoven sonata in public, that all great players have been "wonder children," and have appeared in public before they were ten: thereby proving that all wonder children should be sent flying from town to town over the American continent as fast as modern railway systems can speed them; that his earnings have raised his family from penury to affluence, and that nothing can exceed the devotion of his father and the self-sacrificing assiduity of his mother. The public will believe it, because they want to hear him play; the agent will believe it, because there is money in the boy; the parents will believe it, because it is best for the boy's own sake that they should lay up a little to finish his education when he is too big to be a wonder child; and the critics can do nothing but lie low and do what they can to make it particularly uncomfortable for the agent and the parents if the boy breaks down.

This, by the bye, reminds me of the concert of Mlle Douste, who was about six years old when I first heard her play a Bach fugue in public, and who does not seem any the worse for it, unless it be responsible for a certain lack of force and freshness, which was apparent at the broader points in the Waldstein sonata, though her very delicate and quiet reading of it economized her physical power to the utmost. She was assisted by M. Ortmans, a violinist, who played with excellent taste.

Mr Bonawitz's Stabat Mater, produced at his recent concert at Prince's Hall, testifies that Rossini is still beloved. An attempt to write out Rossini's Stabat from memory by a man in whom that faculty was rather confused and inaccurate, but whose musical feeling was intact, might result in something very like Mr Bonawitz's work. The weak part of it is the "Amen." Rossini's imitation of a choral fugue is irresistible. Its air of grandeur and erudition is worthy of the king of musical *farceurs*; but Mr Bonawitz cannot carry it off so magnificently: one half suspects him of taking the thing seriously. I must confess that I esteem Mr Bonawitz rather for the public service of keeping a little choir together than for his fluent and tuneful, but not original, vein as a composer. Another Prince's Hall concert was that of Miss Amy Sherwin, a Tasmanian *prima donna*, whose intonation will never, I fear, carry conviction to expert London audiences, but whose voice, appearance, and obviously good intention will secure her a following among those who are not fastidious on that point.[U]

BEETHOVEN'S NINTH
The World, 23 July 1890

It is a pity that a statistical department cannot be started at St James's Hall to ascertain how many of the crowd which the Ninth Symphony always draws really like the work. If a question to this effect were supplemented by another as to whether the catechumen had studied the symphony for himself or had derived his knowledge of it wholly from public performances, I am afraid that the answers (in the unlikely event of their being unaffectedly true) would shew that the line of cleavage between those whom it puzzles or bores, and those who cherish it among their greatest treasures, coincides exactly with that between the concert students and the home students. That terrible first movement is the rub. At the Richter concerts we are convinced but unsatisfied; at the Crystal Palace grateful but hardly convinced; at the Philharmonic wearied and embittered. The whole cause of the shortcoming in Richter's case is insufficient rehearsal.

Wagner assures us that the perfect performances which he heard in Paris by the Conservatoire orchestra under Habeneck in 1838 were achieved, not in the least by Habeneck's genius, for he had none, but because he had the perseverance to rehearse the first movement until he understood it. This took two years; but, in the end, the band had not only got hold of the obviously melodic themes, but had discovered that much of what had at the first blush seemed mere figurated accompaniment, to be played with the usual tum-tum accents, was true and poignantly expressive melody.

[126]

My own conviction is that if any band gets hold of this melody, the melody will get hold of the band so effectually that the symphony will play itself if the conductor will only let it, to ensure which it is necessary that he, too, should be equally saturated. But since the process does not pay as a commercial speculation, and the only national provision for orchestral music in this country is made by merely securing to every speculator full freedom to try his luck, a good performance of the first movement is never heard in London.

Richter himself is duly saturated and super-saturated; but in spite of all he can do in the time at his disposal, the perfect balance, the consentaneous inspiration, the felt omnipresence of melody in its highest sensitiveness, remain unachieved: you find the strings stumbling over the *forte* passages in a dry excited way, detaching themselves angrily from the turbid uncertain song of the wood and horns, and producing a worry which suggests that the movement, however heroic by nature, is teething, and cannot help going into convulsions occasionally. Richter strained every nerve to get it as nearly right as possible at his last concert, and he certainly got the uttermost that his material and opportunities admitted; but the uttermost was none too good. The rest was comparatively plain sailing. The *scherzo* went perhaps a shade too slowly: he took it at from 110 to 112 bars per minute; and I stand out for 115 at least myself.

It was remarkable, by the bye, to hear the young people bursting prematurely into applause at the end of the *presto*, before the repetition of the *scherzo*. The reason was that the repeat is omitted in the familiar Peters edition arrangement of the symphonies as pianoforte duets; and these enthusiasts thought accordingly that the movement ended with the little rally at the end of the *presto*. Nothing could be more welcome than a blunder which shewed that young England is not depending on the Philharmonic for its notions of Beethoven. The performance attained its highest pitch during the slow movement. Obvious as the relation between the *adagio* and *andante* sections seems, I have heard it misconceived in all manner of ways by conductors, from Mr Manns, who only misses it by a hair's breadth, to Signor Arditi, who, on being confronted with it for the first time one night at a "classical" Promenade Concert, went at it with the greatest intrepidity, taking the *andante* at a supernaturally slow *lento*, and rattling the *adagio* along at a lively *allegretto*, the whole producing the effect of a chastened selection from Il Barbiere for use on Sundays. Richter made no such mistakes. At the *reprise* of the *andante* the movement was going so divinely that when the first violins went at a passage with an unmistakable intention of overdoing it, Richter flung out an imploring hand with a gesture of the most appealing natural eloquence; and they forbore. There was one other magical instant— the announcement of the choral theme by the bass strings in an ethereal *piano*. Then the choir was unchained and led forth to havoc, in which I am bound to add that the four soloists, who began merrily enough, did not escape scathless. But badly as it was sung, this great hymn to happiness, with its noble and heartfelt glorification of joy and love, was at least better than an oratorio.

It may be that the tempest of evil passions roused by the word oratorio disposes me to be unjust to Mr Lloyd, who is so much associated with that dismal and immoral entertainment: anyhow, I do not think he struck exactly on the vein of Lohengrin's declaration to the Brabanters and the farewell to Elsa, although Richter averted a repetition of last year's flatfalling by enlarging the selection which proved so ineffective then. Somehow,

Mr Lloyd started sentimentally; tried a touch of jingoism at the climax, "Lohengrin's my name"; rose to genteel piety for a moment; and finally relapsed into sentimentality. He sang well, and elicited shouts of "Bravo!" (imagine anybody daring to say "Bravo!" to a real knight of the Grail!); but he was not Lohengrin. Mr Max Heinrich delivered the two bits of public oratory from The Mastersingers (the speeches of Pogner and Hans Sachs) admirably, his enunciation being distinct and full of point. But I take the liberty of warning Mr Heinrich that much singing in that open sharp-edged way will soon cut off a couple of his top notes and damage the quality of the rest; indeed, there are warning signs of wear on them already. So fine an artist as he will easily find how to make a lighter touch and a rounder tone effective, instead of sacrificing himself to his ideal of force and distinctness. There was a tremendous ovation to Richter at the end of the concert.

I have actually only heard one pianist since last week. That one was Madame Madeline Schiller, who has execution in great abundance, but not of the first quality. Banging through a string of Lisztian "studies of transcendent execution" does not make amends for simplifying the *prestissimo* of the Waldstein Sonata by playing the octave passages in single notes.

The performance of Così fan tutte by the pupils of the Royal College at the Savoy was much better than an average performance of Don Giovanni at Covent Garden. It had been assiduously rehearsed from beginning to end; and the performance was a great occasion for a company of greenhorns, instead of a worn-out bit of routine for jaded professionals. The despised book, after all, has some fun in it, though quite as good plays have often been improvized in ten minutes in a drawing room at charades or dumb crambo. The Royal College shewed progress in the orchestral department. Last year, at The Taming of the Shrew, ordinary professional aid was largely drawn on; but this time there were only two outsiders and one member of the teaching staff in the orchestra, the rest being students. And they played very well, the romantic charm of the scoring for the wind in *Soave sia il vento* and the aria *Smanie implacabili* coming out with all possible delicacy. Indeed, Mr Villiers Stanford seems to have applied the smoothing-iron rather too diligently, for the point of the humorously majestic exordium to the overture was quite missed. The notes were played accurately enough; but the whole fourteen bars should have been declaimed so as to arrest the attention of the house at once. Surely Mr Stanford can see more in them than a mere conventional strum of chords by way of prelude.

I cannot say so much for the singing as for the playing. In academies, conservatoires, colleges of music, and the like, the instrumentalists are usually taught by professors publicly known as accomplished players on the instruments they teach. Bassoon and clarinet players get taught by Wootton and Lazarus, and pianists by Clara Schumann and Sophie Menter; but singers are as often as not handed over to gentlemen who, having tried in vain to make themselves sing, continue their experiments with undiminished ardor on others. I have come across a good many singing masters in my time—delightful fellows, with the finest critical taste, full of enthusiasm—sympathetic accompanists, physiologists enough to have an original theory about the function of the so-called false vocal chords, overflowing with good advice about the mischief of tight-lacing and tobacco, tremendously down on all forcing and straining of the voice, and yet quacks, every man of them. Each could see that all the others were quacks, but each firmly believed too that he himself had discovered the true Italian method as taught by Porpora.

When I call them quacks, I mean that they were mere theorists—a reason which would have greatly astonished them, as they all held that the theorist is the capable teacher, and the empiricist the quack. I remember one* who taught very well until he came to London, where he found that good teaching did not pay, because the only people who could afford to pay ten guineas for twelve lessons could not be induced to take more than the twelve. So he told them that he would in six weeks shew them how to sing like Patti; and he took care that at the end of their dozen lessons they should be able to make a much louder noise than at the beginning, which caused their friends to declare that their voices were immensely improved. One day I asked him how he learned the method he had discarded. At first he told me that he had arrived at it by an elaborate study of "the physiology of the vocal organs"; but I scoffed, and said that Huxley and Foster had done the same, but were not, as far as I knew, authorities on singing. He then told me that he had been thrown on his own resources by the discovery that the singing masters to whom he proposed to serve an apprenticeship knew no more about the matter than he; whereupon, he added "I pottered over anatomy, and experimented on myself and my pupils until I could tell by watching a singer exactly how he was doing it. Then I watched all the opera singers, and found that those whose voices wore badly sang differently from those whose voices wore well. I heard old Badiali, when he was nearly eighty, sing with the freshness of a young man. Accordingly I taught my pupils to produce their voices as Badiali did, and to avoid doing what the others did. The plan answered perfectly—except in London, where they dont like it and wont do it, and expect to learn in a

* Vandeleur Lee.

[131]

month what takes four or five years' hard work." I do not know whether it was all true or not; for my late friend had the artistic temperament; but the process he described was a perfectly scientific one. After this I am rather at a loss as to the most delicate method of harking back to the Royal College of Music and Così fan tutte; for I do not know any of the professors of singing at that institution, and should be sorry to criticize them in ignorance. But somehow I cannot quite believe that the plan pursued by those six operatic pupils of the College is Badiali's plan. Of course I cannot be positive, for I never heard Badiali; and, anyhow, I am only a critic, and therefore do not profess to speak authoritatively on such questions. Besides, I do not wish to discourage the six, who came off very creditably.

HAMLET: A FOOLISH OPERA
The World, 30 July 1890

[U] If I take the trouble to criticize the Covent Garden performance of Hamlet (the opera, not the play), my object must be understood to be vindictive rather than artistic. Nobody wanted to hear the thing: many critics earnestly desired not to hear it. I suppose M. Lassalle wanted to sing it: if so, he might have done it privately, without dragging us to listen to him. I really never saw such a foolish opera. Imagine buying a book labelled Hamlet, and finding this sort of thing inside:

> "Such crime, good mother, were as bad
> As kill a king and marry with his brother."

I have long since learnt to leave my commonsense at the door when I go to the Opera; but I cannot help taking in a few of my literary prejudices with me; and when they are outraged, I resort, as aforesaid, to vindictive criticism. The title of the work ought to be changed. Since Ambroise Thomas has honestly done his very best not to remind us of Shakespear, why should the subject be dragged in by calling the people in the libretto Ophelia, Hamlet, Laertes, and so on? If this were altered, and the fifth and sixth acts cut out as the seventh has been, there would be time to have another ballet, and get the whole performance over by half-past eleven. It would also be necessary to sacrifice the moving and original episode of Horatio and Marcellus (or Rosencrantz and Guildenstern: I am not quite sure which) rushing in to inform the chorus that *le spectre du feu roi* is walking; but I believe the audience would take the excision as good-humoredly as the chorus takes the ghost story. Then Mlle Richard would no longer have to be abstractly tragic, by which expression I mean tragic for tragedy's sake in the absence of any intelligible grievance.

Mlle Richard's playing reminds me of old times, which I thought—in fact, hoped—were gone for ever. She never faces the other *dramatis personæ*, but tacks round them, looking at them out of the corners of her eyes and agitating her bosom with a tireless persistence that must be the result of long practice. Lassalle, in black, and distressingly conscious of something rotten in the State of Denmark, does not tack so much; but he begins his phrases flat, as a rule, which Mlle Richard never does. Madame Melba sings chromatic *roulades* very prettily, smiling at the nobility and gentry in the pit and grand tiers, who applaud her with that air of thorough connoisseurship in operatic execution of the *haute école* which imposes on everyone who does not know by practical experience how easy it is to take them in. Then she goes to the water and drowns herself, in token whereof her "double" presently appears supine on a sort of toboggan car, and shoots along feet foremost through the bulrushes to the prompt side. It is all as absurd as it can be; and I, dead beat at the end of the season, have hardly energy enough to make fun of it even on this cheap scale. My comfort is that there are only two more nights on which I can possibly be expected to be present—Miss Russell's turn as Valentine in Les Huguenots, and the appearance on the last night of De Reszke and Lassalle as Don José and Escamillo in Carmen, both which occasions will have duly come off by the time this appears in print. After that I must have a thorough rest; so I shall rush off to Oberammergau, and go to every opera I come across *en route*.

Little Max Hambourg gave a second recital last week at Prince's Hall. He quite confirmed the opinion of his capacity which I expressed last week, and which was shared by those critics who know something more about playing than the difference between wrong notes and right ones. I protest as vehemently as ever against the project of exploiting his talent in the market which these recitals shew to be on foot, and I should not help it by mentioning the boy again were it not for the statement which has been circulated that he is about to be taken in hand by Paderewski. Now as Paderewski carries to the verge of caricature all the faults of violence and exaggerated *rubato* effects which the boy shews a tendency to imitate, I have no hesitation in saying that a worse master for such a pupil could not be found in Europe. The only possible good that could come out of the arrangement is that Paderewski might possibly learn something from Max. The last pianist of the season was Miss Sybil Palliser, not many years older than young Hambourg, and fortunate in having parents who will not force her into professional life until the proper time comes. I must not pretend that the announcement that she was to play Beethoven's First Concerto at the

Meistersingers' Club induced me to spend Saturday afternoon in town; but at least I did not abstain on account of her youth. I have no objection whatever to children singing, playing, acting, doing anything they please in the way or art, provided there is no money made by anybody out of them.

It has been such a tremendous season for pianism that, having nothing better to do, I may as well look back for a moment to find whether I remember any of the legion of *virtuosos* who have devasted my afternoons for months past. At once, without any prompting from past articles or programs, I see, among the thoughtful players, Madame Backer-Gröndahl as the foremost woman, and Stavenhagen as the foremost man. On the other side, where I place the pianists whose music is the expression of their strength and joy in life, the leaders are Sophie Menter and Sapellnikoff. I cannot help admiring my own catholicity as a critic when I recall how exquisitely I felt Madame Gröndahl's noble interpretation of Beethoven's Fifth Concerto, and how intensely I enjoyed Sophie Menter's playing of Soirées de Vienne. But I do not forget all I have had to suffer from players who are not great; and if they come back in the wake of Madame Essipoff in October, what am I to do? Hear it all over again? No: rather sweep a crossing—write novels—anything sooner than have my afternoon nap disturbed again by the patent effects, *fortissimo con esplosione*, of such stupendous executants and indifferent interpreters as De Greef, Paderewski, *et hoc genus omne.* Next to the very best, I prefer, as Grétry said (to the intense indignation of Berlioz), *la musique qui me berce.* He who wakes me up, with playing that I dont want to hear, is the man I hate above all others.

Still, with all drawbacks, it has been a fine season. To recapitulate: the fine, delicate, serious, sensitive people have had Madame Schumann replaced from Norway by Madame Backer-Gröndahl, with Stavenhagen thrown in. The warm-blooded races have rejoiced in the *naïve* force of the Russian Sapellnikoff, and the puissant Austrian fire of Sophie Menter, not at all *naïve*, but irresistible. The average sensual man has been astonished by the terrific dexterity of the Belgian De Greef and of Paderewski, both no mere acrobats, but bright, alert, clever men in the general sense. And for those who take a simple delight in dainty melodies and rhythms, neatly and intelligently played, who could be better than Albéniz, not to mention Schönberger? Here are eight first-class players, two to each of the four departments, with an unfortunate but highly gifted small boy thrown in at the end, so as not to leave the season without its *Wunderkind.* And there still remains unclassed such a player as Madame Teresa Carreño, whose playing is nevertheless of exactly the same quality and degree as that which earned an immense reputation for Arabella Goddard.

One thing is clear about the host of artists in the wake of the ones I have mentioned. They have certainly not lived on the proceeds of their well-papered recitals at Steinway and Prince's Halls. The particular London carcase about which the eagles have gathered in such multitude must, I fancy, be the great number of musical clubs which now engage artists for private concerts. A considerable section of the huge middle-class population of London consists of people who are not satisfied to dance in drawing rooms eleven feet by thirteen to the jingling of a cottage pianoforte, or to stand against the walls of the same apartment whilst Miss Smith, who has just had her second lesson at the Guildhall School, warbles Some Day to her sister's accompaniment. But if they cannot afford to rent mansions in Park Lane, or to engage De Soria, Belle Cole, Johannes Wolff, and Hollmann for their "at homes," with Signor Ducci to accompany; and if they have no chance in the world of being invited by those who can, what are they to do? Simply do without until they get sense enough to take collective action, and club together for dances at the Kensington Town Hall and concerts at the Royal Institute. The dances will not turn society upside down: the spare guineas of South Kensington cannot buy better dances and suppers than Mayfair provides for itself within its own boundaries; but when music is the bait, the big fishes begin to rise. The collective purse of Bayswater and Brompton, or, for the matter of that, of Brixton and Holloway, can command Melba, Ysaÿe, Paderewski, or whom it will. More that that, it can procure a smart secretary, on terms with a few first-rate people who are glad to come round and hear their favorite artists for nothing in any convenient place where the company is inoffensive. Thus the omipresent Nobody, by making common cause with a few hundred other Nobodies, escapes from the eleven-foot drawing room and the cottage piano, to become the patron of world-reputed artists, and entertain dukes and ambassadors in marble halls.

To be sure, the dukes and ambassadors do not know his name; but neither, probably, would they if he turned up, a duly invited guest, at one of their own crushes. These cooperative concert stores carry their audacity even to the length of inviting *me* to their evenings; and I do not stay away from any feeling of exclusiveness; for I can honestly say that I am not proud: I stay away partly because I cannot, as I have repeatedly said, be in more than three places at the same time, and partly because unrehearsed miscellaneous programs seldom contain anything that I need hear or have not already heard a dozen times. Secretaries, especially those who do not send programs with their invitations, will please accept this explanation of my apparent indifference to

a development in social organization which I have really
followed with deep interest.[U]

A BACKWARD GLANCE AT THE
OPERA SEASON

The World, 6 August 1890

[U] What may have happened in London last week is
best known to those who were there to hear: for my part,
I left on Tuesday, having only waited (in vain, as it
turned out) to hear the last of the opera on Monday.
Whether I shall be lucky enough to hit on a Wagner
night under Levi at Munich, remains to be seen; but is
it not beyond all reason that I, coming from London at
the end of a season of exceptional musical activity, must
go to Bavaria to hear Die Walküre or Tristan, as a cheap
tripper from Little Peddlington hurries to Madame
Tussaud's? Suppose Levi calls on me to ask what
novelties we have been producing in our great city of
London, where land is worth a million an acre, and the
subsidy for the opera comes from people who can afford
to hide the fabric of their wives' dresses under a crust of
diamonds, what shall I say to him? how meet his calm
rabbinical eye? If I mention Roméo and the Meistersinger he will say "Yes, you had both last year; but what
have you added to your repertory?" Must I tell him of
that startling novelty Gounod's Faust, and assure him
that the soldiers' chorus is very pretty? Will gently-
introduced allusions to Trovatore, Traviata, Carmen,
Les Huguenots, Don Juan, and Le Nozze sufficiently
prepare him for those two climaxes of managerial
enterprise, the revivals of La Favorita and Hamlet? or
had I better pave the way still more carefully by
mentioning Rigoletto and La Sonnambula? Then to

dazzle him with Le Prophète, finish him with Esmeralda, and triumphantly ask him how soon poor Munich intends to wake up and follow our enterprising example! After all, I shall not make such a bad show, especially if I refrain from describing the Verdi and Mozart performances too closely, and invent a Wagner cycle and a run through Otello for the honor of Old England.

But if I were speaking the sober truth to an Englishman, instead of bragging to a foreigner, I should have to say that beyond brushing up last year's successes, and perpetrating the usual scratch performances of hackneyed operas, nothing has been accomplished except the Frenchifying of Esmeralda, and a monstrous waste upon Le Prophète of the time and money that would have sufficed for any of the half-dozen greater works, from Fidelio to Tristan, with which London really wants to become better acquainted. Indeed, this Prophète affair was mere *fainéantise* on the part of the leading artists concerned; for Mlle Richard, the De Reszkes, and Cobalet must know their parts in it backwards. And here let me say that, whilst I fully appreciate the vocal excellence of the Lassalle-De Reszke combination, we shall pay far too dearly for it if these gentlemen are to be allowed to save themselves all trouble by simply transferring the routine of the Paris Opéra to the Covent Garden stage. I must not dwell on the subject, because I am unfortunately unable to keep my temper when I think of that gilded sink of all the absurd conventions and shams which degraded opera to the level of Richardson's Show in the bad old times. No one can doubt that Mlle Richard, Lassalle, and Brothers Jean and Edouard are naturally as capable of intelligent study of their business as Miss Russell, Miss de Lussan, or Valero. Why is it, then, that there was more brainwork in any five minutes of the Valentine, Carmen, and Don José of the three last-named than in Lassalle's Hamlet and Rigoletto, Mlle Richard's Favorita, and Jean de Reszke's whole repertory taken together? Simply because Paris has decreed that three insufferable attitudes, an engagement at the Grand Opéra, and a *tremolo*, are sufficient to hallmark an operatic artist as finished, and absolve him or her from all further thought. I can remember the time when Jean de Reszke was really alive and growing—when he worked at his parts as earnestly as he could. I still look back to his Don Giovanni (immature as it was) and his Valentin in Faust with pleasure; but now there is nothing of him left except the native grace and fine musical instinct that not even Paris can extirpate. Still, I am not without hope in this matter. London has made a stand against the *tremolo*; and it can make an end of the three attitudes if it will only insist on taking Covent Garden more seriously than Covent Garden takes itself, and stubbornly refuse to be Paris-ridden. Even the Cook's tourist ought to see by this time that in music, as in most other things, Paris is still in the year 1850; wheras our Royal Italian Opera is getting well on for 1876. That ineffable empty swagger, that neglect of everything except ecstatic self-assertion, that ridiculous grimace as of a haughty soul struggling with an irrepressible sneeze, would not be tolerated for a moment from an actor or a public speaker in England. Why in the name of commonsense should it be tolerated from an opera singer? I believe it is our insular contempt for the foreigner and the musician that makes us so prone to indulge him as an irresponsible infant, instead of holding him to account as a grown man, our full equal.

A particularly humiliating feature of the season has been the artistic deadness of the orchestra. The peculiarity of the typical London band is that, whilst it is better equipped, and more to be depended on in emergencies than most others, it never displays artistic qualities spontaneously. It has the British shyness of betraying feeling (which is the essence of artistic expression) lest it should seem to be playing the fool. If the conductor will take the responsibility of the display by insisting on it, he can have it: the men are paid to do what he wants; but if he leaves the matter to them, he might as well turn the handle of a street piano: the mere business of the evening will be done, and nothing more. I shall never forget the face of Grieg one morning at a Philharmonic rehearsal as he folded his arms and stared at the famous orchestra when they began the *pianissimo* of the Aase's death prelude from the Peer Gynt music in a stolid and comfortable *mezzo forte*. When Grieg explained that he expected a good deal more than that, he got it—better than he could have had it anywhere else in the world, perhaps, as those who remember the wonderful *pianissimo* achieved at the concert will admit. But the moment Grieg left the desk and was replaced by Dr Mackenzie, back went the band again to their normal empty undemonstrativeness, as if they had never dreamt of anything better in their lives.

At the Opera the story is the same. Bevignani pulls them through rather more successfully than Randegger, because they are for some reason evidently more willing to be pulled through by him; but neither of the two has once screwed them up to the artistic standard of Messrs Imhoff and Mukle's best orchestrions. Mancinelli fails to make himself understood: at least I infer as much from the fact that he managed to get from the Italian orchestra, which he brought together for Mr de Lara's concert, much finer work than he ever did from the Opera band. What is wanted at Covent Garden is a conductor of the calibre of Richter or Faccio. Failing him, I would suggest that the veteran Arditi might relieve Randegger of a duty for which he has no special vocation. It is true that Arditi is some seven years the elder of the twain, being, in fact, exactly as old as August Manns; but he is a fresher conductor than Randegger by a very great deal.

There has been no great making or marring of reputations among the singers. Montariol certainly lost ground: his David in the Meistersinger was not so good as before; and his appearance as Fernando was unlucky. The place which he held in his first season here was captured by Valero, whose southern vivacity, intelligence, and engaging appearance and manners disarmed those who, like myself, do not admire the Gayarré school of voice production. Ravelli also came bravely to the rescue of the management when all the new tenors except Valero had been discreetly dropped; and had he been as much at home in such distinguished parts as Raoul as he was in Elvino, he would have been almost as popular with the gallery as Jean de Reszke. But I must say that when, in that situation in the third act of Les Huguenots, where the Queen reveals to Raoul the truth about Valentine's indiscreet visit to Nevers, I saw him turn round to Mlle Pinkert, with a sweet reassuring smile that said, as plainly as looks could speak, "O, pray dont mention it, your Highness," I felt that Jean's supremacy was safe. Jean, by the bye, did not attempt Raoul this year. His position forbids him ingloriously to shirk the C sharp in the duel septet as Ybos did (Ravelli bawled it like a man); but, position or no position, the note is too dangerous for him: the terror of its approach quite unnerved him during the first half of the opera last year, when he played Raoul to the Valentine of—what was the name?—Madame Tony [Toni] Schläger, I think. He still holds his own as the unapproachable Walther of Walthers in Die Meistersinger. He may miss points in the story, and botch bits of stage business in a way that old Gudehus, for instance, would never be guilty of at Bayreuth; but when he begins singing to the

Masters about the fireside in winter and the woodlands in spring, Gudehus becomes unthinkable. Lassalle as Sachs, too, makes you forget Lassalle as Hamlet and Rigoletto, which is a good deed. Mention of Bayreuth reminds me to ask Mr Harris why he does not look after Van Dyck, the Parsifal of 1889, an irresistible young hero, whose abounding energy would be the best possible foil to De Reszke's inertia. The truth is that Brother Jean wants a competitor to wake him up; and Van Dyck is the man to do it.

Mlle Richard, if her style were not so hopelessly old-fashioned, would be useful enough for parts like Ulrica, Fidès, and Azucena. But as Un Ballo was not played, and Azucena is the property of Madame Scalchi, whose voice is still in great part thick and effective, and whose adroitness in dodging through what she cannot sing straightforwardly is one of the wonders of Covent Garden, Mlle Richard was only wanted for Fidès. Miss Ella Russell kept ahead of most of her competitors by taking her work very seriously. Her Violetta was admirable; her Valentine the other night, if not a consummate achievement, shewed strength and ambition, which means consummation by and by if she perseveres, which she will probably do, as she seems a determined young lady. To encourage her I shall make bold to tell her some of her faults. The first comes from her being of a strong nature, not easily excited or overwrought: not subject to sentimental hysteria, in short. One result of this is that her normal condition, like that of the British orchestra, is prosaic; and so her performances, instead of being of sustained poetic quality throughout, contain long intervals of prose, during which I must confess that the spell which holds me is rather that of her comeliness than of her art. Second—and here I must be brutally frank—Miss Russell pronounces Italian vilely. I do not mean that she would pronounce Azucena as Azoósina, or Civita Vecchia as Siveetar Vetchyar, things which her compatriots have been known to do; but her vowels are shocking. I can assure her that *pietoso ciel* is not capable of phonetic analysis in English as "pyaytoazoaw chayeel," and that *supremo* is not pronounced "soupraymoaw," or anything like it. I exonerate her from the arch-English crime of making the Italian "o" "ow"; but her "e" is the "a" of the four-mile radius: that is, a thumping diphthong, which an Italian would write down as "ei." Third—but if I am to catch the Friday performance at Munich, I must be off at once. My apologies to Madame Melba, Madame Tavary, Madame Nordica, and all the artists I have not mentioned; and—*au plaisir!* [U]

OPERA AND OBERAMMERGAU

The World, 13 August 1890

[U] Did you ever hear an opera with cornet *obbligato*? If you would like to, then do as I have just done: that is, arrive in Frankfurt a day too late for Lohengrin and a day too soon for Tannhäuser, catching Nessler's Trumpeter of Säkkingen in between. Opera in Germany now wavers between Wagner and Der Trompeter, which is the cheerfulest, sentimentalest commonplace imaginable. But it was better fun, by a good deal, than Covent Garden with Rawner and Tetrazzini in Trovatore, or Favorita with Montariol and Mlle Richard. Besides, the opera house at Frankfurt is immensely more commodious than the one in Bow-street. The *foyer* and balcony are as pleasant as those of the Paris Opéra; prices are from eight shillings to sixpence; programs cost a penny;

you can get an ice for sixpence or a glass of seltzer-water for a penny; hours are from half-past six to half-past nine; and everybody is at home there. Girls come in pairs and manipulate their hairpins in the corridor, as if the occasion were a prize-giving at a high school; and the boxes have not the slightest air of Burlington Arcade about them. The Jew rules in Frankfurt even more than in London; but he is much less flashy there than here. Perhaps Frankfurt has forestalled London in discovering that since people who wish to display their gold lace and plush must admittedly hire men to wear them, and on no account use their husbands and sons for that purpose, so people who wish to display diamonds should not make jewelers' showcases of their wives and daughters, but hire suitable-looking maids, and bring them round as part of their retinue.

I had hoped to catch Wagner's Die Feen at Munich before going on to Oberammergau; but, as it is, I have seen the Passion Play, and Die Feen is still three days off. I may not live to witness it, as I failed to secure covered seats for the play, and it rained all Sunday. Imagine going to the theatre at eight, not in the evening but in the morning, and sitting in your stall in the open air from eight to twelve, and from one-fifteen to half-past five, in a steady downpour, with umbrellas, of course, barred. Fortunately I had a mackintosh and a sou'-wester; but what I may have tomorrow I know not—catarrh, rheumatic fever, anything or nothing. I had heard much about the "quaint old music" of the Passion Play. Long ago I learnt what "quaint old music" is, from a certain Shakespear Society, which gave a concert of Shakespearean music once a year. That is, it engaged "a musician," usually an organist, and supplied him with the necessary funds to pay three third-rate concert singers to come and do some Elizabethan glees and madrigals. These unfortunates would find them-

[145]

selves seated round a table, whereon was a sheet of paper on which the four parts of a madrigal were printed so as to face north, south, east, and west respectively. The organist took the bass, not because he had a voice of that or any other quality, but because the tenor was too high for him; and his three retainers plunged after him into the sort of promiscuity which is called reading at sight. To anyone who knows how long glee parties must work together before even the best of them can produce a tolerable result, the results need not be described. To those who do not know it they cannot be described, language being insufficiently vituperative. But the literary audience liked them, applauded them, gloated over them. The more horribly the parts were out of tune, the more preoccupied each singer became with the desperate necessity of keeping his or her place, the more did the eyes of the Society glisten over the "quaintness" of the entertainment.

And such, too, is the quaintness of the Oberammergau orchestra, if not of the singers. The music is no more medieval than Regent-street: it is, at its worst, in the style of the "Italian" masses of Mozart and Haydn; whilst, at its best, it suggests the Zauberflöte and The Creation. It is full of platitudinous Spohrlike paraphrases of With verdure clad, *La dove prende*, the Benedictus from Mozart's Twelfth Mass, and so on. The leading tenor, during the tableau of Tobias, treated us to the policeman's song from The Pirates of Penzance, *alla capella*, and freely translated. The quaintness comes in with the orchestra, in which the strings are nearly in tune, the woodwind moderately out of tune, and the horns miles away from the key. When the effect rises from mere unpleasantness to excruciation, the choir screw up their faces a little; and the American and English visitors (the audiences are the scum of the earth) whisper "How medieval!"

By the choir I mean the twentyfour guardian angels, who play the part of Greek chorus, and serve the same purpose as carpenters' scenes in an ordinary melodrama. There are seven sopranos, seven contraltos, five tenors, and five baritones. Bass voices are apparently not appreciated at Oberammergau; for none of the men attempt to bring their lower registers into full play; indeed, all the singers, men and women, have been taught to sing simply from the throat, with a clear *naïve* effect that is satisfactory except when a high note has to be strained at. The choragus is a baritone. In speaking to an orchestral accompaniment or *mélodrame*—a thing extraordinarily hard to get properly done—he is quite the best artist I ever heard; and he passes from speaking to singing with a naturalness which would be impossible to a more artificially trained singer. The chief tenor, who is a younger man that the choragus, has a pleasant voice and sings sympathetically. The two have a sort of apostolic beauty of face which is not shared by the women. The chief soprano is downright plain; the chief contralto is not particularly goodlooking; the second contralto, the only one who sings persistently out of tune, has a *laideur de diable* which only Mr Ford Madox Brown could admire; and the attractiveness of the third soprano is discounted by her complexion, which, like that of all her colleagues, has been prepared for public exhibition, village fashion, by a merciless scrubbing with a soap that would fetch not only the grime, but the paint as well, from the roof of King's Cross Underground Station. The second baritone is an elderly man whose voice has lost its quality; and the second and third tenors are unfledged and a little discordant. Howbeit, considering that the population of the village is only thirteen hundred, they have not done badly in producing a choir of twentyfour, eleven of whom can be trusted with solos, and four with important singing parts. The twentyfour, however, are not the only vocalists in the place. Everybody sang in the Hosanna scene, though, as there was no conductor, the performers were soon at sixes and sevens. They did not seem in the least concerned, each probably concluding that the rest were at fault. On the whole, the music would have been admirable but for the confounded orchestra.

Though the play is outside my province, yet I may say a word about it, since I tried in vain to persuade William Archer to accompany me. Last year he went to Bayreuth fast enough, though mere dramatic critics have obviously no special business in that sacred place; but when I suggested Oberammergau he recommended me to stay at home and save the money to buy a bicycle. However, a musical critic, having incomparably the most complex and difficult of all critical functions, must know art as it comes fresh from the peasant, just as the dairyman must know milk as it comes fresh from the cow (fourpence a glass at Oberammergau, though there are more cows than men there); so I went, and I am bound to say that I have since found during my wanderings in the Pinakothek here (in Munich) that I have picked up more about early German pictures from the Passion Play than about the modern theatre. The current accounts, though some of them are very good pieces of descriptive writing, are founded on the romance of peasant life as understood in Fleet-street, and not in the least on the actual performance. If the Play were treated in the spirit of the modern realistic movement in art, fortified with modern historical research, it would be extraordinarily impressive. If, on the other hand, it were treated according to village tradition, it would be fresh and interesting. But when it is trimmed to the measure of an exploded artistic convention—when the Christ is neither the Christ of the elder Holbein nor of Von Uhde, but the Christ of

Ary Scheffer and Sir Noel Paton,* then I submit that the people whom it stirs most must be chiefly those who are too pious to go to the theatre ordinarily, and who are therefore easily hypnotized by the effect of the unaccustomed stage illusion on their own fanaticism. Meyer [Josef Mayr], the celebrated Christ, is highly skilled in his perpetual pose as The Man of Sorrows; but then everybody in the place can pose quite miraculously: their *tableaux vivants*, in spite of the effect of daylight on stage scenery (with real Alps visible over the wall for comparison), are superb. Meyer has no idea beyond maintaining that pose: his voice has no sympathetic inflexion in it; he quotes texts instead of holding human intercourse; he never has even the wish to let himself go; he scourges the moneychangers without indignation, speaks to John and to his mother without feeling, tells Judas to do quickly what he has to do without meaning; and is altogether such a cold, unnatural, self-absorbed specimen of the superior person, that the wonder is, not that he is eventually crucified, but that he should ever have been tolerated by any socially disposed human being for half an hour.

The same criticism applies in a minor degree to the Maries and St John. They are just a little more natural than the figure whose notion of being divine is to avoid being human by simply not being anything at all; but they, too, only pose as they have been taught to pose, and declaim as they have been taught to declaim. Far be it from me to complain of their having learnt to stand and speak, since I have suffered so mightily from people who have learnt neither, and are just as void of internal

---

* Ary Scheffer (1795–1858), a Dutch-born French artist, and Sir Joseph Noël Paton (1821–1901), a Scottish painter, frequently dealt with religious subjects. Shaw's criticism of Scheffer was that he painted "operatic Christs."

initiative as the Ammergauers; but it is one thing to appreciate the village actors' skill and diligence, and another to pretend that they are original tragedians. Still, many of those whose parts allow them to act in earnest without compromising their sanctity, play much better than any substitutes which the London stage could provide for them at short notice. Caiaphas is good; so is Pilate; so is Nathanael; several little bits of business by the soldiers and executioners are done with spirit and verisimilitude; and Judas produces a memorably intense effect, in spite of the way in which his part, traditionally a serio-comic one culminating in a scene with the devil, has been watered down for the sake of gentility. In fact, the whole play has been brought to its present complexion by leaving the devil out, and putting nothing in to replace him. There is no adequate motive left for the treachery of Judas, or the fatalistic inertia of Jesus before Pilate. The story, carefully as it is told, has no momentum until the incidents of the final scenes of the Passion produce a sensational interest.

I have missed Die Feen after all: it has been postponed beyond my utmost opportunity of waiting. Instead, I have heard Der Freischütz, with Vogl, Fuchs, Gura (as the Hermit), and Fräulein Dressler. The spirit and earnestness of the performance were admirable; and the orchestra played the overture "*à la* Wagner," and preserved the artistic atmosphere throughout. And yet the clarinet players had cut their reeds as only street players cut them in England; the brass lacked finesse and dignity; and the quality of tone was in no department equal to what is to be had for the asking in London, if only anyone will take the trouble to ask for it. And not one of the singers, famous as some of them were, could execute a scale or a *gruppetto* neatly; though they could speak well, act well, and co-ordinate their efforts for the sake of the story, which they evidently knew by heart. Why, with so much better material, do we fall so far short of them? [U]

ITALIAN OPERA AND THE FRENCH DICKENS

The World, 20 August 1890

[U] There is so little doing in my department just now that it became a question the other evening whether I should go to a Promenade Concert, or, like my distracted colleagues, write a long essay on Signor Lago's announcement of an October season of Italian opera. However, as I do not know exactly what Signor Lago intends to do, and am even doubtful as to how far he knows himself, I have nothing to say except that the low prices are a move in the right direction. Still I would not, if I were an *impresario*, build too much on the success of October seasons and cheap seats in bygone days. Several things have happened since then. The development of English opera at the Savoy, Prince of Wales's, and Lyric theatres has accustomed the public to have dramatic music served up to them daintily in houses of moderate size, and sung by *prima donnas* on the right side of fortyfive, and considerably under nineteen stone in weight, supported by tenors free from any appearance of gaining their livelihood precariously between one engagement and another by retailing penny ices.

There was a time when I did not greatly mind seeing Violetta laid up with consumption in a small bed in the middle of an apartment rather larger than Trafalgar Square, and consequently worth about six thousand a year in a fairly good neighborhood in Paris. I accepted it, as I accepted her going to bed in white kid boots with high heels, or getting up in the middle of a faint to acknowledge the applause, or retaining all her vocal powers with her lungs in ribbons, or any other trifle that might save trouble. But as I get on in life my powers of make-believe fail. After seeing La Dame aux Camélias on a well-appointed stage of the proper size, La Traviata in the Brobdingnagian *salons* of Covent Garden suddenly becomes ridiculous. Esmeralda's broad acres of garret; poor Gretchen's gigantic cell, into which the Russian Government would think nothing of putting four hundred prisoners down with Siberian fever; the Count's bedroom in La Sonnambula, three times as large as the inn which contains it appeared in the first act, and exactly the same breadth as the cathedral of Münster in The Prophet: all these things stuck in my throat last season as they never did in times past. In vain you tell me that I still put up with greater incongruities, and that it is illogical to strain at a gnat and swallow a camel. It may be illogical to strain at a cat and swallow jugged hare; but men are not made to conform to syllogisms; and just as the restaurateur has to jug hares and keep cat carefully out of his *menu*, so the *impresario* who wishes to please me must serve my camel without gnats, however inconsequent my repugnance to them may be.

It is this growth of squeamishness which makes it dangerous to argue from the past to the present in speculations which turn on the public toleration of Italian opera. Unless Signor Lago is prepared to engage artists who will draw the town under any circumstances, he had better not depend too much on the fascinations of Il Barbiere, L'Elisir, and Lucia. If he really means to produce Otello he will find that Les Huguenots and the eternal Faust will be the safest companions for it in the absence of any serious new departure. The project for reviving Gluck is not a very hopeful one. Gluck, as "le classique" *par excellence*, has bored many generations of Frenchmen, just as Handel has bored many generations of Englishmen. Much as I hate "le classique," I have a great regard for Gluck; and if an afternoon performance of one of his operas were got up in the style of Dr Todhunter's Greek plays, I should enjoy it with academic serenity, and even with a touch of genuinely appreciative emotion. But at night, in a big theatre, before an unprepared, impatient, unlettered crowd, with little Latin and less Greek, and accustomed to richer and more sensational fare, I fear that a Gluck opera, unless consummately handled, would be voted slow and old-fashioned. My own admiration for the composer of Orfeo, Alceste, and the two Iphigenias may be a piece of old-fashionedness on my own part; for I do not mind confessing to a growing misgiving that I am falling behind the times. One night this season I got talking, between the acts of Il Trovatore, to a young violinist—a man, as I guess, some fifteen years my junior, and *très fin de siècle*. "What can you do with such stuff as that?" he said, contemptuously indicating the page of rum-tum on the desk before him. "Ugh! it's like the Messiah." Like the Messiah!—a work the greatness of which I had never dreamt of questioning in my life, in spite of my implacable contempt for oratorio as a *genre*. And nothing happened to the ribald: the earth did not yawn, nor the roof fall and crush him. I felt my hair turning grey and the ploughshare passing along my wrinkles as the august Handelian score came up before my mind's eye, and I had to confess that there was a terrible deal of rum-tum in it, and that sawing through those mechanical violin parts must be truly a dreary job to young giants nursed on Tristan and Die Meistersinger. Granting that my fiddler friend, who had a sprightly wit, was a bit of a *farceur*, would he have amused himself in that fashion—recognizing his game in me, as it were—if he had not considered me a bit of a fogey?

In truth, he so alarmed me that I tried to bring myself up to date on my way to Oberammergau by reading a French novel, feeling that my habit of taking up a volume of Dickens on the rare occasions when I have time to read anything would no longer pass muster with the new generation. I consulted a friend as to what I should read; and he, having ascertained that my knowledge of French fiction was derived from Manon Lescaut, an odd volume of Les Misérables, and the works of Alexandre Dumas *père*, confidently prescribed a writer named Daudet,* of whom I had never heard, but whom he guaranteed to be the modern French Dickens. So I went three francs fifty on a Daudet novel, and found that Dickens has rather fallen off in his latest incarnation. Nevertheless, there is in it a capital description of a reception by a Minister of Fine Arts in Paris, who entertained his guests with a program of music, starting *en vrai classique*, with the solemn chorus at the beginning of the first act of Gluck's Orfeo. I have always had the greatest respect for that chorus; and yet Daudet's account of the desperate *ennui* produced by it at the reception carried conviction to me. I was pleased to find the French Dickens explaining it on the ground, not that Gluck is dull, but that Paris remains, as she always has been since she was invented, incapable of high art. When I say the same thing I am accused of mere perversity and paradox. But since my encounter with the violinist I feel no confidence in Orfeo faring any better in London. Perhaps a course of the splendacious tedium of Versailles before the Revolution is

* Alphonse Daudet, contemporary French novelist and poet, was a gentle satirist in his fiction. His Sapho later inspired the Massenet opera (1897). The novel Shaw had been reading was Numa Roumestan (1881).

needed to make Gluck seem the innovator and sensationalist his contemporaries took him for. Perhaps, too, he has been superseded by Mozart, who did everything that he had done, and did it better, exception being made as to spurious Greek tragedy, which nobody greatly wants. Anyhow, there was a Gluck Society in London some dozen years ago; for I can recall with pleasure an excellent performance of Alceste, in which Mr Theo. Marzials sang the part of Hercules: yet I do not think the performance was a financial success; nor has Mr Malcolm Lawson, the conductor of the society, been able to keep it afoot. On the whole, I cannot believe—though I wish I could—that there is much money in Gluck for Signor Lago, unless his Viennese *prima donna* is exceptionally magnetic.

As to the Promenade Concerts, I actually did go to the first "classical night" (save the mark!), arriving too late to hear that masterpiece of respectable emptiness and decorous triviality, Cherubini's overture to Anacreon. In fact, I missed several high-class works, such as the prelude to Massenet's Hérodiade, which bears about the same relation to what is usually understood by classical music as Mr Pettie's pictures do to Raphael's or Mr Lewis Morris's poetry to Goethe's.* Still, I have no sort of objection to the inclusion of *entr'actes* and preludes in programs of which the chief use is to break serious music gently to the novice. When I entered, Madame Marie Roze was singing *Deh vieni, non tardar*, and, I am bound to say, singing it very indifferently. But then she always did sing indifferently, even when

---

* John Pettie, Scottish artist who favored historical and genre paintings, took many romantic subjects from Sir Walter Scott's novels. Lewis Morris, a Welsh attorney, published a number of volumes of verse, including A Vision of Saints (1890).

her voice, as far as its quality was concerned, was in its prime. Whenever I go to criticize Madame Marie Roze, I shut my ears and open my eyes, with the happiest results. That is hardly what one would do in the case of Madame Belle Cole, who sang Weber's enchanting *O Fatima!* and brought down the house; so that she had to sing Gounod's Whither thou goest for an *encore*.

This reminded me of Ulm Cathedral, into which I fled the other evening to escape from seeing an obscene steeple which some rascally "restorer," whetted by the disfigurement of the Dom at Cologne, has clapped on the tower. Ulm Cathedral ranks with some half-dozen others among the most beautiful things ever made by the hand of man; and I have seldom been more content than when, as I sat down in one of the curious old stalls at the pew corners to take in at my ease the beauty of the clustered columns that divide the place into lines of poetry in stone, a woman began to sing that great old air of Bach's, *Mein gläubiges Herze*, known in England as My heart ever faithful. The violin *obbligato* was played, too; and the voice and the sound of the fiddle, as they soared through the arches, were wonderful, though the violinist fetched a note or two appallingly flat. Then the organist extemporized on the theme of the song, to shew off his instrument (the largest in Germany), with all manner of ingenious stops and shutters; so that he could either thunder in a fashion that made the elbows of my stall tingle, or else lift up his music until it died away in the highest heaven. Unlike Madame Marie Roze, it bore listening to better than looking at, did this organ. If the architect had been alive to see an ugly kist of whistles deliberately stuck right across the rose window over the porch, he would certainly have gone for it with a hatchet. Now the connexion between Madame Belle Cole at Covent Garden and Fräulein Marie Brackenhammer in Ulm Cathedral is that the refrain of Gounod's Whither thou goest is virtually this same air, My heart ever faithful. The reminiscence made me rather impatient of the architectural features of Covent Garden; and when the band attacked a symphony of Dvořák's, my attention wandered so hopelessly that I went home. [U]

BALLET AT THE ALHAMBRA
The World, 27 August 1890

There is no month like August in London. I know nothing more soothing than a walk down Regent-street with all the social pressure off. A horrible story in the papers the other day told us about a marine excursion for the purpose of gratifying idle curiosity as to the sort of fishes that live in the profounder depths of the sea. Needless to add, the marine excursion called itself a scientific expedition, a title which covers a multitude of sins, especially that of unscrupulous cruelty. It has long been known that a Londoner, when suddenly relieved in August of the enormous pressure under which he has lived during the season, exhibits certain curious phenomena. He casts his gloves; his coats change from broadcloth to Scotch tweed; the gleaming black and white cylinders disappear from his head and wrists; and his appearance, considered as the index of his income, deteriorates by at least two hundred a year. The scientific gentlemen yearned to see what would happen to fishes in similar circumstances: hence the expedition. A netful of flattened-out creatures was hauled up from the bottom of the ocean, where they lived with the weight of the whole Atlantic on their backs, to the deck of the scientific ship, where the pressure was light as air. The fishes all burst; and it is now an established fact that the fish is inferior to the Londoner in capacity for adapting itself to circumstances. Let us hope that nothing will happen to that ship, lest the relatives of the exploded martyrs to science be tempted to burst themselves in another way without coming to the surface at all. However, this is somewhat of a digression. What I am trying to say, in as long a way as possible, is that August has set me free to do what a journalist ought to do all the year round—that is, wander in search of something interesting to write about, instead of, as at the height of the season, cramming his column with records of thousands of insignificant things for no better reason than that they are happening, and that people are supposed to want to know everything that is going on, whether interesting or not. That is why the papers now set to work in earnest to tell us in an artistic way the pick of the news between China and Peru, instead of mechanically choking us with the whole of the news between the Griffin and Hyde Park Corner, condensed in the style of the Exchange Telegraph tape.

The other evening it suddenly came into my head that a musical critic could not do better than go to a music hall. The difficulty in the way was the memory of previous experiments in that direction, which had thoroughly convinced me that what makes one man merry makes another melancholy mad; and that I, as far as music halls are concerned, belong to the melancholy mad section. Finally I compromised the matter by going to see the ballet at the Alhambra, and enduring a few of the preliminary "turns" with a view to observing the progress of the music hall school of singing. For it is a distinct school, and in some respects a very striking one. Whether it has any regular teaching professors I do not know: possibly there may be Porporas, Bordognis, Romanos, Behnkes, and Lampertis who preserve the traditional renderings of What cheer, Ria? and Arsk a

P'liceman; who teach pure Whitechapel English; and who are experts in developing that amazing *voce di petto*, five minutes of which would finish Patti's career for ever.

But more probably the music hall *prima donna*, like the literary man, picks up her profession imitatively and intuitively. If a novice came to me for advice, I should recommend her to make the chest register of her voice strong and coarse by using it vigorously and constantly— even vituperatively on occasion—in public and private speech. The rest I take to be a matter of main strength. That chest voice has to be forced, with the utmost resonance of which it is capable, an octave higher than the point at which the well-trained opera and concert singer drops it and betakes herself to her middle register. The thing is impossible; but, like many impossibilities, it can be accomplished at certain sacrifices—sacrifices which would disqualify an opera singer (which *have* disqualified several, in fact), but which do not matter in a music hall.

For instance, the effort cannot be sustained for long: two successive songs *con tutta la forza* can hardly be achieved without such restful devices as speaking, or rather shouting, several of the lines through the music, and occasionally subsiding into the comparative tranquillity of a step-dance. Again, the singer must forgo all power to use her voice sanely; for even if she could fall back on the artistic method, she dare no more face the tremulous squeaking sound of her own ruined upper registers than Edouard de Reszke dare chant Marcel's doxology in Les Huguenots in his head voice. She must vanquish her songs by going at them as if each verse were a round in a very fast glove-fight—which, by the bye, would be slightly less fatiguing to the performers, and, on the whole, decidedly less brutalizing to the audience. There are, however, certain gifted women who have mixed voices, shrill and ringing at the top, intensely telling in the middle, and flexible all over. With such an organ as this, a good ear, and such an abundance of *la joie de vivre* as may raise vulgarity to the pitch of genius, the lowliest lass (the lowlier the better, in fact) may become a veritable *diva* of the London Pavilion, and enter into the closest relations with the Peerage.

I was not fortunate enough to come across such a star at the Alhambra; yet I heard artists who shewed an amazing capacity for taking infinite pains over any musical feat, provided only that it was clearly not worth doing. In the most eccentric ways and with stupendous virtuosity they played trashy tunes on all manner of unmusical instruments, from sticks and sleigh bells up to banjos and mandolins. Where they live, and how they induce the neighbors to stand their practising, baffles my acutest conjecture. If they amused me more than the singers, they gave me less food for professional reflection. I have spoken of the music hall singer's reliance for effect on the ardent abuse of a mere corner of the voice, at the cost of the destruction of the rest of it; but I had no need to go to the music halls to learn that trick. Italian opera familiarized me with it long before I ever knew what the inside of a music hall is like. If you study the scores of Handel, who knew how to treat the human voice, you will find that when he was not writing to suit individual peculiarities he recognized practically only two sorts of voices for each sex, and that he insisted on an effective range of from an octave and a sixth or thereabout to two octaves, the different registers relieving and contrasting with oneanother so as to get the greatest variety of effect with the least fatigue. Turn then to a score by Verdi, and see how the effective compass demanded from a singer has been reduced to a minor sixth at the extreme top, within which narrow

[160]

bounds, however, the most unreasonable and monotonous strain is mercilessly enforced.

Anyone who knows how to sing can go through all the solos proper to his or her voice in the Messiah, and feel not only free from fatigue, but much the better for the exercise. The same experiment on Il Trovatore or Un Ballo would leave them tired and, as regards a considerable part of their compass, almost toneless. The *reductio ad absurdum* of the Verdi style is the music hall style, which is simply the abuse of a particular part of the voice carried to its furthest possible limit. Signor d' Andrade at Covent Garden, who can shout all the high G's of the Count di Luna with the greatest gusto, fails as Figaro in Le Nozze, exactly as the vivacious lady who sang Woman, Poor, Weak Woman at the Alhambra the other night would fail if she were to try *Eccomi alfine in Babilonia*, or Return, O God of Hosts. No doubt she would protest that Rossini and Handel did not know how to write for the voice, quite as vehemently as the Verdi screamers did when Wagner went back to the old plan and revived the art of singing for us.

The ballet, wherein we passed at a bound from the Utter Popular to the Ultra Academic—from the toe and heel crudities of the step-dance to the classical *entrechats* of the grand school—was dramatically weak. A ballet without a good story and plenty of variety of scene and incident is much like one of Handel's operas, which were only stage concerts for shewing off the technical skill of the singers. Now the deftest shake and the most perfect *roulade* soon pall unless they are turned to some dramatic purpose: we put up even with the nightingale only by giving it credit for poetic fancies that never came into its head. It is the same with dancing when somebody else is doing it: we soon weary of the few *pas* which make up the dancer's stock-in-trade.

We demand, first, a pretty dance (and composers of

[161]

good dances are no more plentiful than composers of good songs); and, second, a whole drama in dance, in which the *pas seul* shall merge, as the aria and cavatina have at last merged in the Wagnerian music-drama. In opera this has been done by a gradual reduction of the independence and consequent incongruity of the soloist's show-piece until it became an integral part of the act. But I cannot say that I see much progress in this direction in the ballet. The solos are still often as absurdly out of place as those of Mr Folair and the Infant Phenomenon*; and the old final *cadenza* and high note, which in opera is now either absorbed into the song structure or abolished altogether, flourishes in its choreographic form in the ridiculous teetotum spin round the stage with which every solo in a ballet ends. It is really a sort of taking round the hat for applause, as undignified in intention as it is unlovely in appearance.

The worst of it is that the only journalistic scrutiny as yet brought to bear on dancing is of a sort now all but obsolete in every other art. The very vilest phase of criticism is that in which it emerges from blank inanity into an acquaintance with the terms, rules, and superstitions which belong to the technical processes of the art treated of. It is then that you get asinine rigmaroles praising hopelessly commonplace painters for their "marvelous foreshortening," their knowledge of anatomy, their "correct composition" (meaning that every group of figures has the outline of a candle extinguisher), and so on; whilst great composers are proved to be ignorant and tasteless pretenders, because their discords are unprepared and improperly resolved, or their harmony full of false relations and consecutive fifths, or because *si contra fa diabolus est*. Why, I have myself been reproached with ignorance of "the science

* Characters in Dickens's Nicholas Nickleby.

[162]

of music" because I do not impose on the public by hoggishly irrelevant displays of ignorance of the true inwardness of musical technology! Now it happens that in an evil hour the technology of the ballet has been betrayed to the critics by a friend of mine. Being a clergyman,* he found it necessary to disabuse his clients of their pious opinion that a ballet dancer is a daughter of Satan who wears short skirts in order that she may cut lewd capers. He bore eloquent testimony to the devoted labor and perseverance involved by the training of a fine dancer, and declared his conviction of the perfect godliness of high art in that and all other forms. To this day you may see in the list of his works the title Art of Theatrical Dancing, immediately following Laws of Eternal Life. All this is much to his credit; but unfortunately his indiscreet revelation of how a critic with no artistic sense of dancing may cover up his incapacity by talking about *ronds de jambe*, arabesques, elevations, *entrechats, ballonnés*, and the like, threatens to start a technicojargonautic fashion in ballet criticism, and whilst it lasts there will be no abolishing the absurdities and pedantries which now hamper the development of stage dancing; for the critics will make as much as possible of any ugly blemish (the teetotum spin, for instance), provided only they can thereby parade their knowledge of its technical name.

I have left myself no room to speak more particularly of Salandra, as the Alhambra ballet is called: let it suffice that it is not so good as Asmodeus; that Legnani, young, intelligent, and not yet in her prime, holds her own against the memory of the superb and magnetic Bessone, more by a certain freshness and *naïveté* than by her execution, which is nevertheless sufficiently brilliant; and that Vincenti, the best male dancer I have ever

* The Rev. Stewart Headlam.

[163]

seen, is as admirable as ever, though this ballet does not shew him at his best.

CAPTAIN THÉRÈSE

The World, 3 September 1890

I am sorry I cannot describe the plot of Captain Thérèse. The outline of it in the "book of words," unbearably bald as it is, would, if quoted verbatim, occupy a column and a quarter of your space. Even then the reader would be no wiser; for though I have read this *précis* with close attention, and seen the performance into the bargain, I can make nothing of it. How much of it is Bisson and how much Burnand I know no more than the babe unborn. No doubt when Mr Monkhouse talks about grasping at the *château* and missing the substance, that is Burnand; and when everybody enters into inconceivable explanations as to the movements of an army which changes from French to Spanish and back again every fifteen minutes, getting a new commander-in-chief each time, and falling at last into such hopeless confusion that it arrests its own officer as a spy, and proceeds to court-martial the entire cast: that, let us patriotically hope, is Bisson. However this may be, one thing is clear: the first thing to do with Captain Thérèse is to cut out the plot. The next step will be to cut out the music, even at the risk of leaving somewhat of a hiatus in an entertainment which is, after all, advertized as an opera. I do not say that one or two of M. Planquette's numbers might not be retained to avoid any injury to his feelings; but he would, perhaps, himself prefer the entire suppression of a score which convicts him in every bar of an exhausted invention and a resourcelessly limited technique.

Surely there was no need to go to France for these qualifications: have we not plenty of native composers who would be only too happy to oblige? Certainly, if any of our young lions were allowed to try their hands, there would be serious danger of the audience being no longer able to remember the music phrase by phrase, progression by progression, as they listened, or to forget it with perfect indifference the moment it ceased; but this might be put up with for the sake of a dash of freshness, youth, spirits, fun, imagination, and possibly even of genuine musical originality. Nor need the work to which our musicians are now condemned be left undone, if they take to light opera. M. Planquette might undertake the oratorios, the symphonies, the cantatas for the provincial festivals: his talent is just ripe for them. Professor Villiers Stanford, Mr Cliffe, Mr MacCunn, and the rest could then follow the example of Sir Arthur Sullivan and fertilize their wasting talents by condescending to do as Mozart did—or as near as they can get to it.

There is nothing else in Captain Thérèse that I could wish to see excised, except perhaps all the incidents and most of the dialogue. The characters may be retained, though the only one who does not seem entirely extraneous, and obviously dragged in for the sake of the performer, is Madame Sombrero, who does not appear. And here let me drop the pretence of treating Captain Thérèse seriously as an opera, and put it on its own ground as a sort of variety entertainment to exhibit the popular aspects of Mr Hayden Coffin and Miss Phyllis Broughton. I say aspects advisedly, for I noticed no attempt to display their artistic gifts. Mr Coffin has evidently a great deal of capacity as a singer and actor; but it is running to seed for want of any real appreciation of its value on the part of the management, or on that of the opera purveyors whom the management delights to honor. Far be it from me to deny the grace of the stupendous flirtations, dancings, and kissings with which he and Miss Broughton gather the roses while they may; but I cannot help asking whether a young artist is to spend his whole life at this sort of thing.

A new American *prima donna* was announced because a similar engagement had been successful in the case of Paul Jones.* So much are the managers creatures of habit. The lady in question, Miss Attallie Claire, has a light soprano voice, not very voluminous, but of pretty and unforced tone. Perhaps it was made a condition of her engagement that she should be a contralto, because Miss Huntington was a contralto: at any rate, Miss Claire has been at some pains to cultivate her voice and extend its range downward rather than upward, not without success, as she sang a contralto song in the first act acceptably. But that does not at all alter the fact that she is neither a contralto nor even a mezzo, but a soprano. Mr Joseph Tapley is not a bad specimen of the English sentimental tenor. He lacks variety, like an organ with only one stop to it, though the one stop in his case is a popular one. As a speaker Mr Tapley breaks down. Vaguely conscious of difficulties in the way, and resolute not to be beaten, he rushes impetuously at his dialogue, and cries it about the stage as if his audience were deaf or a hundred yards away. His vocal tone in speaking, too, is poor, nasal, undignified, altogether out of the question, as if it had never occurred to him that quality of sound is as important in speech as in song. If the Daly Company were still in London, I should say to him "Go to Miss Rehan, thou sluggard [if Mr Tapley will excuse that expression—not my own]: consider her

* Paul Jones, a comedietta with music by Robert Planquette, had recently completed a run of 370 performances at the Prince of Wales' Theatre.

ways, and be wise." But the sequel would have been a month's study with some competent guide, by which I do not mean an elocutionist of the Wopsle* school, who makes his victims give speeches from Shakespear "off the chest," nor yet a pedant under the impression that it is correct to pronounce organ as "Orr Gann." Still further is it from my mind to find a job for any gentleman who may have had the misfortune to discover the universal principle which underlies all beauty. But if Mr Tapley can find a counselor with the knowledge of an expert in phonetics, and the feeling of an artist for beauty of sound, he will be well repaid for a little attentive study by a considerable reinforcement of his own position. What is more—and this, of course, is what I am interested in bringing about—he will raise the artistic standard for his class of work, and make an end of the notion that a young opera singer who can get his one or two cheap ballads encored every night has nothing more to learn.

Those who know how slavishly the members of provincial touring companies copy their metropolitan prototypes, and how apt the provincial amateur is to buy the touring tenor's songs and imitate his ways, also know how appallingly true it is that theatres like the Prince of Wales', the Lyric, and the Savoy are more important as centres of artistic influence than St James's Hall and Covent Garden. Mr Tapley's national responsibility as an artist, in fact, is heavier than that of Jean de Reszke. However, if Mr Tapley must be taken exception to as a singer who is no speaker, what am I to say of those colleagues of his who are speakers but no singers? The barbarities which Mr Ashley inflicts on himself and his audience in the course of his experiments as a *basso cantante* are not to be described, and hardly to

* Character in Dickens's Great Expectations.

be endured. Mr Monkhouse's long *scena*, Two years ago, you understand, is so depressing that I could not help feeling that it would have been better for me had Mr Monkhouse never been born. But this feeling gave way to one of intense gratitude when I found that he was not going to make love to the elderly canoness who disguised herself as a soldier. I had mortally feared an attempt to revive the detestable Lurcher and Priscilla business from Dorothy; and it is something to be able to say that my fears were groundless. The comic business, if it is sometimes unnecessarily silly and vulgar, is at least not odious.

Somebody has sent me a cutting from which I gather that a proposal to form a critics' club has reached the very elementary stage of being discussed in the papers in August. Now clearly a critic should not belong to a club at all. He should not know anybody: his hand should be against every man, and every man's hand against his. Artists insatiable by the richest and most frequent doses of praise; *entrepreneurs* greedy for advertisement; people without reputations who want to beg or buy them ready made; the rivals of the praised; the friends, relatives, partisans, and patrons of the damned; all these have their grudge against the unlucky Minos in the stalls, who is himself criticized in the most absurd fashion.

People have pointed out evidences of personal feeling in my notices as if they were accusing me of a misdemeanor, not knowing that a criticism written without personal feeling is not worth reading. It is the capacity for making good or bad art a personal matter that makes a man a critic. The artist who accounts for my disparagement by alleging personal animosity on my part is quite right: when people do less than their best, and do that less at once badly and self-complacently, I hate them, loathe them, detest them, long to tear them limb from limb and strew them in gobbets about the stage or platform. (At the Opera, the temptation to go out and ask one of the sentinels for the loan of his Martini, with a round or two of ammunition, that I might rid the earth of an incompetent conductor or a conceited and careless artist, has come upon me so strongly that I have been withheld only by my fear that, being no marksman, I might hit the wrong person and incur the guilt of slaying a meritorious singer.)

In the same way, really fine artists inspire me with the warmest personal regard, which I gratify in writing my notices without the smallest reference to such monstrous conceits as justice, impartiality, and the rest of the ideals. When my critical mood is at its height, personal feeling is not the word: it is passion: the passion for artistic perfection—for the noblest beauty of sound, sight, and action—that rages in me. Let all young artists look to it, and pay no heed to the idiots who declare that criticism should be free from personal feeling. The true critic, I repeat, is the man who becomes your personal enemy on the sole provocation of a bad performance, and will only be appeased by good performances. Now this, though well for art and for the people, means that the critics are, from the social or clubable point of view, veritable fiends. They can only fit themselves for other people's clubs by allowing themselves to be corrupted by kindly feelings foreign to the purpose of art, unless, indeed, they join Philistine clubs, wherein neither the library nor the social economy of the place will suit their nocturnal, predatory habits. If they must have a club, let them have a pandemonium of their own, furnished with all the engines of literary vivisection. But its first and most sacred rule must be the exclusion of the criticized, except those few stalwarts who regularly and publicly turn upon and criticize their critics. (No critics' club would have any right to the name unless it included—but the printer warns me that I have reached the limit of my allotted space.)

MODERN MEN: SIR ARTHUR SULLIVAN

The Scots Observer, 6 September 1890; unsigned

If a boy wishes to waste his life by taking himself too seriously, he cannot do better than get educated in a cathedral choir with a view to winning the Mendelssohn Scholarship and devoting himself thenceforth to the cultivation of high-class music. Once fortified with a degree of Mus. Bac. and a calm confidence in his power to write a Magnificat in eight real parts, to "analyze" the last movement of the Jupiter Symphony, and to mention at any moment the birthday of Orlandus Lassus, he enters life as a gentleman and a scholar, with a frightful contempt for Offenbach and a deep sense of belonging to the same artistic caste as Handel. Not that he thinks himself as good a man as Handel; but his modesty is of the *anch' io son pittore* kind—for he, too, can write a fugue. Presently he finds that nobody wants fugues— that they are never asked for, nor properly relished when offered gratuitously. Publishers issue them at the composer's expense only: a rule which applies also to Magnificats, Tantum Ergos, and other fearful wildfowl. He begins to feel the force of that old professorial "wheeze": "Learn to write a fugue; and then dont do it." Hereupon he asks himself, How is a man to live? Well, there are still young people who have not yet realized the situation; and these want to be taught to write fugues. Accordingly, the Mus. Bac. takes pupils and a church organ, which is a highly serious instrument, lending itself to counterpoint by its construction, and reserved for music of the exclusive kind—Jackson in B flat, Goss in F, Handel's anthems, and the like. Then, there is the prospect of promotion to a church with an important musical service, perhaps to a cathedral. The provincial festivals may commission an oratorio once in twenty years or so; and the Philharmonic might even rise—(such things have been!)—at an overture. An occasional Christmas carol (or even anthem) to keep one's hand in is sure, on attaining a hearing in his own choir, to create that acceptable awe with which an impressionable public regards the man who understands the "theory of music."

This is no bad life for one whose turn for music does not include inventiveness, nor grace of workmanship, nor humor (creative originality is here left out of account, as it must always fight and conquer as best it can). But if he has these three gifts, his proper sphere is the theatre—not the "Royal Italian Opera," but the Savoy, the Prince of Wales', and the Lyric. Now the pedigree of such houses will not bear investigation: in vain do they imply that they are first cousins to the Opéra Comique: their common and all too immediate ancestor was the Bouffes Parisiennes; and he who composes for them must risk being cut by the decorous and eminently gentlemanly remnant of the Sterndale Bennett set, and must mix with that of the profane and scandalous Offenbach. Anyone who knows the number of footpounds of respectability under which an organist lies flattened can imagine the superhuman courage required for such an act of self-declassation. Not even the present writer, though shrouded in anonymity and wholly independent of the organ, dares positively assert that Offenbach was a much greater composer than Sterndale Bennett, although he submits that the fact is obvious. Grove's Dictionary of Music gives nine columns of eulogy, tombstone-like in its fervor and solemnity, to Bennett; whilst Offenbach has one shamefaced column, recalling by its tone an unspeakable passage in Robertson's history of Queen Mary, in which apology is made for the deplorable necessity of mentioning one so far beneath the dignity of history as Rizzio. Grove—the institution, not the individual Sir George—owes it to society not to mention that La Grande Duchesse, as an original and complete work of art, places its composer heavens high above the superfine academician who won rest and self-complacency as a superior person by doing for Mendelssohn what Pasteur has done for the hydrophobia virus, and who by example and precept urged his pupils never to strive after effect. This counsel, worthy of the best form of Mrs General,* was not only, as Wagner remarked, "all very well, but rather negative": it was also a rebuke to Offenbach, who was always striving after effect, as every artist who is not ashamed of his calling must unceasingly strive from his cradle to his grave.

The reader is now in a position to understand the tragedy of Sir Arthur Sullivan. He was a Mendelssohn Scholar. He was an organist (St Somebody's, Chester Square). He wrote a symphony. He composed overtures, cantatas, oratorios. His masters were Goss and Sterndale Bennett himself. Of Magnificats he is guiltless; but two Te Deums and about a dozen anthems are among the fruits of his efforts to avoid the achievement of an effect. He has shewn his reverence for the classics in the usual way by writing "additional accompaniments" to Handel's Jephtha; and now he has five columns in Grove and is a knight. What more could a serious musician desire? Alas! the same question might have been put to Tannhäuser at the singing-bee in the Wartburg, before

* Character in Dickens's Little Dorrit.

he broke out with his unholy longing for Venus. Offenbach was Sullivan's Venus as Mendelssohn was his St Elisabeth. He furtively set Cox and Box to music in 1869, and then, overcome with remorse, produced Onward, Christian Soldiers and over three dozen hymns besides. As the remorse mellowed, he composed a group of songs—Let Me Dream Again, Thou'rt Passing Hence, Sweethearts, and My Dearest Heart—all of the very best in their *genre*, such as it is. And yet in the very thick of them he perpetrated Trial by Jury, in which he outdid Offenbach in wickedness, and that too without any prompting from the celebrated cynic, Mr W. S. Gilbert. When Offenbach wrote Orphée aux Enfers he certainly burlesqued *le classique*; but he spared Gluck: it is no parody of *Che farò* that he introduces in the Olympus scene, but the veritable air itself; and when some goddess—Diana?—says an affectionate word of recognition, one feels that for the moment *opéra bouffe* has softened—has taken off its hat to the saintly days of yore. But Sullivan wantonly burlesqued *D' un pensiero* in the quintet with chorus beginning A nice dilemma. Had it been *Chi mi frena* or *Un di se ben* one might have laughed; but the innocent, tender, touching, beloved-from-of-old *D' un pensiero*! Nobody but an irreclaimable ribald would have selected that for his gibes. Sullivan murdered his better nature with this crime. He rose to eloquence again for a moment in setting certain words—

> I have sought, but I seek it vainly,
> That one lost chord divine.

No wonder. This was in 1877, when he was thirtyfive. But no retreat was possible after A Nice Dilemma: not even a visit from the ghost of Sterndale Bennett could have waved him back from the Venusberg then. The Sorcerer belongs to 1877 as well as The Lost Chord; and everybody knows Pinafore and The Gondoliers and all that between them is; so that now the first of the Mendelssohn Scholars stands convicted of ten godless mockeries of everything sacred to Goss and Bennett. They trained him to make Europe yawn; and he took advantage of their teaching to make London and New York laugh and whistle.

A critic with no sense of decency might say out loud that in following Offenbach Sir Arthur has chosen the better part. The Mendelssohn school—with all its superficiality of conception, its miserable failure to comprehend Beethoven or even Weber, and the gentlemanlike vapidity which it deliberately inculcated as taste, discretion, reticence, chastity, refinement, finish, and what not—did undoubtedly give its capable pupils good mechanical skill. Their workmanship is plausible and elegant—just what it should be in comic opera. And the workmanship of our comic operas is often abominable. The technical work of Planquette, for instance, compared to that of Sullivan and Cellier, is crude, illiterate, hopelessly inept. Auber himself could not have written the concerted music in Patience or Pinafore without more effort than it is worth. The question remains, would the skill that produced these two works have been more worthily employed upon another oratorio, another cantata? When all our musicians are brought to their last account, will Sullivan dissemble the score of the Pirates with a blush and call on the mountains to cover him, whilst Villiers Stanford and Hubert Parry table The Revenge, Prometheus Unbound, and Judith with pride? With which note of interrogation let us pass.

LA CIGALE

The World, 15 October 1890

And so we inaugurate the winter season by a comic opera at the Lyric! My first comment on the performance must be that not often among upwards of two dozen artists do we see a single comparatively subordinate player, during a bare ten minutes' traffic of the stage, and without having a word to utter, all but make a three-act opera a one-part piece, and that one part his own. But no intelligent critic will deny that this feat was performed on Thursday night by the donkey in the second act. If the tenor had only had that animal's self-possession and sagacity—if the second tenor had only imitated his golden silence—if Mr Brough, welcome as he was after the tedious and unconvincing drolls who have vainly tried to fill his place these many months, could have come up to his asinine competitor in grave elderly humor, La Cigale would run half a lifetime. The audience did not disguise their longing for some more of this gifted ass. The gentleman who sat in the stall next mine rent the air with maniac screams of laughter long after it had vanished.

The fable of the Grasshopper and the Ant is, to say the least of it, somewhat extraneous to La Cigale, having, in fact, no deeper connexion with it than Millais' Bubbles has with Pears' soap: consequently, the annexation of La Fontaine not only causes the action to drag heavily in the last act for the sake of interpolating a farfetched sentimental *tableau vivant*, but causes also a certain instability of *genre* throughout the whole work, which repeatedly threatens to turn serious, and then thinks better of it. Audran's rhythms are hackneyed, his tripping melodies rather shortwinded, and his relapses into threadbare waltz tunes much too frequent; but his workmanship is smart, his orchestration vivacious, and his musical vein harmlessly abandoned, as that of a comic opera writer should be. The *finale* contributed by Mr Caryll would be the best dramatic number in the score if only a dash of humor could be given to the music; for though the gradations which lead to the climax are not quite satisfactorily balanced, and there are a few disappointing bits of padding in it here and there, it is, on the whole, a success. I need hardly add that Mr Caryll discharged his responsibility as conductor in the most honorable artistic spirit. The work had been rehearsed to perfection; and it was a pleasure to hear his band. Miss Geraldine Ulmar made a tremendous hit as Marton. She would not rank as a *prima donna* at Covent Garden (though I have heard worse artists in that position) any more than Miss St Cyr, Miss Mabel Love, and their colleagues would be classed *assoluta* at the Alhambra; still, at the Lyric, with a trifle of natural facility, well backed by good looks, one passes easily for a Cabel or a Bessone. Miss Annie Rose tried to make Mr Scovel act by acting expressively herself; but he did not know his business well enough to respond effectively— and I admit that hardly any address could have saved the absurd situation in the third act, where the dramatic scene of Bernheim's confession is cut down in its prime by the twain suddenly walking off the stage to conclude it behind the scenes. But the fact remains that the easy expertness of Messrs Eric Lewis, Lionel Brough, and E. W. Garden stood out in merciless contrast to the amateurish posturing and unscholarly diction of the two operatic gentlemen, who will both need to polish themselves very assiduously if they mean to keep their places on the London stage.

CHILDREN AND COPYRIGHT

The World, 22 October 1890

I forget the name of the distinguished actress who said, when the Infant Roscius* was carrying everything before him at the theatres, that she began to see some excuse for poor Herod after all. Whoever she was, she was a woman of sense. Threatened as we are with a revival of the pianoforte mania of last season, it was some comfort to be promised a grownup artist like Essipoff to begin with. In her stead we were offered Master Isidore Pavia, warranted only fifteen, of "wonderful talent" and "extraordinary abilities," and withal English born, taught by English masters, and free from all taint of foreign travel. Now I admit that Master Pavia's friends are right in looking on the career of a pianist as "a life not bad for a hardy lad"† in the present dearth of opportunities: my only fear is that he will prove too hardy for the business until his youthful superabundance of stamina has found a more natural vent in the cricket and football field. On Wednesday afternoon he went at the Waldstein sonata like a young avalanche, *fortissimo sempre crescendo e prestissimo sempre accellerando*, keeping his feet cleverly over the

---

* William Henry West Beatty, a child prodigy, who for a season (1804–5) was a London sensation, playing at Covent Garden and Drury Lane, at the age of 13, all the celebrated tragic *rôles* in Shakespear. More than two dozen infant prodigies sought to duplicate his fame before the craze evaporated. Dickens capitalized on the phenomenon in Nicholas Nickleby.

† Gilbert and Sullivan, The Pirates of Penzance (When Frederick was a little lad).

[177]

straightforward bits, staggering gamely through the syncopated passages, going head over heels up and down the flights of octaves, and finishing, flushed but unbeaten, after a recordbreaking neck-or-nothing "reading" that would have made Rubinstein gasp and Madame Schumann faint. When he got up to make his muscular bow, straight from his shoulder, how could an audience whose battles had been won on the playing fields of Eton refrain their applause? For my part, I am glad to see that Mr Pavia (he is really too manly to be called Master Isidore) can come in to try the strength of his youth on a higher plane that that of the athletic barbarian; but though his natural turn for music, unspoiled and unforced as it is, is a gift upon which he and his acquaintances are to be sincerely congratulated, he has not yet developed that depth of feeling and keenness of artistic sensibility which alone can justify even the youngest of us in coming forward at St James's Hall as an interpreter of Beethoven. As to technique, let him take the next opportunity of studying the Liszt technique as mastered by Sapellnikoff or Sophie Menter; or if, as is unfortunately quite possible, his English teachers have told him that Liszticism is mere charlatanry, he has only to hear what the Thalberg-Kullak-Wieck school has exacted from young Mr Borwick and gained from Madame Schumann and Madame Backer-Gröndahl to realize that, among European experts, he would be described as having no technique at all. In short, Mr Pavia, like most English beginners, will have to turn his back on his first counselors, and abandon premature recitalling for some years of hard study abroad.

The appearance of young Max Hambourg at the Pavia recital reminded me that I had not exhausted the subject of La Cigale last week. I want to know why the manager of the Lyric Theatre, after making a parade of his sense of social obligation by opening the season with a performance of the National Anthem, proceeded to fill the stage with a troop of children under ten, whose borrowed rouge and bedizenments must, behind the scenes, have presented as grim a contrast to their own pallor and shoddy as their unhealthy excitement and delight did to the natural play of childhood. I warn the Lyric management and my undiscerning fellow critics that if these senseless child shows be not stopped by the friends of the theatre, they will be stopped by the theatre's enemies, whose vigilance committees are busily collecting evidence which may be employed not merely to establish the beneficent sway of the factory inspector, but to substitute for him the Puritan censor.

I defy any person to invent a valid excuse, however farfetched, for the presence of a single child on the stage in La Cigale. No doubt the ladies were charmed to see the little pets enjoy themselves as if at a splendid children's party; for what mother will not allow her darlings to dress in their best and sit up late at a children's party "just for once"? Unfortunately, as La Cigale promises to have a long run, it will provide a children's party not just for once, but for hundreds of consecutive nights—perhaps until the inevitable hour when the Children's Employment Act will be shorn of that convenient clause by which a magistrate can license a child exceptionally in order that Shakespear's immortal masterpiece, Richard III., may not have to be presented without a sufficiently little Duke of York, and that Ibsen's Doll's House, so popular with the cultured classes in England, may not be lost to us by legal inhibition of the three tots of Nora Helmer's nursery.

Our magistrates have cheerfully accepted that clause as an express injunction to license as many children under ten as the stage will hold. No matter how unnecessary, how incongruous, how destructive to dramatic illusion their introduction may be, they are dragged in, in a sort of frenzy of wantonness, into every pantomime, every comic opera, every ballet, every circus, every spectacular display, as desperately as if the Act bound managers, under heavy penalties, to provide theatrical employment for all applicants of tender years; so that everybody who knows anything about the history of this sort of legislation now foresees that total and unconditional prohibition of the employment of children under ten (if not under twelve) as wage earners will follow in a year or two as certainly as the stringent Factory Act of 1853 followed the loose one of 1848. And unless that result, as far as it concerns the stage, comes as a victory of the playgoers and of the critics over the managers, it will be a victory of our modern Jeremy Colliers over the theatre.

But I see no signs of action from either pit or press. As to the critics, they are hopeless novices in such questions. I verily believe that if they knew that the Factory Acts prevent a benevolent employer, under heavy penalties, from putting Morris wallpapers on the rooms where women's work is carried on, and forbid him to serve up afternoon tea to relieve the toil there, they would be shocked into a clamor for immediate repeal. I am afraid they will leave me to play Cassandra singlehanded until they suddenly find all their theatres under the control of a committee of the County Council, with Mr Hugh Price Hughes* in the chair, and a *police des mœurs* commanded by Mr McDougall.†

Another matter which I may as well say my say about, before the gathering rush of performances reduces me to a mere chronicler of insignificant passing events,

* Nonconformist preacher and earnest social worker, radical in his politics.

† John McDougall, a member of the London County Council who became its chairman.

concerns all those singers, conductors, and managers who are either bewildered or indignant because French composers, whose music they have hitherto been able to lay hands on without payment, are now politely asking whether the Berne Convention, the International Copyright Act of 1886, and the Order in Council of 1887 do not mean that in future English bands must not play their music without paying a share of the *droits d'auteur*, or, if not, what they do mean? Mind, I do not express an opinion on the point myself: that would be contempt of court, as a decision is pending. I simply wish to remind the upholders of the old system that it is doomed in any case; for if his Honor Judge Martineau finds that the Act does not protect the foreign composer, then most assuredly further legislation will. What is more, Mr Alfred Moul, to whom the Literary and Artistic Congress accorded a vote of confidence, will not be in the smallest degree discredited if the decision goes against him. I am no great admirer of our system of providing for the subsistence and encouragement of producers by giving them property rights, which cost frightful sums to maintain and never work fairly; but I am, I flatter myself, all the better qualified to point out that there is a very important distinction between the man who would abolish the property system altogether as we have done in the case of our turnpike roads and bridges—and the man who holds on to his own property rights whilst disregarding those of other people. The first is a Communist: the second is a thief. It was one thing to abolish the toll-bars on Waterloo Bridge: it was quite another to sneak under them whilst other people were paying. If communism in works of art is to be the order of the day, let us by all means agree to allow our composers a reasonable subsistence out of the Consolidated Fund, besides compounding with the foreigner for a lump sum annually (no doubt Mr Moul will be happy to arrange terms), and then make all musical compositions common property; but, pending that readjustment, let us in common honesty give composers the same rights of property in their products as we claim for ourselves. What is to be said of the *impresarios* who want to produce the operas of MM. Massenet and Gounod without paying either of them a farthing, and then screw the top price out of the public for admission to the performance? And why do the theatrical and musical papers sympathize quite tenderly with projects of this description; whilst they imply, as clearly as they dare, that the man who seeks to enforce the author's claims is a blackmailer, a freebooter, an encloser of commons, a blocker of rights-of-way, a spoiler of the widow and orphan of the hardworking British bandmaster who "never paid nothink to no Frenchman for playing the Soldiers' Chorus from Faust, and aint agoing to begin now"? The sober fact is that the Société des Auteurs, Compositeurs et Editeurs de Musique is as necessary an institution as Stationers' Hall*; and I presume Mr Alfred Moul was entrusted with its business in England because he was known to a sufficient number of reputable persons, as he certainly was to me, not only as a business man of capacity and credit, but as a musician and a gentleman. That it does not pay the society to sell its repertory in pennyworths is no more to the point than that Messrs Fortnum & Mason refuse to sell ham by the slice, or that the musician who buys The World only to read my criticisms has nevertheless to pay for those of W. A., Theoc, Q.E.D.,† and the rest of my

* From the XVI century all British books upon publication were "entered at Stationers' Hall," *i.e.*, registered for copyright in the records of the Stationers' Company in London.

† "W.A." (William Archer, theatre), "Theoc." (Theodore Child, Paris correspondence), and "Q.E.D." (Lady Colin Campbell, art).

colleagues into the bargain. And yet in a report of a test action, not yet decided, brought by Mr Moul against Herr Franz Grœnings, bandmaster of the West Pier at Brighton, I find our best musical paper, apparently convinced that Moul and Mephistopheles must be aliases of the same person, describing the demand for the *droits d'auteur* as a fact that was "admitted in cross-examination." This is exactly as if W.A., to whom I mentioned that a box for Aïda was placed at my disposal the other evening, were to state in his next article that "it has been elicited from the musical critic of The World that he made his way into Covent Garden Theatre without paying." I cannot believe that the critics and writers who have allowed themselves to be misled by the moans of their friends in the profession and the publishing trade can have ever given ten minutes' serious thought to the economic and social bearings of the copyright question. As soon as they do they will tell their indignant correspondents to pay and look pleasant, lest the Act of 1886 be amended by a more stringent one, which the French composers will be able to enforce without any of the timidity they evidently feel at present. In any case, I shall be able to say "I told you so," which is one of the chief joys of a wise man's declining years.

P.S.—I was present at the opening of Signor Lago's opera season on Saturday, but I prefer to wait and watch for another week before committing myself to an opinion. Besides, Sunday is hardly the day for one or two of the remarks I shall have to make on the treatment poor Verdi received from his compatriot Bevignani.

SIGNOR LAGO'S OPERA SEASON

29 October 1890

Signor Lago's enterprise at Covent Garden looked unpromising on the first night. The opera was Aïda: but the artists were nervous and unwelcomed; the dresses misfitted horribly; the chorus of Egyptian priests looked more like a string of sandwich-men than ever; the carpenters' department was so short-handed that the audience whistled "We wont go home till morning" and the Marseillaise whilst the last scene was being built; and there was a perfect plague of interruption from a contingent of Italians, who insisted on shouting *Brava,* and drowning the orchestral endings of all the songs by premature applause, in spite of smoldering British indignation. And Bevignani, as I hinted last week, did no more for Verdi than barely keeping the band and the singers together. In vain such written entreaties as *p p p p p, estremamente piano,* and the like appealed to him from the score: the bluff *mezzo forte* never varied two degrees the whole evening. For *crescendos* we had undignified little hurry-scurries of *accelerandos*; and for the deep rich flood of harmony, which should sometimes make itself felt rather than heard through the silence, and sometimes suffuse everything with its splendor, we had shallow, blaring street music and prosaic *mezzo forte* as aforesaid. Once or twice the real Verdi color glowed for a moment through the fog: for instance, in the accompaniment for three flutes in the fourth act; but that was due solely to the initiative of the players. When the conductor's guidance was needed, as it was very conspicuously by the gentleman who played the *obbligato* to *Gia i sacerdoti adunanzi* on a saxophone, and who quite missed the pathetic dignity of its tragic measure, the conductor galloped placidly after him as if the saxophone were doing all that could reasonably be expected of it. As to the majestic but tremendously grave and self-contained address of the captive Ethiopian King to his Egyptian conqueror, I turn in despair from Bevignani to Galassi, and ask him to consider the words—to listen for a moment to the music—and then to say whether he really considers that Verdi intended Amonasro to behave like a bedlamite Christy Minstrel. When one remembers Faccio and the Scala orchestra, it is hard to have to go back to the drum-slammings and blarings and rantings of the bad old times, which can only be mended now by their survivors, Signori Bevignani and Galassi among others, taking warning by the bankruptcy in which they ended. I hoped that fairer treatment might have awaited Il Trovatore; but I am afraid I shall appear smitten with Bevignanophobia if I dwell on what actually occurred. Whether the conductor had made a bet that he would get through the opera in the shortest time on record or not, I do not know: certain it is that the concerted music was taken at a speed which made all artistic elaboration, all point, all self-possession, even bare accuracy, impossible. Bevignani only drew rein once, and that was when, at the end of the first scene of the second act, his eye suddenly caught the word *velocissimo* in the score. At first the slipping, scrambling, and bewilderment of the artists amused me; then I became indignant; and at last the continual jarring and baulking got on my nerves, so that I fled, exhausted and out of temper. But for the relief afforded by the solos, during which the band followed the singers, I should not have held out so long. And I need hardly add that the burden of my grumbling as I went home was that it is all very well to appeal to the critics to encourage cheap opera, but that opera without artistic

[185]

interpretation is dear at any price, and will soon drive the eighteenpenny god back to the Lyric, where Audran as handled by Mr Caryll seems a great composer in comparison with Verdi as handled by Bevignani, who should really devote himself for the future to English oratorio.

On Monday night there was a vast improvement. Arditi, as alert as the youngest man in the band, and, what is more, quite as anxious, conducted Les Huguenots, which only needs a little better stage-management to be as presentable as it is in the summer season. For instance, when Marcel enters in the Pré-aux-Clercs scene, and the Catholics insist that he shall take off his hat, whilst the Huguenot soldiers maintain that he is right to keep it on, it is hardly reasonable in the Catholics to remain covered whilst the soldiers carefully take off their helmets, under a vague impression that somebody ought to do something of the sort. I am no bigot, and have never complained of the Catholics first joining in the Rataplan Chorus, with its gibes at *i Papisti*, and then returning to the bosom of their church for the Ave Maria. Still I do not think that these things should be done when there is no musical gain thereby. Perhaps I am inconsistent; but it is odd how one strains at a gnat and swallows a camel at Covent Garden. In Il Trovatore, for instance, it seemed quite natural to me that a horde of bloodthirsty feudal retainers should break into a convent yard without causing the assembled nuns to exhibit the faintest concern; because, after all, the thing occurs every season. But when the gypsy blacksmiths the other night deposited a glowing bar with its red-hot end on a wooden chair, where it lay during the rest of the act without either cooling itself or damaging the furniture, I could not help feeling that the illusion of the scene was gone.

On the pecuniary prospects of Signor Lago's enterprise I have only to say that if it fails, the failure will be due to the superstition that the primary function of Italian opera is to provide a means of passing the evening for a clique of deadheads in evening dress. The Covent Garden house is a vast auditorium to which hosts of people would willingly pay from two to five shillings a head to be admitted. But these persons would drive out the deadhead, and cause his stalls and boxes to be replaced by plebeian chairs or even benches. On the other hand, ten "commercial gents," each with his missis or young woman, at two shillings a head, would bring in £2 solid cash (*non olet!*) into the treasury; wheras the one languid deadhead, who keeps them out at present, brings nothing. As to that crow's nest in the roof, where you can now swelter and look at the crowns of the performers' hats for eighteenpence, that is not cheap: it would be dear at a shilling: sixpence is the proper price for such a place. It seems to me that Signor Lago, like all his forerunners in this direction, is trying to sit down between two stools. A cheap imitation of the regular fashionable season is impossible. It never pays to charge exclusive prices except when the West End guarantees the inevitable loss for the sake of the exclusiveness. Let me clinch the argument with one statistical fact. Only thirtynine out of every thousand of us die worth as much as £300, including the value of every stick and shred we possess. The moment you propose to do without the West End subsidy this fact forces you back to Drury Lane prices, no matter what the "traditions" of your entertainment may be.

Signor Lago's vocal artists are by no means ill selected. If he were as lucky in his stage managers and conductors as in his singers, his performances would be rather better all round than three out of four of last season's subscription nights. Perotti is a vigorous and intelligent tenor, prompt and to the point with his stage business to a degree which contrasts very favorably with Jean de Reszke's exasperating unpunctuality and irresolution, and gifted with ringing high notes of genuine tenor quality. And if he would but reconsider his pink-and-white makeup, and tone down the terrible smile with which he expresses amorous sentiments, he would escape those incongruous reminiscences of the ballet which one or two passages of his Raoul evoked. Giannini is unsuited to heroic parts, much as Mr Tupman* was unsuited to the costume of a bandit. He can shout high notes without wobbling; but he has so far shewn absolutely no other qualification for his eminent position. The sisters Giulia and Sofia Ravogli are two children of nature who have, by dint of genuine feeling for their art, contrived to teach themselves a great deal; but their Tuscan is full of nasal and throaty intonations abhorred of the grand school; and they indulge in unheard-of *naïvetés* (especially Giulia—Sofia has more *savoir faire*) when they come out of their parts to acknowledge applause, which they are apt to do at the most absurd moments. Further, they trust to luck rather than to skill for getting over florid difficulties; and their metrical sense is particularly untrained: they hardly ever sing a scale with the accents on the right notes. Giulia, the worse offender in this respect also, sang *Strida la vampa* as if every two bars of the three-eight time were one bar of common time. These are matters, fortunately, admitting of remedy. The main point is that Giulia thinks out her parts for herself and acts them courageously and successfully. Her Azucena was a striking performance, though I advise her to give up such little originalities, new but not true, as frankly presenting herself as a fine young *contadina* of eighteen, and laughing ironically as she repeats *Strana pieta! Strana*

* Character in Dickens's Pickwick Papers.

[188]

pieta! Her voice is an ample mezzo-soprano, a little hollow and disappointing in the lower registers, where one expects the tone to be rich, but sympathetic all over, and very free and effective at the top. Sofia is a soprano, with much less spontaneity of utterance and dramatic expression, though she, too, feels her business strongly. Her voice, too, is smaller: indeed, it is hardly enough, used as she uses it, for so large a theatre. She was nervous in Aïda and overweighted in Trovatore; so that she cannot be said to have done much more than hold her own; wheras her sister has made a decided success. Madame Stromfeld, who appeared as Marguerite de Valois in Les Huguenots, is blonde, plump, and over thirty. She has a phenomenal range upward, and is apparently a highly cultivated musician and experienced singer. It is a pity to have to add that the freshness of the voice is gone, except at the top, where some of the more impossible notes are remarkably brilliant. Mlle Maria Peri, aided by youth, screamed her way through Valentine, barely holding the C in the duet with Marcel for half its appointed duration, and occasionally forcing her chest register up to middle A, a fourth higher than she can afford, if she wishes to keep her voice. And here I must drop the Opera for this week, as I have other matters to record.

Sarasate, set up by the autumn holiday, left all criticism behind him at his first concert on Saturday week. He also left Mr Cusins behind by half a bar or so all through the two concertos, the unpremeditated effects of syncopation resulting therefrom being more curious than delectable. Bertha Marx gave a recital on Thursday. It was very brilliant, and brilliant in a sympathetic way; but O, Miss Bertha, if you would only mix just a little thought with the feeling now and then! Essipoff gave her first concert at Steinway Hall on the same evening. I see that Mr Kappey is going to give a lecture today (Tuesday) at the Chelsea Town Hall on military music. I hope he will, with Colonel Shaw-Hellier's assistance, succeed in wakening people up to the importance of having plenty of good wind bands among us. That is the sort of music that really attracts the average Briton to take up an instrument himself.

LA GIOCONDA

The World, 5 November 1890

I cannot say that the Covent Garden repertory has been reinforced by La Gioconda, a mere instance of the mischief which great men bring upon the world when small men begin to worship them. Shakespear set all the dramatic talent in England wasting itself for centuries on bombast and blank verse; Michael Angelo plunged Italian painting into an abyss of nakedness and fore-shortening. Handel plagued our serious music with a horrible murrain of oratorio; Ibsen will no doubt open up the stage to all the Pecksniffery and Tartuffery in Europe with his didactic plays; and Verdi is tempting many a born quadrille composer of the South to wrestle ineffectually and ridiculously with Shakespear and Victor Hugo.

To me, the kinship between La Gioconda and Ernani or Rigoletto is hardly closer than that between Vortigern and Macbeth; and I feel as comfortably superior to the critics and musicians who cannot see much difference between Ponchielli and Verdi as I do to those who could not see any at all between the boyish forger Ireland and Shakespear. It would have been kinder, even when Ponchielli was alive, to tell him frankly that all his strainings at the bow of Ulysses were not bending it one inch—that Donizetti's Lucrezia and even Marchetti's

Ruy Blas are better than his far more elaborate and ambitious setting of Angelo. The choruses and ballets in La Gioconda sound well: but they would sound equally well and be more congruously placed among the strings of Chinese lanterns at the French Exhibition. As for the dramatic music, it is conventional, short-winded, full of used-up phrases thinly disguised by modulations that are getting staler and staler every year, and will soon stir nobody's pulse; whilst the orchestration is invented rather than musically imagined, and therefore, like much of the harmony, remains absolutely inorganic; so that if the score were to be lost, and someone—say Mancinelli—had to reconstruct it from the voice parts alone, with the first violin copy thrown in, there is not the slightest reason to suppose that the result would be any worse than the original. Indeed, as Mancinelli writes for the orchestra better than Ponchielli did, it would most likely be better.

Imagine the effect of such an experiment on a work of Verdi's, or Gounod's, or Meyerbeer's, not to mention the inconceivable case of one by Wagner! Perhaps it is a providentially appointed compensation for the Ponchiellis, Ambroise Thomases, Drs Blank, and Professors Dash that their works need never be lost whilst any fragments of them remain. It is not from any wish to bear hardly on these gentlemen that I offer such observations; but I cannot forget that the enormous expenditure involved by operatic performances makes it imperative that we should insist on getting the best value for our money, which is hardly to be done by shelving the works of the great masters to make room for undesired resuscitations of Giocondas, Hamlets, and the like.

Having thus conveyed my opinion that La Gioconda was not worth doing, I am free to add that it might have been worse done. Miss Damian's *début* in opera was successful. She plays upon one string only, and that one is no *chanterelle*; but its tone is free and penetrating, a little lacking in color perhaps, but still capable of considerable intensity of expression. Suane, the tenor *à la* Gayarré without which no opera company is now complete, is thoroughly in earnest about his work, and shews much artistic feeling as a singer and actor. Those notes of his which are steady enough to have any recognizable pitch are by no means unmusical. But he is so afflicted with goat-bleat (*vibrato* is all nonsense—quite a different thing) that the house loses patience with him.

One lady,* describing his Edgardo to me, averred that if he had sung the part of Faust to the accompaniments of Lucia, it could have made no difference in the effect, as it would have been impossible to say what notes he was singing in any case. I think the lady was a little too hard on Suane; but he would do well to take the criticism to heart; for no tenor will ever conquer England if he cannot keep his voice from splitting twenty times in every second. Let him listen to Patti singing Home, Sweet Home, or to Sarasate playing an adagio, and ask himself whether they could improve the effect by making the notes wobble. This much, however, I will say: Suane's Gayarré wobble is not so bad as Peri's "dramatic" wobble, which is one of the crudest Italian vulgarities, and should never be heard in Covent Garden. Giulia Ravogli and Fiegna were unable to do much with their parts, which are as cheap as even dramatic music can be made in Italy. The *forlana* was the best thing yet done by the *corps de ballet*, headed by Miss Loveday and Miss Smiles, one of whom is, I suspect, only a step-dancer promoted from the music hall, whilst the other, though no great artist, comes off

* Shaw's mother, who attended the performance with him.

with credit. Under these circumstances I am sorry that I have not the remotest idea of which is Miss Loveday and which Miss Smiles. For the Dance of the Hours Signor Lago wisely called in Madame Katti Lanner, who brought twentyfour of her pupils, and was, as usual, immensely equal to the occasion. The work had been fairly rehearsed; and Bevignani was good enough this time to give it a fair chance.

I hear that Meyerbeer's Robert the Devil, with Miss Moody and Mr Manners in the cast, as well as Perotti and Mlle Stromfeld, drew a full house on Saturday week; but I was not in London that evening. Of La Traviata, which served for Madame Albani's entry on Thursday, I also hear encouraging accounts. I was in my stall punctually enough; but the stall was in the St James's Theatre. That, however, need not prevent me from giving a perfectly accurate description and sound criticism of Albani's Violetta, if I run short of matter lower down the column.

Master Brahm Van den Berg is the latest infant pianist. He is nearly as big as Pavia; but he dresses for his part in a white sailor costume which would not be out of place in a kindergarten. A hoop and a toy gun, with a gushing lady confederate in the room to hand him a box of bonbons at the end, would have made the illusion complete. If I were Brahm's age, and could play as well, I would buy a tailed coat, and assert myself as a man in the teeth of parents and agents. All this infantile tomfoolery may amuse the ladies who support afternoon recitals in such hosts; but it puts me out of humor, and turns me crusty when I ought to be specially considerate. Young Van den Berg has a capital technique of the Brussels Conservatoire type, made familar to us by such pianists as De Greef. Ambidexterity apart, he is not an extraordinary player. Essipoff, who is giving concerts at Steinway Hall, now has a rival in the first rank in the person of Paderewski, who on Saturday played Schumann's concerto at the Crystal Palace. And a very fine performance it seemed, coming so soon after Sophie Menter's reckless and unsympathetic onslaught last April on this most sensitive of concertos. Not a single point was missed throughout: Paderewski varied his touch and treatment with the clearest artistic intelligence for every mood and phase of the work, which could not have been more exhaustively interpreted. In the orchestra the great ebullition before the *cadenza* in the first movement was worked up magnificently, and Mr Manns did not conceal his delight at a success so perfectly after his own heart. It certainly was a concert of which he had every reason to feel proud.

The two volumes of Schumann's Letters, just issued by Bentley and translated by May Herbert, ought to be a fearful warning to critics and those who believe in critics. I once heard William Morris, on being suddenly asked why Haydon* shot himself, reply promptly "Because he found himself out." If I am ever asked why Schumann killed himself, I shall steal that pithy explanation. His case was more tragic than Haydon's, because it is not easy to believe that Haydon, even had he started with all possible enlightenment from without as to the true nature of art, would ever have succeeded in drawing a beautiful line or laying a square inch of lovely color; but Schumann was a genuine artist before his restless intellect made him a quack and a pedant.

In these letters we find him again and again recommending some nostrum or another to young musicians— "pure four-part harmony," doses of Bach, and what not—or picking out trivial technical points from the scores of his composer friends, and gushing about them

* Benjamin Robert Haydon (1786–1846), English historical painter.

in the style of an analytical program. On the very next page he will be desperately trying to explain away the fact that the modern works which move him most also violate all his patent methods. He "analyzes" a score of Wagner's, and immediately describes it to Mendelssohn as by a man who cannot write four bars that are melodious or even correct. There are consecutive fifths and octaves in it: Wagner lacks capacity for pure harmony and four-part choral composition: no permanent good can come from such a state of things. Then he goes to the theatre to *hear* the music whilst looking at the stage, and at once admits that he must retract; that he is impressed; that there is much that is deep and original in the work. Yet he learns nothing from this failure: the next time he delivers his opinion he explains as carefully as ever that though Wagner's music produces emotion, and has a mysterious charm that captivates the senses, yet it is demonstrably poor, repulsive, amateurish, and meaningless, because Wagner is "not a good musician," and lacks feeling for form and harmony.

Again, when a fine piece of poetry rouses the artist in him, he promptly sits down and writes to the author, asking him, not for a poem to set, but for something that can be finished up with a double chorus, because Handel has shewn in Israel in Egypt that double choruses are an infallible recipe for sublimity. Decidedly, if ever I write Advice to Young Musicians, the first precept in it will be, Dont take Schumann's. Indeed, the beginning and end of it will be, Dont take anybody's; for I had as soon wear another man's hat as take his advice, whatever other use I might find for it.

WILL GLUCK CONQUER LONDON?

The World, 12 November 1890

Is Gluck, the conqueror of Paris, at last going to conquer London? I hope so; for the man was a great master, one for whom we are hardly ready even yet. Hitherto our plan of sweeping together a sackful of opera singers from Milan, Vienna, Montevideo, Chicago, Clapham, China, and Peru, and emptying them on to the Covent Garden stage to tumble through Trovatore or Traviata as best they can, has not succeeded with Gluck. This Orfeo, for instance! Anyone can see before the curtain is half-a-minute up that it grew by the introduction of vocal music, not into chaos, but into an elaborate existing organization of ballet. The opening chorus, *S' in questo bosco*, sounds nobly to people who are looking at groups of figures in poetic motion or eloquent pose, at draperies falling in graceful lines and flowing in harmonious colors, and at scenery binding the whole into a complete and single picture.

Under such circumstances, our old friend Monseigneur of the Œil de Bœuf, when he had a taste that way, no doubt enjoyed himself. But when we, to wit, Smith and Jones, with our suburban traditions, going to the Opera full of that sense of unaccustomed adventure which the fine arts give us, are dumbfounded by the spectacle of our old original choristers appealing with every feature and limb against the unreasonableness of asking them to look like classical shepherds and shepherdesses—when their desperate Theocritean weeds have the promiscuity of Rag Fair without its picturesqueness—when even Katti Lanner's young ladies move awkwardly and uncertainly, put out of step by these long-drawn elegiac strains—when the scene suggests Wimbledon on a cold day, and Euridice's tomb is something between a Druidic cromlech and a milestone, bearing the name of the deceased in the tallest advertizing stencil—then it must be confessed that *S' in questo bosco* affects its new acquaintances far from cheerfully.

These drawbacks were in full force at Covent Garden last Wednesday; but Orfeo triumphed in spite of them. Gluck and Giulia Ravogli were too many even for the shabby sofa, apparently borrowed from a decayed seaside lodging, which was shamelessly placed in the middle of the stage, just outside the mouth of Hades, for Euridice to die conveniently on. It was the stage manager's last insult; and when it failed, he collected all his forces behind the scenes and set them talking at the top of their voices, so as to drown the singing and distract the attention of the audience. What a thing it is to live in the richest capital in the world, and yet have to take your grand opera, at its largest and most expensive theatre, with the makeshifts and absurdities of the barn and the booth! And to add to the exasperation of it, you are kept waiting longer between the acts for the dumping down of this miserable sofa on the bare boards than would be required for the setting of the most elaborate stage picture at the Lyceum or Drury Lane.

I am not sure that Gluck is not in a better way to be understood now than he has been any time since the French Revolution. Listening to the strains in the Elysian Fields the other night, I could not help feeling that music had strayed far away from them, and only regained them the other day when Wagner wrote the Good Friday music in Parsifal. No musical experience in the journey between these two havens of rest seems better than either. The Zauberflöte and the Ninth Symphony have a discomforting consciousness of virtue, an uphill effort of aspiration, about them; but in the Elysian Fields, in the Good Friday meadows, virtue and effort are transcended: there is no need to be good or to strive upward any more: one has arrived, and all those accursed hygienics of the soul are done with and forgotten. Not that they were without a priggish ecstasy of their own: I am far from denying that. Virtue, like vice, has its attractions. It was well worth while to slip through the Elysian hedge into the domain of Klingsor, and be shewn the enchantments of his magic gardens by Weber, plunged into his struggles and hopes by Beethoven, introduced to polite society in his castle drawing room by Mendelssohn, besides being led by Mozart through many unforgettable episodes of comedy and romance—episodes producing no bitter reaction like that which was apt to follow the scenes of tragic passion or rapturous sentimentality which Meyerbeer, Verdi, and Gounod managed so well for Klingsor. I do not forget these for a moment; and yet I am glad to be in the Elysian Fields again. And it is because I have also been in the Good Friday meadows that I can now see, more clearly than anyone could before Parsifal, how exactly Gluck was the Wagner of his day—a thing that would have been violently disputed by Berlioz, who was, nevertheless, almost as good a critic as I. Listen to Orfeo, and you hear that perfect union of the poem and the music—that growth of every musical form, melodic interval, harmonic progression, and orchestral tone out of some feeling or purpose belonging to the drama— which you have only heard before in the cantatas of Bach and the music-dramas of Wagner. Instead of the mere opera-making musician, tied to his poem as to a stake, and breaking loose whenever it gives him an excuse for a soldiers' chorus, or a waltz, or a crashing *finale*, we have the poet-musician who has no lower use for music than the expression of poetry.

Though it is easy to see all this in Orfeo during such numbers as *Che faro?* it might not have been so apparent last Wednesday in the ballet music, although that never loses its poetic character, but for Giulia Ravogli, about whom I now confess myself infatuated. It is no longer anything to me that her diction is not always so pure as Salvini's, that her *roulade* is inferior in certainty and spontaneity to Signor Foli's, that the dress in which I first saw her as Amneris ought to have had ever so many yards more stuff in the train, that she would not put on the grey eyebrows and wrinkles of Azucena, and even that she is capable of coming out of a stage faint to bow to the applause it evokes. Ah, that heart-searching pantomime, saturated with feeling beyond all possibility of shortcoming in grace, as Orfeo came into those Elysian Fields, and stole from shade to shade, trying to identify by his sense of touch the one whom he was forbidden to seek with his eyes! Flagrant ballet girls all those shades were; but it did not matter: Giulia awakened in us the power by which a child sees a living being in its rag doll. Even the *première danseuse* was transfigured to a possible Euridice as Giulia's hand, trembling with a restrained caress, passed over her eyes! And then the entry into Hades, the passionate pleading with the Furies, and, later on, the eloquence of the famous aria in the last act! I was hardly surprised, though I was alarmed, to see a gentleman in a stage box, with frenzy in his eye, seize a substantial-looking bouquet and hurl it straight at her head, which would probably have been removed from her shoulders had not the missile fallen some yards short of its mark. Her success was immense. Nobody noticed that there were only two other solo singers in the whole opera, both less than nothing beside her. She—and Gluck— sufficed. In the singer, as in the composer, we saw a perfectly original artistic impulse naïvely finding its way to the heart of the most artificial and complex of art forms.

Of the performance generally I have little to say. I intended to remonstrate about the Meyerbeerian *cadenza* which sounded so incongruously at the end of the first act; but I leave the remonstrance unspoken: Giulia shall do what she pleases, even if her next whim be to receive Eros in the first act with a strophe of *L'Amour, ce dieu profane*.* But I submit as a matter for Bevignani's consideration—whilst acknowledging the care and thoroughness with which he has rehearsed the work—that the chorus *Che mai dell' Erebo* is hopeless at Covent Garden as an *andante*. His motley forces are utterly incapable of the Titanic tread with which this giant measure should march—*ben marcato*, each crotchet a bar in itself. Under the circumstances it would be better to take it at exactly the same speed, and with the same strength and precision of accent, as the first movement of the Eroica Symphony. At this rate the groups of three *sforzandos* for the basses would sound like three gruff, fierce barks from the three-headed dog at the gate of hell (which is what Gluck intended), wheras at present they only suggest that Orpheus is a stout sluggish gentleman, giving his boots three careful scrapes outside the door *pour se décrotter*.

I will not chide Katti Lanner's maidens for being no more able than the chorus to move as gods to the noble measures of Gluck, which baffled "the many twinkling feet" even in the times of the old order in France, when the grand school was much grander than it is now. The tone from the strings in the orchestra left a good deal to be desired: it was sometimes weak and whining, and sometimes rough and obstreperous, never pure and dignified. Fewer instruments and finer playing would

* An aria in Ambroise Thomas's Le Caïd (1849).

have produced a much greater effect. More justice was done to the scoring for the wind, which, far from growing old-fashioned, only becomes more admirable by the light of recent developments in orchestration. The oboes, of course, occasionally found it impossible to double the violin parts; but this mere *ripieno* function is no longer necessary or desirable, and the remark is only interesting as a technical record. On the whole, I must congratulate Signor Lago on a performance which gave me me more pleasure than any I have tried this year. Maurel, by the bye, has arrived, and has begun his campaign by making a speech on the art of operatic singing. I shall have a word to say on his views when he delivers himself into my hands as Rigoletto next week.

Señor Albéniz, at his first concert at St James's Hall last Friday, got together not only a good band, led by Hollander, and recruited from the Crystal Palace and Richter orchestras, but also brought into the field a new conductor, one Tomas Breton, born at Salamanca forty years ago, who at once shewed himself able to make our men do their best. Unfortunately the program was insanely long, containing practically three concertos, six orchestral movements, and a symphony by the conductor—an ingeniously horrible work, lasting fortyfive minutes, full of what the program glozingly called syncopations, but which were in fact Procrustean torturings of two-four themes into three-four time. The programist further remarked, of the slow movement, that "there is just here a good deal of polyphony for the careful ear to distinguish." As if people went to concerts to sit carefully distinguishing polyphony! The whole affair, it appears, was only a *tour de force* in the style of Beethoven, produced by the composer as an exercise in his student days. It is as a capable conductor that I welcome Señor Breton; for we are at our wits' end here for men able to get first-rate work out of our bands, wheras we can all write symphonies. Albéniz was monotonously pretty in Mozart's Concerto in D major, playing without warmth, vigor, or variety of treatment. Then he tackled Schumann, but hardly did more than supply the orchestra with a very sweet and dainty accompaniment. In his solos he played some compositions of his own with his usual skill and charm.

A DISMAL SATURDAY
The World, 19 November 1890

As a rule, a musician in London, when he has had enough of chamber music from the Neruda quartet, cannot spend his Saturday afternoon better than at the Crystal Palace concert, if he can afford the six or seven shillings which the expedition costs. But he should take heed lest he stumble on one of those penitentiary Saturdays when they get Mr Edward Lloyd down, and turn on Mendelssohn; for then the land brings forth the oratorio public, who swarm over the room, with Novello scores in all their borders. The orchestra, too, becomes a precipitous landslip of choristers, slanting up to the ceiling as if they had been conveyed in four cartloads of soprano, alto, tenor, and bass to the brink of the organ gallery, and successively tipped over into the abyss beneath. They shove the violins out on to the platforms, and squeeze the basses into the middle of the orchestras, where there is hardly room for a man's elbows, besides insulting the brass and drums for making a deafening noise in their ears. And they sing so woodenly that if the very benches were to cry out—and I sometimes wonder that they dont—the tone of that cry could not be more ligneous. Had oratorio been invented in Dante's time, the seventh circle in his Inferno would have been simply a magnified Albert Hall, with millions of British choristers stolidly singing All that hath life and breath, sing to the Lord, in the galleries, and the condemned, kept away by demons, in the arena, clothed in evening dress.

It was on one of these dismal Saturdays that I went to Sydenham to hear Madame Schmidt-Köhne, of the Royal Opera, Berlin. She patriotically sang a song of Mozart's at the Berlin pitch, whilst the orchestra accompanied her at that of the Crystal Palace organ; so that really, as far as the effect was concerned, she might almost as well have sung out of tune. Then, after a few snatches of harvest tunes worked up into a heavy overture by Grieg, and a "new tone-picture" by Mr Cliffe, which contained nothing that was new to me, we fell to at the Lobgesang, and sat out that dreadful dreary symphony in the sure hope of attaining a condition in which Watchman, will the night soon pass? would exactly express our feelings. But in my opinion the game was not worth the candle. I am for cutting out the symphony and the first four numbers *en bloc* (there is no need to wait for the last three when the Lobgesang is at the end of the program). The rhetoric of the progra-matical analyst cannot much longer hypnotize people into imagining that Mendelssohn succeeded in making a great symphony out of materials barely sufficient for a sentimental pianoforte piece, by merely stretching them on the orchestral rack. That abominable platitude for the trombones with which the thing begins, and which is never dropped until you are bored and worried out of your senses by it, will be cited in times to come as a conclusive proof that there must have been a pseudo-Mendelssohn: they will not believe that the composer of Fingal and the Midsummer Night's Dream music could possibly have perpetrated the Lobgesang.

There is an old story to the effect that the first time the

symphony was rehearsed the trombone player desperately tried to convert this platitude into music by introducing a *gruppetto*. The criticism was lost on Mendelssohn, who, deeply scandalized, sat upon the trombonist; and the story is now always told as instancing the severity and superiority of the composer's taste. As the man was perfectly right, I am glad to take this opportunity of doing him tardy justice in the matter. The truth is that the symphony would have been weak under any circumstances; but coming as it did after Beethoven's Ninth Symphony, it was inexcusable. As to following it up by going to the Albert Hall on Wednesday to hear Elijah, I would rather have died.

When I got to the Opera on Monday week, I found a troop of people coming out in the worst of tempers. Maurel was indisposed, and had retired in favor of Galassi, whose Rigoletto is not exactly a novelty. I stuck manfully to my post for half an hour or so to hear Dimitresco, the new tenor, who, without conspicuous qualities or conspicuous faults, sings acceptably in a style which is none the worse for owing something to the drawing room as well as to the theatre. After *Questa e quella* I left Rigoletto for the Monday Popular Concert, where I heard the last few bars of Paderewski's Schumann solo, and a trio by Rubinstein which made me wish myself back at Covent Garden. Paderewski's recital on Wednesday was much more entertaining, though there was certainly plenty to complain of. For instance, instead of giving us a poetic interpretation of the trio in Chopin's Funeral March, he used it in the most barefaced manner solely to shew how much tone he could get with one finger. Again, he threw himself so violently into Liszt's Erlkönig transcription that he not only made mere rampagious melodrama of it, swamping all the finer distinctions between the plaintive appeals of the terrified child, the grave reassurances of the anxious

[204]

father, and the wanton fairy music of the Erl King, but actually came to grief manually at one point. Every piece in the program suffered more or less from a hurricane of superfluous energy which Paderewski will later on learn to use to the last inch, instead of letting half of it run to waste with a distracting roar through the safety-valve. He finished his recital by the Don Juan fantasia of Liszt, a work too composite to be described in a single phrase. In so far as it is a transcription it is only spoiled Mozart. As a set of variations it is redundant and over-elaborated. But as a fantasia it has some memorable points. When you hear the terrible progressions of the statue's invitation suddenly echoing through the harmonies accompanying Juan's seductive *Andiam, andiam, mio bene*, you cannot help accepting it as a stroke of genius— that is, if you know your Don Giovanni *au fond*. And the riotous ecstasy of *Finch' han dal vino* is translated from song into symphony, from the individual to the abstract, with undeniable insight and power in the *finale*, which Paderewski carried through triumphantly. If he plays it again— and he might do worse—I hope he will not put it at the end of the program, lest other duties should prevent me from waiting to hear it.

Maurel's Rigoletto, which came off in earnest on Thursday, will stand with Giulia Ravogli's Orfeo among the glories of Signor Lago's management. It utterly effaced Lassalle's heavy, stilted, egotistic, insincere attempt of last season. An operatic tragedian may be easily overrated at a period like the present, when it is still possible to follow a whole season attentively without meeting with any convincing evidence of even a superficial knowledge of the stories told in the operas on the part of singer, stage manager, scene painter, or anyone else in the house except those members of the public who bewilder themselves by referring to one-and-sixpenny books, containing an Italian and an

English version, differing almost as widely from oneanother as from the stage version. Therefore, if I were to say that Maurel is a great actor among opera singers, he might well retort "Thank you for nothing: in the country of the blind the one-eyed is king." So I will put it in this way—that his Rigoletto is as good a piece of acting as Edwin Booth's Triboulet*; whilst the impression it makes is deeper, and the pleasure it gives greater, by just so much as Verdi is a greater man than Tom Taylor, which is saying a good deal.

As to his singing, he does more with that French method which all baritones copied from Faure twenty years ago than I ever thought possible; and though he blurs the outline of the melody, and often, instead of striking the exact pitch of an E or an F, drags his voice laboriously up to just a hair's breadth under it, he has a remarkable command of the sort of vocal effects he aims at. If they are not the effects that please me best, yet I am not going to prove that they are "wrong" in the manner of a disciple of Maclise criticizing Monet or Monticelli.

Mlle Stromfeld's Gilda changed my opinion of her for the worse. When I heard her for the first time, as Marguerite de Valois, I confess I took her for an old hand, and a very clever one, making the most of a worn-out voice. I now perceive that her voice has never had a chance, and that her master, whoever he may be, has turned out, not a singer, but only an exponent of his method, which is, like most methods, a very bad one. Instead of teaching her to produce her voice freely, and leaving her to place it here or there according to the dictates of her instinct for musical beauty or dramatic

---

* Booth had appeared in London in December 1880 in a revival of Tom Taylor's The Fool's Revenge (1859), adapted from the opera Rigoletto, which in turn had been based on Victor Hugo's drama Le Roi s'amuse.

expression, he has evidently proceeded on the theory that the voice "ought" to be placed just behind the upper teeth, and has not taught her to produce it at all. The result is that Mlle Stromfeld, in her constant effort (with which her whole artistic nature is at war) to pin every note to her hard palate, squeezes her throat and frays all the middle of her voice threadbare. Of what use was it to be able to finish *Un di se ben* with a high C that cut through the house like a knife, when she could not accurately pitch the preliminary G, which any soprano in the chorus could have managed without trouble?

Though this be method, yet there is madness in it. I am sorry to have to say these hard things; but if I refrain, what will happen? Why, a dozen young ladies who read this column, concluding that Mlle Stromfeld is an exemplary singer, will find out who taught her; go to him or his pupils for lessons; and be sacrificed to his views on the subject of the hard palate. That, among other things, is what comes of the "kindly" criticism which sees good in everything. I prefer to see sermons in stones—and to throw them. Let me therefore add, before dismissing Rigoletto, that no human quartet could have made anything of *Un di se ben* as Bevignani conducted it; and that though Dimitresco no doubt honestly thought that he was singing *La donna è mobile* in B natural at its final reprise behind the scenes, he actually sang it in B flat and a quarter, the audience writhing with anguish meanwhile.

Students of that curious disease, pianomania, which fills St James's Hall with young ladies every afternoon during the season, and puts countless sums into the pockets of teaching *virtuosos*, will find such a treat in Bettina Walker's My Musical Experiences, just published by Bentley, as they have not enjoyed since Miss Fay's Music Study in Germany. Miss Walker, like Miss Fay, went to Liszt, and, on finding that he had no patent process for turning out great players, went to Deppe, who had discovered that arcanum. Then she hurried—rather inconsequently—on to Henselt, of whom she gives an interesting account. It is easy to see that Miss Walker's impression of Henselt (giving a lesson in Si oiseau j'étais as "rising up in all his greatness—suggesting to me a city rising by enchantment out of the dust of ages," is as purely hypnotic in its origin as Miss Fay's estimate of Liszt as "a two-edged sword." And to think that of all those wonderful young fellow students, with such mysterious fascinations in their eyes and manners, who were so sure to be Menters and Rubinsteins in ten years, more than ninetynine per cent. must have been dowdy hobbledehoys and hobbledehoydens who will spend their lives as obscure organists, casual accompanists, suburban teachers, quadrille conductors, or highschool teachers getting up performances of the overture to Zampa on six pianos for prize-days! Still the books are none the less worth reading—perhaps all the better—especially if you know how much of them to take seriously.

MISCHIEVOUS PATTI

The World, 26 November 1890

There are few things more terrible to a seasoned musician than a miscellaneous concert. A ballad concert, a symphony concert, a pianoforte recital: all these are welcome when they are not too long; but the old-fashioned "grand concert," with an overture here, a *scena* there, and a ballad or an instrumental solo in between, is insufferable. Besides, it creates a discomfiting atmosphere by assembling a vast crowd of people without definite musical ideas, loosely strung good-natured creatures who are attracted solely by the names of the performers, and can distinguish between Edward Lloyd and Sims Reeves, but not between a Donizetti cavatina and a Bach fugue.

Now of all miscellaneous concerts a Patti concert is the most miscellaneous. Imagine *Ernani involami*, with Robin Adair as a *ritornello*, or Within a Mile tacked on to *Ombra leggiera*, or Home, Sweet Home introduced by *Il Bacio*! We had all three—I mean all six—at the Albert Hall last week; and that huge audience did not mind a bit—took these abysmal transitions with a complacency which shewed that all music was alike to them. Once upon a time there was some excuse for this. Though Patti has never been convincing or even interesting as a dramatic singer in the sense in which, for instance, Giulia Ravogli excels, yet in the old days we could not help wanting to hear those florid arias of the old school on that wonderful vocal instrument, with its great range, its birdlike agility and charm of execution, and its unique combination of the magic of a child's voice with the completeness of a woman's. And what a woman, too! A consummate artist, able to vanquish every technical difficulty as perfectly as Sarasate on his violin, and withal a shrewd and wilful negotiator, able to secure the full "rent" of her voice to the last farthing without ever letting herself be seen in any character but that of the spoiled darling of Europe, the petulant, capricious little *diva*, singing, as the canaries do, without knowing a crotchet from a quaver or a sovereign from a sixpence. To earn five-hundred-pound notes with the skill and diligence of a Duran, to bargain for them with the tenacity of a Rothschild, and to pocket them with the fascinating *insouciance* of Harold Skimpole*—surely this was the perfection of

*Character in Dickens's Bleak House.

[209]

work and play, the highest achievement of *savoir vivre*. In those days it did not matter how a concert program was made up, provided the name of Patti headed the list of singers. But the extent to which this was taken advantage of to save the trouble of devizing something better than the senseless hotchpotch program of the miscellaneous order always rubbed good musicians the wrong way; and for my part, I must say that I did not like it any the more because I felt how futile all protest must be in the face of immense commercial success.

But time is coming to my assistance at last. Patti now has to evade the full weight of *Ombra leggiera*, much as Mr Sims Reeves, who is just old enough to be her father, economizes his forces in The Message. There are dozens of young sopranos before the public who can sing *Ah, non giunge* better than she can count on singing it next time. Now that the agile flights up to E flat in alt have become too hazardous to be attempted, Patti, deprived of her enchantments as a wonderful florid executant, is thrown back, as far as operatic arias are concerned, upon her capacity as a dramatic soprano, in which she is simply uninteresting. Fortunately she has another string to her bow—one that has for a long time been its best string. She is a great ballad-singer, and I have no doubt that twenty years hence I, as a fogey of the first order, shall hear her sing Home, Sweet Home to an audience whose affectionate veneration I shall compare sadly with the ardent enthusiasm of the days when the black hair was not yet tinged with the hues of sunset. And I shall tell the youngsters, with the mellow goodnature of my age, how she was the prettiest woman in Europe, and made fabulous heaps of money, and never learnt any new songs, and compelled even me to rave about her sometimes, though I always had it upon my mind that she had done no more than she could help for the art that did everything for her. But for the present all I can do is to say that I have been to the Albert Hall to hear her again, and that whilst I would not give twopence to hear *Ernani involami* and *Ombra leggiera* sung in that way and under those circumstances, in the ballads she has still no rival, except in our remembrances of herself. None the less do I insist that for the future the interest in Patti may as well be reinforced by the attraction of good music and artistically composed programs.

I must not omit to mention how Miss Gomez made amends for selecting an arrant piece of trash to begin with by a delivery of Hatton's Enchantress which melted all the criticism out of me, and was decidedly the greatest success of the concert, except perhaps Sims Reeves's introduction of a novelty entitled Come into the garden, Maud. As to the Chevalier Emil Bach's performance of Liszt's paraphrase of Weber's Polonaise in E, I will only say that I doubt whether I could have played it much better myself; and those who know my attainments as a pianist will need no further clue to my opinion.

The London Symphony Concerts began last Thursday. For one reason or another I have not been able to follow them very closely from their foundation. A glimpse of them in the earliest stage left on me the impression that the orchestra was somewhat under-manned and the conductor overparted. So, as the concerts were very much wanted, I decided, since I could not speak strongly in their favor, to let them alone and await developments. Returning on Thursday last to reconnoitre, I found matters quite changed. The band was fit for anything; and Mr Henschel was conducting without any of that nervousness about details and narrowness of survey which somewhat disabled him when he first left the drawing room piano stool for the conductor's desk. He still falls so far short of a complete command of the situation that sometimes, in approaching the grandest moments in a composition, when the steadiest calm is required to keep down all haste and excitement as the music broadens to the most imposing amplitude of tone and elevation of style of which the band is capable, he hurries in spite of himself, allows the impetus of the movement to carry him off his feet, and misses the imperturbable massiveness which Richter has taught us to expect at certain crises. I do not, of course, in the least mean that Henschel will not be complete until he is another Richter: on the contrary, the marked dissimilarity in their temperaments cannot but produce a differentiation of the most welcome kind if Henschel proves equal to Richter in originality and independence. We do not want that dead level which is so earnestly deprecated by the people who all wear the same shiny black hats and shiny white cuffs, who utter the same shiny moral sentiments, who keep the same hours, eat and drink the same foods, live in the same sort of houses in the same neighborhoods, marry the same class of lady, ride in the same class of railway carriage, and dare no more be seen deviating by a hair's breadth from this routine when anyone is looking than they dare carry a leg of mutton wrapped up in a newspaper from St James's Palace to the Royal Institution. They would be down on me at once if I were to lose sight for a moment of the value of independent thought, individual initiative, active and free life, and even of occasional eccentricity; and I am bound to avoid offending them, for I assure you they are very influential. Therefore let me hasten to explain that I do not want Mr Henschel to slavishly adopt Richter's interpretation of, for instance, the Flying Dutchman overture; but I do want him to keep the hurry and tumult of the storm out of the Salvation *motif*—to hold back his forces like grim death just when they have rushed up to it, so that they may give it its proper sublimity of expression, instead of having barely time to scramble over it before the storm is on them again. Richter keeps himself in hand on such occasions by never letting a movement run away with him; never confounding *crescendo* with *accellerando*—indeed, he rather leans to *allargando* in such emergencies; and never flurrying himself by giving two beats in a bar when one would suffice, as in a two-four Mozartian *allegro*, for example. On points like these there is all the difference in the world between taking a wrinkle from a rival and imitating him. And now, lest I should quite overbalance my criticism by dwelling too long on what is, after all, only one particular, let me hasten to say that the Henschel performance was of remarkable excellence, far superior to anything ever heard now at an ordinary Philharmonic Concert, more finished in the details of execution than the Richter performances have been lately, and, on the whole, promising eventually to equal the Crystal Palace Concerts in musical value, and to surpass them in social value through their greater cheapness and accessibility. Even Mozart's Prague Symphony, a masterpiece which would have been a vapid failure anywhere else in England except under Richter, came nearer than I expected to suggesting what it might be if played by a whole band of Mozarts.

During the performance of an old overture composed by one of the minor Bachs I was annoyed by what I took to be the jingling of a bell-wire somewhere; but it turned out to be Dr Parry playing the cembalo part on a decrepit harpsichord. As, though the overture is a hundred years old, it was not written for a harpsichord of that age, Dr Parry might almost as well have played the Emperor Concerto on a Broadwood dated 1809.

At the Crystal Palace we have had two new concertos, one by Hollmann for the violoncello and one by Paderewski for the pianoforte. Hollmann's was the better, because Hollmann is a violoncellist in a sense in which Paderewski is not a pianist. He finds music for a beloved instrument, without which he cannot satisfy his artistic impulse; wheras Paderewski uses the piano merely as a means to appease his musical rage or gratify his fancies, handling it with all the license of a master who has hired it for his pleasure, and cares not a scrap for its feelings. He is a young man of prodigious but most uncompassionate ability, this Paderewski: a sort of musical Richard III. Hollmann, on the other hand, has been rather too effectually tamed in our drawing rooms; but Hercules is still Hercules, distaff or no distaff. If I have not much respect for composer Popper and his Papillons, I can at least appreciate the way in which Hollmann plays that air of Bach's from the Suite in D. After the tranquil boredom of Spohr's Consecration of Sound symphony, Bach was magnificent.

I have seen nothing of the Opera since Miss Russell's appearance as Elsa in Lohengrin, on which occasion I am glad to say that Arditi amended some of the most disgraceful cuts in the score—notably the fanfare behind the scenes in the introduction to the second act, and the dawn music. It is true that the restored pieces were execrably performed; but that can be remedied. They tell me that there have been rare doings since that night's performance of Tannhäuser, introducing Venus on Euridice's sofa, and so on: but the matter was carefully concealed from me until too late, perhaps wisely. So I am not in a position to do more than chronicle the event from hearsay.

THE NEED FOR A STATE OPERA

The World, 3 December 1890

I must say that, after Signor Lago's exploits, I see
nothing for it but a State Opera. Private enterprise is
clearly not able for the work; and it remains for the
critics and musicians to make everybody conscious that
public opera houses are as reasonable institutions as
public picture galleries and art museums. At the same
time I by no means pretend that the resources of private
enterprise were exhausted by Signor Lago. To begin
with, though the experiment was supposed to be in
cheap opera, the performances, as I took occasion to say
at the outset of the season, were only cheap to Signor
Lago, not to the public. Even allowing for the fact that
better dresses and more dancers were introduced as
money began to come in, the staging of the operas,
except in so far as it was borrowed from Mr Harris, was
ridiculous. The preparation was so perfunctory that for
the first week we had Bevignani rushing the performances through by racing the orchestra against the
singers; whilst Arditi, who made the best of matters
with astonishing tact and patience, must have been
exhausted after every performance by the wear and tear
of the vigilance required by his task. After seeing him
pull Lohengrin through, I felt that he could be trusted
to drive twelve horses tandem-fashion from Charing
Cross to the Bank in the busiest hour of the day; and I
am somewhat indignant at the brutalities of the little
party which, for inscrutable reasons, is trying to
persuade the public, by disparaging Arditi, that Bevignani is the operatic conductor *par excellence.*
But though Arditi succeeded in preventing the big

operas from coming to open and irretrievable grief before the public, he was unable to secure anything approaching to steady and satisfactory performances. And I must add that, much as the adroit and sympathetic accompanist was to be preferred to the stolid and impatient one, a conductor in the full sense of the term would have been better than either. Under all the circumstances, it is odd that matters came off as well as they did. Without rehearsal, without stage management, without organization, without authority, without definite artistic aim—in short, without time, money, or leadership, the performances tumbled through with a degree of success that was really amazing. When people are working together for individual but compatible ends frank anarchy is always lucky, because everyone may make an omission or a mistake without throwing the rest out of gear, or even particularly surprising them. But the result produced by a mob of artists, each bent solely upon getting through his or her part without an obvious breakdown, and incidentally picking up as much applause as possible on the way, falls very far short of the artistic whole which a complete operatic representation should present. That can only be achieved by highly disciplined cooperation; and this cannot in artistic matters (or indeed in many others) be established by the methods of the drill-sergeant, but only by spontaneous obedience to the authority of a convincing artistic purpose manifested by some central member of the company.

Thus, when Maurel was on the stage in Rigoletto, there was none of the chaotic disorder of Il Trovatore, in which the chorus looked on at the principals much as a crowd outside a soup kitchen looks on at an altercation in which the parties are too respectable to take to their fists. Maurel seized their attention, and riveted them upon the drama with an authority that needed no reinforcement from the temporal powers that controlled the treasury. Giulia Ravogli did the same thing under ludicrously unfavorable circumstances in Orfeo. But neither Rigoletto nor Orfeo, as wholes, did credit to the management. Had there been a conductor with Maurel's strength and Giulia Ravogli's intensity, the season might have turned out differently, though no conductor can do as much with a scratch company, kept going on the hand to mouth system, as he could with the prestige, the permanence, and the assured resources of an opera house supported by public funds and controlled in the public interest. And what likelihood is there of really great conductors preferring precarious jobs here to the safe berths, with pensions attached to them, available abroad? If Mr Harris, with his subvention from Mayfair, could not tempt Levi from Munich, Richter from Vienna, or Faccio from Milan, what chance have second-rate enterprises which begin with only barely enough money and credit to keep the chorus above the level of worsted tights and tinfoil daggers? This, let me add, is of course not the fault of Signor Lago, who will probably prosper on his provincial tour, to the rehearsals for which London has just had the privilege of paying for admission.

Last Thursday it happened that I was thinking of these things, and wondering whether we should ever have "the poor silly millions," as Marx called them, rescued from operatic imposture by a demand for a better state of things from the artists themselves. The vein was not a very hopeful one. My earliest reminiscence of an eminent operatic artist off the stage dates from a certain performance of Lucrezia Borgia, at which I, then in my teens, managed to get behind the scenes. The tenor was a fine young man from the sunny South, who was going to be the successor of Mario. At that time everybody was going to succeed Mario. The particular child of Nature in question made a deep impression on me as he went on to sing the interpolated aria *Deserto sulla terra* between the last two acts. As he passed me he cleared his throat demonstratively, and in the most natural and spontaneous way imaginable spat right into the midst of a group of women who were seated chattering just behind the proscenium. Immediately the question presented itself, Can a man look like Lohengrin, sing like Lohengrin, feel like Lohengrin, raise the Donizetti-ridden stage to the level of Lohengrin before he has himself reached the phase of having misgivings as to the considerateness of promiscuous expectoration? Since that time I have seen many other Italian successors of Mario—in fact, nearly all those who appeared between Mario and De Reszke—but I can hardly remember one who had any more of Lohengrin, or even of Raoul de Nangis, in him than this early Gennaro of mine. Anyhow, I made up my mind that no demand for a more serious view of the lyric stage would come from the Italian tenors.

As to looking to the enormously expensive star *prima donnas* for a move in any direction except that of an additional hundred a night, and a few fresh cuts to lighten their work, no such Utopian extravagance ever exercised my imagination. I should almost as soon have expected the critics to take the matter up. There was nothing for it but to wait for the whole Gye-Mapleson-Costa *régime* to collapse from inanition, which, to my savage satisfaction, it eventually did very completely. Judge, then, whether I had not some ground for the skepticism with which I pursued that train of thought on Thursday last.

Thursday, it will be remembered, was a dark day, cold as the seventh circle. I presently found myself prowling about a great pile of flats, looking for a certain number at which I had to make a call. Somebody else was prowling also; and I no sooner became convinced that he was looking for the same number as I, and was probably going to call on the same person, than I resolved not to look at him; because to look at a man under such circumstances is almost tantamount to asking what the devil he is doing there. Consequently it was not until we got inside, and were introduced, that I recognized in the stranger no other than Maurel.

Imagine my feelings when I found that the business upon which he was bent was the formulation in some fashion of his demand as an artist for a more earnest treatment of his work and mission. "Of what value is your admiration of my Iago or Rigoletto" he said, in effect "if you do not regard the opera as a serious entertainment? Besides, one of the conditions of a really admirable performance is that it shall be an organic part of a whole in which all the other parts are equally excellent in their due degree; and how can such a whole be organized except in a place where opera is taken seriously, both before and behind the curtain?" Maurel, having gone up and down upon the earth in search of such places, has wisely come to the conclusion that they do not exist readymade, and that the artists must themselves set to work to create them everywhere, by rousing the critics and educating the public to appreciate theatrical art.

As a beginning, he wishes to submit his theory of art to criticism; to give skeptical dramatic critics illustrations of the dramatic resources of stage singing; and finally to assert the claims of operatic actors to weighty social considerations, founded on a sense of the importance and dignity of their function in society, instead of the capricious fashionable vogue which they now enjoy only when they happen to be phenomenal executants. This explains the speech he made at the Hôtel Métropole the other day. He is anxious to enlarge that after-dinner sketch into a carefully considered address, giving practical examples of what he meant by saying that one should not sing the part of Rigoletto with the voice of Don Juan, and to deliver it to a select body of the critics of London, who, as profound thinkers thoroughly conversant with their subject on its philosophic, technical, and social sides, and brimful of general culture to boot, would at once seize his meaning and help him to convey it to the public.

Modesty, and loyalty to my colleagues, restrained me from warning him not to generalize too rashly from the single instance with whom he was just then conversing; so I merely hinted that though the London critics are undeniably a fine body of men, yet their *élite* are hardly sufficiently numerous to make up a crowded and enthusiastic audience. To which he replied that an audience of two would satisfy him, provided the two had his subject at heart. This was magnificent, but not war: we at once agreed that we could do better for him than that. However, prompt measures were necessary, as he has to leave London next week. So we then and there constituted ourselves an executive subcommittee, fixed the date of the lecture for the afternoon of Monday next, and chose for our platform the stage of the Lyceum Theatre, on which, as Iago, he inaugurated a new era in operatic acting. It was a cool proposal, especially as Maurel altogether declined to proceed on a commercial basis, and would only hear of putting a price upon admission on condition that the proceeds should be given to some charity. But the upshot shewed that we knew our Irving, who promptly not only placed the theatre at Maurel's disposal, but charged himself with the arrangements. To the Lyceum, therefore, I refer the critics, the students, the amateurs, the philosophers, and the experts, as well as those modest persons who only wish to hear Maurel sing again, and to be shewn

how he changes the voice of William Tell into the voice
of Don Juan.

THE MANCHESTER ORCHESTRA
The World, 10 December 1890

Sir Charles Hallé has been unlucky this season so far.
When I got to his last concert, on one of those horrible
nights that nail a critic to his ain fireside, unless he is
fonder of music than of vulgar comfort, I found the
Manchester band gravely playing the Oberon overture
to an audience every member of which might have
stretched himself at full length along his bench without
incommoding his neighbor in the least. Still, it was a
picked audience: only enthusiasts would have braved
such villainous weather. It will be a misfortune for us
here if the Manchester orchestra is not supported
sufficiently to ensure our hearing it from time to time.
In London we are rather apt to think that one orchestra
is the same as another; for, as we hear the same players
wherever we go, we conclude that the differences must
be all due to the influence of the conductors. The widest
variation you get is between the Philharmonic band,
which represents orchestral gentility, and the Richter
band, which represents orchestral genius; yet their
members are constantly playing with oneanother at the
Crystal Palace and elsewhere; they cut their oboe reeds
in the same way; they use the same delicate drumsticks;
in brief, they shape the physical features of their
performances so exactly alike as to make them common
to all orchestral concerts in London, just as Coquelin's
turned-up nose is common to all his impersonations.

The public is as capable of appreciating physical
differences in music as the experts are, although it

cannot give a precise account of them as the experts can. Every man with an ear is differently affected by the oboe-playing of Horton and the piping of a pifferaro; by the clarinet of Egerton or Lazarus and the dingy boxwood instrument of his rival in the street, who produces a sound between that of a cheap harmonium and a cornet; by the drum-playing of Chaine or Smith and the flourishes of the trooper who "lets the kettle to the trumpet speak." Such differences are not necessarily those between good playing and bad, but between one sort of playing and another; both extremes, with all the intermediate gradations, have their peculiar emotional suggestiveness, and therefore their special artistic value. In Germany clarinet players use reeds which give a more strident, powerful, appealing tone than in England; and the result is that certain passages (in the Freischütz, for example) come out with a passion and urgency that surprise the tourist who has only heard them played here by Egerton, Lazarus, or Clinton. But when it comes to the Parsifal prelude or the slow movement in Beethoven's Fourth Symphony, one misses the fine tone and dignified continence of the English fashion.

Again, the son of thunder who handles the drums in the Manchester band could hardly, with those mighty drum sticks, play the solo passage in the *finale* to Beethoven's E flat Pianoforte Concerto as delicately as Chaine does whenever the pianist gives him a chance; but then Chaine is equally at a loss when he comes to that final *crescendo* roll, with its culminating stroke upon the last note of the Trold King's dance, in the Peer Gynt suite, a moment which would be one of the highest in the life of his Manchester rival. Thus, though music be a universal language, it is spoken with all sorts of accents; and the Lancashire accent differs sufficiently from the Cockney accent to make the Manchester band a welcome variety, without counting the change from

Cowen or Cusins to Hallé. Besides, the trip from the provinces to London freshens up the men, and does away with that staleness which so few conductors can supply stimulus enough to overcome without external aid from a change of circumstances. And it must not be omitted that the band, at home or on tour, is an excellent one. In *forte* passages it is superior to the Crystal Palace orchestra in power and to the Richter in quality, an advantage which enables it to produce certain effects in the scores of Berlioz which neither of the others can make much of. This alone would be sufficient to guarantee it a footing side by side with its rivals in London, if our amateurs had attained any real connoisseurship in the matter. It is true that Hallé's domain is that of "absolute music," whilst the fashion has been running of late strongly towards tone-poetry and music-drama. But this cannot last; every concert cannot consist of selections from the Niblung's Ring. And you never quite know where to have Hallé. When he conducted the Eroica Symphony last season for all the world as if it were a suite by Handel, nobody would have supposed him capable of coping with Beethoven's later works; and yet at this recent concert he finished with a performance of the Seventh Symphony as good as any I have heard—and I have heard Richter at it repeatedly. Earlier in the evening he had handed the *bâton* to Mr Willy Hess and taken his old place at the piano for Dvořák's concerto, which he played with enviable ease and spirit. The mere fact of his having in his repertory a long and elaborate work by a man twentytwo years his junior shews what sort of votary art has found in him. If Patti or Sims Reeves had been born pianists instead of singers, they would still be playing Mendelssohn's G minor Concerto at every concert, with Thalberg's Moïse fantasia for a solo, and an easy impromptu of Schubert's for an *encore* piece.

[223]

The day after the Hallé concert I heard Brahms's concerto played by Mr Leonard Borwick, the youngest representative of the Hallé school. He is a finished pupil, and can now play whatever any practical composer chooses to write down, however difficult it may be. So far, however, he has nothing to add: the composer's spirit does not attain reincarnation in him. No doubt that will come in time; and in the meantime there is no denying that his quick musical feeling and diligently earned technical accomplishment entitle him to take his place with credit among our foremost concert players.

The latest infant phenomenon is a Belgian violoncello player aged twelve, one Jean Gerardy, concerning whom I am compelled to own, at the risk of encouraging the agents to speculate in the phenomenon business, that he is one of the best players I ever heard. His instrument, though the maker has evidently spared no pains to make it as perfect as possible, is new, and has the faults of that quality. Gerardy, however, makes the best of it with a tact which is perhaps his most surprising quality, considering his age. His execution is finished, his intonation hardly ever at fault, his touch on the strings delicate and firm, and his taste irreproachable; whilst his ways and manners are as thoughtful and dignified as a boy's can be without making him insufferable. Another violoncellist now busy in London is Julius Klengel, who executes *tours de force* with great rapidity and accuracy, but whose dry tone shews that he has cultivated his left hand at the expense of his right. He was warmly applauded at Essipoff's concert last Friday.

The performance of the Norwich Festival setting of Milton's L'Allegro ed il Pensieroso at the Crystal Palace last Saturday did much to soften the feelings with which I have regarded the composer for some time past. Dr Parry is so genuine an enthusiast, so thorough a workman at his craft, so engaging an essayist, and, in short, so unexceptionable a musical fellow creature, that Judith was a hard blow to bear from him. Perhaps he was right—as a doctor of music—to dissemble his artistic feeling; but why did he write an oratorio? I have hardly alluded to him with common civility since; but now that his genius, released from an unnatural and venal alliance, has flown back to the noble poetry that was its first love, let the hatchet be buried—and Judith with it as soon as possible. This new cantata of his is happy, ingenious, as full of contrapuntal liveliness as Judith was full of contrapuntal deadliness, and genuine in feeling throughout. The performance was admirable on the part of the orchestra, and as good as could have been expected on the part of the chorus. Mr Henschel did justice to Dr Parry if not to Milton; but Miss Amy Sherwin displayed a virtuosity in the art of singing flat which no stretch of critical indulgence would justify me in ignoring. In her first contribution to the concert, *Dove sono*, she shewed that in slow melodies, with simple and carefully prepared modulations, she can keep fairly in tune; but when it came to Dr Parry's brisk movements and sudden modern transitions, she lost her way. As her voice is one of exceptional range and quality, it is a pity that she should be practically disabled for work of this class by what may be only a bad habit, acquired in regions where people are rather more easily pleased in the matter of intonation than we in London.

As to Mr Hamish MacCunn's Cameronian's Dream, which was also performed under the composer's *bâton*, I must frankly say that a man might go on setting ballads in that way for a lifetime without making any real progress. Any ardent young musician can pick up those tricks of being solemn on the trombone, pastoral on the oboe, and martial on the side-drum easily enough nowadays. My comment on the Cameronian's Dream is that of the Sheffield gentleman at the Garrick Theatre: "Ive heard that before"; and I may add, as to Mr MacCunn's setting of line after line to the measure of *Esperto nocchiero*, that I have heard it quite often enough. The fiery chariot business at the end, with the ridiculous post-horn flourishes on the cornet, supported by a mechanical accompaniment which is as empty of poetic meaning and as full of prosaic suggestion as the tintinnabulation of an electric alarm, will probably end its days in ashes on Mr MacCunn's hearth, when he has come to see that when we all applauded Lord Ullin's Daughter so heartily we never intended him to make a habit of it.

JACK-ACTING
The World, *17 December 1890*

One cannot but admire Mr Richter Temple's independence and enterprise in trying back to Gounod and Molière as a relief to Cellier and Stephenson. His Mock Doctor company, however, shews how superficial are the accomplishments of the artists (save the mark!) who run about the country in light-opera companies. To perform all the latest works in their line no very great technical skill is needed: good looks, a certain felicity of address, and sufficient natural aptitude for music qualify any young person to play principal parts. At the Savoy we are highly amused by what we indulgently call the acting; but we have only to pronounce the magic word Molière, and think of the Théâtre Français, to recognize at once that this "acting" is nothing but pure tomfoolery—"jack-acting," the Irish call it—wittily turned into a stage entertainment by Mr Gilbert.

I was at the gala performance of The Gondoliers the

other night, and noticed two things: first, that the music was much more familiar to the band than to the composer, who conducted on that occasion; and second, that the representation did not involve a single stroke of skilled stage-playing. Mr Frank Wyatt's success as the Duke of Plaza-Toro does not afford the faintest presumption that he could manage three minutes of Sganarelle: Mr Courtice Pounds and Mr Wallace Brownlow might win unbounded applause as Marco and Luiz a thousand times without knowing enough to enable them to walk half across the stage and make a bow in the character of Leandre. I do not say this as an advocate of the French system: I have always maintained that the English actor who grows his own technique is much to be preferred to the drilled French actor with his borrowed regulation equipment. But if the finished English actor's original art is better than the French actor's conventional art, the Frenchman has still the advantage of the Englishman who has "gone on the stage" without any conception of art at all—who has not only an untrained body and a slovenly tongue, but who, having walked and talked all his life without thinking about it, has no idea that action and speech are subjects for artistic culture. Such innocents, though they do not find engagements at the Garrick or the Haymarket, unfortunately get before the public in light opera very easily, if only they can achieve anything that will pass for singing. Indeed, I need not confine the statement to light opera.

The vulgarities and ineptitudes of Carl Rosaism pass unrebuked at Drury Lane, although, if the culprits were only actors, Mr Harris would scornfully recommend them not to venture north of the Surrey or west of the Pavilion until they had made themselves commonly presentable. Light opera gets the best of it; for all the pleasantest, funniest, and most gifted novices get snapped up by the Savoy, the Gaiety, the Prince of Wales's, and the Lyric, leaving the second-rate aspirants to the provinces for rough wear in grand opera (in English) or lighter work on tour with comic operas, according to their robustness and capacity. Under these circumstances I do not blame Mr Temple for failing to find a company capable of handling The Mock Doctor with the requisite skill and delicacy. No doubt he has done the best he could; but the result is not satisfactory. And I must say, even making the largest allowance for the incapacity of the performers, that I cannot see why so much of the concerted music should be absolutely discordant. It is always possible to be at least smooth and tuneful. Surely Mr Temple could obtain a more musicianly performance of that sextet if he cared enough for it to assert his authority. Still, on Thursday last, when I dropped unobtrusively into the pit, the audience, put in good humor by the irresistible flavor of Molière which hangs about Kenny's libretto, were very willing to be pleased. If Mr Temple's enterprise fails, it will not be the fault of the piece.

Maurel's lecture was, as everybody by this time knows, a great success. That is to say, everybody was there, and everybody seemed delighted. Nevertheless, my private opinion is that very few of the audience appreciated the situation sufficiently to feel the least urgency in what Maurel had to tell them. A certain eminent dramatic critic [William Archer] whom I consulted as I left the Lyceum said, with the air of a man who does not wish to be unkinder than he can help, that the lecture was "free from paradox." By this he meant that it struck him as truistic, not to say platitudinous. Happy man! to have to deal with a department of art in which the petty warfare of the critic is fully accomplished, leaving him free to devote his energy to the demand for a higher order of subject now that there is no further question of the necessity for intelligent and unified treatment of that subject, no matter what its order may be. After his round of the Lyceum, the Princess's, Haymarket, the Criterion, the Alhambra, the Olympic, and Drury Lane this pampered scribe hears Maurel insisting that operatic actors should study the psychology of their parts, and that the designers of stage costume and scenery should aim at producing an appropriate illusion as to the place and period assigned by the dramatist to the action of the piece; and his only comment is "Who disputes it?" How I should like to see him doing six weeks Italian Opera without the option of a fine! There he would find only one period, "the past," and only two places, "an exterior" and "an interior." In costume the varieties might prove more definite and numerous. I have often seen Marta, in which Queen Anne is introduced alive, with the ladies in early Victorian Archery Club dresses, the Queen's retinue in the costume of feudal retainers of the Plantagenet period, the comic lord as Sir Peter Teazle, the noblemen in tunics and tights from Il Trovatore, and the peasants with huge Bavarian hats beneath their shoulders, reminding one of the men in Othello's yarns. As to La Traviata, with Violetta in the latest Parisian confections, and Alfredo in full Louis XIV. fig, that is familiar to every operagoer. Yet this by itself might matter no more than the Venetian costumes in Paul Veronese's Marriage in Cana, if it were ignorance, *naïveté*, convention, poetic license, or anything but what it is: to wit, sheer carelessness, lack of artistic conscience, cynical conviction that nothing particularly matters in an opera so long as the singers draw good houses.

When a special effort has to be made in the case of a practically new work, such as Romeo, The Mastersingers, or Othello, the exception only brings the rule into more glaring prominence; and too often the exception is in point of scenography (as Maurel puts it) rather than of psychology: that is, the scenepainter and costumier, stimulated by lavish managerial expenditure, think out their part of the opera, whilst the principal singers and the stage manager (if there is one) jog along in their old grooves. Clearly, then, Maurel's appeal, granted that from a dramatic critic it would be a mere knocking at an open door, is in the opera house a sort of Childe Roland's blast on the slughorn.

So much I have said to spare the feelings of the dramatic critics. Now I may add privately to Maurel that average dramatic criticism here is simply confusion made articulate, expressing the critic's likes and dislikes unintelligently and therefore unsystematically. It is all very well to say to Maurel "Well, what then? We knew all this before you were born." Suppose Maurel were to produce a sheet of paper, in the manner of Mephistopheles producing his bond, and to say "In that case, oblige me by allotting a hundred marks to Mr Beerbohm Tree, or any other actor whom you have criticized, in such a manner as to shew the proportion between his technical, his psychological, and his scenographic accomplishments; and append an estimate of the allowance to be made for your idiosyncratic bias for or against him." How many dramatic critics would be able to do more than exclaim piteously with Barnacle junior,* "Look here: you have no right to come this sort of move, you know"? If these gentlemen as much as suspected the existence of half the things that I have to pretend to know all about, and that Maurel has actually to do, they would transpose their remarks a tone or so down at future performances.

For my own part, I have no fault to find with the lecture, except on a point of history. All that about the

* Character in Dickens's Little Dorrit.

Dark Ages and the barbarous Middle Ages is a modern hallucination, partly pious, partly commercial. There never were any Dark Ages, except in the imagination of the Blind Ages. Look at their cathedrals and their houses; and then believe, if you can, that they were less artistic than we who have achieved the terminus at Euston and the Gambetta monument. And to think that Maurel, of all men—Maurel, who was an architect before he went over to the lyric stage—should believe such a thing! However, he does not really believe it; for instead of following it up in the sequel, he turned right round in his tracks, and practically assumed that art has been going to the deuce ever since the Renascence.

I have no other exception to take to the lecture or to the vocal illustrations. The *rôle* of lecturer was never better acted since lecturing began. As far as one man, limited by a peculiar vocal technique and a strongly marked meridional temperament, could make his case complete he made it complete. The Verdi *nuance* he utters as if he were native and to the manner born; the Wagnerian *nuance*, like the Mozartian, he has to translate; and intelligently and skilfully as the translation is done it is to me still a translation. Iago and Rigoletto, with their intense moods and swift direct expression, come to life in him; but Wolfram and Don Juan, with their yearning northern abstract sentiment flowing with endless inflexions, only find in him a very able proxy.

I must return to the subject of the Hallé orchestra to chronicle a magnificent performance of Berlioz's Fantastic Symphony. At present no London band can touch this work at all, because no London band has learnt it thoroughly. We can get the notes played, and we sometimes do; but, as in the case of the first movement of the Ninth Symphony, only confusion and disappointment come of the attempt. Now the Manchester band, knowing the work through and through, handles it with a freedom, intelligence, and spirit which bring out all its life and purpose, and that, too, without giving the conductor any trouble. It is especially to be hoped that the orchestral students of the Royal College of Music who had a turn at the Harold Symphony in St James's Hall two days before were at this concert. If so, it must have helped them to realize how completely they were beaten, in spite of the highly praiseworthy degree of skill they have attained in using their instruments, and the excellent drill they are getting in *ensemble* playing.

The singing of the Royal College pupils bore eloquent testimony to the fund of negative advice available at the institution. One could see with half an eye how earnestly the young vocalists had been told what not to do—as, for instance, not to press on the notes with their breath, not to force the tone, not to sing with effort, and so on. If the College only succeeds presently in securing some teacher who can also tell the pupils what to do, they will soon begin to shew signs of knowing how to sing. At present they seem to me to be hardly more advanced than M. Jourdain was in fencing after his instructor had informed him that the two main points in practising that art are—first, to hit your adversary, and second, to avoid being hit by him.

Mr Boscovitz's recital at Steinway Hall last week was unusually well worth hearing. He had a spinet and a harpsichord, both of them really fine instruments of their sort; and on them he played a number of old pieces, from Bull's Carman's Whistle to the Harmonious Blacksmith, occasionally repeating one, with detestable but interesting effect, on a Steinway grand, which is about as like a harpsichord as an oboe is like a Boehm flute, or a bassoon like a euphonium. If Mr Boscovitz repeats this recital, or lecture, he will do well to complete it by also using a clavichord, if he can get one, as well as by securing a double harpsichord for Bach's Italian

Concerto. His omission of the last two movements from this work considerably astonished the audience, in whose powers of endurance he seemed suddenly to lose faith. The *pianos* and *fortes* marked by Bach can only be produced on a harpsichord with two manuals. If Mr Boscovitz cannot obtain such an instrument, he should explain the matter in defence of his own playing; for I confess I did not know what was wrong until Mr Fuller Maitland told me; and without this warning I should certainly have ignorantly pitched into Mr Boscovitz for not attending to Bach's directions.

CIRCENSES
The World, 24 December 1890

The musical season is turning out badly for orchestral concert givers. Mr Henschel, who began by declaring that he would trust the public, and venture without a guarantee, has now sorrowfully announced that he is beaten, and cannot complete his series of symphony concerts unless more stalls are subscribed for. And Sir Charles Hallé was abandoned at his first two concerts in a way really discreditable to London amateurism. Hereupon Mr Arthur Symons,★ in the Pall Mall Gazette, endeavors to sting London into doing its musical duty by declaring that we can no longer pretend to be a musical nation. As to that, it cannot be said that symphony concerts have ever been much of a national matter: so long as St James's Hall suffices for our needs in that department, it is hardly worth discussing its fullness or emptiness from the national point of view.

★ Poet and literary critic, one of the leaders of the esthetic movement in England.

But for the few of us who require good music as part of our weekly subsistence, the cutting off of our opportunities by no less than two concert series out of a total of four is not to be borne without remonstrance. No doubt the weather has been partly to blame: thick boots and a warm coat buttoned up to the neighborhood of the chin are indispensable in St James's Hall just now for people who wish to enjoy their music without a castanet accompaniment from their own teeth; and as the ordinary patron of the stalls is condemned by custom to garnish himself with indoor fireside wear, he naturally shirks his concerts unless the attraction is exceptionally strong. Still, I do not see why the subscriptions should not be forthcoming, whether the subscribers attend or not. Many very rich people in London seem to me to suppose that they have nothing but their own private whims to consult in the disposition of their incomes. I demur to this, and contend that they are as much bound to support orchestral concerts by their subscriptions as they are to support hospitals. That they may dislike music and never go to a concert when they can help it is clearly no more to the point than that they dislike being ill, and would not go to a hospital on any terms. If concerts of high-class music are vitally necessary, as I believe they are, and if they cannot be kept on foot without the support of the rich, why, the rich must do their duty.

As a plebeian, I demand *circenses*, if not *panem*, to that extent. And it cannot be urged that there is at present any difficulty in finding worthy enterprises to support. Hallé has long been above suspicion in this respect; and though Henschel is comparatively a beginner, the value of his concerts is already beyond question. And it must be remembered in estimating the general effect of their labors that they have only asked the public for a shilling where Richter has demanded half-a-crown, whilst the scale of their performances is equally expensive.

The Bach Choir gave a concert on the 16th. I was not present. There are some sacrifices which should not be demanded twice from any man; and one of them is listening to Brahms's Requiem. On some future evening, perhaps, when the weather is balmy, and I can be accommodated with a comfortable armchair, an interesting book, and all the evening papers, I may venture; but last week I should have required a requiem for myself if I had attempted such a feat of endurance. I am sorry to have to play the "disgruntled" critic over a composition so learnedly contrapuntal, not to say so fugacious; but I really cannot stand Brahms as a serious composer. It is nothing short of a European misfortune that such prodigious musical powers should have nothing better in the way of ideas to express than incoherent commonplace. However, that is what is always happening in music: the world is full of great musicians who are no composers, and great composers who are no musicians.

In his youth, Brahms when writing songs or serenades, or trifles of one kind or another, seemed a giant at play; and he still does small things well. I listened to his cleverly harmonized gypsy songs at the last Monday Popular Concert of the year with respectful satisfaction, though I shall not attempt to deny that fifteen minutes of them would have been better than twentyfive. This last remark, by the bye, shews that I am full of malice against "holy John," as Wagner called Brahms, even when he does what I have admitted his fitness for. Consequently my criticism, though it relieves my mind, is not likely to be of much value. Let me therefore drop the subject, and recall the attention of the Bach Choir to a composer of whom I entertain a very different opinion, to wit, John Sebastian Bach himself. It is the special business of this society to hammer away at Bach's works until it at last masters them to the point of being able to sing them as Bach meant them to be sung. For instance, there is the great Mass in B minor. The choir has given several public performances of that; but all have been timid, mechanical, and intolerably slow. And when the elderly German conductor who got up the first performances was succeeded by a young and talented Irishman, the Mass became duller and slower than ever. The public did not take to the work as performed in this manner. It satisfied its curiosity, received an impression of vast magnitude, yawned, and felt no great impatience for a repetition of the experience. If the society thinks that this was the fault of Bach, it is most unspeakably mistaken.

Nothing can be more ruinous to the spirited action of the individual parts in Bach's music, or to the sublime march of his polyphony, than the dragging, tentative, unintelligent, half-bewildered operations of a choir still in the stage of feeling its way from interval to interval and counting one, two, three, four, for dear life. Yet the Bach Choir never got far beyond this stage with the B minor Mass. Even at the great bicentenary performance at the Albert Hall no attempt was made to attain the proper speed; and the work, as far as it came to light at all, loomed dimly and hugely through a gloomy, comfortless atmosphere of stolid awkwardness and anxiety. The effect the slow movements would make if executed with delicacy of touch and depth of expression, and of the quick ones if taken in the true Bach major mood, energetic, spontaneous, vivid, jubilant, was left to the imagination of the audience; and I fear that for the most part they rather declined to take it on trust. All this can be remedied by the Bach choristers if they stick at it, and are led with sufficient faith and courage. There is more reason than ever for persevering with their task at present; for Bach belongs, not to the past, but to the future—perhaps the near future. When he wrote such works as *Wachet auf!*, for example, we were no more ready for them than the children for whom we are now buying Christmas gift-books of fairy tales are to receive volumes of Goethe and Ibsen. Acis and Galatea and Alexander's Feast, the ever-charming child literature of music, were what we were fit for then.

But now we are growing up we require passion, romance, picturesqueness, and a few easy bits of psychology. We are actually able to relish Faust and Carmen. And beyond Faust there is Tristan und Isolde, which is at last music for grown men. Mr Augustus Harris has never heard of it, as it is only thirty years old; but as he goes about a good deal, I cannot doubt that in the course of the next ten years or so he will not only have it mentioned to him by some ambitious *prima donna* who aspires to eclipse Frau Sucher, but may even be moved to try whether a performance of it would not be better business than a revival of Favorita. Now the reaction of Tristan on *Wachet auf!* will be a notable one. The Bach cantata, which seemed as dry and archaic after Acis and Galatea as Emperor and Galilean* would after Cinderella, will, after Tristan, suddenly send forth leaves, blossoms, and perfume from every one of its seemingly dry sticks, which have yet more sap in them than all the groves of the temple of Gounod. Provided, that is—and here I ask the ladies and gentlemen of the Bach Choir to favor me with their best attention for a moment—provided always that there shall be at that time a choir capable of singing *Wachet auf!* as it ought to be sung.

Messrs Richard Gompertz, Haydn Inwards, Emil Kreuz, and Charles Ould, honorably associated as "The

* A dual play by Ibsen (1873).

[237]

Cambridge University Musical Society's String Quartet," have given a couple of concerts at Prince's Hall, at the second of which I enjoyed myself without stint until they began to play Brahms, when I precipitately retired. Mr Edward German's symphony, performed at the last Crystal Palace concert, shews that he is still hampered by that hesitation between two distinct *genres* which spoiled his Richard III. overture. If Mr German wishes to follow up his academic training by writing absolute music in symmetrical periods and orderly ingenuity of variation, let him by all means do so. On the other hand, if he prefers to take significant *motifs*, and develop them through all the emotional phases of a definite poem or drama, he cannot do better. But it is useless nowadays to try to combine the two; and since Mr German has not yet made up his mind to discard one or the other, the result is that his symphonic movements proceed for awhile with the smoothness and regularity of a Mendelssohn scholar's exercise, and then, without rhyme or reason, are shattered by a volcanic eruption which sounds like the last page of a very exciting opera *finale*, only to subside the next moment into their original decorum. I can but take a "symphony" of this sort as a bag of samples of what Mr German can do in the operatic style and in the absolute style, handsomely admitting that the quality of the samples is excellent, and that if Mr German's intelligence and originality equal his musicianship, he can no doubt *compose* successfully as soon as he realizes exactly what composition means.

At the last Monday Popular Concert of the year Madame Neruda distinguished herself greatly in the slow movement of the Mozart Quartet (No. 3 in B flat) and in Grieg's Sonata in F. In the quick movements of the quartet poor Mozart was polished off with the usual scant ceremony. Madame Haas, who is always happy with Beethoven, played those variations on an original theme (in F), an affection for which is a sure sign of tenderness and depth of feeling in a player. The audience acted wisely in recalling Madame Haas twice, as her only fault is an occasional timidity in expressing herself fully—a timidity which must be caused by doubt as to whether her relations with Beethoven are being understood or appreciated.

SUNDRY PARCELS OF MUSIC
The World, 31 December 1890

The music publishers of London owe me their acknowledgments for having devoted Christmas Day to examining sundry parcels of music with which they have from time to time favored me of late. It was a rare way of enjoying the season. I cannot say with Shelley that

> I sang of the dancing stars,
> I sang of the dædal earth,*

but I sang of the love of yore, and the coming years, and the whispered prayer, and the twilight shadows, and the sweet long ago, and the parting tear, and the distant bells, and the old cathedral, and the golden gates, and the moon shining o'er Seville, and the hour before the battle, and the eager eyes looking out for Jack, and a floating home on the world of foam being the home of homes for me, and goodness knows what else. Most of them had waltz refrains, except Seville, which was a bolero, and the pious ones with harmonium *obbligato* culminating in shouts of "Hosanna" or "Miserere, Domine." When I finished it was late in the evening,

* Hymn of Pan, in Posthumous Poems (1824).

and I felt that I had done something to avenge the unfortunate cows and turkeys of whose blood I at least am guiltless.

When I came to turn it all over in my mind, satanic glee at the sufferings I had inflicted on my gormandizing neighbors gave way to wonder as to why these ditties had been sent to me. At the first blush it seemed as if the publishers expected me to review them, and yet how could any sane man of business suppose that there was the faintest chance of my recommending the public to sing:

> Will he come? Will he come? O, my heart!
>   I am waiting and watching in vain.
> Ere twilight's soft shadows depart,
>   O, come to me, come once again!

Waltz Refrain

> Just (*tum tum*)
> Once (*tum*) a-
> Gain (*tum tum*),
> (*Tum*) When the, &c. &c.

One publisher sent me, not this particular song, but some dozens exactly like it, without one redeeming piece to save me from feeling that my time had been utterly and wantonly wasted. Yet I should not be surprised if he feels positively swindled because this column does not contain the titles of all his detestable compilations, with a note certifying them as "a tuneful melody to flowing words, compass G to D, for soprano or tenor, or E flat to B flat, for contralto or baritone." It is certain that space is cheerfully given up to "reviews" of this sort by editors who would fall into convulsions if they were asked to as much as mention the literary equivalents of such songs in their columns. What is more, these reviewers' verdicts are heartily indorsed at hundreds of suburban pianos, where Sullivan is shirked as difficult, Blumenthal given up as abstruse, and Schumann repudiated as hideous and bewildering. For my part, however, I must say once for all that there is no use in asking me to take that point of view at Christmas or any other season. People in search of trash will get no assistance from me, unless I take to composing it myself.

The Doctor of Music who sent me the full score of his motet for double chorus to a couple of phrases from the Psalms, all done in strict Mendelssohnese with the meaning carefully extracted, and beginning with two vigorous minims to the words Lord Howe, must have meant to have a rise out of me. He may esteem himself fortunate that he has failed. Messrs Chappell send a couple of songs by Battison Haynes, one of which, Hey nonny no, is being popularized by Mr Plunket Greene. The music is full of point; but the words, described as "of the Elizabethan period," are almost as void of sense as if they belonged to the Victorian period. They will suit any *basso profundo* who wishes to enliven a drawing room by a *fortissimo* upon such couplets as

> Is't not fine to dance and sing
> When the bells of death do ring?

although, after all, that is a matter of taste. A French serenade, by Francis Thomé, is on the usual lines— three-eight time, *pizzicato* accompaniment, minor mode changing to major, *si tu savais, ma toute belle*, &c. It served the turn of so good a singer as Liza Lehmann at the Crystal Palace the other day. Of songs which claim more serious consideration I have four sets. The first, a couple of songs by Mr Goring Thomas (Chappell), and the second, a series of settings of Tennyson by Mr Alfred Cellier (Metzler), are in the politest vein, delicate in sentiment, elegant and finished in workmanship, shewing the influence of Sterndale Bennett, modified in Mr Thomas's case by the fascinations of Gounod. Nothing could suit Tennyson better. The other two are much fresher. One is a little cycle of songs by Marshall-Hall, with a rhymed preface containing some strong observations as to the sort of encouragement the author received in this country, "where Truth and Art seek bread and home in vain." Australia has now offered Mr Marshall-Hall a professorship, which will, it is to be hoped, establish some sort of truce between Truth and Art and their natural enemies, the baker and the landlord. But these songs will not make Mr Marshall-Hall so popular in Australia as Mr Milton Wellings, for they are no simple tunes with every strain repeated and furnished with an obvious complement. They run into dramatic monologue of the latest Wagnerian type, rather a serious matter for the ordinary amateur. Two or three of the songs, however, can be turned to account by any really cultivated amateur. They are published by Mr Joseph Williams.

The Album for Song, by Agathe Backer-Gröndahl, the Norwegian pianist, published by Warmuth of Christiania and Breitkopf & Härtel, is full of that steadfast poetic feeling and beautiful taste which so ennobled her playing. The pianist's hand is apparent in the vocal parts of the songs; not that pianoforte traits are anywhere substituted for vocal traits, but that a considerable demand is made on the performer for pure *cantabile* singing and delicacy of vocal touch, wheras there is little conceded to what may be called the personal conditions of singing. Pure soprano voices, capable of being used in the upper register pretty continuously without fatigue, will find in Madame Gröndahl's songs just the opportunities they need. Tito Mattei, from whom I dreaded some unscrupulous *pièce de salon*, has surprised me with a song, Treasured Violets

(Doremi & Co.), remarkably happy in its sincerity of expression and the perfect relation between its musical form and Mr Oxenford's little poem. The same merit, though in an absurdly trivial degree, may be claimed by M. Piccolomini for his Madelina (Osborn & Tuckwood). Le Portrait (Metzler) is one of those quaintly sweet and *naïve* old French songs with which singers like Mrs Henschel and Miss Lehmann can score so effectively against the gushing modern drawing room song, of which I have received a fair example in Mr Lawrence Kellie's Sleeping Tide, which goes on to a most fervent and effective climax about nothing that I can discover. Of a couple of songs by Kate Elston, the earlier, For Dear Love's Sake (Marriott), is cruder in workmanship than On the Moonlit Sea (Reid); but it is also more deeply felt and forcibly expressed, an advantage which is well worth the sacrifice of a little conventional smoothness in the harmony. Mary Carmichael's songs (Metzler) are still daintily pleasant, but they are losing all pretence of thoroughness. Charles Ernest Baughan, on the other hand, in setting some lines of Lowell's entitled A Lover's Dream (Hopkinson), has elaborated his harmonies to the point, as it seems to me, of producing a discrepancy between them and the melody, most of which belongs clearly to the old tonic and dominant school. Nevertheless, the song is a promising one. Roeckel's Breton Slumber Song (Enoch) is a tender and pretty lullaby, in which Mr Baughan's error and his promise are alike avoided.

Bad as most of the vocal music sent me has proved, it is classic in comparison to the instrumental pieces. Most of these are waltzes and quadrilles introducing the refrains of all the silliest and most hackneyed of the songs. I believe it would be found quite easy to train circus horses to compose dance music of this sort, if any ringmaster could infatuate himself into the belief that the public would care two straws about such an accomplishment. I do not say that the stuff should not be written if it is wanted; but why send it to be reviewed? Of what interest can it be to anybody to know that I find the picture on the cover of The Chappies' Polka passably comic? In the whole bundle I find just one Valse Caprice, by Hamilton Robinson (Joseph Williams), which I can play without a sense of extreme indignity. There is absolutely nothing else, except Mr Isidore de Lara's Rêveuse (Mocatta), which has a definite poetic intention adequately and characteristically expressed. All the same, it is emptily sensuous, lacking in the intellectual vigor which goes, as a matter of course, with the higher kinds of artistic vigor; and I altogether decline to do violence to my own temperament by celebrating these languors, however featly they may be expressed in tone-poetry. Finally, I have to ask the publishers who send me arrangements of famous works for "the Liszt organ" to be kind enough to send the instrument as well, as otherwise it is impossible for me to say whether the transcriptions are effective or not.

I forgot to mention that Mr James Fleming sends me a number of a magazine entitled The Violin, published at 71 Paragon Road, Hackney, and containing a couple of photographs of a beautiful long-pattern Stradivarius violin, with—considering the subject—some unusually sensible letterpress concerning it.

PANTO IN BRISTOL

The World, 21 January 1891

Christmas being the season of mirth, music, the great English killjoy, with its intolerable hypocrisies, is gladly put away until it is time to return to work and duty and mental improvement and other unpleasantnesses; consequently my critical machinery has got out of gear somewhat. I might have kept off the rust by attending the regulation Christmas performance of the Messiah; but I have long since recognized the impossibility of obtaining justice for that work in a Christian country. Import a choir of heathens, restrained by no considerations of propriety from attacking the choruses with unembarrassed sincerity of dramatic expression, and I would hasten to the performance if only to witness the delight of the public and the discomfiture of the critics. That is, if anything so indecent would be allowed here. We have all had our Handelian training in church, and the perfect churchgoing mood is one of pure abstract reverence. A mood of active intelligence would be scandalous. Thus we get broken in to the custom of singing Handel as if he meant nothing; and as it happens that he meant a great deal, and was tremendously in earnest about it, we know rather less about him in England than they do in the Andaman Islands, since the Andamans are only unconscious of him, wheras we are misconscious. To hear a thousand respectable young English persons jogging through For He shall purify the sons of Levi as if every group of semiquavers were a whole bar of four crotchets *a capella*, or repeating Let Him deliver Him if He delight in Him with exactly the same subdued and uncovered air as in For with His stripes we are healed, or lumbering along with Hallelujah as if it were a superior sort of family coach: all this is ludicrous enough; but when the nation proceeds to brag of these unwieldy choral impostures, these attempts to make the brute force of a thousand throats do what can only be done by artistic insight and skill, then I really lose patience. Why, instead of wasting huge sums on the multitudinous dulness called a Handel Festival does not somebody set up a thoroughly rehearsed and exhaustively studied performance of the Messiah in St James's

Hall with a chorus of twenty capable artists? Most of us would be glad to hear the work seriously performed once before we die.

However, if I did not go to the Messiah, I ventured on a pantomime, although in London we are unable to produce an endurable pantomime for exactly the same reasons that prevent us from achieving an endurable performance of the Messiah. Therefore I did not make the experiment in London. I found myself one evening in Bristol with nothing better to do than to see whether pantomime is really moribund. I am bound to say that it seems to me to be as lively as it was twentyfive years ago. The fairy queen, singing In Old Madrid with reckless irrelevance at the entrance to the cave where Aladdin found the lamp, was listened to with deep respect as an exponent of the higher singing; and in the cave itself The Bogie Man, in about fifty verses, took immensely. A street scene at night, with Chinese lanterns and a willow-pattern landscape, were stage pictures with just the right artistic quality for the occasion; and the absurdity of the whole affair on the dramatic side was amusing enough from an indulgent holiday point of view. There were no processions presenting one silly idea over and over again in different colored tights, until a thousand pounds had been wasted in boring the audience to distraction. And—though here I hardly expect to be believed—there was not a single child under ten on the stage. I told Mr Macready Chute, the manager, that he should come to London to learn from our famous stage managers here how to spend ten times as much money on a pantomime for one-tenth of the artistic return. I bade him, if he thirsted for metropolitan fame, to take for his triple motto, Expenditure, inanity, vulgarity, and that soon no spectacular piece would be deemed complete without him. With these precepts I left him, assuring him that I felt more than ever what a privilege it was to live in a convenient art centre like London, where the nearest pantomime is at Bristol, and the nearest opera at Bayreuth.

Stavenhagen, about whom I need say nothing pending his concert on Thursday, was the pianist at the Monday Popular Concerts from the New Year until last Monday week, when a wild young woman named Ilona Eibenschütz made her first appearance. Coming on the platform immediately after Miss Marguerite Hall, whose *savoir faire* is so superb that nervous people secretly long to throw things at her head, the newcomer, stumbling hastily up the stairs, and rushing at the piano stool with a couple of strange gestures of grudging obeisance, as if she suspected some plot among us to be beforehand with her, produced an unmistakable impression on the matronhood of the stalls. Backs were straightened, elbows drawn in, lips folded: in that moment Ilona, it seemed to me, was friendless in a foreign land. But when she touched the first chord of Schumann's Etudes Symphoniques, the hand lay so evenly and sensitively on it, and the tone came so richly, that I at once perceived that I was wasting my sympathies, and that Ilona, however ingloriously she might go to the piano, would come away from it mistress of the situation. And she certainly did. She is too young to have yet acquired the *sang-froid* necessary for the complete management of her great musical energy: she has to use that energy itself for self-control; but in spite of her not being yet at her best, she left the platform amidst such a storm of applause that, after two more outlandish bows, she dashed at the piano again and gave a brief but terrific sample of her powers of mechanical execution. As to Miss Marguerite Hall, I got laughed at by a critic of a younger generation for admitting that I had never heard her before; but the loss was my own; she uses her voice admirably.

By ill luck, I was performing in public myself on the night of Mr Henschel's first London Symphony Concert of the year; and as he did not come to hear me, I do not think he can reasonably complain of my not having been to hear him.

THE STAVENHAGENS

The World, 28 January 1891

The thaw came just in time to make Stavenhagen's concert comfortable for the nobility and gentry. Nevertheless, as the audience hardly outnumbered the ordinary Stavenhagen recital attendance far enough to cover the extra expense of the band, we all, I hope, felt that we were to some extent sponging on his preference of artistic satisfaction to pecuniary profit. And even the artistic satisfaction must have been qualified by the impossibility of getting a good performance of a concerto out of a scratch orchestra, however well manned, with a casual conductor, however eminent. Only those orchestras which, like the Crystal Palace, the Richter, the Henschel, and the Manchester, are organized by a permanent conductor as going concerns, can achieve really good work in this department. All that could be said was that Stavenhagen was as well served as the circumstances permitted. His old fellow-student in the Lisztian school at Weimar, Arthur Friedheim, himself a pianist of exceptional ability, conducted with a knowledge of the works in hand sufficient to enable him to dispense with a score throughout; and the band was of the best. Poor Madame Stavenhagen had to face the English public for the first time under rather nervous conditions. It was bad enough to brave the personal criticism provoked by her having ventured to carry off one of the few marriageable young men of genius in Europe, without also being compelled by circumstances to assume the character of Potiphar's wife, and sing a tremendously long dramatic soliloquy demanding powers of tragically passionate expression which are foreign to her temperament. This soliloquy, too, was her husband's maiden effort in the sublimely romantic style of composition, so that her anxiety as to her own reception was complicated by uncertainty as to how the composer of Suleika would strike the critics in his new capacity. And I cannot help thinking that there were other misgivings at work. Stavenhagen's hair had been carefully brushed for this concert for the first time within the memory of man; and if I know anything of human nature, he had been lectured on his inveterate habit of putting his hands in his pockets the moment he gets away from the piano. Now, as the evening wore on, his hair visibly fell out of cultivation into its primitive condition; and whenever his hands were idle they wandered in the forbidden direction, and once or twice went all the way. Add to these preoccupations a doubt about the stability of the bow of his tie, which caused Madame Stavenhagen, in the very midst of a sustained high note—and a very sweet one, as it happened—to steal an anxious glance at his neck, and it will be apparent that our minds were confused by two incompatible planes of consciousness—one of being *en famille* with the Stavenhagens, and the other of wandering with Potiphar's wife in the desert under the eye of the eternal Sphinx. However, the music, which is in the Niblung's Ring manner, and contains nothing of which the composer need be ashamed, was well received, and Madame was encored. Later on she sang *Leise, leise*; but here she certainly did not do herself justice. The Adagio—that incomparable Adagio—should never have its steady, tranquil movement disturbed by the slightest *rubato*; but Madame Stavenhagen, I am sorry to say, pulled the latter half of it about badly. And she gave an illustration of what Diderot was driving at in his paradox by almost losing her self-control at the approach of the *finale*. Far be it from me, nevertheless, to complain overmuch of this. I only wish some more of our singers ran any risk from an excess of sensibility. Stavenhagen, whose reception may be described as affectionate, played the C minor Concerto of Beethoven, but hardly succeeded in getting quite back to its date. He did not take it seriously enough. The first movement, which made hardly any effect, is, when properly handled, grand in the old-fashioned way; and the Largo is anything but trivial, though it sounded a little so on Thursday. He was more at home in the Liszt Concerto in A, its genuine organic homogeneity being particularly welcome after the formal incoherence of the earlier work. In The Erl King transcription he did not hit off the heavy father happily. Let him play me that gravely tender and reassuring phrase, *Mein Sohn, es ist ein Nebelstreif*, as Schubert intended it, and I will not ask to hear his present interpretation of the piece further improved upon; for the rest was admirable—far better than the blind passioning of Paderewski, who is yet, in some respects, the riper man of the two. Indeed, Stavenhagen, with all his strength, intelligence, skill, fine taste, and artistic sensibility, is by no means full grown as an artist; the last word cannot be said about him for some years more.

One or two of the comments on Santley's condition after his Australian tour, as displayed at the Popular Concert of the 19th, shew the dangers of becoming the idol of unintelligent critics. When a singer attains fame in England, the person whom *naïfs* mortally offend by describing as "the reporter" proceeds without further consideration to praise him or her for every conceivable excellence that a singer can possess. The raptures of the knowing critics over Ravogli's dramatic depth are picked up and reproduced at second hand in the next puff of Patti; whilst the authentic descriptions of Patti's *roulade* and Marimon's shake are boldly laid at the feet of Ravogli, whose powers of florid execution are hardly greater than mine. This goes on until the advancing age of the famous one makes the critic feel that it is time to discover a falling-off somewhere; and then you have him gravely remarking that Patti no longer sings with her old fire and grandeur, just as he will tell us some day that Ravogli's superb voice, though the hand of Time has impaired its once faultless flexibility, still remains, &c. In the same way we are now being informed that Santley has left behind him in Australia merits that he never possessed. I was conscious of no such deterioration on Monday week as others pretend to have discovered. Certainly the voice is not so smooth and young as it once was: he no longer, for instance, sings G with the ease of a tenor. But that was the case long before he went to Australia. Again, the rough Lancashire diction, the nervous haste, the ineptitude of his attempts to throw himself from one character into another in such dramatic narratives as The Erl King: these shew that he is no Coquelin; but when was he ever a Coquelin? On the other hand, the qualities to which he owes his great reputation—the perfectly placed voice, the unforced, unspoiled tone, the fine vocal touch, the natural quality of his typical (and therefore exceptional) baritone: all these were as conspicuous last week as they were when he sang the same songs just before his departure. To shut our ears persistently to all a singer's imperfections in order to proclaim him a phœnix, and then to take advantage of his going to Australia to suddenly open them and proclaim him a wreck, is neither generous nor sensible. As far as my judgment goes, the voyage has

[251]

done him much more good than the lapse of time has done him harm.

A desperate attempt has been made to get an autobiography out of Rubinstein by setting a shorthand writer at him. The idea was that he should make a full confession to the stenographer, who should, on his part, maintain an impassive attitude and take him down verbatim. Now Rubinstein is an impatient man, and withal so uncommunicative that his own account of his private correspondence is: "It has absolutely no existence. I am not partial to the pen; and I particularly dislike writing letters." Consequently, though the stenographer escaped with his life, the autobiography is not a success. Still, its failure has a certain characteristic value. As might be expected from Rubinstein's work as an artist, he reveals himself as a hugely energetic man, of no great breadth of sympathy or clearness of intelligence; behind our time (and indeed hardly up to his own) in musical development, though extraordinarily intense in that development as far as it goes; and deeply convinced of the religious nature and function of art. "If the theatre is to be a means of education" he says "let it be above the people." And again: "It needs no prophet to foretell the beneficent influence of a permanent opera in the provinces. The standard of morality cannot fail to rise." The much discussed passage about our musical backwardness runs as follows: "Of the German people at least fifty per cent. understand music; of the French not more than sixteen per cent.; whilst among the English—the least musical of peoples—not more than two per cent. can be found with any knowledge of music. Even the Americans have a higher appreciation of music than the English. I speak frankly, but without malice; for I have always been most hospitably received in England. But whilst I am deeply sensible of this kindness, I cannot refrain from saying that their ignorance of music is only exceeded by their lack of appreciation. The children of Albion may resent this candor. Perhaps it would have been wiser to have reserved my opinion." Do not dream of apologizing, friend Rubinstein: your remarks may do the children of Albion some good.

A SUPPRESSED NOTICE OF IVANHOE
The World, 4 February 1891

On second thoughts I have resolved to suppress my notice of Ivanhoe. I was upon my high horse last week when I wrote it; and when I went on Saturday, and saw how pleasantly everything went off, and how the place was full of lovely and distinguished persons, and how everybody applauded like mad at the end, and, above all, how here at last was an English opera house superbly equipped for its purpose, I felt what a brute I had been to grumble—and that, too, after having been indulged with peeps at the proofs of the score, admission to rehearsals, and every courtesy that could pass betwixt myself and the management, without loss of dignity on either side. Just as a sort of penance, and to shew what I am capable of, I give a couple of paragraphs from the discarded notice. Here they are:

"Proceeding then at once to the faults of Ivanhoe, I maintain that it is disqualified as a serious dramatic work by the composer's failure to reproduce in music the vivid characterization of Scott, which alone classes the novel among the masterpieces of fiction. It would hardly be reasonable to demand that Sir Arthur should have intensified the work of Scott as Mozart intensified that of Beaumarchais and even of Molière; but he might at least have done as much for him as he has done for Mr

Gilbert in Patience and its forerunners: that is, before the Savoy operas became machine-made like The Gondoliers. Take for example Scott's Bois Guilbert, the fierce Templar, the original 'bold, bad man,' tanned nearly black, disfigured with sword cuts, strong, ambitious, going on for fifty, a subject for Verdi or Velasquez. Is it possible to sit patiently and hear the music of the drawing room, sensuous and passionate without virility or intelligence, put into the mouth of such a figure? Not with all the brass and drum sauce in the world. Then there is that gallant scamp De Bracy, for whom we all have a sneaking fondness because he broke down ignominiously when Rowena began to cry, and then went out and stood up like a man to King Richard's terrific horseplay. Did he deserve nothing better than to be treated as a mere fop out of Princess Ida? And Richard himself, whose occasional attempts to behave like a king were so like Mr Pickwick's famous attempt to sneer: surely, though it is quite conceivable that he should be singing the same sentimental ballad whenever he is neither drinking nor killing anybody, yet the ballad should not be a mere paraphrase of the Wandering Minstrel song in The Mikado, as if Cœur de Lion had picked up that subtle strain by ear, and not picked it up quite accurately. As to Cedric singing the most arrant modern tum-tum in honor of the Crusaders—no, Sir Arthur: it may be very pretty and very popular; but it is not Ivanhoe.

"I have here condemned the composer, and not the book-maker, because, with Scott's novel to work upon, it was clearly the composer's business to dramatize it musically himself, resorting to a librettist's aid only for the filling in of the lyrics, and of such speeches as could not be taken verbatim from Scott. The task would not, I grant, have been an easy one; for though the material of the story is dramatic enough, yet, being a story, it is told with a disregard of stage conditions which no playwright's ingenuity could entirely overcome. It is true that the resources of music-drama surpass those of narrative in some respects: the castle of Torquilstone might have been exhibited in three compartments, with the scene between Rowena and De Bracy in one, that between Bois Guilbert and Rebecca in another, and Front de Bœuf and the Jew in the cellar, all three couples proceeding simultaneously to the point at which they are interrupted by the horn of the besiegers. Some polyphonic skill would have been required in the composition of the music; and only a comprehensive *coup d'œil* and *coup d'oreille* could have taken it all in; but then Sir Arthur is an accomplished contrapuntist, and the London public has had some training at Barnum's in the practice of watching several shows at the same time. Yet this disposes of but one difficulty. The tournament—and what would Ivanhoe be lacking the tournament?—is obviously impracticable without adjourning to the Agricultural Hall. Still, though the jousting must perforce be done by description, it is hard to have to exchange the inimitable commentary of Isaac of York—'Father Abraham! how fiercely that Gentile rides!' &c.—for alternate characterless fragments of *recitative* from Locksley and Friar Tuck, officiating as a pair of bawling showmen. This, however, is but a trivial sample of the way in which the story has been gutted of every poetic and humorous speech it contains. Here is a piece of Scott's dialogue in the scene in the lists in Templestowe, with Mr Sturgis's 'restorations' (in the architectural sense) of the same:

'REBECCA. Say to the Grand Master that I maintain my innocence, and do not yield me as justly condemned, lest I become guilty of mine own blood. Say to him that I challenge such delay as his forms will permit, to see if

God, whose opportunity is in man's extremity, will raise me up a deliverer; and when such uttermost space is passed, may His holy will be done!

'GRAND MASTER. God forbid that Jew or Pagan should impeach us of injustice! Until the shadows be cast from the west to the eastward will we wait to see if a champion shall appear for this unfortunate woman.

'BOIS GUILBERT. Rebecca, dost thou hear me?

'REBECCA. I have no portion in thee, cruel, hardhearted man.

'BOIS GUILBERT. Ay, but dost thou understand my words? for the sound of my voice is frightful in mine own ears. I scarce know on what ground we stand, or for what purpose they have brought us hither.... But hear me, Rebecca: a better chance hast thou for life and liberty than yonder knaves and dotards dream of. Mount thee behind me on my steed—on Zamor, &c. &c.

"Mr Sturgis 'adapts' the above to the stage as follows:

'REBECCA. I am innocent. Now, if God will, even in this last dark hour He will appoint a champion. But if no champion come, I bow before His holy will and am content to die.

'GRAND MASTER. Sound trumpets! ... Now, since no champion makes answer here, draw near and bind the maiden to the stake, for surely she shall die.

'BOIS GUILBERT. It shall not be! Fools, dotards, will ye slay the innocent? Butchers and burners, she is mine, I say! I say she shall not burn! Back, as you hope to live! ... Swear to be mine, and I will save thee now. My horse is nigh at hand, &c. &c.'

If the noble dialogue of Scott is not more suitable for English music than the fustian of Mr Sturgis, then so much the worse for English music. Purcell would have found it so. I protest, in the name of my own art of letters, against a Royal English Opera which begins by handing over a literary masterpiece for wanton debasement at the hands of a journeyman hired for the job."

Now all this was evidently mere temper. Poor Mr Sturgis, I suppose, knew no better: he unquestionably meant to improve on the book; and if, when he came forward hand in hand with the composer amid thunders of applause on Saturday night, nobody had a brickbat to break on him for love of Scott, why should I spoil the harmony of the occasion by striving to belittle him? But the fact is, I must have been possessed by a demon when I wrote that notice, for I find lower down in it that even the building did not please me.

"The scenepainters" I wrote "have alone dreamt of going to Scott for inspiration; and they stand forth as gods in consequence; though even to them I will say that if Mr Ryan will go round to the front, and look at that pointed doorway under the Norman arch in the scene where Rebecca describes the siege from the window, he will agree with me that it was not a happy thought. Otherwise, the Torquilstone architecture contrasts most favorably with the curious absence of any architectural idea in the auditorium. The view of the stage from all parts of the house, as far as I was able to test it, is capital; and the acoustical conditions are of the happiest. Also the upholstery and materials are luxurious and costly to excess; but as to any beauty of form or individuality of design, I have been in hydraulic lifts of much higher excellence in these respects. Even the exterior has been disfigured by a glass and iron rain-shelter, which I can hardly believe to be the work of human hands, so utterly destitute is it of any trace of the artist's sense. But people who are not particular about these matters will find every comfort and convenience that money can buy; and the majority, I fear, will find that a sufficient recommendation. Indeed, I should not go out of the way to complain myself if it were not for the ostentation of artistic effort everywhere, challenging me at all points to give my opinion—as a musical critic—whether the building is not really handsome."

But enough of this unsociable document. The truth is that the theatre is very pretty; and so is the opera. I do not say that the ceiling is equal to that of Henry VII.'s chapel in Westminster, or that the score is in any essential point an advance upon that of Macfarren's Robin Hood, which had a long run at Her Majesty's thirty years ago; but who ever said they were? My business is to praise them for what they are, not to disparage them for what they are not. Ivanhoe, then, has plenty of charming songs in it; and the crash-bang and the top notes in the exciting situations are as stirring as heart could wish. The score is as neat as a new pin. The instrumentation, from the big drum upwards, is effective, practised, and stylish, with all the fullness given by the latest improvements; the tone-colors, though rich, are eminently gentlemanly; there is no Bohemian effervescence, no puerile attempts at brilliancy or grandiosity; all is smooth, orderly, and within the bounds of good breeding. There are several interesting examples of that coincidence of inspiration which is so common in music. For instance, the third act of Ivanhoe begins like Berlioz's Faust, with a scene before sunrise for the tenor. And the musical expression found by both composers is practically identical. Again, when Rebecca presently comes in, and sings Ah! would that thou and I might lead our sheep! we hear through the music a delightful echo of that other *pastorale* in the first act of Orphée aux Enfers. Then the hag Ulrica no sooner begins her invocation of Zernebock than we recognize her as first cousin to Ulrica in Un Ballo, with her *Re dell' abisso affretati*. The rousing prelude to the Friar's drinking song might be a variation on *Vivat Bacchus* from Mozart's Seraglio. The chief stroke of humor in the opera is the patriotic chorus in the tournament scene, to which, with a sly reference to Mr Macdermott, Sir Arthur has imparted an unmistakable music hall swing, which must have sorely tempted the gallery to join in.

As there is a double cast, I must be careful not to fall into such an error of taste as to draw comparisons; for, after all, a critic is expected to be a gentleman. Therefore I shall keep to myself my opinion that Miss Macintyre is a stronger and more intelligent Rebecca than Miss Thudichum, who is, on the other hand, more sympathetic and yields more readily to musical inspiration than Miss Macintyre, besides having the more suitable voice in point of tone-color. Nor must I hint that Miss Lucile Hill, if her performance was looked forward to with less curiosity than that of Miss Palliser, is a much more credibly Saxon Rowena, in voice as well as in appearance, interesting as Miss Palliser is in her own way. And if I permit myself to remark that Mr Norman Salmond is a more congenial Richard than his gloomy and remorseful rival [Franklin Clive], it is not that I wish for a moment to contrast the two to the disadvantage of either.

As to Mr Ben Davies, the robust and eupeptic Ivanhoe, who sets to with the mailed Bois Guilbert at Templestowe in a comfortable immensikoff of the period, and gets beaten because he is obviously some three stone over his proper fighting weight, his obstreperous self-satisfaction put everybody into good humor. But unless he tones himself down a little at future performances, Mr O'Mara, from the artistic point of view, will leave him nowhere. I do not care how good a voice a man has: I object to his rushing out of the stage picture and bawling at me—not to mention that it sets everybody else bawling too. The Templar of Mr Sturgis's version is a pirate king sort of personage, of whom nothing sensible can be made. Mr Noijé did not dress at the rehearsal at which I saw him play; and as Mr Oudin was in full warpaint both at rehearsal and of course at the first performance, it is not surprising that I have a penny plain impression of Mr Noijé, and a twopence colored one of Mr Oudin. But I applaud them both for their struggles with the worst and most difficult part in the opera. Further comment I must defer until I have seen a public performance by the second cast. I may, however, confirm the good reports of the chorus and the orchestra, especially the orchestra.

Several other performers and composers—Albéniz, Henschel, Mozart, Wagner, &c.—may be safely postponed to next week, their lasting qualities being better ascertained than those of Ivanhoe.

MAID MARIAN AND IVANHOE

The World, 11 February 1891

Maid Marian, the new opera at the Prince of Wales' Theatre, is a good deal better than anyone dared to expect after Captain Thérèse and its forerunners. Naturally we all dreaded that the book would prove an incoherent series of pretexts for exhibiting the principal favorites of the company as nearly as possible in the costumes and business of their previous successes. In devizing these things, men of established literateness have over and over again fallen into such abysses of futility and wearisomeness as to make outsiders doubt whether they knew how to read and write, much less to invent and compose. If I were a manager, I would harden my heart against all veterans who know the stage and know the public and know the people they have to write for. When a man has eaten of that tree, the sooner he is driven out of the garden the better. It will always be found that his reputation is based on triumphs achieved when he was a novice, and dreamed that the public wanted to forget themselves in a pleasant story at the theatre, and not to yawn over stale theatrical gossip illustrated by *tableaux vivants.*

All my hopes of Maid Marian were founded on the fact that I had never in my life heard of Mr H. B. Smith, the librettist, or Mr Reginald de Koven, the composer—though so jealously do I guard my innocence of such matters that this by no means argues them unknown. The result justified my attitude; for seldom has man been less bored of late years by a comic opera than I on Thursday last. Mr de Koven's selection from the general stock of tunes and rhythms has been made with taste and intelligence—always with ease and vivacity, and sometimes with real feeling. The song of the bells in the third act is quite charming: in spite of the lateness of the hour, the double *encore* was endured without the slightest impatience; and Miss Violet Cameron sang it with artistic grace of which I confess I had hardly thought her capable. Indeed, to see Miss Cameron for once in an opera in which the author has not deliberately treated her as a mere beauty in a shop window, forcing vulgarity upon a talent that is naturally quiet and sympathetic, and exploiting her beauty in such a fashion as to betray an utter lack of any true artistic sense of its great value: this alone would be worth a visit to Maid Marian, even if Allan-a-Dale were the only pleasing figure in it.

But none of the artists have this time to brazen out a struggle against degrading and dehumanizing parts. The fun is not unbecoming to those who make it: even where the play is flimsiest there are none of the arid wastes of inanity, feebly favored with blackguardism, which have made many a modern comic opera depressing even to those who were beneath being revolted by it. Mr Coffin appears to greater advantage than ever in a part which allows him to be natural and manly without incongruity; and Miss Attalie Claire as Annabel does far better than was possible in the odiously silly *rôle* in which she made her first appearance. Miss Manola keeps Marian going with credit, though, as the part is the weakest in the opera, and she not particularly well fitted by it, she is unable to make as much of the occasion as her colleagues, who are suited to a hair's breadth. Mr Monkhouse, as the Sheriff of Nottingham, succeeds in shewing that he has a touch of the true comedian in him; and if Mr Le Hay does not venture beyond tomfoolery, it is not for lack of opportunity. Madame Amadi and the gentlemen who fill the minor parts are all efficient. The numbers which proved most popular in the score are the tinkers' chorus, the burlesque glee, a capital quartet in the second act, a serenade warbled by Mr Coffin in his most seductive *mezza voce*, and the song of the bells as aforesaid. Mr Clement Scott has contributed a lyric which begins:

> O, promise me that some day you and I
> Shall take our loves together to some sky,

and goes on prettily about "those first sweet violets of early spring which come in whispers."

I am sorry to have to add that Mr Sedger again permitted Mr Charles Harris to send a handful of unfortunate little children on the stage at the latest possible hour. They were not pretty children; they could only dance in the most childish fashion; they were in the way of the other dancers; they detracted instead of adding to the artistic effect of the stage picture; in short, Mr Harris's motive in allowing them to be present was clearly a philanthropic desire to give them some money to take home to their parents. However, as the children can be withdrawn from the stage and paid all the same, he can easily gratify the humanitarian instincts of the public in this matter without stifling his own.

I ventured on a couple of acts of Ivanhoe again last week; and I must say I saw no sign of the falling-off in public interest which was said to have been apparent on the second night. The house seemed to me as good a one as any manager could reasonably expect or desire. The only reaction that has really occurred is a reaction in feeling after the extravagant hopes raised by the puffery with which the Royal English Opera was inaugurated. A comparison of the newspapers of 1876 with those of 1891 would lead anybody who knew no better to conclude that the opening of the Bayreuth Festpielhaus with The Niblung's Ring was an insignificant event in comparison with the opening of the Shaftesbury Aven-uehaus with Ivanhoe. The innocent people who believe whatever they see in print—and among these are still a considerable section of the playgoing public—are convinced that something magnificent and momentous beyond all parallel in the annals of music has just happened. And no wonder! Editors have given their space, critics their superlatives, with reckless profusion, apparently for the sake of Mr Carte's *beaux yeux*. Dissentients have been intimidated by the unanimity of the cheering; and the fuglemen have been shameless in their disposition to make themselves agreeable. There has never been anything like it since first the press began to notice music.

And now to improve the occasion. First, I would ask Mr Carte whether all those silly columns which soddened the Monday papers have convinced anybody that Ivanhoe is a greater work than Don Juan, than Les Huguenots, than Der Freischütz, than Faust, than Die Meistersinger—and I contemptuously submit that if they do not mean this they mean nothing. Well, the adept, who knows that on these terms they must mean nothing, is justly incensed at being trifled with on so gigantic a scale; whilst the novice, who swallows the stuff and rushes to the theatre, comes away deeply disappointed, wheras if he went with any sort of reasonable expectation he would find a good deal to please him. The truth is, Mr Carte is not a master of the art of advertisement. With all his experience he has fallen into the beginner's error of thinking that praise cannot be overdone, and that nothing else is of any use.

Now it is quite true that over-puffery is impossible; but overpraise is not puffery at all, because it neither interests people nor convinces them. I yield to no man in the ingenuity and persistence with which I seize every opportunity of puffing myself and my affairs; but I never nauseate the public by getting myself praised. My favorite plan is to select some gentleman who has a weakness for writing to the papers, and who writes rather well when his blood is up. Him I provoke, by standing on his tenderest corn, to write to the papers saying that I have no sense of humor, of morals, of decency, of art, of manners, or what not. This creates an impression that the national feeling on these points runs so strongly the other way as to require urgent correction; and straightaway many people who never heard of me in their lives become ashamed of their ignorance. Then all the enemies of my assailant constitute themselves my partisans; and so I become famous to a degree that goads those who see through the whole puff to write fresh letters and paragraphs denying that I am famous at all, thereby making me more famous, or infamous, or what you will; for any sort of notoriety will serve my turn equally. All this would be the easiest thing in the world did not so much depend on the adroitness and opportuneness of the original provocation; and here, no doubt, my wellknown critical insight, developed by profound economic, historic, artistic, and social studies, gives me an advantage. But if Mr Carte will study my method, he will, I think, profit by seeing how the damaging recoil after the Ivanhoe boom might have been avoided, and much ineffective fulsomeness converted into invaluable stimulant, if only an element of attack and controversy had been provided.

There is another point in the recoil which specially concerns Sir Arthur Sullivan. The score of Ivanhoe is far superior to the libretto; and if it be true, as I affirm, and as even the most abandoned of the laudatory critics hint between the lines, that nearly half the second and third acts—that is, the last two scenes of all, and the second scene of the second act—would be better out than in, the fault is entirely Mr Sturgis's (although I still think it serves Sir Arthur right for not having constructed his own libretto). But, according to the press, Mr Sturgis has risen to the full height of the occasion, and has given the composer the utmost opportunity of exercising his powers. Consequently Sir Arthur has not only been baulked in his artistic effort by the weakness of the libretto, but he has to bear the blame of the shortcoming himself in order that nothing may be said against his colleague. It really does not do to spread butter on both sides of the bread. However, the balance of dramatic criticism will soon be redressed. Next Monday week there will be performed, for the first time in England, Rosmersholm, one of the masterpieces of Henrik Ibsen. We shall see how the papers which have just proclaimed Mr Sturgis a great dramatic poet will take it out of Ibsen. The dramatic critics sometimes jibe at us, their musical brethren, because we came so frightfully to grief over Wagner. I should not be surprised if we found a *tu quoque* presently to console ourselves with.

I see that Reményi, whose eminence as a violinist is

almost as great a secret as Dante Rossetti's eminence as a painter was for a long time, announces an afternoon concert for Thursday, just before his departure from England. As it is to take place at Colonel North's, at Eltham,* and the tickets are a guinea apiece, inclusive of special train, I am afraid the news is of little interest to the general public.

BACH AT ST ANNE'S

The World, 18 February 1891

On the 10th, the Bach Choir, which has improved as a singing body since I last heard it, gave us rather more Bach than it was quite able for. The cantata, *Ich hatte viel Bekümmernis*, went well; and I can hardly believe that even the densest Philistine in the room was left quite unmoved by the religious love-duet—just such another as that in *Wachet auf!*—and by the *trio* and chorale following. But the motet was a mere exhibition of incompetence. It is true that the physical difficulty of getting through a long and complicated unaccompanied work without breaking down or dragging the pitch into impossible depths was triumphantly mastered; but the preoccupation caused by the arduousness of the feat hindered all attention to beauty of tone or sensibility of treatment. For the first minute or two all the buzzing noises which attend awkward and hasty singing rose to such a din that a blind listener might have guessed that only a dozen of the choir were singing through an animated conversation carried on in whispers by the rest. Further on the tone became a little cleaner; and the

* Colonel John T. North was a millionaire noted for genial benefactions and high living.

tenors and basses occasionally sang up spiritedly in the true English choral fashion, as if to call attention to their being a fine body of men; but the motet might just as well have been a bare exercise in counterpoint for anything else that the performance brought out.

The Whitsuntide cantata, *O, Ewiges Feuer*, finished the concert, which was too long, considering the great strain made on the attention by music of such fulness and subtlety of detail. Mr Morrow attacked the original first trumpet part with the greatest gallantry; but it was too high for him. The strain was obvious, and the tone forced and hard. Still, it would be a pity to give up the highest register of the trumpet as a bad job again. Julius Kosleck's performances have shewn us the great orchestral value of those silvery ringing notes which seem to come from the sky; and he is a living proof that a XIX-century trumpeter able to touch high D, and to hold out through a performance of a long work like the Mass in B minor, is not an impossibility. Who has not occasionally heard an amateur of the posthorn display powers of lip sufficient to cope with the most unreasonable demands of "the heroic art," as kettledrum and trumpet-playing used to be called? Mr Morrow, though he falls short of Kosleck, is able at least to improve on the effects produced by re-scoring the trumpet parts for clarinets, or transposing them. The solo singers were Mrs Hutchinson, who excelled herself in the soprano part; Mr Hirwen Jones, who, with a little more practice at Bach, would soon supply that want of quality in the lower part of his compass which was the chief drawback to his performance of the tenor music; Mr Plunket Greene, who was fairly equal to the occasion in the wonderful duet; and Miss Hilda Wilson.

On the following Friday I went to St Anne's, Soho, at half-past seven, to hear the St John Passion. These services take place every Friday evening, and will continue until Good Friday. Let me, by the bye, counsel a careful avoidance of tickets marked "Special," and conferring the privilege of admission between a quarter and half-past seven at the Dean-street door; for they also confer disabilities of the most exasperating character. On presenting mine, I was admitted by a policeman to the almost empty church, and referred to a churchwarden for a seat. I should have preferred dealing with a pew-opener, whom I could have corrupted by a tip. The churchwarden, with the natural human impulse to part with his dearest treasures last, deliberately selected the worst seat in the church, and told me I must sit there. Sit there accordingly I did until half-past seven, when the unspecialized ticketholders entered riotously and spread themselves over the seats which I had idiotically supposed to be reserved. Then the bell began to din a certain keynote into our heads; and when, after half an hour's ding-dong, it was firmly fixed there, the organ stole upon our ears with a soft melody in a key exactly a tone and three-quarters sharp to that of the bell, which still jangled solemnly on. Never since I was baptized have I felt less in harmony with consecrated walls than whilst listening, with my teeth on edge, to that execrable discord.

When the bell stopped, I found myself, not a worshiper, but a critic. As such, I cannot refrain from informing the gentleman who intoned the service that he has not the most elementary notion of how to do it. He produced his voice from the throat much as Mr Penley* does, but without that gentleman's eye to humorous effect, and also without his intelligible articulation; for I could not distinguish a solitary word.

* W. S. Penley, a prominent stage comedian, soon to achieve his greatest success starring in Charley's Aunt (1892) under his own management.

I recognized the Lord's Prayer by the help of the choir, and noted that it fell about half a tone as it went on. The lesson was read quite distinctly by another gentleman: he was no artist; but he gave it out like a man who was not disposed to stand any nonsense. On the whole, I must say that the service was treated in a way that shocked me. Granted that the paganism of my profession has so got into my bones that I cannot help looking at a service just as I look at an opera (and I should be a very poor critic indeed if I did not take my function to be as religious a one as man can discharge, and one which, if it is not fit to be exercised in a church, is not fit to be exercised anywhere), yet surely I ought not to be asked to tolerate from a clergyman at the altar a wilful neglect of the technical part of his business that I should never be expected to tolerate from a ballet dancer. Have these clerical gentlemen ever noticed how the noblest music becomes ridiculous and noxious when uttered by the sort of amateur who is too self-satisfied or too slovenly to cultivate his powers carefully.?

If so, has it ever occurred to them to consider what effect a chapter of the Bible may produce under the like treatment—and I estimate the difficulty of doing justice to a chapter of Isaiah as about equal to that of singing an aria by Gluck? Why, Talma said it required eighteen years' work to finish him as a master of diction. There was only one really impressive passage in the entire service at St Anne's; and that was the singing of It is finished, by a boy—a profane, unordained boy with an alto voice. If my recollection serves me aright, the Church has some warrant beyond my word for admitting that even babes and sucklings may make better ministers than gentlemen who do not seem to know the difference between a collect and a gargle. I may add—though this matter is less important—that the St John Passion, or what they did of it, has been carefully rehearsed, and is as well done as the artistic material available admits of. It contains some curiously jejune flights of fancy on Bach's part, and is, as I presume all the world knows, almost trivial compared with the great St Matthew Passion.

Arbos, the Spanish violinist introduced to us by Albéniz, has made no very deep impression on London so far. At his first appearance he tried over the Kreutzer Sonata, and did not seem to think much of it, though here and there a passage evidently struck him as rather good. Then he polished off Bach's Chaconne in D minor very neatly, but yet in a take it or leave it sort of manner that half provoked the audience to leave it. He is a player of no mean address and general intelligence, this Señor Arbos; but he has no intention of giving himself away to the public or to the composers, and I am afraid that they, being by this time rather spoilt in that respect, will return his coldness. Joachim is back again in much better preservation than he was two years ago. He played the E major Partita at the Bach concert admirably; and at the Popular Concert the night before nothing could have been more enjoyable in its way than the pretty Brahms trio which he played with Miss Davies and Paersch, whose horn-playing is fine enough to raise rents in any really musical capital. The concert ended with the Beethoven septet, always popular. But though I can enjoy it still with the youngest, I fled precipitately on this occasion before the end of the first section of the *allegro.* Whether Joachim was impatient of the staleness of the work, or in a hurry to get home, or too tired to do anything but fall back on the habits of his shallow-genteel school, I cannot say; I can only vouch for the fact that he took that broad, free, elate theme with an empty haste that made the whole movement impossible from the outset. There were no such reverses at Reményi's concert at Eltham on the 12th.

It is useless to compare Reményi with Joachim: they are both fiddlers, it is true; but then John the Baptist and the late Archbishop Tait* were both preachers, yet to weigh one against the other was always admittedly out of the question. If there is to be a comparison at all, Sarasate must be the other term of it. In negative excellence—freedom from blemish—Sarasate's playing is certainly superior. In academic qualities of execution, too, the prolonged serenely perfect note that Sarasate makes his violin utter with a single delicate stroke of the bow would take a gold medal from the white-hot sound that Reményi sends whirring at you with at least four full strokes, much as Wilhelmj used to. Again, Sarasate, in his quiet and certain mastery of every sort of passage, shews himself the more highly trained player. But in the intensity of life in the tone—and this affords a cardinal test of a player's force—in vigor and originality of conception, in alertness of interest and unhesitating belief in his own way of doing it, Reményi often makes Sarasate appear a mere musician by contrast. In the concerto (with a piano for orchestra) he woke up Mendelssohn out of his customary pale Philharmonic politeness in an astonishing way. His playing of the last movement which Sarasate treats as a mere record-breaking exhibition of speed, was a masterpiece of creative execution; he transfigured it with innumerable broken lights touched in with infallible judgment.

To declare Sarasate a better or worse violinist than Reményi is about as sensible as declaring Claude a better or worse painter than Constable; but I am not sure that it might not be worth while to open the question—not here or now, though, if you please—whether in Reményi the artist has not gained as well as the man by his refusal

* Campbell Tait was Archbishop of Canterbury from 1869 until his death in 1874.

[271]

to sacrifice all other interests and activities to the cultivation of his violin-playing machinery. His very appearance among musicians is stimulating: he has nothing of "the professional" about him; he might be anything active, from a Chancellor to a shoemaker. Colonel North wound up the concert by a blunt and warrior-like speech, in which, after remarking that this classical music was all very well, but that we wanted something that we knew something about, he called upon Reményi to give us Home, Sweet Home, which was accordingly done with imperturbable complaisance, and with a penetrating charm that would have consumed Patti with jealousy. Our millionaire host could hardly conceal his emotion at the line, Be it ever so humble, of his favorite air.

THE WAGNER SOCIETY
The World, 25 February 1891

I have to announce an important move on the part of the London branch of the Wagner Society, which has almost led to a reconciliation between me and that body. The misunderstanding came about in this way. I once gave them a guinea for the good of the cause; and they spent thirteen shillings of it on a horrible evening party. Then, to appease me, they bought a ticket for a Richter concert, and made me a present of it—a pretty treat for a man who was almost dead of concerts, and was throwing half a dozen tickets per day into the wastepaper basket. Naturally I received an application for a second guinea with speechless indignation. It may be asked what they did with the other eight shillings. Well, they sent me four numbers of their quarterly, The Meister, for half of it—and I admit that The Meister was good value for the money—but they sent the remaining four shillings to the Bayreuth people, who had just cleared a profit out of a series of performances to which I had contributed four pounds. This was enough to make any man mad; and as there was nothing to prevent me from getting The Meister from Messrs Kegan Paul for four shillings paid across the counter (not to mention that I always get review copies), I forswore the Wagner Society, as I thought, for ever. Now, however, the Society makes a fresh bid.

The translations of Wagner's writings in The Meister have deservedly proved a success; for they are good Wagner and good English, being made by men who understand the language of the philosophy of art in both tongues. But as The Meister does not run to a hundred and twenty pages a year, it would take half a century to complete a translation of Wagner's ten volumes in such quarterly doses. Therefore the Society proposes to issue, besides The Meister, six instalments per year of translation, in separate numbers, which can be bought for a shilling apiece by outsiders. And this raises the question, Shall I subscribe again to the Society, or shall I simply pay five shillings a year to Kegan Paul for the translations (there is to be a reduction of a shilling when you buy six together), and four for The Meister, thereby saving eleven shillings a year? I wish I could make up my mind about it. As to the evening party, I object to that entirely: the sort of recruit that gets caught in such traps now goes to the Meistersingers, the Ballad Singers, the Grosvenor Club, &c., where he can have half a dozen lively concerts for every one dull evening which the Wagner Society can offer him. The German subsidy I also repudiate, because we are immeasurably worse off than the Germans in musical matters. I have to sit in our vulgar diamond-show at Covent Garden, listening to scratch performances of Faust and Les Huguenots, while Mottl is producing Les Troyens in Karlsruhe, Levi conducting Siegfried at Munich, and Richter using his left hand at Vienna to conduct Carmen, because his right is fatigued with perpetual Wagner. Next autumn I shall have to pay £20 to hear Tannhäuser properly done at Bayreuth because I have not the remotest chance of hearing it even decently done at home. Of course there is Ivanhoe; but even Ivanhoe is not everything. I shall have to subsidize not only the Festspielhaus at Bayreuth, but the London, Chatham and Dover, or Great Eastern Railways, with other lines whose names I forget—except that vile Links-Rhein-ischer with its string of joggling dustbins—and the hotelkeepers of Brussels, Cologne, Mayence, Nuremberg, and Bayreuth itself. Now there is no fun in all this for me. The sea passage makes me ill; Cologne Cathedral, as "restored" by the German empire, brings on a relapse; and the carnivorous *table d'hôte* which wiles away the Rhine for those who have been there before, fills me with nothing but loathing. And in the meantime I am spending all my holiday time and money, without getting a holiday. The moral is obvious. If there were a Festspielhaus on Richmond Hill, charging fifteen pounds for admission to the regulation Bayreuth cyclus of four performances, I should pay willingly and consider myself a gainer by the transaction. And since there must be many others of the like mind, why in the name of commonsense does not this London branch of the Wagner Society declare itself an autonomous English Wagner Society, and save up the fifty pounds a year which it now spends in sending coals to Newcastle, to form a fund for placing a Wagner Theatre on Richmond Hill? The only objection to it is that it is impossible. What of that? The Bayreuth theatre was ten times as impossible when it was first conceived; yet it has been an accomplished fact these fifteen years. Besides, it does not become gentlemen who propose that the English people should keep their Wagner theatre in Bavaria to talk about impossibility. The arrangement to which they are contributing 4s. per head per year is not only impossible, but impracticable, which is a real objection.

On the whole, I am inclined to conclude that I can do no good by holding one opinion and backing the other to the extent of 12s. a year. I had rather give the money to Mr Grein's Théâtre Libre, which is likely to help Wagnerism more than all the £20 pilgrimages in the world. When the Bayreuth reserve fund is replaced by the Richmond Hill reserve fund, then it will be time enough to open my hand.

Whilst I am on the subject of Bayreuth, I may as well give the particulars of the autumn arrangements. There will be twenty performances—ten of Parsifal, seven of Tannhäuser, and three of Tristan—from July 19th to August 19th, both inclusive. It will, therefore, be possible to see either Parsifal or Tannhäuser twice within four successive performances, but not Tristan. The first and last sets contain two Parsifals, with a Tristan in each; and the two beginning July 26th and August 9th each contain two Parsifals and two Tann-häusers. It is by no means too soon to secure seats now. The Festspielhaus is so admirably constructed that people are apt to think that it does not matter where their seats are, so perfect is the view from all parts of the auditorium. But the distance of the back seats from the stage makes a considerable difference to all but very long-sighted persons. If you want to see the facial play of the artists, take my advice and secure tickets in the front half of the house.

The Crystal Palace concerts began on the 14th with an overture by Miss Ellicott—a pretty piece of writing which left no impression. The symphony was Schumann's in D minor, about which one hardly knows exactly what to say. It is a failure, like most of Schumann's orchestral works; but it is too interesting to be left always unheard on that account. Here and there, indeed, it surges up to momentary success. The beginning is imaginative and full of promise; but at the end the abuse of the full wind, and the general want of clearness and variety in the instrumentation, make the last chord more welcome than it ever could be in a work with sufficient matter in it. The Carmen suite was, perhaps, the most satisfactory number of the program. It consists simply of the preludes to the acts taken in reversed order, except that the working up of the jealousy motive from the end of the first prelude is placed at the beginning of the whole as an exordium. The suite was most delicately played; and the prelude to the fourth act, usually omitted in the theatre, proved, as might have been expected, a particularly poetic little tone-picture.

At the concert last Saturday, Stavenhagen invited us to enter into his recent fancy for Beethoven's early concertos by playing the second, just as he selected the third for his own concert. Of course it is easy for a Lisztian champion to execute these works with prodigious smartness; but if he has no respect for them—if he is only indulging a passing fondness for children of a bygone age, he can make no effect with them. I dare not say that Stavenhagen has no respect for the early concertos; but I do say that it is only a theoretical respect: it does not get into his fingers; and the net result is a depreciative misrepresentation of every part of them except the pretty final rondos. Stavenhagen, by the bye, must not be judged by his performances this season. When he was last over here, though he was very ill on the day of his recital, he played at least six times as well as at his recital the other day, when there was nothing specially the matter with him. I have heard many second-rate players handle the Chopin polonaise in A flat better than he did. The transcription of Isolde's death song brought him up to the mark for a moment; but The Erl King, which he had given brilliantly a few days before, went to pieces so absurdly that he could hardly help laughing at himself. He really owes it to us to pull himself together and give another recital in something like the form he displayed when last he played the Todtentanz at the Crystal Palace. Returning to that institution, I have to record that Neruda, having played the Mendelssohn concerto with great glory at the Hallé concert on Friday (which I was unable to attend— to my loss, as I am told and can well believe), declined to venture again for Mr Manns on the following afternoon. Ilona Eibenschütz accordingly came to the rescue with Chopin's F minor concerto, in which she more than justified all the favorable things I said of her on the occasion of her first appearance at the Popular Concerts. At the back of the room, however, the instrument she used was felt to be not quite what was wanted for the concerto. I say this with the less reserve because it is no longer true of the Broadwoods, as it was twelve years ago, that they had fallen so far behind the time as to make their then virtual monopoly of the concert platform a nuisance to themselves, to the public, and to the artists, upon whose gratitude they had strong and perfectly honorable claims. The monopoly is now broken down; the full force of the competition of Steinway, Erard, Bechstein, and Pleyel has been brought to bear on them; and the result is that they have enormously increased the power of their instruments without sacrificing the artistic individuality and homogeneity of tone which always distinguished their pianofortes from the massive overstrung machines which first put them out of countenance. Nevertheless, it did happen on Saturday that Miss Eibenschütz would have been better equipped, as far as her more remote hearers were concerned, with a good Steinway than with the instrument she had. The orchestra was not at its best except in the quieter parts of its work. In the climax of the first movement of the eighth symphony, and in the Tannhäuser overture, it flagged and fell short just at the very points where a miss was as bad as a mile. Miss Rosina Isidor followed up the Chopin concerto by *Com' e bello* from Lucrezia. Poor old *Com' e bello!* If Miss Isidor had only realized how ridiculous a figure it cut between Chopin and Beethoven, she would have thought twice before bringing it down to the Crystal Palace. The trumpery Italian vocal waltz with which she subsequently favored us was still more out of place. Miss Moody and Mr Manners were more judicious in confining themselves to Gounod and Meyerbeer at the previous concert.

SEÑOR ALBÉNIZ
4 March 1891

On Wednesday afternoon last I went into St James's Hall at one minute before three o'clock to hear the Albéniz concert, intending to have the usual twenty minutes or so over the evening paper before business began. To my amazement Albéniz appeared at the stroke of three as if he had been sent up on the platform by electric wire from Greenwich. This is the sort of thing I have been resolving to do all my life without having succeeded in any single instance; and I shall henceforth regard Albéniz not only as one of the pleasantest, most musical, and most original of pianists, but as a man of superior character. These concerts of his deserve support. They are short; they are cheap; they are enjoyable; the music is light and varied enough for afternoon digestion without any compromise as to artistic quality; and the programs, which strike the happy medium between the bare list of pieces and the heavily manufactured "analysis" with quotations (so useful in keeping your eyes on the music and your ears off it), are given without fee. If the experiment fails, it will only shew that the public has not as much good sense as Albéniz. On the afternoon in question Arbos played the Mendelssohn concerto with pianoforte accompaniment, which, played by Albéniz, was by no means the least interesting part of the performance. Arbos is a smooth, finished executant, seldom at fault in his intonation. Once it is understood that he is not a first-rate player, such as Ysaÿe, Sarasate, or Reményi, he will disappoint no reasonable person. Madame Belle Cole and Mr Hirwen Jones sang the charming old duet from Spohr's God, Thou art Great; and Albéniz played Chopin's Berceuse and Impromptu in his own manner, dainty without triviality. Why, I wonder, has he dropped those Brassin transcriptions of the rainbow bridge in Das Rheingold, and the fire charm and Valkyrie ride in Die Walküre, which the Wagner Society made him get up? His performances of these were highly effective; and Stavenhagen's success with the Liszt transcription of Isolde's last song shews that the public appetite for Wagner is so sharp for the moment that they would rather have transcriptions than nothing; whilst the hit Paderewski made with the Don Juan fantasia suggests the possibility of reviving that form of composition. I fancy that this is the field in which Albéniz might find the largest and freshest scope for his peculiar talent. He has not the temperament for Beethoven and Schumann, nor the inhumanity to visit Brahms upon us. With Mozart he is not at home except when bringing out the exquisite prettiness of the shallowest end of his work. I almost wish he would try a fantasia of Thalberg's just to see how a modern audience would stand it. I mean, of course, one of his own audiences, and not a crowd of those aborigines who unexpectedly descended on St James's Hall last year, when Madame Teresa Carreño began to slash away at Gottschalk's Pasquinade, Tremolo, &c., as though some superb Junonian contemporary of Arabella Goddard's had shared the fate of Rip Van Winkle. They say that Madame Carreño is so pleased with her success that she is coming back to us this season. If so, I shall be happy to go to see her play.

In spite of all the precautions that have been taken to keep the news from me, I accidentally discovered, in the course of a walk up Bow-street the other night, that Mr Harris has been secretly performing oratorios at Covent Garden. My attention has been kept off these pious orgies by a skilful parade of masked balls. Would I could hope to be treated always with the consideration shewn me in this matter! I am spared the oratorios, in deference to the wellknown inadequacy of my constitution to sustain such penitential exercises; but next season, when Mr Harris changes his mind about producing Siegfried, and serves up La Favorita instead, with Mlle Richard to give matronly propriety to the title part, I shall be led to a stall in the front row like a lamb to the slaughter. I have no faith in that lazy Parisian contingent taking the trouble to get up anything that has not been a stock dish at the Opéra for the last ten years.

There are many ways of proving that the social atmosphere of West London is unhealthy; and I have most of them at my fingers' ends. But the most convincing to me is the baneful effect upon musical artists of a run through the drawing rooms. Young Gerardy, who was quite a wonderful artist when he first came, shewed a melancholy falling-off at his last recital.

Not that the execution of the ornamental passages was less finished than before; it was rather more so: all the pretty bits were prettier than ever. But the normal playing—the lengths of straightforward work between these delicacies—that was where the deterioration shewed itself. The tone then became comparatively common, careless, valueless—as different as possible from the thoughtful, sensitive touch on the strings that was so remarkable before. Perhaps it only set his private admirers chattering and yawning; anyhow, the boy is the worse for his London experience—more shame for London.

Let me here say determinedly that if we are to have any more cello virtuosos, someone must really compose a little new music for the instrument. Goltermann and Popper are all very well; but they are not Mozart and Beethoven. What with Hollmann, Klengel, and Gerardy, I have heard that Mazurka Caprice of Popper's not less than fourteen thousand times within two seasons. It has been encored each time; and the *encore* piece has always been Popper's Papillons—a pleasing title, but one which now strikes terror into me. Kol Nidrei is quite a novelty after Popper; but even Kol Nidrei palls as the years roll on. I am now always in two minds as to putting myself in the way of hearing Hollmann. On the one hand, there is the chance of his playing a melody by Bach or Schubert, a chance not to be lightly lost. On the other hand, one never can feel sure that those Papillons will not pop out at the last moment and make me wish I had never been born.

Henschel has just brought his six symphony concerts safely into port, having judiciously kept the public up to the mark by announcing shipwreck when he was halfway across. At the fourth concert he tried the attractions of Albani, with great success as far as the filling of the hall was concerned. No doubt the lady was expensive; but Henschel certainly took it out of her (pardon the expression) by putting both the great aria from Der Freischütz and Isolde's death song in the program. The *Leise, leise* got pulled about as usual; and the other would have fared no better had it not been too difficult to take many liberties with. But on these great occasions, when Albani is rapturous, and almost everybody is near enough to see the shining of her eyes, she gets on the very softest side of her audience; and criticism only mutters between its teeth when she drawls down the scale of E natural like a woman who will not come downstairs sensibly because she wants to shew off her diamonds. At this concert there was produced a symphonic poem by Mr Percy Rideout, modestly entitled Epipsychidion. It begins with some vague extracts from Tristan, and presently settles down into a sentimental ballad refrain, in the manner of Mr Milton Wellings, set forth with a surprising but second-hand splendor and effusiveness of orchestration. Mr Rideout, though he is younger than most symphonic poets, is man enough, I hope, to excuse my frankness if I tell him that Epipsychidion is not worth a rap, though it is quite the right thing for him to have begun with. The fifth concert, at which I was not present, was a Wagner concert; and so, indeed, was the last one, as far as I heard it. The orchestra has not improved during the season. I do not think the wit of man could move such players to a worse performance of the Tannhäuser overture than that with which the final concert ended. Henschel was in his most perverse humor, beating the pilgrims' march in an impossible fashion, and rushing the rest through headlong, besides deliberately urging the trombones to blare most horribly. Altogether, the performance would have done admirably in the Malay Peninsula. The applause it gained was correctly estimated by an amateur critic, who informed his companion, as I passed him on the stairs, that "You can always fetch 'em if you make a jolly row." The Good Friday music was better; though even here the trombones, in giving out the Parsifal motive at the beginning, were allowed, and had no doubt been instructed, to force their power to a point of sinister coarseness which turned Parsifal into Klingsor at once. In the Siegfried Idyll the conductor at first worried his band more than he inspired them; but later on Wagner got the upper hand of both; and the result, if not thoroughly satisfactory, at least led to some happy moments. On the whole, though the London Symphony concerts have gained ground absolutely, they have lost it relatively, owing to the fact that the orchestra's most immediate competitor this time has been no longer the Richter band, which, for excellent reasons, will always share its defects, but the Manchester men, whose recent exploits have been tremendous. In certainty of execution, and the rare combination of intimate knowledge of their repertory with unimpaired freshness of interest in it, they have distanced even the Crystal Palace orchestra. When they played Berlioz's difficult and complicated Fantastic Symphony they gave Hallé less trouble than Henschel would have with the overture to the Calife of Bagdad. I do not see how Henschel can improve matters greatly as long as he has to be content with seasons of six concerts spread over three months.

What is wanted is a weekly orchestral concert at St James's Hall practically all the year round, conducted by Henschel from October to May, and thence to the end of the season by Richter. If the scheme does not pay at first, it should be taken over by the County Council, which could meet the loss by at once confiscating the entire property of the Duke of Westminster, as a judgment on him for signing a petition to prevent the schools of London being provided with pianos, on the ground of "extravagance." If this thrifty nobleman were worth his thousand a day to us he would long ago have put a Steinway grand into every Board School in London at his own expense.

Before quitting the subject of the Gerardy recital I should have chronicled the first appearance thereat of Mr Oudin, Sir Arthur Sullivan's Templar, as a concert singer. He revived *Le Vallon*, one of Gounod's best settings of Lamartine, and an old warhorse of Santley's, with success. His school is French; and he has the chief virtue of it, a charming *mezza voce*. But he has also its radical vice, a *tremolo*, which, though not very pronounced, is yet sufficiently so to occasionally obscure the pitch of his notes. With a little more humanity and variety of mood he would be a welcome figure on the platform. At present he seems unable to discard the Templar sufficiently to make himself at home there. As to Miss Kate Rolla, who also sang, she has two accomplishments: she can sing very well; and she can scream like a steam siren. When she screams she pleases herself: when she sings she pleases me. I recommend her to confine herself in future to pleasing me.

ENGLISH TO THE BACKBONE
The World, 11 March 1891

The Philharmonic Society, English to the backbone, never knows when it is beaten. It has repeatedly shewn itself capable of going on for years in a chronic state of ignominious defeat, without for a moment losing a sense of superiority which Napoleon at the height of his fortunes probably never enjoyed. At such times the critics always flatter it with smooth sayings; for otherwise they would have to attend the concerts, and take infinite pains to find out exactly what is wrong. Consequently no rally is ever made until the people who support the Philharmonic from mere habit die in such numbers that it becomes necessary either to recruit or to carry on the Society at an unbearable loss. Then the directors make good resolutions, and get a new conductor. They once, as all the world knows, got Wagner, who, with the strong commonsense to which he then owed his reputation as an unpractical madman, told the directors that their programs were too long, and that no conductor could do better for them than make his choice between thoroughly rehearsing one or two things, leaving the rest to tumble through anyhow, and having everything only half prepared. This was as much as to say that the Philharmonic performances were not the very best and highest and most respectable in the world, an ignorant, ill-bred, presumptuous opinion, which at once stamped its holder as radically unfit for the position of Philharmonic conductor. Exit Wagner accordingly.

This is an old story; but it remains true to the present hour that whenever anything is well rehearsed for a Philharmonic concert, nothing else thereat is rehearsed at all. For the last season or two we have seen certain composers—Grieg, Moszkowski, Benoît, &c.—all engaged to conduct their own compositions. At the rehearsals, they were of course accorded the first turn; and they naturally kept the band at their works until they had got the effects they wanted. Then there was the concerto player to be attended to: he or she, an artist of European reputation, was not going to be kept waiting for anybody. By the time composer and *virtuoso* were half satisfied, the men were hungry, impatient, due at other engagements: in short, the rehearsal was virtually over. Mr Mackenzie or Mr Cowen could at most approach the Society's illustrious guests with a polite request for just five minutes at the end to run through

Beethoven's Ninth Symphony, or any other trifle that might have been announced. The effect of this was of course to make the unfortunate official conductor, in contrast with the composer who had appropriated all his opportunities of rehearsing, seem only half as competent and conscientious as he really was. But this was no ground for relieving him of the full blame. It was his business to insist on adequate artistic conditions, or, failing them, to resign. Besides, there was no alternative: it was useless to pitch into the Philharmonic directors, who pride themselves on keeping the outside public in its place, and not pampering it with concessions to clamor.

Under these circumstances it is not surprising that Sir Arthur Sullivan did not find it worth his while to retain the *bâton*, and that Mr Mackenzie soon followed his example. Then came Mr Cowen, under whom matters came to such a point that Mr Edward Carpenter, having innocently paid hard cash to hear the Ninth Symphony done by the famous Philharmonic band, wrote to the papers indignantly describing the sort of value he had received. I, still thinking the Philharmonic worth a remonstrance, added a mild word or two; and I think the feeling got fairly afloat among those most concerned that Mr Cowen must either succumb to these attacks or else do away with the foundation for them. Happily he seems to have chosen the latter course. The performance of Beethoven's C minor symphony on Thursday night was not the heartless, vapid, perfunctory affair it might have been if Mr Carpenter and the rest of us had pocketed our wrongs. A strenuous effort was made to rise to the occasion and sustain the reputation of the band; and the difference for the better was hardly to be described, so vast is the gulf between supercilious indifference and even the hastiest and least carefully concerted activity with a purpose in it. If Mr Cowen and the band keep on their mettle throughout the season, they may yet avert the periodic artistic crisis in the Society's affairs which seemed so imminent last year.

There is, however, another direction in which reform is necessary. On Thursday a new work was produced. It was an overture by Rubinstein, entitled Antony and Cleopatra, a great heaping-up of pompous and luxurious commonplaces into a pretentious tone picture—or rather tone oleograph. In purely mechanical bustle, in redundant platitudes out of Czerny's Etudes de la Vélocité, in shameless repetitions and complacent confident shallowness, it surpassed the padding of a Rossini overture. That might have been forgiven if Rubinstein had shewn in it the genius upon which Rossini presumed; but I doubt if anyone will have the hardihood to put forward such a claim on his behalf. Even if it had been thoroughly rehearsed, and smoothly and homogeneously executed, it would not have been worth the trouble. Still less was it worth while under the Philharmonic conditions, which tend to develop to the utmost that habit of relying on the adroitness of our players in making their way through new compositions at first or second sight without a breakdown, which is the bane of instrumental music on London. Were it not for the Crystal Palace band, it would be quite correct to say that we have no orchestra just because we have the cleverest players in the world.

We astonish foreign composers by the way we play their music at the first rehearsal. When they find out that we make this an excuse for doing everything with only two rehearsals, they generally thank their stars for the slower methods of the Continent. However, that is not my present point. I want to know why the Philharmonic Society nowadays deliberately devotes itself to the encouragement of cheap and showy music. The best novelty it has lately given us is Mancinelli's

Venetian Suite, a very pretty piece of promenade music, admirably adapted to the purpose of Dan Godfrey or Strauss, but out of place at concerts solemnized by the elevation of Beethoven's bust before the orchestra. I do not want to draw the line too high up, still less to drive the Society back on its worn-out Mendelssohn, Spohr, Sterndale Bennett repertory; but I do emphatically suggest that such unknown works as the first three scenes of Schumann's Faust are fitter for the Society's efforts than the mock heroics of Peter Benoît; that Berlioz wrote, besides the eternal Carnaval Romain, some overtures which we want to hear at least as much as Antony and Cleopatra; that dozens of English musicians can turn out as much Moszkowski ware as may be required; and that unperformed works by Bach, Haydn, Mozart, and Beethoven, of greater interest for Philharmonic audiences than the Venetian Suite, are to be counted by the dozen. I am all for living in the present rather than in the past, as far as works on the same artistic plane are concerned; but between the treasures of the past and the trivialities of the present there should be no hesitation in a society like the Philharmonic.

Mr Manns, who is what the Philharmonic ought to be, and pretends to be, and is not, has produced a pianoforte concerto by Burmeister, a young Hamburger, now settled at Baltimore. The solo part was played by Madame Burmeister in a cheerful, wifely, willing way, but, as it seemed to me, quite inartistically. The work should be thoroughly revised and condensed, and then played again for us by a powerful Lisztian pianist with no domestic interests in the work to distort his or her artistic attitude towards it. It will then be possible to say with more confidence whether the concerto has any real stuff in it. At present it certainly has a great air of life and interest; but I failed to catch the content of all those strenuous climaxes; and the only judgments on it which I do not suspend are the unfavorable ones as to its want of conciseness and coherence in its present state. Madame Burmeister Petersen will, I hope, give us an opportunity of hearing what she can do apart from her husband's music. The rest of the concert was exceptionally interesting. Berlioz's Death of Ophelia and Funeral March of Hamlet, both perfect compositions of their kind, were finely executed; and the last act of Tannhäuser was given with an effect which cannot be imagined by those who have only seen it with the Covent Garden accessories. The orchestral features could not have been made more of, except at one point, the accompaniment to Venus's invitation, in which the woodwind produced nothing but a dry clucking, appropriate enough to Telramund's defiance in Lohengrin, but extremely unsuggestive of the voluptuous breathings of the Venusberg zephyrs. The chorus of younger pilgrims, too, did not swim along so tranquilly as it might have done; and Wolfram, after singing his opening lines very well, misplaced his voice in shifting to his upper register at the words *Da scheinest du,* and, failing to recover himself, gave *O du, mein holder Abendstern* flat throughout. The rest was beyond cavil. Miss Thudichum, a very carefully trained singer, who shews herself more and more worthy of the pains taken with her, doubled the parts of Elisabeth and Venus; and Mr Edward Lloyd was the Tannhäuser.

I am not a very regular frequenter of the students' concerts at the Guildhall School of Music. They begin at the unreasonable hour of half-past six; and the surroundings always give me an uneasy sense of having been summoned before the Lord Mayor's Court for some misdemeanor. Nevertheless, I looked in at one last week, and found the huge room, as usual, crowded. There was the inevitable child violinist performing prodigies; there was the regulation young lady with the flexible voice, the high range, and the unawakened artistic sense, mechanically using the mad *scena* from Lucia as a stalking horse; there was the intelligent young gentleman cautiously playing the flute *obbligato*; and there was the harmless necessary assortment of students' original compositions, the pretty firstfruits of them that are Corporation Exhibitioners. I was unable to stay very long; and the most enjoyable thing I heard was a Mendelssohn prelude and fugue played by Miss Ethel Barnes, who shewed, before she played six bars, that she had been stimulated artistically as well as finger-trained mechanically. That prelude and fugue consoled me inexpressibly after Lucia; and as the next thing in the program was *Il Segreto*, I fled away into the night, lest a worse thing should befall, leaving Miss Ethel Barnes, as far as I was concerned, mistress of the situation.

BUILD ANOTHER OPERA HOUSE
The World, 18 March 1891

The blizzard put back my arrangements on the 10th so far that I was late for Mr Somervell's Mass. When I arrived at the Bach Choir concert, Miss Eibenschütz and Mr Borwick were playing a masterly Bach concerto for two pianos, the more vivacious sections of which went capitally. The slow movement, unfortunately, was passed over as undemonstratively as possible, and went for nothing. Madame Schumann's novices do not know what to do with music of this kind; but they at least do not vulgarize it, as immature Lisztians are apt to do. On the whole I think I shall in future advise young pianoforte students to divide their apprenticeship between Madame Schumann and Sophie Menter, in order that they may lack neither the refinements of art nor "the joy of life." Those who stick to one school exclusively are apt to come out with slovenly habits of mind on the one hand, or ill-nourished hearts on the other.

The last two numbers at this Bach concert were curiously contrasted. One was an Offertorium and Tantum Ergo by Schubert, the other the Choral Fantasia. Beethoven's genuinely religious music, without a shadow of fear or mistrust on it from beginning to end, fit for happy and free people to sing with the most buoyant conviction, came with an extraordinarily refreshing effect after the hypochondriacal tromboning which Schubert, in a perverse fit, devized to set miserable sinners grovelling. It would be too much to suspect the Bach Choir of any satiric intention in the arrangement of its program: in fact, I suspect it of thinking the Tantum Ergo rather a fine piece of music. If that is so, I will take the liberty of urging them to remember that it is not the cowl that makes the monk, and that some of the most frivolous, the most inane, and even the most wicked music in the world is to be found in such forms as the oratorio, the Mass, the anthem, or the like. Any musician can turn out to order as much church music as you please, from a whole service to a Christmas carol, just as a domestic engineer can turn out a heating apparatus; but how is it likely to compare, as religious music, with Mozart's Die Zauberflöte, for instance, which professes to be no more than a mere profane Singspiel?

Among the pianoforte recitals which are helping to keep an exceedingly dull season going are those of Miss Douste at Steinway Hall, and of Max Pauer at Prince's Hall. Then there is that excellent artist Miss Zimmermann, who gave a recital last week; and Miss Janotha, whose concert on Friday I was unable to attend. There is little to be said on such occasions except to repeat old compliments; but they are none the less important, although the Paderewskis and the Sapellnikoffs get the lions' shares of notice. Naturally an orgy gets talked of more than a plain meal; but the fact remains that orgies can be dispensed with for longer than meals. Strongly as I sympathize with the gentleman* who said that he was prepared to do without the necessities of life if the luxuries were guaranteed to him, I must warn the inexperienced that they will poison themselves in rather less than no time if they attempt to live on any such principle without a very high discrimination between spurious and genuine luxuries. For instance, a man who should come to idolize Paderewski or Rubinstein, and to lose all appreciation of Max Pauer, would be in a parlous state.

This word discrimination reminds me that our plutocratic opera patrons have just bought their pig in a poke, by which vulgar observation I would convey that Mr Harris has sold out his pit and grand-tier boxes for the season without pledge or prospectus. So at least I am told by those who habitually regard themselves as well informed. And, in this instance, I do not doubt them in the least.

Nobody can recognize more fully than I do that if Mr Harris produces any new works, or in any way raises the artistic standard of the Covent Garden performances, he is actuated by no fear of the progressive instincts of his subscribers. All they ask is that the Italian Opera shall be fashionable. Even from the gallery the forward pressure is not very strong. All the arts are now experiencing the first effects of the wide diffusion of literate tastes caused by the operation of compulsory

* The historian John Lothrop Motley, quoted in Oliver Wendell Holmes's The Autocrat of the Breakfast Table (1858), VI.

education in this country. Whole classes which formerly did not know what an opera was are now full of curiosity to see one; and as they have to begin at the beginning, they turn *impresario*'s capital away from the satisfaction of the old opera-going class which has worn Italian Opera threadbare, to the primary education of *naïfs* who find Donizetti's *finales* abstruse, and his instrumentation strangely impressive. What does this point to? Is it to a struggle between two sections of the same audience as to which is to be bored to death—the adepts by Trovatore, or the inepts by Tristan? Clearly not: what we want is separate opera houses for elementary and advanced musicians, with a supplementary one for the display of diamonds, constructed so as to allow the public to promenade down the middle, in the style of the Burlington Arcade.

Differentiation is already in progress on these lines. The Savoy, Prince of Wales', and Lyric theatres provide for comic opera: and now we have the Royal English Opera for musical melodrama. Opera is thus provided with its Criterion and its New Olympic. It has also got its Lyceum at Covent Garden; though here, I admit, the analogy suffers severely from the difference of about a century in the stage of evolution reached by drama and opera. But on one vital point it holds good. Both houses leave the most advanced section of the public out in the cold. I go to see Irving play Charles I.; and my critical sense is highly gratified by his now consummately cultivated artistic sense and perfect certainty of execution. I go to hear Jean de Reszke as the Prophet, or as Romeo, and am as keenly pleased, if not nearly so completely satisfied, as by Irving. But now comes the difficulty. Charles I. interests me so little as a drama that the actor cannot, with all his art, make it affect me one-tenth as strongly as a play of Ibsen's acted by novices who have not a twentieth part of Irving's skill. And I would not go out of London to hear the finest performance of Roméo et Juliette that Europe can produce; wheras I have gone a long way out of England to hear complete performances of Wagner's works by quite stupendously unattractive singers. Now since there is no regular theatre in London which provides me with what I want, I am compelled to make the most unjustifiable assaults on Manager Irving and Impresario Harris in order to force them to attend to my wants for a night or two at the expense of their contented patrons. If I succeed, I know I shall get both gentlemen into no end of trouble. The proper solution is to build another opera house for the advanced party, where it can have the music-dramas it likes without ousting those who dont like them.

Of course, this would not settle the question for the critics, who have to go to all the opera houses, and who, in mere self-preservation, struggle desperately against any movement that takes them out of their depth; but even this might be settled by the newspapers appointing double sets of critics. For example, Class A, the advanced critic, for realistic novels, naturalist painters, Wagner and Ibsen; and Class B, the bourgeois critic for Besantine novels, Royal Academicians' pictures, the old Covent Garden repertory, and the dramas of a gentleman whose name I shall save up until I have fresh occasion to get a letter written to the papers about me.

What is really stopping the way to a new opera house is the usual Utopian notion that nothing can be done without a capital of £100,000, and the patronage of eminent plutocrats. Allow me to say, as a practical person, that a representation of the Nibelungen tetralogy may cost anything from the hire of a barn by a knot of amateur enthusiasts, and a set of pasteboard placards indicating the scenery, up to any sum you like to spend on it. Mr Grein's example in the manner of the

Independent Theatre is a highly instructive one. He first conciliated the demand for "something practical" by putting before the public a complete working scheme for an endowed theatre, with a huge capital and the Prince of Wales as President. The impression produced was admirable: here was none of your cracked-brained impracticable enthusiasts' dreams, but a sensible, well thought out, solid, business scheme on familiar lines, with money in it. Meanwhile, pending the subscription of the huge capital and the waking up of the Prince of Wales, Mr Grein tried what he could do under his own presidency with a handful of faddists and a matter of two-pound-ten or so. He took the nearest thing to a barn left in Tottenham Court Road, and organized a performance of one of Ibsen's greatest plays for the few people who cared about it. Result—barn too small; performance transferred gloriously to a real theatre, with Mr Augustus Harris surveying the proceedings in ineffable awe from a stage box; Ibsen's mortally wounded enemies filling London with their screams of anguish; and Mr Grein the most famous manager in Europe, bar M. Antoine of Paris, also of barn antecedents.* And now, gentlemen of the Wagnerian persuasion, what are you going to do after this? Give another *conversazione* at the Royal Institute, no doubt. That is so like what Wagner himself did at Zurich, is it not?

* André Antoine was the founder of the celebrated Théâtre Libre in Paris. Jacob Thomas Grein, a London dramatic critic, was the founder of the Independent Theatre, modelled after Antoine's enterprise. It had just offered Ibsen's Ghosts as its inaugural production on 13 March.

ROYAL COLLEGIANS

The World, 25 March 1891

Looking back from Easter to Christmas, I pray, now it is all over, that it may be long before I again have to make such a tale of bricks without straw as during this most barren period. No doubt the early winter appeals *ad misericordiam* of Hallé and Henschel for audiences were discouraging to musical enterprise, and the frost was benumbing; but still, it ought to be impossible for a musical critic in London, even during a bombardment, to be compelled to fall back, as often as I have had to, upon him who finds mischief still for idle hands to do. This last week I have hardly heard a note of music, except the Crystal Palace concert, at which Ysaÿe played, on Saturday. I am told that there was a Philharmonic concert on Thursday; but the directors thought it better not to mention it to me; and I, on my part, was unwilling to intrude at the risk of making the conductor nervous.

One of the good works done by the Royal College of Music has been the evangelization of Kensington, which I take to be the home of the submerged nine-tenths of the Art-affecting middle class, by a guild of young fiddlers, ex-students of the College, and ready for anything in the way of chamber music. The vigor and skill they shew always astonishes me. It may be that my early experience of amateur and apprenticed violinists, especially young women, was unfortunate; but I cannot help thinking that there has been an enormous improvement in them since my boyhood. At that time the sight of a fiddlecase in a drawing room filled me with terror: it boded all that was insufferable, infirm, and ridiculous in amateurism. But it was not alone the amateur that was to be dreaded. Even in good professional orchestras, a few bars of solo for the leader, the *obbligato* to *Salve dimora!* or the like, was an infliction which you bore sitting back, with your teeth set, and a grin of indulgent resignation on your drawn lips. I can remember thinking the violin a noxious instrument, and wondering why people played it. My astonishment when somebody took me to hear Sivori was boundless: I perceived that the thing could be played after all, but concluded that it took a magician to do it.

As time went on, I became familiar with the feats of the *virtuosi*; but the orchestra leaders were the same as ever, except insofar as they got worse as they got older. Amateurism I kept clear of altogether, nothing doubting that it, too, was its old self. I suppose I grew belated and benighted by allowing an old conclusion to fossilize in this way. At all events, when, only a few years ago, I happened to hear a strong quintet played by five young Royal Collegians led by Miss Holiday, I was secretly amazed at the ease, the freedom, the boldness, the certainty of their execution. They did not seem in the least preoccupied by technical difficulties which would have kept players of their standing in former generations cramped and miserable from the first note to the last. The other day I heard some members of the same little band, now led by Miss Donkersley (it was at a concert given by that young lady at the Kensington Town Hall), play a couple of movements from a Mendelssohn quartet which I had heard at a Monday Popular Concert very shortly before. And I was sorry that I had not time to hear the quartet out; though at St James's Hall I could have left without remorse at any point. Between my Miss Holiday and Miss Donkersley experiences I had begun to understand better the marked effects of the reinforcement of our orchestras with young men whose offhandedness over Wagnerian scores takes away the breath of their elders; and I had even been at a concert where the *virtuoso* who obliged us with Beethoven's Concerto was far inferior, as a player, to the two men who sat at the leader's desk accompanying him—Hollander and Seiffert, to wit. The progress has been immense; and, if it has left us more dissatisfied than ever, that is because our sense of artistic shortcoming has grown faster than the skill of the violinists, thereby guaranteeing further progress.

But now for the other side of the matter. All this refreshing boldness of execution was not as unknown everywhere as it was among lady amateurs before the era of Miss Donkersley and her fellow-students. Long before that time third-class travelers on the Underground Railway were subject to invasion by itinerant artists, who, fiddle and bow white from a monstrous excess of resin, played the popular tunes of the moment with reckless speed, tolerable intonation, and piercing stridency of tone. In circuses, too, a pair of violin demons would enter the ring and go through all sorts of antics without intermitting a *moto perpetuo* of the liveliest character. These experts were better than the old-fashioned amateurs; but they were not so good as Sivori, or Sarasate, or Reményi, or Ysaÿe. They had a quick left hand, and an ear for pitch; but when once a note was fairly in tune, they had no further concern about its quality, and were quite satisfied when their right hand was merely rasping and rubbing the bow up and down on the strings. Now, to be a great executant one must have not only an exquisitely delicate ear for quality of tone but a fine right hand trained to touch the strings with the bow (the really difficult instrument) with the marvelous legerdemain necessary to produce the tone one's ear demands.

The old masters—men like Baillot for instance—kept

comparatively commonplace pupils for years trying to acquire this power of bowing by slow practice, leaving them in the end spirit-broken, timid, footling pedants, with irresolute touch, uncertain intonation, and thin tone, lacking the assurance of the itinerant third-class carriage troubadour on the one hand, and the special subtle mastery of which their instructor had been dreaming on the other. It was a case of Better being the enemy of Well. Nowadays, it appears, we let our students rasp themselves into familiarity and confidence, and then, having accomplished the first step of making them fiddlers, try to refine their tone and make them artists. It is undoubtedly a huge improvement on Baillot's plan of trying to make them artists before they were fiddlers—a plan which never succeeded, except where Nature had done what Baillot omitted; but it has for the moment the disadvantage that our young fiddlers, comparing themselves with the old fogies who were dropped in their youth between the two stools, are apt to feel sufficiently glorious in their handicraftsman's smartness to lose sight of the step that lies beyond them.

And the modern orchestra, in which the violinist plays in unison with from sixteen to twenty others, no more encourages delicacy of tone in the individual player than choral singing encourages it in the individual singer. Therefore I warn this new generation, wonderfully handy as it is with the instrument which so puzzled its fathers, that much as I rejoice in its exploits, I intend to continue protesting very strongly against mere lefthand playing, especially at the opera, where the younger hands, when they are confronted with those "big guitar" accompaniments which are no longer "interesting," contemptuously refuse to try to make them beautiful—obviously because their ears are too hasty and their right hands too heavy and clumsy.

For the life of me I cannot see why the recent

suggestion that the score of Parsifal may find a place on Signor Mancinelli's desk at Covent Garden should be scouted as "profane." I leave out of the question the old-fashioned objection, founded on the theory that all playhouses and singing-halls are abodes of sin. But when a gentleman writes to the papers to declare that "a performance of Parsifal, apart from the really religious surroundings of the Bayreuth Theatre, would almost amount to profanity," and, again, that "in the artificial glare of an English opera house it would be a blasphemous mockery," I must take the liberty of describing to him the "really religious surroundings," since he admits that he has never seen them for himself. In front of the Bayreuth theatre, then, on the right, there is a restaurant. On the left there is a still larger restaurant and a sweetstuff stall. At the back, a little way up the hill, there is a café. Between the café and the theatre there is a shed in which "artificial glare" is manufactured for the inside of the theatre; and the sound of that great steam engine throbs all over the Fichtelgebirge on still nights.

Between the acts the three restaurants are always full, not of devout Wagnerites (the Meister advocated vegetarianism), but of Spiers & Pondites, who do just what they will do at the Star and Garter when my Festspielhaus on Richmond Hill is finished. The little promenade in front of the theatre is crowded with globetrotters, chiefly American and vagabond English, quite able to hold their own in point of vulgarity, frivolity, idle curiosity, and other perfectly harmless characteristics, with the crowd in the foyer at Covent Garden or the Paris Opéra. When they have seen every celebrity present pass and repass some twenty times, they become heavily bored, and are quite excited at seeing a small contingent from the orchestra, with the familiar German-band equipment of seedy overcoat and brass instrument, assemble under the portico and blare out a fragment of some motive from whatever music-drama is "on" that evening. This is the signal for entering the theatre, but nobody moves, as everyone knows that it is only the third blast that means business, when you do not happen to be at a distance—in which case, however, you hear nothing, unless you are dead to windward, with a strong gale blowing. Inside, the "honorable ladies" are requested by placard to remove their towering headgear; and not one of them is sufficiently impressed with the really religious surroundings to do so. Then the famous "Bayreuth hush" is secured by a volley of angry sh-sh-sh-es, started by the turning down of the lights; and the act begins. What sanctity there is in all this that is not equally attainable at Boulogne or Bayswater remains to be explained.

Mr Charles Dowdeswell's position on the subject is safer than that of his fellow-correspondent. He claims special sanctity, not for Bayreuth, but for Parsifal, and says (what is perfectly true) that the Bayreuth Festpielhaus is the only existing theatre in which justice can be done to the work. But as to his practical conclusion— that for the immense majority here who cannot afford to go to Bayreuth it is better that they should never see any performance of Parsifal at all than see one even as good as the Covent Garden Meistersinger—no practical Wagnerite critic can endorse it. Let us build a Wagner Theatre, by all means, as soon as possible; but if, in the meantime, Mr Harris will produce even the second act of Parsifal—and he could quite easily do it—I, for one, will forgive him for La Favorita, and applaud his artistic enterprise to the skies the whole season through.

OH, AINT IT AWFUL!

The World, 1 April 1891

The world has suffered many things through Grieg's experiments in the grand style of composition; but assuredly the climax was reached on Saturday week, when his setting of three scenes from Björnson's Olav Trygvason was performed—wantonly performed—at the Crystal Palace. I have no idea of the age at which Grieg perpetrated this tissue of puerilities; but if he was a day over eighteen the exploit is beyond excuse. Possibly it would pass muster better in the theatre than it did at Sydenham; yet I cannot think that even the most innocent pit and gallery could be imposed on by the intonings of the sacrificer, with the weird interludes on the closed notes of the horns. But for these Simon Tappertit* solemnities and turnip-ghost terrors we might all have caught the 4·55 train and saved half an hour.

A prominent feature in the instrumental treatment recalled to my mind the attempts I have made from time to time to sample the music halls. On one of these expeditions I heard somebody—Mr Herbert Campbell, I think—sing a ditty of which I remember nothing except that the refrain, delivered in a tone of the strongest expostulation, always began with the exclamation, Oh, aint it awful! And each time the trombone would indignantly echo, Awful. At the other extreme of dramatic orchestration I have heard the cry of Donner echoed back from the clouds in Das Rheingold, as he swings his hammer to fashion the rainbow bridge into

* Character in Dickens's Barnaby Rudge.

Valhalla. That was also done by the trombones. Grieg makes the trombones echo his dreary Sacrificer again and again; and the effect always reminds you of Mr Herbert Campbell, and never of Donner.

Ysaÿe's performance of Weiniawski's concerto in D, of a Bach fugue and prelude, and of Saint-Saëns' Rondo Capriccioso, gave a tolerably comprehensive display of his extraordinary accomplishments as a violinist. His terrific technique, his fondness for the intensely French Saint-Saëns, his self-assertiveness, his readiness to sacrifice higher artistic qualities to the speed of a dazzlingly impossible *presto*, his combination of a Latin finesse of execution with a German solidity of tone, and occasionally with a German obtuseness of intonation, all stamp his share of original sin as distinctively Belgian. That is not altogether a compliment: the nation which municipalized the Wiertz Museum has a good deal to apologize for in the way of art; but Ysaÿe's individual force is of European volume: he is Sarasate's only serious rival among players of his own generation. We seem to be waking up but slowly to the idea that he is anyone in particular; but we will compensate him by making an idol of him years after he has lost all claim to that distinction. His selection of the Bach fugue may have been partly prompted by our habit of saying that nobody can play Bach but Joachim.

Ysaÿe's power of polyphonic playing enables him to challenge any comparison on this score as far as technical mastery goes. For the rest, one need not commit the folly of making the one man a standard for the other, especially in view of the admirable performances with which Joachim has this year retrieved the one or two unlucky occasions on which he did himself some injustice in 1890 over Bach; but there is no harm in coupling the two names for the purpose of discouraging the people who are never satisfied until they have hallmarked somebody as the best player in the world. There is no such thing as the best player in the world, never was, and never will be, unless music falls so far out of cultivation that some one-eared person can claim the throne of the kingdom of the deaf. The rest of the program was of no special interest. Madame Emily Squire gave us one of those airs from La Clemenza di Tito which anybody with the requisite range can sing in a fashion, but which can only be made interesting by an artist who has acquired all the essential qualities of the old classical style. The overture to Rienzi suited the martial vein in Mr Manns: he exulted in it much as he used to in the third movement of Raff's Lenore symphony, which, by the bye, is curiously neglected just now, considering that popular taste is passing through the very phase to which it ministers. Miss Dora Bright, who appeared on the following Saturday, is a pianist who writes her own concertos better than she plays them. She is dexterous and accurate, and a thorough musician to boot; but her talent has not the pianist's peculiar specialization. I do not know that she plays any better than I do, except in respect of her fingering scales properly, and hitting the right notes instead of the wrong ones. Her concerto is remarkable— apart from its undeniable prettiness—for its terse, business-like construction and its sustained animation. Somehow, there is an appalling soundness of the head and heart about our young English lady composers which prevents them from getting into the depths of tone poetry; but they certainly swim very engagingly on the surface.

The Good Friday performance of the Messiah at the Albert Hall reminds me that the Handel Festival will take place on the 22nd, 24th, and 26th of June, with the customary Messiah on the first day, Israel on the third, and a selection on the second. Mesdames Albani,

Nordica, Belle Cole, Emily Squire; Miss Macintyre and Miss McKenzie; Messrs Lloyd, McGuckin, Bridson, Brereton, and Santley will be seconded by four thousand choristers. Mr Manns will conduct; and the result will be regarded by some as "sublime," by others as an effective *reductio ad absurdum* of the principle of monstrosity in art. For my part, as I do not wish to spoil sport, and had much rather see the Crystal Palace Company doing this than merely not doing it, I shall reserve my opinion until after the festival.

I have just received the first part of the Wagner Society's translation of the Meister's prose works. It is well printed and got up, and contains the much-quoted autobiographic sketch which Heinrich Laube got from Wagner in 1843 for his Elegant World's Times. Also the introduction and beginning of Art and Revolution, which is one of the two essays on art that everybody is expected to have read, the other being Art and Religion. The translations, by Mr Ashton Ellis, are excellent. The publishers are Messrs Kegan Paul & Co.

Messrs Sampson Low send me a biography of Gounod by Marie Anne de Bovet, the oddest imaginable mixture of impertinence and information. She makes it impossible for you to get a word in edgeways with her rapturous chatter about the nature of genius, not to mention her explanations to the effect that Planquette does not consider himself the equal of Handel, and that those who prefer Les Cloches [de Corneville] to the Messiah are no judges; that the big drum does not occupy so important a place in the orchestra as a Stradivarius; that "it is well that Bach should have written the St Matthew Passion, and Beethoven the Ninth Symphony, though it was not wrong for Mozart to have written *Deh vieni alla finestra* or Gounod the lark duet in Roméo." I would not stand ten minutes of this in private conversation from the prettiest woman that ever walked; but I forgive Madame de Bovet for the sake of the charming portrait of Gounod which can be divined like a face in a cloud through her irresponsible but spiritual prattle. For Gounod's music I have never found any better words than heavenly and angelic, in the simplest, childish sense. Imagine, then, my delight on learning from Madame de Bovet that when Gounod was studying in Vienna, he wrote on the margin of one of his scores the words: *O heiliger Fra Angelico: wo ist die Musik deiner Engeln!*

L'ENFANT PRODIGUE
The World, 8 April 1891

I can only describe L'Enfant Prodigue, at the Prince of Wales', as touching. I was touched when I laughed no less than when I retired in tears at the end of the third act. But my emotion was not caused by the music. That is simply conventional French ballet music and *mélodrame*, elegantly fitted with all the latest harmonic refinements. And I must add that if the piece is going to have anything like the vogue here which it enjoyed at the Bouffes Parisiens, M. André Wormser had better lose no time in rescoring it for a full band. Accompaniments played by a pianist and eked out by a handful of wind players and a string quartet are tolerated in Paris, where you will see Offenbach's operas treated in this way even at the Eden Theatre; but here such makeshifts stamp a performance as cheap and provincial, and that, too, on good artistic grounds.

The pianoforte is so convenient a substitute for an orchestra where no orchestra is to be had, that a good deal of money and trouble might be saved by employing it in all cases. But its monotonous repercussions and unalterably false equal-temperament tuning soon make it so tiresome that only a great artist, using a first-rate machine, and playing a varied program of music of great intrinsic interest, highly specialized for the peculiar qualities of the instrument, can induce audiences to sit out lengthy recitals. Even at the most modest suburban dance people crave for at least one fiddle to relieve the eternal strum of the piano. If M. Wormser thinks he has got over this difficulty in L'Enfant Prodigue, I can feelingly assure him that he is mistaken. Three-fourths of the pianoforte part have all the air of being a mere transcription from score; and if they had been played by Sapellnikoff on one of the best Steinways ever built, the transfer of at least those three-fourths to the orchestra would have been a gain. For the remaining fourth the piano can be retained if M. Wormser thinks that the one or two special effects it produces are worth the room it occupies. My own opinion is distinctly that they are not: indeed, I think I might safely venture upon an offer to replace them myself with orchestral effects without any loss of piquancy.

For the rest of this most entertaining dumb show I have nothing but praise. The service rendered by the music in making the drama intelligible is not great: there is only one point which would not be as intelligible to a deaf man as it was to me. That was the stipulation made by Phrynette that the Baron must marry her, a point which could easily be conveyed by pantomime, but which was more concisely and amusingly intimated by the introduction of the opening strain of Mendelssohn's wedding march in the orchestra. And nothing could be funnier or more felicitous than the humorous allusion to the same theme when the Baron is left alone. His shake of the head, accompanied by that mocking little *scherzando*, tells, better than the most elaborate pantomime could without music, that he has not the smallest intention of keeping his promise.

I noticed during the sad last act that the domestic incidents repeated from the cheerful first act were now accompanied by the same music changed into the minor mode; but I cannot say that this device interested me much. I was even conscious of resenting it somewhat for obtruding its extreme staleness between me and the much more original and distinguished art of the actors. On the stage there was not a dull moment. If a cat had been present, I believe it would have purred with tickled satisfaction to see old Pierrot sitting there reading his newspaper, from the political article to the account of the latest duel, and from that to the newest impropriety. Madame Pierrot, too, was beyond praise: it will be a technical education to some of our own people to see how Courtès and Madame Schmidt keep the audience interested in the simplest domestic commonplace. Pierrot's part is the one which requires the subtlest play; and Jane May is quite equal to the occasion: she has a quick sense of the character, and puts it into action with a high degree of stage skill. Francesca Zanfretta, a gorgeous brunette, produces the effect of a figure by Phillips introduced in a picture by Watteau. In spite of her eminently continental name, I cannot help suspecting her of being a particularly clever and jolly British columbine. She bounces through her part with much spirit and enjoyment; and though there is a conspicuous want of finesse in her play, and even of punctuality in her relations with the orchestra, I am not sure that she does not relieve and enliven the performance in a valuable way. Gouget, as the Baron, is as funny as possible; and yet he is artistic discretion itself.

In estimating the value of these eulogies, it must be remembered that although the satisfaction of seeing a simple thing consummately well done is most joyful and soothing after a long and worrying course of complex things imperfectly done, the simple success must not therefore be placed above the complex half success. A drama consisting of a series of emotions, so obvious in their provocation and so conventional in their sequence that they can be made intelligible to a general audience by pure phenomena is child's play compared to ordinary drama, or opera, although no actor can venture upon it without a degree of skill in pantomime which most speakers and singers think (erroneously) that they can afford to do without. This much being admitted, I may safely proceed to say that on the chance occasions when I descend from the opera house to the theatre I am often made to feel acutely that the play would be much more enjoyable if the dialogue were omitted. To me the popular dramatist always appears as a sympathetic, kindly, emotional creature, able to feel and to imagine in a pleasantly simple and familiar groove, but almost destitute of intellect, and therefore unable to think or to write. Whilst he is merely emotioning he is the best of good company for an easygoing hour of sentimental relaxation; but the moment he opens his mouth he becomes insufferable; you feel like the policeman in one of Wilkie Collins's novels,* who, when the butler collared him, could only say patiently "You dont know how to do it in the least." If the *dramatis personæ* would only love and languish and storm and despair in dumb show and "do it beautifully," as Hedda Gabler enjoined upon her lover when he consented to shoot himself, then all the valuable parts of the play would be brought into full prominence, and all the rubbish eliminated. L'Enfant Prodigue proves triumphantly that this is quite practicable. Therefore, to those wellknown dramatists of ours who have immense hearts but no brains

* Sergeant Cuff, in The Moonstone.

worth mentioning—I cannot give names, as I never know one from the other, the drama not being my regular department—I most earnestly recommend the adoption of the dumb show form in future. Let them, as Hegel would have said, remain in the stage of consciousness without attempting to advance to that of scientific understanding. Or, as someone else actually has said—I forget who; but it was not Hegel—let them "cut the cackle, and come to the 'osses."

There is one point which, "in the present excited state of public feeling" (here I quote Mr Nupkins),* may expose Mr Horace Sedger to severe animadversion for producing this wordless drama, and may even cause him to be threatened with a withdrawal of his license or a prosecution under Lord Campbell's Act. Like the parable after which it is named, and like that charming novel Manon Lescaut, L'Enfant Prodigue is not, in the accepted sense, "moral." Many of our most sensitive critics must have blushed continuously through the second act; and the spectacle of a young man robbing his father, having his fling with the money; and refilling his pocket by cheating at cards when that is spent, without once forfeiting our sympathies or coming to a bad end, is surely enough to provoke the virtuous indignation of any gentleman who deals in the article. Mr Sedger should really be more careful: comparatively puritanical dramatists, also of foreign origin, have quite recently made a most painful impression, without for a moment going so far as Michel Carré *fils* has gone in L'Enfant Prodigue.

At the Crystal Palace on Saturday we had Dr Mackenzie's Dream of Jubal, or, rather, Jubal's dream of Dr Mackenzie, with Miss Nordica, Mr Iver McKay, Miss Hannah Jones, and Mr Vernon Taylor in the

* Character in Dickens's Pickwick Papers.

principal parts, and Mr Charles Fry as narrator. Jubal is our old friend the first-cousin of Tubal Cain, and the father of all such as handle the harp and pipe (it used to be the harp and organ in my day). Jubal, like Hermes, finds a natural lyre formed by a tortoiseshell, and at once begins, like any Englishman, to try his hand at picking out a tune. An angel is immediately sent to shew him what that sort of thing will inevitably lead to in the course of ages. Under the impression that the angel is proposing to give him a great treat, he allows himself to be transported to a cathedral, where they are singing a Gloria by the Principal of the Royal Academy of Music, concluding with a fugue on the words Cum sancto spiritu, with *stretti, point d'orgue,* and everything complete.

After this depressing glimpse into the future, Jubal becomes a prey to settled melancholy; but the angel relentlessly continues the torture, successively inflicting on him a solo and duet in the oratorio style, an ode, a battle hymn, and a rustic ballad with chorus—all of quite stupendous factitiousness, and relieved only by a funeral march which has some rich and handsome, if not very novel, tone-coloring. Like poor Jubal, I was bored beyond all description; but I had the advantage of him, inasmuch as the composer could not put rapturous compliments into my mouth. If Dr Mackenzie had employed me to write either his libretto or his analytical program, instead of giving both jobs to the same brother critic, no doubt I should have been able to give a more polite account of his cantata. Unless some arrangement of this kind is made, or Dr Mackenzie becomes as a young student again, working at his composition instead of playing at it, I am afraid I shall always be a marplot when there is a new choral *magnum opus* in the wind.

GLUCK'S ORFEO

The World, 15 April 1891

At Covent Garden there is nothing new before the curtain except a lining of mirror to the walls of the corridors; so that on diamond nights boxholders who are tired of being admired by the audience can go outside and admire themselves. When the season began on Monday last week with Giulia Ravogli in Orfeo, we were all in a state of high expectancy, thinking, not unnaturally, that if Gluck's masterpiece was so entrancing with that desperate fit-up of Lago's, what would it not be with the splendid staging of Harris? Even I had my hopes—why should I deny it?—though I had my doubts too, particularly after the mirror arrangement in the corridors. And I admit that if money could have made Orfeo an artistic success, an artistic success it would have been. But the fact that want of money failed to wreck the work last year with Signor Lago should have warned Mr Harris not to depend too much on his purse in dealing with Gluck. Unfortunately the warning was thrown away: Mr Harris has trebled the expenditure and spoiled the opera. It is true that Euridice's tomb, formerly a packing-case on end, with her name stencilled in the only direction it would fit in, is now a medieval milestone, surprisingly old-established considering the recent interment. No longer in a desolate corner of Victoria Park, it stands now about two miles below Bingen on the Rhine, a spot all sunshine and pleasant hillside paths, in one of which Madame Bauermeister, tripping as she retired backwards from the boards, unintentionally sat down, and, somewhat stunned by the concussion, amazedly contemplated Orfeo, who surveyed her with speechless consternation.

The Elysian Fields have been shifted from the Bois de Boulogne, which at least looked infinitely spacious, to a villainous classical Monte Carlo, whither Orfeo comes straight out of the Mediterranean by a flight of stone steps, which land him amid an ill-arranged crowd of temples and columns. Not until the third act does the scenepainter, having exhausted the possibilities of making matters worse than last year, come to his senses and better them. As to the exploits of Madame Palladino and the ballet, I really cannot describe them adequately with any sort of reasonable goodnature. To combine such senseless noddings and trippings and kickings with Gluck's noble measures was a profanity from which Offenbach would have recoiled: it was indecent, not in Mr McDougall's sense—though Madame Palladino was certainly not dressed with any special consideration for his feelings—but in the true artistic sense. I could not look at it; and I could not go out into the corridors because of the mirrors; so I furtively watched the hands of the lady next me, which, as it happened, were expressively artistic hands, until Giulia Ravogli entered and shewed us the sort of movement that should be associated with such music. But even Giulia's pantomime, saturated with feeling as it still is, did not produce its former effect.

Last year the Elysian shades were shabby, certainly; but they all knew what they were there for; and Orfeo, in the focus of their breathless attention, made us forget their ridiculous makeshifts of costumes. This time the costumes are rich enough; but half the heros are girls in tights with long ostrich feathers drooping from their helmets to their calves—girls who, like their colleagues of the ballet, stand listlessly where they have been told to stand, and trouble themselves no more about Orfeo's

feelings than about mine. I do not propose to pursue the
subject further than to note that Sofia Ravogli's voice is
thicker and richer than it was, and to assure Mancinelli
that he only makes matters worse by worrying the
music; for the sources of the flagging and unsatisfac-
toriness which annoy him are not in the orchestra but on
the stage. Mr Harris has the remedy in the hollow of his
hand. If he does not care to fall back on the Lago Elysian
Fields, he can order a new scene with a far remote
horizon, in the style of Martin's* Plains of Heaven. He
can reserve Madame Palladino for modern romantic
operas, and either prepare a classical ballet or else leave
out the dancing altogether. And he can banish from the
stage the people who cannot be induced to take any
interest in the action. Anything short of this will leave
the opera what it is at present, the greatest disappointment of the season, so far.

Faust on the following night was a very different
affair. Miss Eames, the newest American soprano, fully
justified her engagement by her performance as Margaret. The middle of her voice is exceptionally satisfactory in volume and rich in quality, enabling her to make
herself heard without effort in all sorts of quiet dramatic
inflexions. The low notes, as might be expected, are also
very good; but the upper register, though bright, does
not come so easily as the rest; and it was rather by a *tour
de force* that she took the final *trio* right through the
third repetition in B natural instead of using the old
Opéra Comique abridgment. However, as it was a
successful *tour de force*, we were all very grateful for it;
for the abridgment spoils the finest passage in the whole
opera. As an actress, Miss Eames is intelligent, ladylike,

* John Martin (1789–1854) was an English historical and
landscape painter, whose work, says the DNB, was "marked
by wild imaginative power."

and somewhat cold and colorless. The best that can be said for her playing in the last two acts is, that she was able to devize quietly pathetic business to cover her deficiency in tragic conviction. As to Mlle Guercia, the Siebel, her sex betrayed her: she was so intensely feminine in every line of her figure, every note of her voice, and every idea in her acting, that, without being at all a ridiculous or incapable artist, she presented us with quite the most comic Siebel on record. Perotti, with his *allures de danseuse* and his popular high notes, kept Goethe effectually at a distance; and the gentleman who took Devoyod's place as Valentin, though he did an admirable back-fall, was in all other respects quite as bad as anyone could be expected to be at such short notice.

Maurel's Mephistopheles cannot be dismissed with the mixture of contemptuous indulgence and conventional toleration with which one lets pass most of the acting at Covent Garden. He challenges criticism as a creative artist, not as a mere opera-singer. In doing so he at once rouses antagonisms from which his brother artists are quite exempt, since his view of the characters he represents may conflict with that of his critics—a risk obviously not run by eminent baritones who have no views at all. His Mephistopheles is a distinct individual character, exhaustively premeditated, and put upon the stage with the utmost precision of execution. As to consistency, it is almost too consistent to be natural. There is no sentimental trace of the fallen son of the morning about it, much less any of the stage puerilities of the pantomime demon (for example, take his original and convincingly right play during the chorale as they break his spell with the cross-hilted swords). It is the very embodiment of that grim Gothic fancy of an obscene beast of prey with the form and intellect of a man. The artistic means by which this effect is produced—the mouse-colored costume, the ashen face and beard, the loveless tigerish voice—could not have been better chosen.

Yet I take some exception to the impersonation, especially in the last two acts, as lacking relief, both vocally and dramatically. This could be best supplied by a touch of humor, in which it is at present entirely deficient. In the scene of the serenade and duel, Maurel is cumbrous and heavy, dragging the serenade beyond all musical conscience, and taking the whole scene as tragically as Faust himself, instead of being the one person present to whom it is pure sport. In the church, too, where Gounod has provided for one of those changes of voice to which Maurel, in his Lyceum lecture, attached so much importance, he sang the pathetic, heart-searching *Rammenta i lieti di*, accompanied by the organ alone, in the same strident tone as the menace with which it concludes as the orchestra comes in at the words *Non odi qual clamor*. The only really effective passage in this scene, which Miss Eames played lachrymosely and without distinction, was his powerfully expressive play at the chorus of worshipers.

The fact that, being seventy-five minutes late, I saw only half of Giulia Ravogli's Carmen, tempts me to announce publicly that it is a mistake to suppose that I am a sort of boy messenger, always in waiting at York-street, Covent Garden, to dash off to any concert or opera immediately on receipt of an invitation. But, after all, invitations are invitations; and those who send them have a right to choose their own time, without reference to my convenience, which points to at least a day's clear notice. However, I saw enough of Carmen, which went off brilliantly, to be able to testify that Randegger conducts it worse than ever; that Lubert, the latest Spanish tenor, is not so handsome as Valera, nor so fearfully afflicted with goat-bleat as Suane, and that his voice is of rather commoner quality than either of theirs, also that he is, like them, careful and intelligent about his stage business, rising even to energy as a melodramatic actor; that Celli, not knowing his part in Italian, and failing to get any help from prompter or conductor, sacrificed himself somewhat dreadfully as the Toreador; that Mlle Janson fitted into the cast very well as Frasquita (or was she Mercedes?); that Sofia Ravogli played Micaela exactly as she would have played Norma; and that Vaschetti as Zuniga, a small but important part, requiring some distinction of manner and finesse of play, especially in the entry in the tavern scene, maintained his reputation for brazen lungs and unalterable but good-humored incompetence. As to Giulia, I gravely doubt whether my opinion of her is worth the paper it is written on. If anybody else were to sing the florid passages in Bertoni's aria in Orfeo, or the lilt in the tavern scene of Carmen, as she sings them, how that person would catch it in this column! But in the presence of such a millionaire in artistic force as Giulia, Bertoni and Bizet lose their rights. So, I may add, does Prosper Mérimée. His Carmen, with all her subtle charm, was only a gentleman's dream. Giulia's Carmen is real; and her reality reduces the catastrophe to absurdity. The idea of poor Lubert killing her was ridiculous: nobody believed that she was dead: she could have taken him up and thrown him at Randegger's head without exciting the least surprise, especially among those who are good judges of conducting. Indeed, the orchestra and the front row of the stalls, delightful as they are when this wonderful Ravogli is on the stage, are not altogether safe at such times. The face of Mr Antoine Matt, the well-known trombone-player, when he realized that the knife which Carmen had just plucked from Don Jose's hand, and sent whizzing down the stage with a twitch of her powerful hand, was coming straight at his jugular vein, expressed a curious alloy of artistic devotion with a rueful sense that she might just as easily have aimed a little higher and made her shot at a critic instead of imperiling a brother artist. On the whole, since there is no denying that Giulia's strength and reality made havoc with the flimsy and fanciful figment she was impersonating, anyone who likes may denounce her as the worst of all the Carmens. I shall merely add a heartfelt wish that her successors may all be as gloriously bad. As to the genius with which she puts into dramatic action not only what is contained in the part written for her own voice, but the contents of the orchestral score as well, I can only say that I wish our conductors had half her insight, or quarter of her courage, promptitude, and vigor in action.

I have only space left to record hurriedly that the Albéniz concerts are deservedly growing in favor, and that at the last one Tivadar Nachéz advanced his status considerably by playing Bach's Partita in B minor and a chaconne by Corelli so well that I could not help wondering what cynical estimate of our musical intelligence has hitherto induced him to waste so many opportunities by persisting in playing claptrap drawing-room pieces, and playing them very badly too. Another series of three Saturday afternoon concerts which promises well has been begun by Willy Hess, the leader of the Manchester orchestra; and Hugo Becker, a cellist well worth hearing, as he proved by his performance last Saturday of Piatti's arrangement of an *adagio* and *allegro* by Boccherini.

THE BROTHERS DE RESZKE
The World, 22 April 1891

I have seen Faust again, and expect soon to be able to whistle all the tunes in this popular opera, having already made the most gratifying progress with the soldiers' chorus. The occasion of my second visit was the appearance of Maurel as Valentin, and his replacement as Mephistopheles by De Reszke—Brother Edouard of that ilk. I confess to a sort of paternal affection, inspiring inexhaustible indulgence, for Brother Edouard; and I believe this feeling is shared by the public. We all like to see him enjoying himself; and he never enjoys himself more thoroughly than in that outrageous crimson and scarlet costume, with two huge cock's feathers twirling in the Covent Garden draughts (exceptionally boreal this year), his face decorated with sardonic but anatomically impossible wrinkles, and a powerful limelight glowing on him through the reddest of red glasses. His firm conviction that he is curdling the blood of the audience with demonstrations of satanic malignity when he is in fact infecting them with his mountainous good humor; his faith in the diabolic mockery of a smile that would make the most timid child climb straight up on his knee and demand to be shewn how a watch opens when blown on; the exuberant agility with which he persuades himself that his solid two hundred and forty pounds of generously nourished flesh and blood are a mere vapor from the mists of the bottomless pit—all these sights are dear to the hearts of stalls and gallery alike.

And then his singing! Singing is not the word for it: he no longer sings: he bawls, revelling in the stunning sound with a prodigality which comes of knowing that he has so much voice to draw on that no extravagance can exhaust it. It is magnificent; but it is not Mephistopheles. The price we have to pay for it is the destruction of all dramatic illusion whilst he is on the stage; that is to say, during about three-quarters of the whole performance. To say the least, it is not cheap. It would be out of all reason if the singing were like the acting. Fortunately, it is not; for the separation between the musical and the intellectual is uncommonly marked in the De Reszke family. In Edouard's case there is more than separation: there is divorce. Not that I would imply for a moment that our pet baritone has no intelligence. I have not the slightest doubt that if he had to live by his brains, as I have, he would find plenty of them—in an extremely rusty condition, no doubt, but still of sufficient quantity and quality. What I do say is that he has found his voice and his musical instinct so entirely adequate to his modest needs, that he never thinks about his work, and never makes any point that is not a purely musical one.

The intellectual vacuity of his king in Lohengrin baffles description: a deaf man would mistake the opera for Donizetti's Anna Bolena, so unlike anybody except Henry VIII. does he look as he stands there making the chandelier buzz with *O sommo Dio*. The contrast between his huge apathy and the restless cerebration of Maurel is almost ludicrous. Even in the not exactly supersubtle part of Friar Laurence, of which, especially in the exquisite potion scene, he shews the most perfect musical comprehension, he cannot divest himself of a puzzleheaded air, as if he were far from sure what was going to come of it all, and were depending rather doubtfully on Brother Jack to see it safely through. Only as Mephistopheles does he wake up, not to the dramatic requirements of the character, but to the opening for a rare piece of sport as the devil in a red dress, with a serenade full of laughs (in which, by the bye, it must be admitted that he sings his rivals' heads off). Jean, whom it is hard to conceive as the big brother, may be presumed to have his mind kept active by domestic cares; for if the two brothers and Lassalle still live together, it is evident that Jean must think for the three. And yet it cannot be said that he overtasks his brain on the stage. Except in a character like Romeo, which proceeds on the simplest romantic lines, he creates very little dramatic illusion.

When I write my musical recollections, I shall probably have to say that the parts I best remember his acting in are Valentin and Don Giovanni. Good tenors are so scarce that the world has always condoned any degree of imbecility for the sake of an *ut de poitrine*, a necessity which has given currency to the phrase *bête comme un tenor*. Now whether Jean, in his anxiety to prove himself a real tenor after he had compromised himself by starting as a baritone, resolved to dissemble the intelligence which made him such a memorable Valentin, is more than I care to decide; but it is certain that he has not fulfilled his early promise as an actor. He is an enchanting Lohengrin; and his Walther von Stolzing, though the very vaguest Franconian knight ever outlined on the stage, makes Covent Garden better than Bayreuth on Meistersinger evenings. But Wagner would have urged Jean somewhat vehemently to make these heros a little more vivid, alert, and wilful, even at the cost of some of their present nebulous grace.

The Tannhäuser on Saturday was a rather desperate business. To begin with, Bevignani made his first bow amid a gust of fiddle-rapping from the band, and proceeded at once to give us a more than sufficing taste of his quality. He treated the unfortunate opera exactly as the Chigwell donkey-boys treat their steeds, literally *walloping* it from one end of the course to the other. I have no doubt that the more he walloped it, the more his unmusical admirers said "Ah, there you are, you see: fine conductor, Bevignani: no mistake about his beat." And unquestionably there was not. It was the neck-or-nothing beat of the man who, unable to guide and control large combinations, crams on all possible headway in order to rush them through, beginning too fast, and ending in a breathless scramble. A choice example of the results of this policy offered itself in the pitch of scurry and confusion into which he had lashed the march in the second act by the time the final section was reached. There was no time to sing—no time to think. Would that there had been no time to listen! It is deplorable to have to complain of a well-intentioned and apparently quite self-satisfied gentleman in this rude fashion; but the waste of enormously expensive opportunities that goes on every season at Covent Garden for want of a conductor to utilize them is still more deplorable.

One can forgive Mancinelli a great deal on the score of his genuine enthusiasm in his work and his artistic feeling for orchestration; but his beat is fatally irresolute: it does not really lead; and the consequence is, that in such pieces as the prelude to Lohengrin, or the bridal march, the parts lose their consentaneousness, a blur of indecision spreads over the whole design, and at last one's memory wanders back almost regretfully to the pointed, steady, unwavering beat of Costa, who, unsympathetic, obsolete, and obstructive as he at last became, never allowed the threads of the orchestral loom to become tangled, and would have his band together on the fourth beat of the bar as well as on the first, wheras nowadays it is considered sufficient if, when the conductor swoops wildly down at the beginning of the bar, everybody who is ahead of that point goes back to it, and everybody who has not got so far skips forward to it. It is necessary to go often to the opera, and to listen attentively there, in order to realize how this gets on the nerves of an unfortunate critic after a time. It arises in the first instance with the singers, who, when they find that the complaisant conductor will follow them, no matter what they do, by pulling the band together at the first beat of every bar, become more and more careless, until at last melodies which are nothing if not symmetrical are delivered as shapeless declamations. Then the vice spreads until the habit of keeping accurate measure—a habit which is consistent with the most sentimental elasticity of *tempo*—is given up as unpractical; and matters go from bad to worse, until somebody with the musical conscience to feel about it as Mendelssohn, Wagner, Berlioz, and other masters have felt, gets angry enough to hit out without respect to persons. To that pass I am fast coming. With one conductor who can do nothing but wait, a second who can do nothing but wallop, and a third who can do nothing at all, life at Covent Garden is getting unendurable.

Let me return for a moment to Tannhäuser, not to speak of Perotti, whom I propose to leave entirely to his own reflections, but to hail the re-entry of the rapturous Albani as Elisabeth, whom she played excellently, though her curious helplessness in using the middle of her voice is rather a grave set-off to her temperamental aptitude for Wagnerian parts. If Maurel was not at all like Wolfram von Eschenbach, he was at least very like Virgil, which did just as well. But he substituted the Maurel nuance for the Wagner nuance in *O du mein holder Abendstern;* and that certainly did not do as well. However, his Wolfram as a whole was an admirable performance, standing out from the rest by its intelligent artistic quality, like his Telramond, his Valentin, and, in short, everything he has done this season. Sofia

Ravogli played Venus in an old-fashioned straight white robe, she being a brunette with a great wealth of black hair, which she allowed to hang straight down her back; so that we were able to compare the black and white in square pieces, much as we should on a draper's counter. It is true that by this method of dressing she gained an air of propriety which made Elisabeth look comparatively abandoned; but she spoiled the opera by turning the Venusberg into an anchorite's cave. With that beautiful hair made into a coronet in the Greek fashion, and a properly designed vestment of flame color, sea-green, orange, bronze, or anything but vestal white, were it even cream color, and her face toned to the right complexion, she would be a perfect Venus. As it is, she only abets the anti-Wagnerism of the stage manager, whose insanities must be seen to be believed. No words of mine can do justice to the Venus episode in the last act: I leave it to abler pens, and content myself with chronicling the appearance of several horses on the stage at the end of the first act in Rotten Row saddles and harness; whilst the hunting music, written for twelve horns, was played enthusiastically by the military band on cornets and saxhorns behind the scenes.

At Mr Manns' benefit concert next Saturday at the Crystal Palace, Ysaÿe will play the Mendelssohn concerto; and the orchestral pieces will include Berlioz's Benvenuto Cellini overture, Schubert's B minor symphony (the unfinished one), and the prelude to Parsifal. Last Saturday Gerardy played, and played very well indeed. Miss Patterson should not have used *Gli angui d' inferno* merely as a stalking horse for her high F. I shall not pretend to blame her for the shocking interpolation of a shake and an extra F at the end, as no doubt that was the work of her teacher. But I hope the result convinced her that Mozart would have been a safer guide; and I must tell her frankly not to attempt the song in public again until she can sing a simple sequence of triplets smoothly and accurately. Rose Softly Blooming was much better: she was justified in trying her fortune with it, though it is by no means an easy song. The performance of Berlioz's Harold symphony was particularly fine, only needing about thirty extra strings in the last movement to make quite sound enough for the size of the concert room, a requirement with which the directors could not reasonably be expected to comply.

ALBANI DWINDLES

The World, 29 April 1891

After a fortnight of Gluck, Gounod, Bizet, and Wagner, Covent Garden relapsed exhausted into the arms of La Traviata; and the audience promptly dwindled. Albani played Violetta on the occasion; and it is proper, if somewhat personal, to say that on her part too there has been a certain dwindling which does much to reconcile the imagination to her impersonations of operatic heroines. Not, of course, that she can by any conceivable stretch of fancy be accepted as a typical case of pulmonary consumption. But one has only to recall the eminent *prima donnas* who began their careers needing only a touch of blue under the eyes to make them look plausibly phthisical, and progressed with appalling rapidity to a condition in which no art of the maker-up could prevent them from looking insistently dropsical, to feel abundantly grateful to Albani for having so trained herself that nobody can say anything worse of her than that she is pleasingly plump. Indeed, in one way her figure is just the thing for La Traviata, as it does away with the painful impression which the last act produces whenever there is the faintest realism about it. Even in the agonies of death Albani robs the sick bed and the medicine bottles of half their terrors by her reassuring air of doing as well as can be expected. Still, I submit that though the representation is not painful, it is in the last degree ridiculous. In saying this I by no means endorse the verdict of those colleagues of mine who are declaring in all directions that the opera is antiquated, impossible, absurd, a relic of the old *régime*, and so on. Verdi's opera is one thing; the wilful folly of the Covent Garden parody of it is quite another. Take any drama ever written, and put it on a stage six times too large for its scenes, introducing the maddest incongruities of furniture, costume, and manners at every turn of it; and it will seem as nonsensical as La Traviata, even without the crowning burlesque of a robust, joyous, round-cheeked lady figuring as a moribund patient in decline. I have no doubt that when Mr Joseph Bennett is commissioned by Mr Harris to found a *libretto* for an opera by Signor Randegger on Hedda Gabler, and it is produced at Covent Garden with Hedda in modern costume, Tesman as a Dutch burgomaster after Rembrandt, Lővborg as a Louis XIII. *mousquetaire*, Brack as the traditional notary, and Thea in black with a mantilla and a convulsive walk, Ibsen himself will be voted antiquated. The truth is that La Traviata, in spite of its conventionalities, is before its time at Covent Garden instead of behind it. It is a much more real and powerful work than Carmen, for instance, which everybody accepts as typically modern.

With this view of the capabilities of the opera, I read the promise of Maurel's appearance as Germont with some hope of witnessing a beginning of reform. Maurel is courageous in matters of costume: his Holbein dress as Valentin, his mouse-colored Mephistopheles, his stupendous helmet in Lohengrin, which reminded us all of the headdress of the Indian in West's picture of the death of Wolfe,★ had proved him ready for any sacrifice of tradition to accuracy. I fully expected to see Germont enter fearlessly in frock-coat, tall hat, and primrose gloves with three black braids down the back. Judge of my disappointment when he marched forward in a magnificent Vandyke costume, without even an umbrella to save appearances. I knew then that he wanted, not to play Germont, but simply to sing *Di provenza*. However, to do him justice, he did not treat the part with utter frivolity. He came in rudely with his hat on; and when he found that Violetta had a noble soul, he took the hat off, like a gentleman, and put it on a chair. I instantly foresaw that Albani, when next overcome by emotion, would sit on it. So breathless became my anticipation that I could hardly attend to the intervening duet. At last she did sit on it; and never would that hat have graced Maurel's temples again if it had been historically accurate. This, then, I presume, is the explanation of the anachronism on Maurel's part. Albani must have refused to give up the business of sitting on Germont's hat, thereby forcing him to adopt one that would bend but not break under an exceptional pressure of circumstances. But the effect on Maurel was finally disastrous. In the fourth act his determination to take himself seriously faltered several times; and at last his tendency to laugh when he caught anybody's eye became patent. Montariol, the most amiable of tenors and swordsmen, did his best with Alfredo, and even brought down the house by an unexpected burst of vocal splendor in the third act.

★ Benjamin West (1738–1820), American painter of historical subjects, who became president of Britain's Royal Academy. His depiction of the death of Gen. James Wolfe in Quebec, 1759, is one of his most famous works.

La Traviata was followed up by Rigoletto on Wednesday; but my stall reached me too late for use. No doubt Maurel's Rigoletto is what it was last winter in Lago's time. It was then sufficiently powerful and interesting. The management, having thus produced two startling novelties, fell back for the further spring of getting out Le Prophète last Monday. I see that Jean de Reszke has explained that he cannot master Siegfried in time for performance this season. It is a pity; for one would rather see him swinging the sledge-hammer and making the sparks fly in Mime's stithy, or conversing with the woodbird in Fafnir's forest, or waking Brynhild on the fiery mountain, than shouting that detestable and dishonorable drinking song in the last act of the most conventional of the historical impostures of Scribe and Meyerbeer. He might at least play Tannhäuser once for us before the end of the season. The music must be pretty well known to him, whether he has studied it or not.

At Mr Manns' benefit at the Crystal Palace on Saturday, Ysaÿe played the eternal but never quite unwelcome Mendelssohn concerto, which cut but a poor figure after the Parsifal prelude and the Benvenuto Cellini overture. The huge audience took Ysaÿe rather coolly when he came upon the platform, as if most of them had never heard of him. But at the end of the concerto the applause burst out *con furore*; not without reason, for the performance was an astonishing one. Miss Adeline de Lara was hampered by a bad pianoforte. Broadwood is not the right maker for a touch like hers: probably Pleyel would suit her better. The particular Broadwood in question so resented her handling that it ruptured a hammer and stopped the performance. When, after much disconsolate contemplation of the interior of the instrument by everybody in the neighborhood, she consented to proceed with one note dumb, the maimed member extemporized a castanet and tambourine accompaniment by clattering and jingling among the strings. Altogether it was fortunate that the music was not of the slightest interest, being pure Rubinstein from beginning to end; so that Miss de Lara, in giving a convincing display of strength and dexterity, was doing all that she could have done in any case with such a composition. Madame Nordica sang *Dich, teure Halle*, from Tannhäuser, in a bright, bumptious, self-assertive, and otherwise quite unmeaning way that was as exactly as possible the opposite of how it ought to be sung; and a Mr E. O. Banemann gave us an inappropriate air from Elijah without making any decisive effect, though his voice is of exceptionally fine quality, and his way of using it artistic and full of promise for its future. Mrs Hutchinson also sang; and there were two new orchestral pieces by J. F. Barrett; but the program was so long that I had to return to town immediately after hearing Ysaÿe inhumanly accept an *encore* for his prodigious performance of Wieniawski's variations on Russian airs.

YSAÿE

The World, 6 May 1891

Ysaÿe's concert last week was the most sensational we have had this season. His determination to cap feats impossible to other violinists by feats impossible to himself, and his enormous self-assertiveness (significantly associated with a marked personal resemblance to certain early portraits of the late Mr Bradlaugh), really broke up and destroyed the Beethoven concerto. Those *cadenzas* of his, monstrous excrescences on the movements, nailed on, not grafted in, have no form, being merely examples of madly difficult ways of playing the themes that have been reasonably and beautifully presented by Beethoven. One's comfort is, that since Ysaÿe could hardly play them himself, nobody else is likely to be able to play them at all. Comparing him with Sarasate, there can be no doubt that at present the sum of pleasure to be had for one's money at a Sarasate concert is greater than at an Ysaÿe concert, even if the excitement be less strenuous. Sarasate, however, is a fully-matured artist; and it is now evident that Ysaÿe is not. His inscrutable age—guessed at as thirty, forty, and even fifty—turns out to be thirtytwo, which is mere adolescence for a man of such prodigiously unmanageable temperament. His technical skill must have cost him prolonged and intense labor. Nature does not make anybody a present of a touch at once so fine and so vigorous, or of that power of playing with perfect smoothness chords in which other players—even very eminent ones—have to make an uncouth skip from string to string. But the very craving after the heroic and impossible (a highly Belgian craving) which nerved him to face this drudgery is now keeping him behind his chief rival. Sarasate never insists on his extraordinary feats: he treats his own skill as a matter of course—as part of his necessary equipment as a first-class workman—as something which only concerns the public through its musical result.

Joachim, whose *cadenzas*, by the bye, are much better than Ysaÿe's, takes his place beside the conductor and his orchestral colleagues as the interpreter of Beethoven, whose supremacy he never obscures for a moment. But who can think of Beethoven, or even of music, whilst Ysaÿe is Titanically emphasizing himself and his stupendous accomplishment, elbowing aside the conductor, eclipsing the little handful of an orchestra which he thinks sufficient for a concert in St James's Hall, and all but shewing Beethoven the door? The fact is, he has

[330]

created himself so recently that he is not yet tired of the novelty of his own consummated self. As soon as he exhausts this theme, and devotes himself without a grudge to music, his position will be beyond all question. At present he is more interesting as a prodigy than delightful as an artist. I may add, with reference to the orchestra, that I was glad to have an opportunity of once more seeing Mr Cowen and several of the Philharmonic band at work together. Somehow, I never hear of a Philharmonic concert now until it is over. This troubles me somewhat; for though I never bear malice towards people who honestly admit that their performances will not bear criticism from my standard, I cannot help thinking that there must occasionally be a Philharmonic program which would pass muster with me.

At the vocal recital given by the Henschels at St James's Hall on Friday last, my equanimity was upset by an outrage perpetrated on me by the concert agent, the same being nothing less than my eviction from the corner seat to which The World has a prescriptive immemorial right, and the sandwiching of me into a place which I could not reach or leave without pushing past a row of people and making a public disturbance. I denounce the proceeding as a revolutionary one, and demand of that agent how he would like it himself if he had to go to thirtythree concerts every afternoon from Easter to Midsummer, and could not possibly avoid either arriving late or leaving early at every one of them. How would he like to feel as I do when I see the eyes of those young ladies who have been told the secret of where the celebrated critic sits, turning with awe and curiosity upon some impostor thrust into the seat which is morally mine? I hope that no personal consideration shall ever induce me to set down a word that is not scrupulously weighed in the balance of Justice; but if an agent deliberately goes out of his way to direct my attention to every fault in the performances he arranges, he has himself to thank for the consequences. I say now—and I defy anyone to contradict me—that Henschel's habit of singing out of tune is growing on him. In the duet *Vedi che bella sera*, he did not sing one solitary note from beginning to end that was not flat; and as Mrs Henschel, instead of singing equally flat to keep him in countenance, repudiated her wifely duty to gratify her artistic self-will (probably she had been misled by Ibsen's plays), and sang in tune throughout, the effect was far from delectable. This false intonation is not the result of a defective ear: it is a habit of which the ear becomes tolerant after a time. That is, be it understood, the ear of the person affected: the general ear retains its rectitude and protests. In some cases, it is true, one gets used to it. Trebelli, for instance, had a way of leaning caressingly on the pitch of a note and depressing it the least bit in the world, so that she hardly ever sang absolutely in tune; but as the fault was too slight to be actually disagreeable, it passed as part of her individuality as an artist.

Albani is beginning to do the same thing; but she is carrying it too far, and will soon, unless she takes the trouble to readjust her intonation very carefully, be unable to sing piano in *cantabile* passages otherwise than quite painfully flat. Henschel is going Albani's way; for it is in sentimental, soft, sustained phrases that he comes to grief: in Crugantino's song and Loewe's setting of The Erl King there is nothing to complain of. The remedy lies ready to his hand. Mrs Henschel always sings in tune. Let him sing duets with her until the two voices blend without the slightest jar, when he may depend on it that he has recovered his musical integrity. If he neglects this he will find his popularity steadily falling off relatively to that of his wife—a state of things subversive of all domestic discipline.

Gerardy's last concert was an improvement on the previous one, at which, it may be remembered, I had to note a certain shortcoming from the perfection of his first public efforts here. This time he was himself again: there was not a trace of carelessness, weariness, or indifference at any point throughout the performance, except perhaps for a moment during the first section of a piece by Radoux, in which no living human being could have taken a very lively interest. The wonder is that a boy, who is not yet old enough to assert his right to choose his programs according to his temperament, should not let his attention lapse more frequently. As it is, the sustained artistic quality of his performances would be extraordinary in an adult. This concert also was the occasion of the first appearance of Eugène Holliday, whose style as a pianist is so foreign to that of Gerardy as a cellist that his appearance at the same recital made a positively unfavorable impression. He had his revenge, however, at his own concert on Saturday last, when, with a heroic program beginning with Beethoven's gigantic Opus 106,* he held his audience throughout almost as if his master, Rubinstein, had come again.

After making my rounds for months past between the exponents of the Madame Schumann training on the one hand, and the Lisztian training on the other, going from Mr Borwick to Sapellnikoff, and from Miss Eibenschütz to Madame Menter, there is an immense satisfaction in this Rubinstein technique, which has the soundness and thoroughness of the one school and the artistic life and power of the other. In some matters—Chopin ballades, for example—Holliday is too young to understand quite what he is about; and in no case is it safe to estimate his rank as an artist by the exploits for

---

* Piano Sonata No. 29 (Hammerklavier).

[333]

which he has been so lately crammed by a great master. But the fact that it has been possible so to cram him, proves extraordinary capacity, resolution, and endurance on his part. Even granting that his admirable playing of Tchaikovsky's Barcarolle was a feat of pure imitation, it is not to be doubted that he is fully sensible of the artistic nuances he reproduces. His occasional violence, which knocks some twentyfive pounds per recital off the value of the instrument he uses (a Broadwood), and his trick of striking the top note of a descending scale as if his little finger were the hammer of a rifle, make the milder Mendelssohnian amateur wince; but they are only exaggerations of genuine executive power, and not the bluster of a weakling. He would do well, if he can afford it, or persuade the agents into the speculation, to give some further recitals, especially as his association with Gerardy was, through the difference of their artistic planes, something of a false start.

Boïto's Mefistofele has been revived with success at the Opera; but I shall let that rest until next week.

A NON-MOZARTIAN DON
The World, 13 May 1891

Ever since I was a boy I have been in search of a satisfactory performance of Don Giovanni; and I have at last come to see that Mozart's turn will hardly be in my time. I have had no lack of opportunities and disappointments; for the Don is never left long on the shelf, since it is so far unlike the masterpieces of Wagner, Berlioz, and Bach, that cannot be done at all without arduous preparation. Any opera singer can pick up the notes and tumble through the concerted pieces with one eye on the conductor: any band can scrape through the orchestral parts at sight. Last year and the year before, it was tried in this fashion for a night at Covent Garden, with d'Andrade as Don Juan, and anybody who came handy in the other parts. This year it has been recognized that trifling with Mozart can be carried too far even for the credit of the Royal Italian Opera.

At the performance last Thursday, the first three acts of the four (twice too many) into which the work is divided at Covent Garden shewed signs of rehearsal. Even the last had not been altogether neglected. In the orchestra especially the improvement was marked. Not that anything very wonderful was accomplished in this department: the vigorous passages were handled in the usual timid, conventional way; and the statue music, still as impressive as it was before Wagner and Berlioz were born, was muddled through like a vote of thanks at the end of a very belated public meeting. But the overture was at least attentively played; and in some of the quieter and simpler numbers the exhalations of the magical atmosphere of the Mozartian orchestra were much less scanty and foggy than last year, when I could not, without risk of being laughed at, have assured a novice that in the subtleties of dramatic instrumentation Mozart was the greatest master of them all. The cast was neither a very bad nor a very good one. Its weakest point was the Leporello of Isnardon. Lacking the necessary weight in the middle of his voice, as well as the personal force demanded by the character, he was quite unable to lead the final section of the great sextet, *Mille torbidi pensieri*, which, thus deprived of its stage significance, became a rather senseless piece of "absolute music." Again, in *O statua gentilissima*, he hardly seized a point from beginning to end.

Now if an artist has neither voice enough nor musical perception enough to interpret forcibly and intelligently such an obvious and simple dramatic transition as that which follows the incident of the statue nodding acceptance of the invitation to supper, he is not fit to meddle with Mozart. Isnardon certainly makes a considerable show of acting throughout the opera; but as he is only trying to be facetious—abstractly facetious, if I may say so—without the slightest feeling for his part, the effect is irritating and irrelevant. Such pieces of business as his pointing the words, *Voi sapete quel che fa,* by nudging Elvira with his elbow at the end of *Madamina,* almost make one's blood boil. Poor old Sganarelle-Leporello, with all his failings, was no Yellowplush*: he would not have presumed upon a familiarity of that character with Donna Elvira, even if she had been a much meeker and less distinguished person than Molière made her. There is one man in Mr Harris's company whose clear artistic duty it is to play Leporello; and he, unfortunately, is an arrant *fainéant,* whose identity I charitably hide under the designation of Brother Edouard, which, I need hardly add, is not that under which he appears in the bills. In Leporello he would have one of the greatest parts ever written, exactly suited to his range, and full of points which his musical intelligence would seize instinctively without unaccustomed mental exertion. And now that I have begun sketching a new cast, I may as well complete it. *Dalla sua pace* is not an easy song to sing; but if Jean de Reszke were to do it justice, the memory thereof would abide when all his Gounod successes were lapsed and lost.

With Giulia Ravogli as Zerlina, and the rest of the parts allotted much as at present, a tremendous house would be drawn. Nevertheless the tremendous house

---

* Charles James Yellowplush: a character created by Thackeray pseudonymously, in The Yellowplush Correspondence, serialized in Fraser's Magazine (1837–8).

would be bored and kept late for its trains unless the representation were brought up to date by the following measures. Take a pot of paste, a scissors and some tissue paper, and start on the *recitativo secco* by entirely expunging the first two dialogues after the duel and before *Ah, chi mi dice mai*. Reduce all the rest to such sentences as are barely necessary to preserve the continuity of the action. Play the opera in two acts only. And use the time thus gained to restore not only the Don's song, *Metà di voi*, which Faure used to sing, but, above all, the last three movements of the second *finale*, thereby putting an end for ever to the sensational vulgarity of bringing down the curtain on the red fire and the ghost and the trapdoor. There are other suppressed pages of the score to be reconsidered—a capital song which gets Leporello off the stage after the sextet, a curiously old-fashioned tragic air, almost Handelian, for Elvira between *Là ci darem* and the quartet, and a comic duet for Zerlina and Leporello, one of the later Vienna interpolations, which, however, is a very dispensable piece of buffoonery.

To return to the actual Don Giovanni of Thursday last, I need say no more of Miss de Lussan, who does not grow more interesting as her voice loses freshness and sustaining power and her manner becomes perter and trickier, than that she is one of those Zerlinas who end *Batti, batti,* on the upper octave of the note written, as a sort of apology for having been unable to do anything else with the song. The effect of this suburban grace can be realized by anyone who will take the trouble to whistle Pop goes the Weasel with the last note displaced an octave.

I am sorry to add that alterations of Mozart's text were the order of the evening, every one of the singers lacking Mozart's exquisite sense of form and artistic dignity. Maurel, though he stopped short of reviving

[337]

the traditional atrocity of going up to F sharp in the serenade, did worse things by dragging an F natural into the end of *Finch' han del vino,* and two unpardonable G's into the *finale* of the first ballroom scene, just before the final *stretto,* thereby anticipating and destroying the climax *Odi il tuon* from the sopranos. Madame Tavary still clings to that desolating run up and down the scale with which she contrives to make the conclusion of *Non mi dir* ridiculous; and Montariol, unable to evade *Il mio tesoro* by omitting it like *Dalla sua pace,* did strange things with it in his desperation. His Ottavio was altogether a melancholy performance, as he was put out of countenance from the beginning by being clothed in a seedy misfit which made him look lamentably down on his luck. Mr Harris would not dream of allowing such a costume to be seen on his stage in a modern opera; and I must really urge upon him that there are limits to the application even of the principle that anything is good enough for Mozart.

Maurel's Don Giovanni, though immeasurably better than any we have seen of late years, is not to be compared to his Rigoletto, his Iago, or, in short, to any of his melodramatic parts. Don Juan may be as handsome, as irresistible, as adroit, as unscrupulous, as brave as you please; but the one thing that is not to be tolerated is that he should consciously parade these qualities as if they were elaborate accomplishments instead of his natural parts. And this is exactly where Maurel failed. He gave us a description of Don Juan rather than an impersonation of him. The confident smile, the heroic gesture, the splendid dress, even the intentionally seductive vocal inflexion which made such a success of *Là ci darem* in spite of Miss de Lussan's coquettish inanity, were all more or less artificial. A Don Juan who is continually aiming at being Don Juan may excite our admiration by the skill with which he does it; but he cannot convince us that he is the real man. I remember seeing Jean de Reszke play the part when he had less than a tenth of Maurel's present skill and experience; and yet I think Mozart would have found the younger man the more sympathetic interpreter.

It seems ungrateful to find fault with an artist who rescues a great *rôle* from the hands of such ignoble exponents as the common or Covent Garden Dons who swagger feebly through it like emancipated billiard-markers; but it would hardly be a compliment to Maurel to praise him for so cheap a superiority. And, indeed, there is no fault-finding in the matter. It is a question of temperament. When all is said, the fundamental impossibility remains that Maurel's artistic vein is not Mozartian. One or two points of detail may be mentioned. He was best in the love-making scenes and worst in those with Leporello, whom he treated with a familiarity which was rather that of Robert Macaire with Jacques Strop than of a gentleman with his valet. The scene of the exposure in the ballroom he played rather callously. Nothing in the score is clearer than that Don Juan is discomfited, confused, and at a loss from the moment in which they denounce him until, seeing that there is nothing for it but to fight his way out, he ceases to utter hasty exclamations of dismay, and recovers himself at the words *Ma non manca in me coraggio*. Maurel dehumanized and melodramatized the scene by missing this entirely, and maintaining a defiant and self-possessed bearing throughout.

And again, on the entry of the statue, which Don Juan, however stable his nerve may be imagined to have been, can hardly have witnessed without at least a dash of surprise and curiosity, Maurel behaved very much as if his uncle had dropped in unexpectedly in the middle of a bachelor's supper party. The result was that the scene went for nothing, though it is beyond all comparison the most wonderful of the wonders of dramatic music. But if the audience is ever to be cured of the habit of treating it as a sort of voluntary to play them out, it must be very carefully studied by the artist playing Don Juan, upon whose pantomime the whole action of the scene depends, since the statue can only stand with a stony air of weighing several tons, whilst the orchestra makes him as awful as the conductor will allow it. Since Maurel let this scene slip completely through his fingers, I do not see how he can be classed with the great Don Juans (if there ever were any great ones). The problem of how to receive a call from a public statue does not seem to have struck him as worth solving.

The Elvira (Madame Rolla), whose B flat at the end of her aria was perhaps the most excusable of all the inexcusable interpolations, was as good as gold, not indulging once in a scream, and relying altogether on pure vocal tone of remarkable softness. In *Mi tradi* she succeeded in being more pleasing than any Elvira I can remember except Di Murska, who understood the full value of the part and played it incomparably, like the great artist she was. Madame Rolla does not act with the force of Nilsson; and in the quartet she failed to bring off the effect at the end, where Elvira gets louder and angrier whilst the wretched Don gets more and more agitated by the dread of making a scene; but I think Maurel was a little unequal to the occasion here too. On the whole, Madame Rolla, whose voice reminds one somewhat of Marimon's, is a useful addition to the company. Mr Harris had better now turn his attention to achieving a really serious performance of Le Nozze di Figaro.

THE LAST OF THE GREAT TENORS

The Sunday World, 17 May 1891 ; signed "Corno di Bassetto"

[U] Sims Reeves bade the public farewell last Monday at the Albert Hall. We thus lose the greatest tenor in England—perhaps the greatest tenor in the world. The rank and file of the musical public feel this to be so; those critics who understand their business know it to be so, and can tell you exactly the points in which his superiority lies; the amateurs and the critics who do not understand their business deny it altogether, and declare that to drag this voiceless old man, who has gone up and down the country for the last half-century maundering through his eternal Come into the Garden, Maud, and Tom Bowling, into comparison with Edward Lloyd or Jean de Reszke is only to make him still more ridiculous than he has already made himself. At seventy, nevertheless, the "voiceless old man" first sings three songs so that every member of a multitude of people in the immense Albert Hall can hear each note perfectly, and then, without the slightest apparent effort, makes a speech which, for clear and telling delivery, surpassed that made immediately before by so eminent an expert as Mr Henry Irving. The notion that Sims Reeves has no voice is founded, paradoxically as it may sound, on the fact that, in a sense, he has nothing else. All the noisiness, the stridency, the "grit," which give ordinary voices their stimulating, rousing, self-assertive effect, and which are therefore pleasant to people who enjoy singing much as a horse enjoys the "Gee-up" of its driver, but which coarsen and debase the voice's tones, and destroy its capacity for depth, intimacy, and purity of expression, by forcing the singer to keep a muscular grip on it: all these Sims Reeves renounced and abjured. He resolutely gave up all the applause, all the appearance of "power" that a free abuse of his ordinary shouting capacity would have brought him; and in the end he succeeded in cultivating himself so perfectly as a singer, that every note consisted wholly of unadulterated vocal tone of the most beautiful and expressive quality, produced without the least violence, and so completely under his control that he could not only pitch it to a hair's breath, but make it respond instantly to every inflexion suggested by the sentiment of the song, almost as if the voice had a separate sympathetic instinct of its own. He was artist enough to know that this was the only "power" worth working for; and his reward was he was able to stand on the same platform with very popular tenors, and when they had sung so that you could hear the tune they were singing and the words they were repeating in the loudest and most unmistakable fashion, he would come and tell his song in a wonderfully beautiful way quite quietly into your ear, no matter how large the hall was, making every note, high or low, give you the greatest pleasure to hear, and moving you with every word. When the applause broke out at the end, you were not goaded into joining by any particular note or trick; even when he introduced special effects, such as the long throbbing echo of a cheer in his last repetition of the refrain of The Bay of Biscay (an effect, by the bye, musically identical with one employed by Wagner in that great orchestral sea-picture, the overture to The Flying Dutchman), you were so preoccupied with each previous line as it came that you never thought of this effect beforehand, and you would have encored the song all the same if he had omitted it.

Nothing like this can be claimed for any other tenor before the public. Singers who can momentarily excite and startle are to be found everywhere; but Sims Reeves could, and can, move and stir you continuously. The value he could give to every note enabled him to pack a song so completely with as much feeling as it could possibly hold, that to hear him sing one of Handel's finer songs, or such an air as Watchman, will the night soon pass? in Mendelssohn's Lobgesang, was a memorable experience, after which the performances of the other tenors, however agreeable, sounded empty and monotonous. If Jean de Reszke be judged by one of his best pieces of work—say Lohengrin's declaration of his name and mission—his enchanting natural grace and the finer quality of his voice seem at first to enable him to defy comparison; but one has only to think of Sims Reeves to feel that de Reszke's treatment, after all, is much less exhaustive, and leaves a far fainter impression of the meaning and emotional content of the music than Sims Reeves's would be.

No artist gets to the very heart of his profession, as Sims Reeves has done, without considerable sacrifices. He necessarily made himself so sensitive to the slightest variation in the physical condition of his voice that he could not bring himself to sing unless that condition was perfectly satisfactory, and he himself in the vein to make the most of it. As he could not arrange beforehand for the occurrence of this happy state of things, he frequently refused at the last moment to keep his engagements. Announcements of his appearance were always received with doubt, and at certain periods, when the percentage of disappointments had been unusually high, they met with incredulity. When he did sing, he very properly refused *encores*, thereby becoming engaged in contests of obstinacy with his audiences, who occasionally shewed as much determination to prevent anyone else from singing if he would not, as he shewed to give them no more than was bargained for in the program. Again, his desire to spare his voice from any strain that was not artistically necessary, and his independence of mere brilliant effects with high notes, induced him to declare war on the monstrously high pitch in use in this country. In this he was not so successful as Nilsson and Patti were subsequently at the opera houses. At the Handel Festivals an alteration in the pitch of the great organ would have cost a large sum, a fact which illustrates the difficulty of remedying an abuse in which capital has been invested. So he gave up singing at the Festivals, and his appearances on the concert platform were thenceforth distinguished by the presence of a second pianoforte, tuned to French pitch, used only to accompany himself and those of his colleagues, who, being able to do something more for the public than split its ears, were glad to follow his example.

Considering how we have all been spoiled in the matter of *encores,* how indifferent our ignorance leaves us to the merits of the question of pitch, how incapable most of us are of appreciating the differences made to a fine artist by an indisposition so slight that a business man would not be even conscious of it, the accusations of caprice and unreasonableness made against Sims Reeves are less to be wondered at than the fact that his popularity was never shaken by them. Only by consummated art could his stale *repertoire* of Handel, Dibdin and Braham, Schubert, Balfe and Donizetti, with Mendelssohn, Blumenthal and Gounod for extreme moderns, be divested of the ancient and fishlike flavor which it must have to our young people who are busy with Wagner and Ibsen. The occasional addition of a flagrant "royalty song" of the most old-fashioned design, to the old stock, can hardly be regarded as a concession to the spirit of the age. It was by beauty of execution alone that Sims Reeves maintained his supremacy, but it was execution in so comprehensive a sense and beauty of such a high order that only the most remarkable force of character and depth of artistic conviction could have nerved him to attain them. He now proposes to devote himself to teaching, and there can be no doubt that his qualifications for such work are extraordinary; but it is equally certain that his private lessons can never carry as much instruction to the public and the critics as the example afforded them by the unique work he has done during the last half century. [U]

SIMS REEVES, GENT.
The World, 20 May 1891

Every schoolboy, as Mr Churton Collins* would say, remembers Macaulay's story of how Voltaire received Congreve's snobbish application to be regarded as a gentleman, and not as a writer for the theatre. "If you were merely a gentleman" said Voltaire "I should not have bothered to come and see you." Yet here is Mr Walter Pollock†, writing one of those curious valentines which are recited at benefits and on other effusive occasions, complimenting Sims Reeves on being a gentleman. There are thousands of gentlemen in England, and there is only one Sims Reeves. And yet Sims Reeves is told to his face that he is a gentleman. Only one worse outrage could have been perpetrated; and that was to have called him a real gentleman, or person who gives a tip of a sovereign when a common

* A literary critic, who had just written A Study of English Literature (1891).

† Editor of the Saturday Review, until succeeded by Frank Harris in 1894.

[345]

gentleman only gives five shillings. My own opinion is that Sims Reeves is no more a gentleman than I am; for I have seen him appear at an afternoon concert in a black velvet coat, lavender trousers, a canary-colored tie, and primrose gloves—an exceptional and therefore essentially ungentlemanly costume. And no gentleman that I have ever met would be capable of singing as Sims Reeves sings. However, Mr Pollock no doubt meant well. Unable, as a merely literary man, to appreciate his hero's singing, he paid him a conventional compliment to shew his general goodwill, and threw in a literary allusion to Edgar and Captain Macheath* by way of local color.

Whether the great farewell of Monday week will prove a last farewell is a point on which I prefer not to hazard an opinion. Certain it is that, though Sims Reeves at seventy has lost his powers of endurance so far that he cannot now count upon getting safely through a trying song like Blumenthal's Message, yet in such Handelian airs as Total Eclipse, in which the instrumental interludes give plenty of time for rest after each strain, he can still leave the next best tenor in England an immeasurable distance behind. Indeed, he does this even in the songs to which he is no longer fully equal; and the general recognition of his pre-eminence is a powerful support to the critic whose counsels of perfection are cavilled at as righteous overmuch.

For if I were to advise a young man to do what Sims Reeves has done I should apparently be advising him to ruin himself. Rejecting all the coarser, baser, more exciting elements in popular singing for the sake of a pure artistic integrity which only a few appreciate fully, and which many rebel against and scoff at as mere

* Characters in Shakespear's King Lear and John Gay's The Beggar's Opera.

[346]

feebleness and affectation; throwing not only your concert engagements, but coveted positions at the opera and the Handel Festivals to the winds whenever their conditions prevent you from doing your very best; allowing rivals to pass you and seize your golden opportunities as if you had eternity at your disposal: these would seem to be infallible methods of securing discredit, failure, and bankruptcy. Fortunately there is Sims Reeves to prove that they land an artist at the head of his profession. Doubtless they require enormous artistic conviction, courage, and selfrespect; but they have left at least one man better off than the methods of vulgar ambition have left any of his rivals.

The concert came off very happily in every respect. Some of us may have begun by feeling a little anxious as to how much was left of Christine Nilsson; but we were soon relieved on that score. Her figure is ampler than of yore; and her eyes are aided by glasses fixed to the end of an exasperating tortoiseshell pole. The features, too, are perhaps more matronly by a line or so than they were twenty years ago; and it cannot reasonably be asserted that her extreme upper notes are as fresh and free as those, for example, of Miss Eames. But Nilsson is Nilsson still, for better for worse. I do not say that she is not a little more dignified than in the old days, when no law, human or divine, restrained her from doing anything that she wished to do, just as the whim took her. Mine eyes have seen her, as Leonora in Il Trovatore, after listening with a critical air to *Ah si, ben mio* sung by a tenor who must have been a veteran when she was in her cradle, slap the patriarch on the back with a hearty bravo at the end.

At the Albert Hall she refrained from slapping Sims Reeves on the back; and her curtsies on entering were of a splendid, courtly, regal kind; but before she had got through ten bars of the Jewel Song she was gesticulating nearly as vigorously as ever she did on the stage; and when *encore* followed *encore,* she pulled off her gloves and sat down at the pianoforte in her old way to give us that same old Swedish ballad of which no critic knows the name, and every critic of a certain age knows the tune. And when that was encored too, she sang a ditty in which she whooped, and laughed, and screamed like any *gamin.* She had previously re-established her old right to do as she pleased by her singing of The Erl King; and oh! the relief of hearing that song sung again by one whose sense of it was as perfect musically as dramatically. If Paderewski and Stavenhagen, who are fond of putting Liszt's transcription on the piano and pounding the life out of it, would only listen to her once as she winds her way into every turn of the melody with exactly the right dramatic inflexion, how much guilt might they not escape in the future? Unfortunately it is only mere composers, like Mozart or Wagner, who are not ashamed to learn from women and singers; no great pianist could so compromise himself.

When it was clear that Nilsson's reappearance was a huge success, curiosity shifted to Irving's chance of making himself heard in that immense amphitheatre, crowded from floor to ceiling. He settled the question by proving, in his first half-dozen words, that he was no less a master of fine vocal tone than any of the singers who preceded him; and the speech was nearly as well heard as the songs. Still, highly cultivated as Irving's voice is, the normal pitch at which he has accustomed himself to speak is artificially low for him, and his method of production is a little too "throaty." It was necessary to listen attentively in his case, wheras when Sims Reeves himself made a speech later in the evening, he was, very unexpectedly, heard with quite startling ease and distinctness. It was a final and remarkable triumph of perfect vocal art. On the rest of the program it is not necessary to enlarge. Mr Manns conducted the band: Arditi, Kuhe, and Ganz were also down as "conductors" in the Miscellaneous Concert sense, and were assisted in that ornamental function by a Mr Maunder, who accompanied Sims Reeves very well.

Janotha played Mendelssohn's G minor concerto at a stupendous pace, but with all her characteristic reserve of sentiment. When I first heard Janotha play I was enchanted: here, I thought, was a truly noble and delicate talent: the best part of Madame Schumann would live again in this pupil of hers. But somehow it was not to be. She was proud, exacting, perhaps shy: at any rate, when her playing lost its freshness it did not gain the warmth and sympathy of the mature artist. She never would give herself away to the public, though she would play always with the utmost skill and refinement. Now the public yearns for more generous treatment; and feels that though Janotha has preserved her dignity and her individuality, she has turned out a somewhat stonyhearted daughter of Music. It is not to Art and to the people that she devotes herself so scrupulously every time she sits down to play; and on behalf of Art and the people, I feel justly jealous.

One word more on this farewell program. Why does Madame Antoinette Sterling play so persistently on the fourth string, so to speak? Nobody could sing We're a' noddin' better than she if she chose; but she clings to her pathetic stop so fondly that she will not give the right accent of joy, relief, and half-hysterical laughter to the refrain. The result is that before the third verse is reached the song has become monotonous and maundering; and I, for one, become rather impatient of hearing any more of it.

Ysaÿe's recital last week was a greater success than his orchestral concert. He was much more in the vein, and shewed unexpected power and insight as an interpreter of chamber music. His treatment of the Beethoven concerto on the previous occasion had left an impression that in this department of his art he was inferior to Joachim; but after his masterly reading of the sonatas by Raff and Beethoven at the recital—not to mention the Bach pieces—there can no longer be any doubt that the leadership of the quartet at the Popular Concerts will be safe in his hands for another generation. He played one Bach prelude decidedly too fast; and he threw a bunch of thistles to the donkeys at the end of the recital in the shape of an atrocious show piece of his own composition; but for the rest he played magnificently in every respect; and one could only wonder that the reputation of such a genius should spread so slowly as to leave the seats as loosely packed as they were.

After Ysaÿe, we all hurried across the street to Prince's Hall to hear a concert given by the Bach Choir at the eccentric hour of half-past five. Unaccompanied part singing was the staple of the entertainment; and I can frankly and unreservedly say that I would not desire to hear a more abominable noise than was offered to us under pretext of Bach's *Singet dem Herrn** and some motets by Brahms. I will not deny that there was a sort of broken thread of vocal tone running through the sound fabric; but for the most part it was a horrible tissue of puffing and blowing and wheezing and groaning and buzzing and hissing and gargling and shrieking and spluttering and grunting and generally making every sort of noise that is incidental to bad singing, severe exertion, and mortal fear of losing one's place. It was really worse than the influenza. Most fortunately there were some pieces which the choir knew well and took quietly, notably a motet by Palestrina—whose music seems to me as fresh and beautiful today as it can ever

---

* Motet for double choir, S.225.

have been—and some old English madrigals. These were done as well as could be expected from a choir with an average age of at least fiftyfive. There certainly used to be no such lack of young people in it. Can it be that there are members who are such cowardly deserters in the hour of need, as to object to appear on the platform at a public concert? If so, they should at once be threatened with ignominious expulsion. If not, then the sooner Mr Stanford begins to recruit vigorously for young blood the better. It is reassuring to see that the great Mass in B minor is to be performed again next winter.

Ysaÿe seems to have stimulated a number of gentlemen who can fiddle a bit to try their luck at concert giving. I have attended two orchestral concerts given by Herr Waldemar Meyer, who is quite the most easygoing *virtuoso* I can remember. He plays anything you please— Brahms, Bach, Beethoven, Mendelssohn—with apparent facility and satisfaction. Such feats are not commonplace; but Herr Meyer contrives to make them appear so. Mr Haddock, an ambitious orchestral player from Leeds, as I understand, has also considerable powers of manipulating his instrument; but I cannot say that I caught anything in his conception and quality of execution sufficiently exceptional to warrant me, as yet, in admitting his claim to the same eminence as a soloist which he is entitled to in the orchestra. Finally, I have heard Max Reichel, who has the good fortune to be supported by a very clever and original singer, Madame Swiatlowsky, a sort of Russian Antoinette Sterling, though with a certain variety and fire peculiar to herself, and with some charming *virtuoso* tricks of *mezza voce*, &c.

The Opera has been mercifully repeating itself. Montariol has retired from the *rôle* of Ottavio in Don Giovanni, his place being taken by the useful Ravelli, who must feel some mild exultation in the inability of the Royal Italian Opera to get on without him.

GARRICK TO THE LIFE

The World, 27 May 1891

Last week will stand as one of the most memorable under Mr Harris's management. On Tuesday, Manon, or The Triumph of Van Dyck; on Wednesday, The Sleeper Awakened, or Jean de Reszke on his Mettle; and on Thursday, The Voice of the Sluggard, with Brother Edouard as Leporello. And now, who was it that named Van Dyck as the man for Covent Garden at a time when the experimental evenings at that house were reserved for Signor Rawner *ec hoc genus omne*? Who prophesied the effect on Brother Jean, and cast Brother Edouard for Leporello? Well, no matter who; but if his counsels are not henceforth treated with respect, there is no such thing as gratitude in the world.

I cannot remember a more complete and unqualified operatic success than that of Van Dyck as Des Grieux. To begin with, the man himself is irresistible. If any lady has been disqualified by her sex from fully appreciating the charm of Ada Rehan's smile, let her go and see it on Van Dyck's virile face. If any dramatic critic has failed to imagine how a man with Garrick's figure could be a model of active dignity, let him hasten to Covent Garden; for Van Dyck is Garrick to the life. Those who were at Bayreuth when he played Parsifal will need no description of the charm of his youth and strength, his rapid, impulsive, spontaneous movements, his enormous unaffectedness and *bonhomie*, and withal his perfectly serious and dignified comprehension of his position as an artist.

On Tuesday the house found out his merits with surprising quickness. There was a small *claque*; but as it had not been retained for him, his entry in the first act was received with dead silence. Before five minutes had passed, the admirable discipline which usually prevails in the gallery was disturbed by ebullitions of applause. At the end of the act Van Dyck was in the position of a lyric Cæsar, having come, and sung, and conquered. I own that I waited for the second act with some apprehension as to the effect of that charming air which Des Grieux sings to Manon at the dinner table, when, regardless of the toothsome appearance of a Vienna roll four feet long, they literally dine off love. It seemed only too likely that a Belgian tenor would resort to the conventional artificial French *mezza voce*, and thus spoil the pathos of the air for English ears. I am happy to say that I reckoned without Van Dyck's genius. Nothing could be more unstudiedly original and natural in conception, more skilful and artistic in execution, than his performance of this number, which brought down the house as domestically as if it had been Sally in our Alley sung by Mr Edward Lloyd at a ballad concert. As to the *scena* in the second part of the third act, with the explosion of ringing high notes at the end, its success was a foregone conclusion.

But far more conclusive than any isolated achievements of this kind were the sustained excellence of the impersonation as a whole, the bright intelligence, the variety, the fine musical sensibility, the invigorating and thoroughly male character of even the tenderest and most playful episodes of his infatuation for Manon, and the utter absence of that detestable blight of bravado and flunkey-like attitudinizing which has spread to Covent Garden from the Paris Grand Opéra. To have such an artist in London without hearing him in Siegfried, which he was surely born to play, is not to be suffered without protest.

[353]

The present project of allowing him to confine himself to Manon and Faust is a wanton belittlement of an opportunity which is all too narrow at best.

I have said that there was a small *claque* in the house; and this reminds me of Miss Sybil Saunderson, who received of flowers six baskets or thereabouts. There can be no objection to Mr Harris varying the scheme of grand opera at his theatre by engaging Miss Saunderson; but why not Chaumont* at once? Long ago I suggested that an experiment in this direction might be tried by engaging Coquelin for Leporello; and not long since, Mr Irving, in a speech before the curtain, hinted pretty plainly that he would not be indisposed to consider an offer for the part of Mephistopheles at Covent Garden if business became unprofitable at the Lyceum. They do this sort of thing systematically in Denmark with satisfactory artistic results. Why not here? Miss Saunderson does not sing so well as Coquelin—very few people do—but she could hold her own with Mr Irving, having a pretty talent for imitating French singing of the Opéra Comique *genre*.

Of the other parts little need be said. The quartet in the second act will go better another time if MM. Ceste and Dufriche will kindly recollect that in singing concerted music it is necessary to listen sympathetically to the singers with whose notes their own are intended to form chords. Their present plan of standing at opposite corners of the stage and—I do not like to call it howling; and I positively refuse to call it singing—say, delivering their parts in a spirit of unbridled competition, has the effect of extinguishing Miss Saunderson, of making it impossible for Van Dyck to save the

* Céline Chaumont, French actress, was a noted exponent of the grand style of acting, celebrated for what William Archer called her "consummate diction".

situation, of spoiling the quartet, and consequently of making themselves highly obnoxious to the public. Dufriche seemed to enjoy his part, playing it not badly, if somewhat roughly; and Isnardon was good as Des Grieux senior. The opera fell quite flat when Van Dyck was off the stage. It is clever, lively, ingenious, and strongly supported by its relationship to one of the most charming stories ever written (I had almost as soon omit The Vicar of Wakefield or The Pilgrim's Progress from my bookshelf as Manon Lescaut); but it made less effect as a whole than at Drury Lane with Carl Rosa. It is too flimsy and too local in its style to make a permanent place for itself on the English stage.

Les Huguenots on the following night drew an immense house, the cast being an exceptionally attractive one. As to Jean de Reszke, he was hardly recognizable. Even the invariable golden beard was gone, replaced by a much sterner and darker arrangement. Had Van Dyck been dressed at the wing, ready to go on and take his place at the slightest sign of indifference, he could not have worked harder at his part. The very attitudes of fifteen years ago came back to him: there was no more irresolute mooning about the stage and thinking better of each languid impulse to do something: he acted with passion and sang with his utmost eloquence and tenderness. Any great brilliancy of vocal effect was put out of the question by the audacious transpositions to which he resorted in order to bring the highest notes of the part within his range; but he was all the better able to handle his music sympathetically, the chief sufferers from the transpositions being the unfortunate bassos, who, in the *stretto* of the duel septet, were growling in their boots in the most uncomfortable way. On the whole, Brother Jean, though Van Dyck has torn away the enchanted veil from his lack of solidity and variety, rallied magnificently against

his terrible rival: the gallery was cheering him enthusiastically as I left the theatre.

Brother Edouard, in a faultless Lincoln & Bennett
hat, distinguished himself, as usual, in the duet with
Valentine, but was otherwise a mere makeshift in the
absence of a true *basso profundo*, finishing his chorale by
singing the *canto fermo* in unison with the trumpet part,
instead of going down into the depths plumbed by
Meyerbeer. The general effect of his voice in Marcel's
music is like that of a bass clarinet part played on a
saxhorn, the characteristic tone-color aimed at being
quite misrepresented. San Bris, and not Marcel, is
Brother Edouard's affair in Les Huguenots. Nevers was
easy work for Maurel, who forced the management to
make a first step in the long-called-for reconsideration
of the mutilations of the score, by restoring the colloquy
with the servant and the *bravura* which follow the Piff-
Paff song. The present Covent Garden version of the
opera is the result of a music butchery perpetrated half
a century ago in order to bring the performance within
reasonable limits of time. In accordance with the taste
of that Rossinian period, the whistlable tunes were
retained, and the dramatic music sacrificed.

Now that the public takes a lively interest in
picturesque descriptive music, and that the whistlable
tunes have in some instances survived their popularity,
the score needs to be recut, so as to bring the acting
version up to date, and to take full advantage of the time
that was gained some years ago when the rags and tatters
of the fifth act were given up as a bad job. The first thing
to do is to gain more time by making further cuts—to
give up the awkward and absurd repetitions of the Piff-
Paff and of the Rataplan, and to do away with the silly
ballet of bathers in the second act, and indeed (saving
your presence, divine Giulia) with that very superfluous
afterthought, the page's No, no, no, no, no, no. Then

the restoration just effected by Maurel in the first scene could be followed by that of the concerted piece *L'Avventura è Stravagante*, and of the really brutal cut of the unaccompanied episode in the scene of the oath-taking before the Queen, whilst the impetuous *finale* could be given in its entirety. In the Pré-aux-Clercs scene, the exciting climax to the duel, in which Maurevert brings a troop of Catholics to the aid of San Bris, and Marcel knocks at the door of the inn and summons the Huguenot soldiers to the rescue with his Lutheran chorale—the omission of all which at present makes the upshot of the duel septet lame and ridiculous—could easily be added. The opera would not then take longer to play than at present; and it would be greatly freshened and strengthened.

To return to Wednesday night, Albani is the only Valentine of whom it can be said that she does not miss a point in the part. If her intonation had been true throughout, which it hardly was, her praise would be unqualified. Mravina, the new Russian soprano, has a voice of such exceptional range and flexibility that she was able to execute all the shakes and *roulades* of Marguerite with a facility which I do not take to be altogether the result of hard work, because there were suspicious lapses into a comparatively familiar and commonplace manner between whiles. However, as her natural musical gifts are great, and she, moreover, an intelligent and sympathetic person, she is unquestionably a happy acquisition of Mr Harris's. She has, by the bye, that very rare accomplishment, a true shake. The superficiality of Giulia Ravogli's vocal training is brought out rather glaringly by the music of Urbano; but her acting is irresistible, aided as it is by that elation which every energetic woman feels when relieved for a moment from the fetters of feminine costume. Lassalle was the San Bris; but the part is not one in which he distinguishes himself specially: his opportunity did not come until Saturday, when he was better than ever as Hans Sachs in Die Meistersinger, in which Albani also was excellent, and Jean de Reszke was wide awake and in earnest for the first time as Walther von Stolzing—the performance, on the whole, being the most deeply enjoyable of the season.

Several other matters must stand over for another week, notably Karl Armbruster's concert in commemoration of Wagner's birthday, which took place at Lord Dysart's (Ham House, close to the site proposed by me for the English Wagner Theatre).*

WAGNER'S BIRTHDAY
The World, 3 June 1891

The Richter concerts opened on Monday week with a program the like of which for thrilling novelty has not been heard in London for a long time. The seventh symphony, the Parsifal and Meistersinger preludes, the Ride of the Valkyries: these, with a suite by Bach, were the pledges of the progressive and enterprising spirit that chafes in its protuberant prison house beneath the great conductor's waistcoat. Seriously—for the finer shades of musical humor are hardly safe with the English public—Richter has no right to stuff a program with the most hackneyed items in his repertory in order to save the trouble of rehearsing. I do not, of course, mean to

---

* William Tollemache, 9th Earl of Dysart, at whose home in Petersham, Surrey, the Wagner commemorative concert was held, was a devoted adherent of the Wagnerian cult. He had been a patron and supporter of the Richter concerts from their inception.

say that the seventh symphony and the rest should be discarded because they have been performed several times already. But I do mean most emphatically that their excution should be elaborated and perfected every time the public is asked to put its hand in its pocket afresh to hear them. Nothing can be artistically meaner than to trade on the ignorance of those who think that the name of Richter is a guarantee for unimprovable perfection. As a matter of fact, the orchestra is by no means what it ought to be; and it has been getting worse instead of better for some years past.

Let me take an instance or two—always worth a ton of general statement. Every Bayreuth pilgrim is by this time familiar with that wonderful throbbing, fluttering, winnowing cloud of sound which the violins make as the Grail descends in Parsifal. That is to say, the violins ought to make it; but without the most patient and critical preparation they make nothing but a muddle in which the scoffer will justly refuse to recognize anything but a confusion of groups of three notes with groups of four. Now, as prices are high at Richter's concerts, and there is no reason whatever why cheap work should be tolerated there, we are, I consider, entitled to call upon his band either to master this effect or let Parsifal alone. On Monday week they did neither; and the enthusiasm created by the performance of the prelude was due entirely to the extraordinary beauty of that large portion of the work which presents no special difficulties of execution. Why it was immediately followed by the Walkürenritt is more than I can explain. Whether Richter, in a frenzy of contempt for the London musical public, resolved to shew that it had no sense of artistic congruity to be shocked, or whether he took just the opposite view, and thought he would indulge himself with a Mephisphelean joke at its expense, is more than I can guess; but certain it is that the last divine strains of Parsifal were still in our ears when the wild gallop of the Valkyries was upon us with a heathenish riot. And I can unreservedly assure Richter that a more villainous performance of it never was heard before in St James's Hall. To offer us such an orgy of scraping, screeching, banging, and barking as a tone-picture of the daughters of Wotan was an outrage to Wagner. Surely Richter does not conceive Ortlinde, Waltraute, and the rest of them as a parcel of screaming, delirious viragos, without grace, strength, majesty, or regard for their steeds. For that is the sort of Valkyrie Ride suggested to me by fiddles rasped as if they were whirling grindstones, and trombones overblown until they sound like cracked cornets. Such treatment degrades Wagner to the level of Wiertz, and makes novices guess that Walkürenritt must be German for "cruelty to animals," which the Meister abhorred with Shelleyan intensity.

I have often enough done justice to Richter's genius as an interpreter both of tone-poetry and of absolute music to claim exemption from all suspicion of ill will towards himself or his school; and I suffer too often from the vapidity of orchestras which, for all their polish, fail miserably whenever sustained tone is needed, to under-value the example set by the Richter band with its magnificent *sostenuto*. But when it comes to depending on the reputation of the band and the conductor to dispense with careful preparation, and to snatch popular victories with pieces like the Walkürenritt by dint of what I can only describe as instrumental ruffianism, then it is time for every critic whose former praise meant anything but acquiescence in the fashion of admiring Richter, to warn him that unless he promptly takes steps to bring the standard of quality of execution in his orchestra up to that set by the Crystal Palace orchestra, and the standard of exhaustive preparation up to that set by the wonderful performances of Berlioz's works achieved here last winter by the Manchester band, he will lose his old pre-eminence in the estimation of all those who really know the difference between thorough work and scamped work in performing orchestral music of the highest class.

The Wagner birthday concert at Ham House was in many respects a huge improvement on Bayreuth. Twickenham Ferry is an excellent substitute for the Channel or the German Ocean; and the reduction of my traveling expenses from £7 or £8 to 1s. 5½d., and of the time wasted in locomotion from forty hours to one, was highly acceptable. As to comparisons between the country about Richmond and the Fichtelgebirge, or Richmond Park and the Hofgarten, or the view from Richmond Hill and that from the Hohe Warte, it would be ungenerous to Germany to press them. On the other hand, I freely admit that not even the expedient of sending the cornet player out into the garden before the second part of the concert, to blow the sword motive from The Niblung's Ring, quite made up for the absence of the Wagner Theatre and Parsifal. Lord Dysart did what a man could: he annihilated the very memory of the Theatre Restaurant by a marquee in which I took my sober Wagnerian meal of brown bread and lemonade next to disciples who were trying reckless experiments with *sauerkraut* and rum custard; and he received us in a house and grounds almost as fit for the purpose of the afternoon as our own place at Hampton Court. Still, a house is a house, and a theatre is a theatre, and I strongly urge Lord Dysart to secede from the useless London branch of the German Wagner Society, and form a really important English society with the object of building a Wagner theatre within ten minutes' walk of his own door.

The concert was not so good as it might have been had the singers been able or willing to avail themselves to the fullest extent of the very favorable conditions for delicate and expressive vocal art presented by a room in which the weakest singer could have been heard without the slightest effort. Unfortunately, most of them seemed rather bent on making a noise; and as the band was equally anxious to avoid doing so, the result was that the orchestral part of the concert was better than the vocal part. Under these circumstances I could not help thinking it rather cool of Mr Henschel to publicly rebuke a momentary roughness in the orchestra by making them recommence the prelude to Wolfram's *Blick' ich umher*, and then to sing it in the strident and savagely self-assertive accents of Klingsor, instead of in the elevated and spiritual style of the poet Wolfram. If I had been that orchestra, I should have stopped Mr Henschel and made *him* begin again. Maurel, a southern Frenchman who puts forward no claim to any special sympathy with Wagner, would never have inflicted such a misreading on us.

If Mr Henschel had not atoned somewhat by a comparatively reasonable performance of *Wahn, wahn*, it would be impossible to pay him the smallest compliment on his share in the afternoon's proceedings. The only excuse for him is that he is a German—I have long since come to the conclusion that the German nation labors under a congenital incapacity to understand the musical side of the universal Wagner. Even Miss Pauline Cramer, whose sympathy with his sentiment makes her a genuine enthusiast, and often leads her to find the right musical expression unconsciously, has failed to see that unless a singer patiently builds up for herself an eloquent, rich, easy middle to her voice, and can attack her notes in all sorts of ways, quietly or vigorously as the case may demand, half the music of a Wagner part will be lost, and the other half will be apt to produce the general effect of a series of screams. Miss Cramer is so much in earnest, and has such excellent natural gifts—especially a voice which has all the brightness which German voices so commonly lack—that there is no reason why she should not treble her present resources as a lyric and dramatic artist. Her singing of the final scene from the Götterdämmerung was by no means bad; but it was deficient in variety, and cost her more effort than it need have done.

The only orchestral piece performed was the Siegfried Idyll, which has seldom been heard under more suitable conditions (Wagner wrote it, not for public performance, but to serenade his wife with). It went very well, except for a few moments in the middle section, when Mr Armbruster, who has the faults as well as the qualities of an intellect of the most restless and discursive kind, hurried along with mechanical regularity whilst he thought out some remote scientific question, which fortunately did not occupy him very long. On the whole, it was a pleasant half-holiday; and if Lord Dysart would like to give another concert on my birthday, which is due in a month or two, I shall not discourage the project.

Van Dyck was unlucky enough to have a baddish cold on Saturday when he appeared as Faust. He had to take the highest notes in the second and third acts in a cautious falsetto, and to work more or less uphill all the evening; but he, nevertheless, was by far the best Faust I have ever seen, making him the central figure in the opera, instead of the sentimental walking gentleman to whom we are accustomed. Little as there is in the part as treated by Gounod, it is surprising to find how far that little can be made to go by an artist of genuine power and abundant vitality. Van Dyck quite startled the house with the reality and intensity of his appeal for renewed youth in the first scene—a point at which no tenor has ever before carried the slightest conviction to me. From this to the final *trio*, to which he gave a tremendous impetus, the interest of his impersonation never flagged. Edouard de Reszke, who has met his match at last in the duet at the end of the first act, played Mephistopheles with fratricidal relish and vigor. In the middle of the garden scene he was so tickled by a monstrous sunflower which Mr Harris had placed among the extremely miscellaneous *flora* in Margaret's flower bed, that he very nearly accomplished the feat known as "queering the pitch" of the quartet by plucking the giant vegetable and replanting it in the dress of Madame Bauermeister, before whose diminutive figure it flourished like an umbrella during the rest of the scene. It is to be hoped that this jape will not become traditional. Lassalle was announced to play Valentin; but it soon appeared that he only wished to prevent anyone else from playing it, as he omitted *Dio possente*, and would not even pretend to act in the death scene, which accordingly fell flat. A Mlle Passama, who appeared as Siebel, was almost as feminine and tearfully tragic in the part as Mlle Guercia. Miss Eames, as Margaret, improved on her old success. The opera is to be repeated tonight (Wednesday) with a newcomer, Plançon, as Mephistopheles.

Some incredibly stupid and unmusical people are setting a fashion of treating the beginning of the great *trio* in the prison scene as a signal to troop out of the house. I suggest to Mr Harris that, though the law on the subject is not defined, it might be worth while to take their names and summon them for "brawling." Even if the interpretation could not be sustained, the shock would probably bring them to their senses.

MUSICAL HERO WORSHIP

The World, 10 June 1891

With Ysaÿe, Sarasate, and Paderewski all at work together among us, the atmosphere of musical hero worship becomes overwhelming. Yet the audiences have not been so large this year as last. In Ysaÿe's case, this is perhaps due to the fact that the public does not yet realize that he is one of the greatest violinists in the world, since it depends so largely for its information upon that inoffensive, considerate, say-nothing-to-nobody sort of criticism which offers Ysaÿe and Sarasate exactly the same polite congratulations which it offered the day before to Herr Waldemar Meyer. Ysaÿe at his second recital came triumphantly through the highest test a violinist can face—a Mozart sonata. He also brought forward a sonata by Gabriel Fauré, the *maître de chapelle* of the Madeleine; but this, however it might have sounded before Mozart, made no effect after.

Sarasate came on the following Saturday, not so fresh as during his last visit. He is never as good in the summer as after the autumn, when he has just had a rest. After Ysaÿe the thinness of his tone and his exclusive attention to the absolutely musical side of his classical repertory, which he carries to the extremity of appearing to be perfectly indifferent whether he is playing Mackenzie or Beethoven, make themselves felt more strongly than on former occasions when he was not brought into immediate comparison with his great rival; but, on the other hand, his extraordinary smoothness and certainty of execution, and the fine quietude with which he performs miraculous technical feats, are no less thrown into high relief. At his recital on Wednesday last, in a *cadenza* which formed part of an *encore* piece, he, without turning a hair, did some things—notably a scale passage against a shake sustained above, and a chromatic run in sixths—with a speed, a delicacy of touch, and an exquisite precision of intonation that would have astonished Tartini's devil.

Mr Cusins gave his annual concert on Monday week; and an excellent concert it was of its kind, with the Ravoglis, Maurel, and Sauret lending a hand. I mention it just in this place because there is a point—a very delicate point—which must be put frankly to Sarasate and Mr Cusins. Mr Cusins, as all the world knows, conducts at Sarasate's orchestral concerts. I venture to ask the twain, are they quite the men for oneanother in this relationship? Sarasate, whatever his failings may be, is an extraordinarily good violinist. Mr Cusins, with a host of excellent qualities, is an extraordinarily bad conductor. The result is that Mr Cusins spoils Sarasate's concerto-playing, and Sarasate exposes Mr Cusins to public execration. Why should they persist in this reciprocity of injury? As one who has not the option of staying away from the concerts, I must press this question somewhat urgently.

At the same time I cannot blind myself to the fact that though Sarasate can hardly hit on a less suitable conductor, he may easily get one who is not sufficiently better to make it worth while to face the friction of making the change. As a solution of the difficulty, I suggest that he should offer the *bâton* to the faithful Cor De Las, who is such an excellent accompanist that he would probably be able at least to keep the band with the soloist in the quick movements of the concertos; whilst if, in attempting a Beethoven overture—say the Coriolan, which was in the program at the first concert—he should lose his way through the score, the band could do for him what it now does in extreme cases with

Mr Cusins: that is, look the other way, or, as I am told the fashionable expression now is, wink the other eye.

After Sarasate's concert came Paderewski's. He gave two concertos—one too many—Beethoven in E flat and Schumann. It was hard on us, and harder on Schumann. I am by no means naturally predisposed to admire Paderewski's style. His master, Leschetitzky, seems to me to have done more to dehumanize pianoforte-playing than any other leading teacher in Europe. When I hear pianists with fingers turned into steel hammers, deliberately murdering Beethoven by putting all sorts of *accelerandos* and *crescendos* into his noblest and most steadfast passages, I promptly put them down without further inquiry as pupils of Leschetitzky.

Paderewski's excessive hardness of touch, which tells even when he is playing with the most exquisite lightness, and which must be referred to his master rather than to himself, would limit him seriously if his exceptional comprehensiveness as a musician did not enable him to seize about ten points of treatment in a composition for every one that comes within the range of the ordinary pianist. He plays the Schumann concerto, for instance, so intelligently that if I were told that he was the composer and did not know to the contrary, I could easily believe it, although I should be surprised at any composer having submitted to such an arduous technical training as he has evidently undergone. In spite of Leschetitzky, then, the concert, though a tiring one from its inordinate length, was real and interesting throughout.

Paderewski treated the orchestra better than they treated him; for he played with an unfailing sense of the relation of the solo part to the rest, wheras they, in their one great opportunity—the first *allegro* of the Beethoven concerto—played roughly and hastily, a misfortune for which the chief blame must lie upon Mr Henschel, who handled this beautiful movement with a want of tenderness which was at times almost brutal. It is a pity that so able and modern-spirited a musician as he should repeatedly provoke remonstrances of this sort from critics who would much rather help than hinder his influence as a conductor and musical *entrepreneur*. As to Paderewski himself, I have only one demurrer to put in. I maintain that the great octave passage which occupies twenty bars or so of the middle section of that first movement, should be given in an unwavering *fortissimo* until the point when it breaks up and melts like a cloud. Paderewski made a marked *crescendo* in all the ascending passages, and thereby reduced the whole trait to a mere commonplace. Save for this Leschetitzkyism, I unreservedly congratulate him on his concert.

Among other pianists whom I have recently heard are Mr Frank Howgrave and Señor de Silka. Mr Howgrave's fluency of execution is so prodigious that it produces an irresistibly comic effect. Why it should have deserted him in the Prometheus variations by Beethoven, of which he made rather a mess, I do not know, since the sly velocity with which it carried him through Bach's chromatic fantasia brought out a facetiousness which has, I suppose, been latent in the composition all these years. He played a piece by Schumann really well; but somehow his face and air, which are those of a born comedian, lead me to doubt whether his future will lie in the more serious walks of pianism. Señor de Silka has done much to consolidate his technique since last year. A further spell of really hard work will place him beyond all risk of relapsing into a mere brilliant drawing room player—a danger of which he is not yet quite clear. On Thursday last he began by playing a couple of pieces by Scarlatti, and Schumann's symphonic studies, with considerable technical vigor, and with certain distinction of style which is as yet rather negative than positive: that is, it is due rather to the vulgarities from which he refrains than to any refinements which he introduces. In the middle of the program he placed Beethoven's Andante in F, and a couple of pieces by Chopin. Here he was decidedly weak. He was not altogether on the wrong tack in his quiet handling of the Chopin polonaise; but when it came to the Ballade in A flat, the introduction to which is surely as eloquent as human speech could be, he entirely failed to interpret it, and, in fact, played the whole ballade in one piece as a trivial gallop. The rest of the program was eked out by his drawing-room repertory, in which he shewed an appropriate charm of musical manner; but if he allows himself for a moment to overestimate the value of work of this sort, or of the applause which it gains from the section of the audience which is impressed by the rumors that he is "a real nobleman," the result will be the spoiling of a very promising player.

At the Albéniz concert on Thursday evening I looked in for a few minutes, and caught the concert giver napping over the A flat polonaise of Chopin, which he really played shockingly—I do not know why. Herr Johann Kruse, the violinist, has improved since he played the Beethoven concerto at a London symphony concert; but he was not completely successful in the Bach piece which he gave when encored for a Tartini sonata. On the previous day a concert was given by Herr Carl Fuchs, a young cellist well known in Manchester. He is a pupil of the Russian Davidoff, and is an unpretentious but excellent player, a trifle modest in tone compared with the greatest masters of the instrument, but by no means a buzzing bore, as cellists are rather apt to be. The second Richter concert was a great improvement on the first, although the program was knocked all to pieces by the influenza. Having bid "Conscience avaunt" the Monday before, Richter was himself again on this occasion.

MIREILLE

The World, 17 June 1891

The most important event in the musical world since
my last article, from my point of view, has been the
influenza catching me, or, as my friends preposterously
insist on putting it, my catching the influenza. Fortunately for me, many cases of critics and singers disabled
by it had occurred under my eyes within a few weeks;
so that by scrupulously doing the very reverse of what
they did in the way of treatment, I managed to come
through without missing a single engagement. I abstained from medical advice and ammoniated quinine;
I treated the fever by enjoying the morning air at an
open window in an entirely unprotected condition for
a prolonged period before finishing up with a cold bath;
I stimulated myself by transitions from the overwhelming heat of the crowded St James's Hall to the chill
coolness of Regent-street at night; I wore my lightest
attire; I kept out of bed as much as possible, and held on
to railings and lampposts when the temptation to seek
a brief repose at full length in the streets became almost
irresistible, as it did once or twice on the day when the
fever was at its height; I fed myself resolutely (though
not on the corpses of slain animals), and took no alcohol
in any form. The result was that I routed the enemy in
a series of pitched battles, in which I was assailed
successively with delirium, with weakness and fever,
with pains in various portions of my person, including
a specially ingenious one in the eyeballs, and, finally,
with a vulgar and abominable cold in the head, which
pursued me with unabated rage for fortyeight hours
before it lost heart. Had I drugged the fiend, coddled

him, inebriated him, and lavished doctors' fees on him, no doubt I should have left The World musicless for three weeks at least. As it was, I did more work in the five days during which the combat lasted than in the five days before that. Singers will now know how to deal with their foe. It is always worth while to fly in the face of that unvenerable survival of witchcraft which calls itself medical science. To recover triumphantly under such circumstances becomes a point of honor.

On my way to hear [Gounod's] Mireille in French at Covent Garden, on Wednesday last week, a rascal offered me for a shilling a book of the opera. But I was too old a bird to be caught in that way. I recognized at a glance the yellow cover of the old Davidson libretto, with the Italian words and the superseded four-act arrangement of bygone Maplesonian days. I did not give the fellow in charge, for he was miserably poor, and perhaps had no very clear idea of the differences between the new and the old Mireille. Instead, I went my way into the theatre, and there purchased, from Mr Harris's official representative, an authorized libretto for eight-eenpence. I hardly expect to be believed when I add that when I got to my stall and proceeded to investigate my purchase, it turned out to be that identical obsolete Italian Davidsonian libretto, disguised with a blue cover. As an art critic I know nothing about the City, and have never troubled myself as to the worth of the rumors that have reached me concerning the authenticity of the Lord Mayor's sermons. But as to the value of the Sheriff's librettos I have now formed a very strong opinion, which is at the service of the next Royal Commission upon the morals of the Corporation.

Why Mireille was performed I do not know. It is about as suited to Covent Garden as L'Enfant Prodigue is. Still more inscrutable is the casting of Miss Eames for the title part, the requirements of which are great range and great flexibility, enabling the singer to shake on high D at her ease. Miss Eames, even with her chief numbers transposed and cut to pieces, only got through, and that in a sufficiently commonplace manner, by the skin of her teeth—if she will pardon the expression. As to any attempt she made to place before us the ideal Mireille, I can only say that she never in her life was more emphatically that very attractive and ladylike person Miss Eames of the Royal Italian Opera—well educated, and with no nonsense about her, as Mr Sparkler* would have been the first to admit. As it is on Mireille that the whole play depends, it is hardly necessary to add that every attempt to give the scenes an air of conviction soon broke down. Isnardon, Miranda, Madame Passama, and the rest were willing enough; and Ceste, who took Maurel's place as Ourrias, was, if anything, rather too willing; but Mireille's propriety and her black silk dress were too much for them: they flagged, and finally gave it up as a bad job. Lubert alone came off with honor: he redeemed the performance from utter flatness by his unaffected and earnest playing as Vincent. The duets in which he took part, with the farandole and the overture, were the only numbers in which the least whiff of the characteristic atmosphere of the piece got across the footlights. On the whole, unless Mravina or Melba is prepared to take Miss Eames's place in the cast, the opera had better go back to the shelf. I am indebted, by the bye, to Mr Fisher Unwin for sending me, just in time for the performance, a neat new edition of Miss Preston's translation of Frédéric Mistral's Mirèio, which I quite intend to read some day.

The orchestral concert given by the students of the Royal College of Music last week was a vast improvement on the preceding one. Mr Henry Holmes, who has taken

* Character in Dickens's Little Dorrit.

Mr Stanford's place as conductor, gets quite a different class of work from his young battalions, who are probably individually better solo players than the members of the best professional orchestra Beethoven ever saw in his life. After hearing Mr Stanford last season driving them mechanically through a Berlioz score of which they had not mastered a single bar, it was pleasant to see Mr Holmes, as the head of a happy family of musicians, leading them through Cherubini's Les Abencérages overture with all the fine taste and genuine musical feeling which distinguished him when he was almost the only English violinist whose praises could be sounded without the tongue in the cheek. They responded to him with affectionate goodwill, and achieved a really excellent performance. All that the instrumental department at the Royal College seems to want now to bring it into line with its Continental rivals is a more vivid artistic life—a fresh charge of electricity. Mr Sutcliffe, for instance, played the Beethoven violin concerto very creditably, but still in a humdrum, sleepy way that would have filled a pupil of the Brussels Conservatoire with disrespectful amusement.

As to the vocal department, it seems as hopeless as ever. Of the two young ladies who sang—both announced as holders of scholarships—one was as ignorant of the artistic use of her voice as it is possible for any naturally musical person to be in a civilized country; and the other, though she had evidently had plenty of warnings and cautions from some musician of considerable taste, seemed to have had no positive instruction worth mentioning. In fact, any second-rate elocutionist could teach both young ladies all they know about the production of their voices. Considering how every innocent young provincial with a voice will henceforth turn to the Royal College and its scholarships as the one trustworthy chance of getting that voice artistically trained, I would suggest that a board with the inscription *Lasciate ogni speranza, &c.,** be placed over the doors of the singing rooms at the College, and a policeman stationed to explain it to novices from the country.

Mr Harris took advantage of his miscellaneous concert at the Albert Hall on Saturday to get another shilling from me for a book which gave the Italian version of a portion of Lohengrin which Van Dyck did not sing. What he did sing he sang in German. The smithy music from Siegfried was merely described as Schmiedelieder, without any words at all; and what that very innocent audience, consisting largely of people with conscientious objections to the theatre, must have thought of it, baffles my imagination. Half-a-crown going bang in one week for useless literature is more than I can afford. At the same time it was mildly amusing to know that the audience which recalled Van Dyck three times to the platform after the Lohengrin number supposed him to have been saying something to which both his manner of declamation and the music were outrageously inappropriate. An arrangement which struck me as especially shabby was the admission of the public to the seats provided for the members of the chorus, who were consequently crowded in a ridiculous fashion on the platform for the Meistersinger selection, and then bundled off. That, I submit, is not the way in which the Royal Italian Opera should treat its artists; and I shall now mention what I might otherwise have passed over— that the shilling book did not contain a third of what the chorus actually gave us, so that the chorale with which Hans Sachs is greeted passed as the trade song of the tailors. The only artist with whom I was not familiar was a M. Plançon, a *basso cantante* of considerable ability, as

* The words inscribed above the entrance to Hell in Canto III of Dante's Inferno: "Leave hope behind, ye that enter."

far as I could judge from his singing of *Au bruit des lourds marteaux.*

At the Richter concert last week we had all the Fidelio overtures, except that in E, one after another. The result was that the first on the list, Leonore No. 2, was magnificently played, wheras the others, by comparison, produced the effect of very carefully executed taskwork. The more artistically alive a band is, the less it can face two heavy Beethoven overtures in immediate succession. Still, the contrast between the two works was interesting. In No. 2 (I am using the customary numbering) the subjects are instrumented with a freshness and charm which is wanting in the more serious and penetrating No. 3; but the imperfect grip, the irrelevant prettiness, and, above all, the long *quasi*-academic working out in the middle, are insufferable when once No. 3 is thoroughly known; and, in my opinion, the work should be presented definitely as a first and *unsuccessful* attempt at No. 3, and not as an independent composition. The distinction made between the two by Richter was most masterly. Any of our ordinary time-beaters would have taken the *allegro* in both at exactly the same speed, because the subjects are identical. Richter, in No. 2, was easy, gracious, slow, almost caressing. In No. 3, starting at a much higher speed, he was decisive, strenuous, full of serious business, with no time or disposition for dallying with the charms emphasized in the scoring of No. 2.

An equally admirable example of genuine conducting was the performance of Mozart's symphony in D—the one which begins with a couple of springs up two octaves by the violins. Perhaps this was why it got above the heads of most of the audience; but the knowing few were duly appreciative. The typical Richter frequenter is hardly up to the mark in absolute music, being more at home with tone-poetry and program music. The rest of the concert was occupied by Mr Lloyd, who sang Tannhäuser's account of the pilgrimage to Rome, and Siegfried's bellows and anvil music, very tunefully and smoothly, without, however, for a moment relinquishing his original character of Edward Lloyd. Max Heinrich was the Wolfram, and Mr Nichols the Mime of the evening.

BRAHMS'S DREARY REQUIEM

The World, 24 June 1891

The admirers of Brahms had a succulent treat at the Richter concert last week. His German Requiem was done from end to end, and done quite well enough to bring out all its qualities. What those qualities are could have been guessed by a deaf man from the mountainous tedium of the unfortunate audience, who yet listened with a perverse belief that Brahms is a great composer, and the performance of this masterpiece of his an infinitely solemn and important function. I am afraid that this delusion was not confined to those who, having found by experience that good music bores them, have rashly concluded that all music that bores them must be good. It raged also among the learned musicians, who know what a *point d'orgue* is, and are delighted to be able to explain what is happening when Brahms sets a pedal pipe booming and a drum thumping the dominant of the key for ten minutes at a stretch, whilst the other instruments and the voices plough along through every practicable progression in or near the key, up hill from syncopation to syncopation, and down dale from suspension to suspension in an elaborately modernized manner that only makes the whole operation seem more desperately old-fashioned and empty.

Brahms seems to have been impressed by the fact that Beethoven produced remarkable effects by persisting with his pedal points long after Mozart would have resolved them, and to have convinced himself by an obvious logical process that it must be possible to produce still more remarkable results by outdoing Beethoven in persistency. And so indeed it is, as Bach proved before Mozart was born. Only somehow it has not come off in Brahms's hands, though he has prolonged and persisted to the verge of human endurance. Yet, as I say, the academic gentlemen like it, and seem pleased even by those endless repetitions, which are only the *rosalias* of the old Italian masses in a heavy and pretentious disguise. I can only say, with due respect, that I disagree with the academic gentlemen.

The fact is, there is nothing a genuine musician regards with more jealousy than an attempt to pass off the forms of music for music itself, especially those forms which have received a sort of consecration from their use by great composers in the past. Unfortunately, such impostures are sure of support from the sort of people—pretty numerous in this country as far as art is concerned—who think that it is the cowl that makes the monk. Any conspiracy between a musician and a literary man to set Wardour-street Jacobean English to Wardour-street Handelian counterpoint will find ready victims in this class, which may be seen at any festival impartially applauding the music of Handel and the profane interpolations of any opera singer who has learned by experience how to turn its ignorant hero worship to account.

Sometimes, of course, we have, for the sake of some respected professor, to put up with performances of honest pieces of pedantry like the oratorios of Kiel of Berlin, or Macfarren, not to mention names of the living. But I altogether demur to making concessions of this kind to Brahms. It will only end in his doing it again; for his extraordinary mechanical power of turning out the most ponderous description of music positively by tons, and the stupendous seriousness with which he takes this gift, are unrestrained by any consciousness on his part of the commonplaceness of his ideas, which makes his tone-poetry all but worthless, or of the lack of constructive capacity which makes his "absolute music" incoherent. He is quite capable of writing half a dozen more Requiems, all as insufferable as this one, if we hail him as "the most prominent living representative of the classical school," as some enthusiastic simpleton did the other day on the strength of a couple of motets which were inferior in every essential characteristic of the classical school to the best bits of part-writing in Sir Arthur Sullivan's comic operas.

These are not gracious things to say of a composer who has written so many really pretty trifles; but self-defence is the first law of Nature; and though I am at this moment lying broiling on the sands at Broadstairs, at peace with all mankind, and indulgently disposed even towards Brahms, I can say no less when I think of that dreary Requiem, and of the imminent danger of its being repeated next season.

After this it may seem rather unhandsome to describe Sgambati, who gave a concert of his own compositions at Prince's Hall last week, as the Brahms of Italy. But I mean to be complimentary, nevertheless; for Brahms, after all, is not without his merits. Besides, Sgambati's friends do not make considerate criticism impossible by claiming that he is another Beethoven; nor does he vie with the codfish in fecundity. Again, he has a certain Italian clearness and reasonableness which save him from the oppressiveness of the German. On Thursday last, with Sauret and Piatti in his quartet, and Mrs Henschel and Franceschetti to sing his songs, he had no reason to complain of the way in which his work was handled. One incident in the concert raised a point of etiquette, which was decided wrongly, as usual, by the audience. When distinguished persons attend concerts in their private capacity, discreet persons do not make public demonstrations of recognition. When the distinguished persons happen to be fifty minutes late, one would think that the least tactful mortal would perceive the advisability of not emphasizing their arrival.

However, there are always a number of people at every concert who, the moment they catch sight of a royal face, spring up as if they saw a chance of being knighted on the spot. This being so, and incurably so, would it not be better to manage these entrances so as to avoid ridiculous scenes in which half the room—the blundering half—rises in the middle of a song, and the vocalist has to stop, curtsy, and begin all over again?

In that part of the Richter concert which was not devoted to Brahms there was a performance of the Tannhäuser overture which ought to have been phonographed as a model of correct and eloquent phrasing in the Pilgrims' March, and of consentaneous execution in the shakes and *tremolandos* of the Venusberg music. Such a model is badly wanted, now that this composition has taken the place in popular favor accorded, in ages which already seem remote, to the overture to William Tell, with the result that our orchestras play it offhand whenever there is a scratch program to be made up. Need I add that playing it offhand means playing it all at sixes and sevens, as they do, with great applause, at Covent Garden for instance. Mr Barton McGuckin, who, being a native of these islands, has the pleasure of spending his spare evenings at that theatre listening to the performances of leading foreign tenors, of whom three out of five are much inferior to him, had a chance in the first scene of Tannhäuser to shew that it is not *faute de mieux* that we have to accept Perotti in the part on the stage. Mrs Moore Lawson, an American singer, who uses with excellent taste and skill the solitary stop with which her organ is provided, was the Venus. This must have displeased the president of the London branch of the Wagner Society, who has, I hear, protested against the employment of any but German singers at the Richter concerts. Why, I do not know, for I have not noticed that Germans sing Wagner's music better than outer barbarians. Perhaps Lord Dysart would rather hear Gudehus as Walther von Stolzing than the Pole, De Reszke, Vogl as Parsifal than the Belgian, Van Dyck, or Theodor Reichmann as Hans Sachs than the Frenchman, Lassalle. If so, I can assure him that his bargain would be a very bad one indeed on the musical side. As I by no means wish to imply that German singers are necessarily worse than others, perhaps I should in fairness compare on the other side such a group of German *prime donne* as Sucher, Malten, and Materna with—well, no matter with whom, for my conclusion would be the same—namely, that since the true Wagnerism is to sing the Meister's works always in a tongue understanded of the people, Richter's preference for English singers and English texts is not only good artistic policy, but orthodox also, in opposition to the rank heresy of Lord Dysart. In fact, I am not sure that the Bayreuth Church does not bind Richter himself to take out letters of naturalization here.

The Handel Festival is in full swing. I hope to have something to say about it next week, and, in the meantime, cordially recommend the Wednesday selection to lovers of Handel, of whom I hope there are still a few left.

A LUMBERING MESSIAH

The World, 1 July 1891

Fundamentally my view of the Handel Festival is that
of a convinced and ardent admirer of Handel. My
favorite oratorio is the Messiah, with which I have spent
many of the hours which others give to Shakespear, or
Scott, or Dickens. But for all this primary bias in favor
of Handel, my business is still to be that of the critic,
who, invited to pronounce an opinion on the merits of
a performance by four thousand executants, must judge
these abnormal conditions by their effect on the work as
openmindedly as if they were only four hundred, or
forty, or four. And I am bound to add that he who, so
judging, delivers a single and unqualified verdict on the
Festival, stultifies himself. The very same conditions
which make one choral number majestic, imposing,
even sublime, make another heavy, mechanical, meaningless. For instance, no host could be too mighty for
the Hallelujah Chorus, or See the Conquering Hero. In
them every individual chorister knows without study or
instruction what he has to do and how he has to feel. The
impulse to sing spreads even to the audience; and those
who are old hands at choral singing do not always
restrain it.

I saw more than one of my neighbors joining in the
Hallelujah on the first day; and if my feelings at that
moment had permitted me to make a properly controlled
artistic effort, I think I should have been no more able
to remain silent than Santley was. Under the circumstances, however, I followed the example of Albani,
who, knowing that she had to save her voice for I know
that my Redeemer liveth, kept a vocal score tightly on

her mouth the whole time, and looked over it with the expression of a child confronted with some intolerably tempting sweetmeat which it knows it must not touch.

But the Messiah is not all Hallelujah. Compare such a moment as I have just described with the experience of listening to the fiercely tumultuous He trusted in God, with its alternations of sullen mockery with high-pitched derision, and its savage shouts of Let Him deliver Him if He delight in Him, jogging along at about half the proper speed, with an expression of the deepest respect and propriety, as if a large body of the leading citizens, headed by the mayor, were presenting a surpassingly dull address to somebody. There may be, in the way of the proper presentation of such a chorus as this, something of the difficulty which confronted Wagner at the rehearsals of Tannhäuser in Paris in 1861, when he asked the ballet master to make his forces attack the Bacchanal in a bacchanalian way. "I understand perfectly what you mean" said the functionary "but only to a whole ballet of *premiers sujets* dare I breathe such suggestions."

No doubt Mr Manns' three thousand five hundred choristers might better his instructions so heartily as to go considerably beyond the utmost license of art if he told them that unless they sang that chorus like a howling bloodthirsty mob, the utter loneliness of Thy rebuke hath broken His heart, and Behold and see, must be lost, and with it the whole force of the tragic climax of the oratorio. Besides which, there is the physical difficulty, which only a skilled and powerful orator could fully surmount, of giving instruction of that kind to such a host. But I see no reason why matters should not be vastly improved if Mr Manns would adopt through-out the bolder policy as to speed which was forced on him after four on Selection day by the silent urgency of the clock, and persisted in to some extent—always with convincing effect—in Israel. Increased speed, however, is not all that is wanted. To get rid completely of the insufferable lumbering which is the curse of English Handelian choral singing, a spirited reform in style is needed.

For instance, Handel, in his vigorous moods, is fond of launching the whole mass of voices into florid passages of great brilliancy and impetuosity. In one of the most splendid choruses in the Messiah, For He shall purify the sons of Levi, the syllable "fy" comes out in a single trait consisting of no less than thirtytwo semiquavers. That trait should be sung with one impulse from end to end without an instant's hesitation. How is it actually done in England? Just as if the thirtytwo semiquavers were eight bars of crotchets taken *alla breve* in a not very lively tempo. The effect, of course, is to make the chorus so dull that all the reputation of Handel is needed to persuade Englishmen that they ought to enjoy it, whilst Frenchmen go away from our festivals confirmed in their skepticism as to our pet musical classic. When I had been listening for some minutes on Wednesday to the festival choristers trudging with ludicrous gravity through what they called Tellit Outa Mongthe Hea-ea Then, I could not help wishing that Santley, who roused them to boundless enthusiasm by his singing of Why do the nations, had given them a taste of their own quality by delivering those chains of triplets on the words "rage" and "counsel," as quavers in twelve-eight time in the tempo of the pastoral symphony. The celestial Lift up your heads, O ye gates, lost half its triumphant exultation from this heaviness of gait.

Again, in the beginning of For unto us, the tenors and basses told each other the news in a prosaic, methodical way which made the chorus quite comic until the thundering Wonderful, Counsellor, one of Handel's mightiest strokes, was reached; and even here the effect

[383]

was disappointing, because the chorus, having held nothing in reserve, could make no climax. The orchestra needed at that point about twenty more of the biggest of big drums. Another lost opportunity was the pathetically grand conclusion of All we like sheep. Nothing in the whole work needs to be sung with more intense expression than But the Lord hath laid on Him the iniquity of us all. Unless it sounds as if the singers were touched to their very hearts, they had better not sing it at all. On the Monday it came as mechanically as if the four entries of the voices had been produced by drawing four stops in an organ. This was the greater pity, because it must be conceded to our young Handel-sceptics that the preceding musical portraiture of the sheep going astray has no great claims on their reverence.

I am aware that many people who feel the shortcomings of our choral style bear with it under the impression, first, that the English people are naturally too slow and shy in their musical ways, and, second, that *bravura* vocalization and impetuous speed are not possible or safe with large choruses. To this I reply, first, that the natural fault of the English when they are singing with genuine feeling is not slowness, but rowdiness, as the neighbors of the Salvation Army know; second, that it would undoubtedly be as risky to venture far in the *bravura* direction with a very small chorus as to attempt the Walküre fire-music or Liszt's Mazeppa in an ordinary theatre orchestra with its little handful of strings. But both these compositions are safe with sixteen first and sixteen second violins, because, though notes are dropped and mistakes made, they are not all made simultaneously, and the result is that at any given instant an overwhelming majority of the violins are right. For the same reason, I do not see why nine hundred basses, even if they were the stiffest and slowest in the world, could not be safely sent at full speed in the *bravura* style through Handel's easy diatonic semiquaver traits, as safely as our violinists are now sent through Wagner's demisemiquavers.

So much for the compatibility of speed with accuracy. As to safety, I need only appeal to the results achieved by Mr Manns on Friday, when he got away from the Messiah, which is too sentimental for him, to Israel, which is far more congenial to his temperament. The only choral number in this which was quite unsatisfactory was I will exalt Him; and here the shortcoming was made unavoidable by the peculiar style of the chorus, since it—like And with His stripes in the Messiah—requires a beauty of execution which would suffice for a mass by Palestrina, and which is out of the question under Handel Festival conditions. The other choruses were spirited and forcible—some of them magnificent. He gave them hailstones, But the waters overwhelmed, and The horse and his rider were tremendous: one felt after them that the festival had justified its existence beyond all cavil.

If these criticisms are to bear any fruit in raising the festival performances of the Messiah to a typical artistic perfection—a result which I believe to be quite possible, and certainly well worth striving for—they must be weighed, not by Mr Manns or the Crystal Palace authorities, but by the local conductors throughout the country, who coach their contingents in the work, and send them up with preconceived ideas as to its execution which Mr Manns is powerless to change or even greatly to modify. Every contingent trained by a mere organist, to whom the Messiah is but a part of the drudgery of his professional routine, is simply a nuisance on the Handel orchestra. And every contingent trained by an artist who ranks the work among his treasures, and part of whose artistic ambition it is to hear at last in

England a really adequate performance of it, is, as Judas Maccabæus says, "a thousand men."

Space hardly permits of a more particular account of the details of the performances. The successes of the orchestra were the Berenice minuet, cleverly reserved by Mr Best so as to give the seventytwo cellos a rare opportunity, and the Bourrée from the Water Music, in which the tenor register of the bassoons came out very prettily. The accompaniments used in the Messiah were Mozart's, including, besides the usual reinforcements of the brass parts, even that beautiful variation on The people that walked in darkness, which has no more business at the Festival than Liszt's Don Juan fantasia would have at a performance of that opera. The solo singers shewed a considerable growth of artistic self-respect as well as of respect for Handel. Even Albani, who at her first appearance at a Festival took appalling liberties, was this time comparatively faithful to the text. She does not shine as a Handelian singer; but except in I know that my Redeemer liveth, and in an air from Rodelinda, both of which were badly sung, she disarmed criticism if she did not exactly satisfy it. Santley was the hero of that occasion, as far as the applause went; and I am not sure that his admirers were not in the right; for, in spite of his curious want of *sang-froid*, and his shots at perfectly safe notes, none of the other voices were quite so sound, so even, so unspoiled, and so telling. Lloyd's greatest successes were gained on Selection day, in a solo from one of the Chandos anthems, and in Love in her eyes, which he sang delightfully. The contralto part in the Messiah was made a success by dint of resolute exertion and clear diction, but when Miss Marian McKenzie reaches Santley's age, she will not find herself able to depend so largely as she does now on physical force. On the last day the principal singers were at their worst. Lloyd was obviously out of sorts, and fought hard but vainly against having to repeat The enemy said. Nevertheless, he fully sustained his reputation, and, with the assistance of Madame Belle Cole, made some amends for the duet between Madame Nordica and Miss Macintyre, which I was about to put down as the worst thing in the Festival, when something in Nordica's expression magnetically conveyed to me that I had better wait to hear the two gentlemen sing The Lord is a man of war before I rushed to any conclusions. And I must confess that Messrs Bridson and Brereton gallantly rescued the two ladies from me. Nordica, having had plenty of opportunities of distinguishing herself previously, was able to afford this reverse of fortune; but Miss Macintyre had to depend on Thou didst blow to retrieve herself, which I hope she will not mind my saying that she entirely failed to do. A Handelian singer really must not drop notes to take breath, like an Irish lilter. On Selection day, Mr Barton McGuckin would have had a very distinguished success with Waft her, angels, if he had refrained from that old-fashioned bid for applause with a prolonged high note, which spoiled the ending. His Love sounds the alarm was excellent.

Of the chorus the tenors were the best among the men, though they collapsed unaccountably during the first part on the Wednesday. The basses were for the most part baritones, the low notes in Israel being comparatively ineffective. The altos were superb: nothing better could have been desired. On the other hand, the sopranos, for their numbers, had but little tone, and that of the most commonplace kind. Mr Manns was at his best on the last day; and I have no quarrel with him except as to an *allargando* which he made at the words There was not one feeble person among their tribes, which should, I maintain, proceed with swift, determined, unslackened step to the very last bar.

THE NAUTCH GIRL

The World, 8 July 1891

On thinking it over I am inclined to conclude that Mr
D'Oyly Carte did not quite accurately measure the
vacancy made at the Savoy by the withdrawal of his
dramatic poet and his tone poet. His wish to continue on
the old lines as closely as possible is obvious; but instead
of trying to find another Gilbert and another Sullivan,
he has tried to find another Mikado, which, I admit, is
exactly what nobody wanted, one Mikado being enough
for any reasonable generation. Perhaps Mr Carte may
have found that another Gilbert does not exist. That
may very well be the case; for Mr Gilbert, at his best,
was a much cleverer man than most of the playwrights
of his day: he could always see beneath the surface of
things; and if he could only have seen through them, he
might have made his mark as a serious dramatist instead
of having, as a satirist, to depend for the piquancy of his
ridicule on the general assumption of the validity of the
very things he ridiculed. The theme of The Pirates of
Penzance is essentially the same as that of Ibsen's Wild
Duck; but we all understood that the joke of the pirate
being "the slave of duty" lay in the utter absurdity and
topsyturviness of such a proposition, wheras when we
read The Wild Duck we see that the exhibition of the
same sort of slave there as a mischievous fool is no joke
at all, but a grimly serious attack on our notion that we
need stick at nothing in the cause of duty

Nevertheless, there was a substratum of earnest in Mr
Gilbert's joking which shewed that he was not exactly
the sort of writer whom Mr Carte could have replaced
by merely going into the Strand in the usual managerial

way and hailing the first librettist he met there. Now, in the case of the musician, matters were on a very different footing. Sir Arthur Sullivan made his reputation as a composer of comic operas by a consummate *savoir faire* which was partly, no doubt, a personal and social talent, but which had been cultivated musically by a thorough technical training in the elegant and fastidious school of Mendelssohn, and by twenty years' work in composing for the drawing room, the church, the festival, and the concert room. In 1875, when he composed Trial by Jury, no manager would have dreamt of approaching him with a a commission for an Offenbachian opera: he was pre-eminently a sentimental and ecclesiastical composer, whose name suggested Guinevere and Thou'rt passing hence, Nearer, my God, to Thee, and Onward, Christian Soldiers, In Memoriam and the additional accompaniments to Handel's Jephtha. When he plunged into the banalities and trivialities of Savoy opera he carried his old training with him. He taught the public to understand orchestral fun; but his instrumental jokes, which he never carried too far, were always in good taste; and his workmanship was unfailingly skilful and refined, even when the material was of the cheapest.

Why, under these circumstances, Mr Carte should have looked to Mr Solomon to replace Sir Arthur is a problem which reason cannot solve. The right man, Mr Villiers Stanford, was ready to his hand—for I presume that the composer of the Irish symphony would not disdain to follow in the footsteps of Mozart any more than Sir Arthur did. He has the technical training and the culture which stood Sullivan in such good stead; and there must be still alive in him something of the young Irishman of genius who wrote those spirited Cavalier tunes, not to mention some numbers from The Veiled Prophet, before he was forced back into the dismal routine of manufacturing impossible trash like The

Revenge for provincial festival purposes, and into conducting, which is so little his affair that when I lately described his Bach choir work in my unliterary way from the point of view of a person whose business it is to use his ears, the only champion who ventured to say a word in his defence did not dare to sign it. But I do not want to force Mr Stanford on Mr Carte. I might have cited Mr Cowen with equal point. He, also, is no more fitted to be a conductor than the majority of brilliant and popular writers are to be editors. My interest in getting both gentlemen back to their proper work, which I take to be intelligent and vivacious dramatic composition, is that it would then become a pleasure to criticize them, instead of, as it generally is at present, a disagreeable duty.

All this may seem rather hard on poor Mr Solomon, the composer upon whom Mr Carte's choice has actually fallen. But then Mr Solomon has been very hard on me. He has given me the worst headache I ever had in a theatre by an instrumental score which is more wearisome than the conversation of an inveterate punster, and more noisy than the *melodrame* which accompanies the knockabout business in a music hall. Mr Carte had better remove the bassoon, the piccolo, the cymbals, the triangle, and the drums, both *timpani* and *tamburo,* from the theatre; for Mr Solomon is clearly not to be trusted with them. If Sir Arthur Sullivan used these instruments in an artistically comic way once in a thousand bars or so, is that any reason why Mr Solomon should use them in an inartistically comic way nine hundred and ninety-nine times in the same period? Besides, Sir Arthur only did it to point an allusion. Mr Solomon does it, allusion or no allusion, out of a mere schoolboyish itching to lark with the instruments. When he has an allusion to excuse him, he does not make it with anything like the neatness which he shewed once or twice in his Penelope.

Sometimes he simply stops the opera whilst the band play a fragment from some familiar work, and then calmly resumes. This is how he manages the phrase from the Hallelujah Chorus which follows the reference to the Salvation Army, a jape which is open to the double objection that the warriors of the Salvation Army never sing the Hallelujah Chorus, and that Mr Solomon ought to have more regard for his own music than to remind people of Handel's whilst it is proceeding. In the end this topical sort of orchestration becomes distracting, worrying, even exasperating. I do not insist on this to disparage Mr Solomon's incessant inventive activity, or to drive him back into routine instrumentation. But I certainly do wish to recall him to the necessity of exercising the activity under strictly artistic conditions, the first of these being that the score shall be at least agreeable to the ear, if it is too much to ask that it shall be beautiful.

Nothing in The Nautch Girl sustains the orchestral traditions of comic opera—the delicacy and humor of Auber, the inimitable effervescence of Offenbach, or the musicianly smoothness and charm of Sullivan and Cellier, all of whom felt that the function of the orchestra was primarily to make music, and only secondarily to make fun. If Mr Solomon ever had that feeling, he has allowed it to become blunted; and for want of its guidance he has now landed himself in mere horse-play, and brought the artistic standard at our leading comic opera house down with a run. The remedy for him is by no means to acquire the polite but unprogressive technique of our Mendelssohn scholars, which, though it would carry him a safe distance, would then stop him dead, but simply to cultivate the sense of beauty in music until it becomes an infallible monitor as to the point at which those twitches on the piccolo, and grunts on the bassoon, and slams on the drum cease to amuse, and become offensive disfigurements of the tone-fabric instead of eccentric ornaments upon it.

Of the opera as an artistic whole I cannot very well speak, because it hardly *is* an artistic whole. The book was evidently selected for the sake of its resemblance to The Mikado, of which it might almost be called a paraphrase if it were not that the secession of Mr Grossmith and his replacement by Mr Wyatt has necessitated the substitution of a second edition of the Duke of Plaza-Toro for the Lord High Executioner. The managerial argument evidently was that since The Mikado had been so unlike externally to any previous Savoy opera, the way to secure a repetition of its success was to produce the most slavish possible imitation of the best known previous Savoy opera. Managers always reason in this way. The result on the first night was that when the rather characterless equivalents of the Mikado opening chorus, and of A wandering minstrel I, and of the three girls' *trio* had been sung, there were signs of the settling down of an ominous dulness, which was only dispelled by the appearance of Mr Rutland Barrington, who changed the fortunes of the evening, and, in fact, saved the opera. At this point, too, the dialogue brightened a good deal; and thenceforth, though there was a plentiful lack of freshness, there was liveliness enough and to spare. Miss Snyders, the only member of the cast whose accomplishments are not too well known to need description, owed her success chiefly to a truly Circassian beauty; for, though she has sufficient taste and address to do her business very presentably, she is not as yet specially interesting as a singer or actress. As usual at the Savoy, the piece has been well rehearsed; the *mise-en-scène* is of exceptional excellence; and Mr Charles Harris, the stage manager, was received with a cordiality which, I hope, convinced him that he has lost nothing by getting rid of the ballets of infants and the interminable processions in which he formerly delighted. As to the music, it is, to say the least, not distinguished; but it is obvious, lively, and easily caught up by the amateur strummer. Those who rejoiced in An everyday young man will be enchanted with *Vive la liberté*; and if here and there a number is a little too stale and vulgar for even such words as It was all my eye, on the other hand the mosquito song, and one or two others in the same vein, are by no means graceless.

It will not escape observation that the utmost that can be said for the The Nautch Girl amounts to no more than can be said for any piece at the Lyric or the Prince of Wales'. In other words, the Savoy has lost its speciality. This, I think, is a misfortune; and if Mr Carte wishes to remedy it, and cannot discover two new geniuses, he had better make up his mind at once to give a commission to Mr Grundy for his next libretto, and to Mr Stanford or Mr Cowen for his next score.

AFFAIRS OF STATE
The World, 15 July 1891

There is nothing that we do in this country more thoroughly and artistically than our authorized denials of statements which everybody knows to be true. From the honorable gentleman in the House of Commons who asks a question about some notorious job, down to the poorest wretch who protests against being worked for seventeen hours a day, we all receive the same crushing denial, the same dignified rebuke for giving currency to silly and vulgar gossip, the same pledges of the highest credit and the best authority that the statement made is absolutely without foundation. And within three weeks everyone concerned, including the unimpeachably respectable deniers, openly admit that the statement was perfectly true, and that they knew it to be perfectly true all along, and, in fact, denied it on that account.

These observations are suggested to me by recent events at the Opera. When the State performance was first announced,*M. Henri Rochefort† said, in effect, to the French members of the company "Do, if you dare." The exact form which the threat took was an assurance to the French public that no French artist would sing a note for the ravisher of Alsace and Lorraine. Our national genius for authorized denial saw its opportunity at once, and seized it. These French artists, it was solemnly declared, were, like the Kaiser, England's guests; and as gentlemen they would know their duty to their hostess and to their distinguished fellow guest. The report of their refusal to sing was entirely false: not one of them had refused: all were indignant at the monstrous suggestion that they could so forget themselves. M. Rochefort being thus snubbed, shut up, and put to public shame, the next event was the publication of the program for the evening, with the parts of Telramund, Capulet, San Bris, and Nevers, which have been played throughout the season by Maurel, Dufriche, and Lassalle, transferred to Messieurs Alec Marsh, Edouard de Reszke, and Franceschetti, and the promised act from Die Meistersinger omitted, evidently because Lassalle could not be replaced as Hans Sachs: in short, with the authoritatively denied report confirmed in every essential particular. Doubtless it would have been highly un-English to have faced the obvious truth in the first instance; but it certainly would have been simpler

* A special performance of the Opera on 8 July was occasioned by the State visit of the German Kaiser. Shaw had received a ticket, but gave it to William Archer.

† French journalist and politician, editor of L'Intransigeant and member of the staff of Le Figaro.

to have admitted frankly that the French artists could not afford to run the risk of offending M. Rochefort and the section of the French public represented by him, instead of leaving it to be inferred that they are either Republicans haughtily refusing to take part in a monarchical pageant, or else patriots on whose hearts the names of Alsace and Lorraine are indelibly graven. The moral of the whole affair for future distinguished visitors is, Go to the Royal English Opera rather than to the Royal French-Italian-Austrian-Spanish-German-Jewish-Polish Opera; and these unpleasantnesses will not arise.

Lest I should myself become the innocent cause of an international misunderstanding, let me hasten to explain that my abstention from acceptance of Mr Harris's invitation on this occasion had no political significance. I have always understood that one of the advantages of not being an Emperor is that you need not go to ceremonies of this kind unless you like; and I availed myself of my privilege. That is all—absolutely all. Those scraps of Wagner, Meyerbeer, and Gounod may have been delightful novelties to the Kaiser: to the critic they were the oldest of old stories; and the critic consequently stayed away, and had a pleasant unprofessional evening.

Meanwhile, the Opera has been pursuing its accustomed routine. The repeated postponements of Otello were accounted for by the regrettable illness of Jean de Reszke, who gave a touching proof of his prostrate condition by playing Don Jose instead, and, I must say, playing it very well. Lassalle was admirable as Escamillo; and if Ravogli's only too powerful Carmen had been substituted for Miss de Lussan's, which has now been seen often enough for one season, the evening would have been quite a memorable one. Melba did not strengthen the cast as much as she might have done: she was Melba, of course; but she was not Micaela. In the smaller details the performance was slipshod and perfunctory. Melba, De Reszke, Lassalle, and Miranda sang in French; Ciampi and the chorus sang in Italian; and Miss de Lussan sang in whatever language seemed to have the best of it for the moment. The night before this, Fidelio was produced; and the brisk sale of librettos betrayed the mournful fact, unspeakably disgraceful to London, that Beethoven's one opera—and how great an opera!—was new to the audience. It cannot be said that the work received any great instalment of the justice for which it has waited so long; for Tavary, though she deserves unstinted credit for the earnestness and the very considerable ability which she shewed, has not the dramatic genius (nothing less than genius will do) for the part of Leonore. Devoyod as Pizarro was confused and incompetent; whilst Mr Alec Marsh, who sang well enough as the Minister, comported himself with uncalled-for irascibility. On the other hand, Ravelli was exceptionally good as Florestan; and Plançon made an excellent Rocco. Madame Bauermeister, probably the most indispensable member of Mr Harris's company, and by no means the least efficient, was Marcellina. The performance of the overtures was disturbed by an unusually copious influx of young barbarians celebrating their first appearance among civilized people at a musical performance by treating themselves to boxes on the pit tier. They chattered and laughed and enjoyed themselves generally, with an unconsciousness which would have been delightful to contemplate if Beethoven had not had prior claims to our attention. I may remark in passing that the extent to which private boxes encourage this sort of misconduct, even among disciplined people, appears to me to form a strong argument for their entire abolition. Always towards the end of the season, when the boxes are frequently let to strangers, Covent Garden suffers more and more from visitors who have never learnt how to behave themselves in an opera house, and who are excited by the novelty of their situation. Things were particularly bad on this Fidelio night. Not only were there two pit tier parties who were behaving quite outrageously, but there was a gentleman next me with a huge stick, with which he beat time mercilessly on his own ankles, whilst a man behind me supported him in the less subtle rhythms by knocking with his boots against the back of my stall. Add to this that Randegger, to whose achievements as a Beethoven conductor I shall not attempt to do justice, hammered his desk freely with his stick—perhaps to relieve his feelings after a slight altercation with the bassoon which graced the conclusion of the first act—and you will understand the difficulties under which I endeavored to taste the full flavor of Fidelio. Still, with all these drawbacks, I could not help noticing that the work was far better understood in the orchestra, and a little better even on the stage, than it used to be.

Marta, which was revived for Mravina, is an opera which one hardly knows what to do with. The first two acts make such a capital piece of *naïve* storytelling, and the rest is so hopelessly dull and artificial, that every experienced critic now knows that the man who is pleased and indulgent in the middle of the performance will be bored and disenchanted at the end. If I were Mr Harris, I think I should boldly transfer Plunkett's beer song from the third act to the Richmond fair scene, and bring Tristan to the rescue after *Dormi pur* with an overwhelming force of courtiers, finishing the perform-ance there and then with the concerted piece from the end of the third act. The evening could be filled up with that one-act opera of Mascagni's*which we were led to

* Cavalleria Rusticana (1890), which had recently had a sensational success in Rome.

expect this season. Mravina's beautiful unspoiled voice was just the thing for The Last Rose; and Giulia Ravogli and Edouard de Reszke (the only Plunkett I ever saw without a huge hat strapped upon his back) enjoyed themselves at their ease, and pleased us all immensely. Ravelli, as Lionel, was less happy; the part is too high and exacting to be successfully attacked in the robust style which he depends on.

Otello reached its third postponement on Saturday night; and the public, having had proof on the State night and on the previous Saturday that Brother Jean can sing if he chooses, reached the conclusion that its desire to see Maurel again as Iago is not taken in good part by our sensitive tenor.

Though the season is not to be compared to last year's for musical activity, and is now, of course, waning precipitously, concerts still occur pretty frequently. Paderewski's recitals, which ended on Saturday, have been crowded in spite of the heat. He has shewn himself proof against hero worship, never relaxing the steadiest concentration on his business as an artist, so that however you may differ with him occasionally, you have nothing to reproach him with. At one of his recitals he played four of Mendelssohn's Songs without Words, which have dropped out of the stock pianoforte repertory lately, ostensibly because they are too easy for our young lions, but really, I suspect, because they are too difficult. If you want to find out the weak places in a player's technique, just wait until he has dazzled you with a Chopin polonaise, or a Liszt rhapsody, or Schumann's symphonic studies; and then ask him to play you ten bars of Mozart or Mendelsson. At the same time I must confess that it was Chopin, in the B minor sonata, who found out the limits of Paderewski's skill on Saturday last. Another Pole, Stojowski, has given one recital at Prince's Hall. He can play, and that very cleverly; but he did not leave the impression that his musical ability is irresistibly specialized for the pianoforte. Schönberger's recital was welcome because he avoided the stereotyped program, omitting Chopin, playing a Weber sonata, and giving Haydn, Mozart, and Mendelssohn a turn. He plays with remarkable elegance and brilliancy; but in simple passages, where elegance and brilliancy are of little use, he appears diffident and uneasy. At such moments his technique becomes his worst enemy, because he seems to have so much more faith in it than in himself that when it drops out of action he loses confidence. If this is really so, his apprehensions are uncalled for, since his musical feeling, as far as he ventures to give it free play, never betrays him. In his appearances with Ysaÿe and other artists throughout the season he has distinguished himself greatly. Simonetti is a young Italian violinist of whom I have formed no adequate judgment, as I arrived at his concert when the room was crowded to suffocation, and had to content myself with hearing a few bars through the doorway. I can only say that the few bars impressed me favorably by their clean, refined execution and sympathetic tone.

JEAN DE RESZKE'S OTELLO
The World, 22 July 1891

I confess to having witnessed with a certain satisfaction the curious demonstrations which enlivened the first performance of Otello at Covent Garden. The first sign of tumult was a disposition to insist on applauding Maurel in season and out of season, even to the extent of causing ridiculous interruptions to the performance. The second was an almost equally strong disposition to disparage—I had almost said to hoot—Jean de Reszke, who was defended by vehement counter-demonstrations, in leading which Lassalle, standing in a box next the stage on the grand tier, was the most conspicuous figure. Fortunately, the majority in an English audience generally declines to concern itself in greenroom politics; and at Covent Garden the majority is so huge that it is not possible to make much of a scene there. By the end of the second act matters relapsed into the usual routine, greatly, I should imagine, to the relief of Maurel. However, partial as the demonstration was, it was far too general to be the work of a claque; and I recommend it to the most serious consideration of Brother Jean. It is to his petulant laziness, and to nothing else, that we owe the frightful waste of artistic resources at Covent Garden on stale repetitions of worn-out operas night after night, when we might have been listening to Siegfried and Otello, not to mention half a dozen other works which are familiar in every second-rate German town, and of which we know nothing in London. The height of his ambition would be attained, as far as one can judge, if he were permitted to maintain his status as leading tenor at the Royal Italian Opera by a single performance of Romeo every year, leaving the rest of the work to be done by Perotti, Montariol, and Ravelli. And yet, at the beginning of this season, he had the— shall I say the ingenuousness?—to favor an interviewer with some observations about his devotion to Art. Can he wonder at the frequenters of the Opera shewing a little temper in the matter at last?

His acting as Otello was about equally remarkable for its amateurish ineptitudes and for its manifestations of the natural histrionic powers which he has so studiously neglected for the last fifteen years. Though he overcame his genius for being late so far as to get on the stage punctually for his first utterance in the storm, it reconquered him when he entered to interrupt the fight between Cassio and Montano; and in his sudden appearance at the masked door in Desdemona's bedroom, which depended for its effect on being timed exactly to a certain chord, he was a good half bar behindhand. His reluctance to determined physical action came out chiefly in his onslaught on Iago, which he managed in such a way as to make the audience feel how extremely obliging it was of Maurel to fall. And at the end of the third act, in simulating the epileptic fit in which Otello's fury culminates, he moved the gods to laughter by lying down with a much too obvious solicitude for his own comfort.

On the whole it may be said that throughout the first two acts his diffidence and irresolution again and again got the better of his more vigorous and passionate impulses. This was intensified no doubt by nervousness; but it was partly due also to his halting between a half-hearted attempt at the savage style of Tamagno and the quieter, more refined manner natural to himself. In the third act, when the atmosphere of the house had become friendly, he began to treat the part more in his own fashion, and at last got really into it, playing for the first time with sustained conviction instead of merely with fitful bursts of self-assertion. Indeed, but for that gingerly fall at the end, this third act would have been an unqualified success for him. As it was, it shewed, like his Don Jose and other post-Van Dyck performances, that when the rivalry of younger men and the decay of his old superficial charm with advancing years force him to make the most of all his powers, he may yet gain more as an actor than he will lose as a singer.

His Otello will never be like Tamagno's; but he need not regret that, as the same thing might have been said of Salvini. The Italian tenor's shrill screaming voice and fierce temper were tremendously effective here and there; but the nobler side of the Moor, which Salvini brought out with such admirable artistic quietude and self-containment, and which De Reszke shews a considerable, though only half cultivated, power of indicating in the same way, was left untouched by Tamagno, who on this and other accounts is the very last man a wise tenor would attempt to imitate.

There is less to be said as to the other principals. It is no compliment to Albani to declare that she was better than Madame Cattaneo, as she could hardly have been worse. Like De Reszke, she redeemed herself in the latter half of the opera. Her intonation improved; and her acting had the sincerity which so honorably distinguishes her from most of her rivals, and which so often leads her straight to the right vocal treatment of purely dramatic music. If she will only forgo that absurd little stage run with which she embraces Otello in the first act, she will have nothing to reproach herself with as far as her playing of the part is concerned. Maurel, tired out as to voice, dropping all the G's, and unable to make the *pianissimo* nuances tell at anything softer than a tolerably vigorous *mezzo forte*, was yet able to repeat his old success as Iago. His playing is as striking and picturesque as ever; but I have come to think that it requires a touch of realism here and there to relieve its somewhat mechanical grace and effectiveness. The excessive descriptiveness which is the fault in his method, and even in his conception of the actor's function, resulting in a tendency to be illustrative rather than impersonative, occasionally leads him to forget the natural consequences of the actions he represents on the stage.

For instance, when Otello half throttles Iago, it is a little disillusioning to see the victim rise from a faultless attitude, and declaim *Divina grazia, difendimi*, with his throat in perfect order. Nothing is easier to produce than the *voce soffocata*; and there are not many operatic passages in which it is more appropriate than here. Apart from these matters of detail, the chief objection to Maurel's Iago is that it is not Iago at all, but rather the Cæsar Borgia of romance. As far as it is human, it is a portrait of a distinguished officer, one who would not be passed over for Cassio when he was expecting his step. I am aware that this view of him falls in with the current impression in artistic circles that Iago was a very fine fellow. But in circles wherein men have to take one another seriously, there will not be much difference of opinion as to the fact that Iago must have been an ingrained blackguard and consequently an (if I may use a slightly Germanic adjective) obviously-to-everyone-but-himself-unpromotable person.

A certain bluffness and frankness, with that habit of looking you straight in the face which is the surest sign of a born liar, male or female, appear to me to be indispensable to "honest Iago"; and it is the absence of these, with the statuesque attitudes, the lofty carriage of the head, and the delicate play of the hands and wrists, that makes the figure created by Maurel irreconcilable with my notion of the essentially vulgar ancient who sang comic songs to Cassio and drank him, so to speak, under the table. There is too much of Lucifer, the fallen angel, about it—and this, be it remarked, by no means through the fault of Verdi, who has in several places given a quite Shakespearean tone to the part by *nuances* which Maurel refuses to execute, a striking instance being the famous *Ecco il leon* at the end of the fourth act, when Iago spurns the insensible body of the prostrate Otello.

Nobody, it seems to me, can escape the meaning of the descent to the rattling shake on the middle F which Verdi has written. It expresses to perfection the base envious exultation of the ass's kick at the helpless lion, and suggests nothing of the Satanic scorn with which

Maurel, omitting the ugly shake, leaves the stage. His performance is to be admired rather as a powerfully executed fantasy of his own than as the Iago either of Verdi or Shakespear. If his successors in the part try to imitate him, their wisdom will be even less than their originality.

It remains to get through the most melancholy part of my task—the criticism of the staging of the opera. I need hardly say that what money could secure in the way of scenery and dresses had been secured, and that amply. But money alone does not go very far in the first act of Otello, which stands or falls by the naturalness of the delightful scene where the storm subsides, the thunder dies out of the air, and there begins that merry scene round the bonfire which is perhaps Verdi's freshest and prettiest piece of descriptive music. Its total failure at Covent Garden was a foregone conclusion. I should be sorry to assail any such hardworked body as the Covent Garden chorus with so ungraceful an epithet as pigheaded; but really if they could have seen themselves standing just clear of the pale flame of that miserable penn'orth of methylated spirit, staring at Mancinelli, and bawling without a ray of feeling for what they were supposed to be doing, they would not venture to defend themselves against any extremity of abuse. The scene was so effectually extinguished in consequence that those who had seen the Scala people at the Lyceum were to be heard in all directions during the interval naïvely declaring that they found the first act very dull now that the novelty of the work had worn off. The final outrage of the stage manager (if there is really any such functionary at Covent Garden) was the turning on in the sky of a most outrageous constellation, intended, I think, for the Great Bear, and consisting of gas lamps of the first magnitude and of aggressive yellowness. I remember believing implicitly in the reality of everything I saw on the stage at my first pantomime; but even then I do not think I should have been taken in by such incredible heavenly bodies as these. They achieved a sort of *succès de rire* by winking at the most rapturous part of the duet which De Reszke and Albani were carrying on below in happy ignorance of the facetiousness of the firmament; but, though I could not help laughing, I strongly recommend Mr Harris to send down to Greenwich for an expert to superintend this part of the opera before he repeats it.

It cannot be said, unfortunately, that the tediousness stopped after the first act, although the stage manager's opportunities ceased then. The tact, steadiness, and—when needed—the authority with which Faccio brought Otello through at the Lyceum without letting it flag for a second was beyond the powers of the amiable and enthusiastic Mancinelli. He shewed his usual feeling for the orchestral points; but, on the other hand, he let things drag terribly, particularly in the third act, by waiting for singers who were waiting for him, and often choosing unnecessarily slow *tempi* to start with. In the second act he astonished Maurel by taking the applause at the end of the Credo as an *encore*—an unheard-of artistic mistake; and, shortly afterwards, he astonished De Reszke still more by doing exactly the reverse after the *Ora e per sempre addio, sante memorie*. On the whole, if he could have borrowed a little of Bevignani's disposition to whack an opera along, without also acquiring his characteristic imperviousness, Otello would have been over sooner, and the audience would have gone home with a better opinion of the work

ADVICE FOR MR DE LARA
The World, 29 July 1891

The announcement that Maurel had at the last moment found it impossible to undertake the principal part in Mr de Lara's Light of Asia, and the consequent withdrawal of that work, were the final disappointments of the opera season; and one may perhaps be excused for mildly suggesting that Maurel might have made up his mind on the subject a little earlier, instead of keeping innocent critics, who might have been recuperating in the country, waiting vainly in town to witness his *début* as Buddha. However, it did not matter to me: I should have been in town in any case; and I am willing to believe that Maurel was justified in concluding that the task of making the work a success was too delicate to be achieved under the rough-and-ready conditions which prevail at Covent Garden. Still, if Mr de Lara was ready to face that risk, the collapse of the project is rather hard on him. I am not, by temperament, one of Mr de Lara's special devotees: his music appears to me to be one-sided; and a little of its one side goes a long way with me. But, for all that, I look with some indignation on the tendency among the Philistines to regard him as fair game for a sort of criticism which means, if it means anything, that an artist, as such, has no right to live in this country. We no longer literally heave half-bricks at strangers; but we certainly do chivy artists occasionally for no other mortal reason than that they are artists. I do not deny that musicians, when they are very young men, make themselves ridiculous, as other very young men do, through mere ignorance of the art of life. It is easy to find excuses for laughing at beginners in any

profession; but we do not laugh fairly all round: we let
the overweening young curate, or doctor, or lawyer off
very easily in comparison with the overweening young
artist, thereby implying that the nature of his profession
is an aggravating circumstance. This does not hurt the
bold, adroit, and witty spirits if they can handle the pen
or use their tongues publicly: all they have to do is to
turn the attacks into advertisements, and live on their
notoriety until the maturing of their powers enables
them to build solidly on that foundation. But the
inarticulate musician has to live it down as best he can.
It is therefore important that it should be dropped as
soon as he does live it down, if only for the sake of the
scoffers; for there is a point in this popular sport of
artist-baiting at which the quarry outgrows the hunters.
If criticism is to pursue a man to the death, it must
carefully calculate the time at which such epithets as
callow, immature, conceited, and the like, must be
exchanged for old-fashioned, obsolete, exploded, and
played-out. In London the upstart fades so quickly into
the superfluous veteran (from the abusive point of view)
that one has to keep exceedingly wide awake lest the
laugh should suddenly change sides. No doubt Mr
Isidore de Lara, some fifteen or twenty years ago, had
about him a certain quantity of the nonsense proper to
his age, emphasized by a style sufficiently pronounced
to rouse the artist-hunting instinct in the Philistines.
Whenever, in the due course of his struggle for
recognition as a singer and composer, he did those
things which (artistically speaking) he ought not to have
done, and left undone those things which he ought to
have done, he was generally pretty promptly and
publicly informed that there was no health in him. Even
the youngest critics wrote of him with all the freedom of
men old enough to be his father. This was all very well
in its day; but I submit that Mr de Lara has now grown

up, and had better either be treated seriously, or else frankly burnt alive as a warning to young gentlemen who dislike city work. I have, I hope, an open mind in the matter; but I doubt whether it would be wise to burn him. He appears to me to stand out with no small distinction from the ruck of our catchpenny ballad manufacturers and barren professors of the art of doing what has been done before and need not be done again. His popularity with a certain section of London society is a perfectly legitimate popularity, arising from the fact that his music exactly expresses the poetic sentiment of that section, and is therefore felt in it to be genuinely inspired and not merely put together for the royalty market. Of course, if you happen to have a violent antipathy to both section and sentiment, the very genuineness of the inspiration may make his music all the more nauseous to you. But to put forward your antipathy for what he expresses as a proof of his incapacity to express it is ridiculous: the fact of the music rousing that antipathy shews conclusively that the music is alive. And it cannot reasonably be contended that its workmanship is deficient in quality. For my part, if Mr de Lara were to leave his Light of Asia in its original form, and try his hand at a new opera in which he would freely express in music those sides of life which appeal to his humor, intellect, and observation, instead of confining himself to a few threadbare disguises of lovesickness, I have no doubt that the result would be awaited with a degree of interest which will certainly never be aroused by the favorite heros of the writers who appear to think that they are under no obligation to treat him with common politeness, much less to criticize him rationally.

Mlle Teleky, whose *début* at the opera on the last night but two of the season had been so long deferred that it was obviously made at last only to give the lady the Covent Garden hallmark, is undeniably clever and attractive. When a young artist is tall, handsome, and unaffected, with fine eyes, black hair, a well-proportioned head, a nose, mouth, and teeth that can be admired both separately and collectively, a good voice, and plenty of musical aptitude, one is not surprised to hear that she is a favorite with the Hamburg public, or any other public. I watched her with pleasure during two acts of the ridiculous spectacle which they describe as Verdi's La Traviata in the Covent Garden bills; and then, as the performance was hackneyed, the cast bad (Maurel being out of it), and my mind sufficiently made up, I withdrew, and so cannot testify as to the degree of success the new *prima donna* met with in the later scenes. Nor was I present at the performance of Otello on Saturday, when Miss Eames and Dufriche appeared instead of Albani and Maurel as Desdemona and Iago.

One of the results of the Military Exhibition of 1890, the musical department of which was taken good care of by Colonel Shaw-Hellier, has just appeared in the shape of a guinea volume, containing a descriptive catalog of the instruments exhibited, illustrated with heliogravures. In producing these, by the bye, the photographer, for the sake of a pretty picture, has occasionally scorned all technical classification. However, as the references are clear enough, and the plates very effective, the work is none the worse. As far as I know, there is no reference book available in any musical library which could supply the place of this catalog. In order to get at the information it gives concerning modern wind instruments, I have sometimes had to hunt through inventors' pamphlets, "methods" written for bandsmen by bandsmen in a style unrivaled for confused illiteracy and set up by music printers in the ineptest of typography, instrument-makers' catalogs of surpassing mendacity, and standard works on "modern instrumentation" containing statements which must have been already obsolescent when Nebuchadnezzar engaged his orchestra.

The difficulty about producing really comprehensive and exhaustive treatises on the subject is that they are not of sufficiently general interest to circulate to the extent needed to make them remunerative to publishers. It took a whole Military Exhibition to make this catalog possible; and if I were not, as a critic, bound to pretend that there is nothing musical in heaven or on earth that I did not know all along, I should not mind confessing that my knowledge was materially enlarged both by this exhibition and "The Inventions" of 1885. In one or two places, notably in Mr Blaikley's essay on pitch, with its valuable and somewhat astonishing table of variations caused by changes of temperature in concert rooms, the catalog is written rather from the point of view of the instrument maker and military bandmaster than from that of the musician who has to keep the interests of the dramatic singer always in sight; and there is a slight survival of the regulation treatises in the old-fashioned passage about "the growing tendency to replace the trumpet in the orchestra by the cornet." This way of putting it is absurdly out of date, the fact being that the cornet *has* completely superseded the trumpet, and that what is now happening is an attempt to reintroduce the trumpet in the shape of the new straight clarino with two valves on which Kosleck played in Bach's B minor Mass so brilliantly and successfully at the bicentenary performance in the Albert Hall in 1885, and which has since been taken up by Mr Morrow.

I cannot find this instrument, which struck me as a very important one, in the catalog: neither is there any mention of the bass trumpet, for which Wagner has written a part in Die Walküre, usually played on an alto trombone at the Richter concerts. It is in such omissions as these (if I am not complaining only of my own oversights) that the military limitations of the Kneller Hall purview of instrumental music make themselves felt; but they are not typical omissions: Colonel Shaw-Hellier and Captain Day have gone to work in a most catholic spirit, and are evidently guiltless of having purposely excluded any wind instrument on the ground of its not having come into use in military bands.

An excellent little book for Bayreuth pilgrims is Smolian's Themes of Tannhäuser, which has just been translated by Mr Ashton Ellis and published by Chappell for a shilling. I am afraid one or two of its interpretations will considerably startle those admirers of the Tannhäuser overture who have innocently accepted most of its details as mere phrases of absolute music; but Herr Smolian's analysis certainly carries conviction. In looking over it I have been somewhat taken aback by the number of points which had escaped me in a work with which I have an acquaintance of some twenty years' standing. *The* commentary on Tannhäuser, however, must always be Wagner's own instructions for its performance, a translation of which is now running through The Meister.

A very important work for Wagnerites is Glasenapp's new Wagner Encyclopedia, recently published by Fritsch of Leipzig. I bought the two volumes at David Nutt's in the Strand for—I forget the exact price; but it made a huge hole in a sovereign. It is not so impossibly thorough as it has been declared by one or two critics (who must, I think, have had complimentary copies); for, after all, the only genuine Wagner Encyclopedia is a complete collection of his works; but still it gives the most striking verdicts of the greatest art critic of the century. It is a pity that an English translation is not available; for our notions of Wagner are still a jumble of superstitions: hardly anywhere do you meet with recognition of the vigorous commonsense, the clear-sighted practicalness, the unfailing grip of the vital and permanent elements in art as distinguished from its fashions, its aberrations, its flights down no-thorough-fares of all sorts, which made him master of the situation in the teeth of all Europe.

SIR AUGUSTUS
The World, 5 August 1891

Europe, it is to be hoped, will understand that Sir Augustus Harris has not been knighted in public recognition of the claims of Music on the English nation. I forget who it was that paid the Order of the Garter the tribute of acknowledging that there was no nonsense about merit connected with it★; but Sir Augustus must have been reminded of that epigram when he received the accolade, not for his services to Art, but for happening to be Sheriff when the Emperor of Germany happened to pay a visit to the City of London, as if it were not easier to find a dozen Sheriffs than one capable operatic manager. There is, however, some satisfaction in the circumstance that the interest created by our *impresario's* elevation is due entirely to his connexion with music and the drama. Before it occurred, I was the only person in London who, in private conversation, invariably spoke respectfully of him as "Mr Harris." Everybody else spoke of him as "Gus." I do not know what warrant they had for the familiarity; but that they did so is beyond all question. Now, had he been merely a Sheriff all his life, nobody would ever have known his first name, nor cared a straw whether he was knighted or not. Nor should I have to go into the question of

★ "I like the Garter; there's no damned merit in it" (Lord Melbourne).

whether he deserved the compliment after his achievements last season.

On the whole, I am inclined to answer that question in the negative. I admit that he has not grudged prodigious sums of money; and in view of his alleged intention to modify his plans next season in the direction of fewer performances it seems probable that he has not recovered as much of that expenditure as he expected; but it partly serves him right, because neither he nor the public got value for what he spent. He made an initial mistake in engaging five leading tenors and no stage manager. For want of a stage manager, Orfeo was murdered. For want of a stage manager, the first act of Otello was laid waste. For want of a stage manager, Tannhäuser was made a laughing-stock to every German who went to see it, except in the one or two passages which Albani stage managed. For want of a stage manager, the first scene in Boïto's Mefistofele remains so absurd that it is to be hoped that when Edouard de Reszke appears at one of the holes in a ragged cloth, and sends a hearty *Ave, Signor,* in the direction of another hole, the audience do not know whom he is supposed to be addressing. For want of a stage manager, no man in Les Huguenots knows whether he is a Catholic or a Protestant; and conversations which are pure nonsense except on the supposition that the parties cannot distinguish oneanother's features in the gloom are conducted in broad moonlight and gaslight. I have been told that the moon in Die Meistersinger has to be superintended by Jean de Reszke in person; but for the truth of this I cannot vouch. As for the prison doors that will not shut, and the ordinary door that will not open, I do not complain of that: it is the stage way of such apertures. One gets at last to quite look forward to Valentin attempting a dashing exit through an impracticable door into his house opposite the cathedral, and recoiling, flattened and taken aback, to disappear ignominiously through the solid wall at the next entrance. I would not now accept any house as being that in which Rigoletto so jealously immured his daughter, unless the garden door were swinging invitingly open before every onset of the draughts, more numerous than the currents of the ocean, which ventilate the Covent Garden stage, and the courses of which have so often been pointed out to me by the horizontal flames of the guttering candles in the first act of La Traviata.

It must be understood that by a stage manager I do not mean merely a person who arranged the few matters which cannot either be neglected or left to arrange themselves as best they may. I mean rather the man who arranges the stage so as to produce the illusion aimed at by the dramatic poet and musician. Such a one, for instance, would begin his preparation for Mefistofele by reminding the scenepainter of Mesdag's Sunrise in the Museum in Amsterdam, and coaxing him to substitute some great cloud region like that for the dingy cloth with the two holes in it which lames the imagination in spite of Boïto's music. He would give some touch of nature to that garden of Margaret's, where, beneath the shade of tall trees, a discordantly gaudy flower bed blazes in an outrageous glare that never was on sea or land; for, if he could not adapt the light to the scenery, he could at least try to adapt the scenery to the light. He would bring his commonsense to bear on La Traviata, his intelligence on Les Huguenots, his reading on Tannhäuser, and his imagination on all operas. And withal, instead of putting Sir Augustus Harris to any additional expense, he would make fifteen shillings go further than a pound goes now. That is what really offends my economic instincts in the business—that so much money should be wasted. I was able to forgive the shabbiness of Signor Lago's Orfeo, because money was scarce there;

but the splendors of the Harrisian Orfeo were infuriating, because the effect was reduced more than the cost was increased.

Whether, if a stage manager who was a real artist were placed in command of the Covent Garden stage, anyone there would pay much attention to him is another matter. In any case, he would need to be seconded by an *impresario* of great authority, who would make up his costs without fear or favor in the interests of the public alone. Perhaps Sir Augustus's newly-won spurs may strike awe next season into his company; but, so far, the contingent from the Paris Opéra seem to rule the roost. Jean de Reszke and Lassalle, who might, with Ravogli, have made Carmen one of the chief successes of the season, and that, too, without any considerable strain upon them, condescended to play in it just once. Jean was especially trying. He shirked Siegfried; he shirked Tannhäuser; he would obviously have shirked Raoul if he had not been startled into alarmed activity by the success of Van Dyck; and he put off Otello to the last moment. Yet nobody dared to remonstrate, as far as one can see. The *impresario's* hand was wanted on other occasions as well. Les Huguenots should have been recast with Plançon as Marcel, Edouard de Reszke as San Bris, and Lassalle omitted; and in Fidelio the part of Pizarro should never have been left to Devoyod.

It is true that we were spared a second resurrection of La Favorita to please Mlle Richard; but the performances of Lucia solely to shew off Madame Melba's singing, and of La Traviata to gratify Madame Albani's weakness for the part of the consumptive Violetta, were probably nearly as hard on the public as they undoubtedly were on the critics. On the other hand, Il Trovatore, which has been inflicted on us season after season with hopeless casts, was dropped this time, apparently because Lago's experiment had shewed that Giulia

Ravogli's Azucena would have made it interesting. Her Carmen, which was a very remarkable performance, was supported by artists who, in this opera at least, were not worth hearing, and was then withdrawn to make way for the hackneyed and trivial Carmen of Miss de Lussan, who learns nothing and forgets nothing. Maurel's Mephistopheles, a striking and well thought out impersonation, far superior to that of his predecessor Faure, was given up to make room for Edouard de Reszke, who, with the utmost good humor, makes the whole drama ridiculous.

It is only fair to say, however, that Brother Edouard did his share of the season's work manfully, seconding Van Dyck with a will, coming to the rescue of Don Giovanni, achieving a success no less artistic than personal as Mefistofele (Boïto's), and throwing in Plunkett in Martha with the best grace in the world. But this was evidently due to his complaisance, and not to the authority of the management. Still, it is hardly conceivable that Mr Harris (as he was then) was content to see his huge expenses squandered so often upon stale performances by the second-rate singers of his company, whilst his most popular artists were, so to speak, eating their heads off; or that he would have permitted it if he could have helped it. There is, in short, no discipline at the Opera.

The reason, I suggest, is that the Opera does not pay as an ordinary theatre pays. The manager has to spend more than he can hope to receive in payments for admission; and the deficiency, plus his profits, must be made up by rich guarantors who require an opera box in the season just as they require a carriage or any other part of their social equipment. They, therefore, have to grant the subvention which, in Paris or Berlin, is granted by the State. It is this system of private subvention that breaks the manager's back, as far as discipline is concerned. His artists are able to go behind him and make friends with the mammon of unrighteousness in the persons of the guarantors; and he soon finds that he cannot afford to offend his idolized tenor, his fashionable soprano, or his pet baritone, without also offending his most influential guarantors, which he, of course, cannot afford to do. Probably the stories that circulate in the foyer between the acts as to casts vetoed by enamored and jealous lady patrons who object to their idols making even stage love to songstresses whom they are suspected of admiring, are all false; but the fact that they might quite possibly be true is as strong an objection to the system as if they actually were true.

The complete remedy is a social rather than an operatic problem; but it is worth pointing out that if the subvention came from public instead of private sources, the manager could deal far more boldly with those of his artists who are favorites in the drawing room, and far more fairly with those who are favorites only on the stage, than he dares at present, whilst the interests of the public would be materially reinforced.

I purposely refrain from saying anything about the praiseworthy points in the past season. The critic who is grateful is lost. Sir Augustus has given us Otello and revived Fidelio. Instead of thanking him, I ask why he has not given us Siegfried. When he gives us Siegfried (which he can do by engaging Van Dyck for it), I shall complain of the neglect of Die Walküre. Let him add that also to his obsolete repertory, and I shall speak contemptuously of an opera house where Tristan is unknown. After that, I can fall back on Das Rheingold, Götterdämmerung, and Parsifal; but by that time, at the present rate of progress, I shall be celebrating my hundred and fiftieth birthday. If even then I say that I am satisfied, let there be an end of me at once; for I shall be of no further use as a critic.

The very last concert of the season was a little affair at Collards' Rooms the other day, at which a few artists gave their services to help a lady who has been unfortunately disabled. There was the usual middle-aged lady who sang rather well, and the usual somewhat younger lady who sang very badly, and the usual youngest lady of all who sang the Donizetti cavatina which her master had been drilling her in for the past two years. A fortnight ago I would have scorned such a concert with the utmost arrogance: on this occasion I was glad to have something to do in the laziest hour of an idle afternoon. The entertainment, luckily, was considerably strengthened by Seiffert, who lent a powerful helping hand with his violin, and Mlle de Llana, who played Thomé's Sérénade d'Harlequin better than we deserved, considering our very feeble numbers. On referring to my program, by the bye, I find that Mlle de Llana is no longer Mlle de Llana, but Madame Seiffert.

VIVA VOCE CRITICISM
The World, 16 September 1891

Not Bayreuth, but Paulus, is the cause of this momentary lifting up of my voice amid the silence of the dead season. As a matter of fact I have not been to Bayreuth. Those who remember how earnestly I warned my readers to secure tickets in good time will not be surprised to hear that I spoke as a man taught by his own incorrigible remissness in the past. When at the eleventh hour, being wholly unprovided, I found that there was not a ticket to be had in Europe—that there were two hundred and fifty names down for returned tickets for every performance, and that the average of returns was not above twentyfive, I became quite mad to go. But in a day or so, resigning myself to the inevitable, I came to the conclusion that Bayreuth was an overrated place, and made arrangements for an excursion of a different sort. No sooner had I done this than the difficulty about tickets vanished: Karl Armbruster offered to manage it for me: Van Dyck offered to manage it for me: Messrs Chappell actually did manage it for me: Europe, in short, had realized the gravity of the situation, and Bayreuth was at my feet. But it was too late: the other arrangements stood inexorably in the way; and I now had to refuse. Nobody will be surprised to learn that the proffered seats were no sooner sorrowfully disposed of to mere ordinary Wagnerians, than circumstances again modified my arrangements so as to remove all obstacles to my going. I braced myself up once more to face that forty hours' rush from Holborn to Bavaria, with its eight hours' *malaise* between Queenborough and Flushing, less deadly in its after effects than a railway journey from Calais or even Ostend to Brussels; its inevitable inspection of the latest improvements in the Cologne cathedral, in which every inch of new steeple adds an ell of insignificance and vulgarity to the whole structure; its endless joggle along the Left Rhine Railway, with the engine depositing a ring of soot between one's neck and collar, and the impermanent way disintegrating into whirlwinds of dust; its two or three hours' wait after midnight at Würzburg for the Bamberg train, or else the push on to Nuremberg, there to pay a mark for every penn'orth of sleep you have time for; and the final entry into Bayreuth within four hours of the trumpet call to the theatre, hoping desperately that the novelty of the place and the stimulus of Wagnerian enthusiasm will enable you to keep awake during the first performance. I had run it so close that no easier stages were practicable. But I was spared after all: the tickets were

[419]

gone this time in earnest. At least the Committee thought so, and telegraphed "Impossible," though it afterwards turned out that they were wrong, as they usually are about everything except lodgings. Howbeit, I took their word for it; and now the Bayreuthites may boast as outrageously as they please about the Tannhäuser: I shall never be able to contradict them. But since it is clear that the Wagner Theatre was filled at every performance by people many of whom must have spent at least twenty pounds in getting there, it seems to me that it is time, from a mere business point of view, to begin building the Wagner Theatre on Richmond Hill. Unfortunately the noble president of the London branch of the Wagner Society, who might be expected to move in the matter, is preoccupied by the question of his seignorial rights over Ham Common. Perhaps he is going to build the Wagner Theatre there. If not, it will be interesting to see whether it will occur to any of the commoners to impeach before the Wagner Society its London president's fidelity to the principles of the illustrious exile of '48.★

However that may be, I have not been out of England, and have indeed heard no good music lately except a brass band of shoemakers, conducted by a compositor, playing for pure love of their art on the racecourse at Northampton one Sunday afternoon, and playing very well indeed. They gave us a Gloria of Haydn's with a delicacy of execution and a solemn reverence for the old master which were extraordinarily refreshing after the stale professional routine playing of the London concert platforms. It was like seeing a withering flower put into

★ In 1848 Wagner was obliged to flee to Paris and later to Zürich to escape an order for his arrest for involvement in the revolutionary cause. He did not return to Germany until more than a decade later.

water. This has been, so far, the only musical episode in my wanderings, which are chiefly devoted to *viva voce* criticisms delivered gratuitously to the man in the street who cannot afford to buy The World. It is a salutary thing after the worry and hurry of a London season to abandon one's typewriter, fly beyond the reach of the endless deliveries of the metropolitan postal service, and deliver one's soul face to face with one's fellow man under the open sky. To take a trap through a countryside, driving from one village green to another, and criticizing by the oratorical instead of the literary method,* rejuvenates me rarely after three months on the treadmill whose well-worn steps are St James's Hall, Prince's Hall, Steinway Hall, and Covent Garden. With good company to keep you merry during the home journey in the dark, there is no pleasanter way of spending a day, except perhaps lying on one's back on a hillside doing absolutely nothing, a luxury which requires an unconscionable deal of preliminary hard work to give it a really fine flavor. Oral criticism in the streets of a manufacturing town at night is not quite so romantically pastoral; but on the fine evening in such a place, there are much duller diversions than hiring an itinerant shooting gallery or the like, strikingly illuminated with a supply of naphtha flares, from some gypsy showman; assembling a crowd under the false pretence of being a cheap Jack; and then firing off your weekly article at them by word of mouth. You can then see for yourself how many people yawn and drop your column before they have half finished it. You can even test its pecuniary estimation by sending or taking round your hat, as, upon sufficient occasion, I have often done. Or, if there

* Shaw had been on a lecture tour that took him to Reading, Oxford and environs, Wolverhampton, Stafford and the potteries regions, Newcastle, and Lichfield.

is no necessity for that, you can mark the degree of emphasis with which the drunken man who persists in interrupting you is finally seized and hurled into the outer darkness. I cannot but think that criticism would be greatly improved if our leading critics were to rub off the illusions and unrealities of London literary life occasionally in this fashion. They are probably restrained solely by a vague impression that something would happen to them if they followed my example—musty eggs, dead cats, the police, social ostracism, and what not? Now it is no doubt true that if they were to bore the public to its face with the platitudes they sometimes inflict on them under cover of anonymous journalism, it is impossible to say to what lengths popular indignation might go. And it might be as well for even those who have opinions of their own, and are not oversensitive to the very solid reasons which exist for hiding them, to clothe them in vernacular English and not in the literary jargon which is considered good enough for print. But with something to say and a reasonably human way of saying it (and without both why should anyone be a critic at all?) a man may take his criticism into the market place with every prospect of an astonishing width of toleration, and considerable benefit to his lungs.

Thus you can roam about for a while at little cost, receiving much—nay, sometimes overmuch—gratuitous entertainment from hospitable enthusiasts, and sampling provincial art by an occasional visit to the theatre, where the latest London success in the way of farcical comedy will generally be found going the rounds in an edifyingly bowdlerized condition. Or you can stop for a few hours at a cathedral town, and see how the dean and chapter have covered the outside of the greatest of our art treasures with figures ordered wholesale from this or that eminent firm of stonemasons; filled exquisite windows with stained glass resembling transparent linoleum; and blocked up the inside with paltry elaborations of the commonest tombstone-makers' ware to the memory of their own sons and nephews killed in some of our unrighteous little market-making colonial wars. One is not surprised to find that these cenotaphs have to be fenced in with iron railings to prevent visitors who know the value of the outraged building from summarily removing them with pickaxes. When I halted on the way from Stafford to Northampton on Saturday week, I could not help asking myself whether it was any great gain to have escaped Cologne only to come to Lichfield.

But from all such reflections I was recalled by the overwhelming artistic importance of the event in London to which I have alluded. Paulus was (and is) at the Trocadero, singing *L'Amant de la Tour Eiffel, Le Père la Victoire,* and so on. I could not catch the whole meaning of his songs; but as I could catch no meaning at all in the English songs of the evening, perhaps there was not much meaning to catch. He has a certain personal force, has Paulus, and so stands out brilliantly among the twinklings of aborted artistic impulse which make up the music hall firmament. It may be said of him, as Marx said of Mill, that his eminence is due to the flatness of the surrounding country. Still, his talent and industry as a comedian would in England soon transfer him to the comic opera houses; his singing conveys the impression that he could refine upon it a good deal before an audience which could be trusted to appreciate the improvement; and he whistles much better than Mrs Alice Shaw. The rest of the program left me more convinced than ever of the need for free trade in dramatic art. Those items which were the direct product of the law for the protection of theatres seemed to bore the audience almost as much as they bored me— were enough, indeed, to drive a man to make himself uncritically drunk in self-defence. Some ballad singing of the ordinary concert type, by Mr Christian and Miss Yeamans, was much relished; but why the lady should have sung Millard's Waiting in a limelight, gesticulating in the manner of a fourth-rate German *prima donna* struggling with Ocean, thou mighty monster, is more than I can undertake to account for, especially as the audience shewed a lively sense of the absurdity of the proceeding.

The success of L'Enfant Prodigue had its inevitable sequel in the production of Yvette at the Avenue Theatre last Saturday. Yvette was not a success in Paris; and it will not be a success here. L'Enfant Prodigue had drollery, domestic pathos, and the charm of novelty. Yvette has nothing but a pretty and refined musical setting by André Gedalge, whose labor has been entirely wasted. For the sake of Mlle Milly Dathenes and the rest, I wish it were possible to be less blunt; for they play as well as it is possible to play under the circumstances; but they cannot save a piece which is so utterly void of interesting ideas that I cannot help suspecting that Michel Carré designed it originally as a libretto for a grand opera by Gounod.

As there seems no prospect of any revival of musical business before the Birmingham Festival next month, I propose to drop round to Venice until then.

THE BIRMINGHAM FESTIVAL

The World, 14 October 1891

I cannot say that I am unmixedly grateful to the Birmingham Festival people. They brought me all the way from Venice by a polite assurance that a packet of tickets awaited my arrival. But when, after a headlong rush over the Alps and far away into the Midlands, I reached the Town Hall, insufferable indignities were put upon me. The stewards on the floor declared that my seat was in the gallery; the stewards in the gallery insisted that it was on the floor; and finally, when it became plain that no seat at all had been reserved, I was thrust ignominiously into a corner in company with a couple of draughts and an echo, and left to brood vengefully over the performance. On the Passion Music day I escaped the corner, and shared a knifeboard at the back of the gallery with a steward who kept Bach off by reading the Birmingham Daily Post, and breathed so hard when he came to the bankruptcy list that it was plain that every firm mentioned in it was heavily in his debt.

Under these circumstances, no right-minded person will grudge a certain vindictive satisfaction in recording that the performance of the St Matthew Passion, which was what I came from Venice to hear, was not, on the whole, a success. No doubt it was something to have brought the chorus to the point of singing such difficult music accurately and steadily. But a note-perfect performance is only the raw material of an artistic performance; and what the Birmingham Festival achieved was very little more than such raw material. In the opening chorus, the plaintive, poignant melody in triple time got trampled to pieces by the stolid trudging of the choir from beat to beat. The violins in the orchestra shewed the singers how it ought to be done; but the lesson was thrown away; the trudging continued; and Richter, whom we have so often seen beating twelve-eight time for his orchestra with a dozen sensitive beats in every bar, made no attempt to cope with the British chorister, and simply marked one, two, three, four, like a drill-sergeant. The rest of the performance did nothing to shew any special sympathy with Bach's religious music on Richter's part.

It is, of course, to be considered that the necessity for having the Passion sung from Sterndale Bennett's edition, no other being available with the English words, may have compelled him to be content with the best performance, according to that edition, attainable in the time at his disposal; so that he, whilst wishing to give the work "*à la* Wagner," as the Dresdeners used to say, may have had to put up with it "*à la* Mendelssohn" in despair of getting anything better. But, then, why did he let those piteous questions from the second chorus to the first come out with a shout like the *sforzandos* in the roughest and most vigorous pages of Beethoven? And why did he allow the remonstrances of the disciples about the pot of ointment to be sung by the same mass of voices, and with the same savage turbulence, as the outbursts of wrath and mockery from the crowd at Pilate's house and Golgotha? Such matters as these might have been quite easily set right. Perhaps the safest conclusion is that half the shortcoming was due to Richter not having taken Bach's Passion Music to heart, and the other half to Sterndale Bennett, to lack of time for rehearsal, and to the impregnable density of that most terrific of human institutions, the British chorus.

For no one who knows Bach intimately will need to be told that our plan of compensating for the absence of some ten or eleven skilful and sympathetic singers by substituting ten or eleven hundred stolid and maladroit ones will not answer with his music, however strong-lunged the ten or eleven hundred may be. One comparatively easy thing the Birmingham chorus could do well, and that was to sing the chorales. These, accordingly, were excellently given. The rest was leather and prunella. Even the thunder and lightning chorus had no electricity in it.

Rather unexpectedly, where Richter failed to make any mark, Mr Stockley, the local conductor, had a brilliant success. The performance of the Messiah which he conducted was the triumph of the festival. Not that Mr Stockley is a greater conductor than Richter; but he knows the Messiah as Richter apparently does not know the St Matthew Passion; and he has the courage of that knowledge, and of his familiarity with the choir. I have rarely been more agreeably surprised than when I began incredulously to realize that Mr Stockley was in the secret which in London is strictly kept between Handel and myself. I need not now repeat what I said on the occasion of the Handel Festival as to the proper execution of the florid traits in Handel's choruses, and as to the vivacious *tempo* which is necessary to bring out their brightness and vigor. Suffice it to say that if Mr Manns or Mr Barnby, or any of our London conductors, had been present (perhaps they were) to hear And He shall purify taken in *my* manner—which is also Mr Stockley's, which is also Handel's—they must have wondered whether this impetuously confident music could indeed be read from the same notes as the dull, lumbering, heavy-footed, choral monster they have so often goaded along at the Albert Hall and the Crystal Palace.

No doubt the younger members of the band and the soloists were a little taken aback by the absolute refusal of the conductor to drag the *tempo* in order to shew off their tone. But if any complaints or deridings reach the committee, let it fortify itself behind the undeniable fact that the performance had a hearty success and a freedom from tedium quite unknown on Messiah nights in London. If ever, during Mr Stockley's time, the committee entrusts a work of Handel's to any strange conductor, however eminent, it will shew itself incapable of understanding when it is well served.

It is not easy to fit Villiers Stanford's Eden with a critical formula which will satisfy all parties. If I call it brilliant balderdash, I shall not only be convicted of having used an "ungenteel" expression, but I shall grievously offend those friends of his whose motto is *Floreat Stanford: ruat coelum!** If, on the other hand, I call it a masterpiece of scholarship and genius, and expatiate on its erudite modal harmonies and its brilliant instrumentation, I shall hardly feel that I have expressed my own inmost mind. Not that I am prejudiced against modal harmonies. I can harmonize themes in keys other than that of C, and leave out all the sharps and flats against any man alive; and though for the life of me I never can remember which of the scales produced in this manner is the mixophrygian mode, and which the hypoionian, or Dorian, or what not, yet I am content to be able to perpetrate the harmonies and to leave more learned men to fit them with their proper names. But what I cannot do is to persuade myself that if I write in this fashion my music will sound angelic, and that if I use the ordinary major and minor scales the result will be comparatively diabolic. I find it works out rather the other way.

I know, of course, that several modern composers, from Handel to Beethoven, and from Beethoven to Bourgault-Ducoudray, have done very pretty things in the modal manner. But when Professor Stanford asks me to admit that his choristers are angels merely because they persistently sing B flat instead of B natural in the key of C major (as the Siamese band used to do when they played our national anthem, to our great alarm, on stone dulcimers), I feel that he is becoming exorbitant. I see no reason why heaven should be behind earth in the use of the leading note in the scale. Perhaps this is not serious criticism; but I really cannot take Eden seriously. From the mixolydian motet at the beginning

* May Stanford flourish though the heavens fall.

to the striking up of Three Blind Mice to the words Sleep, Adam, Sleep by the Archangel Michael at the end, I caught not a single definite purpose or idea at all commensurate with the huge pretension of the musical design. That pretension is the ruin of Eden. There is one interlude which I should applaud if it were a piece of hurdy-gurdy music for a new setting of [Donizetti's] Linda di Chamounix; and there are plenty of other passages which would be acceptable on similar terms.

But in a work which stands or falls as a great musical epic, they only made me wonder what Mr Stanford would think of me if I took advantage of my literary craftsmanship to write inane imitations of Milton's Paradise Lost with all the latest graces of style, and got my friends to go into raptures over its grammar and its correct scansion. However, who am I that I should be believed, to the disparagement of eminent muscians? If you doubt that Eden is a masterpiece, ask Dr Parry and Dr Mackenzie, and they will applaud it to the skies. Surely Dr Mackenzie's opinion is conclusive; for is he not the composer of Veni Creator, guaranteed as excellent music by Professor Stanford and Dr Parry? You want to know who Dr Parry is? Why, the composer of Blest Pair of Sirens, as to the merits of which you have only to consult Dr Mackenzie and Professor Stanford. Nevertheless, I remain unshaken in my opinion that these gentlemen are wasting their talent and industry. The sham classics which they are producing are worth no more than the forgotten pictures of Hilton and epics of Hoole.*

* William Hilton (1786–1839), whose Christ crowned with Thorns had recently been purchased by the Royal Academy out of the Chantrey Fund. John Hoole was an XVIII century playwright whose three tragedies were produced at Covent Garden.

Dvořák's Requiem bored Birmingham so desperately that it was unanimously voted a work of extraordinary depth and impressiveness, which verdict I record with a hollow laugh, and allow the subject to drop by its own portentous weight. Besides, I do not wish to belie that steward who introduced me to his colleague on Thursday morning (when I was looking for a seat) as "one of these complimentary people."

Considering the mass of work to be prepared, the execution was, on the whole, highly creditable, though I doubt if Dvořák thought so, as most of the fatigue, the bad intonation, and the blunders of band, chorus, and principals fell to his lot on the Requiem day. All the English music was well done. The band achieved a splendid performance of Brahms's Symphony in F (No. 3); of Beethoven's Seventh Symphony, especially the last three movements; of the Walkürenritt, concerning which our gifted Hans must be slightly mad, considering the outrageous position he gave it in the program; and of the accompaniments to the last act of Tannhäuser, and to the concertos played by Joachim. Of the solo singers, only Lloyd and Santley did their work with any great distinction. Miss Anna Williams, in the Messiah, took But Thou didst not leave out of the mouth of the tenor—a proceeding which I can gasp and stare at, but not criticize.

Of the Crystal Palace Concerts, which began last Saturday, more anon. Popper duly made his appearance, and proved quite as fine a violoncellist as his great reputation had led us all to expect.

CHEAP OPERA

The World, 21 October 1891

The reaction after the feverish musical activity of last year seems to continue. Last week London had to live until Saturday on the expectations raised by Signor Lago's prospectus, and on the rival enterprise of Sir Augustus Harris. The most interesting point about the Lago enterprise is the transfer of Italian opera to a theatre of reasonable size—one in which such a work as Donizetti's Elisir d'Amore might possibly come to life again if any sort of serious trouble were taken with it. The spread of musical knowledge and cheap pianos must sooner or later produce a crop of cheap editions of the non-copyright operas of the old repertory; and that in turn must lead to a revival of that repertory, not at Covent Garden, but on stages like those of the Lyric and Prince of Wales' Theatres. The notion that the march of modern music has left Rossini, Donizetti, and Bellini hopelessly behind, because their palmy days at the Royal Italian Opera are gone by, is like the illusion that prevails in literary circles to the effect that nobody now reads the novels of Grant, James, Fenimore Cooper, or Alexandre Dumas *père*,* because they have ceased to be reviewed or discussed by literary experts.

When the day comes—and it is surely coming—when opera singers at ten pounds a week or less will be more competent in every way than those who now demand

---

* James Grant, a Scot; G.P.R. James, an Englishman; James Fenimore Cooper, an American; and Alexandre Dumas *père,* a Frenchman: all were prolific writers of historical romances early in the XIX century.

from thirty to a hundred, plenty of small theatrical capitalists, who now would as soon think of running an empire as an opera house, will try the effect of the enchanting old tunes and the inspiriting old rum-tum on the social strata which are being lifted into the region of dramatic music by the great social upheaval of the School Board. Depend upon it, Signor Lago, in moving from Covent Garden to the Shaftesbury, is marching in the track of evolution, and is leaving Sir Augustus, as far as so-called cheap opera is concerned, behind him. If he fulfils his promise of producing Wagner's Flying Dutchman there, he will have the advantage of working on the same scale as Carl Rosa at the Lyceum in 1876. And the Flying Dutchman had a success on that occasion, both artistic and financial, which it has never attained elsewhere in London.

The subject of cheapness in musical and other literature was forced upon me yesterday by the spectacle, in Ricordi's shop window, of the vocal score of Mascagni's Cavalleria Rusticana, published by Sonzogno of Milan, price ten shillings net. Having already seen this score at Milan offered for the Italian equivalent of ten shillings, and refused to pay any such monstrous price for a one-act opera, I passed on, musing on the enormous stupidity of Italian shopkeeping from the English point of view. In Venice the other day a friend of mine went into a shop and asked the price of a certain article. Twentyfive francs was the answer. My friend bid three, an offer which was waved off as a pleasantry on the part of the English gentleman. He, however, made no move until the shopkeeper came down to four, when he bid three-and-a-half, at which figure the transaction was closed to the satisfaction of both parties. Now, far be it from me to pretend that if that child of the South had been an Englishman, with an establishment in Oxford-street, he would have been one whit

[432]

honester. But he would have found, first, that my friend's time, being worth so many guineas an hour, was too valuable to admit of his patronizing shops where it took longer than two minutes to make a purchase; and, second, that the shopkeeper who makes money in London is he who sells twenty articles at a profit of a halfpenny each, instead of selling one at a profit of sixpence. Hence, though we can hold our own in commercial dishonesty with any foreigner ever born, we have *unico prezzo* in all our shops, and we can buy Professor Stanford's Eden in vocal score, mixolydian motets and all, for half the price of Cavalleria Rusticana, though the latter does not contain one-third as much new copyright music as the former. I do not profess to be a man of business (though musical criticism includes business, as the whole includes the part), but I respectfully submit to Ricordi, Sonzogno, and continental music publishers generally, that vocal scores are not in any country the luxuries of the rich, and that the way to make money by them is through low prices and large sales. Such prices as sixteen shillings and twenty shillings for scores of Boïto's Mefistofele and the last seven works of Wagner are not remunerative; they are simply prohibitive. The astonishing thing is that Novello, or some other London and American firm, does not purchase these copyrights from the present holders, and make a large haul by reversing the greedy and shortsighted policy at present in force.

Although I have not, at the moment of writing this, seen Cavalleria Rusticana, my refusal to buy the score has not left me in total ignorance of the work. Do not be alarmed, I am not going to perpetrate an "analysis." Those vivid emotions which the public derive from descriptions of "postludes brought to a close on the pedal of A, the cadence being retarded by four chords forming an *arpeggio* of a diminished seventh, each grade serving as tonic for a perfect chord," must be sought elsewhere than in these columns. It is perhaps natural that gentlemen who are incapable of criticism should fall back on parsing; but, for my own part, I find it better to hold my tongue when I have nothing to say. Yet I cannot help chuckling at the tricks they play on their innocent editors. An editor never does know anything about music, though his professions to that effect invariably belie his secret mind.

I have before me a journal in which the musical critic has induced the editor to allow him to launch into music type in order to give a suggestion of a certain "fanciful and suggestive orchestral design" in Cavalleria Rusticana. The quotation consists of a simple figuration of the common chord of G sharp minor, with "&c." after it. If a literary critic had offered this editor such a sample of the style of Shakespear as

"Now is the," &c.

he would probably have remonstrated. But he is perfectly happy with his chord of G sharp minor, which is ten times more absurd. And yet that editor devotes a column of his paper to criticizing me in the most disrespectful manner. Can he wonder that my sense of public duty does not permit me to remain silent on the subject of his utter incapacity within my special province?

The fact is, I have heard the music of Cavalleria Rusticana, and can certify that it is a youthfully vigorous piece of work, with abundant snatches of melody broken obstreperously off on one dramatic pretext or another. But, lively and promising as it is, it is not a whit more so than the freshest achievements of Mr Hamish MacCunn and Mr Cliffe. The people who say, on the strength of it, that Verdi has found a successor and Boïto a competitor, would really say anything. Mascagni has shewn nothing of the originality or distinction which would entitle him to such a comparison. If he had, I am afraid I should now be defending him against a chorus of disparagement, instead of deprecating a repetition of the laudatory extravagances which so often compel me to take the ungracious attitude of demurring to the excesses of the criticism instead of the cordial one of pointing out what is good in the composition. Already I have read things about Cavalleria Rusticana which would require considerable qualification if they were applied to Die Meistersinger or Don Giovanni.

Max Bruch's new violin concerto, No. 3, in D minor, was played for the first time in public in England by Mr Hans Wessely on the 11th, at the South Place Sunday Popular Concerts. Sarasate had the second turn at it on Saturday last, with the advantage of an orchestra. I did not hear either performance. I take the opportunity, however, of mentioning the admirable way in which things are kept going at South Place, where a concert of the best chamber music, on the lines of the Monday and Saturday Popular Concerts, is open every Sunday evening at seven to anyone who chooses to walk in and listen. The programs are in no way less severe than those at St James's Hall; but the Finsbury working man comes in, sits it out, and puts what he can into the plate to help to keep the concerts going. If one of our prosperous westenders would go down some Sunday and put into the plate the same percentage of his week's income as that contributed by his Finsbury neighbor, he would make the committee's mind easy for the rest of the season.

In mentioning Herr Popper's performance at the Crystal Palace I forbore to deal specially with his concerto, because, to tell the truth, I was puzzled by its abruptly ending after what I had supposed to be only the first movement. I now find that I was right. Popper, through no fault of his own, did not succeed in getting

[435]

to the Palace in time for rehearsal; and it was thought better not to venture on the last two movements at first sight. Mr Manns was anxious to explain to the audience; but Popper has an objection—rather unusual in the profession—to have a fuss made about him. At last Saturday's concert Hans Sitt conducted an overture of his own, composed for a play Don Juan d'Austria, a play by Leschivo,* of whose fame I confess myself wholly ignorant. The overture is clever and interesting, steering, somewhat in the manner of Berlioz, between the Wagnerian tone-picture and the formal "absolute music" overture. On the purely musical side, and especially in its rhythmic structure, it shews that Mendelssohn's influence is not dead yet. Mr Barton McGuckin sang Lend me your aid very well, and afterwards gave us a couple of songs by Mr Bemberg, the composer of Elaine, the forthcoming novelty at Mr D'Oyly Carte's opera house. Mr Bemberg, like Mr Goring Thomas, follows the French school, even to the extreme of calling his Hindoo chant a "Chant Hindoo." It is much in the style of Massenet, and throws no more light on Elaine than that the composer can utter with sufficient taste and address any inspiration that may come to him. Miss Adeline de Lara played Rubinstein's concerto in D minor. Considering that Miss de Lara's frame is not of the most powerful build, and that her technique is rather that of Henselt than of Rubinstein, her performance may fairly be described as extraordinary. On her last appearance at the Palace her fingers were startlingly rapid and accurate; but the hardness of her touch, and the nervous tension at which she played, shewed that the effort demanded by the manual execution left her

* Alma Leschivo was the pen name of Klara Fahrig (1848–1905), a German poet and dramatist, one of whose three plays was *Don Juan d'Austria*.

little energy to spare for artistic treatment. She was able to play the piano, but not to play with it. On Saturday her finger-work was as brilliant as before; but it seemed to be much further within her utmost resources, and to leave her comparatively at ease. Her class as a pianist cannot, however, be determined until she lets us hear her play the concertos of greater masters than Rubinstein.

CAVALLERIA RUSTICANA

The World, 28 October 1891

If experience had not convinced me these many years that theatre managers of all kinds, and operatic *impresarii* in particular, retain to the end the madness which first led them to their profession, I should be tempted to remonstrate with Signor Lago for getting a good thing like Cavalleria Rusticana, and tying [Ricci's] Crispino e la Comare round its neck. As a member of a Northern race, I refuse to have patience with Crispino. Any grasshopper with a moderately good ear could write reams of such stuff after spending three months in Italy. Offenbach's lightest operetta looms in intellectual majesty above this brainless lilting, with its colorless orchestration and its exasperatingly lighthearted and emptyheaded *recitatives*, accompanied by sickly chords on the violoncello with the third always in the bass. Perhaps Coquelin might make the farcical adventures of the shoemaker amusing; but Ciampi is not Coquelin: he is not even Ciampi in his prime. The simple-minded Italians of Soho, if they could obtain a *biglietto d'ingresso* for a shilling, would no doubt bless Signor Lago for restoring to them, in a foreign land, a sort of entertainment which gratifies their love of strumming and singing without for a moment disturbing that sunny stagnation of mind, the least disturbance of which they hate worse than cold baths. But in England the climate, the national character, and the prices of admission, are against such entertainments. When I spoke, last week, of the possibilities of a revival of the old repertory, I was thinking, as far as comic opera is concerned, of such works as Il Barbière, Don Pasquale, Les Deux Journées, Fra Diavolo, or La Grande Duchesse, and by no means of the second-hand wares of Cimarosa or Ricci. The operas which did not cross the Italian frontier when they were young, will not do so now that they are old. I also stipulated that they should be fairly well done; and, to be more particular, I may say that one of the conditions of their well-doing is that the buffo, however comic, shall sing instead of quacking, and that the tenor who revives *Com' e gentil* for us shall not have a shattering *tremolo*. This last remark is not, I assure you, a side-thrust at Crispino, which consists of two hours of Ciampi's buffooneries with no tenor at all, and is, indeed, so childish an affair that I really think that any party of musical boys and girls could improvize something just as clever and funny, just as one improvizes a charade or a game of dumb crambo. In a very comfortable country house (if such a thing exists), or out picnicking in the woods on a summer day, the Crispino style of entertainment would not come amiss; but in a crowded theatre, with one's mind made up to have some value for money paid at the doors, it is not good enough. In all friendliness to Signor Lago's enterprise, I recommend him to get rid of Crispino with all possible expedition, and either to give Cavalleria Rusticana by itself, without any padding, or else have it followed by a single act of one of Wagner's operas, played without cuts. Why not, for instance, the second act of Parsifal?

Of the music of Cavalleria (with the stress on the penultimate vowel, if you please: it is a mistake to suppose that the Italians call it Cavvlearea) I have already intimated that it is only what might reasonably be expected from a clever and spirited member of a generation which has Wagner, Gounod, and Verdi at its fingers' ends, and which can demand, and obtain, larger instrumental resources for a ballet than Mozart had at his disposal for his greatest operas and symphonies. Far more important than that, it has a public trained to endure, and even expect, continuous and passionate melody, instead of the lively little *allegros* of the old school, which were no more than classically titivated jigs and hornpipes; and to relish the most poignant discords—tonic ninths, elevenths, and thirteenths, taken unprepared in all sorts of inversions (you see, I can be as erudite as anybody else when I choose)—without making a wry face, as their fathers, coddled on the chromatic confectionery of Spohr and his contemporaries, used to do when even a dominant seventh visited their ears too harshly.

Even today you may still see here and there a big, strong, elderly man whimpering when they play the Tannhäuser overture at him, and declaring that there is no "tune" in it, and that the harmony is all discord, and the instrumentation all noise. Our young lions no longer have this infantile squeamishness and petulance to contend with, even in Italy. They may lay about them, harmonically and instrumentally, as hard as they please without rebuke: even the pedants have given up calling on them to observe "those laws of form to which the greatest masters have not disdained to submit"—which means, in effect, to keep Pop Goes the Weasel continually before them as a model of structure and modulation. Consequently, opera now offers to clever men with a turn for music and the drama an unprecedented opportunity for picturesque, brilliant, apt, novel, and yet safely familiar and popular combinations and permutations of the immense store of musical "effects" garnered up in the scores of the great modern composers, from Mozart to Wagner and Berlioz. This is the age of second-hand music. There is even growing up a school of composers who are poets and thinkers rather than musicians, but who have selected music as their means of expression out of the love of it inspired in them by the works of really original masters. It is useless to pretend that Schumann was a creative musician as Mendelssohn was one, or Boïto as Verdi, or Berlioz as Gounod. Yet Schumann's setting of certain scenes from Goethe's Faust is enormously more valuable than Mendelssohn's St Paul; we could spare La Traviata better than Mefistofele; whilst Berlioz actually towers above Gounod as a French composer.

And this because, on the non-musical side of their complex art, Mendelssohn and Gounod were often trivial, genteel, or sentimental, and Verdi obvious and melodramatic, whilst Schumann was deeply serious, Berlioz extraordinarily acute in his plans and heroic in his aims, and Boïto refined, subtle, and imaginative. The great composer is he who, by the rarest of chances, is at once a great musician and a great poet—who has Brahms's wonderful ear without his commonplace mind, and Molière's insight and imagination without his musical sterility. Thus it is that you get your Mozart or your Wagner—only here we must leave Molière out, as Wagner, on the extra-musical side, is comparable to nobody but himself. The honor of the second place in the hierarchy I shall not attempt to settle. Schumann, Berlioz, Boïto, and Raff, borrowing music to express their ideas, have, it must be admitted, sometimes touched an even higher level of originality than Schubert, Mendelssohn, and Goetz, who had to borrow ideas for their music to express, and were unquestionably superior only in the domain of absolute music.

But nobody except the directors of the Philharmonic Society will claim any higher than fourth place for those who have borrowed both their ideas and their music, and vulgarized both in the process—your Bruchs, Rubinsteins, Moszkowskis, Benoîts, Ponchiellis, and other gentlemen rather more likely to see this article and get their feelings hurt if I mentioned their names. Brahms, as a unique example of excess in one department and entire deficiency in the other, may take his place where he pleases, provided I am out of earshot of his Requiem.

I offer these illustrations to explain the difference between my critical method and that of the gentlemen who keep only one quality of margarine, which they spread impartially over all composers of established reputation; so that you shall not detect one hair's breadth of difference in their estimates of Beethoven and Meyerbeer, Wagner and Sir Arthur Sullivan, John Sebastian Bach and the President of the Royal Academy of Music. As they speak today of Mascagni, and will speak of Mozart at the forthcoming centenary celebration, they spoke yesterday of Dvořák and Villiers Stanford, four months ago of Handel, and a year ago of Moszkowski and Benoît.

The worst of it is, that the public judgment has become so pauperized by this butter bounty that although I habitually stretch goodnature to the verge of weakness in extenuating and hushing up all manner of avoidable deficiencies in the performances I criticize, yet I find myself held up as a ruthless and malignant savage because, in spite of all my efforts to be agreeable, a little perspective will occasionally creep into my column, and will betray, for instance, the fact that I consider Ivanhoe as hardly equal in all respects to Lohengrin, and am a little loth to declare offhand that Dr Parry's oratorios are an improvement on Handel's.

Some day I think I will go further, and let out the whole truth; for since I get no credit for my forbearance, it often comes into my mind that I may as well be hung for a sheep as a lamb.

All this is a mere preamble to the remark that Mascagni has set Cavalleria Rusticana to expressive and vigorous music, which music he has adapted to the business of the stage with remarkable judgment and good sense. That is the exact truth about it; and so, Mascagni being disposed of with this very considerable eulogy (implying that he is a man in a thousand, though not in a million), I go on to say that Vignas, the tenor, is completely satisfactory, both as singer and actor, in the part of Turiddu; that there is no fault to be found with Mlle Brema and Miss Damian in the mezzo-soprano and contralto parts; that Signorina Musiani, who is not a bit older or stouter than Miss Eames, has some genuine pathos and a voice of fine natural quality to offer as a set-off to a rather serious *tremolo*; and that Signor Brombara is so afflicted with the same complaint that he would be better advised to resort to dumb show, since he acts with much conviction.

The conclusion of the duet *Vendetta avrò*, which consists of several melodramatic exclamations delivered simultaneously, *fortissimo*, by Miss Musiani and Signor Brombara, was the most trying moment in the opera, as neither of the voices was steady enough for any pitch to be discernible. Brombara is, I fear, incurable, and must look for fame to countries where the *tremolo* is popular. Miss Musiani might possibly get the better of hers, though I am not very sanguine as to her losing her taste for it. However, all five principal artists do their work in the most artistic spirit, and succeed in justifying the credible side of the reputation of the opera—which is saying a good deal, considering how loudly the trumpet has been blown. If the body of tone from the ladies of the chorus were a trifle richer and stronger, and the harmonium in the church less remote in pitch from the band, there would be nothing but the *tremolos* to complain of. Would it be an impertinence on my part, by the bye, to remark that *tremolo* and *vibrato* are not synonymous terms? There is not even the most distant relationship or resemblance between them. One is a defect of the gravest kind: the other is one of the most precious graces a dramatic singer can acquire—if it can be acquired at all. There is no difficulty in acquiring the *tremolo*. No doubt these facts are well known: still, on looking over the papers lately I thought I would just mention them.

I hear that a few operatic performances are given every week at Covent Garden; but I presume they are of no particular importance, as my attention has not been specially called to them.

OPERA ON THE CHEAP

The World, 4 November 1891

I must say that I think Signor Lago has gone just a little past bearing in his mounting of The Flying Dutchman. I know very well that it is not within the power of any scenic artist, however lavishly supplied with capital, to put upon the stage the picture of the ocean which Wagner has conjured up with the orchestra. The tossing seas of the stage are but sorry makeshifts, whether they are revolutions of huge green canvas corkscrews, as at Covent Garden; or flat painted boards swinging to and fro from frankly visible ropes, as in the William Tell tempest at the same home of stage realism; or small boys industriously jumping up and down under a billowy

carpet, as in the Halliday version of David Copperfield.*
The wind can never roar at the wing with the mighty
volume and infinite compass which makes even Margate
sublime in a storm; and though the advance of
civilization has made the more expensive qualities of
stage lightning as smokeless as the newest gunpowder,
and may some day even evolve an Italian chorus capable
of turning up smartly on the deck of a tempest-tossed
ship and hauling and hoisting with something approaching a hearty Yo heave Ho, yet no stage sea will ever bear
that ship along, or rush seething past into her white
wake as it rushes past Daland's ship in the orchestra at
the end of the first act of the Dutchman.

Therefore, I can imagine Lago pleading that, since
adequate staging of the work is impossible, and since a
miss is as bad as a mile, matters would have been no
better if he had spent ten times as much money and
taken a hundred times as much pains. And, indeed, had
he on this ground frankly abandoned all pretence, and
reverted to the Elizabethan method of placarding the
stage in the first and last acts, I should have heartily
applauded his courage, and watched the result with
interest. But the moment he committed himself to doing
anything whatsoever, he committed himself to doing it
as well as it could be done with the resources at his
command; and the smaller the resources, the greater the
occasion for making the most of them. Now, I do not
think that any person can pretend that as much is done
at the Shaftesbury as might be done without the
expenditure of one extra penny. All the energy of the
management seems to have been exhausted by the effort
of procuring a small copy of the Victory at the Naval

* Andrew Halliday, essayist and dramatist, did an adaptation of David Copperfield for the stage, produced as Little
Em'ly (1869).

[444]

Exhibition, and rooting it so monumentally in the Shaftesbury stage that even I could ride out the storm in her without a qualm. This desirable vessel is allotted to Daland. The Dutchman is provided with the butt-end of a very poor imitation of a fishing lugger with impracticable ropes. The Victory also is furnished with unpatent immovable rigging. Besides these craft, there is one *prima donna's* spinning-wheel (practicable) out of Faust, for Miss Damian, and three broken and incomplete ones (desperately impracticable) for the chorus.

Signor Lago has virtually gone to Miss Macintyre, and said: "If I place these properties at your disposal, and undertake to abstain from repeated rehearsals and to scrupulously violate all Wagner's stage directions, do you think you can make The Flying Dutchman a success for me?" It says much for Miss Macintyre's courage and devotion that she appears to have answered in the affirmative. If so, Signor Lago has certainly kept his agreement to the letter. I could not pledge myself to train a choir of St Bernard dogs in the three rehearsals to sing the sailors' choruses as accurately and intelligently as Signor Lago's choristers sang them on the first night; but nobody who has ever enjoyed the friendship of an intelligent dog would have been quite incredulous if Mr Heinrich Mehrmann had made some such offer. The simple rollicking chorus at the beginning of the last act, and the Ho-yoho-yoho, as easily picked up as a street cry: not a bit of either could they sing decently. They did not even rise to the dance, perhaps because the timbers of the Victory were too frail to stand the stamping; but it might easily have been stagemanaged so as to take place on the quay if there had been any capable person in command. As to the miserable travesty which accompanied such mutilated fragments of the scene between the two crews and the girls on shore as were attempted, it would be waste of time to pretend to take it seriously. And yet, properly done, that episode would draw all London.

Everything in the last act was of a piece with the initial absurdity of making the scene identical with that of the first act. Even when the principal singers came on to rescue us from the chorus, the tenor got an attack of goat-bleat which nearly incapacitated him; and the curtain came down amid roars of laughter at the apotheosis of Senta, who had no sooner plunged into the deep in the person of Miss Macintyre than she rose resplendent from her dip in the person of a soft, plump, smiling, golden-haired lassie, whose extravagantly remote resemblance to Miss Macintyre took in nobody but the ghost of Vanderdecken, which hugged her with enthusiasm.

If the members of the orchestra had not known their business better than the stage manager and the chorus, the performance would have been impossible; but for all that, they did not greatly distinguish themselves. It was evident that there had been little rehearsal—probably the instruments were only used at one repetition, at which there was, of course, no time to pay any special attention to the band. All the men simply got through anyhow they could, and went away thankful at having earned their salaries without an actual breakdown.

As to Arditi, his position was only appreciable by experts. There he sat for three mortal hours, incessantly active, desperately anxious, bothered by discrepancies between the score and the band parts which eventually drove him to conduct from the pianoforte copy, feeling his way after a careless singer here, pulling the band together for a dash out of a difficulty there, rescuing somebody from destruction every two minutes or so, expecting every bar to be the last, and yet keeping a clear beat to meet every glance at his *bâton*. If he had been thirtysix, instead of sixtysix, and if he had felt sure of the sympathy of the whole house, instead of having too much reason to believe that he was more likely to get the blame of all the shortcoming, the ordeal would still have been a cruel one.

As it was, I think Arditi should at once receive a pension from the Civil List so as to relieve him from the necessity of wasting his skill in saving scratch performances from the fate they deserve. I wonder what would happen if Signor Lago had a conductor like Costa, whom I once saw dealing with a hitch in the ball scene in Don Giovanni by putting down his stick with ineffable contempt, freezing the whole stage and orchestra by refusing even to look at them, and then quietly resuming after an awful pause. But I doubt whether, if that were done at the Shaftesbury, any human power could set the frozen works going again.

Fortunately for Signor Lago, the second act of The Flying Dutchman requires no staging worth mentioning, and lies almost altogether in the hands of the two principal artists. Blanchard, who played Vanderdecken, has the music at his fingers' ends. He was thoroughly in earnest, and did his best all through. He has a sufficiently powerful voice, remarkably equal from top to bottom (an immense advantage for this particular part); and though its steadiness and purity of tone have been much impaired by his continental training, still, as he did what he could to minimize his defects, it carried him through with a very respectable measure of success. His acting was too sentimental: he was rather the piously afflicted widower than the obstinate and short-tempered skipper who declared, in profane terms, that he would get round the Cape in spite of Providence if he had to keep trying until the Day of Judgment. But this fault, again, was relieved a little by his substantial stage presence and effective makeup.

Artistically, I think he had more to do with such effect

as the work was able to make under the circumstances than Miss Macintyre, who was, nevertheless, the favorite of the evening. She is undoubtedly an interesting young lady; and the pit, captivated by her auburn hair and her Scottish beauty, resolved, to a man, to see her triumphantly through. And they did. Whenever she threw herself at the footlights in the heroic elation of youth, and sent a vigorous B natural tearing over them, the applause could hardly be restrained until the fall of the curtain. But whether it is that I have seen so many stage generations of brave and bonnie lassies doing this very thing (and too many of them have since lost the power of doing that without ever having acquired the power of doing anything better), or whether because my own hair is more or less auburn, the waves of enthusiasm broke over me as over a rock, damping me without moving or warming me. I can see that Miss Macintyre is a true Scot in her susceptibility to a good story, especially a legend. Tell her all about Gretchen, Senta, or Rebecca, and you find her intelligence and imagination on the alert at once, wheras many an Italian *prima donna,* under the same circumstances, would barely tolerate the information as an irksome and not very important guide to her stage business.

So far, so good. But the storyteller's instinct may be keen enough in a young lady to make her vividly imagine incidents and emotions, without raising her an inch above the commonplace in her power of imagining and realizing beauty of musical tone, eloquence and variety of musical diction, or grace and dignity of movement and gesture. And here it is that Miss Macintyre breaks down. Her notion of dramatic singing at present hardly goes beyond intensely imagining herself to be the person in the drama, and then using the music to relieve her pent-up excitement. This is better than no notion at all; but, all the same, it is the notion of a schoolgirl, and not

[448]

of an experienced artist. In unstrained situations it leaves her without ideas; in strenuous ones it results in her simply singing excitably, or standing with every muscle, from her jaw down to her wrists, in a state of tension as utterly subversive of grace as the attitude of a terrified horse, which is a perfect example of sincerity of conception without artistic grace of expression.

I would ask Miss Macintyre to go and see Miss Ada Rehan* in the latest variety show devized by Mr Daly for the squandering of that lady's exquisite talent, and to ask herself whether it is possible to imagine Miss Rehan standing for an instant on the stage—or indeed anywhere else—as Senta stood the other night for several minutes on the entry of Vanderdecken. I shall not do her the injustice of asking her whether she is satisfied to rely on the fact that her person, apart from what she does with it, has a pleasant appearance, just as her voice, apart from her artistic use of it, has a pleasant sound; for beyond a doubt she would indignantly answer, No. But where, then, are the original acquirements which she should by this time have added to the laborious work of her teacher? Are they only those vigorous high notes with which, in the strength of her youth, she exhilarates the gallery, and that conventional *piano* which, being produced with a rigid chin, inevitably ends flat? Surely these are a small store of graces for a singer who claims the most ambitious parts in grand opera. They did not avail with Handel at the Crystal Palace, or with Bach at Birmingham. No: Senta may be a popular success; but I shake my head, and shall continue shaking it, auburn locks and all, until Miss Macintyre plays the part better—much better—than that.

I have only space for a word as to Paderewski, who

* Shaw had seen her perform in The Last Word at the Lyceum on 12 October 1891.

seems to have kept his head and stuck to his work in spite of lionizing; for his playing is positively better, technically, than when he last played in London. It is quite true that he has cut his hair, but only a little. After his farewell recital I shall have something more particular to say concerning his performance of the Waldstein sonata. Mr Henschel gave the first of his London Symphony Concerts on Thursday. I was unable to be present; but from what my deputy reports of the fullness of the room and the impression produced, the prospects of the enterprise seem satisfactory. The remaining concerts are fixed for the 12th and 26th of November, the 14th of January, and the 11th and 25th of February.

THE BASOCHE

The World, 11 November 1891

The Basoche is so good an opera of its kind that I am quite at a loss to explain how it succeeded in getting itself trusted to the mercy of London. The plan of the work is almost perfect: the dainty combination of farce and fairy tale in an historical framework could hardly be more happily hit off. The farce is void of all vulgarity; the fairy tale proceeds by natural magic alone, giving us its Cinderellas and its princesses without any nursery miracles; and the pie-crust of history is as digestible as if it had been rolled by the great Dumas himself. Add to this that the music has a charming liveliness, and that whilst Messager, the composer, has avoided the more hackneyed and obvious turns of the modern operatic stock-in-trade in a fresh, clever, cultivated, and ingenious way, yet he does not presume upon his ability. The man who knows his place as well as this is scarce in French art, where the colder and less humorous talents waste themselves on bogus classicism, and the lighter-hearted throw away all self-respect and take to what polite policemen call gaiety. Paris encouraged Meyerbeer in posing as the successor of Mozart and Beethoven, as it encourages Saint-Saëns and Massenet in posing as the successors of Meyerbeer; whilst it allowed Offenbach and Lecocq openly to play the fool with their art. And London, unfortunately, never had any proper accommodation for the works of Auber, who kept his self-respect without losing his head. Our operatic stages were always either too large or too rowdy for his dainty operas.

Now that Mr D'Oyly Carte has at last given us the right sort of theatre for musical comedy, it is too late for Auber: we have had enough of the serenade in Fra Diavolo and the Crown Diamonds galop, and can no longer stand the Scribe libretto which sufficed to keep our fathers from grumbling. We want contemporary work of the Auber class. The difficulty, so far, has been to find a contemporary Auber. The Gilbertian opera did not exactly fill the vacancy: it was an altogether peculiar product, extravagant and sometimes vulgar, as in the case of the inevitable old woman brought on to be jeered at simply because she was old, but still with an intellectual foundation—with a certain criticism of life in it. When the Gilbert-Sullivan series came to an end, the attempt to keep up the school at second hand produced the old vulgarity and extravagance without the higher element; and Savoy opera instantly slipped down towards the lower level. Sir Arthur Sullivan, meanwhile, made a spring at the higher one by trying his hand on Ivanhoe, which is a good novel turned into the very silliest sort of sham "grand opera." I hardly believed that the cumulative prestige of Sir Walter Scott, Sir Arthur Sullivan, Mr D'Oyly Carte with his new English Opera House, and the very strong company engaged, not to mention log-rolling on an unprecedented scale, could make Ivanhoe pay a reasonable return on the enormous expenditure it cost. Yet it turns out that I either overrated the public or underrated the opera. I fancy I overrated the public.

Now La Basoche is exactly what Ivanhoe ought to have been. Though it is a comic opera, it can be relished without several years' previous initiation as a bar loafer. The usual assumption that the comic-opera audience is necessarily a parcel of futile blackguards, destitute not only of art and scholarship, but of the commonest human interests and sympathies, is not countenanced for a moment during the performance. The opposite, and if possible more offensive and ridiculous, assumption that it consists of undesirably *naïve* schoolgirls is put equally out of the question: you can take your daughter to see it without either wishing that you had left her at home or being bored to death. You attain, in short, to that happy region which lies between the pity and terror of tragic opera and the licentious stupidity and insincerity of *opéra bouffe*.

Now comes the question, what is going to happen to The Basoche? The opera-goers who support the long runs upon which Mr Carte depends for the recoupment of his princely expenditure, must be largely taken from the social strata upheaved by popular education within the last twenty years. These novices have only just learned, partly from glimpses of Wagner, but mostly from the Savoy operas, that music can be dramatic in itself, and that an opera does not mean merely the insertion of songs like When other lips into plays otherwise too bad to be tolerated. Only the other day they were encoring The flowers that bloom in the spring, tra la, I forget how many times every evening, with a childish delight in frank tomfoolery and tum-tum which a digger or backwoodsman might have shared with them. In Ivanhoe they found plenty of old rum-tum, with sentimentality substituted for the tom-foolery, and a huge stage glitter; and it is these, and not the elegance of the musical workmanship or the memories of Scott's story which have kept the work on the stage so long—for it is still flourishing: it was revived last Friday, with Mr Barton McGuckin in the title part.

I begin to think that Mr Sturgis was right in concluding that the first thing to do with Scott, in order to adapt him to the Cambridge Circus audience, was to remove his brains. Now, on the plane of The Basoche there is neither tomfoolery nor sentimentality: the atmosphere is that of high comedy, of the very lightest kind, it is true, but still much cooler, wittier, finer, more intelligent than that of either Ivanhoe or The Nautch Girl. It remains to be seen whether the admirers of these works will respond to the new appeal. If they do not—if Mr D'Oyly Carte is forced back on the normal assumption that the respectable opera-goer must be catered for as at best a good-humored, soft-hearted, slow-witted blockhead, void of all intellectual or artistic cultivation, then the critics may as well abandon English opera to its fate for another generation or so. There is no use in our making ourselves disagreeable to the managers by clamoring for higher art, if the managers can simply retort by shewing us rows of empty benches as the result of complying with our demands. Deep as is the affection in which I am held by most of our London *impresarios*, they can hardly be expected to ruin themselves solely to carry out my ideas.

Mr Carte, in mounting the piece, seems to have had no misgiving about its running powers. He has not only spent a huge sum of money on it, but he has apparently got value for every penny of his outlay. This sort of economy is so rare among managers—for instance, Mr Irving, in a Shakespearean revival, generally contrives to spoil a scene or two; whilst Sir Augustus Harris will occasionally slaughter a whole opera, like poor Orfeo, by dint of misdirected expenditure—I say it is so rare, that I strongly suspect that Mrs Carte comes to the rescue at the Royal English Opera just at the point where the other managers break down. However that may be, the only disparaging criticism I have to offer on the staging of The Basoche is that the dance at the beginning of the third act is a pointless, poorly invented affair, and that the scene, considering that the audience consent to wait half an hour to allow time for its setting, ought to be a wonder of French Gothic, best of the best, which can hardly be said for it at present, handsome as it is.

However, the fact that things have progressed far enough to set me complaining that the scenepainters have not saturated the stage with the architectural beauty of the Middle-Ages, proves the attainment of something like perfection from the ordinary standpoint. Bianchini's dresses are admirable; and the movements of the crowds engaged in the action are free alike from the silly stage-drill of *opéra bouffe* and the hopeless idiocy and instinctive ugliness of our Italian choristers. As the work has been thoroughly rehearsed, and the band is up to the best English standard of delicacy and steadiness, I think it must be admitted that, incredible as it may sound, we have at last got an opera house where musical works are treated as seriously and handsomely as dramatic works are at the Lyceum. Mr Carte has really put London, as far as his department of art is concerned, in a leading position for us; and the acknowledgment of that service can hardly be too cordial. The "dram of eale" in the matter is that The Basoche is the work of a French author and a French composer. Such drawbacks, however, cannot be helped as long as we abandon high musical comedy to the French, and persist in setting men who are not dramatists to compile nonsensical plays of the obsolete Miller and his Men* type, in order that popular musicians, of proved incapacity for tragedy, may pepper them with sentimental ballads, and make royalties out of them when paragraphists have puffed them as pages of grand opera.

For the principal performers in The Basoche I have nothing but praise, as they are all quite equal to the occasion, and do no less than their best. A prodigious improvement in the diction and stage manners of the company has taken place since the opening of the theatre. Even Mr Ben Davies conquers, not without evidences of an occasional internal struggle, his propensity to bounce out of the stage picture and deliver his high notes over the footlights in the attitude of irrepressible appeal first discovered by the inventor of Jack-in-the-box. Being still sufficiently hearty, good-humored, and well-filled to totally dispel all the mists of imagination which arise from his medieval surroundings, he is emphatically himself, and not Clement Marot; but except insofar as his opportunities are spoiled in the concerted music by the fact that his part is a baritone part, and not a tenor one, he sings satisfactorily, and succeeds in persuading the audience that the Basoche king very likely was much the same pleasant sort of fellow as Ben Davies.

Miss Palliser is to be congratulated on having a light, florid vocal part instead of a broad, heavy one, in which she would probably knock her voice to pieces through her hard way of using it; but the inevitable association of the light music with comedy is less fortunate for her, as her dramatic capacity evidently lies rather in the expression of strong feeling. On the other hand, Miss Lucile Hill, who was thrown away as Rowena, has in

* Melodrama (1813) by J. Pocock, at Covent Garden, with music by Sir Henry R. Bishop.

Colette a part which exactly suits her genuine humor, her quiet cleverness, and her—well, whatever is the feminine of *bonhomie*. And then she affords one the relief of hearing a singer whose method of producing her voice is not also a method of finally destroying it. Nine times out of ten, when a *prima donna* thinks I am being thrilled through by her vibrant tones, I am simply wrestling with an impulse to spring on the stage and say "My dear young lady, pray *dont*. Your voice is not a nail, to be driven into my head: I did not come here to play Sisera to your Jael. Pray unstring yourself, subdue your ebullient self-assertiveness, loosen your chin and tongue, round the back of your throat, and try to realize that the back of the pit is not a thousand yards beyond ordinary earshot." Miss Hill, far too sensible to need such exhortation, gets her *encores* as trumphantly as if she shortened her natural term as a singer by two years every time she sang a song in public. And her acting, for the purpose of this particular part, could hardly be bettered. Mr Burgon, Mr Bispham, and the rest, down to the players of the smallest parts, make the most of their tolerably easy work. Altogether, if we do not take kindly to The Basoche, we may make up our minds to ninetynine chances in the hundred of having to fall back on something worse in its place.

WHICH PITCH?

The World, 18 November 1891

I see that an association of pianoforte manufacturers in New York, the headquarters of the Steinway pitch, which is the highest standard pitch in the world, has decided to adopt French pitch for its instruments in future. Now here, at last, is a move worth all the platonic discussions that have ever been held at the Society of Arts and in St James's Hall, as far as immediate practical results are concerned. Whether this step has been taken by the New York reformers in pursuit of an ideal, or whether it is simply a market operation of the usual American kind, need not be too curiously considered. It is sufficient that the pitch question is again being talked about; that the more it is talked about, the better; and that most of my readers depend on me to put them in a position to talk intelligently about it.

Let me explain, then, for the benefit of the bewildered outsider, what French pitch means. If, in composing a piece of music, I write down the note A, meaning the A in the middle of the pianoforte, nobody knows the exact pitch of the musical sound I want to have played. All that can be said is that I mean it to be a third higher than the note I write down as F, and a fourth lower than the note I write down as D; but this is like saying that an omer is the tenth part of an ephah, which, however explicit, does not get rid of the question of how much an ephah is (further than that it is obviously ten omers). Now, in 1858, the French Government appointed a commission, of which Rossini, Berlioz, Meyerbeer, Auber, Halévy, and Ambroise Thomas were members, to settle what this A should indicate. They fixed on the note produced by 435 vibrations per second; and that pitch (A = 435) is what is called French pitch to this day. Costa, however, did not agree with the French commission, and ordained that, whatever the French might choose to mean by A, the London Philharmonic Society should mean by it a note produced by 452 vibrations per second—about two-thirds of a semitone higher than the 435-vibration A.

The utterances of the Philharmonic Society being deeply respected throughout Great Britain by all responsible citizens who are entirely ignorant of music, it was thereupon set forth in the Queen's regulations that the Philharmonic pitch should be adopted by our military bands. Therefore $A = 452$ is the regulation pitch at Kneller Hall, where our military bandsmen are trained; and from that centre it has spread over India and the Colonies. But the American eagle treated the British lion as the British lion had treated the French commission. It soared six vibrations higher. Steinway, the king of pianoforte makers, turned up to $A = 458$; and the Theodore Thomas orchestra used very nearly this pitch, that is to say $A = 456$. The complete liberty of the individual to choose his own pitch being thus triumphantly established, we have every organ builder setting up a fancy "concert pitch" and a fancy "church pitch", and calling both of them "standards" (all other makers' pitches being spurious); so that a church organ will have any pitch from about 441 up to the St Paul's pitch of 445, whilst concert organs are made a little sharp or flat to Philharmonic pitch, the makers seeming not to care whether they tune to 453 or 451 so long as it is not 452, which is what it ought to be on Philharmonic principles.

Now try to conceive in your mind's ear a grand international concert in the Albert Hall, with the St Paul's organ lent for the occasion to reinforce the permanent one, and the band assisted by contingents of players, civil and military, from America and the Continent. Imagine the process of tuning—the Albert Hall organ leading off with an A at concert pitch, the church organ responding, horribly flat, with an A at church pitch, the French and German oboists following a good ten vibrations flatter, the Philharmonic men asserting the dignity of England two-thirds of a semitone sharp, and the Americans and the military coming in with a crash, sharp even to the Philharmonic. Let us now suppose that, after sufficient wrangling, Philhar-

[458]

monic pitch carries the day, and the instruments which cannot reach it are silenced.

The ninth symphony of Beethoven is put in rehearsal. The sopranos complain bitterly of the strain of the repeated high notes in the choral section. Up jumps the ghost of Beethoven to declare that his music is perfectly singable, but that his symphony has been transposed up from the key of D to that of E flat, and is nearly a quarter of a tone sharp even at that. He then returns to the shades, execrating the folly of a generation which tries to give his works and those of Handel and Mozart the vulgarest sort of cavalry-band shrillness. So Beethoven is abandoned; and the closing scene from Götterdämmerung is put into rehearsal, only to half-kill the unfortunate *prima donna*. Whereupon the ghost of Wagner explains that, though he did not contemplate so low a pitch as Beethoven's, he certainly did mean his music to be sung at French pitch, and not at Philharmonic. Consequently the arrangements have to be altered, and the pitch changed to French.

This is no sooner done than Dr Mackenzie and Professor Villiers Stanford declare that they cannot now permit either the Dream of Jubal or Eden to be played at the concert, as the low pitch would destroy all the brilliancy of their instrumentation. It being felt that no really great musical festival would be complete without these works, the whole scheme falls through; and the agitation for a uniform pitch proceeds with renewed vigor.

The opponents of reform lay great stress on the commercial difficulties of any change. These difficulties arise from the fact that the various pitches come into play not only in performances, but in the manufacture of instruments. Every instrument which produces notes of definite pitch at all is constructed to be at its best at a certain pitch; and though it may be lengthened or

[459]

shortened, or screwed up or let down within narrow limits to some other pitch, yet the change will be for the worse both as to quality of tone and (in keyed wind instruments) accuracy of intonation also. A Stradivarius violin cannot be safely screwed up to concert pitch in England and America without certain structural fortifications which can hardly leave the tone unaffected; and old hands declare that the effect of the violoncellos in the orchestra is quite altered by the substitution of the modern thin strings for the thick ones formerly used at the old low pitch. Still, with stringed instruments, the change is at least possible: a new pitch does not mean a new fiddle.

With keyed wind instruments it is often said that a change so great as that from Philharmonic to French is impossible; and as first-rate instruments of this class are quite as dear as the best cottage pianofortes, the opposition of the players to any change involving the purchase of new instruments might be expected to be very strong, and to be counterbalanced by a corresponding anxiety on the part of the manufacturers to promote the change. Both players and manufacturers seem, however, to be so little concerned about the matter that I am emboldened to relate my earliest experience of the alleged impossibility of French pitch for the woodwind. When I was a small boy I had a sort of family interest in a casual operatic performance, at which the singers and the conductor very much wanted French pitch. The band, though extremely sympathetic and obliging, pointed out that this could not be. The strings would have been only too happy; the brass could have managed at a pinch; there was no question about the alacrity of the drum in sinking; and the flute, oboe, and bassoon did not deny that they could do something to meet the conductor's views.

But the clarinet was the difficulty. It was, they all

said, a universally admitted fact, familiar alike to the musician and the physicist, that the pitch of a clarinet is an unalterable and eternal natural phenomenon. And the more the poor conductor struck his "diapason normal" tuning-fork at the beginning of the first rehearsal, the more the clarinettist (there was but one) blew a melancholy response nearly half a tone sharp to it. So the conductor sighed; and the rehearsal went forward at Philharmonic pitch. That evening the conductor privately interviewed the clarinettist. He suggested that if the instrument could be altered (for the occasion only) at a cost of, say, a guinea, he would willingly place that sum in the artist's hands for the purpose. A pause ensued, during which the clarinettist steadfastly and solemnly contemplated the conductor, and the conductor, with equal gravity, contemplated the clarinettist back again. Then the guinea changed hands; and the twain parted.

At the second rehearsal the conductor took out his fork as before, and, disregarding an impatient groan from the band, sweetly said "Do you think, Mr Blank, that if you were to insert a washer in that clarinet, you could get down to my fork?" At this apparently *naïve* suggestion the band could hardly refrain from open derision. Laughter, and cries of "Yes, Joe: try the washer," lasted until Mr Blank, after a brief manipulation of his instrument, responded to the fork by an A dead in unison with it. With the fury of the betrayed band, and the quantity of spirits Mr Blank probably had to buy for them out of his guinea before recovering their trust, I need not here occupy myself. Suffice it to say that I never read the declarations of impossibility which recur regularly as often as the pitch controversy is renewed, without thinking of Mr Blank and his simple device of the washer which cost a guinea. I do not suggest that Mr Blank is typical of the London orchestral

[461]

player of today. A large proportion of Mr B.'s colleagues were either illiterate persons, or tipplers, or both. Today they would be self-respecting members of the community, classed as artists and gentlemen, not to mention that they would be also more skilful and refined, if not steadier or more accurate, in their playing.

But I see no reason to believe that orchestras have at all got the better of their old reluctance to take any avoidable extra trouble, or of their readiness to allege impossibility to any conductor or singer who can be put off with such a plea. Consequently it is not surprising to find that when the conductor wants the high pitch for the sake of orchestral "brilliancy"; when basses and contraltos want it to ease their low notes; when high baritones of the Count di Luna school, and "dramatic" sopranos with just four notes at the tip-top of their voices and all the rest of their compass a wreck, want it so as to have as much screaming and as little singing as possible, it is no wonder that French pitch is found "impossible." But will someone kindly explain—for, like Rosa Dartle,* I only want to know—why when Patti at Covent Garden and Nilsson at Her Majesty's declined to sing at the Costa pitch, the impossible was achieved and the pitch came down? Also why, at a festival, when the low-pitched church organ commands the situation one day, and the high-pitched concert organ usurps its place on the morrow, the band manages to be equal to both occasions? Why, again, is it that members of the Philharmonic band are also members of the Queen's private band, where French pitch is the rule? Why, in short, the alleged impossibilities are so often got over when it becomes apparent that they *must* be got over? I really do not know the right answer to these questions.

It may be that the impossibilities are in fact not got

* Character in Dickens's David Copperfield.

over, except by elderly players whose instruments were originally made for the low pitch—that the results are never quite satisfactory—that the younger players keep a second set of instruments for the opera—that they raise their pitch a little and transpose their parts half a tone down instead of attempting to flatten their instruments—that some woodwind players, in correcting their upper octaves in the blowing, are less put out by a strange pitch than others. A hundred considerations beyond my ken may be patent to men with a more detailed knowledge of the subject than I possess. But of one thing I am certain; and that is, that "can't," when delivered *sans phrase*, always means, in this connexion, "wont."

My own opinion is that of six hundred out of the seven hundred musicians consulted by the Society of Arts. In all the respects as to which one pitch can be said to be better or worse than another, I believe—in fact I know—that there is every possible objection to Philharmonic pitch, and no objection to French, except that it is a trifle too high for XVII and XVIII century music, including the works of Handel, Bach, Haydn, Mozart, and Beethoven. Both pitches, I understand, are obnoxious to calculators as presenting fractional vibration numbers; but as I find that the results of my own attempts at calculation are equally inaccurate whether I deal with whole numbers or fractional ones, I have left that consideration entirely out of account.

PHILÉMON ET BAUCIS

The World, 25 November 1891

Last Wednesday, whilst Eden was in progress at the
Albert Hall, I resisted the fascination of Professor
Stanford's mixolydian minstrelsy like another Odysseus,
and was about to devote the evening to my neglected
private affairs, when I happened to pass through Bow-
street on my way home. To my surprise, I found Covent
Garden all alight and alive, as if in the middle of the
season. So I stopped to read the bills; and there, sure
enough, was the announcement that Gounod's Philémon et Baucis was at that moment just going to begin,
and that Bruneau's Le Rêve would be given the next
night.

Conceive the situation. When the summer season
begins I shall be invited on the opening night to witness
Gounod's Faust, with A. as Faust, B. as Mephistopheles,
C. as Valentin, and Z. (first time) as Margaret. My next
invitation will be to see Faust with B. as Valentin and C.
as Mephistopheles, but cast otherwise as before. Third
invitation, Gounod's Faust, as before, except for the
début of Miss Y. as Siebel. Fourth invitation, Gounod's
Faust, cast as before, except first appearance for the
season of the champion tenor as Faust, a part I have
heard him play fifty times. On arriving at the theatre I
shall find a printed slip on my stall to say that the
champion tenor is indisposed, and that Signor A. has
kindly consented to oblige the management by taking
the part of Faust at very short notice, my indulgence
being therefore requested for him. After that, to prevent
Faust growing on me like brandy, I shall positively
refuse to go any more. The management will then put

me through a precisely similar course of Les Huguenots, with an occasional Carmen (Miss Zélie de Lussan and the useful A. again) by way of variety. All this I must suffer because my criticisms help Sir Augustus Harris to stand up against the tyranny of his "princely tenors" and their all-powerful guarantor-patrons. But now that he is master of the situation, with something new and interesting to shew, he leaves me to find it out from placards, musical criticisms, and other forms of advertisement. Such is managerial gratitude.

However, I must confess it was a luxury to find my old stall obtainable for five shillings, and when I went in, I found them, to my intense astonishment—I suppose that there is no place in the world but Covent Garden where such a thing would be done—actually eking out the prelude to Philémon et Baucis with the overture to Tannhäuser, which was being conducted with immense spirit by a French gentleman who did not understand one bar of it, but who "worked up" the finish with a truly Gallic glitter and grandiosity. Only, shallow and mundane as M. Jéhin's conception of the work was—and it was both to the verge of downright desecration—he did not at all fail to get his conception executed, and that, too, with much more refinement and precision than Signori Mancinelli, Bevignani, and Randegger obtain from the same players in the season. With Gounod, being no longer out of his depth in German waters, he was quite successful; and I should have nothing but praise for him but for that unlucky and ridiculous notion of making a *lever du rideau*—and what a malapropos one!—of the Tannhäuser overture.

Philémon et Baucis is a charming work, all pure play from beginning to end, but play of the most exquisite kind—a tranquilly happy recreation for really hardworked and fine-strung men and women. I say "hardworked" with intent; for I know well the sort of objection that is always made to these quiet little art luxuries. It is an age, we are told, of stress and strain, of fierce struggle for existence, in which men come to the theatre exhausted by work, and requiring something stimulating, exciting, amusing, and easily intelligible. If you search for a typical apostle of this view, you will generally find him to be a gentleman some six stone over his proper weight, who, not being permitted by his wife and housemaids to lounge about the house after breakfast, goes down in a first-class carriage to the City, where he receives a number of illiterate letters, and dictates equally illiterate answers to his clerks; goes out and eats confectionery enough to make a schoolboy blush; writes one private letter (an appointment with his doctor about his liver); meets his fellow citizens, and tries to get the better of them in the dull sort of whist without cards which he calls "business"; takes a snack and two glasses of sherry to sustain him while he loafs at a bar and brags in whatever his particular line of brag may be; tries a little more whist; takes a heavy meal called lunch; orders something new to wear; goes to his club for afternoon tea and the evening papers until it is time to pay visits or go home to dinner; and finally turns up at the theatre, under compulsion of his fashionable wife and daughters, in the character of a victim of brain pressure, as aforesaid. That man does not do as much real work in ten years as I have to put into every five lines I write; yet, whilst his clerks swelter willingly in an uncomfortable crow's-nest for half-a-crown during four and a half hours of Die Meistersinger, he yawns in his box for an hour or so, secretly wishing that the opera were a dog fight, and only imperfectly consoled by the advertisement of his money afforded to polite society by his wife's diamonds. Real work cultivates a man instead of brutalizing him; and what we want at present is more recreation for cultivated men, and less sacrifice of all our artistic resources to the stimulation of underworked or wholly idle persons, with all their higher appreciatory organs in an advanced stage of fatty degeneration. Who ever heard a capable and active individual in sound health complain of a good play or opera as overstraining his or her faculties?

Philémon pleased me so well that I went to see Le Rêve on the following night. With Gounod to shew how to write angelic music, Zola to provide a poem exactly suited to the exploitation of Gounod's discovery,* and Wagner to shew how to weave the heavenly strains into a continuous tissue from end to end of each act, Bruneau has been able to compile an opera which would have ranked as a miracle fifty years ago. Verily, our young composers are entering into a magnificent inheritance— though do not forget that it requires a large natural endowment to enter into that inheritance as fully as Bruneau has done. The score is full of the most delicate melody; and the harmonies and orchestral coloring are appropriately tender and imaginative.

Like all Frenchmen, Bruneau vindicates his originality by a few *hardiesses*, as, for instance, the introduction of the washerwoman's dance at the close of the first act in bloodcurdling defiance of the harmony, the senseless drum business at the words *Le voilà! mon rêve de bonheur* at the end of the procession scene, and the clever and wonderfully successful imitation of the effect of a peal of bells by the wind instruments earlier in the same scene. Only a French audience could thoroughly relish the sentimentality of the bishop, which reaches a climax in the melancholy tootlings of the woodwind when he says,

* Bruneau's opera is based on Zola's novel of the same name.

Laisse-moi te parler, mon fils, avec douceur,
  Au nom de ta mère adorée,
  Toujours présente, tant pleurée, &c.

Indeed, the whole affair is frightfully sentimental; but the bishop is the only character who goes a little too far for British patience in this direction.

As to the performance, it was so good that I forgot that I was in Covent Garden until, at the end of the last scene but one, the band got up and went home, leaving the opera unfinished and the audience sitting wondering whether the entertainment was really over, and, if so, whether they would get back as they went out an eighth of the money they had paid for admission. But nobody gave them a farthing; and Sir Augustus Harris consequently owes me sevenpence-halfpenny, which, as far as I can see, he has not the remotest intention of paying. Except for this sufficiently flagrant omission, there was nothing to complain of. Mlle Simonnet's soprano voice, well produced as it is, would completely conquer any English audience if she would only aim, in forming her upper notes, at the round tone which we—rightly, as I think—prefer to the shriller, thinner quality which the French like. The lady is otherwise well graced, and is an excellent artist in all respects. Engel imitates Jean de Reszke too obviously, and in energetic moments his voice trembles; but in the quieter and tenderer passages of Felicien and Philémon he sang unexceptionably. As to Bouvet and Lorrain, the *tremolo* often made it impossible to distinguish the pitch of their notes. In the parts of Jupiter and Vulcan they wobbled so inveterately that the only perceptible difference between their shakes and their ordinary notes lay in the fact that in the first case they shook on purpose, and in the second they did it because they could not help themselves. But the *tremolo* is not so much a vice in them as a mistaken point

[468]

of honor; and I found myself ready to forgive almost any defect of style in my delight at the artistic spirit in which the whole company worked together. Certainly, nothing could have been less like the inorganic proceeding of the summer companies.

THE MUSIC SEASON IN LONDON

The Bradford Observer, 30 November 1891 ; unsigned

The musical season here demands a long-delayed word from me. We have had three opera houses at work, and an extraordinary supply of *virtuosos* of the first rank: Sarasate, Ysaÿe, Popper, Paderewski, for instance. The operatic experiments have ended rather variously, financial success and artistic excellence having been attained in the inverse ratios. Signor Lago, who closed his doors at the Shaftesbury Theatre the other day, is said to have made some money by the success of Cavalleria Rusticana, a clever and vigorous, straightforward bit of work, which could have been as well done by one of our young lions. Signor Lago has produced a few miserably-mounted fragments of worn-out Italian operas by way of *levers de rideau* for Cavalleria. He has tried to revive his old success with Gluck's Orfeo, without Giulia Ravogli; and he has ventured, with the most desperately inadequate equipment, upon Wagner's Flying Dutchman. But the only possible criticism of these efforts is that he had much better have confined himself to Cavalleria. Sir Augustus Harris, meanwhile, has "exercised his right of legitimate competition" by opening Covent Garden with a capital French company, which, by dint of cooperative artistic spirit rather than individual excellence, has won and deserved golden opinions from all sorts of critics. He has produced

Gounod's Philémon et Baucis and Bruneau's setting of a dramatic idyll founded by Gallet on Zola's Le Rêve. This is a charming piece of work, full of delicate and noble themes in what I may call the celestial style of Gounod, and woven together in the fashion of Wagner, as far as such a very French composer as Bruneau is either capable or desirous of acquiring the unmatched German craftsmanship of the composer of Die Meistersinger. Sir Augustus has certainly triumphed over Lago on the artistic side, but he is said to have lost money on the experiment. Mr D'Oyly Carte, too, has at last given up the struggle to recover his large expenditure on Sir Arthur Sullivan's Ivanhoe, and disbanded his company, except as to those artists who are playing in Messager's La Basoche, which is likely to have a long run. He has also given up his attempt to screw up prices, and has adopted the ordinary scale for first-class theatres, of half-a-guinea for the stalls and half-a-crown for the pit. La Basoche is just the work for the English Opera House, elaborate and polished in style, without being pretentiously and emptily heavy, and amusing without being slangy or vulgar. It is exceptionally independent of any extraordinary powers on the part of the performers and, as great pains have been taken by Mr and Mrs Carte with its preparations, it is uncommonly well done.

London is still as badly off as ever for orchestral concerts; for the Crystal Palace concerts are too far away, and cost too much to count for much with amateurs of modest means. Sir Charles Hallé and Mr Henschel, encouraged by the advertisement they obtained from their ill-success at the beginning of last season, when the whole press overflowed with sympathy, have returned to the charge. Hallé, unfortunately, began with the Eroica symphony, which is quite the worst card in his hand. If he had chosen one of those works of Berlioz of which the Manchester has an unrivaled knowledge, he would have drawn a much larger audience. Henschel, with his London Symphony Concerts, is gaining ground. He still worries the orchestra by too often handling his *bâton* as if he were actually executing the passages with it; but there is a marked improvement in finish of execution at his concerts, and it looks as if the Henschel band were destined to become the classical band of London, as Richter is not adding to his old laurels, and Mr Manns' retirement cannot, in the strength of nature, be very remote now, since, vigorous as he looks, he is nearer seventy than sixty. Ysaÿe, the Belgian violinist, played Mendelssohn's concerto lately for Henschel better than any other living violinist could have played it, as far as London knows. He has been leading the quartet at the Popular Concerts, where Mr Chappell has at last awakened to the fact that his stock players were becoming what vestry politicians call an old gang. Popper, the famous violoncellist, the other evening took the place of the veteran Piatti, as Mr Edward Howell has also done on several occasions; in fact Piatti has not taken his old seat on the platform this season. Popper gave a concert on Wednesday, and played several compositions of his own, all somewhat slight, but elegant and finished, occasionally reminding one of Bizet, though without Bizet's originality. Popper's playing more than justifies his great reputation.

As young Gerardy is playing in London again, the violoncello cannot complain of being neglected at present. Another boy prodigy, Max Hambourg, a pianist, gave a recital recently at Steinway Hall, where he again shewed, by his faults and his qualities, that he has real genius as a player and has not merely been coached up for the prodigy market. Paderewski, during his recent visit, played technically better than before, and with, of course, the same largeness of artistic comprehension which is the secret of his success—for his rivals would have no difficulty in doing his fingerwork if only they could do his brainwork. His immense vogue has made matters difficult for all later arrivals. Stavenhagen is making a bold bid for his old place as first favorite among the younger pianists; but since Liszt's death he has been all astray, oscillating between affected little exhibitions of crisp dexterity, for which he uses Beethoven's early concertos as stalking-horses, and wildly violent wrestlings with Chopin polonaises and Lisztian fantasias. In both moods he wastes much energy and technical accomplishment, and steadily loses ground, without, however, quite forfeiting the interest which his earlier visits aroused.

STAVENHAGEN *CONTRA* PADEREWSKI

The World, 2 December 1891

Although, like my fellow critics, I have been wallowing in virtuosity for weeks past, I have fallen so behindhand with the mere chronicle of the season that I hardly know where to pick it up again. It is clearly too late to hark back to Paderewski, who has had time to make what they call a colossal success in New York since he played here. I am reminded of him chiefly by the fact that, after an interval during which nobody ventured to play the pianoforte, Stavenhagen has come and measured himself against his supplanter, challenging comparison in every line of his programs, which are full of Beethoven, Chopin, Liszt, and so on. This was only to be expected; for Stavenhagen is not deficient in perseverance; and he was first-favorite among the young lions until Paderewski came. He had the advantage of coming from the school of Liszt, a much nobler, if a less muscle-hardening, one than that of Paderewski's master Leschetitzky, some of whose superficialities and vulgarities cling to his most famous pupil to this day, as you may hear in his reading, for instance, of the Appassionata sonata. However, when Paderewski's pupilage came to an end, and Liszt died, the more Paderewski forgot his master the better player he became, whilst the more Stavenhagen forgot his the worse player he became. When Stavenhagen came over last year he was positively silly. Instead of his old Titanic victories over Liszt's sonatas, Todtentanzes,* and the like, he was shewing off fatuous little crispnesses and neatnesses of execution with childish exultation, poor Beethoven's earlier concertos serving as hobby-horses for the occasion. It was amazing to see a young man's musical soul shrunk that much in so short a time. But we put up with him smilingly—pretended that he was as wonderful as ever— and why? Simply because the case was made romantically delightful by the fact that he brought a bride with him, and that any other condition than one of abject infatuation would have been unpardonable in him. Did he not give an orchestral concert, and make her sing to us huge *scenas* of his own composition, vast in conception, instrumented with tone-colors of oceanic depth, sounding like veiled echoes of the last act of Götterdämmerung? Not for all the solar system would I have hinted then that Beethoven's early concertos were never meant to be rapped out, *staccatissimo*, like a succession of postman's knocks. As to the musical public, need I say that it was charmed—that Stavenhagen and his wife threatened for a moment to eclipse the popularity of Mrs Kendal and her husband? For in England there is nothing so popular in a public performer as perfect domesticity, except perhaps the extreme reverse. But

* Liszt's Todtentanz, a paraphrase on Dies Iræ, is Op. 24.

this could not last always: it was plain that Stavenhagen must presently get back to the serious business of his profession.

The question was whether he would be able to do so—whether he had in himself the inspiration that never failed him whilst Liszt was at his elbow. That was what was in my mind when I went to the Crystal Palace last Saturday week to hear him play Beethoven's fourth concerto. Would it be again a series of variations on the postman's knock, or would it be Beethoven? As usual, the facts turned out to be neither snow-white nor jet-black, but grey, and sometimes rather a dark grey. It was, to begin with, an advance on last year that the concerto chosen was the fourth, and not the third. But there was too much—a great deal too much—of the postman still; and I should almost have lost patience, and given up Stavenhagen as hopelessly lapsed and lost, but for his recital on the following Tuesday, when, though he partly failed, he failed more heroically.

His long selection from Chopin brought him fairly into the lists against Paderewski; and his onslaught on the A flat polonaise (an *encore*) was terrific. He went at it like a thousand blacksmiths; and if he could only have combined his tremendous ebullition of nervous excitement with the *sang-froid* needed to hold and control it, he might have brought his fine Lisztian reading off successfully. As it was, he maintained the combat to the end with such smashing energy that he was encored a second time, and returned to the piano to play a nocturne, and to find the instrument worth about thirty pounds less than before the polonaise began. Later on, he shewed us the fruits of his Weimar "studies in transcendent execution" by playing a prodigious series of pianoforte presentments of *Suoni la tromba*, which were announced as "for the first time," but which, if I mistake not, he had played once before in St James's

Hall. He may take my word for it, however, that no amount of transcendent execution alone will regain for him the position he has nearly let slip through his fingers.

What is the matter at present is that he has taken serious and beautiful works of Beethoven, and played them frivolously and boyishly because they are technically easy to him; wheras Paderewski has played us a few of Mendelssohn's Songs without Words, still easier from the technical point of view, and brought back all their almost forgotten delicacy and poetic beauty. After that, it is vain to point out that Paderewski once came to smash in Liszt's Erl King transcription after Stavenhagen had played it without missing a note, or that he was beaten by a certain passage in Chopin's funeral march sonata which Stavenhagen could possibly have mastered. These are mere accidents, as indeed we have seen by the fact that the last time we had The Erl King from Paderewski it was faultless; whilst Stavenhagen's last attempt at it was nearly as unlucky as the earlier one of Paderewski.

So long as Paderewski can take a simple piece of music in which any schoolgirl can be made finger-perfect by her teacher, and can play it for all that it is worth as tone-poetry, whilst Stavenhagen trips over it only to shew how much easier it is to him than to the schoolgirl, so long can Stavenhagen never be mentioned in the same breath with Paderewski as a player. But surely a young man of such capacity as Stavenhagen has shewn can retrieve a position so simple as that is. Let him abandon the postman's knock at once and for ever, and cap Paderewski's Mendelssohn by a Mozart sonata—say that noble one in A minor, which certainly requires something more than a thrashing left hand and a flying right one, but which, with much less than half Stavenhagen's manipulative skill, and ten fingers with feeling and song in them, could be restored to its rightful place high up among the highest pianoforte classics.

I had almost forgotten Madame Stavenhagen, who sang us several songs at the recital. She has a very good voice and a very good ear: what she lacks is sensibility of vocal touch. If she would only cultivate that quality, and then communicate it magnetically to her husband's left hand, the future would be a golden one for both of them.

By ill luck, I have been unable so far to get to a single Popular Concert this season, and consequently only know by hearsay of the revolution there—the substitution of Howell and Popper for the veteran Piatti, and of Ysaÿe for Madame Neruda. I will not deny that, when changes of this kind are made, I am glad to see them made too soon rather than too late. Of all the duties of a critic, there is none harder than giving a hint to the veteran who lags superfluous. To have to say "My dear Sir, or Madam: when you play or sing I can hear the old tone, the old style, the old expression, just as well as you can; but, if you dont mind my saying so, I am afraid the young people are beginning to disagree with us on the subject"—that is far worse than to have to perform a surgical operation, because you dont get thanked for it, and chloroform is out of the question. Suppose, for instance, that some day down at the Crystal Palace I were to detect, with a sudden heartstroke (even critics get such things), some ominous sign that would send me to Grove's Dictionary to see how long ago Mr Manns was born, what would I be expected to do then? Well, I am afraid I should either hold my tongue or prevaricate like a police witness on the subject. Meanwhile, let me congratulate Mr Manns on being still far better than the next best man, and on having, among many other recent feats which I have not had space to chronicle, conducted only ten days ago a most brilliant performance of the last three movements of Beethoven's seventh symphony (the

[476]

band slept through the first *allegro*), and on Saturday last an equally fine performance of Mendelssohn's Scotch symphony, in which, however, I contend for a more sympathetic transition from the middle section of the first movement to the recapitulation. In passing, by the bye, I would like to ask the advocates of the high pitch how they like it in the *allegretto* of the seventh symphony. I know no more flagrant instance of a beautiful piece of music spoiled to propitiate the ghost of Sir Michael Costa.

The Third London Symphony Concert was given on Thursday last; but the only one of the series I have heard has been the second, at which I found a great improvement in the orchestra in point of finish and delicacy of detail. The mass of tone from the full band is brighter and purer than before; and Henschel conducts better, although he still retains enough of the habits of the player and singer to make him occasionally flurry himself and prevent the band from looking at him by cutting at every crotchet in the bar with his stick, instead of simply keeping his hand on the *tempo* with as few beats as possible. At this concert Ysaÿe played Mendelssohn's concerto magnificently: Sarasate and Joachim rolled into one could have done no more. Popper gave a concert on Wednesday last, at which he performed a good deal of his own music, which is elegant and fanciful in its lighter phases, and elegiac on its sentimental side. He is as unlike his rival Hollmann in appearance and temperament as his violoncello is unlike an ophicleide, so that there is no lack of novelty about his style to Londoners; and he is, on his own plane, the best player in the world, as far as we know here. Gerardy, hugely petted by the public, needs a good deal of indulgence both for himself and his instrument after Popper. Another prodigy, young Max Hambourg, gave a pianoforte recital at Steinway Hall, and once more played Bach better than any other composer on his program. With such a training as Eugene Holliday has had from Rubinstein, this Russian lad might astonish the world some day; but he does not seem to be exactly in the way of getting it at present.

MOZART'S FINALITY
The World, 9 December 1891

The Mozart Centenary has made a good deal of literary and musical business this week. Part of this is easy enough, especially for the illustrated papers. Likenesses of Mozart at all ages; view of Salzburg; portrait of Marie Antoinette (described in the text as "the ill-fated"), to whom he proposed marriage at an early age; picture of the young composer, two and a half feet high, crushing the Pompadour with his "Who is this woman that refuses to kiss me? The Queen kissed me! (Sensation)"; facsimile of the original MS. of the first four bars of *Là ci darem*, and the like. These, with copious paraphrases of the English translation of Otto Jahn's great biography, will pull the journalists proper through the Centenary with credit. The critic's task is not quite so easy.

The word is, of course, Admire, admire, admire; but unless you frankly trade on the ignorance of the public, and cite as illustrations of his unique genius feats that come easily to dozens of organists and choirboys who never wrote, and never will write, a bar of original music in their lives; or pay his symphonies and operas empty compliments that might be transferred word for word, without the least incongruity, to the symphonies of Spohr and the operas of Offenbach; or represent him as composing as spontaneously as a bird sings, on the

[478]

strength of his habit of perfecting his greater compositions in his mind before he wrote them down—unless you try these well-worn dodges, you will find nothing to admire that is peculiar to Mozart: the fact being that he, like Praxiteles, Raphael, Molière, or Shakespear, was no leader of a new departure or founder of a school.

He came at the end of a development, not at the beginning of one; and although there are operas and symphonies, and even pianoforte sonatas and pages of instrumental scoring of his, on which you can put your finger and say "Here is final perfection in this manner; and nobody, whatever his genius may be, will ever get a step further on these lines," you cannot say "Here is an entirely new vein of musical art, of which nobody ever dreamt before Mozart." Haydn, who made the mould for Mozart's symphonies, was proud of Mozart's genius because he felt his own part in it: he would have written the E flat symphony if he could, and, though he could not, was at least able to feel that the man who had reached that pre-eminence was standing on his old shoulders. Now, Haydn would have recoiled from the idea of composing—or perpetrating, as he would have put it—the first movement of Beethoven's Eroica, and would have repudiated all part in leading music to such a pass.

The more farsighted Gluck not only carried Mozart in his arms to within sight of the goal of his career as an opera composer, but even cleared a little of the new path into which Mozart's finality drove all those successors of his who were too gifted to waste their lives in making weak dilutions of Mozart's scores, and serving them up as "classics." Many Mozart worshipers cannot bear to be told that their hero was not the founder of a dynasty. But in art the highest success is to be the last of your race, not the first. Anybody, almost, can make a beginning: the difficulty is to make an end—to do what cannot be bettered.

For instance, if the beginner were to be ranked above the consummator, we should, in literary fiction, have to place Captain Mayne Reid, who certainly struck a new vein, above Dickens, who simply took the novel as he found it, and achieved the feat of compelling his successor (whoever he may be), either to create quite another sort of novel, or else to fall behind his predecessor as at best a superfluous imitator. Surely, if so great a composer as Haydn could say, out of his greatness as a man "I am not the best of my school, though I was the first," Mozart's worshipers can afford to acknowledge, with equal gladness of spirit, that their hero was not the first, though he was the best. It is always like that. Praxiteles, Raphael and Co., have great men for their pioneers, and only fools for their followers.

So far everybody will agree with me. This proves either that I am hopelessly wrong or that the world has had at least half a century to think the matter over in. And, sure enough, a hundred years ago Mozart was considered a desperate innovator: it was his reputation in this respect that set so many composers—Meyerbeer, for example—cultivating innovation for its own sake. Let us, therefore, jump a hundred years forward, right up to date, and see whether there is any phenomenon of the same nature in view today. We have not to look far. Here, under our very noses, is Wagner held up on all hands as the founder of a school and the archmusical innovator of our age. He himself knew better; but since his death I appear to be the only person who shares his view of the matter. I assert with the utmost confidence that in 1991 it will be seen quite clearly that Wagner was the end of the XIX century, or Beethoven school, instead of the beginning of the XX century school; just as Mozart's most perfect music is the last word of the

XVIII century, and not the first of the XIX. It is none the less plain because everyone knows that Il Seraglio was the beginning of the school of XIX century German operas of Mozart, Beethoven, Weber, and Wagner; that Das Veilchen is the beginning of the XIX century German song of Schubert, Mendelssohn, and Schumann; and that Die Zauberflöte is the ancestor, not only of the Ninth Symphony, but of the Wagnerian allegorical music-drama, with personified abstractions instead of individualized characters as *dramatis personæ*. But Il Seraglio and Die Zauberflöte do not belong to the group of works which constitute Mozart's consummate achievement—Don Juan, Le Nozze di Figaro, and his three or four perfect symphonies. They are XIX century music heard advancing in the distance, as his Masses are XVII century music retreating in the distance. And, similarly, though the future fossiliferous critics of 1991, after having done their utmost, without success, to crush XX century music, will be able to shew that Wagner (their chief classic) made one or two experiments in that direction, yet the world will rightly persist in thinking of him as a characteristically XIX century composer of the school of Beethoven, greater than Beethoven by as much as Mozart was greater than Haydn. And now I hope I have saved my reputation by saying something at which everybody will exclaim "Bless me! what nonsense!" Nevertheless, it is true; and our would-be Wagners had better look to it; for all their efforts to exploit the apparently inexhaustible wealth of musical material opened up at Bayreuth only prove that Wagner used it up to the last ounce, and that secondhand Wagner is more insufferable, because usually more pretentious, than even secondhand Mozart used to be.

For my own part, if I do not care to rhapsodize much about Mozart, it is because I am so violently prepossessed in his favor that I am capable of supplying any possible deficiency in his work by my imagination. Gounod has devoutly declared that Don Giovanni has been to him all his life a revelation of perfection, a miracle, a work without fault. I smile indulgently at Gounod, since I cannot afford to give myself away so generously (there being, no doubt, less of me); but I am afraid my fundamental attitude towards Mozart is the same as his. In my small-boyhood I by good luck had an opportunity of learning the Don thoroughly, and if it were only for the sense of the value of fine workmanship which I gained from it, I should still esteem that lesson the most important part of my education. Indeed, it educated me artistically in all sorts of ways, and disqualified me only in one—that of criticizing Mozart fairly. Everyone appears a sentimental, hysterical bungler in comparison when anything brings his finest work vividly back to me. Let me take warning by the follies of Oulibicheff, and hold my tongue.

The people most to be pitied at this moment are the unfortunate singers, players, and conductors who are suddenly called upon to make the public *hear* the wonders which the newspapers are describing so lavishly. At ordinary times they simply refuse to do this. It is quite a mistake to suppose that Mozart's music is not in demand. I know of more than one concert giver who asks every singer he engages for some song by Mozart, and is invariably met with the plea of excessive difficulty. You cannot "make an effect" with Mozart, or work your audience up by playing on their hysterical susceptibilities.

Nothing but the finest execution—beautiful, expressive, and intelligent—will serve; and the worst of it is that the phrases are so perfectly clear and straightforward that you are found out the moment you swerve by a hair's breadth from perfection, whilst, at the same time, your work is so obvious, that everyone thinks it must be

[482]

easy, and puts you down remorselessly as a duffer for botching it. Naturally, then, we do not hear much of Mozart; and what we do hear goes far to destroy his reputation. But there was no getting out of the centenary: something had to be done. Accordingly, the Crystal Palace committed itself to the Jupiter Symphony and the Requiem; and the Albert Hall, by way of varying the entertainment, announced the Requiem and the Jupiter Symphony.

The Requiem satisfied that spirit of pious melancholy in which we celebrate great occasions; but I think the public ought to be made rather more sharply aware of the fact that Mozart died before the Requiem was half finished, and that his widow, in order to secure the stipulated price, got one of her husband's pupils, whose handwriting resembled his, to forge enough music to complete it. Undoubtedly Mozart gave a good start to most of the movements; but, suggestive as these are, very few of them are artistically so satisfactory as the pretty Benedictus, in which the forger escaped from the taskwork of cobbling up his master's hints to the free work of original composition. There are only about four numbers in the score which have any right to be included in a centenary program. As to the two performances, I cannot compare them, as I was late for the one at the Albert Hall.

The Jupiter Symphony was conducted by Mr Manns in the true heroic spirit; and he was well seconded by the wind band; but the strings disgraced themselves. In the first movement even what I may call the common decencies of execution were lacking: Mr Manns should have sent every fiddler of them straight back to school to learn how to play scales cleanly, steadily, and finely. At the Albert Hall, there was no lack of precision and neatness; but Mr Henschel's reading was, on the whole, the old dapper, empty, *petit-maître* one of which I, at

[483]

least, have had quite enough. Happily, Mr Henschel immediately redeemed this failure—for such it was—by a really fine interpretation of the chorus of priests from the Zauberflöte. This, with Mr Lloyd's delivery of one of the finest of Mozart's concert arias, Mr Norman Salmond's singing of a capital English version of *Non più andrai*, and the Crystal Palace Band's performance of the Masonic Dirge, were the successes of the celebration. I should add that Mr Joseph Bennett, fresh from throwing his last stone at Wagner, modestly wrote a poem for recitation between the Requiem and the Symphony. He appeals to Mozart, with evidently sincere emotion, to accept his lines, in spite of any little shortcomings,

> Since tis from the heart they flow,
> Bright with pure affection's glow.

Perhaps Dr Mackenzie or Dr Parry, in view of a well-known observation of Beaumarchais,★ may set Mr Bennett's ode to music some of these days. Mr Herkomer, too, has helped by drawing a fancy portrait of Mozart. I have compared it carefully with all the accredited portraits, and can confidently pronounce it to be almost supernaturally unlike the original.

THE MOZART CENTENARY

The Illustrated London News, 12 December 1891

Wolfgang Mozart, the centenary of whose death on December 5, 1791, we are now celebrating, was born on January 27, 1756. He was the grandson of an Augsburg bookbinder, and the son of Leopold Mozart, a composer,

---

★ Beaumarchais, in his play Le Mariage de Figaro (1784), advises: "That which is too silly to say may be sung."

author, and violinist of good standing in the service of the Archbishop of Salzburg. When he was three years old he shewed such an interest in the music lessons of his sister, four and a half years his senior, that his father allowed him to play at learning music as he might have allowed him to play at horses. But the child was quite in earnest, and was soon composing minuets as eagerly as Mr Ruskin, at the same age, used to compose little poems. Leopold Mozart was a clever man up to a certain point, "self-made," untroubled by diffidence or shyness, conscious of being master of his profession, a practical, pushing man, ready to lay down an ambitious program for his son and bustle him through it. Seeing that Wolfgang had talent enough to qualify him for the highest attainable worldly success as a composer and *virtuoso*, he at once set about founding a European reputation for the future great man by making a grand tour through Vienna, Paris, London, Amsterdam, and many other towns, exhibiting his two children at Court and in public as "prodigies of nature." When the boy made a couple of tours in Italy in 1769–71, he knew everything that the most learned musicians in Europe could teach him; he became an unsurpassed harpsichord and pianoforte player; and as an organist he made old musicians declare that Sebastian Bach had come again. As a violinist he did not succeed in pleasing himself. Leopold insisted that nothing but self-confidence was needed to place him at the head of European violinists; and he may have been right; but Mozart never followed up his successes as a concerto player, and finally only used his skill to play the viola in quartets. On the whole, it must be admitted that the father, though incapable of conceiving the full range of his son's genius, did his utmost, according to his lights, to make the best of him; and although Mozart must, in his latter years, have once or twice speculated as to whether he might not have managed better as an orphan, he never bore any grudge against his father on that account.

Mozart's worldly prosperity ended with his boyhood. From the time when he began the world [*sic*] as a young man of twentyone by making a trip to Paris with his mother (who died there) to the day of his early death, fourteen years later, he lived the life of a very great man in a very small world. When he returned to settle in Vienna and get married there, he burst out crying with emotion after the ceremony. His wife cried too; and so did all the spectators. They cried more wisely than they knew, considering what the future of the couple was to be. Mozart had three means of getting money—teaching, giving concerts, and using such aristocratic influence as he could enlist to obtain either a Court appointment or commissions to compose for the church or the theatre. None of these ways were fruitful for him, though between them all, and a good deal of borrowing, he just managed to die leaving his wife in possession of £5, exactly £15 short of what they owed to the doctor. As a teacher, he got on very well while he was giving lessons for nothing to people who interested him: as a fashionable music master he was comparatively a failure. The concerts paid a little better: he wrote one pianoforte concerto after another for them, and always improvized a fantasia, and was overwhelmed with applause. But there was then no great public, as we understand the term, to steadily support subscription concerts of classical music. His subscribers were people of fashion, inconstant except in their determination only to patronize music in "the season." His failure to obtain anything except a wretched pittance at Court for writing dance music was due to the extreme dread in which he was held by the cabal of musicians who had the ear of the Emperor. Salieri frankly said afterwards "His death was a good job for us. If he had lived longer not a soul would have given us a crumb for our compositions." Mozart was badly worn out by hard work and incessant anxiety when his last fever attacked him. He even believed that someone had poisoned him. A great deal of false sentiment has been wasted on the fact that the weather was so bad on the day of his funeral that none of the friends who attended the funeral service at St Stephen's Church went with the hearse as far as the distant graveyard of St Mark's. The driver of the hearse, the assistant gravedigger, and a woman who was attached to the place as "authorized beggar," were the only persons who saw the coffin put on top of two others into a pauper grave of the third class. Except to shew how poor Mozart was, the incident is of no importance whatever. Its alleged pathos is really pure snobbery. Mozart would certainly not have disdained to lie down for his last sleep in the grave of the poor. He would probably have been of the same mind as old Buchanan,* who on his deathbed told his servant to give all the money left in the house away in charity instead of spending it on a funeral, adding, in his characteristic way, that the parish would have a pressing reason to bury him if they left him lying there too long.

It must not be supposed, however, that Mozart's life was one of actual want in the ordinary sense. He had immense powers, both of work and enjoyment; joked, laughed, told stories, talked, traveled, played, sang, rhymed, danced, masqueraded, acted, and played billiards well enough to delight in them all; and he had the charm of a child at thirty just as he had had the seriousness of a man at five. One gathers that many of his friends did not relish his superiority much more than

* George Buchanan, Scottish humanist and author of tragedies, was the teacher of Montaigne and tutor to James VI. of Scotland.

Salieri did, and that, in spite of society and domesticity, he, on his highest plane, lived and died lonely and unhelpable. Still, on his more attainable planes, he had many enthusiastic friends and worshipers. What he lacked was opportunity to do the best he felt capable of in his art—a tragic privation.

It is not possible to give here any adequate account of Mozart's claims to greatness as a composer. At present his music is hardly known in England except to those who study it in private. Public performances of it are few and far between, and, until Richter conducted the E flat symphony here, nobody could have gathered from the vapid, hasty, trivial readings which were customary in our concert rooms that Mozart, judged by XIX century standards, had any serious claim to his old-fashioned reputation. One reason among many for this mistake may be given. Leopold Mozart undoubtedly did his son the great harm of imposing his own narrow musical ideal on him, instead of allowing him to find out the full capacities of the art for himself. He taught the boy that when a piece of music sounded beautifully, and was symmetrically, ingeniously, and interestingly worked out in sonata form, nothing more was to be expected or even permitted. Mozart, if left untutored, would probably have arrived at the conclusion that a composition without a poetic or dramatic basis was a mere luxury, and not a serious work of art at all. As it was, he was trained to consider the production of "absolute music" as the normal end of composition, and when his genius drove him to make his instrumental music mean something, he wasted the most extraordinary ingenuity in giving it expression through the forms and without violating the usages of absolute music, bending these forms and usages to his poetic purpose with such success that the same piece of music serves as a pet passage of tone-poetry to the amateur who knows

[488]

nothing of musical formalism, while the pedant who is insensible to poetry or drama holds them up as models of classic composition to his pupils.

This combination of formalism with poetic significance has been much applauded, not only for its ingenuity, as is natural, but as a merit in the music, which is perverse and absurd. Mozart apologizing to his father for some unusual modulation which he could not justify except on poetic grounds cut but a foolish figure. If he had written his G minor quintet, for instance, in the free form contrived by Liszt for his symphonic poems, the death of his father, which immediately followed the composition of that work, would, no doubt, have been attributed to his horror on reading the score; but there is not the slightest ground for pretending, with Wagner's works to instruct us, that the quintet would have been one whit less admirable. Later on, when Mozart had quite freed himself, and come to recognize that the forbidden thing was exactly what he was born to do, he still, from mere habit and mastery, kept to the old forms closely enough to pass with us for a formalist, although he scared his contemporaries into abusing him exactly as Wagner has been abused within our own time. The result is that since Mozart, under his father's influence, produced a vast quantity of instrumental music which is absolute music and nothing else, and since even the great dramatic and poetic works of his later years were cast mainly in the moulds of that music, we have hastily concluded that all his work is of one piece, and that an intelligent dramatic handling of his great symphonies would be an anachronism. In his very operas it is hard, nowadays, to get the most obvious dramatic points in his orchestration attended to, even the churchyard scene in Don Juan being invariably rattled through at Covent Garden as if it were a surprisingly vapid quadrille.

Fortunately, the persistence with which Wagner fought all his life for a reform of orchestral execution as to Mozart's works, the example set by the conductors inspired by him, and such authoritative utterances as those of Gounod on the subject of Don Giovanni, not to mention social influences which cannot be so simply stated, are at last letting the public into the important secret that the incompetence and superficiality of Mozart's interpreters are the true and only causes of the apparent triviality of his greatest music. Properly executed, Mozart's work never disappointed anybody yet. Its popularity is increasing at present, after a long interval. The appetite for riotous, passionate, wilful, heroic music has been appeased; and we are now beginning to feel that we cannot go on listening to Beethoven's Seventh Symphony and the Tannhäuser overture for ever. When we have quite worn them out, and have become conscious that there are grades of quality in emotion as well as variations of intensity, then we shall be on the way to become true Mozart connoisseurs and to value Wagner's best work apart from its mere novelty. The obstacle to that at present is the dulness of our daily lives, which makes us intemperate in our demands for sensation in art, and the bluntness of mind which prevents us from perceiving or relishing the essentially intellectual quality of the very finest music. Both these disqualifications are the result of deficient culture; and while that lasts Mozart will have to lie on the shelf. But that is so much the worse for the uncultured generation—not for the composer of Don Juan.

CORNELIUS'S BARBER

The World, 16 December 1891

The thirtythree years that have elapsed since Cornelius composed his Barber of Bagdad, which the Royal College students introduced to England last Wednesday at the Savoy Theatre, have taken all the point out of its defiant Wagnerisms. The younger generation simply do not recognize them, so commonplace have they become. Older hands will have noted one or two progressions, which were copied, with controversial intention, out of Wagner's scores at a time when they were to be found nowhere else. But nowadays it is hardly conceivable that there should ever have been such a fuss about the work as that which ended in Liszt's withdrawal from the Weimar Theatre. In listening to it one catches a reminiscence of Meyerbeer here, or an anticipation of Goetz there; but Wagner is the last composer suggested, although, on reflection, it is easy to see that in 1858 there was nobody else from whom a man with so little musical originality as Cornelius could have learned how to compose an opera which was at that period so unconventional.

Its late arrival here is due, not to any peculiarity in the work itself, but to the poverty of our operatic resources, which has limited us for so many years to grand opera on the one hand, and *opéra bouffe* on the other, with no intermediate theatre for the higher artistic forms of light and comic opera. I need not now repeat all that I said on this point when La Basoche was produced. Suffice it that The Barber of Bagdad—very different from our threadbare old acquaintance, once so prosperous, the Barber of Seville—is an excellent specimen of comic opera taken seriously in an artistic sense. The concerted music is remarkably good, especially a quintet, Oh, Mustapha! in the second act, which is, besides, highly comic. The weakest parts are the patter solos of the barber, which are too ponderous in their movement and heavy in their style for any country on earth except Germany. Such doggerel as Lore academical, physical, chemical; Learning grammatical; Facts mathematical; Rules arithmetical, trigonometrical, &c. &c. &c., if they *must* be set to music for the hundredth time, had better still be set in the time-honored lilt which Sir Arthur Sullivan, following the example of Mozart and Rossini, chose for the lists of accomplishments of the Major-General in The Pirates or the Colonel in Patience.

The performance at the Savoy was of the usual Royal College sort, carefully prepared as a task by the principals, and enjoyed as a rare bit of fun by the chorus and band, but uninspired and amateurish. The tenor, Mr William Green, had to struggle not only against the irrational but uncontrolable nervousness of a novice, but against the rational nervousness caused by his having neither been taught how to produce his voice nor succeeded in finding out a safe method for himself. He was anything but happy during the first act, singing mostly flat; but in the second, when the worst was over and he was beginning to feel more at ease, he rallied, and came off with glory. I still hold to my opinion that in none of these large music-teaching institutions is there, as yet, any instruction to be had in the physical act of singing. When I see a set of pupils among whom there is a certain clearly evident agreement as to aiming at certain graces and avoiding certain blemishes of style, I conclude that they have had some common teaching on these points.

But when I find, at the same time, that one of them will produce his voice as if he were trying to crack a walnut between his vocal cords, whilst his neighbor depends on spasms of the diaphragm for vocal execution, and yet another regards the judicious use of the nose as the true secret of tone-coloring, then I naturally conclude that the motto of the professorial staff is "Make yourself a singer as best you can; and we will then give you excellent precepts as to what a singer should and should not do." Fortunately, most of the cast of The Barber of Bagdad were clever enough to have come to no serious harm under this system. Mr Sandbrook and Mr Magrath are comparatively old hands; the first much improved, the second not so much so. Mr Magrath has the misfortune to be an Irishman, with all that musical facility and native genius which have prevented so many of his countrymen from going on to acquire a seriously cultivated artistic sensibility.

Let no Englishman regret what in Ireland is called his stupidity—meaning his congenital incapacity to talk brilliantly about subjects and practise adroitly arts of which he knows next to nothing. This observation might, perhaps, from Mr Magrath's point of view, have been more appropriately made in the course of an essay on national characteristics than in a notice of his performance as Abul Hassan Ali Ebn Bekar; but it explains why I decline to give him as much credit for his accomplishments as I should had he been born on a soil where they do not, like Mr Scadder's* public buildings, "grow spontaneous." Miss Bruckshaw, as Margiana, was perhaps the most completely satisfactory member of the cast, though Mr William White, who played the Cadi, might, by his freedom from the awkwardness which all the rest shewed, more or less, have borne off that distinction but for his rather thin voice, which was certainly outclassed by Miss Bruckshaw's.

* Character in Dickens's Martin Chuzzlewit.

Miss Pattie Hughes made a bouncing old woman, full of youth; and the orchestra was good in a pleasant, juvenile way, and would have been better had Mr Stanford conducted them with a broader, freer hand, instead of checking their every attempt to get fairly into their own stride. The austerities of the mixolydian mode are out of place when romping through a comic opera overture with a young orchestra.

I have nothing to offer as to the host of concerts last Thursday except my apologies. I should explain that wheras other men have fixed hours of work and Sundays' off, I am compelled to adopt the simpler plan of going on until I drop; so that I have sometimes been tempted to petition the House of Commons to pass a special Factory Act to deal with my case. On Thursday, having worked without intermission since the 4th of October, I surveyed the awful weather, and determined that I had rather die than do another stroke of work. I longed to sit in a very easy chair and do absolutely nothing but lazily watch another person working hard in some interesting way entirely unconnected with music. After a moment's reflection I went to my dentist's. There is nothing that soothes me more after a long and maddening course of pianoforte recitals than to sit and have my teeth drilled by a finely skilled hand. But my dentist's complexion was yellower, and his eyes wearier than my own as he informed me that not for any human patient would he do a stroke of work that afternoon. So I went home disappointed. This, observe, is the literal truth, and not an extravaganza invented for the occasion. I add this assurance because, though I can always make my extravaganzas appear credible, I cannot make the truth appear so.

The Saturday afternoon concerts at the Crystal Palace are now over for the year, to be resumed on February 14th. As usual, the last one was conducted, not by Mr

Manns, but by Mr Cowen, who gave us his Scandinavian symphony, a pretty piece of work, although, like the Robertsonian drama, it is not quite so fresh as it was. Miss Clotilde Kleeberg succeeded in reviving the youthful enchantments of that charming early work of Beethoven's, his second pianoforte concerto, known as No. 1. Miss Louise Douste is giving a series of concerts, as are also Messrs Nicholl and Septimus Webbe. Mr Max Heinrich, too, is recitalling lyrically at Steinway Hall, with the assistance of Madame Heinrich and Herr Benno Schönberger, who must excuse my saying that his little hands were never made to treat Schubert's Wanderer-Fantasie in a style so foreign to its genius and to his own as he adopted at the last recital. I regret having missed Mr Stephen Philpot's Zelica at Prince's Hall on Tuesday; but the tickets did not reach me until the performance was nearly over. Messrs Besson, the instrument-makers, invited me to hear a recital to demonstrate the capacities of their newly invented "pedal clarinet," which must surely be a contrabass clarinet. As they fixed the recital for the Barber of Bagdad afternoon, I was unable to hear this *contrabasso profundo*; but I note its advent for the benefit of composers who may have felt the want of a woodwind deep bass with the single-reed quality of tone. Let me hasten to add that I neither assert nor deny the absolute novelty of the invention. I admit there never was an instrument made yet that had not been invented by somebody else years before the inventor was born. Whenever I speak of an instrument as new, I mean new to me.

BRAHMS, BEETHOVEN, AND THE BARBER OF BAGDAD

The World, 23 December 1891

The admirers of Brahms are to be congratulated on the set of vocal quartets which have just been sung at the Popular Concerts for the first time by Mrs Henschel, Miss Fassett, Mr Shakespeare, and Mr Henschel. For once in a way, Johannes has really distinguished himself. In these quartets we have, it goes without saying, the extraordinary facility of harmonic workmanship which Brahms shews in everything he does, from the colossally stupid Requiem, which has made so many of us wish ourselves dead, to those unmitigated minor bores, the Liebeslieder Waltzes. But we have also in them a feeling which is thoroughly roused—a vivacious, positively romantic feeling—graceful, tender, spontaneous— something as different as possible from his usual unaroused state, his heavy, all-pervading unintelligent German sentimentality. Besides, they shew good handicraft in another sense than that of doing easily what other men find very difficult. Brahms has always had the mere brute force of his amazing musical faculty. No one can deny that he all but equals our most famous native orators in respect of having a power of utterance that would place him above the greatest masters if only he had anything particular to say. But this time he has shewn imaginative workmanship, especially in the play of color of the four voices, which are combined and contrasted and crossed and interwoven in a delightful way. Much of the effect was, no doubt, due to the four singers, each of them a soloist of distinguished merit; but that does not account for everything, since quite as much has been done for previous compositions of Brahms without for a moment producing the same charm. He evidently composed the quartets in one of those fortunately-inspired moments to which we owe all that is valuable in his work.

I wish I could go on to say that the instrumental quartet (Beethoven's in E flat, Op. 74) was as well rehearsed as the vocal ones. But had that been so, the first movement would not have been the scramble it was. Madame Neruda's solo was Mozart's Adagio in E, which she played, it seemed to me, as well as she could possibly have played it even in her prime, in justice to which golden period I must not pretend that she can now secure her former rapidity and boldness of execution in quick movements without some sacrifice of the old delicacy of hand and purity of intonation. Miss Adeline de Lara earned the tremendous applause she got for her performance of Schumann's Symphonic Studies by the not too common feat of holding the attention of the audience unwearied from the first bar to the last. Nevertheless, the element of nobility of style, which is essential to a completely adequate interpretation of Schumann's intention in this composition, was lacking in Miss de Lara's romantic reading of it. Brahms's Sonata for violoncello and pianoforte, Op. 38, a long elaboration of nothing whatever, was played by Miss de Lara and Mr Howell. It may seem an impertinence to tell an artist of Mr Howell's experience that he is improving; but the change from the orchestral desks in St James's Hall, at which there is no chance of asserting one's individuality except when the overture to William Tell or the accompaniment to *Batti, batti* comes into the night's work, to the Popular Concerts, where the whole audience have often to be held by the cellist single-handed, is one to which the most hardened veteran could not conceivably be insensible. The fact is that the orchestra, though it levels many players up, levels down others, who retain for a long time their power of rising to the occasion when the occasion comes. Unfortunately, it too often never comes—at least, not in the focus of London criticism. Only in the suburbs or the provinces can our many excellent orchestral players get a taste of the bracing responsibility of solo-playing.

I paid the Royal College students the very considerable compliment (from a critic) of going a second time to see their performance of The Barber of Bagdad. The improvement from the elimination of stage fright was enormous; and I am disposed to retract something of what I said about the absence of evidence of training in voice production. Mind, I do not retract it altogether; but I now believe that the tenor's habit of thickening his tongue at the root until he might almost as well have a potato there is one against which his teachers have vainly warned him, because he fought with it successfully all through his first song. Not until he rose from his couch and was fairly upon his legs did it get the better of him. Will he believe me that, if he would only cultivate his sense of beauty in vocal tone, and then face the ordeal of listening to himself with manly fortitude, he would never need any warning beyond that of his own ear? Like all the rest, he sang much better on the 16th than on the previous occasion. Mr Villiers Stanford also was less anxious, and gave his forces their head when they were disposed to make the pace lively. Under these bettered circumstances, The Barber of Bagdad revealed itself as a lighter and more fantastic work than it seemed before. Several passages, of which the shape and intention were obscured on the first occasion by timidity of execution, came out as burlesques of particular points in the reigning grand operas of thirty years ago, Meyerbeer being the chief victim of these pleasantries. Thus, the Barber's long *cadenza* on the word Margiana, which sounded at the first performance like a somewhat overdone parody of the operatic *cadenza* in general, became recognizable as a gibe at Peter's elaborate *cadenza* on the name Caterina in the tent scene in L'Etoile du Nord, from the last act of which opera, by the bye, Cornelius borrowed the leading phrase of Noureddin's first song. An odd coincidence of this kind occurs in the first act, after the Barber has driven away the servants, when Noureddin, flattering him, breaks out mellifluously with a stave of In happy moments, day by day, from Maritana. The clever *trio* at the beginning of the second act, He comes! he comes! oh, blessed be the day! is an unconscious echo of Daland's entry in the *trio* at the end of the second act of The Flying Dutchman. Many other points illustrate Cornelius's way of assimilating music in all directions, and adapting it in a thoroughly artistic way to his own purpose. If Mr D'Oyly Carte in course of time amasses a repertory at the Royal English Opera, he might do worse than include The Bagdad Barber in it. I am quite prepared to listen to it a third time: in fact, I am in the stage of going about the house fitfully bawling out scraps of "Sally Maleikum" (or whatever it is), to the astonishment of my people, before whom I seldom unbend in this way.

The students of the Royal Academy of Music gave a concert on Thursday afternoon at St James's Hall. The program was an extremely liberal one, consisting of a composition of symphonic proportions, in four movements, for pianoforte, chorus, and orchestra, by Raff, entitled Die Tageszeiten, with three concertos, a *suite de ballet*, and four airs. I held out until after the second concerto; and everything that I heard was well prepared and creditably executed. The orchestra was more heavily reinforced by first-rate professional players than that of the Royal College—too much so to be taken as a genuine students' orchestra; but the tone from the string band, which was largely manned by the pupils, was excellent. The only performance which rose above student level into the region of beautiful execution and sympathetic interpretation was that of Beethoven's fourth concerto by Miss Ethel Barns, who very far surpassed Staven-hagen's recent performance of the same work at the Crystal Palace. The Rubinstein *cadenzas* were, of course, beyond her physical powers; but she succeeded in suggesting their effect vividly to those who recollect Rubinstein's style. Next in order of interest came Goldmark's violin concerto, one of the many composi-tions of this kind which are not worth the time and trouble of listening to them. It was played by a young gentleman named Philip Cathie, who has not as yet developed any style, but whose touch and intonation are remarkably good. In fact, his fine quality of tone and natural musical feeling would be a sufficient equipment on the technical side for a violinist of considerable eminence. But such a position is not to be attained by mere fiddling. Every generation produces its infant Raphaels and infant Rosciuses, and *Wunderkinder* who can perform all the childish feats of Mozart. But if they are commonplace in character and general capacity, nothing ever comes of their phenomenal excess of special faculty; unless, indeed, they are pretty *prime donne*, in which case they make a world-wide reputation with a surprisingly small share of artistic honor and conscience. Mr Philip Cathie must, then, take it to heart that having made a fiddler of himself everything now depends on his success in making a man of himself.

I cannot say that I was favorably impressed with the singing at this concert. I heard three very good voices, a soprano, a contralto, and a *basso cantante*. But they were all trained more or less on the old system of grinding the voice to a fine edge, and controling it by steady pressure. I am a hopeless infidel with regard to that system. No doubt, gifted dramatic singers have made reputations with it in spite of the disadvantage it put them at. I have even heard a singer or two to whom it seemed natural—who could sing in no other way, and could produce a free, rattling tone with it, and be none the worse. But all the cases I have met with of prematurely worn-out voices, and patients whose doctors have had to forbid them to sing, are due to vocal grinding, which begins so promisingly with a great increase in the "strength" and clearness of the voice. And, on the other hand, I have found that veterans like Sims Reeves, who are proof against everything except old age, avoid it as if it were the plague. Fortunately, it has lost much of its old authority, especially of late years, when the superiority of rival methods has been so repeatedly demonstrated by the success of American singers. The Royal College teaching staff evidently warns its pupils not to depend on the old formula of "tension of cords and force of blast," which is, at least, a valuable negative counsel. But at the Academy the grindstone is not wholly discarded yet. However, my opinion on the subject is only my opinion. The Academy tradition claims descent from the great Garcia, whom I am not in a position to criticize, as he died sixty years ago at the age of fiftyseven. No doubt he was a famous teacher; and his son, our Royal Academy Garcia, born in 1805, was his pupil. But if I find by observation that certain ways of singing produce, with persons of average capacity, premature deterioration and failure, whilst opposite ways give the vocal powers their full natural lease of life, I am forced to draw my conclusions without respect of persons or institutions. Therefore, though I do not question the value of the instruction that is to be obtained on many important points in Tenterden-street, much less pretend that individual professors on

the staff do not make highly beneficial departures from
the typical Academy teaching, yet, on the whole, I am
not in the habit of advising novices to lay the foundations
of their vocal methods in the R.A.M. And I cannot say
that the concert the other day did much to disarm my
prejudices in that respect, although I recognize the
natural talent shewed by the three young singers,
especially the lady who sang the Inflammatus from
Dvořák's Stabat Mater.

THE SUPERIORITY OF MUSICAL TO
DRAMATIC CRITICS

The Players, 6 January 1892

I suppose no one will deny the right of the fully
accomplished musical critic to look down upon the mere
dramatic critic as something between an unskilled
laborer and a journeyman. I have often taken a turn at
dramatic work for a night merely to amuse myself and
oblige a friend,* wheras if I were to ask a dramatic critic
to take my place, I should be regarded as no less
obviously mad than a surgeon who should ask his
stockbroker to cut off a leg or two for him, so as to leave
him free for a trip up the river. Clearly, I may without
arrogance consider my dramatic colleagues—I call them
colleagues more out of politeness than from any genuine
sense that they are my equals—as at best specialists in a
sub-department of my art. They are men who have

* Shaw had served on several occasions as substitute
dramatic critic for William Archer on The Manchester
Guardian, A. B. Walkley on The Star, and R. J. Lowe on The
Scottish Leader. He had also written a few dramatic reviews
for The Pall Mall Gazette and Our Corner.

failed to make themselves musical critics—creatures with half-developed senses, who will listen to any sort of stage diction and look at any sort of stage picture without more artistic feeling than is involved in the daily act of listening to the accent and scrutinizing the hat of a new acquaintance in order to estimate his income and social standing. Their common formula for a notice is as follows. First, they trace the origin of the play to any previous foreign work which happens to contain similar incidents—as, for example, the unexpected reappearance of a long-lost husband just in time to rescue his young and beautiful grass widow from the toils of a villain, or a complication arising from one character being mistaken for another extremely like him. Next, they tell the story of the play, more or less accurately. Then they offer some remarks, in their best taste, on the moral to be drawn, and its probable reaction on the domestic purity of the nation. If the conclusion arrived at in this section is harsh to the author, they easily avoid all unpleasantness by assuring him privately that they agree with every word he says, but that people are such fools that it would hardly do to avow as much. Finally, a run through the names in the playbill enables them to do any little good turns or pay off any old scores that may be outstanding. This last section is the only one which is common to both the theatrical notice and that higher art form, the musical criticism.

All this is such child's play that I once formed the design of becoming a dramatic critic myself, in order to shew how the thing might be done by a really competent hand; and I actually sacrificed my dignity to the extent of telling the editor of a new journal, who had asked me to contribute, that I should like to become his dramatic critic. He replied that he had had applications for the post from the entire literary profession in London (not a single member of which would have dreamed of presuming to consider himself qualified for the post of musical critic), and that, foreseeing this, he had promised the post beforehand to a veteran journalist whose pre-eminent claims would excite no ill feeling, since they were founded entirely on prescription. A young man could only have been selected on the ground that he was the best man, an implication that would have cost the editor all his friends at one blow. So the veteran was duly appointed; and when he found, as he soon did, that he had neither time nor inclination to do the work, an able junior unobtrusively slipped into his berth without offense to anyone, the vacancy being forgotten by that time. As for me, I resolved to effect my purpose in another way by some day taking apprentices and teaching them the whole critical business, which comprehends writing, esthetics, and technique of the various arts. This is the more necessary, since even in my own superior branch the dignity of the profession is too often compromised by *littérateurs* who have no ears and musicians who cannot write, both varieties being often so destitute of analytic faculty and training that when, after protracted and desperate writing round and round a performance, they are forced at last to give an account of its quality, they have to fall back on the most helpless generalities of praise or blame, and can no more *describe* an artist than a tailor can dissect his customer. Any of these defects, and *a fortiori* all three of them, will lame a critic to such an extent that unless he is magnificently endowed with the superb quality which we dishonor by the ignoble name of Cheek—a quality which has enabled men from time immemorial to fly without wings, and to live sumptuously without incomes—he becomes diffident and deferential in his style. Now, a critic cannot be anything worse than deferential. To aggravate the mischief, the deference is shewn less to the performers than to the *entrepreneurs* who speculate in their attractions; so that the actor who takes a theatre of his own instantly receives from the press a huge unearned increment of consideration far beyond what is due to the sense of advertisements to come.

In consequence, these men of business are rapidly sinking to the level of the artists they employ; and the *impresario*, manager, or agent of the future, instead of being a reasonable man of the world, with a good knowledge of art from the business point of view, promises to be a vain, petulant creature, regarding the critic as a poor dependant to whom he dispenses a magnificent hospitality, and reading press notices with a morbid susceptibility to their bearing on his own personal vanity. Nothing but a timely revival of uppishness on the part of the critics can check this demoralization of the *entrepreneur*; and how can a man be uppish if he is a mere scribbling play-goer, an amateur who can be replaced at a moment's notice by dozens of incipient barristers or *dilettanti* from the upper division of the Civil Service with a taste for complimentary first night stalls?* Dramatic criticism has fallen to the level of an amusement for gentlemen: musical criticism remains the scarce product of highly-skilled labor. Between the Richter and the Crystal Palace concerts, the musical critic has opportunities of hearing at least once a week the masterpieces of musical art executed by highly trained performers; whilst the theatrical critic, from lack of familiarity with the masterpieces of dramatic poetry, becomes at last so illiterate that when he is forced, once in a blue moon, to endure a night of Shakespear (performed mostly by actors who deliver blank verse much as a *ripieno* cornet

* This is a sly dig at A. B. Walkley, Shaw's erstwhile colleague on The Star, who was a Civil Servant turned dramatic critic.

from a Salvation Army band might play one of Handel's trumpet *obbligati*) he cannot conceal his dislike, his weariness, his disparagement, his longing to be back at his usual work of discussing plays that only prove how the old reproach has passed from music to the drama, since it now needs no Beaumarchais to discover that when a piece is too silly to be read one acts it.

It is conceded that a musical critic who was nothing but an opera-goer would be a gross impostor; and yet no man could go to the opera for ten years and be as ignorant of "absolute music" as a dramatic critic may be of absolute literature (if I may so transfer the term) after twenty years of play-going. And accordingly, we find that even the great mistakes of the musical critics are far less discreditable than the great mistakes of the dramatic critics. Take, for example, the apparently cognate cases of the failures to appreciate Wagner and Ibsen. The opposition to Wagner was provoked by the extreme strangeness of the sound of his music to the ears of critics saturated with Handel, Haydn, Mozart, Beethoven, Schubert, and Mendelssohn. Clearly the musical critics were misled by sheer intensity of culture, just as Spohr and Weber were betrayed into attacking Beethoven. But the anti-Ibsenite dramatic critics cannot allege that Ibsen staggered them with unwonted tonic discords and unprepared major ninths—that his words were unknown to dictionary makers and his syntax to grammarians. No critic saturated with Goethe (the dramatic contemporary and peer of Mozart and Beethoven) could possibly have come so desperately to grief over Ibsen as most of our dramatic critics now rue having done. The proof is that the two dramatic critics who most triumphantly escaped the pitfall—and that without at all accepting the Ibsenist philosophy—were not only accomplished literary critics, but one of them had practiced musical criticism as well, and the other was the author of a life of Wagner.* They were in no more danger of taking the "suburban egotist" view of Ibsen than I, through my poor opinion of most of Brahms's music, am of mistaking that composer for an organ grinder. Besides, compare the anti-Wagnerite documents with the anti-Ibsenite ones. Read Hanslick,† Edmund Gurney, or even the belated Mr Statham on the hopeless subject of the fallacy of Wagner's art theory. Set against their criticisms the best of the current indictments of A Doll's House and Ghosts; and then deny, if you can, that even in making an ass of himself the musical critic towers majestically over the little specialist of the playhouse.

One important point of inferiority which the dramatic critic cannot very well help, considering the limits of his experience, is his gullibility on the subject of "the palmy days" of theatrical art. As it happens, the palmy days are in full swing at the opera still. I know all about them. At Covent Garden the bill changes every night, and always from one heroic work to another: coats and waistcoats are as unfamiliar to me on the stage as they were to Mrs Siddons. The artists to whom I am accustomed do not play the same little bit of ephemeral comedy for five hundred nights at a time, and find their wigs becoming grey before they have played one classic part. No: they receive that "thorough all-round training," and acquire that "readiness of resource" which is only to be gained by playing a fresh leading part in a great work every night, as actors used to do in such famous old schools of acting

* William Archer in his nonage had written a biographical study of Wagner; it was never published. The other dramatic critic apparently was A. B. Walkley.

† Eduard Hanslick (1825–1904) was an eminent Viennese musical critic of strong prejudices, who bitterly opposed Wagner and championed Brahms.

as the provincial stock companies, mostly extinct at present, and deeply regretted by all those who are too young to know at first hand what they are talking about. And the strong opinion I have formed from my experience is, that of all the —— but I find that I have no room left. I am very sorry; but I am strictly limited in point of space, and really cannot go on any longer.

GILBERT SANS SULLIVAN
The World, 6 January 1892

Need I say anything more in justification of The Mountebanks, a Gilbert opera with Cellier as composer *vice* Sullivan, retired, than that it made me laugh heartily several times. The brigands whose motto is "Heroism without Risk"; the alchemist who pays his bills with halfpence, accompanied by a written under-taking to transmute them into gold as soon as he discovers the philosopher's stone; the girl who thinks herself plain and her lover handsome, but has to confess to him that she finds herself in a hopeless minority on both subjects; the unsuccessful Hamlet who so dreads to be ever again laughed at by the public that he has turned clown; the mountebank who, pretending that he has swallowed poison and is in the agonies of stomach ache, is forced to swallow an elixir which has the magic property of turning all pretences into realities; the transformation by this same elixir of the brigands into monks, the clown and columbine into automatic clockwork figures, the village belle into an old hag, the heroine into a lunatic, and the rustic hero into a duke: if all these went for no more than one laugh apiece, the opera would come out ahead of many of its rivals in point of fun. With them, however, the merit of the piece stops: every line that goes a step further is a line to the bad.

Mr Gilbert has gone wrong in his old way: he has mixed his *genres*. In this Shakespear-ridden land one cannot be a stickler for the unities of time and place; but I defy any dramatist to set the fantastic and the conventional, the philosophic and the sentimental, jostling one another for stage room without spoiling his play. Now The Mountebanks begins in an outrageous Sicily, where the stage-struck people want to play Shakespear, and where impossible brigands, prosecuting farcical vendettas, agree to hold a revel for twentyfour days on wine ordered from the chemist's, and not to cheer during all that time above a whisper, because of a bedridden alchemist upstairs, shattered by the repeated explosions which have attended his researches into the transmutation of metals. As aforesaid, brigands, mountebanks, and everyone else become enchanted by drinking a magic potion, and are restored to their natural, or rather normal, condition by the burning of the label of the bottle which contains the philtre.

Clearly there is no room here for the realism of Ibsen or the idealism of Drury Lane. That a man so clever as Mr Gilbert could have supposed that the atmosphere of such a Sicily could be breathed by a figure from the conventional drama is a startling example of the illusions of authorship. He undoubtedly did suppose it, however; for one of the characters, a girl who loves the hero and is cordially detested by him, might have been turned out by Tom Taylor himself. When Alfredo impersonates the duke, and is caught in that assumption by the action of the elixir, she impersonates the duchess and shares his fate, thereby becoming his adored wife. Incidentally she delays the action, bores the audience, and, being quite unfancifully conceived, repeatedly knocks the piece off its proper plane. In the second act, she goes to the incredible length of a sentimental *dénouement*. She "relents" at the entreaty of the heroine, not in the fashion of the Pirate of Penzance on learning that his prisoner is an orphan—the only variety of ruth conceivable in Gilbertland—but actually in the orthodox manner of Hubert in King John.

I am afraid that Miss Lucille Saunders will think me grossly inconsiderate when I say, as I must, that if her part were completely cut out, the opera would be vastly improved; but that is certainly my opinion. Alfredo could quite Gilbertianly be represented as devoted to an absent duchess whom he had never seen; and the incident of Pietro losing the charm might easily be managed otherwise, if not wholly omitted. Under these circumstances, it is little to be thankful for that Ultrice, though she is ugly, is at least not old. The old woman of the play is happily not a new Lady Jane or Katisha, but a young maiden who takes the elixir when simulating octogenarianism, and pays the penalty like the rest.

Another weakness in the scheme is that there is no dramatic action in the second act—nothing but a simple exhibition of the characters in the plight to which the elixir reduced them at the end of the first. They walk on in twos; sing comic duets recounting the anomalies of their condition in Gilbertian verse; and go off again, all except the incorrigibly malapropos Ultrice, who sings a tragic *scena* which nobody wants to hear. And nothing else happens except an incident planned in the first act and deprived of its *raison d'être* by the charm, and the sentimental *dénouement*, which is dragged in by the ears (if I may so mix my metaphors) when the fun begins to wear out. The result is that the opera is virtually over ten minutes before the curtain falls; and this means that the curtain falls rather flatly, especially as the composer signally failed to come to the rescue at this particular point.

Cellier's strength never lay in the working up of *finales*; but this one flickers and goes out so suddenly that one can almost hear ghostly muffled drums in the orchestra. The rest of the score is what might have been expected from the composer—that is, better than the occasion required it to be; and in this very superfluity of musical conscience one recognizes his want of the tact which has saved Sir Arthur Sullivan from ever wasting musical sentiment on Mr Gilbert. Musicians will not think the worse of Cellier for this. There are many points, such as the graceful formalism of the little overture, with its orthodox "working out," and the many tender elaborations in the accompaniments, all done from sheer love of music, which will shield Cellier more effectually than his new dignity of *de mortuis* from that reproach of musical unscrupulousness which qualifies every musician's appreciation of the Sullivanesque *savoir-faire*.

But from the more comprehensive standpoint which is necessary in judging an opera, it must be confessed that, since Sullivan is spontaneously vivacious where Cellier was only energetic—and that, too, with an effort which, though successful, was obvious—and since Sullivan is out of all comparison more various in his moods, besides being a better songwriter, Mr Gilbert cannot, on the whole, be said to have changed for the better when he left the Savoy for the Lyric. Only Cellier's master, Sterndale Bennett, would not have thought the worse of him on that account; nor do I set it down here as any disparagement to him.

In speaking of Cellier as generally less vivacious than Sullivan, I do not of course imply that he is behindhand in those musical facetiousnesses which tickled the public so hugely at the Savoy. The duet for the automata with the quaint squeaking accompaniment, the clockwork music, and the showman's song with big drum *obbligato*

[511]

by Mr Monkhouse, are quite up to the Savoy standard—if, indeed, that does not prove too modest an appreciation of the popularity of Put a penny in the slot. The old and easy expedient of making the men sing a solemn chorus and the women a merry one successively (or *vice versa*, as in Patience), and then repeat them simultaneously, is achieved in the second act to the entire satisfaction of those who regard it as one of the miracles of counterpoint.

One of the operatic jokes is the best in the whole Gilbertian series. The monkized brigands receive the Duke with a mock ecclesiastical chorus on the syllable La. He expresses his acknowledgments by an elaborate *recitative* in the same eloquent terms, and, having to finish on the dominant, and finding himself at a loss to hit that note, explains that he is "in want of a word," whereupon they offer him La on the tonic. He shakes his head, and a monk gives him La on the dominant, which he immediately accepts with an air of relief, and so finishes triumphantly. Not to damp my readers too much, I may add that anybody with an ear can appreciate the joke when they hear it without in the least knowing what "the dominant" means.

Mr Gilbert has not much to complain of in the way his work is given to the public. Miss Aida Jenoure makes a hit as the dancing girl who becomes an automaton. She is clever, funny, pretty, a sufficient singer and dancer, with the only woman's part in the opera worth having. Poor Miss Lucille Saunders does her work earnestly, in spite of the fact that the better she does it the more heartily the audience (through no fault of her own) wish her at the Adelphi. Miss Geraldine Ulmar can do little except clothe herself in the dignity of leading lady, and get through her part as prettily as possible. She rather declines to be mad in the second act, mistrusting, as I surmise, the effect of vociferous lunacy on the voice. Miss Eva Moore, as one of a subsidiary pair of lovers, brings in a second tenor, Mr Cecil Burt,* who, though condemned to impersonate a particularly fatuous brigand, and to answer to the name of Risotto—all of which he does without apparent reluctance—looks like an early portrait of Daniel O'Connell by Sir Thomas Lawrence. Mr Robertson, the leading tenor, retains all his freshness, even to the extent of an occasional rawness of voice which suggests that it has not yet attained full maturity, and an air of unfamiliarity with the stage which often clings for long to men who are not mummers by natural temperament. The comedians are as funny as could be desired. Mr Monkhouse's Bartolo is a genuine creation: he shews a thoroughly artistic perception of the fact that as the pseudo-Ibsenite clown with drum and pipes he has to make his part funny, wheras in the automaton scenes his part makes him funny, and he has only to be careful not to spoil it by trying to help it too much. Mr Brough gets everything that is to be got out of the business of the chief mountebank; and Mr Wyatt is in the highest spirits, dancing less than usual, but executing every step with all his old air of receiving the most exquisite anguish from the exercise. Furneaux Cook, as the innkeeper, describes the alchemist with an unembarrassed conviction which sends the fun well across the footlights. And the band, under Mr Caryll, is excellent. I am bound to mention, though, that I am writing all this before the first public performance, on the strength of a dress rehearsal. But I do not think I shall have occasion to change any of my judgments, however the cat may jump.

The death of Cellier has diverted public attention from that of Weist Hill, who was chiefly remarkable, as

---

* The second tenor, Cecil Burt, who resembled the early portrait of the great Irish nationalist leader, was Shaw's brother-in-law Charles Butterfield. See **I**, 780 n.

far as my knowledge of him went, for what he did as a conductor. The set of concerts he conducted for Madame Viard-Louis, when orchestral music in London was at its lowest ebb, can hardly yet be forgotten by the survivors of that famine. Had he been lucky enough to find a capitalist of sufficient staying powers, he would undoubtedly have anticipated Mr Henschel's London Symphony enterprise. He knew that the London orchestral forces of his day were capable of extraordinary feats of combined speed and precision; and he saw, what everybody has since learned from Richter, the need for enlarging the orchestra and insisting on the importance of broad handling and sustained tone. It is not altogether to the credit of English musical enterprise that it should have been possible for him to give such signal proofs of capacity as he did with Madame Viard-Louis without succeeding in finding another backer when that lady's resources were exhausted.

THE ABSENCE OF ORCHESTRAS

The World, 13 January 1892

Professor Riseley, conferring with an assembly of professional musicians at Newcastle, complains of the absence of orchestras in England. I have often complained of this myself, without receiving any encouragement to believe that my grievance received the smallest attention. Mr Riseley, I see, appeals to Church and State for aid; and it is just possible that persistent hammering away in this direction might get something done in the course of half a century or so. At present every parish in England has a parish church in which instrumental and vocal music is performed at least once a week, and in which the congregation, however impatient of serious and elevated art on weekdays, resigns itself on Sunday to countenance the highest pretensions that music can make. Unfortunately, most of these churches are provided with nothing better in the way of instrumental music than a huge machine called an organ, which, though capable of great things in the hands of a first-rate player dealing with solo music specially written for it, is in many ways highly objectionable for accompanying choral music, and a quite atrocious substitute for orchestral accompaniments. The manipulator of this mechanical monster is generally selected by a sort of open competition, one applicant after another playing before a few gentlemen who bring a trained judgment of horses, crops, groceries, or dry goods to the assistance of the clergyman, who may perhaps know the difference between the Greek β and B flat, or perhaps may not. Every organist will tell you stories of the games he has had with these tribunals, and of the ingenious dodges, wholly irrelevant to his musical fitness, with which he has borne off appointments from less adroit competitors. Once accepted, an organist is underpaid; his authority in directing the services is jealously limited by the clergyman; and he is relegated to a social status intermediate between that of a gentleman and an organ-blower or gravedigger. Clearly, then, a church which has only an organ in the hands of an organist of no more than ordinary force of character will do little or nothing for music, and will presumably do less for The Church (as distinguished from the church) than it might if its services were musically decent. For my part, I have hardly ever heard a service at a country church without wondering at the extraordinary irreverence of the musical arrangements—the gabbling and bawling of the boys in the psalms, the half-hearted droning of the congregation in the hymns, and the trumpery string of modulations and tunes played by the organist, with perhaps a flight into comparative classicism with a number from Mozart's Twelfth Mass, the Cujus Animam from Rossini's Stabat, or the march from Le Prophète, to play the people out. When there is anything better than that, you always find, either that the incumbent (not the organist) is a musical enthusiast, or else that there are several churches in the neighborhood which compete hotly with the parish church for worshipers. Deplorable as this state of things is, and deeply corrupted as the ears of most English people become by their being trained from youth up to listen patiently to bad music once a week, it is not easy to see where the remedy is to come from so long as no musical qualification is expected from those who have the supreme control of a service that is half music. This is hardly to be wondered at in view of the fact that many bishops will ordain men who, though they can satisfy the chaplain of their ability, under stress of preparation, to blunder through the Gospels in Greek, cannot read a chapter of the Bible aloud in English intelligibly. And indeed I do not pretend that The Church could fill its pulpits if its ministry were to be made musical as well as spiritual. The artistic part of the service should be placed under the separate control of a capable artist, just as the heating arrangements are placed in the hands of a capable plumber. But since only those few clergymen who are themselves artists can recognize or even understand this, present circumstances offer no chance of the emancipation of the organist from the despotism of the rector. The organist is, and will always be, a slave. But if there were an orchestra in the church the organist would have to be a conductor, capable of inspiring some degree of confidence in a whole band; and the most inveterately obtuse incumbent could no longer make him feel that he might be replaced by any person who knew enough about the organ to strum through a service, pending whose appointment one of the young ladies from the rectory could keep things going for a week or two. Besides, the artistic conscience of a band is a stronger resisting force than that of an individual organist. It is always easier to say "We object" than "I object." The parish church bands would give the orchestral nuclei which Professor Riseley wants. As a first step in reconciling public opinion to them, let everyone of musical pretensions do his or her best to discredit the notion that the organ is a specially sacred kind of music machine. It is, as a matter of fact, quite the reverse; for I doubt if there is any instrument which so frequently and irresistibly provokes the player to profanity. Indeed, organists are far from being the majestic and self-contained men their office might lead outsiders to expect.

As to Mr Riseley's other suggestion, of bands maintained by the municipalities, or at least subventioned by them, I have urged that also, being quite unable to see why a County Council or Town Corporation should refrain from providing bands in parks when they provide flower gardens. However, we must first educate the rate-paying classes on the subject, as they seem at present to have no idea of the plain fact that people who are bred in towns where there is no good theatre, no good picture gallery, and no good orchestra, are ill-bred people, and that this is the reason why provincial society consists so largely of men who, though they are positively wallowing in money, are, with the best intentions, the dreariest boors imaginable. The twenty thousand bandsmen of Lancashire (I do not guarantee the figure, which I quote from an old number of the British Bandsman) are all men who work for weekly wages.

There was a time, as any instrument manufacturer will inform you, when gentlemen also broke into spontaneous musical activity of this kind, and amateurs of the key bugle, cornetto, serpent, and other musical weapons were not uncommon. My own father, armed with a trombone, and in company with some two dozen others of ascertained gentility, used to assemble on summer evenings on a riverside promenade on the outskirts of my native town, and entertain their fellow citizens with public-spirited minstrelsy. In fact, my father not only played his trombone part, but actually composed it as he went along, being an indifferent reader-at-sight, but an expert at what used to be known as "vamping." What my father's son might have said had he been compelled to criticize these performances in his present capacity is a point upon which I shall pursue no unfilial speculation: suffice it that such music must have been infinitely better and more hopeful than no music at all. At any rate, it did not encourage that sort of materialism which makes England a desert wherein music has to resort to the most degrading shifts for a living. We are all very angry when anyone calls us an unmusical nation; but let the holder of that opinion come from the general to the particular by proposing a rate of half a farthing in the pound for musical purposes; and he will soon have plenty of documents to support his contention.

Meanwhile, we have, outside London, just one first-class orchestra, the result of Hallé's life work at Manchester. And all the music in London last week was its two performances of Berlioz's Faust. One of the advantages of being a critic in London is that at all seasons of rejoicing and holiday making, Music vanishes from the critical sphere and takes to the streets, where she is very vociferous between eleven and two at night. The drunken bachelor sings, four or five strong, beneath my window; and the drunken husband passes doggedly on his way home, with his hardly sober wife one pace behind, nag, nag, nagging, except at such crises of screaming as are produced by the exasperated husband proving himself unworthy the name of a British sailor. This is a leading feature of our English Christmas, with its round of slaughtering, gorging, and drinking, into the midst of which this time comes Hallé with his orchestra, and finds his stalls anything but well filled, though the gallery is faithful even to "standing room only," and not too much of that.

When he first introduced The Damnation of Faust here, there were no rival performances to compare with that of the Manchester band. Now the work is a stock piece at the Albert Hall and the Richter concerts; and it has been heard at the Crystal Palace. The result is that London is utterly eclipsed and brought to naught. In vain does Mr Barnby guarantee metronomic regularity of *tempo* and accurate execution of every note in the score: the work is usually received at the Albert Hall as an unaffectedly pious composition in the oratorio style. Richter, by dint of incessant vigilance and urgency, only gets here and there a stroke of fancy, power, or delicacy out of his orchestra in its own despite. Mr Manns conducts Faust conscientiously, but without opposing any really sympathetic knowledge to the blank ignorance of the orchestra. Hallé simply indicates the quietest, amblingest *tempos* at his ease; and the score comes to life in the hands of players who understand every bar of it, and individualize every phrase.

The Hungarian March, taken at about half the speed at which Lamoureux vainly tries to make it "go," is encored with yells—literally with yells—in St James's Hall. Nobody mistakes the Amen parody for a highly becoming interlude of sacred music, nor misses the diabolic *élan* of the serenade, the subtler imaginative qualities of the supernatural choruses and dances, or the originality and pathos of the music of Faust and

Margaret. Here is the experimental verification of my contention that no precision in execution or ability in conducting can, in performing Berlioz's music, supply the want of knowledge on the part of the band of the intention of every orchestral touch. Victories over Berlioz are soldiers' victories, not generals'. The long and short of the matter is that our London men do not know the works of Berlioz and the Manchester men do; hence the enormous superiority of the latter on such occasions as the one in question.

The principal parts were taken by the Henschels, Herr Georg of that ilk singing on this occasion better, if less prettily, than his wife. The gentleman who sang Brander's music only needs to raise his standard of accuracy of intonation to gain my unqualified approval. During the recent fog, when Messrs Besson were cheering me up one afternoon by the pipings of their new contrabass clarinet, they also submitted a new compensating piston, by which they have improved certain false notes in the scale of the cornet. If this compensating piston can be applied successfully to English bass singers, I do not hesitate to pronounce it the greatest invention of modern times.

Mr Barton McGuckin had to take Mr Lloyd's place, at the disadvantage of a very superficial acquaintance with a difficult part. His words were quite unintelligible; and in the invocation, at the very climax of the tremendous burst into C sharp major, he altered the cadence in a way that robbed me of breath. I see no reason why Mr McGuckin should not some day make an excellent Faust—quite as good as Mr Lloyd, who is not at his best in the part—as soon as he learns it. Pending which event, I reserve further criticism.

MUSIC FOR THE THEATRE

The World, 27 January 1892

I have seldom been more astonished than I was last week, when the manager of the Haymarket Theatre offered me an opportunity of hearing the music which Mr Henschel has just composed for Hamlet. Not only had I never heard of a tragedian regarding incidental music as having any interest separable in the remotest degree from his own performance, or as being a less mechanical part of that than the last touch of paint or limelight, but I had been brought up to believe that Hamlet in its natural state consisted musically of the march from Judas Maccabæus for the entry of the Court, and the Dead March in Saul for Hamlet's death, the *entr'actes* being selected from no longer popular overtures such as La Sirène, &c. My opinion of Mr Tree* consequently rose to such a pitch as to all but defeat the object of my visit to the last rehearsal; for instead of listening to Mr Henschel's interludes, I spent the intervals in explaining to Mr Tree exactly how his part ought to be played, he listening with the patience and attention which might be expected from so accomplished an actor. However, I heard enough with one ear to serve my purpose.

What Mr Henschel has done with his opportunity cannot be described offhand to those who have never thought over the position of the composer in the theatre. For him there are two extremes. One is to assume the

---

* Herbert Beerbohm Tree, wellknown actor-manager, made his first appearance in London as Hamlet on 21 January, with the greatest success.

full dignity of the creative musician, and compose an independent overture which, however sympathetic it may be with the impending drama, nevertheless takes the forms proper to pure music, and is balanced and finished as a beautiful and symmetrical fabric of sounds, performable as plain Opus 1000 apart from the drama, as satisfactorily as the drama is performable apart from it. Example: Egmont, in which Beethoven and Goethe associate as peers in their diverse arts, Beethoven not merely illustrating Goethe's masterpiece, but adding a masterpiece of his own on the same subject. The other extreme is to supply bare *mélodrame*, familiar samples of which may be found in the ethereal strains from muted violins which accompany the unfolding of transformation scenes in pantomimes, the animated measures which enliven the rallies in the harlequinade, or the weird throbbings of the ghost melody in The Corsican Brothers.*

The production of these is not musical composition: it is mere musical tailoring, in the course of which the *mélodrame* is cut and made to the measure of the stage business, and altered by snipping or patching when it comes to be tried on at rehearsal. The old-fashioned actor got his practical musical education in this way; and he will tell you that certain speeches are easy to speak "through music" and frightfully hard without it; or, as Richard III., he will work himself up to the requisite pitch of truculence in the "Who intercepts me in my expedition?" scene, partly by listening to the trumpets, and partly by swearing at them for not playing louder.

Beyond this he is so untutored that he will unhesitatingly call upon the *chef d'orchestre* to "stop that music"

* Classical romance by Dion Boucicault, from the French play adaptation of the Dumas novel.

in the very middle of a suspension, or with a promising first inversion of the common chord, or on a dominant seventh or the like, quite unconscious of the risk of some musician rising in the theatre on the first night and saying "I beg your pardon for interrupting you, sir; but will you kindly ask the band to resolve that four-to-three before you proceed with your soliloquy?" The idea that music is written in sentences with full stops at the end of them, just as much as dramatic poetry is, does not occur to him: all he knows is that he cannot make the audience shudder or feel sentimental without music, exactly as the comedian knows that he cannot make the audience laugh unless the lights are full on. And the music man at the theatre seldom counts for more than a useful colleague of the gas man.

This state of things at last gives way to evolutionary forces like other states of things. The rage for culture opens a career for cultivated men (not merely cultivated players) as theatrical managers and actors; and the old-fashioned actors and managers find themselves compelled by stress of competition to pose as connoisseurs in all the arts, and to set up Medicean retinues of literary advisers, poets, composers, artists, archeologists, and even critics. And whenever a masterpiece of dramatic literature is revived, the whole retinue is paraded. Now the very publicity of the parade makes it impossible for the retinue to be too servile: indeed, to the full extent to which it reflects lustre on the manager can it also insist on having a voice in the artistic conduct of his enterprises.

Take the composer, for instance. No actor-manager could tell Sir Arthur Sullivan to "stop that music," or refuse to allow Mr Henschel to resolve his discords. On the other hand, no manager will engage an orchestra of from eighty to a hundred performers for an overture and *entr'actes*; and no actor will sacrifice any of the effectiveness of his business in order to fit it to the music; whilst at the same time the actor-manager expects all the most modern improvements in the way of "leading motives," which make excellent material for press cuttings. The situation being thus limited, the composer submits to become a musical tailor as far as the *mélodrame* is concerned, but throws over the manager completely in the overture and *entr'actes* by composing them with a view to performance as "an orchestral suite" at the Crystal Palace or London Symphony concerts, laying himself out frankly for a numerous orchestra and a silent audience, instead of for a theatre band contending feebly with the chatter of the dramatic critics. Clearly he might venture upon a great overture like Egmont or Coriolan but for the modern improvements—the leading motives—which are an implied part of his contract. The tragedian must have his motive; and the leading lady, even when she is not the most influential person in the theatre, is allowed to have one also as a foil to the tragedian's. Macduff, Richmond, and Laertes will soon advance their claims, which are obviously no more valid than those of high-reaching Buckingham, Duncan, Polonius, and Claudius.

Mark my words: as actors come to understand these things better, we shall have such scenes at rehearsal as have never before been witnessed in a theatre—Rosencrantz threatening to throw up his part because his motive is half a bar shorter than Guildenstern's; the Ghost claiming, on Mozart's authority, an absolute monopoly of the trombones; Hamlet asking the composer, with magnificent politeness, whether he would mind doubling the basses with a *contrafagotto* in order to bring out the Inky Cloak theme a little better; Othello insisting on being in the bass and Olivia on being in the treble when their themes are worked simultaneously with those of Iago and Viola, and the wretched composer finally writing them all in double counterpoint in order that each may come uppermost or undermost by turns.

Pending these developments our composers lean towards compromise between the leading motive system and the old symphonic form. At first sight a double deal seems easy enough. Use your bold Richard motive or your tragic Hamlet motive as the first subject in your overture, with the feminine Ophelia theme as the second subject ("happily contrasted," as the analytic programist is sure to say if he is a friend of yours), and then proceed in orthodox form. Unfortunately, when this formula comes to the proof, you find that a leading motive is one thing and a symphonic subject another, and that they can no more replace oneanother than drawings of human figures in dramatic action can replace arabesques. It is true that human figures can be expressed by curved lines, as arabesques are; and there are arabesques composed of human figures, just as there are pictures in which the figures are decorations. In the hands of the greatest masters the success of the combination of decorative and dramatic seems complete, because every departure from perfect grace and symmetry produces a dramatic interest so absorbing that the spectator feels a heightened satisfaction instead of a deficiency.

But take a picture in which the epic and dramatic elements have been wrought to the highest pitch—say Ford Madox Brown's Lear and Cordelia—and contrast it with a shutter decorated by Giovanni da Udine.* Imagine Giovanni trying to tell the story of Lear in his own way as convincingly as Madox Brown has told it, or Madox Brown attempting to give his picture the symmetry of Giovanni's shutter. The contrast at once reveals the hollowness of the stock professorial precept

* Giovanni Nanni of Udine (1487–1564) was an Italian painter and sculptor, pupil of Raphael.

about uniting the highest qualities of both schools, which is seen to mean no more than that a man may reasonably prefer Tintoretto's Annunciation in the Scuola di San Rocco because the flight of angels shooting in through the window is more graceful than Giovanni's designs, whilst the story of the virgin is as well told as that of Cordelia. But in subjects where flights of angels are unworkable, Tintoretto had, like Brown, to fall back on qualities of beauty not in the least arabesque.

Bring up a critic exclusively on such qualities, and he will find Giovanni vapidly elegant, empty, and artificial; wheras if you nurse him exclusively on arabesque he will recoil from Madox Brown as being absolutely ugly and uncouth. In fact, though Madox Brown is no less obviously the greatest living English epic painter than Mr Burne-Jones is the greatest decorative painter, his friends are at present collecting a thousand pounds to get him out of pecuniary difficulties which are no fault of his own, but a consequence of the nation being still too exclusively addicted to arabesques and pretty sentimentalities. Just as pictorial storytelling, having a different purpose from arabesque, has necessarily a different constructive logic, and consequently must seek a different beauty; so the dramatic composer must proceed differently from the composer of absolute music. If he tries to walk with one foot in each way, he may be as fine a musician as Sterndale Bennett was, and yet not be safe from producing futilities like Paradise and the Peri.

Take, for example, the overture to Richard III., which Mr Edward German, a musician of considerable talent, composed for Mr Mansfield. In this work the first subject begins as a genuine Richard motive; but in order to adapt it to sonata treatment it is furnished with an arabesque tail, like a crookbacked mermaid, with the result that the piece is too clumsy to be a good overture,

and yet too trivially shapely to be a fitting tone symbol
of Richard III. It is far surpassed by Grieg's Peer Gynt
music, which consists of two or three catchpenny
phrases served up with plenty of orchestral sugar, at a
cost in technical workmanship much smaller than that
lavished on Mr German's overture. But the catchpenny
phrases are sufficiently to the point of the scenes they
introduce, and develop—if Grieg's repetitions can be
called development—according to the logic of those
scenes and not according to that of Haydn's symphonies.
In fact, Grieg proceeded as Wagner proceeded in his
great preludes, except that, being only a musical
grasshopper in comparison with the musical giant of
Bayreuth, he could only catch a few superficial points in
the play instead of getting to the very heart and brain of
it.

Mr Henschel has wisely taken the same course,
avoiding arabesques, and sticking to the play and
nothing but the play throughout, except in one passage
where he casts the oboe for the part of "the cock that is
the trumpet [not the oboe] to the morn." This bird is
usually *persona muta*; and Mr Henschel had better have
left him so. Save in this one bar, the *mélodrame* is the
simplest and most effective I can remember. Then there
are preludes—Hamlet tragic but irresolute for Act I,
Ophelia a trifle gushing for Act II, Hamlet ferocious
and deaf to Ophelia's blandishments for Act III, Dirge
for the Drowning for Act IV, and Pastorale (with real
birds) for Act V. Of all which I shall have more to say
when I hear them in full orchestral panoply at the
postponed London Symphony concert. For the present,
suffice it to say that they go deeper than Grieg, besides
confining themselves, as aforesaid, strictly to their own
business, without any digressions into arabesque.

BURNS NIGHT

The World, 3 February 1892

When I received an invitation to a Grand Scotch Festival at the Albert Hall on the Burns anniversary, I was a little staggered; but I felt that a man should have the courage of his profession, and went. The population of the Albert Hall was scanty and scattered, probably through crofter emigration. I had no sooner entered when bang went two saxpences for a program! Now I am not a Scotchman—quite the reverse: my nature is an exceptionally open and bounteous one; and a shilling more or less will neither make me nor break me. All the meaner is the conduct of those who take advantage of my lavishness. And at the Albert Hall they always do take advantage of it. I look at this matter as a political economist. The charge made for a program is exactly a hundred per cent. on the charge for admission at the margin of cultivation—I mean in the gallery. This program is not, like the sixpenny program at the Crystal Palace or the Popular Concerts, full of elaborate analyses, quotations in music type, latest historical discoveries concerning the compositions performed, and so forth. It is a bare list of the names of the pieces played, with the words of the songs more or less accurately copied, and spread out as widely as possible over sixteen quarto pages. Now in a huge building like the Albert Hall, where a couple of thousand copies could be easily sold if the price were reasonable, it would be possible, without any help from advertizers, to sell a sixteen-page program, quite sufficient for the purposes of the evening, at a penny, and make a profit on the transaction. At twopence the profit per cent. would be huge. I am a sufficiently old hand at pamphleteering to know this offhand, without the trouble of making inquiries. Fancy my feelings, then, on being compelled to disburse a whole shilling for the sixteen quarto pages aforesaid, made to that size for the more effective setting forth, on a dozen other pages, of the excellencies of Quinine and Iron Tonics, Dental Institutes, Scientific Dentifrices (with seductive illustration), Voice Production Studios based on the purest Italian methods, Parisian diamonds, Steinway pianos, and Yorkshire Relish. Of course, not one Scotchman in twenty will buy a program on such terms. This means that the price is too high to extract the largest obtainable booty from the audience. It is obviously more profitable to receive from ten people a penny apiece than to receive eightpence from one person, when both operations fit equally into the night's work. And this is why I, as a critic, meddle in the matter.

I cannot say that the concert was particularly Scotch in anything but the name. The part-songs given by Mr Carter's choir were so primly British in their gentility as to suggest that the native heath of the singers must be Clapham Common at the very wildest. Perhaps the highest pitch of emotional excitement was reached in that well-known Caledonian *morceau*, the Miserere from Il Trovatore, with military accompaniments from the band of the Scots Guards, in which Madame Giulia Valda expressed the distraction of the heroine by singing convulsively out of time. The effect of the entry of the organ and side drum *ad lib.* on the concluding chord was sublime; and the idea of having Manrico imprisoned in the cellar instead of in the tower was not unhappy in its effect; but, on the whole, I should not like to answer for Verdi's unqualified approval of the performance.

Most of the songs were in the last degree unlike themselves. I presume Mr Dalgety Henderson is a Scotchman; for only a Scotchman could have been so bent on making the vengeful Macgregors' Gathering into a sentimental English ballad. From Sims Reeves it was memorable—almost terrible; but when Mr Henderson sang Give their roofs to the flame and their flesh to the eagles, with his most lackadaisically pathetic *nuance* on "eagles," I felt that the whole Macgregor clan might be invited to tea with every confidence in the perfect propriety of their behavior. Miss Rose Williams's nationality is unknown to me. She is a contralto of the school of Madame Antoinette Sterling, singing very slowly and with a steady suffusion of feeling (physically a steady pressure of chest voice), which only admits of the most mournful expression. Her song was A man's a man for a' that; and she sang it exactly as if it were The Three Fishers. It was pretty; but it would have damped a whole revolution had there been one on at the moment.

Even Miss Macintyre was not in the least racy of the soil in her cosmopolitan rendering of Mary Morison. In short, the only singer who hit the mark in the first part of the concert (I did not wait for the second) was Mr Norman Salmond, who, having nothing Scotch about him, sang—and sang to perfection—what a cockney printer next morning described as Green grow the rashers O. The only other item in which any sense of the beauty and romantic dignity of Scotch folk music was shewn by the artist was a movement from Max Bruch's Scottish Violin Fantasia, finely played by Mr Seiffert (a Dutchman), under the heavy disadvantage of a pianoforte accompaniment and a silly misdescription in the program, which led the audience to believe that he was to play a simple transcription of a Scotch melody. On the whole, I would not ask to hear a less Scotch concert.

The London Symphony Concert on the 26th was none the worse for its postponement as far as the band was concerned, though it unluckily found Mrs Henschel on the sick list. The Lohengrin prelude and Schubert's unfinished symphony in H moll were played *con amore*, and went splendidly, in spite of a rough detail or two. Mr Górski gave a respectable performance of Max Bruch's first violin concerto. The Hamlet music, eked out a little by some illogical repeats, was naturally much more effective in its stormier phrases than it is when played at the Haymarket by a band of forty thrust under the stage. In dramatic force and consistency it is undoubtedly better than anything which our great theatrical revivals have yet produced. The impetuous interlude (No. 3), in which occur the remarkably graphic passages for the piccolo which laugh away the Ophelia motive, is, on the whole, the best number. The pastorale, the march, and the dirge would probably have been better done by Sir Arthur Sullivan or any of our "absolute musicians."

The Hamlet music reminds me of the Haymarket conductor, Mr Karl Armbruster, and of a lecture on Wagner which I heard him deliver the other evening at the London Institution. It is my special merit that I have always seen plainly that in this Philistine country a musical critic, if he is to do any good, must put off the learned commentator, and become a propagandist, versed in all the arts that attract a crowd, and wholly regardless of his personal dignity. I have propagated my ideas on other subjects at street corners to the music of the big drum; and I should not hesitate to propagate Wagnerism there with a harmonium if I were sufficiently a master of that instrument, or if the subject were one which lent itself to such treatment. Failing that, Mr Armbruster's lectures, under the auspices of educational bodies, with magic lantern and vocal illustrations, are clearly the next best thing. Of course the modern Arcedeckne, being unable to say "You should have a

[531]

piano, Thack,"* will say "You should have an orchestra, Armby"; but in view of the impossible expense, the conclusive reply is "Dont you wish you may get it?" Once or twice I thought Mr Armbruster was more ornate than candid in his descriptions. It is all very well to represent Bayreuth as a quiet spot where Nature invites the contemplative peace in which Wagner's message comes to you with the full force of its deepest meaning (or words to that effect); but in solemn truth the place is such a dull country town that the most unmusical holiday-maker is driven into the theatre to avoid being bored out of his senses.

The proper way to enjoy Parsifal is to step into the temple straight out of the squalid rush and strain and vulgar bustle of London, with every faculty in keen activity, instead of loafing up a country road to it in a slack, unstrung, vagabondizing, overfed and under-worked holiday humor, when a stroll through the pines seems better than any theatre. I once, on a Parsifal night, when there was a wonderful sky outside, spent the last act on the hills pretending to terrify myself by venturing into pitchy darknesses in the depths of the woods. You do not suppose, probably, that I would have wandered about Drury Lane under the same circumstances.

However, it is no use complaining of the absurd things people will say about Bayreuth. It is a European centre for high art mendacity; and Mr Armbruster, who is always professionally busy inside the theatre, and so

* Andrew Arcedeckne was an eccentric member of the Garrick Club, who fancied himself as a comic entertainer, and who bedevilled W. M. Thackeray at every opportunity after the latter satirized him as Foker in Pendennis. At the end of Thackeray's first lecture in a series on The English Humourists of the Eighteenth Century, in Willis's Rooms on 22 May 1851, Arcedeckne cried out from the rear as he departed "Ah! Thack my boy! you ought to ha' 'ad a pianner."

carries his London activity thither with him, has never realized what the genuine tourist-suited Bayreuth pilgrim experiences at the shrine of the Meister. The lecture, however, unmistakably roused considerable interest and curiosity; and although I doubt if the London Institution audience quite knew how well Miss Pauline Cramer sang Isolde's death song, they were left well on the way to a state of greater grace.

Mr D'Oyly Carte has withdrawn The Nautch Girl at the Savoy, and put on The Vicar of Bray. Mr Rutland Barrington is very funny as the Vicar; but in the work as a whole there is no life. It is, at best, a tolerable stop-gap.

WAGNER NOT A WAGNERITE

Remarks in a discussion following a lecture by
E. Algernon Baughan on The Development of Opera,
9 February 1892. Proceedings of the
Musical Association 1891–92

[U] I have listened to this debate with a good deal of interest. When I heard Mr Baughan deliver his lecture I knew what was going to happen. Mr Baughan, I am afraid, is a Wagnerite, and, to a certain extent, Wagner himself was not a Wagnerite, and I think we have arrived at that period when no person should be a Wagnerite. This Wagner cult is all very well and very touching, but if it be carried out with too much enthusiasm, the enthusiasm becomes a nuisance. Mr [E. F.] Jacques very aptly remarked in opposition to our lecturer that it was possible to regard the matter from another point of view. There is musical inspiration which is really absolute musical inspiration. To the individual who has no taste for dramatic music, most of

[533]

Wagner's compositions will appeal in vain. So long as music is absolute, he likes it; but the moment the musical element becomes subordinate to the dramatic, it no longer has any attraction for him. You must remember that there are all sorts of men between the two extremes. I have found that a large number of Wagner's admirers have very little musical faculty whatever. I have also been struck with the number of scientific men who do not in the least care for absolute music, and cannot endure opera, who, on witnessing the performance of Wagner's operas, have said "Ah, here at last is something that I can understand and appreciate." They simply ignore the musical element altogether, and address themselves to the dramatic alone. Those individuals, to my mind, are no more to be respected than are Wagner's opponents. I should say that there are few great composers whom one would not put second to Wagner. I think he stands as high as any composer who ever lived. I would like to remind the lecturer that he rather lets slip his argument when he says that sometimes you have the same air which has served for a love scene in an opera used as a religious air in an oratorio, and there you find a change was made in the rhythm, and, perhaps, in the accompaniment. No such thing, and no such change occurs in Handel's airs, except in the words themselves.

[*Mr Baughan asks: "Are they sacred in effect?"*]

Perfectly, and on your shewing. The emotion expressed by music must necessarily be abstract, and only becomes a concrete and specific thing when defined by words. As to concerted music: in the first act of Siegfried, where they ask each other riddles, concerted music would be absurd, and, consequently, at that particular point they speak alternately. At the end of the act, however, when the two men pursue a similar train of thought, they naturally speak together. In such a wonderful way does Wagner weave all the separate themes together, that to denounce concerted music would be to fly in the face of his own writings. The Italian quartets, &c., so often found in Donizetti and Verdi, to my mind shew how much superior opera is to the spoken drama, and our lecturer's hostility to Italian opera can only be accounted for on the assumption that he holds a brief on behalf of German *versus* Italian opera. I think that he should reconsider this question.[U]

CHARITY AND THE CRITIC

The World, 10 February 1892

The musical season is still very dull. Miss Macintyre's charity concert was quite an event last week, though it was of the miscellaneous order, with *Ah, fors' è lui* on top of *O luce di quest' anima*, and *Un di se ben* to finish up. Such concerts always give me an uneasy sensation of being still a boy of twelve, just wakened from a mad dream of maturity. And my impulse most decidedly is to add, Ah, do not wake me: let me dream again! to the program. There is, perhaps, a faint critical interest in hearing how Miss Fanny Moody makes the provincial *dilettanti* think that she is a great *prima donna*, and in watching the result of Miss Macintyre's original and very modern views as to how Verdi's music should be treated. Mind, I do not imply any sort of disparagement, or the opposite; no miscellaneous concert can stimulate me to face the risk and effort of forming a critical judgment, much less expressing it. I greatly enjoyed the performance of the Meister Glee Singers, and admired the success with which Miss Macintyre brought off her enterprise; but I mention the subject chiefly as an excuse for saying a word or two on the subject of charity concerts generally, concerning which I have often to act with apparent callousness to the claims of the poor and ailing. Every lady who has any turn for getting up such entertainments is keenly aware that a few lines in this column, costing me no more than a turn of the wrist, may help to feed many hungry persons, clothe many shivering children, and provide an extra bed or so at the hospital for some suffering and indigent fellow creature. An announcement beforehand will sell tickets for any concert which is to provide funds for these purposes; whilst a word of notice afterwards will gratify the artists, and make it easier to get them to sing or play again for nothing next year.

Under these circumstances, it cannot but appear the height of wanton hardheartedness in me to withhold my help and receive all appeals for it in stony silence. But the very ease with which I might help if I chose is so obvious that the idea of asking for it occurs to someone or other at least twice a day during the crises of charity-concert organization which occur from time to time. If I were to comply, my compliance would soon defeat its own object; for what I wrote would cease to be read, nothing being less interesting than strings of puffs preliminary, however pious their objects may be; whilst as to criticizing the performances subsequently, I always think it as well not to look gifthorses in the mouth, particularly when the verdict might be anything but gratifying to the donors. In short, it is impossible for me to notice on charitable grounds concerts which I should not mention if they were ordinary commercial specu-lations; and I appeal to the charitable not to make me feel like a monster by writing me touching and artful appeals, which I must, nevertheless, disregard. All I can say is, that if a concert is musically important, I shall not be deterred from noticing it by the fact that the aims of its promoters are philanthropic.

The closing of the New English Opera House has elicited a chorus of indignant despair from us all as to the possibility of doing anything for a public which will not support The Basoche. It does not appear to be certain that The Basoche is stark dead—I see it stated that it is only speechless for the moment; but, assuming that it has had its utmost run, let me point out that it is not true that it has received no support. There are many degrees of failure. If I compose an opera, and get Mr Carte to produce it at his theatre, with the result that not a single person is found willing to pay to hear it, that will undoubtedly be a failure.

Suppose, however, that Mr Carte, bent on surpassing all previous examples of managerial enterprise and munificence, spends £1,000,000 sterling in mounting my opera, and that it is played for a thousand nights to a thousand people every night with the free list entirely suspended, that will be a failure too. Failure means simply failure to replace the capital expended with a fair profit to boot in a single run; and this may be brought about by the manager spending more than the first run is worth, as well as by the public paying less. The fact is, there is no grand opera in the world which will run long enough in one capital to pay for a complete and splendid *mise-en-scène*. On the other hand, such a *mise-en-scène* will last for years as part of the stock of the house.

What Mr Carte wants is a repertory, and a position in the social economy of London like that occupied in Germany by such opera houses as those of Frankfurt or Munich, where works like [Nessler's] The Trumpeter of Sakkingen or The Barber of Bagdad may have a prodigious vogue without the manager dreaming for a moment of running them exclusively and leaving the town for months bereft of all opportunity of hearing

[537]

Der Freischütz, or Fidelio, or Die Walküre, or Le Nozze di Figaro. And here Mr Carte will recoil, and ask me whether I seriously propose that he should attempt to recover his outlay on Ivanhoe and The Basoche by mounting half a dozen grand operas to sandwich them. Certainly not, if the mounting is to be as sumptuous as that of these two operas. But why should it be? Of course, it is impossible to insult gentlemen like Messager and Sir Arthur Sullivan with less than the best of everything; but there is no need to be particular with Mozart, Beethoven, Weber, and Wagner. They are all dead; and when they were alive they had to put up with what they could get. Signor Lago has shewn that the way to make money out of the classic masterpieces of lyric drama is to practise the severest asceticism, not to say downright mortification, in respect of scenery, dresses, and everything in which Mr Carte is habitually extravagant.

Not that I would have Mr Carte too slavishly copy Signor Lago, who, perhaps, overdoes his Lenten severities a trifle; but there is no avoiding the conclusion that if the expensive ventures of the Royal English Opera are to be spread over the full period needed to produce a reasonable return on them, their runs must be broken by performances of attractive operas mounted neatly but not gaudily, and perhaps performed on "popular nights" with lower prices than when the stage is *en grande tenue* for Ivanhoe, &c. I see nothing else for it, unless Mr Carte by chance discovers some individual performer whose magnetism may do for The Basoche what Mr Irving's does for the Lyceum plays. The smallness of the cultivated section of our population is the disabling factor in all these costly schemes for performing musical works of the best class. London, artistically speaking, is still a mere village.

Meanwhile, Sir Augustus Harris is said to be about to

modernize the Covent Garden repertory to the extraordinary extent of introducing world-famous operas which were composed as recently as 1860 or thereabouts, and which have not been familiar to the German public for more than fifteen years. This is not bad for an *impresario* whose musical education consisted in watching the spectacle of post-Rossinian Italian tragic opera slowly dying of Madame Titiens at one house, without any serious attempt at rescue by Madame Patti at the other. I do not say these things by way of a fleer at Sir Augustus Harris; for I also am an old subject of the Titiens dynasty.

Imagine being inured from one's cradle to the belief that the sublime in music meant Titiens singing the Inflammatus from Rossini's Stabat Mater; that the tragic in operatic singing, far overtopping anything that Mrs Siddons could ever have done, was Titiens as Lucrezia Borgia; that majesty in music-drama reached its climax in Titiens tumbling over the *roulades* in Semiramide; that Valentine in Les Huguenots, the Countess in Le Nozze, Pamina in Die Zauberflöte, all weighed eighteen stone, and could not be impersonated without a gross violation of operatic propriety by anyone an ounce lighter. I was brought up in these articles of faith; and I believe Sir Augustus Harris was brought up in them too. Nothing will persuade me that he was not moved by some desperate yearning to recall the ideals of his boyhood when he allowed Mlle Richard, who is more like Titiens than any living artist, to play La Favorita at Covent Garden a couple of seasons ago.

What I am not so sure of is whether Sir Augustus Harris ever found Titiens out—whether he ever realized that in spite of her imposing carriage, her big voice, her general intelligence, and, above all, a certain good-hearted grace which she never lost, even physically, the intelligence was not artistic intelligence; the voice, after the first few years, was a stale voice; there was not a ray of creative genius in her; and the absurdity of her age, her pleasant ugliness, and her huge size (which must have been to at least some extent her own fault), the public got into a baneful habit of considering that the end of opera-going was not to see Lucrezia, Leonora, Valentine, or Pamina, but simply Titiens in these parts, which was tantamount to giving up all the poetry of opera as a mere convention, which need not be borne out by any sort of artistic illusion. The first time I was taken to the opera, I was so ignorant of what the entertainment meant that I looked at the circle of resplendently attired persons in the boxes and balcony with a vague expectation that they would presently stand up and sing.

But when I was an experienced young opera-goer, and had seen Titiens—the great Titiens—a dozen times, I believe I was far more hopelessly astray on the subject than I had been on that memorable first night before the curtain so astonished me by going up. For such experience only tended to make me a connoisseur in this pseudo-opera which was nothing but a *prima donna* show, and to train me to regard the *impresario* as one whose sole business it was to engage the most famous performers in that spurious *genre*, and to announce them at the beginning of the season in a long prospectus which was equally remarkable for the absence of any allusion to the artistic conditions under which the operas were to be performed, and the presence of names of artists whom the manager had not engaged, and whom he had no reasonable prospect of being able to engage.

Sir Augustus Harris has reformed that prospectus altogether; but for the life of me I can never quite divest myself of a suspicion that the great Wagner Reformation has never convinced him, and that he regards people like myself as heretics and renegades. However, if the

Nibelungen tetralogy and Tristan really reach Covent Garden or Drury Lane this year—nay, if even one of them, say Siegfried or Die Walküre, comes off—that will be the best answer to me.

THE BAYREUTH HUSH

The World, 17 February 1892

The first packed audience of the year at St James's Hall was drawn on Thursday last by the Wagner program, plus the Eroica, at the London Symphony Concert. Wagner, nevertheless, failed to get the room settled by half-past eight. I was late; but that would have made no disturbance worth mentioning had not about a hundred other people been late too. Our struggle, or rather scrimmage, to get into the room when the doors were opened after the first piece, and our persistence in wandering in search of our seats in the wrong direction when we did get in, necessitated a longish interval between the first and second numbers; and later on it became evident that the concert could not be finished by half-past ten without cutting the customary interval between the two parts very short indeed. This Mr Henschel accordingly did, with the result that when, by dint of repeated rappings, he succeeded in getting a perfect "Bayreuth" hush for the Parsifal prelude, he was paralyzed by the discovery that the tuba was absent. After a period of intensifying suspense the artist duly appeared, and took his place with the solid calm of a man who knew that we could not begin without him. Up went Mr Henschel's stick again; and we were once more breathless with expectation when the fresh discovery was made that the orchestra lacked its apex in the familiar and conspicuous person of the eminent drummer, Mr Smith. Hereupon the Bayreuth hush, overstrained, broke into ripples of laughter and a chatter of questions from those who did not understand the delay, and explanations by those who did. Finally, Mr Smith hurried in, and was received with an ovation which took him aback for the first time in the experience of the oldest concert-goer. Somehow, the Bayreuth hush seems to be an unlucky institution, even in St James's Hall. In the Bavarian Festspielhaus, of course, it is, and always has been, quite hopeless: somebody inevitably drops an opera-glass, or slams a seat, or rushes in all but late out of the sunshine without, and remarks before the solemn influence has had time to operate, "Oh my, aint it dark! however are we to tell our seats?" But hitherto I have been able to boast that there is never any difficulty in getting the London hush, about which, by the bye, no Briton is patriotic enough to gush. After last Thursday I fear I shall have to confess that the malign influence of Bayreuth has reached and corrupted us at last. What used to be a spontaneous piece of good sense and good manners has now become, when Parsifal is in question, a "put-up" solemnity. Naturally, the Powers that rule over Art are angered by this, and have made Mr Smith, formerly the most punctual of drum players, their scourge and minister to bring the ways of Bayreuth to confusion.

The performance proved afresh that Mr Henschel has now got hold of the art of orchestral conducting, and that the bringing to perfection, humanly speaking, of the London Symphony Concerts is only a question of time and perseverance. The performances come right in the mass; the due balance of tone, the color, and, above all, the intelligent and imaginative execution which is produced by playing steadfastly to fulfil the poetic purpose of the composition, are now so far achieved that

Mr Henschel's battle for a place as a conductor is nine-tenths won. The remaining tenth, depending on purity of tone, subtlety of *nuance*, and delicacy and precision of touch in the details, he is not likely to cease striving for, since it was, in fact, a premature attempt to achieve these that caused him at first to worry his band and waste his time at rehearsals by beginning at the wrong end.

At present, whilst this tithe is still in arrear, it is instructive to compare the Henschel band with the Philharmonic band, which exactly lacks what the London Symphony band has, and has what the London Symphony band lacks. For my own part, though I insist on the necessity of the combination of the qualities of both, I cannot understand the taste of the man, if such a one lives, who would not rather a thousand times have the interesting roughness of the new band than the empty elegance of the old. At the same time, it must be understood that the interest does not lie in the roughness, any more than the emptiness lies in the elegance; and my criticism on the performance of the Eroica symphony is, therefore, that it will take five years more work to make the vigorous sketch of Thursday last into a finished picture. The violin work which accompanies the Grail motive in the Parsifal prelude also requires a tremendous application of elbow-grease to make it in the least like the wing-winnowing which it should suggest. For the rest, there was nothing to complain of and much to be thankful for. The Siegfried Idyll, in particular, shewed a huge improvement on last season's performance of it. Madame Nordica, always courageous to the verge of audacity, and strong in that technical skill in the management of her voice which seems to be now almost a monopoly of American *prima donnas*, attacked Isolde's death song in superb black velvet and diamonds, and survived it, not without deserved glory; though there is all the difference in the world between Madame Nordica's bright impulsiveness and the seas of sentiment in which Isolde should be drowned.

One of the curiosities of this concert was the analytic program by Mr Joseph Bennett, who, as everyone knows, consecrated his life, rather unfortunately, to the cause of Anti-Wagnerism. Now, when you are engaged to write a program for a concert commemorative of Wagner, you cannot—at least without risking a certain friction with the *entrepreneur*—take the opportunity to demonstrate to the audience that what they are listening to is a series of outrages on all the true principles of musical art. Even the story of Wagner's milliner-made dressing-gowns would hardly be in place on such an occasion, since it is held to be fatal to his pretensions as a composer. Mr Bennett, thus hard put to it, yet came off triumphantly, like a man of resource as he is.

First, he got over the difficulty of singing the praises of the composition under analysis by quoting them from his enemies, thus: "Mr Edward Dannreuther, than whom no one knows better what he is talking about when Wagner comes up for discussion, declares," &c. Or: "The following admirable notes upon the prelude to Wagner's last and, and as many believe, greatest music-drama are from the pen of Mr C. A. Barry, than whom no better authority," &c. &c. The ground being cleared in this fashion, Mr Bennett gave the analyses the slip no less ingeniously. Die Meistersinger was eluded by the remark that "technical discussion here of so elaborate an overture would serve little purpose." Of the Siegfried Idyll we were told that "it would serve little purpose, even if confusion could be avoided, were we to follow Wagner's working of the themes through all its elaborate details."

Tristan was treated in the same way. "This music" said Mr Bennett "evades analysis: indeed, it is intended to be felt rather than submitted to any process of scientific inquiry." In the reference to the prelude there was, for those behind the scenes, a rich double meaning in the following artful passage, which to the outsider appeared remarkable for nothing but its extraordinary recklessness of metaphor. "The movement, as a whole, will be best understood and enjoyed by him who most clearly perceives the connection of its various parts with the theme which is its germ. Mere verbal commentary cannot contribute to this end in the slightest degree, since there is no form to define, and there are no salient features serving as milestones on the road for the identification of stage after stage." Amusing as all this is, it is extremely provocative of a discussion on the modern system under which the critic joins the retinue of the *entrepreneur* as writer of his program, or his catalog preface, or what not.

When Macfarren used to do the programs for the Philharmonic Society, he allowed his opinions of modern music to appear pretty plainly between the lines, and even openly sneered at Goetz's overtures as examples of the effect of consecutive sevenths. Yet he did not say all that he would have said had his hands been perfectly free, although he was in a stronger position than any critic, and had behind him the Philharmonic Society in a stronger position than any private *entrepreneur* like Mr Vert or Mr Henschel. It is not surprising, then, to find the most remarkable difference between Mr Bennett's Wagner programs and those articles of his which contain his whole mind on the same subject. Without pretending to be deeply scandalized by the discrepancy, I still think it sufficiently awkward to make its avoidance desirable if it can be managed. Of course, it is not easy; for if analytic programs are to be written at all, they must come from musicians who can write; and all scribbling musicians now turn an honest penny by criticism. But the same man need not write every article in a program any more than every article in a magazine.

In the Crystal Palace programs the signatures of Sir George Grove, Mr Dannreuther, Mr Manns, and Mr Barry may occur in one and the same Saturday sixpenny book; so that none of these gentlemen need say smooth things about compositions which he dislikes. If Mr Henschel were to ask me to write a program for Brahms's Requiem, for instance, I should as a matter of course send him to Dr Parry, who has an unquenchable appetite for pedal points, of which delicacies this colossal musical imposture mainly consists. Surely that would be better than suppressing my own opinion of the work, and stringing together between inverted commas the opinions of those who differ from me, with a prefatory observation to the effect that they are the people to consult if you want a favorable view of the Requiem. How could I feel sure that they would not resent my annexing their work and getting paid for it, even though they might, as a matter of politeness or magnanimity, consent to the operation at my request? The distribution of the articles among different writers would meet this difficulty, though it would leave untouched the graver question of what musical criticism will be worth when all the men who write it are programists in the pay of the persons criticized.

It seems to me that if we musical critics ever get tired of the irresponsible freedom of odd-jobbing, and make ourselves into a regular guild of workers with a recognized professional status, we shall have to establish a pretty strict etiquet on one or two points of this kind.

Herr Jan Mulder's concert at Mrs Jackson's last week was more important than drawing-room concerts generally are, as it brought forward a capital cello sonata by the Rev. J. Ridsdale, who composes unambitiously, but with genuine feeling and grace, in the old formal arabesque style, of which Spohr was the last famous exponent.

The Crystal Palace concerts, I may remind my readers, were resumed last Saturday.

CHAMPION OF A LOST CAUSE

Review of H. Heathcote Statham's My Thoughts on
Music and Musicians. Illustrated London News,
20 February 1892

[U] Mr H. Heathcote Statham's Thoughts on Music and Musicians is a heroic book. When a cause is so utterly lost as anti-Wagnerism is—when our concert programs and opera bills are so be-Wagnered that one meets an alarming number of young people to whom music means Wagner and nothing else, Haydn and Mozart being mere names to them—when even the daily papers believe and tremble, there is something fine in the spectacle of a single figure standing immovable amid the general rout, and, with unabated crest, hurling at his victorious enemy all the defiance and scorn of the old days when the fortune of war went the other way. And how uncompromisingly Mr. Statham does it! It is not so much that he sums up Wagner as "the most remarkable charlatan that ever appeared in art," adding that the characteristic qualities of charlatanism are "brag and insincerity"; nor that he extends this summing up by describing the composer as "one of the most vain, vulgar, selfish egotists that ever lived"; nor that he taunts him with the money he borrowed from Liszt; nor that he holds up his hands in horror at Siegfried's father and mother, in the Nibelungen Lied, marrying within our prohibited degrees of kinship; nor even that he returns,

[547]

in his extremity, to the worn-out jibes at "the wretched dragon that spouts steam out of its nostrils and is killed by a lath sword, the Valkyrie maidens drawn across the top of the scene on rocking-horses, and the still more absurd 'real horse' that acts as Brünnhilde's charger, and is lugged in and out with a pertinacity which suggests Scenes in the Life of a Cabhorse as a subtitle for the last two plays." For all this is the outcome of a foregone conclusion that Wagner is a dog, and any stick, therefore, good enough to beat him with. It reflects on the writer's temper and commonsense, not on his musical sensibility.

But when, after quoting the first mournful strain of the shepherd's pipe in the third act of Tristan, he adds, "Compare this tuneless and tortured form of jodel with the Ranz des Vaches phrase in the overture to William Tell," all remonstrance, all amazement, give way to hearty admiration of the writer's dogged courage and devoted self-sacrifice. One's only impulse is to go up to him—to shake his hand—to pat him on the back. It is magnificent; but it is not criticism. Even in his little popular lesson on harmony at the beginning of the book, he does not hesitate to suggest that the extremest discord which any competent musician would use without preparation as the first chord in a composition is a diminished seventh, or at most an added sixth—an implication too desperate to be fully appreciated by anyone except a musician well acquainted with modern dramatic music. The explanation, of course, is that Wagner frequently began an act with harsher discords. There is little reason to doubt that if Mr Statham were to write a treatise on pure acoustics, he would somehow state the physical laws of musical sound in such a way as to exclude all the notes in Wagner's scores from his definition.

It need hardly be added that the critical portions of

Mr Statham's essays on Mozart and Beethoven are hopelessly disabled by his determination to extol absolute music at the expense of dramatic and descriptive music. Although Mozart is a hobby of his, he belittles him by ignoring the greatest side of him, and dwelling with the detail of a program writer on his mere ingenuity, besides repeating old stories about the composition of overtures in a single night, &c., founded on the fact that Mozart, unlike Beethoven, elaborated his works "in his head," and did not take up the pen until they were finished; so that he once composed a prelude while he was writing out the fugue for it. Mr Statham actually mentions this incident, thereby conclusively disposing of the childish tale which he quotes about Mozart's composing the overture to Don Juan the night before the performance, whilst he was so tired that he dropped off to sleep in spite of his wife's efforts to keep him awake by telling him stories and giving him punch. Obviously he was simply copying the overture, not composing it. The chapter on Beethoven, again, is spoiled by the intentional surcharging of the laudation of the "abstract" symphonies in order to give relief to the inevitable anti-Wagnerian strictures on the choral symphony, the Eroica, and the Pastoral, in criticizing which last Mr Statham descends to such schoolmasterly objections as that the thunder in the storm movement is wrong, because it is irregular for some of the basses to be playing five notes whilst others are playing four. Somewhat more quarrelsome in manner are the exceptions he takes to such colloquialisms in the articles of Wagner's admirers as can be made to pass for solecisms, he himself, be it remembered, writing meanwhile with all imaginable freedom, using adjectives for adverbs in the most conversational manner, and, for instance, informing his readers in quaint English-Italian that kettledrums are called "tympani." Mr Statham should remember that the one thing that is not permitted to the champion of a lost cause is too small a style of fighting.

Fortunately, there are considerable portions of the book which the author, forgetting Wagner for the moment, wrote with his temper undisturbed and his critical faculty unbiased. On these occasions he appears as a musician of intensive, if not extensive, knowledge and clear judgment, and as a writer with a certain vigorous self-possession and commonsense not always to be found in the literature of the fine arts. He is justifiably boastful of the sanity of his admiration for Mendelssohn; and his counterblast to Sir George Grove on the subject of Schubert, though there is, perhaps, a little too much made in it of the personal slovenliness of the composer, and of his preference of the servants' hall to the drawing room at Count Esterhazy's, is, in the main, a sound and timely piece of criticism. The essay on Chopin is an appreciative one (which is no small praise for it); whilst that on Liszt, considering Mr Statham's violent antipathy to Liszt's school, is, in intention, a very generous one. But the best chapters are undoubtedly those on the organ and on Bach, especially that part which deals with the organ fugues. If readers will bear in mind always that Mr Statham is an architect, and criticizes music chiefly from his professional point of view, they will be able to learn something from his steady eye, his clear head, and his straightforward and effective literary style.[U]

THE STOCK EXCHANGE CONCERT

The World, 24 February 1892

The Stock Exchange orchestra is not, as I firmly believed up to Thursday last, composed entirely of stockbrokers. If it were, probably an orchestral concert by it would be impossible. The performance of the simplest overture requires an immense power of business organization and knowledge of business method on the part of the composer and conductor, as well as absolute punctuality and high efficiency on the part of their staff of players. In fact, the strain on a musician's business capacity tires it out so, that his reluctance to exercise it in the intervals between performance and performance often leads to more confusion in his pecuniary affairs than is common in the case of men of quite ordinary capacity in the City, although City business means chiefly the systematizing of want of system and waste of time. I often pause to contemplate with melancholy amazement the "man of business" wasting the lives of innumerable clerks, at great expense to himself, in counting over his money, as if counting it, even in the most inaccurate manner, could add a single sovereign to the pile, or in making reduplicated records of millions of insignificant and immemorable transactions, knowing well that not five out of each million will ever be referred to again, and that the absence of any record even of these five would not cost a half per cent. of what it costs to register the remaining 999,995. The Chinaman burning down his house to roast his pig* is nothing to this. One's impulse

* Charles Lamb's A Dissertation upon Roast Pig, in Essays of Elia (1823).

is to exclaim "Give these men, not a fiddle, since they could not play it, but at least a big drum or a pair of cymbals, and let them have just one run with an orchestra through the overture to Il Seraglio to shew them what business really means."

But I should not hope to derive any enjoyment from such a performance; and this is the real reason why I have hitherto always steadfastly refused to go to the Stock Exchange concerts. The likelihood of every man, on City principles, making a point of coming in several bars late, and playing thirty notes for every one set down for him, seemed so strong that I pooh-poohed the newspaper accounts of the achievements of Mr Kitchin's band. Yet I had a certain curiosity about the affair, too, which eventually helped a friend of mine to break down my prejudice. This friend is a stockbroker for whom I have always had a great admiration, softened by a feeling of compassion for a chronic affliction which has embittered his whole existence. He is what they call brilliant—imaginative, vivacious, full of humor and dramatic perception, a man who might still make his mark if he pleased, in literature or the drama, who might even have made a good musical critic if he had been caught young and trained to the work. But he is the victim of a chronic successfulness which forces him, in spite of strong social sympathies, to become continually richer and richer, and threatens finally to cut him off from human society, and leave him a solitary Monte Cristo. When I first knew him he was comparatively poor: I doubt if his income was much more than forty times as large as mine; and I think, in spite of his generous temperament, he envied me my poverty. Since then he has struggled with his unfortunate propensity as earnestly as any man could; but his efforts are vain: every time I go to see him he is in a more magnificent house than the former one; and as I glance significantly over the palatial environment he looks at me with a mutely pleading eye, which says plainly: "I know, old chap; but dont reproach me: I cant help it: you mustnt drop me for having failed to stave off an extra thousand or two." What can I do but make myself as comfortable as possible on the spot in order to reassure him? The other day he demanded, as a crowning proof of my undiminished friendship, that I should go to the Stock Exchange concert in order to convince myself that Art does not utterly wither in the atmosphere of Capel Court. I confess I suspected him of having taken secretly to playing the cornet, and of having a design to astonish me by appearing before me as a performer. But, being afraid to refuse him lest I should seem to be casting in his teeth my entire freedom from his complaint, I went; and I do not mind admitting that more than I could have considered possible can be done with a squad of musical stockbrokers if you sandwich them between two thoroughly trustworthy professional veterans. I will go further: I will confess—nay, proclaim—that the combination of the professional steadiness and accuracy with the amateur freshness, excitement, and romance, produces a better result than an ordinary routine performance by professionals alone; and I would rather hear this Stock Exchange band at work than hear the best of our professional orchestras playing under a mediocre conductor.

For, in the profession, the better the men are, the staler they are, and the more formidable and inspiring must be the energy and devotion of the leader who rouses them. The symphony on Thursday was an old one by Gade, the last movement of which was mere filigree-work of the Mendelssohnian pattern, requiring nothing but extreme prettiness and precision of execution, which I can hardly say it got, though the performance was creditable on the whole. Before the

[553]

symphony Miss Alice Schidrowitz and the leader of the band made a very elegant display with voice and violin respectively in Hérold's *Jours de mon enfance*, which reminded me of the *jours* of my own *enfance*. It sometimes seems odd that Hérold's sort of music should be going on still, and that there are plenty of young people to whom it is as novel and romantic as ever. After the symphony we had Beethoven's violin concerto; and this proved something of a find for me, the young lady who played the solo part—Miss Lilian Griffiths—being decidedly an artist of considerable talent. Except for a trifling slip or two in the last movement her technical success quite justified her ambitious selection; and her execution was remarkably firm and dainty, all the phrases, besides, being rhythmically placed to a nicety. She should, however, have chosen Mendelssohn's concerto instead of Beethoven's; for she is a graceful rather than a poetic or eloquent player: indeed, her fourth string verges on the prosaic, a bad fault when Beethoven is in hand. Only, as increase of knowledge in this direction generally means increase of sorrow, I am far from grumbling because a young Englishwoman is not absolutely Beethovenian at her *début*. All I say is, why not choose Mendelssohn? For the rest of the concert I cannot answer, as I left whilst Miss Lilian Griffiths was bowing to the gallant and enthusiastic plaudits with which Capel Court, as one man, saluted her. By that time, I am sorry to say, it was too late to hear Beethoven's posthumous quartet in A minor and Mr Algernon Ashton's new violin sonata at Mr Gompertz's concert over the way in Prince's Hall.

Miss Osmond, who appeared at Steinway Hall on the 16th, is a young English pianist who has studied in England from first to last, which is at present, I am sorry to say, a course rather patriotic than wise. Miss Osmond has exceptional agility of finger; and this has led her, apparently, to depend for success chiefly on her ability to strike all the notes in florid compositions of the Balakireff type with great rapidity. But I recommend Miss Osmond to go abroad for a while, after all. Not that she will find better teachers there; but she will find places where a young lady can, without excessive expense or scandal, spend enough of her life in the opera house and the concert room to educate herself musically—an end not to be gained by any quantity of pianism alone. For her fault now is that her pianism has outstripped her musicianship; and it is but too likely that this is due to her misfortune in living in a country where you cannot have even a cheap piano provided for the children to march to in a Board School without some mean millionaire or other crying out that the rates will ruin him.

Messrs Longmans have just published the most interesting book I have opened for a long time—the late Ferdinand Praeger's Wagner as I Knew Him. It is an account of Wagner by a man who was not ashamed of him as he really was, and who was not afraid of being denounced for exposing the failings of a gentleman recently dead, as Sir Augustus Harris would call Wagner. A more vivid and convincing portrait than Praeger's was never painted in words: even the bluntest strokes in it are interesting. No doubt the author, with all his vigor of mind and strong commonsense, was too matter-of-fact to see all the issues that presented themselves to Wagner's very subtle mind. For instance, Wagner wrote in 1876: "In my innermost nature I really had nothing in common with the political side of the Revolution [of 1849]." Praeger's comment on this is simply: "Max von Weber told me that he was present during the Revolution, and saw Wagner shoulder his musket at the barricades."

A deeper experience of revolutionary politics would

have taught Praeger that the very speech on The Abolition of the Monarchy, which he quotes, shews that Wagner's vehement hatred of the gross military despotism of that time, though it made a revolutionary orator and a barricader of him, never made him a really able politician. Wagner found this out eventually; and the discovery was sufficient to alter his tone as to his exploits in 1849, of which he had previously been sufficiently vain. No doubt the usual demand for a coat of perfectly respectable whitewash for all great men when their turn comes to be hero-worshipped has led some of Wagner's later disciples to try very hard neither to know nor to let the public know that "The Master" was once a colleague of Bakoonin,* with whom he helped to organize the barricading affair in Dresden in 1849; and Praeger's flat refusal to countenance any such feebleminded suppression is altogether to his credit; but he hardly appreciates the grounds Wagner had for coming at last to think of himself as having taken a comparatively commonplace, superficial, and amateurish part in the political side of the Revolution of which, on the artistic side, he was the supreme genius.

But since Praeger has given the facts, it matters little that he has once or twice missed their exact significance; and I only wish I had space to quote a few dozen of the anecdotes and pregnant instances with which he makes us see his extraordinary hero as genius, buffoon, coward, hero, philosopher, spoilt child, affectionate and faithless husband, king of musicians, execrable pianist, braving poverty and exile, wearing silk dressing-gowns and sending for confectionery in the middle of a barricading affray—in short, defying all the regulation categories by

* Mikhail Bakoonin [Bakunin], Russian extremist, was from 1861 until his death in 1876 the leading anarchist in Europe.

which we distinguish admirable from despicable characters, and yet throughout all standing out consistently as a great and lovable man. Praeger, by the bye, mentions an autobiography which Wagner left for publication on his son's majority. Will someone ask Siegfried Wagner, who was born in 1870, how soon we may expect this book, which is likely to prove the most interesting autobiography since Goethe's Dichtung und Wahrheit?

MR HENSCHEL IN A BAD LIGHT

The World, 2 March 1892

The winter series of London Symphony Concerts came to an end on Thursday last; and Mr Henschel celebrated the occasion by making a speech. It was just before the Schumann symphony (in D minor), and what he said was: "Ladies and gentlemen, I feel it to be my duty to inform you that although any defects in the performance are, no doubt, altogether my own fault, yet the light here is so bad that it is hardly possible for the orchestra to distinguish a flat from a sharp." The band rubbed in this protest with vigorous applause; and the audience smiled vaguely, and fell to counting the incandescent lights above the platform—six to each pendant, five pendants on each side: total, sixty lights, and sharps nevertheless indistinguishable from flats. It seemed hardly reasonable; but Mr Henschel was right for all that.

Most amateurs have found out by experience that in a room which is lighted sufficiently for all ordinary purposes the pianoforte candles are indispensable if music is to be read comfortably. There was certainly not light enough on the orchestral desks on Thursday for any but very young eyes. Of course the parts were read

accurately enough; but a first-rate orchestral performance uses up the executants so thoroughly that the
slightest uneasiness or preoccupation tells on its artistic
quality; and I have no doubt that the mess which was
made of the accompaniments to Hugo Becker's last two
solos were due to lack of candle power overhead. Becker
himself, playing from memory, was sufficiently illuminated from within. The repeated calls which followed his performance were partly due to Stradivarius,
who would, I think, be famous on the strength
of that violoncello alone, even if he had never made a
violin.

I cannot pay Becker a higher compliment than to say
that he is worthy to be the trustee of such an instrument.
I say the trustee; for I flatly refuse to recognize any right
of private property in such a treasure. If he played it
badly I should advocate its immediate and forcible
expropriation, no matter what it had cost him. I live in
constant dread of some Chicago millionaire purchasing
the best twelve Strads in the world; having them altered
into glove boxes; and presenting them to the bridesmaids
at his daughter's marriage with an English peer.

When E. M. Smyth's heroically brassy overture to
Antony and Cleopatra was finished, and the composer
called to the platform, it was observed with stupefaction
that all that tremendous noise had been made by a lady.
But the day is not far distant when everything that is
most passionate and violent in orchestral music will be
monopolized by women just as it is now in novel-writing.
I shall not say that there is any likelihood of our ever
seeing a female Mozart or Wagner, lest I should hurt the
feelings of many male composers who are nothing like
so clever as Miss Smyth or Miss Ellicott; but surely
nobody who is not imposed on by the bogus mysteries
of musical composition will deny that there is no reason
why we should not have a female Moszkowski, a female

[558]

Rubinstein, or a female Benoît, and find the change of sex rather an improvement than otherwise.

In fact, if the chief of the Royal Academy of Music does not carefully avoid composing in the style of that *entr'acte* from Colomba which was performed at the close of this very concert, we shall have female Dr Mackenzies by the score. When the whole mass of strings and the harp began that strum! strum! strum! strum! to a tune on the cornet which had all the vulgarity of a music hall patriotic song without its frankness and simplicity of metre, I distinctly saw the ghost of Sterndale Bennett looking at me just as he looks out of Millais's portrait. And when I told him that the composer of the cornet *morceau* was his successor at Tenterden-street, he disappeared with a shriek before I could assure him that though the composer once thought this *allegro giovale* (*giovale* is Italian for rowdy) good enough for the theatre, and was, perhaps, even a little proud of the elaborate inconvenience of the rhythm, it is not up to his standard academic mark.

The Schumann symphony might have been more delicately played; but the result, as far as I am concerned, would have been much the same in any case. I cannot understand why we take ourselves and Schumann seriously over a work the last half of which is so forced and bungled as to be almost intolerable. I wish someone would extract all the noble passages from Schumann's symphonies, and combine them into a single instrumental fantasia—Reminiscences of Schumann as the military bandmasters would call it—so that we might enjoy them without the drudgery of listening to their elaboration into heavy separate works in which, during three-quarters of the performance, there is nothing to admire except the composer's devoted perseverance, which you wish he had not exercised. We all have a deep regard for Schumann; but it is really not in human nature to refrain from occasionally making it clear that he was greater as a musical enthusiast than as a constructive musician. If he had only had Rossini's genius, or Rossini his conscience, what a composer we should have had! I drag in Rossini because he was born on the 29th of February, 1792, and so gained the distinction of having a concert all to himself on Monday last at the Crystal Palace—too late for description here.

The Saturday concert brought forward Becker again. He was to have repeated the Saint-Saëns concerto; but he thought better of it, and gave us instead a harmless concert piece by Bazzini, which soothed me to such an extent that I have no very clear recollection of the details. Becker was rapturously encored for the tarantella of the inevitable Popper, whereupon he inhumanly sat down again and inflicted on the Popperites an "old master" of the severest type. One of the novelties of the concert was a *scena* by a Mr Herbert Bunning, being the soliloquy of Lodovico il Moro in prison.★ Mr Oudin sang this as well and sympathetically as the most sanguine composer could have desired; but as the *scena* began with a spirited breakdown for the whole orchestra, which recurred whenever Lodovico's dulness, or perhaps the coldness of his cell, drove him to seek relief in the dance, the whole composition acquired a serio-comic flavor which was not, I imagine, intended by Mr Bunning. Still, in the words of Mr Leland's judge "I like to see young heros ambitioning like this"†; and though I must pronounce Mr Bunning's emotional matter too commonplace, and his modes of expression too cheap

★ Lodovico Sforza (1451–1508), called Il Moro, was duke of Milan until defeated and imprisoned in 1500 by Louis XII. of France.

† The judge was Carey, of Carson, in Brand-New Ballads (1885) by Charles Godfrey Leland, a popular American humorist.

and obvious to entitle him to the rank he seems to challenge, yet the same criticism might have been justly made of Wagner himself up to a later period of development than I take Mr Bunning to have reached as yet. Mr Oudin also gave us a piece of the Templar in Ivanhoe.

The overture of The Barber of Bagdad, with which the concert opened, made another step forward in popularity. I should like to hear the whole opera again; and, *a fortiori*, the general body of our amateurs, less jaded than I, must be of the same mind. Why does not Mr Carte turn his attention to Cornelius's most popular work, and to the Beatrice and Benedict of Berlioz, the nocturne from which, by the bye, was sung by Mrs Henschel and Madame Hope Temple at the London Symphony concert?

The comparative roughness of Mr Henschel's band on that occasion heightened the effect of the finished execution of Mendelssohn's Italian symphony by the Crystal Palace Orchestra, which was in its best form on Saturday. I am far from having grown out of enjoying the Italian symphony; but I confess to becoming more and more disagreeably affected by the conventional features of the instrumentation, especially the trumpet parts in the first movement.

I think it must be admitted that even in Beethoven's symphonies the trumpet parts are already in many places mere anachronisms. Perhaps the dots and dashes of trumpet which we learn from "the study of the best masters" between the Bach period of brilliant florid counterpoints for three trumpets, and the modern Berlioz-Wagner style based technically on the essentially melodic character of our cornets and tubas, were always ridiculous to ears unperverted by custom and the pedantry which springs from the fatal academic habit of studying music otherwise than through one's ears.

People would compose music skilfully enough if only there were no professors in the world. Literature is six times as difficult an art technically as composition: yet who ever dreams of going to a professor to learn how to write? Anyhow, when Mr Manns next performs the Italian symphony I hope he will either omit the dots and dashes, or else have them played on those slide trumpets which are always produced with such solemnity when that august classic, the pianoforte concerto in G minor, is in the bill.

THE ROSSINI CENTENARY
The Illustrated London News, 5 March 1892

Fifty years ago Rossini would have been described as one of the greatest of modern composers, the equal, if not the superior, of Beethoven. At present, such an estimate of him seems as ridiculous to us all as it seemed then to Berlioz and Wagner; and the danger now is that all the centenary notices of him which are not mere compilations from the musical dictionaries will revenge upon his memory the excesses of the Rossinian age, when even scholarly musicians regarded him as an Italian Handel. Mendelssohn himself was captivated by his genius, although it is not too much to say that Rossini never produced a single secular composition of any length without padding or spicing it with some gross claptrap which Mendelssohn would have hanged himself rather than put before the public as his own work. Indeed, Rossini was one of the greatest masters of claptrap that ever lived. His moral deficiencies as an artist were quite extraordinary. When he found the natural superiority of his genius in conflict with the ignorance and frivolity of the public—and the musical ignorance and frivolity of the Venetians and Neapolitans can hardly be overstated—he surrendered without a struggle. Although he was so able a man that it was easier and pleasanter to him to do his work intelligently than to conventionalize it and write down to the popular taste, he never persevered in any innovation that was not well received; and it is hardly possible to doubt that the superiority of William Tell to his other operas is due solely to the fact that it was written for the Grand Opéra in Paris, where the public had been educated by Gluck to expect at least a show of seriousness in an *opera seria*. He rose to the occasion then as a matter of business, just as he would have sunk to it had the commission come from Venice; and it was characteristic of him that he did not rise an inch beyond it: in fact, he adapted all the old claptrap to the new conditions instead of discarding it. This may be seen plainly enough in the overture which every reader of these lines probably knows by heart. Rossini's previous overtures had all been composed according to a formula of his own. First came a majestic and often beautiful exordium, sometimes extending, as in Semiramide, to the dimensions of a slow movement. Then he fell to business with an irresistibly piquant "first subject," usually a galop more or less thinly disguised, working up into the conventional *tutti*, with the strings rushing up and down the scales and the brass blaring vigorously. Then a striking half-close, announcing a fresh treat in the shape of a "second subject," not a galop this time, but a spirited little march tune, leading to the celebrated Rossini *crescendo*, in which one of the arabesques of the march pattern would be repeated and repeated, with the pace of the accompaniment doubling and redoubling, and the orchestration thickening and warming, until finally the big drum and the trombones were in full play, and every true Italian was ready to shout *Viva il gran' maestro!* in wild enthusiasm. And then, since everybody wanted to hear it all again, the whole affair, except, of course, the introduction, was repeated note for note, and finished off with a Pelion of a *coda* piled on the Ossa of the *crescendo*, the last flourish being always a rush up the scale by the fiddles, and a final thump and crash for the whole band. As Rossini's invention never flagged in the matter of galops and marches, he was able to turn out overtures of this sort without a second thought. They soon overran Europe; and those to Tancredi, L' Italiana in Algeri, La Gazza Ladra, and especially Semiramide, are still as familiar to military bandsmen as God Save the Queen. When William Tell was ordered, Rossini understood that Paris would expect something more than a mere reshaking of his old box of tricks; but he knew better than to risk his popularity by giving them any really novel or profound work. All he abandoned was the wholesale repetition and the *crescendo*. By way of repudiating all noisy pomp in the exordium, he made it a charming concerted piece for the violoncellos alone. The galop and the *tutti* he presented in the most ingenious metamorphosis as the approach and final bursting of a tremendous storm. The second subject was a charming pastorale, with variations on the flute which no schoolgirl could misunderstand. Suddenly came a trumpet call, and then such a quickstep as the world had never heard before. Not one of his old galopades or *crescendos* could keep pace with it for a moment: it was the very quintessence of all his claptrap. Hackneyed as it has become, it is hard to this day to keep an audience from encoring it when it is well played. The whole opera bears the same relation to his other operas as the overture to his other overtures. It was meant for an audience which included a certain percentage of serious and cultivated musicians. He just surpasses himself far enough to compel the admiration, if not the respect, of these few, without losing his hold of the rest. Had the percentage been higher, he would have taken a little more trouble: if it had been lower, he would have taken less. The success of William Tell, added to the results of a prudent marriage, and the friendship of the Rothschilds, who looked after his savings for him, secured his future pecuniarily. From that time, although he had not turned thirtynine, he wrote no more operas. For the forty years of life which remained to him he could afford to be idle, and he was idle, except that he composed a mass and a Stabat Mater, in which again he rose with consummate ease just to the requirements of his church, still without sacrificing a jot of his popularity. The Stabat, with its Cujus animam set to a stirring march tune, its theatrically sublime Inflammatus, and the ingenious sham fugue at the end, shews that he was the same man in the church as in the theatre. Insofar as he was ever great, he was great in spite of himself. When he was a lad learning counterpoint, his master one day disparaged him as only knowing enough to compose mere operas. He immediately replied that all he wanted was to compose operas, and refused to carry his studies a step further. Among musicians, therefore, his name is famous, but not sacred. He was captivating and exhilarating; he was imposing to the last degree in his splendid moments; he was clever, and full of fun; his practicality was largely due to good sense; he did not settle down to offering the public frivolous work until it had snubbed him for taking himself more seriously; he may be credited with some sincerity in his admissions that he was not a great composer as Mozart was a great composer; and it cannot be denied that he was exceptionally unfortunate in respect of the illiteracy, the Bohemianism, the ignorance, narrowness, and squalor of his environment during childhood. On all these grounds, and some others, there is a case to be made out on Rossini's side which cannot be adequately stated here; but when the utmost has been made of it, it will not entitle him to pre-eminence even among modern Italian composers, whilst as to a place in the hierarchy of the greatest modern masters, from Bach to Wagner, that is quite out of the question.

ROSSINI REDIVIVUS
The World, 9 March 1892

The Rossini Centenary passed without any celebration in London (as far as I know) except an afternoon concert at the Crystal Palace, whither I went, partly for the sake of old times, and partly because the concert afforded me an opportunity, now very rare, of hearing Rossini's overtures, not from a military band, or from a careless promenade-concert orchestra with an enormous pre-ponderance of string quartet, but from a first-rate wind band, balanced by about as many strings as the composer reckoned upon. The program was made up of no fewer than four overtures—Siege of Corinth, La Gazza Ladra, Semiramide, and William Tell—with an admirable arrangement of the prayer from Moses for orchestra and organ by Mr Manns, and two vocal pieces, *Di piacer* and *Una voce*, curiously chosen, since one is almost an inversion of the intervals of the other. There was, besides, a selection from William Tell, arranged for the band alone.

This was rather too much for the endurance of the orchestra, which became a little demoralized towards the end. Rossini's band parts consist mostly of uninter-esting stretches of rum-tum, relieved here and there by some abominably inconvenient melodic trait; for he was the most "absolute" of musicians: his tunes came into his head unconnected with any particular quality of tone, and were handed over to the instrument they would sound prettiest on, without the least regard to the technical convenience of the player—further, of course, than to recognize the physical limits of possibility, and not write piccolo parts down to sixteen-foot C, or trombone parts up to C in *altissimo*. Consequently, though the scores of Berlioz and Wagner are in a sense far more difficult than those of Rossini, you do not hear during performances of their works any of those little hitches or hairbreadth escapes which are apt to occur when a player has to achieve a feat, however trifling, which is foreign to the genius of his instrument.

It is true that what I call the genius of the instrument varies with the nationality of the player; so that a French horn, though most refractory to a compatriot of its own, or to an Englishman, will be quite docile in the hands of a German; or twelve violins played by Italians will have less weight in an orchestra than five played by Englishmen, not to mention other and subtler differences. Yet the fact remains that we have at present a sort of international school of orchestration, through which an English player, whatever his instrument may be, finds much the same class of work set for him, whether the composer be the Italian Verdi, the French Gounod or Massenet, the Jew Max Bruch, the Bohemian Dvořák, the Norwegian Grieg, the Dutchman Benoît, and so on to the Irish Villiers Stanford, the Scotch Hamish MacCunn, and the English—well, perhaps I had better not mention names in the case of England. Rossini's scores, especially those which he wrote for Venice and Naples, run off these lines; and the result is, that at a Rossini concert there is more likelihood of actual slips in execution than at a Wagner or Beethoven concert; whilst the eventual worrying, fatiguing, and boring of the executants is a certainty when the program is a long one.

The Crystal Palace band held out brilliantly until the final number, which was the overture and selection from William Tell, in the course of which it occurred to most of them that they had had about enough of the Swan of Pesaro. Yet the Swan came off more triumphantly than one could have imagined possible at this time of day. *Dal tuo stellato soglio* was as sublime as ever. Mr Manns conducted it as he had arranged it, with perfect judgment and sympathy with its inspiration; and in spite of myself I so wanted to hear it again that after a careful look round to see that none of my brother-critics were watching me I wore away about an eighth of an inch from the ferrule of my umbrella in abetting an *encore*. Another *encore*, of which I am guiltless, was elicited by the *cabaletta* of *Una voce*, which, however, Miss Thudichum did not sing so well as *Di piacer*. The repeats in the overtures were, strange to say, not in the least tedious: we were perfectly well content to hear the whole bag of tricks turned out a second time. Nobody was disgusted, *à la* Berlioz, by "the brutal crescendo and big drum." On the contrary, we were exhilarated and amused; and I, for one, was astonished to find it all still so fresh, so imposing, so clever, and even, in the few serious passages, so really fine.

I felt, not without dread, that the nails were coming out of Rossini's coffin as the performance proceeded; and if I had been seated a little nearer the platform, there is no saying that I might not have seized Mr Manns' arm and exclaimed "You know not what you do. Ten minutes more and you will have this evil genius of music alive again, and undoing the last thirty years of your work." But after the third overture and the second aria, when we had had six doses of *crescendo*, and three, including one *encore*, of *cabaletta*, I breathed again. We

[568]

have not heard the last of the overture to Semiramide; but we shall not in future hear grave critics speaking of it as if it were first cousin to Beethoven's No. 3 Leonore. The general opinion, especially among literary men who affected music, used to be that there was an Egyptian grandeur about Semiramide, a massiveness as of the Great Pyramid, a Ninevesque power and terror far beyond anything that Beethoven had ever achieved. And when Madame Trebelli, as a handsome chieftain in a panther-skin, used to come down to the footlights, exclaiming "Here I am at last in Babylon," and give us *Ah quel giorno*, with a *cabaletta* not to be distinguished without close scrutiny from that to Rosina's aria in Il Barbiere, we took it as part of the course of Nature on the operatic stage. We are apt to wonder nowadays why the public should have been so impressed at first by the apparent originality, dramatic genius, depth and daring of Meyerbeer as to be mystified and scandalized when Mendelssohn, Schumann, and Wagner treated him with no more respect than if he had been an old clo' man from Houndsditch.

But the explanation is very simple. We compare Meyerbeer with Wagner: amateurs of 1840 compared him with Rossini; and that made all the difference. If we are to have any Rossini celebrations during the opera season, the best opera for the purpose will be Otello, partly because the comparison between it and Verdi's latest work would be interesting, and partly because it is one of the least obsolete of his operas. When it was last played here at Her Majesty's, with Nilsson, Faure, and Tamberlik, it proved highly bearable, although Faure was then almost at the end even of his capacity for singing on his reputation, and Tamberlik was a mere creaking wreck, whose boasted *ut de poitrine* was an eldritch screech which might just as well have been aimed an octave higher, for all the claim it had to be received as a vocal note in the artistic sense. The only difficulty at present would be to replace Nilsson, who sang Desdemona's music beautifully.

William Tell, of course, we may have: Sir Augustus Harris's attempts with it have always ranked among his triumphs from the artistic point of view, probably because (like Rienzi) it is an opera not of heros and heroines, but of crowds and armies. He is therefore able to deal with it as he deals with his pantomimes and melodramas, which he takes so much more seriously and artistically than he is able to take those unfortunate operas in which his spoiled children of the Paris Opéra, lazier than Rossini himself, have to be petted at every turn. However, enough of Rossini for the present. I cannot say "Rest his soul," for he had none; but I may at least be allowed the fervent aspiration that we may never look upon his like again.

Before quitting the subject of the opera season let me express a hope that the statement lately made as to the likelihood of Nessler's Trumpeter of Säkkingen being produced at Covent Garden may not be borne out. The Trumpeter, to begin with, is not a trumpeter at all, but a flagrant amateur of the *cornet-à-piston*. The opera is a pretty but commonplace work of the long-lost-child order of plot and pathos; and there is not the smallest reason why it should be dragged across the frontier, seeing that we have half a dozen native composers who could furnish an opera of equal interest provided some reasonable care were taken to engage the services of a competent librettist. I heard The Trumpeter once at Frankfurt, and have no desire to hear it again, especially on a stage which should be reserved for the best of the best, and not for the Adelphi commonplaces of musical melodrama. If it need be heard here at all, it is more in Mr Carte's line than Sir Augustus Harris's. That is, if I rightly understand Sir Augustus Harris as aiming at the consecration of Covent Garden to works of the highest grade, leaving what I may call semi-grand and cottage opera to the house at Cambridge Circus. Nessler's opera is no more a first-class work than The Basoche is; and it is much less witty.

The death of Lady Jenkinson—the Dowager Lady Jenkinson as she had been for only five weeks—ought not to pass without a word of notice from the musical chroniclers. She founded a scholarship at the Royal Academy in memory of her friend Thalberg; and she gave a yearly prize for pianoforte-playing at the Guildhall School, thereby setting an excellent and much-needed example. Lady Jenkinson was an Irishwoman, early famous for her pianoforte-playing and her personal beauty, the tradition of which reached me through my mother, who was a neighbor of hers at Stillorgan Park, near Dublin, in her young days, when she was the beautiful Miss Lyster.

On one occasion I happened to explain in this column, à propos of Paderewski's playing of Mendelssohn's Songs without Words, that the real reason why they are so seldom played nowadays is not that they are out of fashion, but that, innocent as they look, they are too difficult for most of our players. It not uncommonly happens that people whose opinions I express in expressing my own, write to me, sometimes assuming that I must agree with them on every other point as well as the one in question. Lady Jenkinson wrote to me on the strength of the word I had put in for Mendelssohn; and her letters shewed that at sixtyfive her enthusiasm for music, her good nature, and her belief in her fellow-creatures, even including critics, were as fresh as ever. Many musicians whom she helped will have solid reasons to regret her loss. May I suggest to the many women in her social position who are at present busily employing their means in such a way as to render their existence a matter of utter indifference to everyone but themselves and their next-of-kin, that if any one of them happens to be looking about for a vacancy, in filling which she could become of some use in the world, there can be no doubt that Lady Jenkinson's death has just created one?

MOZART'S SCANDALOUS NEGLECT
The World, 16 March 1892

I am unable to give any account of Mr Hamish MacCunn's Queen Hinde in Calydon, because the first performance was unreasonably fixed for the day of the polling for the County Council. Municipal bands were at stake at that election, and I threw myself into it with ardor, my candidate* having pledged himself not only to vote steadily for municipal music but to agitate for giving citizens a really effective power of moving street pianos out of earshot instead of to the next house but one. His opponents never once alluded to music, confining themselves to political matters of entirely secondary importance. The result was that we brought him in by a most tremendous majority, which will, I hope, serve as a lesson to all politicians and parties who identify their cause with that of the enemies of music. Yet I did not quite neglect Mr MacCunn. I made a dash for the Crystal Palace between the canvassing of two streets, but arrived just too late for Queen Hinde, and had to be contented with a wantonly dismal Wagner selection. Rienzi's prayer was first sung by a tenor who was much bothered by the *gruppetto* on the second note. The lugubrious prelude to the third act of Tannhäuser followed. Miss Fillunger then extinguished the last ray

* Sidney Webb, at Deptford.

of vivacity left in us by Elizabeth's prayer; after which the band, with a forced and ghastly merriment, attacked the bridal prelude to the third act of Lohengrin, which sounded like the clattering of bones and skulls. Even canvassing was a relief after it.

For some years past the Wind Instrument Society has been giving concerts for the performance of chamber music for wind instruments, which generally proves attractive whenever it is tried at the Popular Concerts. Last year difficulties arose between the Society and the little group of players known as "Clinton's wind quintet," consisting of Mr G. A. Clinton, the well-known clarinetist, Mr Borsdorf (horn), Mr Malsch (oboe), Mr Griffiths (flute), and Mr Thomas Wotton (bassoon). Preparation for the Society's performances cost these gentlemen so much time that, to secure an adequate return, they found it necessary to stipulate that they should be engaged for all the concerts.

The Society, naturally wishing to keep its platform open to other wind-instrument players, demurred, and offered Mr Clinton four concerts out of six. The quarrel was a pretty one, as both parties were perfectly reasonable in their demands—Mr Clinton, for concerts enough to make it worth his while to keep his quintet in harness; and the Society, for freedom to engage what artists it pleased at its own concerts. Finally, they agreed to differ; and Mr Clinton has now resolved to give concerts on his own account at Steinway Hall. The first of these was announced for Tuesday the 8th; and I have no doubt it duly and successfully came off. The program included Hummel's septet and Spohr's nonet, pretty works both of them, but no longer magnetic enough to draw me to Steinway Hall in such an abominable east wind as prevailed on the 8th. On April the 6th, when Mozart's clarinet trio in E flat will be in the bill, and on May 3rd, when there will be a Beethoven serenade, not

[573]

to mention some new works at both concerts, I shall perhaps venture. Meanwhile the Wind Instrument Society's concerts are in full swing at the Royal Academy of Music, mostly on Friday nights, when it is quite impossible for me to attend them.

It is important that both enterprises should receive sufficient support to keep them going, for the sake of the opportunities they afford for turning mere bandsmen into artists. At present the dearth of first-rate wind players is such that important concerts and rehearsals may be made impracticable by the pre-engagement of two or three players—a ridiculous state of things in a city like London. But men will not, as a rule, face the labor of acquiring extra skill unless there is extra credit and remuneration to be got for it; and there will always be a marked difference between the orchestral routine hand and the artist who has occasionally to step out from the rank-and-file before an audience and acquit himself of a difficult task with all the responsibility and prominence of a soloist. The multiplication of concerts at which this occurs means the multiplication of wind players of the class of (to name veterans alone) Lazarus and the elder Wotton.

And we want, besides these Wind Chamber Concerts, as Mr Clinton calls them, an awakening on the part of our conductors to the fact that it is rather more important, on the whole, that the best players in their bands should sometimes have a chance of playing a concerto, than that young ladies and gentlemen with a crude relish for instrumentation should have their overtures and symphonic poems tried over in public for them. Not long ago a young player of my acquaintance asked a London conductor for such a chance. The conductor replied that he could not think of allowing a performer who had previously occupied a desk in his orchestra to appear at his concerts as a soloist. If that conductor had realized how very strongly such a declaration was bound to prejudice him in the minds of all the intelligent critics and amateurs to whom it was repeated, it is possible that he would have thought twice before making it.

The Philharmonic, I am glad to say, rose to the occasion on Thursday last, when it devoted its first concert of the season to the works of Mozart, whose bust, wreathed with laurel, had the same dissipated air which I remember seeing a lady instantaneously produce in the living Wagner by crowning him, too, with a wreath which had not been made for him. The concert was a great success. The music had been thoroughly rehearsed; the band was on its mettle, the strings going with extraordinary brilliancy and precision; and Mr Cowen did his very best. The result was one of those performances during which, if you happen to turn to the program of the next concert, as I did, and find that the symphony there announced is Beethoven's seventh, you feel that you really cannot listen to such clumsy and obvious sensationalism after Mozart.

For my part, I heartily wish that the Philharmonic Society would devote not merely one concert but a whole season to the commemoration, with a view to educating our London amateurs. These ladies and gentlemen, having for years known Mozart only by vapid and superficial performances which were worse than complete neglect, or by the wretched attempts made to exploit Don Giovanni from time to time at our opera houses, have hardly yet got out of the habit of regarding Mozart's compositions as tuneful little trifles fit only for persons of the simplest tastes. I have known people to talk in this fashion whilst they were running after every available repetition of the Walkürenritt, the Lohengrin bridal prelude, or the *finale* to Beethoven's seventh symphony—all of them glorified bursts of rum-tum, which any donkey could take in at the first hearing—firmly believing them to be profound compositions, caviare to the general. Much as if a picture-fancier should consider Gustave Doré's and Leon Gallait's work finer and deeper than Carpaccio's, or a literary critic declare Victor Hugo the great master of masters, and Molière an obsolete compiler of trivial farces.

I do not deny that there has been an improvement in popular taste in the last few years, and that mere musical stimulants, from the comparatively innocent whisky-and-water of the Beethoven *coda* and the Rossini *crescendo* to the fiery intoxicants of Liszt and Berlioz, are beginning to be recognized for what they really are—that is, excitements which have their use on the stage, in the dance, and in flashes of fun and festivity, but which are as much out of place in the highest class of music as a war-dance would be at a meeting of the Royal Society. The notion that the absence of such stimulants from the symphonies and the chamber music of Mozart is to be counted against him as a deficiency, is precisely analogous to the disappointment which a sporting collier might experience at going to the Lyceum Theatre and finding that the incidents in Henry VIII. did not include a little ratting. And if no such notion has prevailed among our Wagnerians, how is it that when you turn over the programs of the Richter Concerts you find such an inordinate proportion of Walkürenritt and seventh symphony to such a paltry scrap of Mozart? in spite of the fact that Richter's conducting of the E flat symphony was one of his highest achievements—if not his very highest—here as a conductor.

When no demand arose for a repetition of it, I could not help suspecting that if Richter had tried his followers with the chorus of Janissaries from Il Seraglio, or with a vigorous arrangement of *Viva la liberta*, he might have hit off their Mozartian capacity more happily. On the whole, I have no hesitation in saying that as soon as our Wagnerians (and do not forget that there is no more enthusiastic Wagnerian than I have shewn myself) have had their eyes opened to the fact that Wagnerism may cover a plentiful lack of culture and love of stimulants in music, we shall hear more of Mozart's symphonies and concertos, scandalously neglected now for a whole generation, and yet far more beautiful and interesting than any of their kind produced since, by Beethoven or anyone else.

To return to the performance, I have to congratulate M. de Greef on having come triumphantly through the ordeal of taking Mozart's own place at the pianoforte in the C minor concerto, and in the *obbligato* to the *scena, Ch' io mi scordi di te*, composed for Nancy Storace in 1786 to words from Idomeneo. Nancy was succeeded on Thursday by Madame Giulia Valda, who sang with her usual vigor and self-possession, but fell far short of the standard of vocal execution and delicacy of style required for Mozart's music. The Philharmonic Society was on its best behavior, and committed only two blunders and one crime. The crime was the singling me out from the general body of critics, and putting me in a seat right between the two doors, in a most glacial draught—a clear attempt to "remove" me from my post in the most permanent and effectual way. Its success will depend on the course taken by the cold from which I am suffering. Blunder number one was the retention of a vulgar old concert *coda* in the overture to Idomeneo, instead of finishing it as written, with the quiet passage leading into the first act of the opera. Blunder number two was the interpolation of Mr Joseph Bennett's extraordinary valentine to Mozart, which Mr Fry recited at the Albert Hall, and need hardly have recited again at St James's Hall. Perhaps Mr Fry thought so himself; for he began to wander towards the end, expressing his astonishment that "Mars's thunder" did not remonstrate about the cheapness of Mozart's funeral, and—if my ear caught the word aright—taking the liberty of transforming Mr Bennett's "strangers" who, "tearless and careless, lay that precious form," &c., into "ravens."

The whole concert, as I have already said, was of notable excellence, though here and there the great excess of string-tone over what Mozart calculated upon caused the violins to enter with a certain *sforzando* effect which was anything but acceptable. On the other hand, Mozart would have been delighted with their vigor and splendor in the broader passages, if somewhat astonished at their screamingly high pitch. The only point which they can be said to have actually spoiled was the demisemiquaver figure in the *andante* of the G minor symphony. This was much too heavily touched; and the blemish was the more apparent because Mr Cowen took the movement a shade too slowly, as musicians are apt to do on the suggestion of the first bar. At least I thought so; but Mr Cowen is entitled to his opinion on the matter; and I will not urge my own now, lest I should seem to disparage the most satisfactory appearance he has yet made as a conductor.

POOR SCHUBERT
The World, 23 March 1892

Some alarm was created at the Crystal Palace on the 12th by the announcement that "Professor Joseph Joachim" was to play Max Bruch's latest violin concerto. At a time when all the best friends of art are striving to turn our professors into artists, it seemed too bad to turn one of our greatest artists into a professor. However, he did not play in the least like one. His artistic conscience is as sensitive and as untiring as ever; his skill is not diminished; and his physical endurance proved equal to a severe test in a quick movement—practically a *moto perpetuo*—by Bach. Bruch's concerto, like most of his works, is masterly in the most artificial vulgarities of the grandiose, the passionate, the obviously sentimental, and the coarsely impulsive. Those partisans of Joachim who contend for his superiority to all other violinists (that is the worst of your amateur critic: he or she always has a Dulcinea whose charms are to be maintained against all comers) are fond of proclaiming the severity of his taste. He knows, they tell us, all the fantasias and the claptrap to which Sarasate and Ysaÿe condescend, and can execute them superbly; but he refuses to play any music in public that is not of the very highest class. Then, I ask, why does he play Max Bruch?

I do not, of course, address the question to Joachim himself, since I know better than to hold any artist responsible for everything that his devotees ascribe to him; but I do ask it of the devotees themselves, with a view to instructing them a little as to qualitative as distinct from formal differences in music. It is true that Joachim does not go down to the Crystal Palace with a set of variations by Ernst, and entertain the audience by mimicking the whistling of the piccolo with his harmonics. But if Ernst's variations were as good as those in a Bach chaconne, Joachim would put them at the head of his repertory. The difference is not in the variation form, but in the quality of the music.

Now, if you overlook the difference in form between Bruch's concertos and the fantasias which Sarasate plays so admirably, and compare the quality of the music only, you will end by exclaiming that a violinist who plays Bruch may play anything—variations on the Carnival of Venice, Home Sweet Home on one string, or what you please. Let us make up our minds comfortably that the writing of a piece in three movements in sonata form does not add a cubit to its stature. Otherwise we shall have every composer who finds himself inspired with barely matter enough for a fantasia, spinning it out into a concerto in order that it may lie upon the same shelf with the work of Beethoven and Mendelssohn, and so come under Joachim's notice. In dramatic literature it is now generally understood that an author is not to rush into five acts and blank verse if he can possibly help it; and the result is that nobody now confuses the born vaudeville writers with the great dramatic poets.

But in music there is still a general impression that the form makes the composer, and not the composer the form. Bruch's Scottish fantasia is much better than his concertos; but it is on the strength of the concertos that he is regarded as a sort of contemporary old master, and played by the severe Joachim. By the way, if we must always have concertos, could we not have a little more variety in them? I seem to be for ever listening to Mendelssohn, Beethoven, Bruch, and Brahms; whilst Mozart, Spohr, and Wieniawski are numbered with the dead.

At the Crystal Palace there is an understanding among the regular frequenters that a performance of Schubert's Symphony in C is one of the specialities of the place. The analytic program of it is one of Sir George Grove's masterpieces; and Mr Manns always receives a special ovation at the end. The band rises to the occasion with its greatest splendor; and I have to make a point of looking interested and pleased, lest Sir George should turn my way, and, reading my inmost thoughts, cut me dead for ever afterwards. For it seems to me all but wicked to give the public so irresistible a description of all the manifold charms and winningnesses of this astonishing symphony, and not tell them, on the other side of the question, the lamentable truth that a more exasperatingly brainless composition was never put on paper. Fresh as I was this time from the Rossini centenary, I could not help thinking, as I listened to those outrageously overdone and often abortive climaxes in the last movement, how much better than Schubert the wily composer of Tancredi could engineer this sort of sensationalism. It was not only his simple mechanism and the infallible certainty with which it wound you up to striking-point in exactly sixteen bars: it was his cool appreciation of the precise worth of the trick when he had done it.

Poor Schubert, who laughed at Rossini's overtures, and even burlesqued them, here lays out *crescendo* after *crescendo*, double after quickstep, gallopade after gallopade, with an absurdly sincere and excited conviction that if he only hurries fast enough he will presently overtake Mozart and Beethoven, who are not to be caught up in a thousand miles by any man with second-rate brains, however wonderful his musical endowment. Much as I appreciate the doughtiness with which Sir George Grove fought Schubert's battle in England, yet now that it is won I instinctively bear back a little, feeling that before any artist, whatever his branch may be, can take his place with the highest, there is a certain price to be paid in head-work, and that Schubert never paid that price. Let that be admitted, and we may play the Symphony in C until we are all black in the face: I shall not be the first to tire of it.

A modern disciple of Schubert—or at least a walker in his ways—is Mr Algernon Ashton, who gave a concert of his own music at Prince's Hall last Wednesday. Mr Algernon Ashton goes in for the delight of creation, stopping short at the point where the intellectual grapple turns that delight into the grim effort which makes the greater sort of creators rather glad when it is over. He is at no loss for pretty themes—who is, nowadays?—and he dandles them in his arms, in at one key and out at another, in a very tender, playful, and fatherly way. This is engaging, and even interesting, for a limited period—usually something short of four movements; but it is not quite the same thing as composing quintets in the sense established by the practice of the greatest masters. It may be that I was lazy and discursive, and did not concentrate my attention with sufficient intensity on Mr Ashton's ideas.

Anyhow, I thought the quintet purposeless and extemporaneous, fluent without being coherent, carefully finished in detail without being elegant or striking on the whole, and generally tending to recall that terrible couplet of Mr Gilbert's which so often runs through my head at concerts:

> Though I'm anything but clever,
> I could talk like that for ever . . .*

At the same time, I do not wish it to be inferred that such quintets should not be composed. They give a great deal of pleasure in musical circles where Spohr and Hummel are venerated, and Schubert's violin sonatas not despised. They help to educate the members of such circles in the latest harmonic developments, and to accustom them not to make wry faces in good company when they hear a dominant eleventh in some other form than the venerable four-to-three of the schools. But my business is to declare concerning chamber music offered at Prince's Hall whether it is of the stuff from which Monday Popular programs are made. All I can say is, that Mr Ashton is far from having touched even the Schumann level, without bringing into question the summit marked by Mozart's G minor quintet. He is far

* H.M.S. Pinafore (Things are seldom what they seem).

more successful in his songs and fantasias, which are pretty, and not lacking in appropriate feeling.

I return for a moment to the Crystal Palace to congratulate the directors on having decided not to waste the thunders of the Handel orchestra this year on Gounod or Mendelssohn. Their selection of Samson was arrived at after some hesitation between Samson and Judas. But why not between Samson and Jephtha? The objection to Samson is that, in its integrity, it depends largely on solos which can only be executed by highly accomplished vocalists. It is humiliating to have always to omit, as a matter of course, such numbers as Then long eternity because no one can sing them, or even understand what Handel meant the singer to do with them.

However, we shall do very well if we hear the choruses in their full splendor; for though Samson is not one of Handel's most deeply felt works, yet it shews him in his brightest, most heroic vein, at the height of his strength, decision, audacity, and mastery. The first four bars of Fix'd in His everlasting seat are alone worth getting up a performance on the festival scale for; and if it were possible to get an English tenor and an English chorus to catch the ring of pagan joy-worship in Great Dagon has subdued our foe, that too would be a memorable experience.

I have also to congratulate the veteran E. Silas on his success at the last Saturday concert with his new pianoforte concerto in B minor, of the brilliancy and cleverness of which we should hear no end if the composer were forty years younger. Had the technical quality of his playing been equal to its spirit and artistic feeling, the reception of the work would have been warmer than it was. Probably Mr Silas will find no difficulty now in inducing some popular pianist to add it to his or her repertory.

THE BACH CHOIR'S WORST EFFORT

The World, 30 March 1892

That light-hearted body the Bach Choir has had what I may befittingly call another shy at the Mass in B minor. When I last had occasion to criticize its singing, I gathered that my remarks struck the more sensitive members as being in the last degree ungentlemanlike. This was due to a misunderstanding of the way in which a musical critic sets about his business when he has a choral performance in hand. He does not on such occasions prime himself with Spitta's biography of Bach, and, opening his mouth and shutting his ears, sit palpitating with reverent interest, culminating in a gasp of contrapuntal enthusiasm at each entry and answer of the fugue subject.

On the contrary, the first thing he does is to put Bach and Spitta and counterpoint and musical history out of the question, and simply listen to the body of sound that is being produced. And what clothes his judgments in terror is that he does not, like the ordinary man, remain unconscious of every sound except that which he is expecting to hear. He is alive not only to the music of the organ, but to the rattling and crashing caused by the beating of the partial tones and combination tones generated by the sounds actually played from in the score; and he is often led thereby to desire the sudden death of organists who use their stops heedlessly. He hears not only the modicum of vocal tone which the choristers are producing, but also the buzzing and wheezing and puffing and all sorts of uncouth sounds which ladies and gentlemen unknowingly bring forth in the agonies of holding on to a difficult part in a Bach chorus. And his criticism of the choir is primarily determined by the proportion of vocal tone to the mere noises.

To the amateur who has heroically wrestled with the bass or tenor part in the Cum Sancto Spiritu of the B minor Mass, and succeeded in reaching the "Amen" simultaneously with the conductor, it probably seems, not musical criticism, but downright ruffianism to tell him publicly that instead of deserving well of his country he has been behaving more like a combination of a debilitated coalheaver with a suffocating grampus than a competent Bach chorister. But the more outraged he feels, the more necessary is it to persecute him remorselessly until he becomes humbly conscious that in the agonies of his preoccupation with his notes he may perhaps have slightly overlooked the need for keeping his tone sympathetic and telling, and his attack precise and firm. The conscientious critic will persecute him accordingly, not giving him those delicately turned and friendly hints which a fine artist catches at once, but rather correcting him with such salutary brutality as may be necessary to force him to amend his ways in spite of his natural tendency to question the existence of any room for improvement on his part.

When the critic has duly estimated the quality of the vocal material, he begins to take Bach into consideration. An untrained singer can no more sing Bach's florid choral parts than an untrained draughtsman can copy a drawing by Albrecht Dürer. The attempts of ordinary amateurs to make their way through a Bach chorus are no more to be taken as Bach's music than a child's attempt to copy one of Dürer's plumed helmets is to be taken as a reproduction of the original. The critic accordingly must proceed to consider whether the ladies and gentlemen before him are tracing the lines of the great Bach picture with certainty, mastery, and vigilantly sensitive artistic feeling, or whether they are scrawling them in impotent haste under the stick of the conductor.

In the first case, the master's design will come out in all its grandeur; and the critic will give himself up gratefully to pure enjoyment: in the second, he will sit in implacable scorn, asking how these people dare meddle with Bach when they are hardly fit to be trusted with The Chough and Crow.* Need I add, that if they happen to have had the unbounded presumption to call themselves by the name of a great man, he will entertain just so much extra contempt for them as we feel for a bad circus clown who aggravates his incompetence by calling himself The Shakespearean Jester.

Although the facts have fallen, as usual, somewhere between these two extreme cases, I nevertheless might now, perhaps, most mercifully leave the Bach Choristers to their own consciences, and say no more about their last performance. It certainly was a very bad one; for the audience, as their coldness shewed, hardly caught a glimpse of the splendor of the work through the cloud of artistic poverty raised by the execution of it. The principal singers were uncomfortable all through, holding on desperately to their books, and never feeling safe until they came to a cadence, when they invariably perked up and delivered it with a confidence and expression so absurdly different from that with which they had been gingerly picking their way to it, that it says much for the politeness of the musicians in the audience and for the ignorance of the rest that every cadence was not received with an ironically congratulatory laugh.

* A glee for trio and chorus, from the musical play Guy Mannering (1816), with music by Sir Henry R. Bishop and lyrics by J. Attewood.

Miss Hilda Wilson was the steadiest of the soloists. As to Mrs Hutchinson, Mr Watkin Mills, and Mr Borsdorf (who played the horn *obbligato* in the very funniest performance of the Quoniam I ever heard), they are far too good artists to expect any compliments from me on a performance concerning which they can have no feeling except one of devout thankfulness that it is over. The Choir's worst effort was in the Kyrie, a number requiring the highest sensitiveness in the voices and finesse in the execution. As it was, the tone was horribly common, and the execution slovenly. The Sanctus, being much easier, was much better. And this relation between the easier and harder numbers held good throughout the performance. The brisk, florid, but comparatively mechanical movements, in which no great delicacy or expressiveness is called for, such as the Et vitam venturi, the Hosanna, and the Gloria, all of which are pretty plain sailing, went fairly well; whilst the Cum Sancto Spiritu, the most difficult number in this class, was an undignified scramble, and the Et Resurrexit was only so-so. The slow numbers, though carefully done, were constrained and unhappy; and some of the more beautiful modulations, notably that into G major at the end of the Crucifixus, were spoiled by being made obvious "points" of by the conductor.

The summary of the above criticism of the choruses is that the work only received about one-third of the necessary rehearsal. And until this deficiency is ungrudgingly remedied, the performances of the Mass can never be brought up to the standard which they attained under Goldschmidt, who, although he altogether lacked the vivacity needed to place him in perfect sympathy with Bach, yet approached the work with a deep German seriousness which ensured strenuous preparation, and banished all triviality and vulgarity from the performances he conducted.

Mr Villiers Stanford conducted the Mass much better than last time. At such work, it is true, he is always more or less the round peg in the square hole; and he was at fault here and there, dragging the *tempo*, managing a transition like that from the jubilant Gloria to the solemnly tranquil Et in terra pax without tact, or obtrusively calling on his forces to mark some *nuance* which ought to have quietly marked itself. And he is not to be absolved from his share of the general responsibility for the insufficiency of the preparation. Still, these shortcomings are not irremediable; and if Mr Stanford's next attempt is as much better than this as this is than the last, there will be little to complain of—always provided that he will discard the flippancy with which he at present tolerates the unpardonably low standard of quality of tone and refinement of execution which satisfies the Choir.

Mr Morrow's success with the principal trumpet part was much more complete than in his former attempt. On that occasion, as his lip tired early in the performance, so that many of the notes above A were missed during the latter half of the concert, the result of the experiment was doubtful. This time his lip was in good condition; and though he did not attain the infallibility of Kosleck, he quite settled the question as to the practicability of the original parts. It is all the more to be regretted that the effect should have been two-thirds spoiled by his colleagues, Messrs Backwell and Ellis. These gentlemen used the old slide trumpets, which they blew sedately into their desks whilst Mr Morrow's uplifted clarion was ringing through the hall, the effect being that of a solo trumpet *obbligato* instead of three trumpets *concertante*.

Now, surely Mr Ellis and Mr Backwell could have procured "Bach trumpets" from Messrs Silvani & Smith without any fear of being unable to play the comparatively easy second and third parts on them. The three instruments would then have been equally well heard, and the characteristic play of the three-part counterpoint fully realized. Until this is done the trumpet parts will in some respects sound actually less like what the composer intended than they used to when played on three clarinets. I believe that it is only in its new-old form that the trumpet has any chance of restoration to the orchestra.

At the Crystal Palace the other day, and at the Philharmonic on Thursday, they played Mendelssohn's Trumpet Overture *without trumpets*, using cornets instead. But who can wonder at the conductors allowing this, in spite of all the protests of the treatise writers, when the choice lies between a cornet of which the player has complete command and a dull hard slide trumpet to which he is so unused that when he has to *filer* a note, as in the opening of the Rienzi overture, he must either fly to his cornet or conspicuously bungle his work? In the hands of a man who can really play it, the slide trumpet is undoubtedly better than the cornet for fanfares, penetrating held notes, and certain florid passages which are meant to ring metallically. But such players, since their skill does not repay the cost of cultivation, are scarce; and even in their hands one never gets even a suggestion of the silvery, carillon-like clangor of the top notes of the clarion. All that is ever required of the slide trumpeter is occasionally to get through the *obbligato* to Let the bright seraphim or The trumpet shall sound, in an amateurish fashion at a festival.

On all other occasions trumpet parts are played on the cornet; and the scores of Wagner, Gounod, and Verdi abound in cornet effects which would come out villainously on slide trumpets. The way to restore the "Bach trumpet," or clarion proper, is simply to induce composers to write parts for it in their scores, and to

[589]

agitate for its introduction into military bands. Until this is done it will be hardly better worth a player's while to learn the clarion than it is now to learn the *viol d' amore* or the harmonica.

I greatly regret that my absence from town last Friday prevented me from taking advantage of the discussion on Colonel Shaw-Hellier's United Service Institution lecture on military music to raise the question of clarions in bands. Anyone who has ever noticed how the peculiar bugling tone of an Italian military band using flugel horns contrasts with that of an English military band using cornets, and compared both with the tone of the clarion as played by Kosleck and Morrow, must have felt how far we are from having fully developed the orchestra on this side.

I gave Dvořák's Requiem one more chance on Wednesday last, when it was performed—and very well performed too—for the first time in London, at the Albert Hall, under Mr Barnby. And I am more amazed than ever that any critic should mistake this paltry piece of orchestral and harmonic confectionery for a serious composition.

At the Philharmonic on Thursday, Sapellnikoff, who was received coldly, like a forgotten man, had his revenge after the concert in a series of recalls and an *encore* which were, for a Philharmonic audience, quite frantic. No doubt we shall have some recitals from him, though the agents have been so timid in that department of late.

ENOUGH OF MERE BALLET

The World, 6 April 1892

The last place a musical critic ordinarily thinks of going to is a music hall. I should probably not know what a music hall is like, if it were not for the transfer of the ballet in London from the Opera to the Alhambra. The effect of this transfer has been to confront music hall audiences, nursed on double meanings, with an art emptied of all meaning—with the most abstract, the most "absolute," as Wagner would have said, of all the arts. Grace for the sake of grace, ornamental motion without destination, noble pose without *locus standi* in the legal sense: this is the object of the tremendous training through which the classical dancer goes before figuring as *assoluta* in the Alhambra program.

Some years ago, a section of the Church of England made the discovery, then rather badly needed in this country, that *laborare est orare* is true of labor devoted directly to the production of beauty—nay, more true of it than of labor devoted to the acquisition of money without regard to ulterior social consequences. This came with the shock of a blasphemous violation of vested interests to the section which had obligingly handed over the whole beauty-producing department of human industry to the devil as his exclusive property.

One discovery generally leads to another; and the clergymen who took up the new ideas had no sooner opened their minds resolutely to the ballet than they were greatly taken aback to find that the exponents of that art, instead of being abandoned voluptuaries, are skilled workers whose livelihood depends on their keeping up by arduous practice a condition of physical training which would overtax the self-denial of most beneficed clergymen. Strange doings followed. Clergymen went to the music halls and worshipped the Divine as manifested in the Beautiful; and a deputation of dancers claimed their rights as members of the Church from the Bishop of London, who, not being up to date in the question, only grasped the situation sufficiently to see that if it is a sin to dance, it is equally a sin to pay other people to dance and then look on at them. He therefore politely and logically excommunicated the deputation and all its patrons, lay and clerical.

Matters have smoothed down a little since that time; and whilst nobody with any pretension to serious and cultivated views of art would now dream of ridiculing and abusing Mr Stewart Headlam as the fashion was in the early days of the Church and Stage Guild, the enthusiasts of that body would not now, I imagine, dispute the proposition that the prejudices against which they fought could never have obtained such a hold on the commonsense of the public had not too many music hall performers acquiesced in their own ostracism by taking advantage of it to throw off all respect for themselves and their art. The ideas of the Guild have by this time so far permeated the press, that the present tendency is rather to pet the halls, and to give free currency to knowing little paragraphs about them, the said paragraphs often amounting to nothing more than puerile gushes of enthusiasm about exploits that ought to be contemptuously criticized off the face of the earth.

Last week I devotedly sat out the program at the Empire; and I am bound to say that I was agreeably surprised to find the *lion comique* and the wearisome "sisters" with the silly duet and the interminable skirt dance quite abolished—for that evening, at all events. Instead, we had Poniatowski's Yeoman's Wedding, I fear no foe, and some of Mr Cowen's most popular drawing room songs. I took what joy I could in these; in the inevitable juggler who had spent his life practising impossibilities which nobody wanted to see overcome; in the equally inevitable *virtuoso*, who, having announced his intention of imitating "the oboy," seized his own nose and proceeded grossly to libel the instrument; and in "the Bedouins," the successors of the Bosjesmen who turned somersaults round my cradle, and of the Arab tribes who cheered my advanced boyhood in flying head-over-heels over rows of volleying muskets.

I heard also the Brothers Webb, musical clowns who are really musical, playing the Tyrolienne from William Tell very prettily on two concertinas—though I earnestly beg the amateurs who applauded from the gallery not to imagine that the thing can be done under my windows in the small hours on three-and-sixpenny German instruments. The concertinas on which the Webbs discourse are English Wheatstones of the best sort, such as are retailed at from sixteen to thirty guineas apiece. There were two frankly odious items in the program. One was a Hungarian quartet, in which the female performers did their worst to their chest registers in striving to impart the rowdiest possible *entrain* to some Hungarian tunes and to *Le Père la Victoire*. The other was Ta-ra-ra, &c.,* sung by a French lady, whose forced abandonment as she tore round the stage screaming the cabalistic words without attempting to sing the notes, was so horribly destitute of any sort of grace, humor, *naïveté*, or any other pleasant quality, that I cannot imagine any sober person looking on without being shocked and humiliated.

* Ta-ra-ra-boom-de-ay! by Henry J. Sayers was a nonsensical song popularized by the music hall entertainer Lottie Collins, initially in the pantomime Dick Whittington (1891) at the Grand, Islington.

Let me now hasten to admit that as the words of the refrain were perfectly harmless, and the lady dressed with a propriety which none of her antics materially disturbed, the most puritanical censor could have alleged nothing in court against the performance, which was nevertheless one of the least edifying I have ever witnessed. I have not had the pleasure of hearing Miss Lottie Collins sing this ancient piece of musical doggerel; but I should be sorry to believe that it "caught on" originally in the unredeemed condition to which it has been reduced at the Empire.

All this, however, was by the way. What I went to see was the ballet. I have already said that classical dancing is the most abstract of the arts; and it is just for that reason that it has been so little cared for as an art, and so dependent for its vogue on the display of natural beauty which its exercise involves. Now the ballet, as we know it, is a dramatic pantomime in which all sorts of outrageous anomalies are tolerated for the sake of the "absolute" dancing. It is much worse than an old-fashioned opera in this respect; for although the repeated stoppages of the dramatic action in order that one of the principal dancers may execute a "solo" or "variation" is not more absurd than Lucrezia Borgia coming forward from the contemplation of her sleeping son, under thrillingly dangerous circumstances, to oblige the audience with the roulades of *Si voli il primo*, yet Lucrezia is allowed, and even expected, to wear an appropriate costume; wheras if the opera were a ballet she would have to wear a dress such as no human being, at any period of the earth's history, has worn when out walking.

But this advantage of the *prima cantatrice* over the *prima ballerina* is counterbalanced by the fact that wheras dancers must always attend carefully to their physical training, singers are allowed, as long as their voices last, to present themselves on the stage in a condition ludicrously unsuitable to the parts they have to play. Twenty years ago or so you might have seen Titiens playing Valentine, just as you may today see Signor Giannini playing Radames or Manrico, with a corporal opulence which is politely assumed to be beyond voluntary control, but which, unless it culminates in actual disease—as of course it sometimes does—is just as much a matter of diet and exercise as the condition of the sixteen gentlemen who are going to row from Putney to Mortlake next Saturday*. Everything in opera is condoned, provided the singing is all right; and in the ballet everything is condoned, provided the dancing is all right.

But, as Rossini said, there are only twelve notes in European music; and the number of practicable vocal ornaments into which they can be manufactured is limited. When you know half a dozen cabalettas you have no more novelty to look for; and you soon get bored by repetitions of their features except when the quality of the execution is quite extraordinary. My recollection of Di Murska's Lucia does not prevent me from yawning frightfully over the *fioriture* of the dozens of Lucias who are not Di Murskas. In the same way, since the stock of *pas* which make up classical dancing is also limited, the solo dances soon become as stale as the *rosalias* of Handel and Rossini.

The *entrechats* of Vincenti at his entry in the ballet of Asmodeus were worthy of Euphorion; but the recollection of them rather intensifies the boredom with which I contemplate the ordinary *danseuse* who makes a conceited jump and comes down like a wing-clipped fowl without having for an instant shewn that momentary picture of a vigorous and beautiful flying feature

* The annual Oxford-Cambridge boatrace, which Shaw viewed at Hammersmith on 9 April.

which is the sole object of the feat. In short, I am as tired of the ballet in its present phase as I became of ante-Wagnerian Italian opera; and I believe that the public is much of my mind in the matter. The conventional solos and variations, with the exasperating teetotum spin at the end by way of *cadenza* and high B flat, are tolerated rather than enjoyed, except when they are executed with uncommon virtuosity; and even then the *encores* are a little forced, and come from a minority of the audience. Under such circumstances, a development of the dramatic element, not only in extent but in realistic treatment, is inevitable if the ballet is to survive at all.

Accordingly, I was not surprised to find at the Empire that the first and most popular ballet was an entertainment of mixed *genre* in which an attempt was made to translate into Terpsichorean the life and humors of the seaside. Maria Giuri, a really brilliant dancer, condescended to frank step-dancing in a scene set to national airs, which, however, included one brief variation on Yankee Doodle which the most exclusive pupil of the grand school need not have disdained. Vincenti himself had an air of being at Margate rather than in the Elysian fields as usual. I am afraid he is rather lost in Leicester Square, where the audience, capable of nothing but cartwheels, stare blindly at his finest *entrechats*; but that is the fate of most artists of his rank. He confined himself mainly to mere *tours de force* in the second ballet, Nisita, in which Malvina Cavallazzi, as the Noble Youth, was nobler than ever, and Palladino, who reminded me of the approaching opera season, hid her defects and made the most of her qualities with her usual cleverness.

Perhaps by the time I next visit a music hall the ballet will have found its Wagner, or at least its Meyerbeer. For I have had enough of mere ballet: what I want now is dance-drama.

THE VICISSITUDES OF CRITICISM

The World, 13 April 1892

At the Philharmonic Concert last week I went down
during the interval to find out from the placards at the
door whether the musical season was really so dull as I
had gathered from the comparatively few concert
invitations which had reached me. For I am never quite
certain as to how much music may be going on behind
my back. The people who only want puffs have given
me up as a bad job; the concert givers who cannot afford
to have the truth told about their performances shun me
like the plague; the spoiled children of the public are
driven by a word of criticism into fits of magnificent
sulking; the soft-hearted, uncritical patrons and patro-
nesses, always regarding me as the dispenser of a great
power of giving charitable lifts to hard-up people who
have mistaken their profession, see plainly that since I
reserve so much of my praise for comparatively well-to-
do artists my favorable notices must be simply the
outcome of invitations, chicken and champagne, smiles
of beauty, five-pound notes and the like (I am far from
wishing to discourage such realizable illusions); and the
genuine enthusiasts, whenever I do not appreciate their
pet artists and composers, will have it that I am an
ignorant fellow, writing musical criticism for the
gratification of my natural hatred of the sublime and
beautiful. In brief, there is always a section of the
musical world thoroughly convinced that, like the
creditor who detained Sam Weller in the Fleet, I am "a
malicious, badly-disposed, vorldly-minded, spiteful,
windictive creetur, with a hard heart as there aint no
softnin." When a person, in passing through this

harmless and transient madness, gives a concert or an opera, I am not invited; and as I never bias myself by reading advertisements or criticisms, I may quite easily, at any given moment, be the worst-informed man in London on every current musical topic except the quality of the performances I have actually attended.

Sometimes it is I who have to stand on the offensive, and exclude myself, in self-defence. The *entrepreneurs* who send me a couple of stalls the week before a concert, and a lawyer's letter the week after it, may be irascible gentlemen who must splutter in some direction from congenital inability to contain themselves, or they may be long-headed men of business who understand the overwhelming disadvantages at which the law of libel places every writer whose subject is completely outside the common sense of a British jury. But the effect on me is the same either way. The moment I understand that the appeal to law is not barred between myself and any artist or *entrepreneur*, I fly in terror from the unequal contest, and never again dare to open my lips, or rather dip my pen, about that litigious person.

No doubt, in the case of an *entrepreneur*, the fact that I dare not allude to the artists he brings forward is a disadvantage to them, to the public, and to myself; but I submit that the remedy is, not for me to defy the law and bring ruinous loss of time on myself and of money on my principals, nor for the artists, who are mostly foreigners and strangers, with no effective choice in the matter, to avoid litigious agents, but for the public, as electors and jurymen, to make criticism legal. Many innocent persons believe it to be so at present; but what are the facts?

Last season an opera singer [Giuseppe Ciampi], of whom I am reminded by an unconfirmed report of his death at Malta, had his performance criticized by my eminent colleague Mr Joseph Bennett in a manner which was almost culpably goodnatured. The artist, however, declared that the effect of the criticism was to open the eyes of *impresarios* to the undisputed fact that he was no longer in his prime; and, the paper in which the notice appeared being well able to pay any amount of damages, he sued it. The case was peculiarly favorable to the critic, as there was no difficulty in making even a jury see that the criticism erred only on the side of leniency. But one of the proofs of its justice was that it had depreciated the market value of the artist's services, as every unfavorable criticism must if it has any effect at all. The jury accordingly gave a verdict for the artist against the critic, putting the damages at a farthing to emphasize the fact that they considered that the critic would have been in the right if his occupation had been a lawful one. And if Mr Bennett had called on me next day, and asked me in the common interests of our profession and of the public never to mention that artist's name again, he could have been indicted for conspiracy and imprisoned.

In spite of the adverse verdict, some critics expressed themselves as satisfied with the termination of the case, on the ground that the artist had a fine lesson, since he had gained nothing, and incurred both heavy costs and loss of reputation, not to mention such press boycotting as arises spontaneously from the *esprit de corps* of the critics without any express concert between them. No doubt this was so, though it does not offer the smallest set-off to the still heavier costs incurred by the defendants. But let us proceed from what actually happened on that occasion to what might have happened. Suppose the artist, instead of depending on his own resources, had been backed by a rich and influential *impresario* who had made up his mind to muzzle the press. If I were such an *impresario* I could do it in spite of all the boasted thunders of the Fourth Estate. First,

I would take the young men; cultivate them; flatter them a little; wave my hand round the stalls, and say "Come in whenever you like—always a place for you— always glad to see you." In this fashion I would make personal friends of them; invite them to garden parties and introduce them to my artists; make them feel themselves a part of the artistic world of which I was the great solar centre; and give them hypnotic suggestions of my intentions in such a way as to create tremendous expectations of the artists I had in my managerial eye. No young man recently promoted from the uncomfortable obscurity of the amphitheatre or gallery, no matter how conceited he may be, knows enough of the value of his goodwill to suspect that a great *impresario* could have any motive beyond pure amiability in shewing so much kindness to a mere beginner in journalism. The old men would give me still less trouble. They would have learnt to live and let live: not a fault in my performances would they find that they had not pointed out over and over again twenty years ago, until they were tired of repeating themselves. I should not quarrel with them, nor they with me. What with the foolish critics who would think everything delightful as long as I made them happy, and the wise ones who would call everything beautiful as long as I made them comfortable, the ground would be cleared for my final *coup*. This, of course, would be struck at the few born critics—the sort of men who cannot help themselves, who know what good work is, crave for it, are tortured by the lack of it, will fight tooth and nail for it, and would do so even if the managers were their fathers and the *prima donnas* their sweethearts. These fellows would presently find their principals figuring as defendants in libel actions taken by my artists. They would learn from bitter experience that they must either hold their tongues about the shortcomings in my theatre, or else find themselves costing more in damages and lawyers' fees than any paper could afford to spend on its musical department alone; and the full accomplishment of this would not cost me a thousand pounds if I managed it adroitly. If one big manager can do this, what could not a ring of managers and concert agents do by organizing a boycott against any obnoxious critic? They could drive him out of his profession, unless his danger roused his colleagues to the need for a counter-organization, which would not be easy in an occupation which employs so much casual and unskilled labor as musical criticism. In short, then, I pursue my present calling by sufferance— by a sort of informal Geneva convention, which puts actions-at-law in the same category with explosive bullets. When a combatant shews the least disposition to violate this convention, I prudently avoid him alto- gether. At the same time, I do not object to retorts in kind. The one manager with whom I feel on perfectly easy terms runs a paper of his own*; and whenever I libel his enterprises in this column to the tune of £500 damages, he does not meanly take an action against me, but promptly fires off a round thousand worth of libels on me in his own paper. I appreciate his confidence as he appreciates mine; and we write reciprocally with complete freedom, wheras, if we suspected any possi- bility of litigiousness, we should never dare allude to one another.

I offer this little glimpse behind the scenes partly to explain to a bewildered public how it is that only the most desperate and ungovernable critics say half what they think about the shortcomings of the performances

---

* Augustus Harris was, at this time, proprietor of the Sunday Times, whose music critic, Herman Klein, served him as an unofficial advisor in the selection of performers for Covent Garden.

they sample, and partly to complete my reasons for going down to the entrance of St James's Hall between the parts of the Philharmonic Concerts to ascertain whether there was a tremendous eruption of musical activity going on unknown to me under the auspices of the gentlemen who shelter their enterprises from criticism beneath the shield of Dodson and Fogg.*

But there was nothing of the sort: the season had not recovered from the discouragement of the failure of the concerts given by the Manchester band, and the recoil after the disastrous over-speculation of the year before last, when the program of each week was as long as the program for the month is now. At the Philharmonic concert in question, the chief attraction was Joachim, who played Bruch's new concerto badly—outrageously, in fact—for the first twenty bars or so, and then recovered himself and played the rest splendidly. The orchestra played Mr Cowen's *suite de ballet*, entitled The Language of Flowers, very prettily, though the audience must have felt that, in the absence of any dancing, the performance was much as if Mr Cowen had arranged the accompaniments of some of his songs for the band, and given them without the aid of a singer.

As to the other pieces, I am sorry to say that their execution shewed a relapse into the old Philharmonic faults from the standard reached at the Mozart Concert. The death song from Tristan, with which Madame Nordica did so well at the London Symphony Concert under Henschel, fell flat: every time the orchestra began to rise at it Mr Cowen threw up his hand in agony lest the singer should be drowned. There was not the slightest danger of that. And, if there had been, she would probably have preferred to risk it rather than have her only chance at the concert spoiled, as it was, by

* A firm of attorneys in Dickens's Pickwick Papers.

being handled like a trumpery drawing room ballad. I call it her only chance; for I am quite sure that Madame Nordica will agree with me that she was not up to her highest standard of brilliancy and smoothness of execution in the polacca from Mignon.

For the rest, nothing but the *suite de ballet*, and perhaps the Cherubini overture, had been sufficiently rehearsed; and the old complaints of superficiality, tameness, dulness, and so on, have begun again. The fact is, that the Philharmonic thinks its band above the need for rehearsing as carefully as its rivals. But since superiority in London means superiority to first-rate competitors, it can only be secured by the hardest workers. And that is why the Philharmonic is the worst band of its class in London, and will remain so until it sets to work in earnest, instead of simply getting one of its directors to write Panglossian puffs for circulation among the audience, assuring them and the "bigoted" critics that the Society is the best of all possible societies, and the conductor the best of all possible conductors. It had much better give its conductor a fair chance, by either shortening its programs or multiplying its rehearsals, and insisting on a full attendance at each of them.

At the Crystal Palace concert last Saturday I heard a new note in the orchestra, and traced it to the first flute, Mr Fransella, whom I have not, as far as I know, had the pleasure of hearing before, but who shewed himself a fine artist, fully worthy of the post he has just taken. Mr Arthur Hervey's Overture in G has a Fate motive and a Love motive, transformable into one another, this being the latest development of double counterpoint, which used to mean merely that two simultaneously played parts would sound equally well when you turned them upside down. It shewed how easily a man of artistic taste and intelligence, with a dash of imagination, can

[603]

turn out imposing tone-poems. Mr Hervey handles the orchestra and manages his themes with such freedom and ingenuity that I hope he will try his hand at something more interesting to me than fate and love, for which, in the abstract, I do not care two straws. The pianist at this concert was Mr Lamond, who played a swinging concerto of Tchaikovsky's in the Cyclopean manner, impetuous and formidable, but a little deficient in eloquence of style and sensitiveness of touch.

Miss Gambogi sang *Mercè, dilette* well enough to justify her in having attempted it, which is no small praise; whilst another singer, a gentleman who had evidently often brought off *Dio possente* with applause on the stage, discovered that the only operatic method known to the Crystal Palace audience was pure singing, which unluckily happened to be his weak point.

WHY DRAG IN VELASQUEZ?

The World, 20 April 1892

At Easter time there is nothing for the musical critic to do but go to church and listen to Bach's Passion Music. This year, I confess to having neglected my duty for the sake of snatching a few days out of London before the season sets in at its worst.

In speaking of the performance of the Brothers Webb at the Empire recently, I paid the concertinas they used the compliment of describing them as "English Wheatstones of the best sort." Here I unwarily fell into the old-fashioned habit of speaking of the English concertina as the Wheatstone concertina, the instrument having been invented by the late Sir Charles Wheatstone. The house of Wheatstone still flourishes; but the manufacture of Wheatstone concertinas is no more peculiar to it today than the manufacture of saxhorns is to the house of Sax, or of Boehm flutes to the representatives of Boehm. Now Mr Jones, of 350 Commercial Road, East, who manufactured the instruments I alluded to, and who claims the Messrs Webb as his pupils, thinks that my way of putting the case confers the credit due to him upon Messrs Wheatstone of Burlington-street.

Accordingly, he not only asks me to correct my statement forthwith, but, I regret to say, deprives my willing compliance of much of its grace by adding that he will place the matter in the hands of his solicitor if I dont. The oddity of this threat lies in the fact that to mistake any English concertina for one made by Messrs Wheatstone, who have much the same prestige among concertina makers as Messrs Broadwood have among pianoforte makers, is to pay it a very high compliment. Possibly Mr Jones feels on this point much as Mr Whistler did when he uttered his celebrated "Why drag in Velasquez?" But I wonder whether if I had by mistake attributed the portrait of Miss Alexander to Velasquez, Mr Whistler would have threatened to place the matter in the hands of his solicitor? I confess I wonder still more what could possibly happen to me if he did? However, if I cannot quite understand Mr Jones's legal position, I can sympathize with his desire to get full credit for his two fine instruments; and I shall in future take due care not to hark back ambiguously to the father of English concertina makers.

The last Monday Popular Concert of the season came off on Monday week with the usual demonstrations. Joachim and Neruda played Bach's concerto in D minor, and were so applauded that they at last returned to play again with a new accompanist in the person of Hallé, who was received with three times three, but who probably retained his own opinion as to the way his Manchester enterprise was treated by the London

[605]

amateurs. Mr Plunket Greene sang three songs by Lully, Cornelius, and Schumann admirably in the first part of the concert; but whether he waited for the second part in a draught, or was disheartened by the trashy quality of the Magyar song which he sang afterwards, certain it is that he made hardly anything of his second opportunity. There were two quintets, the great G minor of Mozart, and the E flat of Schumann, one of the best of his works. Miss Fanny Davies, who accompanied Joachim in some of his arrangements of Brahms's Hungarian dances, was full of those curious tricks and manners of hers which so often suggest wicket-keeping rather than pianoforte-playing; and Miss Agnes Zimmermann played the pianoforte part in the Schumann quintet like the excellent artist she is. Piatti gave us Kol Nidrei, and retired covered with glory, as who should say "Well, ladies and gentlemen: you have been making remarks on my age, and listening to Popper, Becker, Hollmann, and all sorts of wonderful people; and yet here I am precisely where I was." Joachim was very warmly greeted indeed; and I am not surprised at it; for he seems to be passing now through a sort of St Martin's summer of his talent. Three or four years ago it seemed to me that he was living more on his reputation than on his current achievements; but this year and last his playing would have made his reputation afresh if it had never been made before.

In answer to a request for my opinion of the new Brahms quintet, I must explain that I did not hear it. Messrs Chappell, probably knowing that I am not to be trusted on the subject of Brahms, forbore to invite me on the occasions of its performance; and I was quite content to know nothing of the important event in progress. If there is one thing of which I am more convinced than another it is the worthlessness of criticisms that have dislike at the back of them. Now I do not exactly dislike Brahms; but I can never quite get over that confounded Requiem of his. Therefore, I am not going to meet the quintet halfway. It will come to me some day, I have no doubt; and I shall do my best to make it prove the validity of the estimate of Brahms as a serious composer which I have so often expressed. Until then, why should we molest oneanother?

WHAT IMPRESSION DO I PRODUCE?

The World, 4 May 1892

Herr Heinrich Lutters, who gave a pianoforte recital at St James's Hall last week, is not what one would call a magnetic player. He is accurate and businesslike, reasonably tasteful and intelligent, and altogether the sort of artist you praise when you want to disparage the other sort. His interpretation of Beethoven and Schumann is commonplace; and his technique, though trim and gentlemanlike, is undistinguished in quality, and particularly deficient in dynamic gradation, his changes from *piano* to *forte* sometimes sounding more mechanical than those of the best sort of clockwork orchestrion.

I seldom now write a criticism of a player without wondering what impression I am producing upon my readers. The terms I use, though they appear to me to be, taken with their context, perfectly intelligible, must suggest the most unexpected and unintended ideas, if I may judge by the way my correspondents take them. For example, on the occasion of Mr E. Silas's performance of his own concerto at the Crystal Palace, I made, in estimating the work from the performance, a certain allowance for what I called the lack of technical quality in Mr Silas's playing. By which I meant that Mr Silas's touch was not that of the trained athlete of the pianoforte, able to bring out upon every step of a rapid scale the utmost and finest tone the instrument is capable of yielding. This power is the foundation of such techniques as those of Paderewski and Rubinstein.

There are plenty of excellent musicians and good teachers who can play very brightly and neatly with their right hands, and thump away with the greatest vigor and spirit with their left—who, besides, will not play in half a year as many wrong notes as I have heard both Paderewski and Rubinstein play in half a minute, and who are invaluable as accompanists and professors, but who are never classed with the great pianists. Mr Silas is a capital player of this class; and as such he was quite well able to play his concerto without bungling, and with a vivacity and agility which would have done credit to a much younger man; but if Paderewski had played it there would have been all the difference in the world in the ringing of the notes. Yet because I expressed this inevitable shortcoming on Mr Silas's part in technical terms only, without explaining elaborately what I meant, I ran the risk of leading the British mother, upon whose fiat the livelihood of the pianoforte teacher depends, to set him down as a blunderer who plays F natural where he should play F sharp, and does not know how a scale should be fingered.

Let me say then, once for all, that players who are not good enough to be above all suspicion of such musical illiteracy never get themselves brought to my notice by means of Crystal Palace concerts; and that if they challenged my verdict by giving concerts of their own I should either give no opinion at all or else give one about which there could be no possible mistake. I may also state, for the information of those who complain that my standard of criticism is too high, that the population of the world is over fourteen thousand millions; and that to speak of any pianist or violinist in superlative terms in London is to declare him or her one of the half-dozen best in that number. Obviously, to be one of the best thousand requires a very high degree of skill, though it does not entitle its possessor to more than a lukewarm compliment in this column. Always bear the fourteen thousand millions in mind; and you will understand the truth of the remark of Dumas *fils*, that it takes a great deal of merit to make a very small success.

Madame Frickenhaus gave a recital on Thursday, and had a large audience, but she was not in the vein for Beethoven, and rattled through that beautiful last movement of the Les Adieux sonata about twice too fast, as if she had a wager to finish it within a given number of seconds. The effect, of course, was to make that short time seem too long. Knowing that Madame Frickenhaus can do much better than this when she chooses, I retired disheartened at the end of the first part, which concluded with those heavy and barren variations by Saint-Saëns for two pianos, on a theme of Beethoven's. In the meantime Mr Norman Salmond had sung Tyrannic Love, accompanied by his wife, who also took the second piano in the Saint-Saëns piece; and Simonetti, the Italian violinist, had played a couple of pieces by Beethoven and Sarasate in his clever, free-and-easy way, just too free-and-easy to be perfectly classical.

Mr Manns' benefit at the Crystal Palace was, of course, a huge success, and would have been made so by the unassailable popularity of the beneficiary if it had been the worst concert ever known. Its only fault was that there was too much of it. It began with Mr Hamish MacCunn's overture, The Dowie Dens o' Yarrow, which has a good musical fight in the middle section, but is otherwise a predestined failure, since it is impossible to tell a story in sonata form, because the end of a story is not a recapitulation of the beginning, and the end of a movement in sonata form is. Mr MacCunn has chosen his subject like a schoolboy, and his form like a pedant, the result being some excellent thematic material spoiled, and another example held up of the danger of mixing *genres* in musical composition, a danger already quite sufficiently exemplified by the follies of Sterndale Bennett in overture composition. Mr Manns might perhaps have given the work a more consistent air by a melodramatic treatment of the opening section; but as this would have been an artistic condescension as well as a forlorn hope, it is not to be wondered at that he did not attempt it.

The most noteworthy event at the concert was the first appearance in England of Gabriele Wietrowetz, who bounded into immediate popularity on the back of Mendelssohn's violin concerto. She has been thoroughly trained, and has abundant nervous energy; but her performance of the work was only a highly finished copy of the best models. It left me quite in the dark as to her unaided original capacity. Not that she is a mechanical copyist: she seizes on her model and assimilates it with an intensity which amounts to positive passion. Whether she can interpret for herself at first hand remains to be seen.

Another artist who was new to me was Madame Marie Mely, whose voice, though somewhat worn, is still one of rare beauty. Unfortunately she does not appear to have learned what to do with her middle register, which is veiled and uncertain; and this defect, with a certain languor in her delivery—possibly the effect of indisposition or nervousness—and the characteristically Italian vein of tragedy in the song she chose (*Pace, pace, mio Dio!* from Verdi's Forza del Destino), rather perplexed the audience, in spite of the peculiarly fine and touching quality of some of the singer's upper notes.

Mr Andrew Black got—and deserved—much applause for Vanderdecken's scene from the first act of The Flying Dutchman, which can only be made effective by one who knows how to handle his voice all over, from top to bottom, like a competent vocal workman. Beethoven's Choral Fantasia, the slenderest measure of justice to which always enchants me, was played by Miss Fanny Davies. To those who cannot understand how anybody could touch a note of that melody without emotion, her willing, affable, slap-dash treatment of it was a wonder.

The Philharmonic concert last Wednesday was better than the previous one. The worst of this admission is that the Philharmonic is certain to presume on it by so neglecting its next program that it will be necessary to invent some exceptionally poignant form of insult to flog it up to the mark again. It is the most troublesome of Societies, this old Philharmonic, without conscience, without manners, without knowledge enough to distinguish between Benoît and Beethoven or Moszkowski and Mozart except by tradition, unable to see anything in its own prestige and its great opportunities except a pretext for giving itself airs. We all do our best to keep it going, sometimes by coaxing and petting it, sometimes by cuffing it when it gets too exasperating, not unfrequently by telling the innocent public lies about it, and giving it the credit that is really due to Manns, Richter, Henschel, Hallé, and others.

There is nothing to prevent the band being the best in the world, and the concerts from leading music in Europe, except the belatedness of the directorate, which at the present time includes a clear majority whose ages range from fiftyseven to seventyone. As none of these gentlemen would have passed as specially advanced musicians thirty years ago, and as since that time there has been something like a revolution in music (the position may be faintly realized by recalling the fact that

Lohengrin, now more hackneyed than Il Trovatore, provoked a furious controversy on its production here as a daring novelty in 1875, when it was twentyeight years old), I think I may fairly say that the placing of them in a majority shews that the Society takes no real thought or trouble about electing its Board, particularly as there are plenty of vigorous and up-to-date members to choose from.

The chief event at this last concert was the playing of Beethoven's E flat concerto by Madame Sophie Menter. Poor Beethoven came out of it better than I expected. When the joyous Sophie lays her irresistible hands on a composer who has anything of a serious turn, he seldom escapes in a recognizable condition. I have seen her leave Weber and Schumann for dead on the platform. To see her play a Beethoven sonata in her puissant, splendid, tireless manner, without any perceptible yielding to its poetry or purpose, and yet presiding over its notes and chords with a certain superb power, is a spectacle that never palls on me. In the concerto, however, Beethoven, though somewhat put out of countenance at first, finally rose to the occasion, and gave her all she could manage of the softly brilliant, impetuous revelry which suits her Austrian temperament and her Lisztian style.

At the end came the usual burst of Menter worship; and the Joyous, exalted by the occasion, returned and played Liszt's Erl King transcription. The symphony was Raff's Lenore, in which a great point was made of the *crescendo* of the march. The opening *pianissimo* was certainly successful enough; but the climax ought to have been much more magnificent. It is not enough for an orchestra to be able to coo: it should be able to thunder as well. The Lenore symphony requires rather more study and stage management, so to speak, than a Philharmonic conductor can be expected to give to it unless it has a special attraction for him; and so I do not blame Mr Cowen for having failed to excite the audience sufficiently to conceal the weakness of the work as a symphony, especially in the last movement, which will not bear cool examination, notwithstanding its one really imaginative theme and the clever picture of the night scene before the arrival of William's ghost.

It is odd, by the bye, that the program-writer never points out that William's appearance is preceded by a Wagnerian quotation of the phrase in which Vander-decken speaks of the resurrection that is to release him from his curse. But your born program-writer is always so much bent on pointing out some marvelous harmonic surprise caused by a masterly resolution of D, F, G, B, into C, E, G, C, that he seldom has time to mention matters connected with the poetic basis of the music. Except in this last movement, which ended rather raggedly, the performance was careful and precise, shewing that its preparation had not been altogether perfunctory. Still, it was far from being as perfect as that of Mr Villiers Stanford's Edipus prelude, in which the composer's imagination occasionally gets the better, for once in a way, of his scholarly trivialities. The Rex theme might have been more broadly handled by Mr Cowen, even at the cost of comparative roughness: otherwise, the band made the most of the piece.

BRAHMS'S VERBOSITY
The World, 11 May 1892

Only the other day I remarked that I was sure to come across Brahms's new clarinet quintet sooner or later. And, sure enough, my fate overtook me last week at Mr G. Clinton's Wind Concert at Steinway Hall. I shall not attempt to describe this latest exploit of the Leviathan

Maunderer. It surpassed my utmost expectations: I never heard such a work in my life. Brahms's enormous gift of music is paralleled by nothing on earth but Mr Gladstone's gift of words: it is a verbosity which outfaces its own commonplaceness by dint of sheer magnitude. The first movement of the quintet is the best; and had the string players been on sufficiently easy terms with it, they might have softened it and given effect to its occasional sentimental excursions into dreamland. Unluckily they were all preoccupied with the difficulty of keeping together; and they were led by a violinist whose bold, free, slashing style, though useful in a general way, does more harm than good when the strings need to be touched with great tenderness and sensitiveness.

Mr Clinton played the clarinet part with scrupulous care, but without giving any clue to his private view of the work, which, though it shews off the compass and contrasts the registers of the instrument in the usual way, contains none of the haunting phrases which Weber, for instance, was able to find for the expression of its idiosyncrasy. The *presto* of the third movement is a ridiculously dismal version of a lately popular hornpipe. I first heard it at the pantomime which was produced at Her Majesty's Theatre a few years ago; and I have always supposed it to be a composition of Mr Solomon's. Anyhow, the street-pianos went through an epidemic of it; and it certainly deserved a merrier fate than burying alive in a Brahms quintet. Quite charming, after the quintet, was Thuille's elegant and well-written sextet for woodwind, horn, and pianoforte, the slow movement of which begins as if the horn had forgotten itself and were absently wandering into See the Conq'ring Hero. Messrs Griffiths, Clinton, Malsch, Borsdorf, Wotton junior, and Oscar Beringer were the executants. Miss Clara Samuell sang one of Dr Mackenzie's best songs admirably; and I could say the same for her Nymphs and Shepherds if she had not made one of those absurd attempts to turn the final cadence into a *cadenza* by altering the penultimate note and hanging on to it—a sort of claptrap which one hardly expects to hear at this time of day, except at third-rate concerts or in the provinces. It is only at the Opera that such things are still perpetrated by artists of first-rate pretension.

The performance of Elijah at the Albert Hall last Wednesday was one of remarkable excellence. The tone from the choir was clean and unadulterated: there was no screaming from the sopranos, nor brawling from the tenors, nor growling from the basses. In dispensing with these three staple ingredients of English choral singing Mr Barnby has achieved a triumph which can only be appreciated by those who remember as well as I do what the choir was like in its comparatively raw state some fifteen years ago. Nowadays he gets the high notes taken *piano* as easily as the middle ones; and the sharpness of attack and the willing vigor and consentaneousness of the singing, when the music in hand is as familiar to the singers and as congenial to the conductor as Mendelssohn's, are all that could be desired.

I sat out the performance on Wednesday to the last note, an act of professional devotion which was by no means part of my plan for the evening; and I did not feel disposed to quarrel with Mr Barnby more than twice. The first time was over the chorus Hear us, Baal, which he quite spoiled by taking *allegro molto*. If he had taken it as Mendelssohn directed, *allegro non troppo*, with the quaver accompaniment excessively detached, and the theme struck out in pompous, stately strokes, the result would have convinced him that Mendelssohn knew quite well what he was about; and the chorus would not have discounted, by anticipation, the effect of the startled Hear our cry, O Baal, or of the frantic Baal, hear and answer. The second occasion was of the same kind.

[615]

The chorus Then did Elijah the prophet break forth like a fire was taken almost twice too fast, in spite of Mendelssohn's instructions. For surely no difference of opinion as to the right *tempo* can extend to making a rattling *allegro* of a movement marked *moderato maestoso*. The consequence was that the unaccompanied phrase And when the Lord would take him away to heaven sounded ludicrously hasty; and there was no sensation at the end like that after Thanks be to God: He laveth the thirsty land, which, taken as Mendelssohn ordered it to be taken, roused the audience to enthusiasm. Madame Albani hardly needed the apology which was circulated for her on the ground of a "severe cold" which she simply had not got, though I have no doubt she was suffering, as we all were, from the abominable east wind. The selection of Mr Ben Davies and Madame Belle Cole for the tenor and contralto parts could not easily have been improved on; and though Mr Watkin Mills began badly, and did not at any time exactly break forth like a fire, he was not too far overparted.

The audience was a huge one, shewing, after all deductions for the numbers of the foolish people who only run after the reputations of the solo singers, that there is no falling off in the great popularity of Elijah. This need not be regretted so long as it is understood that our pet oratorio, as a work of religious art, stands together with the pictures of Scheffer and Paton, and the poems of Longfellow and Tennyson, sensuously beautiful in the most refined and fastidiously decorous way, but thoughtless. That is to say, it is not really religious music at all. The best of it is seraphic music, like the best of Gounod's; but you have only to think of Parsifal, of the Ninth Symphony, of Die Zauberflöte, of the inspired moments of Handel and Bach, to see the great gulf that lies between the true religious sentiment and our delight in Mendelssohn's exquisite prettiness.

The British public is convinced in its middle age that *Then shall the righteous shine forth as the sun* is divine, on grounds no better and no worse than those on which, in its callow youth, it adores beautiful girls as angels. Far from desiring to belittle such innocent enthusiasm, I rather echo Mr Weller's plea that "Arter all, gen'lmen, it's an amiable weakness."

At the same time, a vigorous protest should be entered whenever an attempt is made to scrape a layer off the praise due to the seraphs in order to spread it over the prophet in evening dress, who, in feeble rivalry with the Handelian prophet's song of the power that is "like a refiner's fire," informs the audience, with a vicious exultation worthy of Mrs Clennam, that "God is angry with the wicked every day." That is the worst of your thoughtlessly seraphic composer: he is a wonder whilst he is flying; but when his wings fail him, he walks like a parrot.

We have now reached the season at which professional ladies and gentlemen are wont to give what they call their annual concerts, and sometimes to take it very ill on my part that I find so little to say about them. But what can I do when the programs contain nothing that I have not described at least forty thousand times already? No matter how charmingly Madame Belle Cole may sing *Sognai* and *O Fatima*, or how featly Tivadar Nachéz may play Raff's rigadoon, there must at last come a time when the public will yawn over my opinion of these performances, however wide awake it may remain during the performances themselves. The same observation must cover the case of Mr Plunket Greene's German Lieder, as it soon will, no doubt, that of the irresistible Irish soldier's song which he sang the other night at Miss Shee's concert at Steinway Hall, to an old tune arranged by Mr Fuller Maitland. Having been a Bayreuth flower maiden (one of the enchantresses of Klingsor's magic garden, and not a vendor of buttonholes), Miss Shee herself rather challenged criticism as an artist of some pretension. She is so young that I am almost afraid to tell her that she has still much to learn—notably two things. Number one, never to sing with that wind pressure which blew out the shake at the end of the Jewel Song like a candle before it was finished, and which is quite able to do for a whole voice in less than four years what it did for the shake in less than four seconds. Number two, to learn the difference between Italian vowels and English diphthongs. "Ei la figlia d' un rei che ognun dei salutarei" is not Italian: neither is "mi troverebbei béla." It is perhaps rather hard on Miss Shee that I should single her out for a fault which sets my teeth on edge almost every time I enter a concert room where English singers are singing Italian songs; but I really must be allowed to break out into protest sometimes, necessarily at somebody's expense. Why on earth cannot they go to my veteran friend, Tito Pagliardini, and get him to set their vowels right? For the rest, Miss Shee's is a pretty talent; and I hope she may succeed in cultivating it to perfection. My evening was divided between her concert and Mr Ernest Kiver's, at which I heard a new string quartet by Reinecke, full of all the composer's engaging qualities. It might have been better played; but this is an inevitable criticism except where the four players have been able to work together for years.

I took an opportunity the other night of acquainting myself with Miss Collins's interpretation of Ta-ra-ra, &c. It is a most instructive example of the value of artistic method in music hall singing, and may be contrasted by students with Violette's crude treatment of the same song. Violette's forced and screaming self-abandonment is a complete failure: Miss Collins's perfect self-possession and calculated economy of effort carry her audience away. She takes the song at an exceedingly restrained *tempo*, and gets her effect of *entrain* by marking the measure very pointedly and emphatically, and articulating her words with ringing brilliancy and with immense assurance of manner. The dance refrain, with its three low kicks on "Ta-ra-ra" and its high kick on "Boom" (with *grosse caisse ad lib.*), is the simplest thing imaginable, and is taken in even a more deliberate *tempo* than the preceding verse.

Miss Collins appears to be in fine athletic training; and the combination of perfect *sang-froid* and unsparing vigor with which she carries out her performance, which is so exhaustively studied that not a bar of it is left to chance or the impulse of the moment, ought to convince the idlest of her competitors and the most cynical of music hall managers that a planned artistic achievement "catches on" far more powerfully than any random explosion of brainless rowdiness. I do not propose to add to the host of suggestions as to the origin of the tune. As it is only a figuration of the common major chord, it is to be found almost wherever you choose to look for it. In the last movement of Mozart's finest pianoforte sonata in F, in the opening *allegro* of Beethoven's septuor, and even in the first movement of Mendelssohn's violin concerto, it will henceforth make itself felt by all those who continue obsessed by it.

NYDIA
The World, 18 May 1892

The other day an actor published a book of directions for making a good play.* His plan was a simple one. Take all the devices which bring down the house in

* Frank Archer, How to Write a Good Play (1892).

existing plays; make a new one by stringing them all together; and there you are. If that book succeeds, I am prepared to write a similar treatise on opera composition. I know quite a lot of things that would be of great use to any young composer. For instance, when two lovers are on the stage together, be sure you make them catch sight of the moon or stars and gaze up rapturously whilst the violins discourse ravishing strains with their mutes on. Mutes are also useful for spinning-wheel business and for fires, as in Marta and Die Walküre.

For dreamy effects, tonic pedals as patented by Gounod and Bizet are useful. When large orchestras are available, broad melodies on the fourth string of the violins may be relied on for a strong and popular impression. When the heroine is alone on the stage, a rapid, agitated movement, expressive of her anticipation of the arrival of her lover, and culminating in a vigorous instrumental and vocal outburst as he rushes on the stage and proceeds without an instant's loss of time to embrace her ardently, never fails to leave the public breathless. The harmonic treatment of this situation is so simple that nobody can fail to master it in a few lessons. The lady must first sing the gentleman's name on the notes belonging to the chord of the dominant seventh in some highly unexpected key; the gentleman then vociferates the lady's name a peg higher on the notes of a more extreme discord; and, finally, the twain explode simultaneously upon a brilliant six-four chord, leading, either directly through the dominant chord, or after some pretty interruption of the cadence, to a flowing melody in which the gentleman either protests his passion or repeatedly calls attention to the fact that at last they meet again.

The whole situation should be repeated in the last act, with the difference that this time it is the gentleman who must be alone at the beginning. Furthermore, he must be in a gloomy dungeon, not larger at the outside than the stage of Covent Garden Theatre; and he must be condemned to die next morning. The reason for putting the gentleman, rather than the lady, in this situation is to be found in the exclusion of women from politics, whereby they are deprived of the privilege of being condemned to death, without any reflection on their personal characters, for heading patriotic rebellions. The difficulty has nevertheless been successfully got over by making the lady go mad in the fourth act, and kill somebody, preferably her own child. Under these circumstances she may sing almost anything she pleases of a florid nature in her distraction, and may take the gentleman's place in the prison cell in the next act without forfeiting the moral approval of the audience. Florid mad scenes, though they are very pretty when the lady's affliction is made to take the playful turn of a trial of skill with the first flute, which should partly imitate the voice and partly accompany it in thirds, is now out of fashion; and it is far better, in dramatic opera, to be entirely modern in style.

Fortunately, the rule for modernity of style is easily remembered and applied. In fact, it is one of the three superlatively easy rules, the other two being the rules for writing Scotch and archaic music. For Scotch music, as everyone knows, you sustain E flat and B flat in the bass for a drone, and play at random in some Scotch measure on the notes which are black on the piano. For archaic music you harmonize in the ordinary way in the key of E major; but in playing you make the four sharps of the key natural, reading the music as if it was written in the key of C, which, of course, simplifies the execution as far as the piano is concerned. The effect will be diabolical; but nobody will object if you explain that your composition is in the Phrygian mode. If a still more poignant effect be desired, write in B natural, leaving out the sharps as before, and calling the mode hypophrygian. If, as is possible, the Phrygian is more than the public can stand, write in D without sharps, and call the mode Dorian, when the audience will accept you as being comfortably in D minor, except when you feel that it is safe to excruciate them with the C natural. This is easy, but not more so than the rule for making music sound modern.

For compositions in the major, all that is necessary is to write ordinary diatonic harmonies, and then go over them with a pen and cross the t's, as it were, by sharpening all the fifths in the common chords. If the composition is in the minor, the common chord must be left unaltered; but whenever it occurs some instrument must play the *major* sixth of the key, *à propos de bottes*, loud enough to make itself heard rather distinctly. Next morning all the musical critics will gravely declare that you have been deeply influenced by the theories of Wagner; and what more can you desire, if modernity is your foible?

But I am neglecting my week's work. Although I repeat that "How to compose a good opera" might be written as easily as "How to write a good play," I must not set about writing it myself in this column, although the above sample will shew every learned musician how thoroughly I am qualified for the task. The fact is, I had been reading the reviews of Mr Frank Archer's book; and it set me thinking of what are called actors' plays, meaning plays which are not plays at all, but compilations consisting of a series of stage effects devised *ad hoc*. Indeed, stage effects is too wide a term: actors' effects would be more accurate. I thought of how hopelessly bad all such works are, even when, as in the case of Cibber's Richard III. and Garrick's Katharine and Petruchio, they are saved from instant perdition by a mutilated mass of poetry and drama stolen from some genuine playwright.

And then I fell to considering which would be the worst thing to have to sit out in a theatre—an actor's play or a singer's opera. Before I could settle the point the clock struck; and I suddenly realized that if I lost another moment I should miss the one-fiftyfive train to the Crystal Palace, where I was due at two-fortyfive to witness the performance of Mr George Fox's new opera, Nydia. And when I sat down just now to write an account of Nydia, it naturally reminded me of Mr Frank Archer, and led to the above tremendous digression on the subject of operatic composition in general.

Nydia is founded on Bulwer-Lytton's Last Days of Pompeii, a novel which I read when a boy. I remember nothing of it except the name Arbaces, and the Roman sentinel, and Pliny—though, indeed, I am not sure that I did not get the last two out of Chambers's Miscellany. At all events, I found the libretto of Nydia as new to me as it is in the nature of any libretto to be to a musical critic of my age. It began with a bustling crowd, singing:

> Water melons, rich and rare,
> None excel them we declare;
> Olives, figs, and honey sweet,
> You will find them hard to beat;
> Here is game, wild mountain boar,
> Oysters too from Britain's shore,
>> Come and buy, come and buy.

This was out of Carmen, tune and all, except the oysters; and even their freshness must have been severely tried by hawking them in the full blaze of an Italian sun.

Then we had a blind girl with a Leitmotif, also rather like the jealousy motive in Carmen, with a heroine, lover, and villain, in due course. The villain, a Pompeian archbishop, held a service in a temple on the lines of the one in Aïda; and the lover came in and dashed him down the steps of the altar, for which exploit he was haled away to prison—very properly, as I thought—in spite of the entreaties of the heroine. In prison he shared his cell with a Nazarene, who strove hard, not without some partial success, to make him see the beauty of being eaten by a lion in the arena. Next came the amphitheatre, with a gladiator fight which only needed a gallery full of shrieking vestals with their thumbs turned down to be perfectly *à la* Gérôme*. Then the hero, kept up to the mark by the Nazarene, was thrown to the lion, whereupon Vesuvius emitted clouds of spangles and red fire. A scene of terror and confusion in the streets followed, the crowd standing stock-still, with its eyes on the conductor, and the villain falling, slain by lightning, and then creeping off on all fours behind the calves of the multitude.

Finally the clouds parted; and we had a pretty pictorial composition of the hero and heroine at sea in a galley with the blind girl, who presently took a deliberate header into the waves, to the intense astonishment of everybody except the hero, who, without making the smallest attempt to save her, set up a thundering Salve eternum just as I was expecting him to break into

> Rosy lips above the water,
> Blowing bubbles soft and fine;
> As for me, I was no swimmer,
> So I lost my Clementine.†

*Jean-Léon Gérôme was a contemporary French historical and genre painter.

† Oh My Darling Clementine is a popular American song, whose authorship is confused. The lyrics first appeared in an 1863 song Down by the River Lived a Maiden, credited to H.

Mr Durward Lely sustained the tenor part with great heroism; and Madame Valda, after innumerable high C's, finished the third act with a big big D which brought down the house.

Mlle de Rideau did her best with the part of the blind girl; and Messrs Clifford, Pyatt, King, Joyce, and the rest did, I imagine, much what the composer expected them to do. The Crystal Palace orchestra played through the score with deadly skill at a serene *mezzo forte*, not paying the smallest attention, as far as I could perceive, to any of the composer's numerous *pianos* and *pianissimos*, though some of his *fortissimos*, notably an astounding series of double knocks on the drum in the second act, received rather more attention than I should have bargained for had I been the conductor. On the whole, though I must compliment Mr George Fox on his industry, his ambition, and his energy, I find that the point of view from which he regards operatic composition is so far remote from mine that I shall continue to esteem him rather as a singer than as a composer.

As to the concerts of last week, I have only space to say that Miss Evangeline Florence, an American soprano with the extraordinary range of three octaves from the B natural below the treble stave upward (the same, allowing for the rise of pitch, as that recorded by Mozart of Lucrezia Agujari), made her appearance at a concert given by that clever and cultivated singer, Miss Marguerite Hall. She fully satisfied the curiosity of the audience as to her high notes, which sound like violin harmonies of ordinary quality. She is a pleasant young lady, with a sufficiently strong turn for music; but she

---

S. Thompson. In 1884 the text was published with the now-familiar tune, words and music being credited to Percy Montrose. Both compositions were issued by the same publisher, Oliver Ditson of Boston, Mass.

did not strike me as being an artist by temperament; and I cannot say that her cheerful, rather domestic kind of musical accomplishment is likely ever to make her independent of her upper octave as a public singer.

Of Elkan Kosman, the new Dutch violinist, and of Sir Charles Hallé, whom I found on Friday in St James's Hall playing Schubert to Mr John Morley* (who was listening with quite a vegetarian air) and a happy and perfectly attentive audience, I must take some later opportunity of writing.

SLIVINSKI AND SAURET
The World, 25 May 1892

Joseph Slivinski, the latest rival of Paderewski, would make an unparalleled *maître d' armes*. Everything that can be said of Eugène Pini's wrist is true of each separate joint of Slivinski's fingers. He is prodigiously swift; and that air of deliberate, undistraught purpose which a man can only maintain when he is at something well within his physical power, sits unmoved on Slivinski when he is doing things that Paderewski or Ysaÿe (on the violin) could not match without some show of desperation. From the purely gymnastic point of view he, and not Paderewski, is the exponent of the Leschetitzsky technique; for in his case it has not, as in Paderewski's, become overlaid by a technique of his own: besides, being natural to him, it does not sound cruel and artistically contradictory from him as it often does from Paderewski. His steely finger is always elastic: it leaves the piano ringing unhurt—indeed, you feel no more

* Writer and M.P., who was Chief Secretary for Ireland 1892–5.

pity for the instrument than you do for a sword that has parried a brilliant thrust, Slivinski's feeling for it being a veritable *sentiment du fer.*

Whenever the piece which he has in hand enables him to bring his extraordinary gymnastic powers fully to bear, it becomes transfigured, sometimes quite dazzlingly. Even in cases where he brings it to bear in flat defiance of the obvious intention of the composer, as he repeatedly does, it is often curiously and not unpleasantly novel. Where it is entirely appropriate, as in Chopin polonaises and Liszt rhapsodies, the effect is tremendous. Nevertheless, I am still tempted to dwell on the *maître d' armes* view of him. He is so simply and unaffectedly masculine that the moment the music becomes clearly womanly—as in Schumann's Romance, for instance—he modestly abnegates his supremacy at once, and plays neatly and gently, with the utmost good feeling—much as an athlete might sew on a button— but without any pretence of being in his element. Paderewski, in such moments, brings into action a wealth of feminine power and delicacy which no woman could surpass.

The two men, indeed, contrast at all points except the high discipline under which both have brought their executive ability. Paderewski has the passionate, nervous, wilful power of the artist in poetry, tonal or other: Slivinski has the cool muscular strength, elasticity, and rhythm that make the artist in bodily exercises. Slivinski is a toughly knit, free-stepping, spare man, with salient cheekbones and closely cropped black hair. Paderewski is a thin, flat man, with a startling turban of the fluffiest red hair on his head. He moves determinedly, but with his chin down and his ankles feeling nervously for the floor, like one walking in darkness. There is no reason to doubt that Slivinski is quite as ambidextrous as Paderewski, if not more so; but he has not his variety of touch, his sympathy with all phases of music, his comprehensive intelligence—in a word, his powers of interpretation as distinguished from his power of manual execution. Nor has he the exquisite though *naïve* musical instinct of Sapellnikoff: his plain, exclusively virile talent seems impatient of the luxuries, dreams, and *enfantillages* of art.

On the whole, though he is unquestionably a player to be heard and studied, and one, too, not easily to be forgotten, he takes his place for the present without supplanting Paderewski or indeed any other player of established eminence. I say for the present, because the whole of the foregoing criticism must be taken as provisional in view of the fact that Slivinski is a very young man, certain to develop largely on the sympathetic side as he matures.

A very different player from Slivinski is Mr H. S. Welsing, who combined his forces with Carl Fuchs, the violoncellist, at a concert in Prince's Hall on Wednesday. Mr Welsing is a lightfingered player with a pretty touch. He patters with terrific rapidity over the lighter scales and *arpeggios*, and presently shoots himself plump into a heavy bit of work at a speed quite beyond its possibilities. His *cheval de bataille* for the occasion was the Waldstein sonata, which is full of such traps; and it is hardly too much to say that he fell headlong into all of them, invariably rescuing himself with great gallantry, but not without moments of confusion during which the notes rolled over one another in the wildest confusion, though I will not venture to assert that any of them escaped him. The fact is, the Waldstein sonata requires a more contemplative and less impetuous temperament than Mr Welsing's to expound it; for in spite of the pernicious old convention to the contrary it is not a mere *bravura* piece, and has never been really successful when so treated. Mr Welsing had a flattering success as a composer, his setting of Shelley's Love's Philosophy, sung by Marie Brema, being enthusiastically encored. As to Herr Carl Fuchs, I can only say that if his right hand were as skilful as his left, he would rank as a first-rate player.

Sauret had the good sense to make a solid concert of his first "recital" at St James's Hall on Thursday last. The Beethoven quartet (F major, Op. 59) was well worth hearing, which means that it had more elbow grease put into its preparation than is commonly spent on such occasions. Sauret also circulated a translated notice of himself from the Neue Berliner Musikzeitung, explaining, in a free English style, that "there is in him a strong 'violin individuality'—not to be mistaken for 'speciality,' like [*sic*] Sarasate." The public will infer that the thing for a violinist to aim at is speciality rather than individuality. What the critic meant, if he had only hunted down his meaning sufficiently to be able to express it accurately, was that Sauret is less of a virtuoso than Sarasate because he has not sunk the man so completely in the violinist—has not specialized his individuality so devotedly. No doubt he gains in fulness and variety of life what he loses in artistic perfection. The critic goes on to say: "In the power which he exercises over his audience he approaches the great Paganini. Sauret's ease in overcoming every imaginable difficulty is fabulous. [This is the reverse of what the writer means; but the intention is obvious.] Thus may the Italian hero of the violin have played." Now it is true that Sauret's command of the violin *is* extraordinary—so much so that if he had concentrated himself on the career of a virtuoso as Sarasate has, he might have justified his German critic's enthusiasm. As it is, violin playing is with him an accomplishment carried to the most brilliant degree, but not a calling. On Thursday he was in an excellent vein, and displayed his best quality

[629]

in leading the quartet. His subsequent performance of a movement from a concerto by Ernst pleased me less, partly because I do not see any adequate excuse, in the presence of so much music of the highest class for violin and pianoforte, for giving concertos with the orchestral parts strummed on a piano, and partly because I detest Ernst's music as the most ignoble stuff known to me in that kind. The only other violinist whose concert came into the week was Miss Winifred Robinson. I only got in for a scrap of a trio by Dvořák, which was not going smoothly enough to make me regret having missed the rest of it. I unluckily did not hear Miss Robinson's solos.

Gaston de Mérindol, who gave a pianoforte recital at Prince's Hall on Friday, is hardly more than a cultivated amateur. He is a fluent executant, and plays with refinement and feeling, but without the trained strength and studied conception which we look for in first-class playing. I had to leave in the middle of his recital to go to Grosvenor House, where Mr John Farmer was shewing what could be done with a choir of young ladies selected from the pupils of the Public Day Schools Company. It may seem a small thing to have made a collection of schoolgirls sing a dozen part songs and canons well; and, no doubt, when the opportunity was once provided, all that was needed was the exercise of Mr Farmer's skill and devotion as a choirmaster. But to provide the opportunity—to carry the musical idea so far into the dense jungle of English middle-class Philistinism as to make such a concert possible—this has meant, in Mr Farmer's case, a lifelong struggle with the powers of darkness. However, he seems to enjoy it; and he is certainly so far successful that wherever you find John Farmer, there also you find some respect paid to music, even if it only goes the length of a general qualm of conscience as to its neglect. Some day I shall enlarge a little on this subject, and on the respective shares of the school timetables allotted to music, and to the comparatively unimportant and revolting subject of mathematics. For the present I can only add that the work done at the concert was unexceptionable as far as I heard it, and that Miss Elsie Hall, who played a couple of movements from an early concerto of Chopin's, and, for an encore, his Berceuse, has improved—I had almost said matured, though she is only thirteen—remarkably since I heard her at Steinway Hall. She is a real, not a manufactured, "wonder child." The concert was for the benefit of the Maria Grey Training College for Teachers. I wonder whether it trains them in the whole duty of a headmistress towards the art on which the college sponges for pecuniary aid.

On Saturday, at Prince's Hall, Mr J. H. Bonawitz began a Historical Recital, which must, I think, be going on still, as I had to leave after the sixteenth piece, and there were eleven, including the Appassionata Sonata, yet to come. Besides, there was a running commentary by the editor of the Musical Times, Mr Edgar Jacques, who, being clever, popular with his colleagues, and well up in the subject, would have been the very man for the occasion, were he not afflicted with a sense of humor, with which he maintained a cheerful struggle throughout the performance. Not that the recital was uninteresting—by no means; nor was it anybody's fault that the harpsichord jingled like a million bell-wires, or that the effect of the Bach clavichord fugue upon it was execrable, or that the Palestrina *ricercate* had to be played on the most modern of American organs, or that the audience, overcome by the association of reading-desk and organ, was ludicrously solemn. Yet these things were; and when Jacques pleaded that the American instrument was "something between" the organ in the Albert Hall and the portable organs of Palestrina's day, and frankly gave up the harpsichord as a bad job after the audience had listened to it for half an hour with unsuspicious awe, the twinkling of his eye betrayed the suppressed convulsions within. At last he disappeared from the platform for a while; and, as I seized the opportunity to slip out, I was conscious of a seismic vibration in the building, which convinced me that Jacques, hidden somewhere among the foundations, was having his laugh out. It does not do to have too clever a lecturer on these occasions unless you have all the other arrangements to correspond.

L' AMICO FRITZ
The World, 1 June 1892

L' Amico Fritz has one strong recommendation from the critic's point of view: there is no trouble in taking its measure. Some of it is fresh, freehanded, bouncing, rather obstreperous, like Cavalleria—was composed before it, perhaps. The rest is more artificial without being in any way better, except that the orchestra is more knowingly handled. High spirits and audacity are jewels in the crown of youth when they are lucky enough to pass with half the musical wiseacres of Europe as strength and originality; but the imposition is one that cannot be repeated. The most striking example I know of a very young composer astonishing the world by a musical style at once fascinating, original, and perfectly new, is Mendelssohn's exploit at seventeen with the Midsummer Night's Dream overture. One can actually feel the novelty now, after sixtysix years. There was nothing whatever of this sort in Cavalleria. The style was the common Italian style of the day; and Mascagni's "originalities" were simply liberties taken with it, liberties consisting of unconventional—I had almost written cheeky—progressions which were exhilarating in their roughness, and freshened up the old musical material wonderfully.

The exactly parallel case of Massenet in France ought to have shewn every critic what to expect from Mascagni's next attempt. However, all this is an old story with me. I was not taken in by Cavalleria; and now that everybody finds L' Amico Fritz obviously deficient in first-rate promise and first-rate accomplishment, I am in the pleasing position of being able to say "I told you so." Let us therefore clear the discussion of all nonsense about genius of the highest order, and of the ridiculous comparisons with Verdi and Wagner which were rife last year, and give Mascagni fair play as an interesting young composer with a vigorous talent, and plenty of courage in asserting it, congratulating ourselves meanwhile on the fact that Bellini has at last found a disciple, albeit one far inferior to his master.

L' Amico Fritz, then, is an opera which will pass the evening pleasantly enough for you, but which you need not regret missing if you happen to have business elsewhere. The libretto is as delightfully free from blood and thunder as that of La Sonnambula: it is more an idyllic picture than a story. The cherry-tree duet ought really to be hung in the Royal Academy. The pretty harmonies of the opening line, changing in the most fashionably petted Tosti manner, belong rather to the drawing room; but when Madame Calvé climbed the ladder with an apron on, and threw down cherries to the tenor on the other side of the wall, I was transported as if on a magic carpet to Burlington House, where I remained in imagination until it suddenly occurred to me that I had paid a guinea instead of a shilling for my stall, when I came to myself in rather a melancholy frame of mind.

For the cherry duet "caught on"; and immediately I

had a vision of Mr Worldly Wiseman* coming from his strongholds in Bond-street and in the Strand theatres to conquer the Opera with his pretty trivialities, his happy endings, his second-hand morals, and his impotent cowardice and superficiality, offering golden opportunities to intellectual and artistic mediocrity, and cloaked indulgence to the sanctimonious people whose appetite for beauty is of such a character that they are themselves ashamed of it. Goodbye, if my vision comes true, to Gluck, Mozart, Weber, Wagner—even to Meyerbeer. The worst of it was that the invader was so horribly well treated. Sir Augustus had taken the greatest pains with that cherry tree, and with the well and bucket, the watering-pot, and the inevitable landau and horses. His "unprecedented combination of the first [and laziest] musical talent in Europe" actually contributes one first-rate artist to help out Madame Calvé and Mascagni, although it is so busy with those startling novelties, Faust and Roméo et Juliette, that a comparatively provincial German company has had to be sent for to do the Nibelungen tetralogy. For that, it appears, is the end of loading our favorites with princely salaries and fulsome praise.

The unprecedented combination puts us off for years by pretending that it is going to learn a new work (meaning a work that has been familiar in every second-rate German town for the last ten years); and now, when the limit of our patience is reached, the unprecedented ones tell us that London had better ask Hamburg to come over and help it out of its difficulty, and offer us another performance of Roméo by way of consolation. I throw the responsibility on the combination rather than on the manager, because I know how helpless he is in the face of his guarantors and their pets, and how, even if this were not so, the progress made with new

* Character in John Bunyan's Pilgrim's Progress.

work would still depend mainly on the devotion of the artists to their work; but, all the same, had I been in his place, I think I could have managed to get at least a Siegfried of my own as well as a Meistersinger and an Otello. If I had in my company such a Siegfried and such a Wotan as Bayreuth never heard, I would make them feel that I was something more than their showman, and that a leading singer should not be content to wallow in the old parts which he picked up by ear when he was a little boy.

However, I am forgetting all about L' Amico Fritz and the cherry tree. The duet, as I said, "caught on" immensely; and there was a frantic *encore* a little later when Madame Calvé and Signor de Lucia finished a number with a sudden *pianissimo* on a sustained high note, the effect—a favorite one with Mascagni—being that of a ravishing caterwaul. Next to the cherry-tree episode, the most effective bits in the opera are the recital of the story of Eleazar and Rebecca at the well ("something out of Dante, I think" said one of my neighbors); the procession of orphans to a jolly music hall tune, said to be an Alsatian march; and the long violin solo played behind the scenes which prepares the entry of Giulia Ravogli so cleverly in the first scene. The last act is preceded by the now inevitable intermezzo, with the equally inevitable and exasperating *encore* (pure affectation on the part of the gallery), and contains a duet in which there is a touch of the dramatic energy of Cavalleria. The story is too happy and sunshiny for more than the touch; and on the whole I think I may compendiously describe the work as having all the merits of a fine bank holiday.

As to the performance, it was more than good enough for the occasion. Signor de Lucia succeeds Valero and Lubert as artificial tenor in ordinary to the establishment. His thin strident *forte* is in tune and does not tremble beyond endurance; and his *mezza voce*, though monotonous and inexpressive, is pretty as prettiness goes in the artificial school. I cannot say that I like that school; but I must admit that its exponents have hitherto set a good example by minding their business and identifying themselves with their parts; and this, considering the lax discipline of the operatic stage at present, is a considerable merit. Giulia Ravogli has evidently been taking lessons somewhere. Strange to say, instead of having had her voice ruined, she has been led to correct the looseness and raggedness of the upper part of it; so that her vocal style has gained in compactness and force. She is as irresistible as ever: else I might venture to tell her that she has not the remotest idea of how a fiddle should be held, much less a fiddle-bow.

Madame Calvé was so affecting in the simple grace and *naïve* musical feeling which exhaust the scope of the part of Suzel that in a tragic *rôle* I should expect a good deal from her. She has a free, even voice of adequate volume, not of the brightest color, but very sympathetic. As a soprano of innate dramatic force, she is the most notable recruit we have had at the Opera for some years. The orchestra had no difficulty with the score, which is vigorous, and supplies all the usual stimulants and luxuries in profusion. The worst orchestral number is the prelude, which is arrant shop stuff. Bevignani conducted; and there was an enthusiastic ovation at the end: Sir Augustus, coy as usual, being dragged out by main force to share in it.

May I, without offence, suggest to the Italian visitors at the Opera that however backward we may be as a nation in musical culture we have at least got beyond the stage at which we can tolerate strident *Bravas* breaking in on the silence of the audience and the flow of the music after every high note and every salient phrase. To me at least, the jar of such an interruption is as irritating as a slap in the face. The chattering from English ladies in the boxes is bad enough; but it does not usually begin until late in the season, when the owners leave town and sublet the boxes to trippers from the provinces; wheras the *Brava* nuisance is in full swing already. I submit it to the good sense of our visitors whether our insular custom of confining such exclamations to political meetings is not, on the whole, to our credit, musically speaking.

On Wednesday there was a grand operatic concert at St James's Hall for the benefit of those who wished to hear the unprecedented combination without entering a theatre. Sir Augustus hospitably invited me; but after a glance at the program I decided to go and hear Mr Lunn lecture at Prince's Hall on singing. It is now thirty years since I first met a singing-master [Vandeleur Lee] who was having a discussion with Mr Lunn; and during that whole period I have met fresh cases at intervals of from eighteen months to five minutes. A more hot-headed, pugnacious, intolerant, impossible controversialist than Mr Lunn does not exist. He will tell you that he is nothing if not logical, and then offer you the most fantastic comparisons and analogies as stepping-stones to his conclusions. Although you may be the most sympathetic of his partisans, or the most innocent and humble-minded of his disciples, he will treat you as if you had personally instructed every bad singer who has appeared at the Opera since Grisi's time.

The scientific world for him is divided into ignoramuses who do not know of his discoveries, and plagiarists who have annexed them without acknowledgment. As to the things he says about teachers of singing, I simply dare not describe them, they are so inhumanly true. On this particular occasion at Prince's Hall he was more himself than ever. He had written out an elaborate and surpassingly bad lecture by way of a tramway to keep

[637]

himself straight upon; but he soon went hopelessly off the rails, to our great relief, and abandoned his manuscript with an appalling threat of publishing it. Do not for a moment suppose, however, that the lecture was not a success. Mr Lunn, in spite of all the difficulties he places in his own way, has the advantage of being desperately in earnest, and of being, in the main, perfectly right. It was, of course, easy for him to ridicule Ravelli's singing of *Il mio tesoro* at the Opera, and to caricature that hurrying of the accompaniment which is always resorted to in order to get a singer over a long-sustained note. But he also produced a pupil of his own who sang the song far better than the average Covent Garden Don Ottavio.

Nevertheless, I cannot admit Mr Lunn's claim that the crucial passage with the long-sustained F was sung exactly as Mozart meant it to be sung. The singer, though he held the F, took breath in the middle of the fourth bar, which was most certainly a violation of Mozart's intention. Any singer who has been taught to hold back the air-current at the larynx like Mr Lunn's pupils, can, if he also distends his pharynx by rounding the back of it, sing the whole five and a half bars through without taking breath. I have often heard it done; and I have half a mind to offer to do it myself, provided the passage be transposed into G to accommodate a limited baritone, and the quality of the execution left out of account. In the minor section of The trumpet shall sound, in the Messiah, there are phrases of ten and eleven bars, the longest containing notes equivalent to thirtytwo crotchets. They can be, and should be, sung in one breath, though they bring a singer nearer to the end of his tether than the twentytwo crotchets, in slower time, of *Il mio tesoro*. If Mr Lunn's baritone pupil, who sang very well, had vanquished For this corruptible, &c., the feat would have been quite *à la* Farinelli.

However, I do not complain; and I hope Mr Lunn will keep pegging away at his most useful mission. Only I can assure him that as soon as pupils really want to sing well, and the public learns to prefer Mozart's sustained F in *Il mio tesoro* to the B flat which Ravelli bawls in its place, there will be no difficulty about the supply of teachers. Mr Lunn himself admits that his pupils are apt to go to fashionable teachers to get "finished." That means that he shews them what good singing means; that they dont like it, and dont believe in it; and that they find the public agrees with them. It needs the authority of genius like that of Sims Reeves to enable a young artist to differ from the public and compel it to admit, for the moment, that fine singing is better than popular bull-roaring. In short, it is the demand, and not the supply, that is lacking; and the quality of the demand, in spite of such aberrations as the revival of the goat-bleat school produced by the success of Gayarré, is improving. Let Mr Lunn, therefore, be of good cheer: he is not quite such an isolated phenomenon as he supposes.

THE FAREWELL OF HENRY LAZARUS

The World, 8 June 1892

On Tuesday last week I found myself with tickets for nine concerts and a speech by Mr Gladstone. At this I lost my temper, and declared that I would not stir out of the house all day. But I have never been a man of my word; and at three I began my round as usual. First there was Miss Clara Eissler at Erards', playing the harp, which is a cool, limpid instrument for a hot day, and almost suggests that some stout pianoforte has realized Sydney Smith's aspiration by getting out of its skin and sitting in its bones.* The particular harp which Miss Eissler used was a very fine one; and she played it as if she appreciated it, instead of pinching it to make it speak in the professorial manner. Unfortunately nobody seems to think of writing anything but the most old-fashioned sort of filigree music for the harp; and as a little of this goes a considerable distance with a critic, however handsomely executed, I was soon on my way to Steinway Hall, where I found Miss Else Sonntag giving a pianoforte recital.

It was a curious freak of fate that made Miss Sonntag, with her frail physique and her characteristic *naïveté*, a pupil of Liszt. To hear her play a Chopin ballade in her master's way is the oddest of musical experiences. She has appropriated his conceptions in her own fashion, mostly by making fairy tales of them. But she has not been able to appropriate his powers of execution; and when she comes to a passage which, from Liszt's point of view, might be arranged as a duet for a lion and a hurricane, it is almost as if a baby mermaid had got into a whirlpool, or had petulantly insisted on trying to shoot the rapids below Niagara. However, she comes out alive, and disports herself prettily, if sometimes rather quaintly, in the smoother waters. On this occasion she was not at her best; for the weather was warm enough to make anybody play wrong notes—almost warm enough to make me play right ones. Even Slivinski, whose recital I next visited, was all but dissolved by the time I got to St James's Hall.

It was amazing to see the smallness of the paying part

* Sydney Smith (1771–1845), canon of St Paul's, reformer, and essayist, "was honored and admired for his honesty, and exuberant drollery and wit" (DNB). The quotation is from Saba Lady Holland, A Memoir of the Reverend Sydney Smith (1855), Vol. I.

of his audience, considering the extraordinary quality of the performance. Of course this will not last for ever. In about fifteen years' time I shall have people rushing up to me to ask whether I have heard the new pianist Slivinski, for whose recitals there is not a seat to be had. But the danger in this system of deferred results is that the greater a player is, the more apt is he to find something better to do than dancing attendance on English stupidity. If Slivinski meets Rubinstein now, Rubinstein will not ask him whether he has succeeded in England, but simply whether the English have failed, as usual, to appreciate him. To which Slivinski will rightly reply in the affirmative. And Rubinstein will remind him that we failed also in his own case and in Liszt's, and that our comparatively prompt recognition of Paderewski must be accounted for by the fact that every intelligent Englishman could see by his head of hair that he was an exceptional man.

If Slivinski does not come back to London in a hurry, the loss will be ours and not his. He unbent somewhat in his last two recitals, and shewed the most astonishing power of making the pianoforte sing in transcriptions of vocal melodies, so that the older people began to compare him to Thalberg. He also gave us a chance of hearing one of those prodigious opera fantasias of Liszt's which few pianists can play and fewer understand. The one selected by Slivinski, that on Robert, is a pungent criticism of Meyerbeer as well as a *tour de force* of adaptation to the pianoforte. To anyone who knows the opera and knows the composer thoroughly, no written analysis of Robert could be half so interesting as this fantasia in which Liszt, whilst vividly reproducing Meyerbeer's cleverly economized and elaborated scraps of fantasy, grace, and power, picks up the separate themes apparently at random, and fits them to oneanother with a satirical ingenuity which brings out in the most striking way how very limited and mechanical the Meyerbeerian forms were.

After Slivinski, there remained only six more concerts, and Mr Gladstone on current London politics. It is commonly held that the finest politeness is needed to enable you to listen quietly to a man when he proceeds to instruct you at great length in a subject which you understand and which he does not. Feeling unequal to this strain, I consigned the Gladstone ticket to the wastepaper basket with all the remaining concert tickets except one; and with that one I went off to St James's Hall to the farewell concert of Henry Lazarus, at which everybody sang, or conducted, or did something in honor of the occasion. Lazarus's age was for long an inscrutable mystery; and I have my doubts as to the value of the latest settlement arrived at. As lately as twelve years ago he was the best clarinet player in England: when you were sitting behind Costa at the Opera you listened for certain phrases from the clarinet just as you did from the *prima donna*, except that you were much less likely to be disappointed in the former case. Lazarus was beginning to look oldish then, though he made no flesh, and was still a trim, neatly proportioned man, with old-fashioned but very unobtrusive whiskers, thin lips, and a perfect mouth for his instrument, with a chronic lift at the corners that looked like a smile, and very readily developed into one. Your neighbor on the right would tell you that he remembered Lazarus as premier clarinet for twenty years. Your neighbor on the left would correct him and say thirty years at least. Some veteran would then pooh-pooh both calculations and declare that he had heard Lazarus before 1840, and that he was then in his prime.

And yet it is only within the last couple of years that Mr Egerton has taken his place at the Monday Popular Concerts when Beethoven's septet is in the program. I may quite safely put it that he has been playing in public for more than fifty years, and that during at least forty of them, dating from the death of Willman in 1840, his pre-eminence was unquestioned, as it would be still if his lip and fingers had their old strength. For, with all due respect for the ability of his successors, I do not know one of them who can pretend to his distinction of tone and style, and his elegant phrasing. He now retires finally, confessing to seventyseven years. We were all a good deal touched when he came up out of the past, as it were, on to the platform at the farewell concert, and sat down to play us a couple of pieces with fingers that trembled a little, but with something of his old habit of assured competence, his old style, and here and there, especially in the *chalumeau* and middle registers, his old fineness of tone.

At the end the applause was tremendous; and when he returned to the platform for the second time, leaving his instrument behind him, he had perhaps some idea of making a speech. Whether this was so or not, he was taken aback by the appearance of a huge wreath poking itself at him over the platform rail; and when, after a moment of bewilderment, he collected himself and took the offering, there was another green monster lunging at him on his right. By the time he had got hold of both, he had given up all idea of speaking, if he had really entertained any. He put his hand on his heart, as all public performers used to do in the days when he was taught to make a bow, and with many mute acknowledgments edged himself to the steps in a quite sufficiently eloquent fashion, and disappeared. The practical object of the concert was the starting of a testimonial fund, of which Mr Charles Coote, of 42 New Bond-street, is treasurer.

At the Philharmonic last week Miss Macintyre sang *Robert, toi que j'aime* and *Ritorna vincitor* with her usual cleverness, and with that invaluable determination of hers to succeed which can only be appreciated by those who know how much talent is wasted in this world for want of will. The orchestra gave itself no real trouble, and was good only in the accompaniments to the Beethoven concerto. In the symphony (Schubert's unfinished) there was no getting a decent *piano*, much less a *pianissimo*, from the cellos; so that the exquisite and quite simple second subject of the first *allegro* was stolidly murdered. The *fortes* in the slow movement were also unsatisfactory, Mr Cowen allowing his attention to be drawn off to the great slashes and accents of the strings, instead of concentrating it on the sustained flow of melody in the wind, with the result, of course, that the melody was not sustained at all, the ends of the notes tailing off in the usual feeble Philharmonic fashion.

Becker played a concerto of Raff's for the violoncello, and was warmly applauded for the first movement. He could do but little with the *finale*, which is trivial, with an ugly solo part. Mr Lamond was the pianist; and he chose that beautiful fourth concerto of Beethoven's, as great in a feminine way as the fifth is in a masculine way. I thought it a curious selection for so rough a player; but I never dreamt that he, or any musician, could miss the grace and tenderness of the opening phrase, even if Beethoven's "*dolce*" were erased from the pianoforte copy. However, Mr Lamond saw nothing in it but a mere battery of chords. He smacked it out like a slater finishing a roof; and I paid no more attention. I remember how exquisitely Janotha used to play that concerto in the latter half of the seventies, when she first came over here. Nowadays she is content to gabble over Mendelssohn's G minor concerto like a schoolgirl; and when I went to her recital the other day, I found her idly displaying her rare dexterity of hand and her capricious individuality of style without a ray of thought or feeling;

[644]

so that I left sorrowfully after sitting out two or three
barren numbers.

SIEGFRIED AT COVENT GARDEN
The World, 15 June 1892

Last Wednesday I was told that Siegfried was to be
produced that evening at Covent Garden. I was
incredulous, and asked my informant whether he did
not mean Carmen, with Miss Zélie de Lussan in the title
part. He said he thought not. I suggested Faust, Les
Huguenots, even Die Meistersinger; but he stuck to his
story: Siegfried, he said, was really and truly in the bills,
and the house was sold out. Still doubting, I went to the
boxoffice, where they confirmed the intelligence, except
that they had just one stall left. I took it, and went away
wondering and only half convinced. But when I reached
the theatre in the evening a little late, fully expecting to
find notices on the seats to the effect that Siegfried was
unavoidably postponed, in consequence of the sudden
indisposition of the dragon, and Philémon and Cavalleria
substituted, I found the lights out and the belated stall-
holders wandering like ghosts through the gloom in
search of their numbers, helped only by the glimmer
from the huge orchestra and some faint daylight from
the ventilators.

The darkness was audible as well as visible; for there
was no mistaking that cavernous music, with the tubas
lowing like Plutonian bullocks, Mime's hammer rapping
weirdly, and the drums muttering the subterranean
thunder of Nibelheim. And before I left the house—to
be exact, it was at half-past twelve next morning—I
actually saw Rosa Sucher and Sir Augustus Harris hand
in hand before the curtain, looking as if Covent Garden

[645]

had been the birthplace of her reputation, and as if he had never heard La Favorita in his life. Perhaps it was all a dream; but it seemed real to me, and does so still. Assuming that I was awake, I may claim that at least one of those curtain calls was not for the manager at all, but for me and for those colleagues of mine who so strongly urged Sir Augustus Harris to try this experiment in the golden years when money was plenty and there was no Dissolution impending, even at the cost of depriving London of the opportunity of witnessing the *début* of Signor Rawner as Manrico.

The performance was vigorous, complete, earnest— in short, all that was needed to make Siegfried enormously interesting to operatic starvelings like the Covent Garden frequenters. The German orchestra is rough; but the men know the work, and are under perfect and willing discipline. In readiness and certainty of execution they are fully equal, if not superior, to the ordinary Covent Garden orchestra. But I cannot say as much for them in the matter of purity and individuality of tone. After making every allowance for the difference between the German orchestral tradition, which is partly popular, and the English, which is purely classic, as well as for the effect, peculiar to the Nibelungen tetralogy, of the rugged and massive ground bass which pervades so much of the score, I still cannot accept this imported orchestra as being up to the standard of tone quality we have been accustomed to expect in London.

In that vast mass of brass, it seemed to me that instead of three distinct and finely contrasted families of thoroughbred trombones, horns, and tubas, we had a huge tribe of mongrels, differing chiefly in size. I felt that some ancestor of the trombones had been guilty of a *mésalliance* with a bombardon; that each cornet, though itself already an admittedly half-bred trumpet, was further disgracing itself by a leaning towards the flügel horn; and that the mother of the horns must have run away with a whole military band. Something of the same doubt hangs over the lineage of the woodwind, the bass clarinet alone being above suspicion. Even in the strings, the cellos and tenors lack distinction, though here the thicker and heavier tone is partly due to the lower pitch, which is in every other respect a prodigious relief. I think it will not be disputed that the Covent Garden orchestra, if it had half the opportunities of the German one, could handle the score of Siegfried not only with much greater distinction of tone and consequent variety of effect, but also with a more delicate and finished execution of the phrases which make up the mosaic of leading-motives, and with a wider range of gradation from *pianissimo* to *fortissimo* than Herr Mahler's band achieved, excellent in many respects as its performance certainly was. This is no mere conjecture: we have already heard the Siegfried blacksmith music and forest music played by our own orchestras in concert selections better than it was played on Wednesday last.

And that is why I still complain that Sir Augustus Harris is no more establishing the Wagnerian music-drama in London than Mr Kiralfy is establishing the gondola.* When he organized the performance of Die Meistersinger by his own company and his own orchestra, he achieved his great feat as an *impresario*. This time he has only sent for a German *impresario* and a German company to help him out of the difficulty; and for that I grudge him the smallest exaltation, as I could have done as much myself if I had the requisite commercial credit.

* Imre Kiralfy was the creator of the spectacle Venice, at the Olympic (1891-3), advertised as an "aquatic pageant and reproduction of the modern city."

The impression created by the performance was extraordinary, the gallery cheering wildly at the end of each act. Everybody was delighted with the change from the tailor-made operatic tenor in velvet and tights to the wild young hero who forges his own weapons and tans his own coat and buskins. We all breathed that vast orchestral atmosphere of fire, air, earth, and water, with unbounded relief and invigoration; and I doubt if half a dozen people in the house were troubled with the critical reflections which occurred to me whenever the orchestra took a particularly rough spin over exquisitely delicate ground, as in the scene between Wotan and Erda. It is not to be doubted that all the women found Brynhild an improvement on Carmen and Co.

I say nothing of the great drama of world-forces which the Nibelung story symbolizes, because I must not pretend that the Covent Garden performance was judged on that ground; but considering how very large a proportion of the audience was still seated when the curtain came down at half-past twelve, I think it is fair to assume that the people to whom Wotan is nothing but an unmitigated bore were in a minority. At the same time, Herr Grengg, with his imposing presence, powerful voice, and perpetual *fortissimo*, did very little to break that ponderous monotony which is the besetting sin of the German Wotan. Lorent, who was on the stage for a few minutes as Alberich, was also earnest, but pointless and characterless. Fortunately Mime (Herr Lieban) saved the situation by his unflagging vivacity. It would be unreasonable to ask for a cleverer representation than his of the crafty, timid, covetous, and, one must admit, unmercifully bullied old dwarf. His singing shewed remarkable artistic ingenuity—exactly the quality which Mime's music requires.

There are two great points in the part: first, that awful nightmare which comes upon Mime after the question-

and-answer scene in the first act, when he curses the shimmering light and falls into a growing terror which is just reaching an intolerable climax when it vanishes as if by magic at the voice of Siegfried in the wood outside; and, second, his attempt to poison Siegfried after the fight with the worm, when he involuntarily talks murder instead of the flattery he intends. Both of these passages were driven home forcibly by Lieban, especially the poison scene, where the effect depends more on the actor and less on the orchestra than in the other. Alvary, though he has something of that air of rather fancying himself in his part which distinguishes some of the most popular impersonations of Mr Wilson Barrett* (whom Alvary rather resembles personally), attained a very considerable level of excellence as Siegfried, especially in the forest scene, the remembrance of which will, I think, prove more lasting than that of the first and last acts when we have seen a few rival Siegfrieds and grown a little more critical. Fräulein Traubmann, as the bird, was energetic, purposeful, human, and, in short, everything that a bird ought not to be. For so nice a stage illusion we need wilder and far more spontaneous woodnotes than hers.

As I have already intimated, Fräulein Heink, as Erda, had her scene rather roughly handled both by the orchestra and by Wotan; but she nevertheless succeeded in rescuing something of its ineffable charm by her expressive delivery and her rich contralto tones. As to Rosa Sucher, she was as prompt, as powerful, as vigorous, as perfect in her drill, as solid and gleaming in her tone as ever. Her efficiency, brilliancy, and strength have a charm that is rather military than feminine; and consequently they will fail to rouse the voluptuous enthusiasm of our devotees of that splendid and

* Wellknown London actor, manager, and playwright.

invariably repentant female, the Womanly Woman; but as Brynhild was no Magdalen, Frau Sucher can hardly be blamed for not making her one. Finally, I have to chronicle several curtain calls for the energetic conductor, Herr Mahler. He knows the score thoroughly, and sets the *tempi* with excellent judgment. That being so, I hope he will yet succeed in getting a finer quality of execution from his band.

The scenery is of the usual German type, majestic, but intensely prosaic. The dragon, whose vocal utterances were managed jointly by Herr Wiegand and a speaking-trumpet, was a little like Carpaccio's dragon at San Giorgio Schiavone, a little like the Temple Bar griffin, and a little like a camel about the ears, although the general foundation appeared to be an old and mangy donkey. As usual, people are complaining of the dragon as a mistake on Wagner's part, as if he were the man to have omitted a vital scene in his drama merely because our stage machinists are such duffers as to be unable, with all their resources, to make as good a dragon as I could improvize with two old umbrellas, a mackintosh, a clothes-horse, and a couple of towels. Surely it is within the scope of modern engineering to make a thing that will give its tail one smart swing round, and then rear up.

The stage effects throughout were punctual and conscientious (always excepting the flagrant exhibition of Brynhild in the last act as the Sleeping Beauty instead of as an armed figure whose sex remains a mystery until Siegfried removes the helmet and cuts away the coat of mail); but they were not very imaginative. The stithy was lighted like a Board School; and the fires of Loge and the apparition of Erda might have been ordered from the gas company, for all the pictorial art they displayed. Sir Augustus Harris need not look to Bayreuth for a lead in this direction. Where Bayreuth surpasses us is not in picturesque stage composition, but in the seriousness, punctuality, and thoroughness with which it looks after the stage business, which is mostly left to take care of itself at Covent Garden.

I am compelled by want of space to postpone until next week my notice of Mr de Lara's Light of Asia, which was successfully produced on Saturday evening. If it is repeated in the meantime, Mr de Lara will do well to withdraw the fourth act, unless the establishment can do something better in the way of staging it. It almost eclipses the absurdities of the Tannhäuser *mise en scène* at present.

BUDDHA SINGS
The World, 22 June 1892

Mr Isidore de Lara, the composer of La Luce dell' Asia, is young and new: he has hardly been fairly in the field as a composer for twenty years. It is remarkable how much faster Italians mature than Englishmen. Mascagni is positively Mr de Lara's senior in the operatic world; and no doubt Mr de Lara will be quite content to survive him. Mr Cowen might almost be Mascagni's father; and yet people still talk of him as "Freddy Cowen," without the smallest sense of incongruity. As to Sir Augustus Harris himself, he is admittedly getting on for middle age; and yet it has taken a knighthood to abolish the general custom of speaking of him by the second syllable of his first name alone. My own immunity from such familiarities I believe to be due less to natural awe than to the fact that my surname is so much easier and shorter than my Christian names, which are happily incapable of abbreviation, that the general use of either of them would involve a serious loss of time to the community.

But even I am often described as callow, and impressively lectured for my immaturity and rashness by critics of from nineteen to twentyfive. Hence I am not surprised to find that the younger section of Mr de Lara's friendly critics condescend handsomely to him, by way of encouraging a young man; whilst the hostile ones speak loftily, as responsible persons who do their stern duty to society by rebuking an upstart.

Among the academic section there is the feeling that since Mr de Lara, having always followed his own artistic bent with perfect sincerity and independence, is not a man of scholarships and professorships, it is just like his impudence to attempt to compose at all. Add to this that his achievements as a drawing room singer have brought about him a remarkably ill-behaved crowd of partisans, consisting, as far as I could judge from what I noticed in the stalls at Covent Garden on Saturday week, of prepossessing and apparently prepossessed ladies who would persist in applauding in impossible places, to the indignation of all beholders and the great prejudice of the unfortunate composer; and you will see that what with patronizing critics, bigoted academicians, and indiscreet adorers, Mr de Lara has much to live down.

It must not be supposed that The Light of Asia is a philosophical opera. It is necessary to say this explicitly, because there are some people who, if I were to write an opera called The Light of Edinburgh, and make Adam Smith the hero, would immediately find that the overture contained a good deal of political economy. Wagner's Nibelung Ring tetralogy may be called a philosophic music-drama, because the characters are dramatic personifications of the forces which are the subject-matter of metaphysics, the Pilgrim's Progress itself not being a more unmistakable allegory. The Light of Asia is a representation of the adventures of the man

Buddha and his mistress, with about as much Buddhism in it as an ordinary oratorio contains of Christianity.

Still, The Light of Asia differs in one vital respect from the general run of modern oratorios. These works are mostly written by men who are or have been church organists; and church organists are, as a class, more utterly void of religious reverence than any other body of men in the world. As Mr de Lara has presumably never played the organ in a Buddhist temple, he remains fresh to the impressiveness of the Buddha legend, and has set Mr Beatty Kingston's poem to music which is remarkably free from professional pedantry, deliberate imitation, claptrap, padding, and vulgarity. Naturally, a work so deficient in all that the professors can teach is not likely to be popular with them. The fact that it is conscientiously finished to the utmost of the composer's ability completes his title to be criticized with entire respect.

Mr de Lara's chief disadvantage at Covent Garden is that the best side of the composition is the worst side of the performance. The centre of the opera is the song, Loosen from thy foot the bangle, which made its mark a few years ago when Miss Ella Russell sang it at St James's Hall, and for which Miss Eames was heartily applauded on Saturday week. It is a languorous, dreamy, half mystical, half voluptuous Oriental love song, as the Oriental love song exists in the English imagination. This sort of seraglio music pervades the whole work, more or less: the second and third acts consist almost entirely of it. Now, in an opera, the creation of an atmosphere so subtle as this requires not only appropriate music but poetic dancing and delicate stage management. I need hardly say that neither of these luxuries were to be had at Covent Garden.

The principal dancer, Miss Mabel Love, whose chronic expression of tragic indignation replaces this season the smile of Palladino, understands what is wanted for the scene in which she appears, and makes a courageous and interesting attempt to supply it; but her powers are not yet matured, and her physical training is still far from thorough; so that she can do but little to soften the ruinously prosaic effect produced by the *corps de ballet*, which accompanies Mr de Lara's swaying syncopations and incense-breathing consecutive fifths with a feeble modification of its ordinary exercises. If the regular ballet was a failure—as, on the whole, it decidedly was—what could be expected from the passages in the third act, where the movements of the chorus of odalisques (if that is the correct expression) should be subdued from positive dancing almost to the abstract poetry of gliding, weaving motion? With this in view, a group of young ladies wandered about in the prompt corner as if some vivisector had removed from their heads that portion of the brain which enables us to find our way to the door; and though the audience, restrained by the presence of Lassalle and Miss Eames, who might have broken into song at any moment, waited patiently, they probably blamed Mr de Lara for maundering.

But Mr. de Lara was not in a position to complain. Everybody on the stage was lending a willing hand to the utmost of his or her knowledge; and the management had been quite princely in the way of expenditure. Unless Mr de Lara had torn out handfuls of his hair and strewn them despairingly on the stage in protest against having his opera stifled with goodwill and hundreds of pounds' worth of silks and precious-looking metals when it was perishing for want of two-penn'orth of skill and fancy, I do not see what he could have done. His feelings in the fourth act must have been particularly unenviable. The persons who appeared therein were mostly supernatural; and this immediately brought out the superstitious side of the Covent Garden stage management. Sir Augustus Harris has been imbued from his earliest years with the belief that the vital distinction between the inhabitants of the other world and of this is that the latter move horizontally and the former vertically. Enter his room through the door and walk across to his chair, and he will recognize you as human. Remove a square piece of the floor and rise slowly into the room on a lift, and he will believe you to be a demon as firmly as if you were a musical critic and had found fault with the Royal Italian Opera. You cannot get this out of his mind: it is part of the faith of his childhood.

No fair-minded critic can doubt that when Signor Miranda was hoisted on to a lift; shot up like a Jack-in-the-box out of a neutral-tinted canvas cloud resembling a photographer's background of monstrous size; and bathed in the fiery glow of a red limelight, Sir Augustus was convinced that only a hardened atheist could refuse to believe and tremble. And yet everybody laughed except Mr de Lara and Signor Miranda, who was standing giddily on the brink of a precipice some twelve or fourteen feet high. As to the siren's cave business which followed, I really have not the patience to describe it, further than to say that it was as like a kitchen fireplace as usual, and that nobody was surprised at the insensibility to its seductions displayed by Buddha, who had been having a nap under a tree in a heavy shower. When he walked off the stage, and the curtain came down for a long pause just at the wrong time, the fortunes of The Light of Asia reached their lowest ebb. Will no friend of Sir Augustus Harris's open his mind gently to the fact that all this machinery of traps and visions is as dead as Queen Anne?

It will be seen that Mr de Lara cannot be said to have had his work performed to the greatest possible advantage. Still, he had much to be thankful for. Lassalle, who

[655]

took the part of Buddha, and comported himself with a sublime self-satisfaction which would have put the very smuggest Indian idol out of countenance, sang magnificently. Miss Eames, though a little matter-of-fact, gave sufficient weight to the part of Yasodhara; and Plançon saved the first scene, which is musically the weakest part of the work. The rather empty motive with which it opens is nearly identical with the refrain of Autolycus's song in The Winter's Tale; the song of Atman is only a pretty piece of troubadouring; and the mock-scholastic choral passages beginning For earth's sake, produce a burlesque effect not unlike that of the Amen in Berlioz's Faust.

One or two of the instrumental interludes are too long: they cause stage waits; and it struck me that the material of the funeral march got just a shade more repetition than it can bear with the best effect. The scene in the fields is much the worse for the transformation of the work from a cantata to an oratorio. But the rest is of remarkable merit; and the whole work abounds in vocal melody of exceptional excellence. When I recall the extravagant praise that was lavished on Ivanhoe, with its refractory voice parts nailed down to a perpetual mechanical rum-tum, I cannot but wonder why so little has been said of Mr de Lara's purely musical, well-phrased, and often eloquent vocal writing. What he lacks at present is more intellectual vivacity; an intenser, more symphonic grip of his musical material; greater variety of mood; and a distinct orchestral style as distinguished from mere taste in orchestral effects.

The best point in the score at present is the use made in Yasodhara's song of the instrument known to military bandsmen as "Jingling Johnny"*—a point that would

* An inverted crescent with dangling bells, called a *pavillon chinois*.

not be worth mentioning in a score of Gounod's. It will be noticed that these are all negative failings, and that I have admitted the opera to be throughout sincere and original. I will not go so far as to say that Mr de Lara is the only English composer of his generation whose feeling for his work is calculated to do his country credit; but there is certainly more hope in The Light of Asia than in those things with the pedal points and the mixolydian angels in them which are composed by our professors for the provincial festivals. I hope Mr de Lara will never condescend to take shares in the mixolydian business. Some of the partners in it began, like himself, as musicians. Let him consider what they are now, and take heed that he follows not in their footsteps.

FROM JUDAS TO RHEINGOLD

The World, 29 June 1892

Some months ago I mentioned that a performance of Handel's Samson, on the festival scale, had been arranged at the Crystal Palace. Then came the news that a substitution of the comparatively hackneyed Judas Maccabæus would save Mr Edward Lloyd trouble. The program was accordingly changed for the worse; and the performance thereby became a gigantic celebration of Mr Lloyd's indisposition to exert himself. Formerly, when musicians wanted to describe the most fatuous depths of stupidity, they used to say *"bête comme un tenor."* Nowadays tenors are clever enough; but they are not energetic. Miss Eames lately told an interviewer, who kept his countenance with heroic constancy, that the severity with which Jean de Reszke studies his work is beyond description. No doubt she was thinking of the fact that he has spent the past year in cerebrating with volcanic intensity over the color of Romeo's beard, as to which he could now probably write us a volume worthy to rank with the famous essay on the character of that master of refined pleasantry, the nurse's husband.* A paper upon his old fair theory and his new dark theory, which may yet give place to a shaving theory or even a no-beard-at-all theory, would draw a huge crowd to a meeting of the New Shakspere Society.

In the meantime the years are flying; and we have not yet heard Brother Jean as Siegfried, or Siegmund, or Loge, or Tannhäuser, though his Walther in Die Meistersinger, which is, as far as I know, the best in the world, shews what he could do for Wagner if he had the will. The age is therefore confronted with two problems: (1) to make Edward Lloyd learn Samson, and (2) to make Jean de Reszke learn Siegfried. I wish there were some legal process by which we could lock them both up in Holloway Gaol until they had taught oneanother the parts. They would get on capitally together; for there is no rivalry between them: to Lloyd, Brother Jean is simply a baritone of exceptional range; whilst to Brother Jean, Lloyd is an admirable *soprano robusto*.

The Judas performance came off last Saturday. The audience was the usual festival crowd, big and extremely barbarous, as the soloists well knew; for unscrupulous alterations of the text in order to finish with the most absurd high notes were the order of the day; and the more outrageous they were the better the audience liked them. The choruses left little to be desired in point of precision and none in point of magnitude. The baritones distinguished themselves specially by the brilliancy and steadiness of their tone. I say baritones advisedly; for there seemed to be very few bass voices among them: the tone, which rose to great splendor above the stave, fell off almost to nothing when they got down below C.

* For note, see Vol. 3, Appendix, p. 783.

The sopranos were very bad: they had a noble opportunity in the first verse of God save the Queen; and all they did was to give us a careless, common, vulgar piece of screaming. The altos were much better; the tenors better still; and the baritones, as I have said, best of all.

Miss Clara Samuell sang some of the soprano music, and made the most of her voice by her good intonation and well-formed tone. As to Albani, Patey, Lloyd, and Santley, it is not necessary to say more than that From Mighty Kings, Sound an Alarm, Arm, arm, ye brave, &c., produced all the customary cheering and clapping. Mr Manns was not in his brightest and most confident vein; but he was none the less equal to the occasion.

After the performance of Das Rheingold last Wednesday at the Opera, I do not think we shall hear much more about the impropriety of beginning the season with Siegfried, which should have come third instead of first. If it be true that it was Alvary who insisted on the transposition, let us admit now that Alvary knew what he was about. Siegfried was a success because there was hardly a moment in the three acts during which Lieban or Alvary, or both, or Sucher and Alvary, were not on the stage to keep things going. Besides, the defects of the orchestra did not matter so much in a score which admits of a certain degree of roughness of treatment. The dullest moment in Siegfried was the dialogue at the beginning of the second act between Wotan and Alberich.

Now imagine our German visitors setting to at a music drama which contains an enormous percentage of Wotan-cum-Alberich, with a score requiring the most delicate handling, and you will be able to understand that the performance of Das Rheingold was none of the liveliest. The band, no longer braced up by the excitement of the first night, did what I hope was its worst. Its playing of the wonderful water music prelude suggested that the Rhine must be a river of treacle—and rather lumpy treacle at that; the gold music was arrant pinchbeck; Freia's return to heaven brought no magical waftings of joy to the audience; and the rainbow music, with its hosts of harps (I distinctly heard one, and was not well placed for seeing whether there were any others), might have been pleasant deck music during a steamboat excursion to Hampton Court, for all the success it attained in providing a splendid climax to the prologue of a mighty drama.

Then the stage arrangements were rather hard to bear. There was nothing to complain of in the first scene, since no better way of doing it has yet been invented. The Rhine daughters waved their arms, and floated up and down and round and round in their aquarium; and if I could only have forgotten the scene as it appeared to those behind the curtain—the three fire-escapes being elongated and shortened and raced round the floor, each with a lady fastened to the top and draped with a modern green skirt of prodigious length—I should have been satisfied. But the orchestra did not make me forget it, nor did Alberich, nor anyone except Flosshilde (Fräulein Heink), who quite fulfilled the promise of her Erda in Siegfried. The really difficult part of the stage management in Das Rheingold is the change from the home of the gods to that of the dwarfs, and the business of Alberich's metamorphoses and final capture.

The way in which these were either bungled or frankly given up in despair shewed with brutal directness what I have so often tried to hint delicately: namely, that if Sir Augustus Harris would dismiss a round dozen of his superfluous singers, and give a fifth of what they cost him to an artistic and ingenious stage manager, he would double the value of the performances at Covent Garden. The attempts of Herr Lissman, who is, to say the least, no harlequin, to disappear suddenly through a trick shutter, the obviousness of which would have disgraced a cheesemonger's shop in a Christmas pantomime, were not made any the more plausible by the piffling little jet of steam which followed. As to the changes into the dragon and the toad, they were simply taken for granted, although Sir Augustus might easily have taken advice on the subject, not from Bayreuth, but from any provincial manager who has ever put the story of Puss in Boots on the stage. The descent from god-home to dwarf-home was avoided by dropping the curtain and making an interval at the end of the second scene; and the change back again, which should be an ascent into the clouds, was a badly managed attempt at the descent which had been omitted. Evidently the scene-plot had got mixed on its way from Hamburg.

The shortcomings in the staging of the work were all the more depressing because, with two conspicuous exceptions, the principal performers were so averagely German that it is only by repeatedly telling myself not to be rude that I can restrain myself from saying flatly that they might as well have been English, so powerfully mediocre were they. Grengg sang his way loudly and heavily through the part of Wotan with both his eyes wide open (one of them should have been removed). Every line he uttered was exactly like every other line. Alberich did not even sing: he shouted, and seemed content if he came within a half-quarter tone of the highest notes he aimed at. His acting, though conscientious, was that of a pirate in a Surrey melodrama: neither in his ghastly declaration to Loge of his ambition to become master of the world, nor in his frantic despair when Wotan wrests the ring from him, did he make the smallest sensation.

Frau Andriessen failed to make Fricka interesting— small blame to her, perhaps, considering the impossibility of getting any variety of play out of Wotan.

Fräulein Bettaque, as Freia, was pretty and pleasing enough to disarm criticism; and the giants, having little to do except to appear clumsy and intellectually and artistically dense, took to their parts with considerable aptitude. But they certainly would not have made the performance endurable but for the two exceptions I have alluded to: namely, Lieban (Mime), whose ten minutes on the stage, including his capital singing of *Sorglose Schmiede*, sent up the artistic level of the performance with a bound during that too brief period; and Alvary, who, as Loge, the northern Mephistopheles, succeeded by his alertness in making the rest of the gods look anything but quick-witted.

On the whole, it was fortunate for the success of the work that most of us are at present so helplessly under the spell of the Ring's greatness that we can do nothing but go raving about the theatre between the acts in ecstasies of deluded admiration. Even the critics lose their heads: you find the same men who are quite alive to the disparities between Jean de Reszke and Montariol, Maurel or Edouard de Reszke and Miranda or De Vaschetti, Calvé or Giulia Ravogli and Melba or Miss de Lussan, losing all discrimination when the German artists come up for judgment; admiring a third-rate Alberich as devoutly as a first-rate Mime; and meekly accepting the German tendency to coarse singing and wooden declamation as the right thing for Wagner, whose music really demands as much refinement, expression, and vivacity as Mozart's.

As to the band, one hardly knows what to say of the revelation it has made of the fewness of the people who know *by ear* the difference between a second-rate German orchestra reinforced by a number of students from the Guildhall College and first-rate ones like those of London and Manchester.

When the public wakes up from its happy hypnotic

trance and resumes its normal freedom of judgment, it will inevitably be bored by Das Rheingold, unless it is smartly and attractively stage-managed and well acted in English. And even then it will remain, like Die Zauberflöte, a mere extravaganza, except to those who see in all that curious harlequinade of gods, dwarfs, and giants, a real drama of which their own lives form part. Herren Wiegand and Litter, raised to gigantic stature on thick-soled boots, and poking at oneanother with huge cudgels whilst the drum is pounded unmercifully down in the orchestra, may look ridiculous; but the spectacle of goodnatured ignorance and serviceable brute force, suddenly roused to lust and greed, and falling to fratricidal murder, is another matter—one that makes the slaying of Fasolt by Fafnir the most horrifying of stage duels.

Wotan is a delicate subject, especially in England, where you do not know whose toes you may tread on if you suggest that the Wagnerian stage is not the only place in which Religion, corrupted by ambition, has bartered away its life-principle for a lordly pleasure house, and then called in the heartless intellect to rescue it from the consequences of its bargain by hypocrisy, fraud, and force. As to Alberich, renouncing love for gold, and losing all fellow feeling in his haste to accumulate it, I question whether it is good taste to exhibit him at Covent Garden on "diamond nights." But I am sure that Das Rheingold must either be read between the lines and through the lines, or else yawned at. Siegfried, Die Walküre, and Götterdämmerung may pass as ordinary dramas, barring a little interruption from time to time by the prolixities of Wotan; but Das Rheingold is either a profound allegory or a puerile fairy tale. Consequently it is hardly worth doing at all unless it is done very well, which is precisely why it was so much less successful at Covent Garden than Siegfried.

THE EFFECTS OF ELECTIONEERING
The World, 6 July 1892

It is only fair to the artists whom I have to criticize in this hour of political battle to ask that a large allowance may be made for the deterioration of my character produced by electioneering. A fortnight ago I still had, I will not say a conscience, but certain vestiges of the moral habits formed in the days before I became a critic. These have entirely disappeared; and, as I now stand, I am capable of anything except a findable-out infringement of the Corrupt Practices Act. A collation of the speeches I have delivered would destroy all faith in human nature. I have blessed in the south and banned in the north with an unscrupulously single-hearted devotion to the supreme end of getting my man in which has wholly freed my intellect from absolute conceptions of truth.* I learnt long ago that though there are several places from which the tourist may enjoy a view of Primrose Hill, none of these can be called *the* view of Primrose Hill. I now perceive that the political situation is like Primrose Hill.

Wherever I have been I have found and fervently uttered *a* true view of it; but as to *the* true view, believe me, there is no such thing. Place all the facts before me; and allow me to make an intelligent selection (always with the object of getting my man in); and the moral possibilities of the situation are exhausted. And now I can almost hear some pillar of the great church of Chadband saying "Faugh! no more of this: let us return to the purer atmosphere of art." But *is* the atmosphere

* Shaw was campaigning for Edward J. Beale, Liberal candidate in the General Election. Beale lost.

of art any purer? One evening I find myself appealing to the loftiest feelings of a town where many of the inhabitants, when you canvass them, still keep up the primitive custom of shutting the door carefully, assuring you that they are "all right," and bluntly asking how much you are going to pay for their vote. The next evening I am at the Opera, with Wagner appealing to my loftiest sentiments. Perhaps Mr Chadband would call that a return to a purer atmosphere. But I know better. Speaking for myself alone, I am as much a politician at a first night or a press view as I am on the hustings.

When I was more among pictures than I am at present, certain reforms in painting which I desired were advocated by the Impressionist party, and resisted by the Academic party. Until those reforms had been effectually wrought I fought for the Impressionists—backed up men who could not draw a nose differently from an elbow against Leighton and Bouguereau—did everything I could to make the public conscious of the ugly unreality of studio-lit landscape and the inanity of second-hand classicism. Again, in dealing with the drama, I find that the forces which tend to make the theatre a more satisfactory resort for me are rallied for the moment, not round the so-called French realists, whom I should call simply anti-obscurantists, but around the Scandinavian realists; and accordingly I mount their platform, exhort England to carry their cause on to a glorious victory, and endeavor to surround their opponents with a subtle atmosphere of absurdity.

It is just the same in music. I am always electioneering. At the Opera I desire certain reforms; and, in order to get them, I make every notable performance an example of the want of them, knowing that in the long run these defects will seem as ridiculous as Monet has already made Bouguereau's backgrounds, or Ibsen the "poetical justice" of Tom Taylor. Never in my life have I penned an impartial criticism; and I hope I never may. As long as I have a want, I am necessarily partial to the fulfilment of that want, with a view to which I must strive with all my wit to infect everyone else with it. Thus there arises a deadly enmity between myself and the *impresarios*; for wheras their aim is to satisfy the public, often at huge risk and expense, I seize on their costliest efforts as the most conspicuous examples of the shortcomings which rob me of the fullest satisfaction of my artistic cravings.

They may feel this to be diabolically unfair to them whenever they have done the very utmost that existing circumstances allowed them; but that does not shake me, since I know that the critic who accepts existing circumstances loses from that moment all his dynamic quality. He stops the clock. His real business is to find fault; to ask for more; to knock his head against stone walls, in the full assurance that three or four good heads will batter down any wall that stands across the world's path. He is no dispenser of justice: reputations are to him only the fortresses of the opposing camps; and he helps to build or bombard them according to his side in the conflict. To be just to individuals—even if it were possible—would be to sacrifice the end to the means, which would be profoundly immoral.

One must, of course, know the facts, and that is where the critic's skill comes in; but a moral has to be drawn from the facts, and that is where his bias comes out. How many a poor bewildered artist, in the conflict of art movements, has found himself in the position of the harmless peasant who sees a shell bursting in his potato patch because his little white house on the hill accidentally happens to help a field battery to find its range. Under such circumstances, a humane artillery officer can at least explain the position to the peasant. Similarly,

I feel bound to explain my position to those in whose gardens my shells occasionally burst. And the explanation is probably quite as satisfactory to the shattered victim in one case as in the other.

Electioneering notwithstanding, I have been at countless concerts during the past few weeks, and am well content to forget a good deal of what I have heard of them. Some were what I may call Cooperative Concerts, each artist guaranteeing the sale of a certain number of tickets in return for the advantage of appearing before the London public. For further particulars I must refer my readers to my Confessions of a Concert Agent, which is to be published when death has placed me beyond the fear of assassination. It will not contain anything scandalous—at least, anything *very* scandalous; but part of it will be sufficiently surprising to the innocent British public to offer some inducement to our *entrepreneurs* to pay me every possible attention with a view to prolonging my life to the utmost. Besides the Cooperative Concerts, there have been a good many concerts of the annual benefit or one-good-turn-deserves-another description, some of them good of their kind, but not critically interesting. We have had two remarkable examples of the value of great masters to finely receptive pupils. Miss Nettie Carpenter, who played Bruch's first violin concerto at the concert given by her husband, Mr Leo Stern, shewed that she had caught everything from Sarasate except the extraordinary strength and endurance, the unremitting and exquisite sensitiveness and vigilance of his right hand. And Miss Szumowska gave a pianoforte recital at which she played so beautifully and intelligently that I think Paderewski would have admitted that she gave his interpretations of the works in her program better than he, in his coarser and more headstrong moods, has often given them himself. We are having a visit now from Reisenauer, a most Boanergetic disciple of Liszt, who has acquired a huge superfluity of technical power, which, doubtless after sufficient consideration, he has resolved to take out in speed rather than in thought. The result is satisfactory in compositions which are meant to excite and dazzle; but I fervently hope I may never again hear the last variation in Schumann's Symphonic Studies as it sounded under the Reisenauer treatment. Max Schwarz, another pianist, or rather a professor of the piano, reminded me a little of Heinrich Lutters. He is Director of the Raff Conservatoire at Frankfurt.

Among the best miscellaneous concerts I have attended were Miss Palliser's and Miss Gambogi's. Miss Palliser produced a child fiddler, Arthur Hartmann, small enough to be Gerardy's little brother, but grave, self-possessed, and capable to a degree which four times his years have not enabled me to attain. Another and more mature young violinist is the girl Panteo, who played one of Wagner's few *pièces de salon* at the last Opera Concert, and triumphed over an orchestral accompaniment that would have disheartened an older performer. We shall probably hear more of her. Dutch violinists still arrive in shoals. They almost all play with remarkable neatness, and seem likely to be favorites at miscellaneous concerts and in drawing rooms; but Henry Seiffert remains the only one from whom there is much to be expected. Unlike most of his compatriots, he excels in the power of his *cantabile* playing, and often executes florid ornaments with reckless roughness. I am bound to add that he never, like some of his smoother competitors, suggests any doubt as to whether he could play his scales if put to it. I return to the subject of Miss Palliser's concert for a moment to say that I was much struck by the singing of Mr David Bispham, who seems to me to be fully qualified to take his place on the stage

as an operatic artist of considerable distinction. No
doubt this has been known and said long ago; but it so
happens that I have only heard him at this concert, and
once before, in The Basoche, when I took him to be a
drier singer than I now perceive him to be. Miss Marie
Brema has sung much this season, and always with
success, notably at one of the operatic concerts, where
her singing of The Erl King completely eclipsed the
clumsy concert-singing of the rank and file of the Covent
Garden company; but at present she is an organ with
one stop, the quality of which will not be improved if it
is too persistently ground at. Miss Brema must be more
versatile than she has hitherto shewn herself (as far as I
have had the opportunity of observing); and if she
succeeds in widening her dramatic scope in the direction
of comedy, and also enlarging her purely musical
resources by occasionally substituting the attraction of
simple beauty of sound in the upper part of her voice for
that of dramatic intensity in the lower, she will take high
rank as a singer. At present she is narrowing her talent
by over-specialization. Miss Gambogi's concert was
abruptly finished, for me, by Miss Ellen Terry, who
projected herself into a recitation with such superb
artistic power that I was quite unable to face the feeble
superficiality of ordinary concert business after it, and
so hurried out of the room. Miss Gambogi is too young
as yet to have much grip of her talent, which is, besides,
by no means precociously developed; but she has natural
refinement, good looks, and an engaging personality,
reminding one occasionally of Trebelli. A young lady
named Leonora Clench spiritedly attacked the last two
movements of Mendelssohn's violin concerto, and came
off with credit. Hollmann also helped, and compelled us
to acknowledge his excellence, now so well proved that
it is an impertinence to praise it.

I am far from having exhausted my concerts; but

space begins to close in, and I have yet a couple of other matters to mention. La Statue du Commandeur is now preceded at the Prince of Wales' Theatre by a musical tomfoolery called Did you Ring? which at first moved me to majestic scorn, and afterwards brought me down off my pedestal (like Le Commandeur), and made me laugh with undignified heartiness. It is by Messrs Houghton and Mabson, and is played by Miss Amy Farrell, Miss Kate James, and Mr Templar Saxe. I saw La Statue for the second time, and enjoyed it more than I had done before. The dancing of Mlle Litini is as good as the singing of Miss Alice Gomez, whom she somewhat resembles; and the Don (M. Burguet), though he gives the Commandant no excuse for taking him so very seriously at the end, is a capital comedian and a skilful pantomimist. The piece needs to be visited twice, because on the first occasion one sees hardly anything but the petrified personality, or rather colossality, of Tarride as the Commendatore. You lose all sorts of good things whilst you are gaping at the huge white marble man.

The second act, as a highly organized artistic achievement, is far superior to anything in L'Enfant Prodigue. The music is a clever piece of *rococo* in the most modern taste, just half in earnest, like the dumb show itself. It is quite understood, however, between Adolphe David and his audience that thinking of Mozart is barred.

I must postpone notice of Die Walküre at the Opera until next week, strongly recommending everybody meanwhile to go and hear the first act, which retrieved for the German company all the credit it lost over Das Rheingold. The rest is not so good. The second act is horribly mutilated; and Reichmann is overparted as Wotan. The Valkyries are good; and Frau Andriessen, though she was not dazzling on the warlike side, played

Brynhild with a sincerity and depth of feeling that greatly advanced her popularity.

MUSICAL LEEDS

The World, 13 July 1892

I have just received the most amusingly frank book I have read for a long time—just the thing for any old musical hand who would like to be led back, without too much detail, over the last thirty years. It is the History of the Leeds Musical Festival, by Joseph Bennett and Alderman Frederick Spark. Which of the twain handled the scissors and which the paste is not stated on the title page; but I think I may venture to guess that Mr Bennett selected the press notices quoted, and supplied most of the pen-and-ink setting for the mosaic of programs, facsimiles, advertisements, letters, balance-sheets, and miscellaneous excerpts of which the volume is composed.

Pray do not suppose that I mention the scissors and paste as a reproach to the authors. On the contrary, they have made the book exactly as it ought to be made. Instead of an essay on the festivals, which would be insufferable, we get all the documents needed to give concert-goers the required information in the form to which they are most accustomed—that of the program and prospectus, which is also the most compact for reference. The statistical particulars are thus packed into a book of 400 pages, which you read easily in two hours, picking out what you are curious about in the programs; skipping the dry records of hours, days, and names of nobodies; abstracting the letters at a glance; and taking the anecdotes and significant bits of narrative at your ease.

Imagine a parcel of Yorkshire manufacturers, trained to go through the world on the understanding that every man with wares to sell is to get as much for them as he can; every man with money to buy to give as little as possible for what wares he wants; and nobody without wares to sell or money to buy with to be considered at all. Conceive these plain dealers suddenly set to bargain with great singers, the highest souled and most sensitive artists of their time, creatures to be approached like princes and princesses, too delicate to name a price, and too proud to endure a bid lower than what they privately think themselves well worth!

Naturally, there was a pretty confusion until Yorkshire discovered that the pursuit of manufacturing profits might pass for disinterested benevolence in comparison with artistic rapacity; that manufacturing competition looked like pure altruism beside musical jealousy; and that manufacturing domineering and push had not a chance against the absolutism of the foreign favorites of the musical public. *Prima donna* number one coolly demanding (and getting), in addition to her salary, the handsome sum she was to subscribe with queenly charity to the Leeds hospitals; *prima donna* number two inserting a clause in her agreement that no artist engaged should be paid more than herself; Costa ordering the committee not to write letters but to send an ambassador to see him, as if Leeds lay within ten minutes' walk of London, and browbeating them out of every proposal to get a little ahead of Rossini; *impresarios* planting unspeakable miscellaneous concerts of operatic bits and scraps on them as choice expositions of the highest glories of musical art: these and cognate matters are recorded with all possible openness in Messrs Bennett and Spark's volume.

The Leeds committee men do not always cut a very dignified figure in its pages. When Charles Hallé treated them politely, reasonably, and unassumingly, in a thoroughly artistic spirit, they immediately proceeded to insult him, and let him know that his Manchester orchestra was not good enough for Leeds—that they were accustomed to a first-rate article from London, conducted by the great Costa. When Costa treated them with contempt, sneered at their ignorance, personally insulted those who dared to argue with him, publicly brought their Yorkshire novelty (Smart's Bride of Dunkerron) to grief in order, I presume, to have an excuse for refusing to have anything to do with novelties in future, and demanded a hundred guineas more for his services than Hallé, they grovelled before him, and only fell back on Sir Arthur Sullivan when their Neapolitan tyrant finally refused to have anything further to do with them. And yet, while Costa was treating them in this way, they had the assurance to write to Liszt asking him whether he would not like to "submit" a work of his for performance at the Festival (of 1877). Which of course elicited the following snub:

"Messieurs,—En réponse à votre lettre du 22 décembre, j'ai l'honneur de vous informer que je suis tout à fait en dehors des *soumissions* auxquelles vous avez l'obligeance de m'inviter. Veuillez agréer, Messieurs, mes civilités.   F. Liszt."
30 décembre '76, Budapest.

Down to 1877 the majority of the committee never got beyond the primitive notion that a great musical event was one at which Tietjens sang and Costa conducted. I should myself have been educated in that superstition if it had been possible to educate me at all, which it most fortunately was not. Poor Tietjens herself, I imagine, believed in it devoutly; and so did Costa: it was not until she died and he repudiated the committee that Leeds at last found out that familiarity with the

Messiah, Elijah, and the overture to William Tell was not the climax of XIX century musical culture. Since then, thanks to the tact of Sir Arthur Sullivan, the Leeds Festival has become a really important musical event. The forthcoming performances in October will be welcomed by all except those who incautiously attended the benumbing fourth day of the 1889 Festival, on which occasion the whole West Riding was plunged into listless gloom by an unprovoked performance of Brahms's Requiem.

On one point this book, which may be obtained at Novello's for a considerable sum of twentyfive shillings, has made me somewhat remorseful. A friend of mine asked me the other evening whether the Opera, at which I am so constantly grumbling, is not far better than it used to be under the *régime* that collapsed so soon after Costa vanished. And I replied, in the words of Matthew Bagnet,* "Yes; but I never own to it. Discipline must be maintained." The memories awakened by the programs in the History of the Leeds Musical Festival bring home to me how great the advance has been, and nerves me to clamor implacably for further progress.

MAUREL'S LECTURE

The World, 20 July 1892

Maurel's lecture at the Lyceum Theatre on Tuesday last week was a much more businesslike affair than the crowded and fashionable reception of 1891. Our aims on this occasion were supposed to be exclusively scientific and artistic; and we did our best to look like a select body of critics and savants. I think, on the whole, we

* Character in Dickens's Bleak House.

kept up appearances fairly well, though a stranger from another planet might have thought it rather a suspicious circumstance that Maurel should have felt it necessary to spend quite half an hour in arranging our ideas for us before he came to the actual business of his lecture. In fact, the first half of his address might have been introduced in the following terms. "Ladies and Gentlemen: Most of you are either musical critics or teachers of singing. A long experience of both classes in the various countries I have visited during my long professional career has convinced me that neither musical critics nor teachers of singing ever think intelligently. It is, therefore, necessary that I should give you a little rudimentary instruction in the art of thinking before I give you something to think about."

Here I think Maurel made a mistake. The attempt was probably entirely unsuccessful in the cases of those who needed it, and was perhaps resented in the cases of those who did not. Besides, in making it, he forgot to allow for the English habit of mind. It is our insular custom to tackle intellectual problems without any preliminary arrangement of the subject matter; and, however slovenly this may seem to a Frenchman, we find that it serves our turn, and are rather proud of it than otherwise.

We admit that they *order* things better in France, but not that they *do* them better on the whole. Mere order for the sake of order is wasted in London: if Maurel had bundled all his practical points into a sack, brought it in a cab to the Lyceum, and simply emptied it out anyhow on the table before us, we should have been quite satisfied that he was setting about the job in the shortest and handiest way, though he would no doubt have felt guilty of a monstrous want of consideration for our intellectual convenience.

The matter of the lecture—which was so excellently

delivered in French that even I, who am the most maladroit of linguists, understood every word of it—consisted of two points. First, an unanswerable condemnation of the *coup de glotte* method of vocal attack, as to which I need say no more than that I doubt whether any practical singer has ever dreamt of using it systematically, though I suppose everybody uses it unconsciously for special effects. Most advocates of the *coup de glotte* mean nothing more than to discountenance the habit of gasping like a grandfather's clock before striking, as many distinguished amateur vocalists do, instead of attacking their notes cleanly and promptly.

The second point excited more curiosity. Every critic knows to his cost that singers take considerable liberties with the vowels which they have to sing, producing the extreme notes of their compass on any sound that is most convenient, without regard to the word they are supposed to be uttering. Singers usually exhort composers not to set unfavorable vowels to high notes; and composers, who want to be as free as possible and not to hear every high A sounding exactly like every other high A, exhort singers to master the art of producing all the vowel sounds on every note, without reference to its pitch.

Maurel declares that it is impossible to do this effectively without injury to the voice; but instead of defending the customary barefaced resort to the Italian *a* or French *â* for every difficult note, he declares that it is possible to modify every vowel so as to accommodate it exactly to the pitch, and yet to deceive the ear so completely that the modified sound will be accepted as unmodified. This art of vocal prestidigitation—of substituting what he calls a *trompe d'oreille* for the true vowel where the pitch is not favorable to the latter, is one of the things that he proposes to explain in his forthcoming book on the art of singing. The need for it

[676]

is also the main theme of his Le Chant renové par la Science, a report of his lecture at Milan, just published by Quinzard & Cie, of Paris. This little book at least settles the question of Maurel's literary competence; for his style is as clear as Tyndall's. His conspicuous urbanity and good taste, qualities almost as ineligible in a musical controversialist as in a Cossack or a Turco, are fortunately counterbalanced by a conscientious sincerity; so that his determination not to talk about himself or to criticize his fellow artists—as I should do most unboundedly if I were in his place—is not likely to lead to the suppression of any material scientific points, however hardly their recognition may bear on living singers and teachers.

Quite another sort of musical demonstration is that of Miss Constance Howard, who has just completed a series of three lectures on Die Meistersinger at Steinway Hall. Miss Howard's plan is to give a verbal description of an act of one of Wagner's music dramas, playing the *motifs* associated with the various points as she comes to them. She then plays the whole act straight through on the pianoforte, declaiming the words as she goes along. This sort of analysis is not altogether novel: Mr Karl Armbruster has sent, from his public lectures and private classes, shoals of carefully grounded Wagnerian amateurs to Bayreuth; but Mr Armbruster has never, as far as I know, limited his demonstrations to what one person, not a singer, can do with a pianoforte and a vocal score alone.

One of the truest practical things Wagner ever said was that the masterpieces of music are kept alive, not at the theatres and concert halls, but at the pianofortes of lovers of music. It is the young people who hammer away at Meyerbeer and Verdi just as other young people read Dumas and Victor Hugo; who get their knowledge of the Bible from Handel and Bach much as Marlbor-

[677]

ough got his knowledge of history fron Shakespear; who, having learnt from Mozart how to appreciate Molière, arrive at the level of epic poetry and Greek tragedy through Wagner, all with the aid of a Bord pianette and a cheap library of Peters editions: these are the people upon the number of whom in a nation its musical prosperity depends.

It is true that the pianette-Peters culture can only be turned to its full account by those who have opportunities of learning by actual comparison the relation the pianoforte score bears to the complete performance. Indeed, pounding through such scores is, with most players, a process that is only tolerable insofar as it suggests or recalls the very different sound of the orchestra; but the fact remains that nobody, not even a critic, can acquire more than a fragmentary musical culture from public performances alone. You may find a veteran who has heard every soprano from Pasta to Calvé, every tenor from Rubini to Van Dyck, every Don Giovanni from Ambrogetti to Maurel, every pianist from Cramer to Paderewski, and yet he may know less of the great composers than the playgoer who never reads knows of Shakespear. There are critics of ten years' experience in London at present who have only just heard the Niblung's Ring performed for the first time, and who have not yet heard two operas by Gluck or Weber, or more than one pianoforte sonata of Mozart's.

Here, then, we have the importance of a lecture like Miss Howard's. It suggests the true use of the pianoforte as a domestic instrument. At present men refuse to learn their notes because they feel that they will never be able to play well enough to be worth listening to. They might just as well refuse to learn to read because they will never be able to recite or declaim the contents of volumes of poetry well enough to delight an audience. Miss Howard illustrates how people may read tone-poetry and music-drama to themselves for their own enjoyment and culture. I wish, however, that the music publishers, who have most to gain by the spread of this idea, would help it by abandoning the absurd scale of charges now in force for copyright works.

Two pounds fifteen for vocal scores of the four numbers of The Niblung's Ring; twelve shillings for Verdi's Otello: what possible sense is there in maintaining these prohibitive prices after the cream is taken off the sale? It is not conceivable that the restricted circulation involved by such charges brings in the largest attainable profit to the publishers and owners; whilst its crippling effect on musical culture is obvious. If I were Chancellor of the Exchequer, I would devote the proceeds of the tax by which spirits are made artificially dear, to making music artificially cheap. I should buy up all the Wagner, Verdi, and Gounod copyrights, and sell vocal scores at the post offices at a uniform rate of half-a-crown.

The Goring Thomas memorial concert was the smoothest of successes. The platform was a perfect bower of white blooms; the room was crowded, and stuffy enough to gratify the most exacting hater of ventilation; and the inordinately long program was drawn out to the utmost by Mr Villiers Stanford, who appropriately converted the *allegro vivace* of the Cambridge Suite into a dead march by taking it at rather less than half its natural pace. The result was that I was unable to wait for the second act of Nadeshda, which is by far the best piece of work Goring Thomas ever turned out for the stage. Goring Thomas's fame will not, I fear, be very long-lived. He always seemed to be dreaming of other men's music—mostly Frenchmen's; so that he spent his life in elaborating, with remarkable facility and elegance, what Gounod and his disciples had done before. Still, there is a good deal to be done in the world by men who are first-rate hands at their work when once they have been shewn how to do it. Goring Thomas, always a little too much of a voluptuary in music, was more completely Frenchified than an islander of grit ought to have been; but he was no bungler: his work could not have been much better without becoming really original and powerful.

In speaking lately of the operetta Did you Ring? at the Prince of Wales' Theatre, I inadvertently put the librettist in the place of the composer, Mr Landon Ronald, to whom I tender my excuses.

THE SEASON EXAMINED
The World, 27 July 1892

The season is practically over now as far as music is concerned; and a very bad season it has been for everyone but myself; for had the General Election been complicated by a really active musical season, I should hardly have been here to tell the tale. As it was, my last visit to the Opera terminated tragically. After contemplating Götterdämmerung for over three mortal hours exactly as I usually contemplate the Calais light during the last half of a rough crossing from Dover, I fled in disorder, leaving Siegfried with about a hundred bars still to live. His death scene and that of Brynhild would have rewarded me for holding out another half hour; but the limit of human endurance was reached; and the season ended then and there for me. Looking back over it, I am bound to say that it has been a discouraging one to musicians. I have always watched the people who fill the stalls in St James's Hall when serious musical business is in hand with certain misgivings as to their sincerity. I have asked myself, Is it love of music that brings them here, or merely social pressure, like that which forces little children into church to listen to sermons that they cannot possibly understand? Obviously this question could only be settled by observing their behavior under circumstances which gave them a valid social excuse for staying away without in the least obliging them to do so if they still craved for music. Such circumstances do not often arise; but they were created this year by the death of the Duke of Clarence. The effect was instantaneous and unmistakable. The music was still there: but the excuse was provided; smart dressing was out of the question; and the audiences vanished.

I do not see how that fact is to be got over. It was sufficiently depressing to have to admit, at the best of times, that St James's Hall sufficed for the morsel of first-rate music required by the largest and richest city in the world; but when even this limited demand turns out to be heavily adulterated with hypocrisy and millinery, I am half driven to drop the subject altogether. We are living, artistically speaking, in a hovel; and yet I am expected to agitate about the condition of the dome.

Undoubtedly the great musical event of 1892 has been the performance in London of Wagner's Niblung's Ring, after an interval of ten years. Das Rheingold, composed thirtyeight years ago, and first performed twentythree years ago at Munich; Die Walküre, composed thirtysix years ago, and first performed also at Munich, twentytwo years ago; Siegfried and Götter-dämmerung, finished respectively twentythree and twentytwo years ago at Bayreuth: London has just heard these world-famous works for the *second* time, not as part of the regular repertory of an English opera house, but, as before, by a German company imported for the occasion.

And our new English Opera House, built last year, is lying there, a failure so far, nobody knowing whether it will be pulled down, or turned into a music hall, or utilized as a carriage repository,* like the old Queen's Theatre in Long Acre. I know these dates; I remember these facts; I understand the value of the Manchester orchestra, which we sent back home the other day as not worth its traveling expenses to us. And I ask any reasonable person whether I can be expected to hurrah, and shake hands, and drink healths, and beam, and congratulate, and pay compliments over a state of things which if it existed in the cotton trade would raise a general alarm of national bankruptcy.

I am half inclined to doubt whether I am in my right mind when I see everybody so unconcerned and satisfied merely because Madame Calvé has touched them with her beautiful singing, or because Die Walküre, which I have known almost by heart for years, cuts and all, has thrown its spell on them for the first time. I remember one day visiting a relative of mine who had shewn a considerable power, rather rare in the family, of making money. His doctors had persuaded him strongly to leave his work, and had been even more urgent with his people to attend closely to him. When I called on him in the course of his vacation, he took me aside into the window, and asked me whether I saw those rooms, and the remains of the meal he had just risen from. I said I did. He then informed me in a whisper that his wife was mad, that they had not a penny in the world to pay for all these costly things, that they were stark ruined. I have been wondering these six weeks whether I have inherited his malady—whether the pressure of the season and the election have not made me imagine

* It is now the Palace Theatre, Cambridge Circus, home of musical comedy, operetta, and rock opera.

disaster and failure whilst the reality is that we are passing through a climax of unexampled musical prosperity. If so, I hope the *impresarios* and concert agents will come forward with their balance-sheets, and have me removed at once to an asylum.

Still, it is considerably to the credit of this season that it has seen the production of Mr Isidore de Lara's Light of Asia, Mr Bemberg's Elaine, Mr George Fox's Nydia, and Signor Mascagni's L'Amico Fritz. The old subscription night routine, with its scratch performances of the worn-out Italian repertory, has all but vanished; and I should be unspeakably grateful for that if I did not know that what Burke said of politics is true also of criticism: there is no room for gratitude in it. And if there were, the gratitude would be due to me, who have so ruthlessly hunted down the old repertory, with its perfunctory Trovatores and slipshod Traviatas.

This year we have had new works tried and old works let alone to an unprecedented degree. We have also had an opportunity of learning something from the German company. The orchestra played Wagner just as the Manchester band plays Berlioz: it knew the works instead of merely spelling through them at sight in the London fashion; and everybody must have been struck with the difference this made, even when the familiarity of the orchestra degenerated into vulgarity. Among the leading artists the one whose success is likely to have the greatest influence is undoubtedly Alvary. I do not mean that Alvary was the member of the company who had the largest share of direct natural gifts for the stage. In that case, his success would have been no more remarkable than that of Frau Klafsky, Fräulein Heink, or Lieban.

Van Dyck's eminence as a tenor is explained at once by his exuberant force and brilliancy, as Jean de Reszke's is by his romantic grace and distortion both of voice and person. Put either of them into a group of half a dozen barristers, and you would single them out at a glance as confidently as you would single out Salvini. Put Alvary there in his habit as he lives off the stage, and you would accept him without suspicion as a sufficiently barrister-istic person, well set up, but with no more of Siegfried about him than there would be of Hamlet about Mr Beerbohm Tree under the same circumstances. His voice is serviceable, but by no means beautiful; and in plucking Nothung from the Branstock, or forging it anew on Mime's anvil, he has no superfluity of physical power with which to exalt and play the Titan. And yet he held the attention and interest of the house whenever he was on the stage, and made a smart Loki, a pathetic Siegmund, and a remarkably handsome and picturesque Siegfried.

Wilkes,* who was one of the ugliest of mortals, used to boast that he was only quarter of an hour behind the handsomest man in Europe; and I can imagine Alvary boasting that, with nothing exceptional to help him except his brains, he could keep pace all through Der Ring with Van Dyck or De Reszke, perhaps falling five minutes behind the one in shouting over the sledge-hammer, and behind the other in singing *Winterstürme wichen dem Wonnemund,* but regaining his ground at other points, and holding his audience to the end as successfully as either of them. He has proved to us that as soon as the development of opera into genuine music drama makes the lyric stage attractive to clever and cultivated men, we shall no longer be dependent on prodigies.

Possibly some of my readers may prefer prodigies, thinking, no doubt, that they are all De Reszkes and

* John Wilkes was a controversial XVIII century political reformer and agitator.

Van Dycks; but if they had seen as much as I have of the results of picking up an Italian porter, or trooper, or gondolier, or ice-barrow costermonger who can shout a high C; thrusting him into heroic *rôles*; and sending him roaring round the world to pass in every capital over the prostrate body of lyric drama like a steam roller with a powerful whistle, they would understand the immense value I attach to the competition of artists like Alvary, who could not retain his place on the stage at all if he had nothing but his lungs to recommend him. The career is now opening to the talented; and the demand for artists of the Alvary type will increase with the number of our music dramas.

For you must not for a moment suppose that Wagner is going to be an isolated phenomenon in art. The peasant who, on hearing of Wordsworth's death, said he supposed his son would carry on the business, was not half such a fool as the man who imagines that the list of Bayreuth dramas closed with the death of Wagner. We have produced our Eschylus: our Sophocles and Aristophanes have yet to come; and very handsomely our Wagnerians will abuse them when they do come for violating the classic traditions of Wagner, and dispensing with his continual melody, his careful regard for form, and his effective but simple and quiet scoring.

ELAINE AND MADAME MELBA
The World, 3 August 1892

A long string of mishaps prevented me from hearing Mr Bemberg's Elaine until last Saturday week, when the second act somehow got omitted. The oversight passed unnoticed, however; and I cannot say that I was greatly disappointed: indeed, I should not have mentioned the circumstance if it did not form a practical criticism of the opera as distinct from its presentation, with which I shall, by your leave, not concern myself. Mr Bemberg is no English composer, but rather a music-weaver who, having served an apprenticeship to Gounod, and mastered his method of working, now sets up in business for himself. In Elaine we have the well-known Gounod fabric turned out in lengths like the best sort of imitation Persian carpet, the potential supply being practically unlimited.

There is one ballad, *L'Amour chaste comme la flamme*, which would probably never have been written if Gounod had not supplied the pattern in Mireille, but which is certainly a charming elaboration of the masters' suggestions. Mind, I do not hurl Mr Bemberg's want of originality at him as a reproach. One of the greatest artists the world has ever seen began in this very way. Raphael mastered Perugino's style before he developed his own. Mr Bemberg may yet leave Gounod as far behind as Raphael left Perugino. But there are no signs of his doing so yet.

I wonder how soon strong men in England will begin to take to musical composition. It cannot be said that the national genius is for the genteel, the sentimental, the elegant, the superficial. When I am asked to name a composer who is to England what Wagner is to Germany, I do not cite our elderly imitators of Spohr and Mendelssohn, or our youthful imitators of Gounod: I have to go back to Henry Purcell, whose Yorkshire Feast suggests that if he were alive today he might give us an English equivalent to Die Meistersinger.

Again, in what I may call epic or dramatic painting, I do not refer the inquiring foreigner to Mr Frank Dicksee, Mr Herbert Schmalz, Sir Noël Paton, or even Sir Frederick Leighton, as typical English painters: I send them to Mr Ford Madox Brown.* And I should certainly never dream of holding up Tennyson's poetry as the verse-mirror of the English spirit. It seems to me quite obvious that if our popular art was really the expression of the national character, England would long ago have been annexed as a convenient coaling station by Portugal. Fortunately, Englishmen take their business and their politics very differently from their art. Art in England is regarded as a huge confectionery department, where sweets are made for the eye and ear just as they are made for the palate in the ordinary "tuck-shop."

There is a general notion that painting tastes better before dinner, and music after it; but neither is supposed to be in the least nutritious. Too great a regard for them is held to be the mark of a weak character, or, in cases like those of Ruskin and Morris, of derangement due to genius. Under these circumstances we are kept well supplied with pretty things; but if we want really national music-dramas we shall have to take art seriously, or else wait for the advent of a genius big enough and strong enough to set himself against us all and cram his ideas down our throats, whether we like them or not.

I am obliged to Elaine for one thing in particular: it reconciled me to Madame Melba, who is to all intents and purposes a new artist this year. I do not mind confessing now that I used not to like her. Whilst recognizing the perfection of her merely musical faculty, I thought her hard, shallow, self-sufficient, and alto-gether unsympathetic. Further, she embarrassed me as a critic; since though I was utterly dissatisfied with her performances, I had nothing to allege against them; for

* Shaw admired Madox Brown as "the most dramatic of all painters," an Ibsenist realist, as contrasted with men like Leighton ("a mere gentleman draughtsman"). See Our Theatres in the Nineties (1931).

you really cannot take exception to an artist merely because her temperament does not happen to be sympathic with yours.

This year, however, I find Madame Melba transfigured, awakened, no longer to be identified by the old descriptions—in sum, with her heart, which before acted only on her circulation, now acting on her singing and giving it a charm which it never had before. The change has completely altered her position: from being merely a brilliant singer, she has become a dramatic soprano of whom the best class of work may be expected.

A little book on Wagner, just published by Messrs Kegan Paul & Co., should be bound up with every library copy of the late Ferdinand Praeger's very entertaining Wagner as I knew him. Mr Ashton Ellis's retort to Wagner as I knew him is practically "Yes; but you didnt know him." Praeger was never at any time able to take in more of Wagner than his natural size enabled him to hold, which was somewhat less than the whole man; and their acquaintanceship began rather later than Praeger, when at the height of his biographic fervor, quite realized.

At any rate, Mr Ellis shews that in the Dresden rising in 1849 Wagner, though he took his share of public duty by managing the business of escorting convoys into the town, and "conducting" the signaling, was not, like Bakoonin, what the Fenians used to call a "head centre" in the affair. The sensational incident of the woman falling shot, and Wagner heading a charge on the Prussian soldiers and capturing them, turns out to be just about as true as might have been expected: that is to say, the woman was not shot; the soldiers were not captured; and Wagner was not present; but the story is otherwise founded on fact. Mr Ellis straightens out the whole narrative very completely, and explains, for the benefit of those persons who have not the revolutionary temperament, how the German sovereigns, unable to conceive how monarchy would in the nature of things be constitutionally limited, forced all the best-informed and most public-spirited of their subjects to resist them.

To me Wagner's conduct needs no apology, since it is plain that every man who is not a Pangloss is bound to be in a state of incessant revolutionary activity all his life long if he wishes to leave things better than he finds them. However, there are unaccountable people who think otherwise; and to them I recommend Mr Ellis's Vindication. .Indeed, I recommend it to all English Wagnerians, who already owe more to its author than to any other man, except perhaps Mr Dannreuther. And when Mr Ellis's translation of Wagner's prose works, which has now reached the 1851 Mittheilung an meine Freunde, is complete, even Mr Dannreuther's claims must give way to those of the editor of The Meister.

THE NEW COMIC OPERAS
The World, 28 September 1892

The light operas which have been running for some time past at the Lyric and Trafalgar Square theatres did not succeed in moving me to break the autumn silence on their account. Cigarette is a work of uncertain *genre*, melodramatic and farcical in alternate episodes, except during one desperately melancholy moment in the second act, when Messrs Collette and Evelyn have to sing a duet with chorus, intended to be comic, but void to a quite stupefying degree of any passable nonsense or fun, not to say sense or humor. I must say that I like opera manufacturers to make up their minds as to the plane they are going to work on, and stick to it. The Marquis de Portale, disowning and cursing his son (who wants to marry for love) in a ranting exit speech of the best Wardour-street workmanship, is all very well in his way; and there is, perhaps, a place in the world for recruits comically labeled Benzoline and Nicotine, though I stipulate that the place shall not be in my neighborhood. Again, there is no general objection to church scenes with sacred music sung behind the scenes to the pealing of the solemn American organ. Nor do these exclude the possibility of Gaiety trios with step-dance refrains. But when the Marquis de Portale and Benzoline, the anthems and the step-dances, jostle oneanother on the same stage on the same evening, the effect, to my taste, is unseemly. And that is what occurs in Cigarette. Its aberrations into commonplace melodrama on the one hand, and unsuccessful burlesque on the other, may harmlessly divert our light opera audiences, which seem to me artistically less intelligent and less cultivated than even the big oratorio audiences at the Albert Hall and Crystal Palace; but they are not worth the powder and shot of serious criticism. The only member of the cast whose performance suggested any comment was Miss Florence Bankhardt, who has apparently had a training as a dancer, and is therefore in a better position than the ordinary comic opera *prima donna* who has had no training at all. Her playing as Cigarette was rather spoiled on the first night by restlessness and exaggeration; but if she has sufficient instinct for her profession to tranquillize her abundant energy and turn it to account in pursuit of softness and ease of style, there is no reason why she should not hold her own in parts like Cigarette.

The Wedding Eve, at the Trafalgar, is at least homogeneous in its triviality. It is much more smartly and tastefully mounted than Cigarette; and the leading parts are both better and better cast. Mr Tapley, whose powers as a tenor singer enabled him to gain a prominent position when he was still rather a rough diamond as to his carriage and diction, has now polished himself into one of the best artists in his line in London, and that, too, without losing the freshness and natural humor which put him on easy terms with his audiences from the first. Miss Decima Moore gets on very prettily in the part of Yvonette, her gift of good looks, good manners, facility, and tact carrying her through in spite of an occasional pettiness of touch and emptiness of play which shew how far she is from having attained the skill and breadth of style which mark the fully accomplished artist. The customary humors of comic opera abounded in the portion of The Wedding Eve which I witnessed; and there was no lack of choral young ladies, all dressed and wigged and complexioned alike, according to operatic custom, which seems to me to be stupid and thoughtless on this point. I would fine a chorus singer half-a-crown for looking like any other chorus singer. For the rest, the management of the new theatre is evidently liberal and tasty—if I may use that revolting expression for want of a substitute that will not overshoot the mark. Of the music of both Cigarette and The Wedding Eve I need say nothing except that it is as neat and plausible as anything in the shop windows of Bond-street. Mr Haydn Parry has supplied the score of the former, and M. Toulmouche that of the latter. Some dances in The Wedding Eve are by "Yvolde,"* a voluminous composer whose aliases are too numerous for mention here.

To a superficial person it may seem that my objection to a mixture of *genres* in opera has been most signally exploded by the huge success of Haddon Hall at the Savoy last Saturday. I do not admit this for a moment. I contend that Savoy opera is a *genre* in itself; and that

* Pseudonym of Hamilton Clarke, theatre and opera conductor, who composed operettas and symphonic works.

Haddon Hall is the highest and most consistent expression it has yet attained. This result is due to the critical insight of Mr Grundy. He is evidently a frequenter of Covent Garden; for he has discovered that what Italian opera desperately lacks is the classic element of comic relief. He has sat out the last acts of Lucia, and has felt, as I so often have myself, that what was wanted there was a comic Highlander with a fling, and a burlesque chorus to enliven the precepts of Raimondo.

He has then gone to the Savoy, and has seen that there, too, relief was wanted—sentimental relief generally, but anyhow relief from Mr Gilbert, whose great fault was that he began and ended with himself, and gave no really congenial opportunities to the management and the composer. He exploited their unrivaled *savoir faire* to his head's content; but he starved their genius, possibly because he did not give them credit for possessing any.

Now The Basoche and Haddon Hall prove that Mr and Mrs D'Oyly Carte have unmistakable genius for management: their stage pictures are as recognizable by the style alone as a picture by Watteau or Monticelli. You do not catch them spending ten guineas on two-penn'orth of show: they are at once munificent and economical, getting their full pound of beauty out of every yard of costly stuff on the stage. As to Sir Arthur Sullivan, he is certainly not a dramatic composer; but he has over and over again proved that in the sort of descriptive ballad which touches on the dramatic his gift is as genuine as that of Schubert or Loewe. In this province he excites a feeling which is as different as possible from the cynical admiration of his adroitness, his tact, his wit, and his professional dexterity, which is all that could ever be evoked by his settings of Mr Gilbert's aridly fanciful lyrics, whether for the stage or the drawing room.

All these observations have evidently been made by Mr Grundy, who has accordingly devized a unique entertainment, consisting of a series of charming stage pictures which at once put you in the mood to listen to episode after episode of descriptive ballad music, full of unforced feeling, and tenderly handled down to the minutest detail of their skilful and finished workmanship. After each of these episodes you are let down into indulgent boredom during a brief would-be dramatic number, in which the principals are consciously ridiculous, and the music suggestive of nothing but a storm in a tin pot. And then, just as you are beginning to feel dull and apprehensive of failure, comes the comic relief—the unspeakably outrageous but unspeakably welcome comic relief. The patter song which Mr Kenningham suddenly fired into the house from a masked battery in the form of a futile "dramatic" trio in the first act, produced, by its mere unexpectedness and contrast, an effect beyond the reach of Mr Grossmith.

Later on, the business of Mr Rutland Barrington and the comic Puritans, who are addicted to Stage Socialism (a very fearful variety), created uproarious merriment; and if Mr Rutland Barrington's elaborate japes on the land question fell somewhat flat, it was probably not so much because the joke was at the expense of the audience as because everybody had got accustomed during the late general election to hear better and fresher fun made out of the subject at every political meeting throughout the country. In the second act the comic business was less happy. The act began with it; so that it did not take the form of "relief"; and the hopes raised by the entrance of Mr Denny in a kilt, playing the bagpipes, were speedily dashed by the discovery that his Scotch dialect was spurious, and that Mr Grundy's treatment of the tempting theme of Social Purityism was cheap and witless, the duet, If we but had our way, being the least successful comic number in the opera.

It is always a mistake to undervalue our friend the enemy; and Mr Grundy had better recognize that unless his social satires are at least as smart as Mr Hugh Price Hughes's sermons, Mr Hughes will get the better of him. The real relief in this act occurs when Sir Arthur Sullivan takes up the running with his romantic setting of the elopement scene as a quartet, or rather as a descriptive ballad for four voices. (By the way, in the previous comic trio Hoity toity, the composer has reproduced the exact movement of For a British tar is a soaring soul from Pinafore, the notes alone being altered.) The following few minutes, during which the stage remains a black void, with hammer-and-tongs storm music and patent lightning flashes recurring with unerring precision in the same four spots, is merely an effective dodge to intensify the brilliancy of the ensuing ballroom scene, which is a Cartesian triumph.

It was the last act, however, which swept away all doubts as to the popular success of the opera. First, a sentimental duet for Mr Green and Miss Brandram brought down the nouse; and then the comic business became irresistible. A song for Mr Rutland Barrington, with a general dance in which he joins after a painful struggle with his conscience, was none the less triply encored because much the same thing had been seen in The Vicar of Bray. Yet it was no sooner over than it was eclipsed by the entry of Mr Denny, in breeks, to sing an absurdly funny musical burlesque of Auld Lang Syne, and dance, and dance again, and yet again—the *encores* seemed endless—a Highland fling, in which he was seconded with remarkable grace and *élan* by Miss Nita Cole. All the critics in the house exclaimed as one man that if something of this sort could be done at Covent Garden with the last act of La Favorita, Il Trovatore,

&c. &c., their lives would be indefinitely prolonged—which, by the bye, is an argument against the innovation.

Of the cast of established favorites I need say little more than that they fully sustained their reputations. Miss Lucile Hill's part is more difficult and less effective than that which she had in The Basoche, but her ability is no less conspicuous. Mr Courtice Pounds, costumed as a harmony in strawberries-and-cream, was nervously screwed up to the tenseness of a compressed spiral spring, in which condition he declared, with convulsive elocution, that Too-Wen'ty cousins should not interrupt his love-making. He also took his high notes flat; expressed his emotions facially in a manner extremely disconcerting to the spectators; and generally did himself injustice. These, however, were clearly mere first-night aberrations, the effect of an unblunted artistic sensitiveness; and he is no doubt by this time as good a John Manners as could be desired.

Mr Rutland Barrington was capital, though his compulsory lapses into melodrama tried the gravity of the audience as severely as they tried his own. If at such moments he were allowed to sing in Italian, the effect would be far finer. It only remains to warn the matter-of-fact theatre-goer that from the hour when, at the beginning of the piece, Sir George Vernon points to the XVI century *façade* of Haddon Hall, and remarks that it "smiled before the Conquest," to the final happy moment when Charles I., having beheaded Cromwell in 1680, or thereabout, restores the property to the evicted parent of the heroine, Haddon Hall, in history, costume, logic, and everything else of the kind, is perfectly impossible.

THE PASSING OF TREBELLI

The World, 5 October 1892

The recent death of Trebelli must not pass without a word of comment in this column, more especially as so many of the obituary notices contain descriptions of her singing which are purely imaginary. In her best days her voice was extraordinarily rich in the middle. Her tribute to Bella Venezia in the opening chorus of Lucrezia Borgia:

> *Men di sue notti e limpido*
> *D'ogn' altro cielo il giorno,*

sounded better than a ripe plum tastes, though the phrase lies round the middle of the treble stave, altogether above the point at which ordinary singers have to leave their chest register, on pain of displacing and ruining their voices. She produced contralto effects in mezzo-soprano and transposed soprano parts more successfully than in contralto parts, in one of which—Amneris, in Aïda—she ground her lower notes so unmercifully for the sake of "dramatic effect" that their old rich purple-velvety quality vanished irrecoverably.

This was one of many exploits of hers which seemed to prove her natural judgment much inferior to her cultivated taste; but I am afraid the truth was that the public were so obtuse to her finest qualities as an artist, and so appreciative of claptrap, that she either lost faith in herself at times, or else gave up the struggle with the public in despair. At Her Majesty's, as Cherubino or Zerlina, she would sing *Voi, che sapete*, or *Batti, batti*, transposed, but without a note altered or a phrase vulgarized, only to find herself written of with much less enthusiasm than Pauline Lucca at Covent Garden, whose treatment of Mozart was—well, I have spent five minutes in trying to find an epithet both adequate and decorous, without success. On the other hand, when, as Maffio Orsini, she turned the *brindisi* into a bad joke by that never-to-be-forgotten shake of hers, which was certainly the very worst shake ever heard in an opera house (it used to get sharper and sharper by perceptible jerks), she was encored and applauded to the echo. She liked Maffio, as she liked Siebel, Urbain, Arsaces, and all parts which freed her from the tyranny of the petticoat, of which, like most sensible women, she was impatient. She never seemed to lose her fresh enjoyment of these parts.

Once, happening to be behind the scenes at the end of the prologue to Lucrezia, I saw her, the moment the curtain fell, throw herself in a transport of excitement into the arms of Titiens, though the two had played the scene together often enough to make it the most hackneyed piece of business in the world to them. Trebelli was at her best in the most refined and quiet class of work. It is quite a mistake to suppose that she fell short as an oratorio singer. I have never heard her singing of He shall feed His flock surpassed: her diction alone put many of her English colleagues to shame. Her Cherubino, her Zerlina, and her Rezia in Oberon were criticism-proof. Her Carmen was, vocally, the most finished we have heard. In the tragic, passionate contralto parts in Verdi's operas she was not good: she played them out of imaginative ambition, just as she sang such things as Offenbach's *C'est l'Espagne* out of high spirits; but the result was commonplace and, by contrast with her fine Mozartean work, vulgar.

Unlike her daughter, she was deficient in agility of vocal execution, and could not manage a shake. She had also a certain mannerism which affected her intonation, and made her one of the many great artists who are always the piquant shadow of a shade out of tune—flat, as I judged it; though I confess that in very minute dissonances I cannot tell flat from sharp. She was, I should say, a much more cultivated musician than most of her colleagues; and she was an eminently goodlooking woman, with a ready smile that did full justice to her teeth. The collapse of the old *régime* at the opera caused the stage to leave her long before she was ready to leave the stage; and she was by no means worn out as a singer when physical infirmity, produced by a paralytic stroke which fell on her some years ago, created the vacancy which remained unfilled until Guilia Ravogli came.

Criticism, of course, knows no gratitude and no regret; but I must say that if all the artists of the Titiens epoch had been as good as Trebelli, my occasional references to that dark age would be much less ferocious than they generally are.

Of the late Emil Behnke I knew just enough to be able to say that his death is a considerable loss to teachers-in-training, speakers, and singers who find themselves stopped by a difficulty which they cannot get round. He was an exceedingly good demonstrator with the laryngoscope, and would shew you exactly what he wanted done instead of making more or less vague suggestions to your imagination. His scorn of the professors who tell you to sing from the head, or the throat, or the chest, or to pin your voice to your hard palate, was immense: he was justly proud of his ability to name with the exactitude of a watchmaker the movement and action he wished you to produce. He knew a great deal about the physical act of voice production; and his principal achievements were the relief of experienced singers from disabilities which their ordinary training had not overcome (or had created), and his cures of stammering.

Everybody who went to him learnt something, though

nobody learnt everything from him; and even those who knew beforehand what he demonstrated to them with the laryngoscope knew it much better afterwards. He was always keenly interested in himself and his work, and would talk about it, rush into controversies about it, and denounce the ordinary commercial singing-master up hill and down dale with unabated freshness at an age which finds most professional men stale routineers. Needless to add, he was not a popular character in academic circles. As to his artistic capacity, I confess I had and have my doubts about it. Besides his scientific interest in voice production, he undoubtedly had a strong practical turn, and hated to hear voices spoiled or wasted or only half turned to account. He wanted to have every throat in first-rate working order.

But whether he had that passion for perfect beauty of vocal tone and perfect dignity and expressiveness of delivery in singing which is the supreme attribute of the greatest singers and teachers of singing, I do not know, though I guess with some confidence that he had little more than the ordinary appetite for them. He once "sang" the notes of the common chord for me when shewing me the action of lifting the soft palate. He then got me to "sing" the same notes whilst he observed that action in me. I use the inverted commas because laryngoscopic vocalism can only be called singing by courtesy: as a matter of fact we simply bawled the syllable "Haw" at oneanother in a manner which would have created the utmost consternation in the theatre or on the platform.

I remember being struck by the fact that though he seemed interested by my success in managing my soft palate, he did not make any comment on the extreme unloveliness of the noise with which I had responded to his invitation to sing, which he had not qualified by any allusion to the impossibility of my complying in the artistic sense under such conditions. The incident by itself proved nothing; but it put me on the track of further observations, which finally left me under the impression (possibly a mistaken one) that his authority was limited to the physical acts involved by ordinary voice production, and did not extend even to the modifications of those acts which have no reasons for their existence except purely artistic ones.

For instance, he had made an elaborate study of breathing, and could teach people to use their diaphragms; but I once heard a pupil of his who had her diaphragm under perfect control, and who yet blew away her voice in the most ineffective way as she sang, because she had not been taught to acquire that peculiar steadying and economizing of the air column which is the first condition of beauty of tone in singing. I am therefore skeptical as to Behnke's having ever trained a complete artistic singer or speaker; though many singers and speakers learnt a good deal from him. I was so convinced on the latter point that at the moment of his death I had arranged with him to take in hand a class of about twenty political speakers, some of whom had already acquired sufficient skill and experience to enable them to teach an ordinary elocution professor his business.

Perhaps the most important thing to make known about Behnke is, that though he elected to take his differences with the majority fighting instead of lying down, and so made enemies of many whose countenance is supposed to be indispensable to musical success, he prospered, as far as I am able to ascertain, quite as well as his more compliant rivals. Although his terms were higher than any but first-rate teachers can venture to ask in these days of Guildhall Schools and Royal Colleges, he was overworked. His Voice Training Exercises sold at the rate of over eight thousand copies a year; and his Mechanism of the Human Voice got into a seventh edition, whilst the better advertized book which he wrote in collaboration with Dr Lennox Browne nearly doubled that record.

It may be, of course, that London, according to its custom with professional men, gave with one hand and took back with the other, and that all the return he got for his labor over and above his bare subsistence was the privilege of collecting money for his landlord, his servants, his tradesmen, and so forth. But this is the common lot of the orthodox and the heterodox alike. My point is that he had not to pay any more for his self-respect than less courageous men have to pay for being humbugs and nonentities. It is a mistake to be too much afraid of London merely because it is much stronger and much stupider than you are, just as it is a mistake to be too much afraid of a horse on the same ground. Behnke, I imagine, was shrewd and resolute enough to know this.

His death is a real loss; for on his weak side (as I judge him) he at least did no mischief, whilst on his strong side he undid a great deal. Besides, he ventilated his profession, which is, if I may say so in a whisper, rather a stuffy one.

INCOGNITA

The World, 12 October 1892

Now that we have five comic operas running, London perhaps feels satisfied. I, for one, do not want any more. Sufficient for me the privilege of living in the greatest city in the world, with five comic operas within easy reach, and not a symphony to be heard for love or money. However, it is a poor heart that never rejoices;

and I have been doing my best to rejoice at the Royalty over The Baroness, and at the Lyric over Incognita. To Incognita especially I must be civil; for is it not financed by that great syndicate which has set about buying up the London press as the Viennese press has been bought up? Do not expect outspoken criticism from me in such days as these: I cannot afford it: I must look to the future like other journalists. Therefore the utmost I dare say against Incognita is that the more you see of it the less you like it, because the first act is better than the second, and the second much better than the third, which produces the effect of being the first act of some other comic opera. The piece has a plot turning upon some maze of Portuguese diplomacy; but I speedily lost my way in it, and made no attempt to extricate myself, though I was conscious of its boring me slightly towards the end of the performance. The music is quite Lecocquian: that is to say, it is cleverly scored, rises occasionally to the level of a really graceful chansonette, is mechanically vigorous in the *finales*, and calculatedly spirited in the frequent Offenbachian rallies, for which the old quadrille and galop prescription has been compounded with the old remorseless vulgarity. It is also Lecocquian in the speedy running dry of its thin fountain of natural grace and piquancy, and the eking out of the supply with machine-like *bouffe* music more and more as the opera proceeds. This remark does not apply to the third act, which is not by Lecocq at all, but by Mr Bunning, who, if I recollect aright, recently had a most tremendous tragic *scena* performed at the Crystal Palace by Mr Hamilton Clarke; and by the composer who conceals his identity under the exasperating name of Yvolde.* I may add that the pretty stage pictures of the first act degenerate into the pecuniary garishness of the second in sympathy with the degeneration of the

* See II, 691 n.

[702]

music; and with this I abandon all attempt at formal criticism, and proceed to discuss the affair at random.

To begin with Miss Sedohr Rhodes, she made all the usual American mistakes. First, by a well-worked battery of puff, she led us to expect so much from her that an angel from the spheres would have disappointed us; and then she arranged an elaborate handing up of floral trophies across the footlights, in spite of the repeatedly proved fact that this particular method of manufacturing a success invariably puts up the back of an English audience. I have never seen the American flower show turned to good account by any *prima donna* except Miss Macintyre. One evening at Covent Garden, when she was playing Micaela to the Carmen of an American *débutante*, the two ladies appeared before the curtain simultaneously; and the contractor's men set to work at once to deliver bouquets and wreaths. Carmen, overwhelmed with innocent surprise at this spontaneous tribute from the British public, gracefully offered a nosegay to Micaela, who quietly turned her back and walked off the stage amid signs of thorough and general approval which ought to have settled the question of flowers or no flowers for all future American *prima donnas*. On Thursday night Miss Rhodes, though she entirely failed to make herself first favorite on the merits of her performance, got so overloaded with trophies that she had to ask Mr Wallace Brownlow to carry the last basket for her. He, being goodnatured, did not there and then inform her publicly that he was not her florist's porter; but if he had done so he would, I imagine, have had the entire support of the house. The puffs and the flowers were the more ill-judged in Miss Rhodes's case because she had exactly that degree of talent which playgoers, with cheap generosity, like to discover and encourage when it is modestly and friendlessly presented to them, wheras if it be thrust pretentiously upon them as first-rate, they delight in taking it down a peg.

When Miss Rhodes stepped out of her sedan chair in the first act she was for a few moments a complete success; for, with her delicate skin, fine contours, slender fragile figure, small hands and feet, and perfect dress, she was sufficiently near the perfection of the ladylike ideal of beauty. Unfortunately, it presently appeared that she not only looked like a Court beauty, but sang like one. Her voice, thin, and with a flexibility which is only a quality of its fault, could not be fitted by her warmest admirer with any stronger adjective than prettyish. In order to substantiate her pretensions as a vocalist, she had to attempt a florid vocal waltz which was much too difficult for her, and which was only encored from a chivalrous desire to console her for the opposition of a party of malcontents who were, I must say, musically in the right, though they would have done wiselier to have kept silent. Her dancing, again, was rather pretty, but not extraordinary. She speaks in the American dialect, which I do not at all dislike; but her diction, though passable, has all the amateurish deficiency in force and style which we tolerate so weakly in our operatic *prima donnas.* On the other hand, the assurance with which she carried off her part in spite of her want of technical grip, and the courage with which she faced the opposition from the gallery, shewed that she is not lacking in force of character. I therefore conclude that she will improve with experience up to a certain point. To pass that point she will require something of the genius for her profession which is displayed so liberally by Miss Jenoure, who quite fulfilled the promise of her performance in The Mountebanks. Her singing, from the purely musical point of view, is commonplace enough; but her dancing and pantomime are capital. Mr Wallace Brownlow made a very decided hit as the hero. He is a vigorous and handsome young man of the type which Kemble made fashionable in "the palmy days"; his voice is a genuine baritone, of good tone all over his range; he sings with fire and feeling, without any suicidal shouting; and he has abundant freshness, virility, humor, and activity. What he lacks is training in speech and movement: he is always off his balance, and is therefore only comfortable when he is hard at work at some stage business or other; and his diction is rough and ready, audible and intelligible certainly, but no more artistic than the diction of the Stock Exchange. Happily, these are eminently remediable faults; and when they are vanquished, Mr Hayden Coffin will have a rival all the more formidable because of the wide difference of style between them.

The tenor is Mr John Child, whose vigorous B flat will be remembered by the patrons of Carl Rosa. It is still in stentorian condition; and though Mr Childs has a strong provincial tendency to bawl occasionally (if he will pardon the expression) and to concern himself very little about his tone and style when using the middle of his voice, the *encore* he won for the catching soldier's song in the first act was the heartiest of the evening. The opera is so strongly fortified by a squadron of comedians of established drollery and popularity that a great deal of thin and childish stuff becomes amusing in their hands. Mr Monkhouse, who has gained remarkably within the last two years in quietude and refinement of play without losing an inch of the breadth of his humor, was seconded by Miss Susie Vaughan in a stale and odious duenna part which she contrived to make not only bearable, but for the most part genuinely funny. The attempt to double the harlequinade in the third act by the introduction of a second comic king (Mr Fred Kaye) and a second comic old woman (Miss Victor) was not a success. Mr Kaye was certainly laughable in his surpassingly silly character; but Miss Victor, who had really no function in the piece at all, and had been engaged solely that she might repeat the vulgar business of her part in Miss Decima—a part entirely unworthy of her—cannot be congratulated this time.

The whole third act, however, is such a desperate and obvious makeshift that it would be mere affectation not to accept it, with its serpentine dance, pastoral symphony with transformation scene, and comic turns for Mr Monkhouse as a gypsy girl, &c., as a brilliant variety entertainment. The band is good, as it usually is at the Lyric; and the chorus, though not up to the Savoy level of refinement, would pass with credit if some of the men could be induced to refrain from shouting. Finally, let me say that the Lord Chamberlain, by licensing the second act of Miss Decima, has completely cleared himself of all suspicion of Puritanical intolerance. When I saw the audience laughing at the spectacle of a father, in nightcap and bedgown, chuckling as he listened at the door of his daughter's bridal chamber, I could not help feeling how vast an advance we had made since last year, when all London was supposed to have shuddered with horror at the wickedness of that scene in Ibsen's Ghosts, where the mother in the drawing room overhears her son kissing the housemaid in the dining room.

Mr Cotsford Dick's Baroness, at the Royalty, is not so well staged as Incognita, the management having evidently been compelled to accept what recruits they could get for the rank and file in the face of a heavy competition. On the whole, they have made the best of their circumstances; and the opera gets a tolerable chance. The book, which begins as a burlesque of King Lear, and proceeds on the lines of the Who's who? pattern of farce, is funny enough, especially in the Turkish-bath scene, until the third act, in which the tangled threads of the plot are unravelled in a rather butter-fingered way. The fact is, Mr Cotsford Dick, who is his own librettist, takes matters too easily and genially to turn out distinguished work; but he always manages to keep on pleasant terms with his audience. The music is lively and pretty, with plenty of Cotsford-Dickian ballads, and much unblushing borrowings from The Mikado and Trial by Jury, not to mention a vocal waltz of which the honors are divided between Gounod and Weber. The verses I need not describe, as Mr Dick's powers in that field are familiar to all my readers. The cast has been selected with a view to having the music sung rather than to having the opera played. Miss Giglio, who makes a considerable display as a vocalist, and is evidently quite conscious of being able to sing the heads off most comic-opera *prima donnas*, hardly seems to know that speech and action on the stage are arts not a whit less important and less difficult than fluent vocalization. Mr William Foxon, too, though rather above the usual stage mark as a tenor singer, is, to speak plainly, such a stick that it is difficult to believe that he has ever seriously studied and practised the business of the stage with a competent instructor. The principal tenor, Mr Charles Conyers, is an agreeably robust and good-looking young gentleman, no great artist dramatically, but a pleasant singer of ballads. Mr Magrath, familiar to us as the old knight in Così fan tutte and the venerable barber of Bagdad in Cornelius's opera, flashes out in The Baroness as a dark-eyed handsome youth who might serve the President of the Royal Academy as a model for a young Italian noble. He was much more nervous over this comparatively trivial job than he shewed himself in his former far more difficult exploits; and his air of melodramatic exaggeration was not always humorously intentional: there was a touch in it of that traditional penny-plain-and-twopence-colored style which has left so many promising young artists fit for nothing better than the boundless absurdities and artistic shams of "English Opera" in the provinces. His drinking song in the last act was loudly applauded; but it would have been a much greater success if it had been sung with the easy self-possession of a gentleman at a ball, and not with the heroic stress of John of Leyden's *Versez* in the last act of Le Prophète. I take Mr Magrath the more specially to task on this point because he has improved in every other respect, and is likely to have an honorable career if he shuns the burnt-cork path along which I have seen so many well-equipped aspirants go down to their destruction. The fun of the opera was kept up vigorously by Mr Lionel Brough, Mr Fred Emney, Mr George Grossmith, junior, and Mr Charles Stevens, a comedian whom I last saw, if I mistake not, at Bristol, where he was for some years a leading member of Mr Macready Chute's company.

I am informed that three other comic operas are in contemplation, in addition to the five already in full swing. I can quite believe it. The one business notion that theatrical managers have is that when the bank flourishes, then is the time to make a run on it.

VISITING THE HALLS

The World, 19 October 1892

On Saturday last the Crystal Palace concerts came to relieve the musical famine. Before saying anything about the music, I may point out that a move has been made at last in the direction of reducing the expenses of attending these concerts. Hitherto the bill has been made up in the following way: railway ticket, two shillings first-class (saving by second-class not worth

making, and third-class barred on special concert train);
program, sixpence; admission to Palace, half-a-crown;
admission to concert room, one shilling, or for a
numbered stall half-a-crown, reducible to two-and-a-
penny-fifthing by booking in advance for the whole
twenty concerts: total, five-and-sixpence at least, and
seven-and-sixpence at most, without counting a probable visit to the tea room for persons addicted to that
deleterious fluid. These charges are absolutely prohibitive for four out of five Londoners; and regular
frequenters of the concerts are, consequently, very
scarce outside the ranks of the season-ticket holders
resident in the neighborhood of the Palace.

In general social value the free orchestral concerts
given on other afternoons, with a smaller band, are
probably much more important than the Saturday ones.
This season, however, the railway companies have
consented to issue twenty first-class return tickets from
London to the Palace, available on concert Saturdays
only, for a guinea to holders of the two-guinea serial stall
tickets. By this arrangement I shall save nineteen
shillings if I go to all the concerts; and even if I only go
to one more than half of them, I shall still save a shilling.
A further concession has been made in favor of those
families who take one or two serial stall tickets and
transfer them from one member of the household to
another according to tastes, circumstances, and the
fortunes of the weekly war for their possession. By
paying an additional guinea the transferable stall ticket
can be made to carry with it admission to the Palace,
which formerly involved twenty separate half-crowns,
since the ordinary guinea season ticket is not transferable.

I make no apology for dwelling on these financial
arrangements. It has always been evident to people who
understand the importance of these concerts, that their
utility is far too much restricted by the necessity of

making charges which cut off, not only the shilling public, but the half-crown public as well. If Mr Irving, Mr Tree, Mr Hare, &c., were to raise the prices at their theatres to a minimum of five-and-sixpence, the stupidest citizen would see that we should have either to endow a theatre or else face the consequences of leaving the mass of the people without any higher dramatic recreation than such as they might extract from the excitement of playing the very mischief by using their votes without the smallest regard to the vital necessity of maintaining a high general level of artistic culture in a country rapidly becoming entirely democratized.

Even as it is, with the Lyceum gallery accessible daily for a shilling, people are asking for an endowed theatre, because the social need for art of the highest order is so inadequately expressed by the effective commercial demand for it: our Philistines being able easily to outbid our Idealists and Realists combined for the use of all the capital that is available for dramatic enterprise. Still, London is never left absolutely without dramatic performances, as it so commonly is without concerts. You can go to the theatre every weekday all the year round; but when there is an orchestral concert once a fortnight in St James's Hall, music is supposed to be in full swing, whilst such a concert once a week indicates the height of the season.

What we want in London is an orchestral concert *every day*, with permanent engagements and pensions for the conductors and players, among whom there should be, in each division, competent soloists, each playing solo once a week or so. Concertos should, on all ordinary occasions, be played by members of the orchestra, and not by wandering "stars" who pay an agent a lump sum to foist them off for three or six months on givers of concerts and parties as distinguished *virtuosos*. All masterpieces should be rehearsed up to

[710]

that point of intimate knowledge which the Manchester band has attained in its Berlioz repertory; and this should be insisted on whether the work in hand were a trifle by Grieg, requiring two or three days' attention, or the Ninth Symphony, requiring two years (*à la* Habeneck).

I say this with deep feeling; for I protest that if there is anything of which I am heartily sick, it is the London no-rehearsal system, under which, with the best players in the world, equipped with the best instruments in the world, we have orchestras that read everything and know nothing; so that the moment we are confronted by works which can only be played properly by a band thoroughly obsessed with every melody and every accent in the score, we are beaten and disgraced not only by our provincial rivals from Manchester, but by a second-rate German band from Hamburg, which supersedes us in our own leading opera house.

I do not make these remarks *à propos de bottes.* A gentleman of benefactorious disposition has offered to endow the Albert Palace to the tune of £10,000. Let us suppose that the Vestry, the County Council, &c., rise to the occasion and complete the endowment of the Palace. It will then remain for some musical millionaire to eclipse all the rest by endowing an Albert Palace orchestra on the lines I have suggested. Who speaks first?

Meanwhile I am forgetting the Crystal Palace concert, which introduced to us two novelties: to wit, Mr C. A. Lidgey's Ballade for Orchestra, Op. 7, after Doré's picture A Day Dream, and Les Lupercales, by André Wormser, the composer of L'Enfant Prodigue. M. Wormser's "symphonic poem" (save the mark) occasionally rises, at second hand, to the level of Offenbach's Orphée. There is one little dance tune in the style of L'Enfant which is tolerable: the rest, with its sham

Greek modes which are simply minor scales without leading notes, is vulgar, noisy, and, except in the dance tunes, ingeniously ugly. Mr Lidgey's Ballade is much better. The first section is very successful in point of form (in the real as distinguished from the common, academic sense of the term). It is well balanced, all of one piece, with gathering movement and a strong climax. But it has no special originality or distinction—if it had, Mr Lidgey would have ranked as an eminent composer after its performance. When the double bar is passed the composition falls off, the working out containing a good deal of stale imagination and instrumentation, and the tremendous outlay of organ and orchestra on the peroration adding nothing to the value of the theme on which it is lavished. Vladimir de Pachmann, pianist and pantomimist, played Beethoven's third concerto and some Chopin, including a juvenile *scherzo* which nobody wanted to hear at full length at five o'clock in the afternoon. De Pachmann is unquestionably a very able pianist, and by no means an insincere one; but now that I have seen, in La Statue du Commandeur, a lady sing a song in dumb show, I want to see a pianoforte concerto played in the same way; and I think there can be no doubt that de Pachmann is the player for that feat. The concert opened with Sullivan's In Memoriam overture, substituted for a number from one of Bach's suites.

Now that the new English Opera House is about to be turned into a music hall, and that the Theatre of Varieties is supposed to be swallowing up all other theatres, I have resolved to keep myself up to date by visiting the halls occasionally. The other evening I went to the Empire, where I immediately found myself, to my great delight, up to the neck in pure classicism, *siècle de Louis Quatorze*. To see Cavallazzi, in the Versailles ballet, walk, stand, sit, and gesticulate, is to learn all that

Vestris or Noblet★ could have taught you as to the technique of doing these things with dignity.

In the stage management too—in the coloring, the costuming, the lighting, in short, the stage presentation in the completest sense—an artistic design, an impulse towards brilliancy and grace of effect, is always dominant, whether it is successful or not; and in some scenes it is highly successful. Now is it not odd that at a music hall to which, perhaps, half the audience have come to hear Marie Lloyd sing Twiggy voo, boys, twiggy voo? or to see Mr Darby jump a ten-barred gate, you get real stage art, wheras at the Opera the stage is managed just as a first-rate restaurant is managed, with everything served up punctually in the most expensive style, but with all the art left to the cook (called *"prima donna"*), helped by the waiters (otherwise the chorus).

Wagner noticed long ago that the supremacy of the ballet masters, who are all enthusiasts in the ballet, made it the most completely artistic form of stage representation left to us; and I think that anyone who will compare Versailles at the Empire with Orfeo at Covent Garden from this point of view, will see what Wagner was driving at, and what I have driven at pretty often without any further effect so far than to extract from my friends many goodnatured but entirely irrelevant assurances that our operatic *impresarios* are the best fellows in the world when you come to know them. As to which

★ Malvina Cavallazzi, Italian dancer, had performed in London since 1879. She later directed a ballet school at the Metropolitan Opera, New York. Teresa Vestris (1726–1808) was a member of the famed Italian dancing family, performing spectacularly with two of her brothers at the Paris Opéra in the mid-XVIII century. Lise Noblet (1801–52), elegant French dancer who appeared in London 1821–4, created many important *rôles* in French ballets, and was a notable performer of Spanish dances.

[713]

I may observe that I am a capital fellow myself when you come to know me.

One performance at the Empire exhibited the audience to pitiful disadvantage. A certain Señorita C. de Otero, described as a Spanish dancer and singer, danced a dance which has ennobled the adjective "suggestive" for me forever. It was a simple affair enough, none of your cruel Herodias dances, or cleverly calculated tomboyish Tararas, but a poignant, most meaning dance, so intensely felt that a mere walk across the stage in it quite dragged at one's heartstrings. This Otero is really a great artist. But do you suppose the house rose at her? Not a bit of it: they stared vacantly, waiting for some development in the manner of Miss Lottie Còllins, and finally grumbled out a little disappointed applause. Two men actually hissed—if they will forward me their names and addresses I will publish them with pleasure, lest England should burst in ignorance of its greatest monsters.

Take notice, oh Señorita C. de Otero, Spanish dancer and singer, that I wash my hands of the national crime of failing to appreciate you. You were a perfect success: the audience was a dismal failure. I really cannot conceive a man being such a dull dog as to hold out against that dance. Shall it be said that though Miss Collins could stimulate us cleverly but mechanically, Otero, an immeasurably greater artist, cannot touch us poetically? If so, then let the nations know that dancing in England is measured simply by the brightness of the scarlet and the vigor of the kicking. But I wax too eloquent.

There was a second ballet, called Round the Town, mostly mere drill and topical spectacle, plus a few excellent pantomimic episodes in which Cavallazzi again distinguished herself, as did also Mr W. Warde, a skilful and amusing comic dancer, who played the swell (archaic name for a Johnny). Vincenti has given up the British public in despair, and treats them to unlimited cartwheels and teetotums instead of to the fine classic dancing he used to give us in Asmodeus. Both ballets, I may remark, became tedious at the end through the spinning-out of the final scenes by mechanical evolutions involving repeats in the music almost beyond endurance.

One other performer must not go unnoticed. Miss Marie Lloyd, like all the brightest stars of the music hall, has an exceptionally quick ear for both pitch and rhythm. Her intonation and the lilt of her songs are alike perfect. Her step-dancing is pretty; and her command of coster-girls' *patois* is complete. Why, then, does not someone write humorous songs for her? Twiggy voo is low and silly; and Oh, Mister porter, though very funnily sung, is not itself particularly funny. A humorous rhymester of any genius could easily make it so.

I am greatly afraid that the critics persisted so long in treating the successes of music hall vocalism as mere impudent exploitations of vulgarity and indecency (forgetting that if this were more than half true managers could find a dozen Bessie Bellwoods and Marie Lloyds in every street) that the artists have come to exaggerate the popularity of the indecent element in their songs, and to underrate that of the artistic element in their singing. If music hall songs were written by Messrs Anstey, Rudyard Kipling, W. S. Gilbert, &c., our best music hall singers would probably be much more widely popular than they can ever become now. Twiggez vous, Miss Lloyd?

A LAGO SEASON

The World, 26 October 1892

It is impossible not to sympathize with the devotion of Signor Lago to the romance and adventure of opera management. When I was a boy I took that view of opera myself: the wildest pirates and highwaymen in fiction did not fascinate me more than the *prima donnas* in Queens of Song, nor could the pictures of their deeds and the tales of their exploits please me as did Heath's gift books with decorative borders and operatic *tableaux*, or the anecdotes in that quite inimitable work, Sutherland Edwards's History of the Opera, which I take to be the most readable book of its kind ever written. I have lived to become the colleague, and to all appearances considerably the senior of Mr Sutherland Edwards; and I tired long ago of paying at the Opera doors and then supplying all the charm of the performance from my own imagination, in flat defiance of my eyes and ears.

Yet I still remember the old feeling of the days when the Opera was a world of fable and adventure, and not a great art factory where I, with wide open eyes and sharpened ears, must sit remorselessly testing the quality of each piece of work as it is turned out and submitted to my judgment. I read Wagner now, and take the theatre seriously to make amends for my youthful profligacy; and I am tremendously down on the slovenly traditions of the old school when they survive apart from its romantic illusions and enthusiasm; but when it survives in such integrity as is possible under existing circumstances, I cannot always bring myself to be hard upon it.

And that is why I always approach a Lago season in

an indulgent humor. I know that the atmosphere of the stage will be one of perfect freedom; so that every individual thereon, down to the hindmost chorister, will be welcome, released from control or direction of any kind, to give the rein to his or her individual genius. I also know that the choristers, hindmost and foremost, will have no individual genius to give the rein to, and that they will stand and look on at the principals, criticizing their solos, and trusting to me as one who has known many of their faces for years, and who ought therefore to be glad to see them all there again, not to try to get the bread taken out of their mouths by a lot of new-fangled girls from the Savoy with Cambridge certificates.

I know, further, that the treasury will not run to downright splendor in the way of dresses and scenery, and that the ballet will have to be made the best of by kind friends in front. In short, that, as in the old times, unless the principal singers are good enough to triumph for the moment over surroundings which at every turn defeat the efforts of the imagination to produce a gratuitous illusion, there will be virtually no opera. I am not sorry to see that the power of the younger generation of critics to put up with these hard conditions is comparatively small, leading them to greatly underrate the value of the Italian operas of the old repertory which they more especially associate with such conditions; but to me submission is not so difficult; for I was broken in to the system when young, and can get back only too easily to my old attitude and concentrate my attention wholly on consent to do this at Covent Garden, where the public position of the enterprise, its pretensions, and the prices charged entitle me to demand that the performances shall in all respects set the highest European standard; but with Signor Lago, playing to his two-shilling pit and shilling gallery, and frankly offering his entertainment on the old lines, I do not feel bound to be so strict.

Besides, Signor Lago discovered Giulia Ravogli and Cavalleria, and in due course had these trumps annexed by his rival, and played against him on his opening night. Who would not sympathize with him under such circumstances?

Eugene Onegin, his latest card, reminded me, I hardly know why, of The Colleen Bawn. Something in the tailoring, in the scenery, in the sound of the hero's name (pronounced O'Naygin, or, to put it in a still more Irish way, O'Neoghegan) probably combined with the Balfian musical form of the work to suggest this notion to me. There is something Irish, too, as well as Byronic, in the introduction of Eugene as an uncommonly fine fellow when there is not the smallest ground for any such estimate of him. The music suggests a vain regret that Tchaikovsky's remarkable artistic judgment, culture, imaginative vivacity, and self-respect as a musical workman should have been unaccompanied by any original musical force. For, although I have described the form of the opera as Balfian, it must not therefore be inferred that Tchaikovsky's music is as common as Balfe's—ballads apart—generally was. Tchaikovsky composes with the seriousness of a man who knows how to value himself and his work too well to be capable of padding his opera with the childish claptrap that does duty for dramatic music in The Bohemian Girl. Balfe, whose ballads are better than Tchaikovsky's, never, as far as I know, wrote a whole scene well, wheras in Eugene Onegin there are some scenes, notably those of the letter and the duel, which are very well written, none of them being bungled or faked (factitious is the more elegant expression; but the other is right). The opera, as a whole, is a dignified composition by a man of distinguished talent whose love of music has led him to adopt the profession of composer, and who, with something of his countryman Rubinstein's disposition to make too much of cheap second-hand musical material, has nothing of his diffuseness, his occasional vulgarity, and his incapacity for seeing when to drop a worn-out theme.

The performance, as far as the principals are concerned, is by no means bad. Signor Lago was particularly fortunate in finding to his hand, in Mr Oudin, just the man for Onegin, dark, handsome, distinguished, mysterious-looking—in short, Byronic, and able to behave and to act in a manner worthy of his appearance, which is not always the case with the Don Juans and Corsairs of the stage. Miss Fanny Moody achieved a considerable dramatic success as Tatiana; and it may possibly interest her to learn, on the authority of no less critical a Russian than Stepniak,* that she so exactly represented the sort of Russian woman of whom Tatiana is a type, that he is convinced that she would make a success in the part in Russia, even if she sang it in English. To my mind, however, it is a pity that Miss Moody's gifts are so exclusively dramatic. If she were only musical—if she could give that hard, penetrating voice of hers the true lyric grace of execution and beauty of sound as unerringly as she can give it convincing dramatic eloquence, she would be a *prima donna* in a thousand. Happily for Signor Lago, he could not have chosen a part better calculated than Tatiana to emphasize her power as an actress and cover her want of charm as a vocalist. Mr Manners scored the hit of the evening in a ballad in the last act, the audience being, to tell the truth, greatly relieved after a long spell of Mr Oudin's

* Sergius Stepniak, a nihilist who had settled in London, was active in the Socialist movement until his accidental death in 1895.

rather artificial style by the free, natural, sympathetic tone of Mr Manners's voice, which is as sound and powerful as ever. Mr Ivor McKay, having been shot with a terrific bang, produced by a heavy charge of anything but smokeless powder, by Mr Oudin, retired from the tenor part, which is now filled by Mr Wareham: how, I know not. Madame Swiatlowsky is good and very Russian as the nurse; and Mlle Selma fits well into the part of the mother. Miss Lily Moody, a vigorous young lady with a strong mezzo-soprano voice which has not been sweetened by her work as a dramatic contralto, is a somewhat inelegant Olga.

The stage management was, I submit, rather worse than it need have been. Granted that there is nobody capable of making the willing but helpless chorus do anything in the quarrel scene except make it ridiculous, and that the two capital dances are utterly beyond the resources of the establishment, I still think that the gentleman, whoever he was, who loaded that pistol with so fine a feeling for the stage effect of the duel, might, if promoted to the post of chief gasman, manipulate the lights so as to make the change from dark to dawn in the letter scene rather more plausible than on the first night. The dresses were quite good enough for all purposes; but the supply ran short, the dancers at Madame Larina's in Act II reappearing in the same costumes at Prince Gremin's in Act III. Onegin fought the duel in a dark coat with two rows of blazing golden buttons, which made him a perfect target; and he would most certainly have been slain if he had not fired first. Years afterwards he came back, a grey-haired man, to make love in that same coat. In fact, Signor Lago might have made a "missing-word competition" out of Onegin's exclamation "I change from one land to another, but cannot change my ——." The missing word is "heart," but would be guessed as "coat" by nine-tenths of the audience. This scrap from the book reminds me that Mr Sutherland Edwards, who knows Russian, has expiated that unnatural accomplishment by translating the libretto, the most impossible of literary tasks, but one which he has managed, with his usual tact, to accomplish without making himself at all ridiculous. Onegin is now being played three times a week; and it is to be hoped that it will pay its way for the better encouragement of Signor Lago in his policy of bringing forward novelties.

La Favorita was played on the following night; but I forebore it. I saw an act and a half of Lohengrin on Saturday, and can certify that the pit got handsome value for its money, although they would do it differently at Bayreuth. Signor Zerni, the tenor, is a representative of that modern Gayarrean school which has raised bleating to the rank of a fine art throughout Europe. He has been carefully warned to keep his voice as steady as the nature of his method will permit; and this he does with sufficient success to save himself from the fate of Suane, Signor Lago's last venture in that manner. Mr Manners will make a good king when he has become thoroughly familiar with the part; and Signor Mario Ancona, as Telramund, is exceptionally good as Telramunds go in London.

Mr Worlock, too, is by no means an everyday herald; and on the whole, if there were only somebody to make the chorus look alive occasionally, especially at the entry of Lohengrin; if Signor Lago would urge the choristers to either let their beards grow or not, but by no means to shave only once a week; and if, further, some of the band would follow the example of Albani, who plays Elsa as scrupulously and carefully as ever she did on the most brilliant night at Covent Garden in the regular season, Signor Lago would be able to boast of having pulled the biggest opera on his list very creditably off. Arditi conducted. Onegin, by the bye, was conducted by Mr Henry J. Wood, who did his work steadily, and, as far as my acquaintance with the music enabled me to judge, chose the *tempi* well; but he did not succeed in getting any really fine execution out of the band, which does not play at all as well as it could if it liked.

Slivinski, who stepped in to replace Paderewski (laid up with rheumatic fever) at Manchester, gave a recital last week at St James's Hall. The altogether extraordinary degree of technical accomplishment displayed by him during his last visit has had its edge very perceptibly taken off by, as I guess, too much drawing room playing, and perhaps by yielding to squeamish complaints of the swordsmanlike quality of his touch.

However that may be, he has certainly been cultivating the feathery execution which Paderewski sometimes uses for Chopin studies; and though he is too skilful a player to attempt any style without some success, he has lost more in force and distinction than he has gained in softness and prettiness. Also he has contracted a habit of slurring over—indeed, all but dropping—the unaccented notes in rapid passages. This was more or less noticeable all through the recital; but when he came to Liszt's transcription of Schubert's Auf dem Wasser zu singen, with its exquisite accompaniment of repeated semiquavers, the ticking of the second semiquavers was not heard until they were played as chords instead of single notes. His deficiency in eloquence of style was very apparent in his playing of that touching and dignified piece of musical rhetoric, Schubert's Impromptu in C minor, which he quite misconceived.

In Schumann's Fantasiestücke, which he played right through all the numbers, he was very good, except in the first, which he gave with a *rubato* which had the worst fault a *rubato* can have—that of sounding as if the pianist, vainly trying to play in strict time, were being baffled by the sticking of the keys. But on the whole the

Schumann pieces proved that Slivinski has advanced as an interpreter. One or two of them were perfectly played; and the whole program was full of evidences of his exceptional powers.

THE THIRD ACT OF ERNANI

The World, 2 November 1892

The young English composer is having a good time of it just now, with his overtures and symphonies resounding at the Crystal Palace, and his operas at the Olympic. Mr Granville Bantock's Cædmar is an enthusiastic and ingenious piece of work, being nothing less than an adaptation of all the most fetching passages in Wagner's later tragic music-dramas to a little poem in which Tristan, Siegmund, Siegfried, Hunding, Isolde, and Sieglinde are aptly concentrated into three persons. The idea is an excellent one; for in the space of an hour, and within a stone's-throw of the Strand, we get the cream of all Bayreuth without the trouble and expense of journeying thither. There is also, for the relief of anti-Wagnerians, an intermezzo which might have been written by the late Alfred Cellier or any other good Mendelssohnian.

The plot, as I understood it, is very simple. A pious knight-errant wanders one evening into the garden of Eden, and falls asleep there. Eve, having had words with her husband, runs away from him, and finds in the sleeping warrior the one thing lacking to her: to wit, somebody to run away with. She makes love to him; and they retire together. Elves appear on the deserted stage, and dance to the strains of the intermezzo. They are encored, not because the audience is particularly charmed, but because Cavalleria has put it into its head that to recognize and *encore* an intermezzo shews connoisseurship. Then the pair return, looking highly satisfied; and presently Adam enters and remonstrates. Ten minutes later the knight-errant is the sole survivor of the three, whereupon he prays the curtain down.

The whole affair is absurdly second-hand; but, for all that, it proves remarkable musical ability on the part of Mr Granville Bantock, who shews a thorough knowledge of the mechanism of the Wagnerian orchestra. If Cædmar had been produced as a newly discovered work by Wagner, everyone would have admitted that so adroit a forgery implied a very clever penman. After Cædmar, Signor Lago put up the third act of Ernani. Strange to say, a good many people did not wait for it.

Just imagine the situation. Here is a baritone singer, Signor Mario Ancona, who has attracted general notice by his performance of Telramund in Lohengrin and Alfonso in La Favorita. Signor Lago accordingly mounts a famous scene, the classic opportunity for lyric actors of the Italian school (baritone variety), a scene which is not only highly prized by all students of Italian opera, but which had its dramatic import well taught to Londoners by the Comédie Française when they crowded to see Sarah Bernhardt as Doña Sol, and incidentally saw Worms as Charles V. In the play Charles is sublime in feeling, but somewhat tedious in expression. In the opera he is equally sublime in feeling, but concise, grand, and touching in expression, thereby proving that the chief glory of Victor Hugo as a stage poet was to have provided libretti for Verdi.

Every opera-goer who knows chalk from cheese knows that to hear that scene finely done is worth hearing all the Mephistopheleses and Toreadors that ever grimaced or swaggered, and that when a new artist offers to play it, the occasion is a first-class one. Yet, when Cædmar was over there was a considerable exodus from the stalls, as if nothing remained but a harlequinade for the children and the novices. "Now this" thought I "is pretty odd. If these people knew their Ernani, surely they would stay." Then I realized that they did not know their Ernani—that years of Faust, and Carmen, and Les Huguenots, and Mefistofele, and *soi-disant* Lohengrin had left them ignorant of that ultra-classical product of Romanticism, the grandiose Italian opera in which the executive art consists in a splendid display of personal heroics, and the drama arises out of the simplest and most universal stimulants to them.

Il Trovatore, Un Ballo, Ernani, &c., are no longer read at the piano at home as the works of the Carmen *genre* are, and as Wagner's are. The popular notion of them is therefore founded on performances in which the superb distinction and heroic force of the male characters, and the tragic beauty of the women, have been burlesqued by performers with every sort of disqualification for such parts, from age and obesity to the most excruciating phases of physical insignificance and modern cockney vulgarity. I used often to wonder why it was that whilst every asphalt contractor could get a man to tar the streets, and every tourist could find a gondolier rather above the average of the House of Lords in point of nobility of aspect, no operatic manager, after Mario vanished, seemed to be able to find a Manrico with whom any exclusively disposed Thames mudlark would care to be seen grubbing for pennies. When I get on this subject I really cannot contain myself. The thought of that dynasty of execrable impostors in tights and tunics, interpolating their loathsome B flats into the beautiful melodies they could not sing, and swelling with conceit when they were able to finish *Di quella pira* with a high C capable of making a stranded man-of-war recoil off a reef into mid-ocean, I demand the suspension of all rules as to decorum of

[725]

language until I have heaped upon them some little instalment of the infinite abuse they deserve. Others, alas! have blamed Verdi, much as if Dickens had blamed Shakespear for the absurdities of Mr Wopsle.*

The general improvement in operatic performances of late years has taken us still further away from the heroic school. But in due time its turn will come. Von Bülow, who once contemptuously refused the name of music to Verdi's works, has recanted in terms which would hardly have been out of place if addressed to Wagner; and many who now talk of the master as of a tuneful trifler who only half-redeemed a misspent life by the clever artificialities which are added in Aïda and Otello to the power and freedom of his earlier works, will change their tone when his operas are once more seriously studied by great artists.

For the present, however, it is clear that if Signor Mario Ancona wishes to interest the public, he must depend on character parts instead of heroic ones. His offer of Charles V. could hardly have been less appreciatively received. This was certainly no fault of his own; for he sang the opening *recitative* and cavatina well, and the solo in the great sestet, *O sommo Carlo*, very well. As a piece of acting his performance was a trifle too Italian-operatic; his fold of the arms and shake of the head when Ernani insisted on being beheaded was overmuch in the manner of Mr Lenville†; and there was too constant a strain throughout, since even in the third act of Ernani there are moments which are neither stentorian nor sentimental. But one does not expect a revolution in operatic acting to be achieved in a single night, especially in a part which is, to say the least, somewhat inflated; and, on the whole, Signor Ancona

* Character in Dickens's Great Expectations.
† Character in Dickens's Nicholas Nickleby.

was more dignified and sincere than any experienced opera-goer had dared to hope.

The applause at the end was only moderately enthusiastic; but this was largely due to the carelessness of the management, which, instead of providing a book of the triple bill, left the audience entirely in the dark as to what the Ernani excerpt meant, and tried to effect separate sales of vocal scores of Cædmar and shilling books of L'Impresario to elucidate the rest of the program. After which you felt that Signor Lago deserved anything that might happen to him in the way of the performance falling flat.

And the chances of Ernani were not improved by the modesty of Charles's coronation arrangements, or by the unkempt staginess of the conspirators, or by the fact that though the music had been rehearsed sufficiently to secure accuracy, no attempt was made to color and enrich the sombre depths of the orchestra. As to the choristers, they were allowed to bawl away in the old slovenly, rapscallionly fashion, on the easy assumption that, if the time came right and the pitch right (or thereabouts), the quality of tone and style of delivery did not matter two straws. When will Signor Lago pay a visit to our comic-opera houses with their English choruses, and realize that Queen Anne has been dead for some time now?

Der Schauspieldirektor, in the version known as L'Impresario, of course put all the rest of the entertainment into the shade. Every number in it is a masterpiece. The quartet would make a very handsome *finale* for any ordinary opera; the overture is a classic; the air *Quando miro quel bel ciglio* will last as long as Pergolesi's *Tre giorni son che Nina*, or Gluck's *Che farò senza, Euridice?* How far its finest qualities are above our heads, both before and behind the curtain, I need not say. The overture was scrambled through post-haste in the old exhilarating slapdash style, expressive of the idea that Mozart was a rattling sort of drunkard and libertine, tempered by the modern and infinitely more foolish notion that he was merely a useful model of academic form for students.

Mr G. Tate sang *Quando miro* in the person of Mozart himself. To shew how thoroughly he grasped the character he altered the last phrase so as to make the ending more "effective," much as, if he were a sculptor instead of a singer, he might alter the tails of the Trafalgar Square lions by sticking them up straight in order to make *their* endings more effective. This public announcement on Mr Tate's part that he considers himself a better judge of how a song should end than Mozart is something that he will have to live down. Unless, indeed, the real explanation be that Mr Tate is too modest, and succumbed, against his own better sense, to the bad advice which is always thrust upon young artists by people who have all the traditional abuses of the stage at their fingers' ends, and know nothing about art. And that is why, on the boards as off them, eminence is only attained by those whose strength of conviction enables them to do, without the least misgiving, exactly the reverse of what all the non-eminent people round them advise them to do. For naturally, if these non-eminents knew the right thing to do they would be eminent.

Of the performance generally, I have only to say that it has been well prepared and is really enjoyable. Mlle Leila, who played Mlle Herz, has a naturally good voice, which has been somewhat squeezed and wire-drawn by an artificial method; but she managed to hold her own in her very difficult part, which is worth hearing not only for its own sake, but for the very fine Mozartian aria which she introduces when asked by the Schauspieldi-rektor (Mr R. Temple) to give a sample of her powers.

[728]

I have to chronicle the resumption of the Monday and Saturday Popular Concerts, and to congratulate Señor Arbos on his playing in the adagio of Beethoven's quartet in E flat (Op. 74) at the opening concert, and Mlle Szumowska on her neat handling of the last three movements of the Pastoral Sonata. The first movement came to nothing, perhaps because Mlle Szumowska had a cold, perhaps because she has not a pastoral turn. Mlle Wietrowetz succeeds Señor Arbos this week as first violin.

THE PISTOL OF THE LAW

The World, 9 November 1892

To Dvořák's Requiem, which was performed last Wednesday at the Albert Hall, I could not be made to listen again, since the penalty of default did not exceed death; and I had much rather die than repeat the attempts I made, first at Birmingham, and then at Kensington Gore, to sit it out. It is hard to understand the frame of mind of an artist who at this time of day sits down to write a Requiem *à propos de bottes*. One can fancy an undertaker doing it readily enough: he would know as a matter of business that in music, as in joiners' work, you can take the poorest materials and set the public gaping at them by simply covering them with black cloth and coffin-nails. But why should a musician condescend to speculate thus in sensationalism and superstition?

When I hear Dvořák's weird chords on muted cornets (patent Margate Pier echo attachment), finishing up with a gruesome ding on the tam-tam, I feel exactly as I should if he held up a skull with a lighted candle inside to awe me. When in the Dies Iræ, he proceeds, as who should say "Now you shall see what I can do in the way of stage thunder," to turn on organ pedal and drum to make a huge mechanical modern version of the Rossini *crescendo*, I pointedly and publicly turn up my nose, and stare frigidly. But the public, in spite of Charles Dickens, loves everything connected with a funeral.

Those who are too respectable to stand watching the black flag after an execution take a creepy sort of pleasure in Requiems. If Sir Joseph Barnby were to conduct with a black brass-tipped *bâton*; if the bandsmen wore black gloves and crape scarves; if the attendants were professional mutes (*sordini*), and the tickets edged with a half-inch jet border, I believe the enjoyment of the audience would be immensely enhanced. Dvořák seems to have felt this. Mozart's Requiem leads you away from the point: you find yourself listening to the music as music, or reflecting, or otherwise getting up to the higher planes of existence. Brahms's Requiem has not the true funeral relish: it aims at the technical traditions of requiem composition rather than the sensational, and is so execrably and ponderously dull that the very flattest of funerals would seem like a ballet, or at least a *danse macabre*, after it.

Dvořák alone, mechanically solemn and trivially genteel, very careful and elaborate in detail, and beyond belief uninspired, has hit the mean. One almost admires the perseverance with which he has cut all those dead strips of notes into lengths, nailed and glued them into a single structure, and titivated it for the melancholy occasion with the latest mortuary orchestral decorations. And then, the gravity with which it is received and criticized as a work of first-rate importance, as if it brought the air of a cathedral close with it, and were highly connected! Wheras, if the same music had been called Ode to Revolution, or The Apotheosis of Ibsen, or Dirge for the Victims of Vaccination, it would have been found out for what it is before the end of the first ten bars, as I found it out at the Birmingham Festival.

That is the way things go in England. Some few years ago Peter Benoît, a much-in-earnest Dutch composer, who is almost as great in music as Haydon was in painting, made his *début* here with an oratorio called Lucifer, containing one pretty song (by Schumann), but otherwise a most barren colossus of a work. The public felt that Lucifer was an integral part of the Church of England, most Englishmen being persuaded that Milton's Paradise Lost is a poetical paraphrase of the book of Genesis; and Benoît was received with deep respect as a too long neglected Dutch Beethoven. Presuming on this success, Peter laid a work called Charlotte Corday at the feet of the Philharmonic Society. That infatuated body, feeling itself traditionally committed to the discovery and encouragement of foreign Beethovens, allowed him to conduct it at one of its concerts. He promptly found out that in England, though Lucifer is respectable, Charlotte Corday is quite out of the question.

The Corday revolutionary scenes were not a whit more mechanical and shallow than the oratorio, and were nearly as bulky, besides being twice as lively (thanks to Ça ira, the Marseillaise, &c.); but the British public would have none of them; and Benoît has not since been heard of in London. I mention the matter to illustrate how easy it is to get taken seriously as a composer if you begin with an oratorio. But if you want to make assurance doubly sure, begin with a Requiem. After Dvořák every musical agent and publisher in Europe will give, as the straightest of tips to foreign composers, the word to write Requiems. I foresee the arrival of shiploads of such compositions on these coasts. When that day comes, I shall buy a broom; select some crossing out of earshot of the muffled drums, and earn

[731]

my bread in a more humane and less questionably useful occupation than that which I now follow. It is true that even then I shall have to see a funeral go past occasionally. But a funeral goes past in less than two minutes, wheras a Requiem takes a matter of two hours. Besides, it is generally understood that funerals are to be avoided as long as possible, wheras Requiems are offered as a sort of treat, whether anybody is dead or not.

I have myself, however, to sing the requiem of Signor Lago's opera season, which expired on Thursday after a performance of Die Zauberflöte, which I did not attend, partly because of the London Symphony Concert, and partly because the disappearance of Signor Lago's advertisements from the morning papers had led me to believe that the end was already come. It is impossible not to sympathize with the defeated *impresario*, who has given us so much fresh music during his brief struggle.

From my personal point of view, I hugely appreciated his unspoiled condition. He had the courage of his profession as well as the enterprise of his business, and always stood up without wincing to the hardest hitting in the way of criticism. He never raised the cry of "personal attack," or invited me to discharge my duties with the pistol of the law of libel held to my ear. He did not expect me to gorge him with impossible flattery, nor did he keep a critic and a paper of his own to supply me with weekly examples of what he considered fair and becoming notices of his enterprises. He may even, for all I know to the contrary, have attained the superlative managerial wisdom of seeing that the only criticism which really helps operatic enterprise is criticism which creates and sustains public interest in music, even when it deals with *impresarios* almost as severely as they generally deserve; and that however agreeable it may be to be extolled daily in terms which would be considerably over the mark if applied to the management of Liszt at Weimar or Wagner at Bayreuth, the end of that must be the same as the end of the old experiment of calling Aristides "the Just" about a thousand times too often.

He belongs, does Signor Lago, to the old days, now for ever fled, it appears, when no critic ever dreamt of alluding to the legal conditions under which his work was carried on, much less to the relations between himself and the managers. The public assumed that there was an unwritten understanding by which its representative was to be absolutely free to pursue his occupation unmolested, both in its legal phase of applauding and its illegal phase of finding fault. Whilst that understanding was observed, every public allusion to it from either side was an impertinence.

But now that it is cast to the winds, and that such verdicts as the one given in favor of the late Signor Ciampi against the Daily Telegraph have proved that even in the cases most favorable to the critic, the public, through its juries, will generally console adversely criticized persons at the expense of newspaper proprietors on the general ground that they can well afford it, I, for one, am forced to remind the said public from time to time that since they will neither protect themselves in the jury-box nor pay enough for their papers to provide for the huge cost and worry of continual litigation, a critic must either give up his work and fall back on some safer branch of literature, or else absolutely refuse to criticize the undertakings of agents and *impresarios* who resort to the law whenever they are dispraised.

Great artists and most interesting performances pass, and must continue to pass, unnoticed in this column because they are under the auspices of gentlemen who have threatened me with actions when I have pointed out imperfections in their enterprises, though, most

[733]

inconsistently, they never sent me a ten-pound note when I praised them. I do not blame them in the least, as they are by no means bound to observe the old truce longer than they see the advantage of it: only, I insist on the public being warned that the truce is no longer general, so that it may be understood that I neither neglect my duties nor slight the artists whose visits I pass by silently; and I also wish artistic *entrepreneurs* of all sorts to know that if they want mere advertisements they must pay for them, and if they want criticism they must take the rough with the smooth.

So, you see, I pay Signor Lago no small compliment when I say that the above observations, the bearings of which lay in the application thereof, need never have been obtruded on the public if his fortitude in facing severe criticism, even when followed by heavy losses, were quite as much a matter of course as it once was.

At the first London Symphony Concert last Thursday the band was very rough; and there must have been something exceptionally unfavorable in the atmospheric conditions, for the wind was badly out of tune. Even the drums could not catch the pitch accurately. Berlioz's King Lear overture sounded positively music-hally. I was curious to hear it; but I did not know it or care for it enough to have found out the right way to play it; and I venture to guess that Mr Henschel and the band were in exactly the same predicament. Anyhow, it made a great noise and gave no sort of satisfaction. At the end of the concert the orchestra had a lively game of football with Wagner's celebrated American Potboiler,* the second and last of his short series of efforts in that fascinating *genre* (the first was Rienzi).

* Festival March (also known as Centennial March), commissioned for the Centennial Exhibition in Philadelphia, 1876.

Mrs Henschel sang Liszt's setting of *Kennst du das Land* cleverly, but without anything approaching the requisite depth of feeling. Szumowska played Weber's Konzertstück, which she has apparently picked up, not quite accurately, by ear, with fewer slips than she made when she played it at the Crystal Palace a fortnight ago. The most successful item in the program was the C minor symphony, in which Mr Henschel shewed sound conductorial instinct by boldly roughing it for the sake of a powerful general effect instead of giving us smoothness and prettiness of detail with no general effect at all. But it is not to the credit of the band that such an alternative should be forced on him.

I especially protest against the way in which those first three notes of the symphony, forming a gigantic *appoggiatura* to Fate's knock at the door, were executed. Some of the band regarded them as a triplet of quavers, some as three ordinary quavers, and some as a quaver and two semiquavers, whilst doubtless there were other views represented which I was not quick enough to catch. The *coda* to the first movement was spoiled by want of crispness; and the second section of the trio was too slow and heavy-footed. However, Mr Henschel has the root of the matter in him. The concerts are interesting and of reasonable length; and the shortcomings are shortcomings of detail which are certain to be remedied in time, and which do not meanwhile interfere seriously with the value of the performances, which is high enough to make it a matter of public importance that they should be well supported.

SPECIALISTS IN SINGING

The World, 16 November 1892

Last season appears to have been a favorable one for
specialists in singing, for volumes and pamphlets on
voice production have been hurled at me from all sides;
and this, I suppose, indicates a wave of interest in the
subject. All such treatises used to be practically identical
as to their preliminary matter, which invariably dealt
with the need for a new departure, so as to get away
from the quackery of the ordinary singing-master and
rediscover the lost art of Porpora. Nowadays, the new
departure is still advocated; but there is a tendency to
leave Porpora out of the question, and to claim for the
latest methods a modern scientific basis, consisting
mostly of extracts from Huxley and Helmholtz. With all
due respect, however, I beg to remark that there is no
sort of sense in attempting to base the art of singing on
physiology. You can no more sing on physiological
principles than you can fence on anatomical principles,
paint on optical principles, or compose on acoustic
principles.

Sir Joshua Reynolds painted none the worse for
believing that there were three primary colors, and that
the human eye was one of the most exquisite and perfect
instruments ever designed for the use of man; nor have
his successors painted any the better since Young
exploded the three primary colors for ever, and Helmholtz scandalized Europe by informing his pupils that if
an optician were to send him an instrument with so
many easily avoidable and remediable defects as the
human eye, he would feel bound to censure him severely.
Again, half a century ago every singing-master firmly

believed that there were in the human body three glands—one in the head, immediately behind the frontal sinus; one in the throat; and one in the chest: each secreting a different quality of voice.

Nowadays even an Italian singing-master must, on pain of appearing a gross ignoramus to his pupils, know that all voice is produced by the same organ, the larynx, and that the so-called three voices are "registers" made by varying the adjustment of the vocal cords. This advance in scientific knowledge does not alter the position of those teachers of singing who study their profession *by ear*, or of the painters who paint *by eye*—who are artists, in short. But it has a good effect on the gentlemen whose methods are "scientific." In the days of the three primary colors, there were teachers of painting who held that the right color for a scarf across a blue robe was orange, because blue was a primary color, and the proper contrast to it was a compound of the other primary colors, red and yellow. The Divine Artist had colored the rainbow on these principles; therefore they were natural, scientific, and orthodox.

There are still gentlemen who teach coloring on natural, scientific, orthodox principles; and to them the discovery that the doctrine of the three primary colors will not do, and that Shelley's "million-colored bow" is nearer the truth than Newton's tri-colored one, no doubt has its value, since their daubs are more varied than before, though the artist-colorist remains no wiser than Bellini or Velasquez. In the same way, the scientific vocal methods based on the latest observations of the laryngoscopists are, on the whole, less likely to be dangerous than those based on the theory of the three glands, although the artistic method is just the same as ever it was.

Now, I am hopelessly prejudiced in favor of the artistic method, which is, of course, the genuinely scientific method according to the science of art itself. On behalf of my prejudice I plead two chapters in my experience of "scientific" methods. When the study of the vocal cords first began, it led straight to the theory that the larynx was a simple stringed instrument, and that singing was, physically, a mere question of varying the tension of the vocal cords, and throwing them into vibration by a vigorous current of air. This was duly confirmed by an experiment, of the physiological-laboratory type, by Müller; and then we had the "tension-of-cords-and-force-of-blast" theory of singing, which all the violent and villainous methods prevalent in the middle of the century, to the ruin of innumerable pupil-victims, claimed as their "scientific" foundation, and which every true artist was able to explode to his or her own satisfaction by the simple experiment of listening to its results.

The second chapter concerns composers more than singers. When it was discovered that musical sounds, instead of being simple, are really enriched by a series of "partial tones," and that the most prominent of these "partial tones" correspond to the notes of the commonest chords, all the professors who could not distinguish between science and art jumped at the notion of discovering a scientific method of harmonizing which should quite supersede the barbarous thoroughbass of Handel and Mozart. A stupendous monument of ingenious folly, in the form of a treatise on harmony by Dr Day, was installed at the Royal Academy of Music, where it reigns, for aught I know, to this day; and the unhappy pupils who wanted certificates of their competence to write music could not obtain them without answering absurd challenges to name "the root" of a chord, meaning the sound that would generate the notes of that chord among its series of "partial tones."

Now as, if you only look far enough through your

series, you can find every note used in music among those generated by any one note used in it, the professors, though tolerably unanimous as to the root of C, E, G, or C, E, G, B flat, could not agree about the chromatic chords, and even the more extreme diatonic discords. The result was that when you went to get coached for your Mus. Bac. degree, the first thing your coach had to ascertain was where you were going to be examined, as you had to give different answers to the same questions, according to whether they were put by Ouseley and Macfarren, or Stainer. (Sir John Stainer finally succumbed to an acute attack of commonsense, and invested Day's system with that quality in the only modern treatise on harmony I have ever recommended anyone to open.) Sterndale Bennett was a convinced Dayite, and sometimes spoiled passages in his music in order to make the harmony "scientific."

Meanwhile Wagner, working by ear, heedless of Day, was immensely enlarging the harmonic stock-in-trade of the profession. Macfarren kept on proving that the Wagnerian procedure was improper, until at last one could not help admiring the resolute conviction with which the veteran professor, old, blind, and hopelessly in the wrong, would still rise to utter his protest whenever there was an opening for it.

Here, then, we have science, in the two most conspicuous cases of its application to musical art, doing serious mischief in the hands of the teachers who fell back on it to eke out the poverty of their artistic resources. Yet do not suppose that I am an advocate of old-fashioned ignorance. No: I admit that a young teacher of singing, if he cannot handle the laryngoscope, and knows nothing of anatomy or physics, deserves to be mistrusted as an uneducated person, likely to offer fantastic and ambiguous suggestions instead of exact instructions.

But I do declare emphatically that all methods which have come into existence by logical deduction from scientific theory can only be good through the extravagantly improbable accident of a coincidence between the result of two absolutely unrelated processes, one right and the other wrong. Practically, they are certain to be delusive; and this conclusion is not the anti-scientific, but the scientific one. And in all books on the subject which I may happen to review here I shall concern myself solely with the practical instructions offered, and criticize them in the light of my own empirical observation of singing, without the slightest regard to the hooking of them on to physiology or acoustics.

First comes the redoubtable Mr Lunn with a reprint (Forster Groom—a sixpenny pamphlet) of the lecture he delivered last May at Prince's Hall, which I noticed at the time. I disagree with him flatly in his denunciation of the vowel *oo* for practice, and am quite of the opinion of the sensible and practical author of Our Voices, and How to Improve Them, by A Lady (Willcocks—a two-shilling manual), who recommends practice on *oo* in the middle of the voice, and points out that the traditional Italian *a* is invariably translated here into the English *ah*, which would have driven the old Italian masters out of their senses.

Mr Lunn's objection is that *oo* sets people "blowing," against which vice his pamphlet gives effective and valuable warning. But if Mr Lunn will teach his pupils to round the back of the throat (the pharynx) as they sing— and this is a trick of the old school which he does not seem to know—he will find that they can "compress the air," as he puts it, just as effectually on *oo* as on Italian *a*; and his well-taught tenor pupil, Mr Arthur, will be able to do in one breath that passage in *Il mio tesoro* which cost him one and a quarter at Prince's Hall.

A Lady might learn something from Mr Lunn as to the importance of not wasting the breath (the skilled singer, in rounding the pharynx, has an imaginary sensation of holding the breath back—of *com*pressing it at the larynx, though the control really comes from the diaphragm). She says "The voice should be directed forward, always forward, until the vibrating air is felt right on the lips."

This is both fanciful and misleading. The phrase "direction of the voice" means really shaping the cavity of the mouth by the disposition of the lips, tongue, and jaw, the voice being immovable; and the attempt to carry out the precept as to feeling the air on the lips would lead in practice simply to "blowing." Dr J. W. Bernhardt, the author of Vox Humana (Simpkin, Marshall—a five-shilling book), gives the proper word of command for this particular emergency in the ten quite invaluable paragraphs (94 to 103) in which he urges the necessity of putting no strain on the geniohyoid muscles—in other words, of keeping your chin loose whatever you do. By his emphasis on this point and his knowledge of the importance of the pharynx, he is able to give some excellent advice; but in suggesting the vowel *o* for practice, he forgot that it would be read as ah-oo, ow, aw-oo, &c., by different readers, Mr Irving being the only living Englishman who makes it a pure vowel.

Dr Bernhardt's plan of beginning it with an aspirate and an *n*, thus, *h'n'o*, is a clever trick as far as the *n* is concerned; but the *h* belongs to his notion (also Mr Lunn's) that the air should be compressed by the vocal cords as by a safety valve. He carries this so far as to advocate attacking a note, not merely by the *coup de glotte*, as Mr Lunn does, but by nothing short of an explosion. I quite agree with Maurel, that the *coup de glotte* is objectionable; and I never heard a good singer who attacked notes explosively. I am convinced that both Mr Lunn and Dr Bernhardt have been misled by the imaginary sensation, described above, of pressing back the air with the vocal cords.

Any good singer can touch a note gently, reinforce it to its loudest, and let it diminish again, without the least alteration of the pitch, and consequently without the least alteration of, or pressure downwards of, the glottis, the *crescendo* and *diminuendo* being visibly effected by the diaphragm. The explosive process produces bawling, not singing; and Dr Bernhardt virtually admits this when he says that the ladies who, when asked to sing louder, plead "I really have no more voice," would scream loud enough to awaken the echoes a mile away if any sudden fright came upon them. If one of Dr Bernhardt's pupils were to apply this remark practically, by beginning to scream instead of singing (as many *prima donnas* do), he would, I have no doubt, pull her up with a remarkably short turn.

But at this point I must pull myself up with equal sharpness, leaving unnoticed many points in these three interesting books, for which I beg Mr Lunn, Dr Bernhardt, and A Lady, to accept my best thanks.

SANTLEY'S REMINISCENCES

The World, 23 November 1892

"I believe" says Santley in his Reminiscences, just published by Mr Edward Arnold, "I would have preferred being an actor of moderate fame to being the most renowned singer on earth." That is the beginning. Now listen to the end. "The stage had proved my great *illusion perdue*, my own enthusiasm and love for it had not abated; but I could not fight almost singlehanded against the lack of earnestness, except for pecuniary gain, which I encountered turn what way I might, and I resolved to quit it." Let me quote a few of the steps of the disillusionizing process:

"I essayed the part of Don Giovanni for the first time at Manchester on September 14th, 1865. As usual, I had one rehearsal the morning of the day of performance. Mario, who was always a late riser, did not come in until we were half-way through the rehearsal.

.   .   .   .   .   .

"Tannhäuser was not produced at all during my Italian career. I always regret this, as I had a great desire to play Wolfr m.

.   .   .   .   .   .

"Queen Topaz might have proved a fair success if some care had been taken in its production. Swift, who played the hero, never knew his part—neither music nor words. There was no attempt at stage management: we all wandered on and off and about the stage as we pleased. The effect produced was very curious: neither players nor audience seemed to have the remotest notion what it was all about. The stage management throughout was the most perfect—of its kind—I ever knew. At one performance of Fra Diavolo matters were so well arranged that principals, chorus, supers, &c., were all left outside the curtain at the end of the first act. At one of the rehearsals of The Amber Witch, the stage manager showed off to peculiar advantage. In the last act, the so-called witch, finding herself menaced by a number of peasants, conceives the idea of acting on their superstitious fears, and sings or recites a Latin prayer. This they take for a spell, and hurry away, leaving her in peace. Mr Stage Manager, hearing the prayer, called out 'Don't you hear? she's praying: down on your knees.' I happened to know the situation from Chorley, the author of the libretto, and took upon myself to point out the mistake. The stage manager merely remarked 'How the devil should I know anything about it? I have never read the book. Here, you Chorus, it's a spell to frighten you; so, as soon as you hear the first words, clear off as fast as you can.'

.   .   .   .   .   .

"We had (at La Scala, Milan, 1865) a rehearsal for the stage business with the stage manager, Piave, the author of several of Verdi's librettos, including that of Il Trovatore.* I was highly amused; for the old gentleman wandered about the dark stage with a coil of wax-taper, directing us. He had evidently forgot all about his own work. He told me to come on from the wrong side for my first entrance, and was highly indignant when I suggested he was mistaken; but he begged my pardon when he found his mistake led to a muddle. . . . For Il Templario we had several rehearsals on the stage with the full orchestra and with a multiplicity of directors—Cavallini directing the orchestra with his fiddlestick, and taking the time from Mazzucato, who, seated in front of the stage, beat the time with his hand, whilst the chorus master stood in front of his regiment, also beating time. Altercations between the conductor and the principal instruments were not uncommon. I remember one which amused me very much. Cavallini turned to the principal cello and bass, and remarked that a certain B ought to be natural, not flat. The professors replied that he was mistaken, upon which a long argument ensued, ending in the doublebass requesting the con-

* Santley may have confused this opera, which has a libretto by Salvatore Cammarano, with La Traviata, for which Francesco Maria Piave was the librettist.

ductor to 'shut up,' as he did not know what he was talking about."

I make these extracts because I have been so often told that my criticisms of the opera are "too cynical," and I am so fully aware of how improbable the truth seems to the innocence of the ordinary opera-goer that I am not sorry to be able to call as a witness to the state of things of which we are at present enjoying "the traditions" our chief baritone, one who has achieved all that is as yet possible for a great English singer, and who speaks, nevertheless, as a disappointed man, driven from the stage by the impossibility of getting any honest work done there.

When my witness says "I can conscientiously say that I never had money-making for an object; my aim and ambition have always been to make the best use of the talent God entrusted to me," I believe he carries conviction of his sincerity to all who remember any considerable portion of his career; and it is not necessary for me or anyone else to supplement that statement by any compliments. The impression he made on me years ago, under the Mapleson *régime*, was that he was not a readymade artist for stage work, and had never been able to get thoroughly finished.

As to his singing, I cannot say how long it took him to perfect that; for the first time I ever heard him (it was as Di Luna in Il Trovatore) he was already fully accomplished vocally. But as an actor he was blunt, unpractised, and prone to fall back on a goodhumoured nonchalance in his relations with the audience, which was highly popular, but which destroyed all dramatic illusion. He was always Santley, the good fellow with no nonsense about him, and a splendid singer; but never (except as Papageno) was he the character in the opera, who was usually a person with a very great deal of nonsense about him. The nonchalance was really diffidence: one could see that a man of his straightforward temperament could only acquire the art of impersonation by years of unremitting and severe practice.

If he had been on the staff of a National Theatre, working his way steadily on to an unassailable position and a secure and sufficient pension, he would have had plenty of thorough rehearsal to train him; and his earnestness and vigor would have been transmuted into dramatic intensity of feeling and grip of character. A National Opera could hardly have had better material to work up. But there was no National Opera; and the opportunities he actually got were of the kind described in the typical passages I have quoted. For example, he may be said to have created Valentin in Faust, as it was considered a minor part until he made it a leading one; yet I heard him, when he was about forty, play it in an unfinished, hail-fellow-well-met way, even to the extent of rattling off *Dio Possente* at the rate of a hundred crotchets per minute or thereabouts; and though he was tremendously in earnest in the death scene, the earnestness was by no means fully incorporated with the part.

Later on, in Vanderdecken, Mikeli, Claude Melnotte, and the Porter of Havre, his dramatic grip was much surer; and at the present moment, on the verge of his sixtieth year, he is a more thorough artist than ever. There can be no doubt that his sincerity of temperament, developed by the Philistine atmosphere of his native Liverpool into bluffness, and his sensitiveness, with nothing to exercise it but the snubs and checks which fall to the lot of a young clerk in a commercial town, were hindrances to him on the stage, where, under honest artistic conditions, they would have helped him. It is noteworthy that when he went to Milan to study, he brought thither a Lancashire eye to which the showy cathedral and beautiful church of Sant' Ambrogio were absolutely indifferent. He describes the services at both without a word to indicate any consciousness of the artistic gulf which separates the one building from the other; and he adds "Picture galleries, museums, libraries, or exhibitions never possessed much attraction for me."

And yet he is beyond a doubt a highly imaginative man. If he had been a romantic humbug and *poseur*, he would perhaps have educated himself in the artifices of the stage by his efforts to look picturesque in private life; but being the very reverse of that, he started as an awkward masquerader, and was received with the usual nonsense about his not being a born actor—a convenient evasion for the critic who feels that there is something wanting, and does not know his business well enough to be able to say what the something is. If Santley's eyes and limbs had been educated from his childhood as his ear was, he would have been as much a born actor as a born singer; for Nature had been as kind to him in the matter of face and figure as in that of voice. As it was, one remembers his performances far better than those of the numerous "born artists," "thorough artists," "artists to the tips of their fingers," and so on, who have played his parts here.

There is much more in Student and Singer which I should like to quote and moralize upon if I had space— all the more freely, as Mr Santley declares that, as a rule, he does not read criticism. His self-criticism is extraordinarily frank; and after reading such remarks as he permits himself on his fellow artists I should set a good deal of store by his opinion if he were to set up in my business. On the subject of singing he says little, explaining that he intends to deal fully with it in a separate work, which will be awaited with interest by many young singers who are curious to know how a man can sing for forty years and then appear at a Handel

Festival with a much fresher voice than most baritones have after forty weeks' run of their first comic opera. I conclude with an extract which may be useful to students bound for Italy:

"I had letters of introduction to several musical and other influential people in Milan, three of which I delivered, and this I regretted having done, as they were the cause of no little persecution for loans, gifts, &c. . . . But I had no need of letters of introduction to make the acquaintance of similar gentry, all bent on plunder. I had journalists, or people who called themselves such, who wanted subscriptions to papers I had never heard of and did not wish to see," &c. &c. &c.

Ma mie Rosette, produced last Thursday at the Globe by Messrs Lart and Boosey, is refreshingly free from the stale vulgarities without which no comic opera is supposed to be complete. It is positively elegant, and appeals throughout to the tastes of people who have not a deliberate preference for baseness in art. Therefore it may very possibly fail. M. Paul Lacome's music is taken from good sources; his reminiscences are those of a fairly cultivated musician and not of a mere music hall frequenter. The numbers interpolated by Mr Caryll fall considerably below this standard: they are thin and trivial, and might have been composed by Mr Solomon in an uninspired moment. The cast is good. Mr Oudin is not mellow and humorous enough for Henri Quatre; but he brings down the house by his singing, especially in an air in the second act, founded, apparently, on Vincent Wallace's Why do I weep for thee? Miss Nesville, whose voice is no larger than the point of a very small pin, is clever enough to please the audience, though, for all her undoubted stage talent, I do not feel disposed to admit that she is in her place as a *prima donna*. Miss Jessie Bond, Mr Wyatt, and Mr D'Orsay are amusing and not oppressive in the comic parts; and Miss Jennie McNulty shews some capacity as Corisande. The opera is prettily mounted; but the electric candles in the second act so dazzle the spectator and kill the costumes in front of them that their miraculous extinction halfway through is a relief. And Mr Courtice Pounds's second dress, which makes him look like Tavannes in Les Huguenots pretending to be a Highlander, is simply inconceivable, even by those who have seen it.

THE BOARD SCHOOL COMPETITION
The World, 30 November 1892

By far the most important musical event in London last week was the annual competiton of the Board School choirs at Exeter Hall for a Challenge Medallion. I spent three mortal hours listening to eight choirs singing, first, See the chariot at hand, then a "sight test," and finally, whatever part-song was the *cheval de bataille* of the particular school in hand. The audience consisted of the judges, Sir John Stainer and Mr McNaught, of a few critics to judge the judges from the reserved seats, and of the Lord Mayor and Lady Mayoress in great honor and glory on the platform, supported by a contingent of the London School Board, including at one extreme the Reverend Chairman Diggle, who listened moderately, and at the other the Reverend Stewart Headlam, who listened progressively. There was, besides, a vast audience of friends, relatives, and partisans of the competitors, who followed the points of the competition with an intelligence unknown at St James's Hall.

Some young ladies behind me were eagerly scanning

the choristers to find "the angel," who, as I gathered from the context, was a boy of seraphic beauty and goodness. I sought him eagerly, but entirely failed to identify him. There were dreamy, poetic, delicate-featured boys and girls; docile, passively receptive ones (with medals—I despised them); little duchesses whom I should have liked to adopt, little dukes who would have been considerably enriched if anyone had cut them off with a shilling; and a sprinkling of Miss Morleena Kenwigs and Bailey junior,* all making points of interest in a crowd of the children of Voltaire's wise friend, Monsieur Tout le Monde. But angel there was none, except all our good and bad angels, who, being two to each member of a crowded audience, must have been kept pretty constantly on the wing to avoid being crushed. Then there were pupil-teachers' choirs, large bodies of picked young women, all of them survivals of the fittest, resolute, capable, and with a high average of good looks. When I look at a fashionable audience of ladies at a recital I always feel, in spite of my profession, as if I were an honest, useful, hard-working citizen; but before the pupil-teachers I quailed, and knew myself for what I really am—that is to say, a musical critic.

The competition, like all competitions, was more or less a humbug, the Elcho shield going eventually to the conductor who had trained his choir single-heartedly in the art of getting the highest marks, which is not the same thing as the art of choral singing. His pupils performed with remarkable vigor and decision, and were the only ones who really succeeded in reading the "sight test" all through; but Mr Casserley's choir from the Great College-street School shewed more artistic sensibility; and Mr Longhurst's boys from Bellenden

* Characters in Dickens's Nicholas Nickleby and Martin Chuzzlewit.

Road were not further behind than all choirs of one sex alone are inevitably behind mixed choirs, both in quality of tone, in which the difference is enormous, and in the address with which girls pull boys out of difficulties, and boys girls, according to their special aptitudes. The decision shewed that the "sight test," which is the most mechanical part of the business, was five-sixths of the battle. And it was not even fairly conducted. I concluded that it was not possible to keep all the later competitors quite out of earshot of the earlier ones; for the reading of the upper part got better as the afternoon wore on, the little pitchers using their long ears to pick up the tune; whilst the reading of the middle and lower parts in the harmony shewed no such improvement. Thus, the winners of the shield, who, as it happened, sang last, must, unless they had been carefully plugged with cotton-wool for some two hours or so, or else kept outside the building, have heard the "sight test" sung no less than seven times before they tried it. This was sufficient to prepare them completely for the chief difficulty presented by the dotted crotchet and five quavers in the ninth bar, which so bothered the early competitors; as well as by the trap into which even the conductors fell, to their great credit, in the tenth, the composer, Mr Roston Bourke, having deliberately truncated the metre by leaving out a bar at that point. If I had been one of the judges I should unhesitatingly have given twenty marks to every choir which made the mistake Mr Bourke intended it to make, and struck twenty off the unintelligent plodders who passed unconsciously and safely through the danger. As to the senseless syncopation on the word "death," I am ready to head a deputation of ratepayers to the School Board about so perfect an instance of the evil inherent in all competition.

Mr Roston Bourke, instead of acting as a musician

desirous to write beautiful music for children, acted as a Jack-o'-Lantern, and did his worst to mislead them. If Haydn had written that "sight test," I believe that the very first symptom of confusion among the children would have sent him out into the Strand to publicly kneel down and beg forgiveness of Heaven for his crime. The sight test was otherwise bad in respect of the minor section, where the greatest difficulty was experienced in reading the notes, being also the only episode calculated to test a choir's power of catching a change in the sentiment of the music.

As might have been foreseen, the result was that the choir which caught the change in sentiment bungled the notes; whilst the winning choir, which alone vanquished all three parts in this section, absolutely disregarded the change in sentiment. As I have already said, the conductor of that choir, Mr J. Harris, a very competent gentleman, knew that if his children came out right upon matters of fact, they might safely disregard matters of taste. And this brings me to the injustice to the children of a competition which depends more on their instructor than on themselves. This is more or less true of all school competitions; but it is especially true of choral singing, the difference between one school and another being mostly a difference in the ability of the conductors, since children, in the lump, are all alike. There is, however, an element of luck in the matter as well, arising out of the existence of specially gifted children.

Every practical musician knows that sight reading is a very rare accomplishment, and that the champion exponents of the Tonic Sol-fa, the Chevé method, Hullah's system, and so forth, are usually persons who have what is called a sense of absolute pitch, and who, in reading from the ordinary staff notation, are guided neither by the intervals from one note to the next, nor by the "mental effect" of the note in the scale, but simply remember the pitch of every separate note, and sing it when they see it written down. These tuneful mortals, if you met them in the middle of the Great Sahara, and asked them to give you B flat, would strike it up like a tuning-fork. The easiest and commonest method of sight reading is to sit next to an absolute pitcher, and sing what he or she sings.

The sense of absolute pitch is rather commoner among children than among adults; and here the school conductor's luck comes in. If he happens to have one absolute pitcher in each division, he may, without having taught a single child to read at sight, get his choir to sing a test on the follow-my-leader plan more successfully than a rival whose singers are all consciously calculating their intervals or Sol-faing. Obviously, this possibility introduces an additional element of chance into the competition. On the whole, I think it would be well to discard the challenge shield from the annual exhibition, and so get rid of the senseless game of winning marks. There is quite incentive enough in the presence of the audience and the Lord Mayor to secure all the benefits which are supposed to accrue from an invidious award of the custody for one year of an absurd signboard to the choir which does the ill-office of humiliating all the rest.

The really tragic feature of the exhibition, however, was not in the pedagogic method, but in the little snatches of sweet and delicate singing which occasionally came from the mass of sound of which, in the main, no musical adjustment could disguise the vulgarity. It was not quite so bad as an ordinary oratorio chorus—the remnants of the charm of childhood saved it from that extremity; but already every child's voice was in far better training for slang and profanity than for poetry.

Children become adepts at what they hear every day

and what they see every day; and the notion that you can educate a child musically by any other means whatsoever except that of having beautiful music finely performed within its hearing, is a notion which I feel constrained to denounce, at the risk of being painfully personal to the whole nation, as tenable only by an idiot. Imagine a country teaching its children for half the day how to read the police intelligence, how to forge, and how to falsify accounts, and the other half how to tolerate, and eventually prefer, uncouth sights, discordant sounds, foul clothes, and graceless movements and manners.

However, I am gratified to be able to announce, by special request, that the Duke of Westminster, who so firmly protested against the extravagance of furnishing each Board School with a pianoforte, has presented the Westminster Orchestral Society with a life-membership donation of ten guineas.

As to Mr Cliffe's new symphony in E minor, composed for the Leeds Festival, and performed some weeks ago at the Crystal Palace, I am disqualified from any fruitful criticism of it by finding that I do not like it. This is not Mr Cliffe's fault: neither is it mine. The general mood of the work is too sentimental for me; and the orchestration, to my taste, is particularly cloying. Mr Cliffe seems to have no respect for the instruments: instead of giving them real parts, or at least firm virile touches to lay in, he uses them only to rouge his themes up to the eyes, and to hang rings on their fingers and bells on their toes, so to speak.

The themes themselves have no backbone: they languish along by diminished intervals whenever they get a chance of leaning on chromatic progressions; and it is quite a relief to come to some commonplace but straightforward prettiness, like that of the serenade, with the affectionate reminiscence of one of Mendelssohn's Songs without Words in the first phrase. Another reminiscence, which is very conspicuous among the thematic materials of the opening movement, is the first bar of Siegmund's spring song in Die Walküre, extended by a sequence through a second bar, and with its intervals altered, but still unmistakable. As to the program of Sunset, Night, and Morning (I need not mention the inevitable Fairies' Revel *scherzo*), all I can say is that sunset, night, and morning never make me feel like that. Evidently a case of deficient sympathy, on which account I do not lay any stress on my impression of the work. Mr Cliffe has apparently done exactly what he aimed at, and done it with great skill and industry, though also, I must reproachfully add, without the least regard for my idiosyncrasy.

Last Saturday we had a new symphonic poem, The Passing of Beatrice, by Mr William Wallace, a young Scotch composer with a very tender and sympathetic talent. I would cite the prelude to Lohengrin as an instance of the successful accomplishment of what Mr Wallace tries to do in his poem, which, if cut down by about nine-tenths, and well worked over, would make a pretty *entr'acte*. The orchestra, by the bye, has rubbed off the rustiness of the beginning of the season, and has been playing admirably these last few weeks.

A LIFE OF CHOPIN
The World, 7 December 1892

At the London Symphony Concert last Thursday, Mr Henschel staked the capacity of his orchestra for refinement of execution on Raff's Lenore symphony, and won. The *crescendo* of the march, from *pianissimo* to *forte*, was admirably managed. It did not quite reach *fortissimo*—not what I call *fortissimo*, at least—and it fell short of the final degrees of martial brilliancy which Mr Manns has sometimes achieved in it; but it was enormously superior to the recent attempt of the Philharmonic band, which began moderately *piano*, tumbled into a *mezzo forte* in the second section, and stuck there for the rest of the movement. The second movement was perfectly executed: it held the attention of the audience from the first note to the last, as slow movements very seldom do. The quick movements would have been equally perfect but for a certain unpunctuality of attack in the vigorous touches, especially in the bass, and an occasional want of weight when the fullest power of the band was needed.

I should explain, however, that I heard the performance, not from my usual seat, but from the extreme back of the room, where, as I went in, I spied a few empty benches suitable for a secluded nap. A long work by Brahms was in the program; so I thought I would go and sit there in case of accidents. It was a concerto for violin and violoncello, with one or two glorious beginnings in it in Brahms's vigorous, joyous, romantic style; but they did not hold out; and there was nothing for it, most of the time, but resignation or slumber. Gorski, the violinist, had not come to much of an understanding with Fuchs, the cellist; and neither of them had come to an understanding with Brahms—at least, it seemed so to me; but then my attention wandered a good deal. Miss Evangeline Florence sang the balcony scene from Lohengrin; and the concert wound up with the overture to Die Meistersinger.

Violoncellists who want to play like Gerardy will be interested by the Cours Préparatoire de Violoncelle of his master, Alfred Massau, of the Verviers school of music. There is an abominable custom among agents of persuading young and unknown artists, however admirably they may have been taught, to prepare for their *début* by taking three months' lessons from some celebrated player, in order that they may be announced and puffed as pupils of the eminent So-and-so. Thus they are taught to begin by being ashamed of their own talent, and ungrateful to the master to whom they owe its cultivation. The master is robbed of the credit due to him; and the eminent one finds Europe full of players claiming to be his pupils on the strength of perhaps a dozen lessons.

Think of the legion of pianists, good, bad, and indifferent, who, because they once loafed about Weimar for a few months, and managed to obtain the not very difficult entry to the famous music-room there, are now "pupils of Liszt." The system is not only a dishonest one, but stupid into the bargain; for the public, as far as it concerns itself with an artist's antecedents at all, judges the master by the player, and not the player by the master. I therefore give Alfred Massau as Gerardy's master neither on his own claim nor on that of his famous pupil, but on the authority of an official certificate from the Communal Administration of Verviers, duly stamped with the town seal, whereupon a lion ramps in a meat safe, with a crown above him, and the motto *L'Union fait la force* below.

The document, dated November 1891, runs as follows:

"I subscribe, declare, and certify that Mr Jean Gerardy, violoncellist, has gone through the regular violoncello course at our establishment (professor, Alfred Massau), from October 1st, 1885, to August 15th, 1889. He has carried off the following distinctions: Competition of 1886 (2nd division), 1st *accessit*; 1887 (*idem*), 1st prize; 1888 (1st division), 1st prize, with distinction; 1889 (higher competition), silver-gilt medal, with the greatest distinction.

"The jury for these last competitions was composed of MM. L. Kefer, Presiding Director; Van der Heyden, violoncellist from Paris; J. de Swert, violoncellist, Conductor at Ostend; Ed. Jacobs, violoncellist, Professor at the Brussels Conservatoire; and Jos. Mertens, Government Inspector of Schools of Music."

Here follow the signatures of M. Louis Kefer and the President of the Communal Administration, solemnly affixed in "our" presence. That is, the presence of the Burgomaster, whose signature, as becomes that of a man with a plural pronoun, is wholly illegible.

I give this document for the sake of its suggestiveness as to the state of affairs in the musical profession. Verviers is a small Belgian town; its school of music is not widely famous; and Massau, though his reputation as a teacher is first-rate, is not known as a *virtuoso* in London and Paris. The consequence is that Verviers and Massau, instead of finding themselves made famous by the brilliant European success of Gerardy, actually have to place official certificates in my hands in order to make it known in London that the five years' training which made Gerardy what he is were not the work of Herr Bellmann or any other *virtuoso* who may have subsequently given him "finishing lessons."

As to the Cours Préparatoire, I can only testify to its completeness and intelligibility. Not being a cellist, I must take Gerardy's playing as evidence of its soundness. It is published by Schott, has its instructions printed in French, German, and English, and is remarkably cheap, considering its bulk and quality, at ten shillings, or in two volumes at six shillings each.

I have received from Messrs Sampson Low & Co. a Life of Chopin, by Mr Charles Willeby, which strikes me as really supplying a want. For some years past the Liszt-George Sand stereo on the subject has been wearing out; and the arrival of an exceedingly cool young gentleman, adequately skilled in music, who gives his own account of the matter without the least regard for the expiring Chopin fashion, is highly refreshing. The older I grow, the more I appreciate the *sang-froid* of early manhood. Middle age makes me sentimental, hot-headed, and withal conscious of the folly of the multitude and the ease with which that folly can be exploited by anybody with a moderate power of self-expression in politics or in any of the popular arts. This I call becoming wise; but if I were anybody else, I should doubtless call it becoming stale.

Anyhow, it is a condition in which I could not write as freshly about Chopin as Mr Willeby; and I welcome his book accordingly; though I cannot refrain from giving utterance to the melancholy conviction that time will mellow his stern judgment of George Sand, and shake his incredulity as to her having boxed her son-in-law's ears and turned him out of the house for smiting one of her guests on the nose. "Were we dealing with children, and the nursery our scene" says Mr Willeby "we might accept this story. But when we think that the parties concerned were men and women of the world, it is laughable, and to accept it seriously, impossible." Alas! alas! it is precisely the men and women of the world who do these things, whilst the novices are furtively studying manuals of etiquet to ascertain the proper use of the fingerbowl.

Mr Willeby, to tell the truth, rather breaks down over George Sand. He says:

"However lenient we may be towards the woman who so worthily added to the art of her country, one cannot deny the fact that she was of a nature the reverse of admirable—a woman who, while stopping at nothing in the gratification of her desires, yet was ever ready with an excuse for herself, and who *posed* before the world as an example of all that was good and upright in womanhood. Moreover, she seems to have been wanting alike in tact, reserve, and dignity of conduct; while by no means the least noticeable feature in her character was the manner in which she succeeded in deceiving even herself."

All of which, though irrefutable from its point of view, is entirely worthless as a description of George Sand, because it would be equally irrefutable of dozens of other eminent women who were not in the least like George Sand. One does not refute that sort of criticism; one repudiates it.
Again:

"One of the vices of George Sand seems to have been not an extraordinary one in women generally, that of curiosity. This fatal feeling," &c.

Observe the implication that "this fatal feeling" is a stranger to the nobler male breast. Only once does Mr Willeby relent:

"Inasmuch as she kept his accounts, wrote many of his letters, and tended him with the greatest devotion in the many trying times when his disease laid him up, *she is worthy of some praise.*"

I should rather think so. I do not hold a brief for George Sand; but Mr Willeby provokes me to ask what would have been said if the shoe had been on the other foot. Suppose Chopin had been George Sand's benefactor. Suppose he had found after a time that she was as exacting as an invalided child; that she spoiled the home life of his other children by quarreling with them; and that he could not spare from his own work as a composer the energy wasted in combating these circumstances. Would any reasonable person have blamed him for refusing to share his home with her any longer? If not, how can any reasonable person blame George Sand, except on the gratuitous assumption that she and her children were Chopin's slaves, with no duty to anybody but to him? For the life of me, I cannot see how she behaved worse than Chopin.

The fact that he appears to have suffered more by the separation than she did is clearly a proof that he gained more than she by their association. Mr Willeby has certainly made out a case of ingratitude against Chopin, as well as one of levity against George Sand; but neither of them is more interesting or convincing than the cases against Salvini for vagabondism, against Mr Hamo Thornycroft for breach of the Second Commandment,* against the Duke of Wellington for rapine and murder, or against any English Mahometan for not attending his parish church. Nothing is more idle and tedious than the sort of criticism which deals with a man who is acting up to his own convictions, right or wrong, as if he was simply violating his critic's convictions, or those of his critic's publisher.

On the whole, Mr Willeby's moral judgments must be taken as a trifle disabled by the very quality of youth which gives value to his book as a whole. To say, for instance, that Chopin was not a man to grasp opportunities merely because he did not jump at a chance of giving a paying concert, is to substitute the business standard of a smart agent for the artistic standard of the critic of a great composer. A man who died of consumption at thirtynine, and yet produced what Chopin has left us, was clearly a man of immeasurably greater energy and practicality than the late Mr Jay

* Hamo Thornycroft, highly reputed English sculptor, was a violator of the commandment not to "make unto thee any graven image."

Gould, who worked far longer than Chopin, and produced nothing.

On musical ground I agree better with Mr Willeby, though even here I am made somewhat restive by such passages as:

"In the Concerto, Chopin's subordination to, and inability to cope with, form was as conspicuous as was his superiority and independence of it in his smaller works."

This implies that form means sonata form and nothing else, an unwarrantable piece of pedantry, which one remembers as common enough in the most incompetent and old-fashioned criticisms of Chopin's ballades, Liszt's symphonic poems, and Wagner's works generally, but which is now totally out of countenance. Mr Willeby himself evidently would not stand by it for a moment. Yet on another page (229) he goes still further in the same direction by identifying music in sonata form with "absolute music," and describing all other music as "program music." Now a Chopin ballade is clearly no more program music than the slow movement of Mozart's symphony in E flat is.

I submit that a definition which makes program music of Chopin's tone poems, and abstract music of Raff's symphonies, clearly wants a little further consideration. However, I must not unduly depreciate Mr Willeby's book by dwelling too much on our differences. A few slips in the critical analyses may very well be condoned for the sake of a readable biography of Chopin which is not nine-tenths a work of pure imagination.

WAGNER'S OPINIONS

Remarks in a discussion following a paper by William Ashton Ellis on Richard Wagner's Prose, 13 December 1892. Proceedings of the Musical Association 1892–93

[U] I may be permitted to express my surprise that what Wagner said about Mendelssohn should be called in question in England, of all places on the earth. I really cannot understand how it is that Wagner should be so misunderstood on the subject. It seems to me that Wagner did strict justice to Mendelssohn, who appears to have treated his music very much in the same way as he conducted it. Anyone whose memory goes back to the time before Richter began to conduct, about twelve or thirteen years ago, will remember what a performance of a Mozart or Beethoven symphony was like. It was so rapid that scarcely one idea of the composer was properly brought out. But when Richter came there was a change; people began to recognize the true music and saw the proper conductor; they began to hear the music of the great composers as it was written.

Now with regard to Wagner's opinion about Brahms. Brahms is a man of most enormous musical power, but he decidedly is not a great thinker or poet as Wagner was. I do not think that his music will suggest that to anyone. His Requiem I take to be a most abominable work, and furthermore it is a work which all cultivated musicians know to be a poor composition. It is intolerably long, and I really cannot understand how people can listen to it. But you find a general tendency on the part of the members of the Press and musical critics to write about Brahms as though he were a great composer. Every contemporary critic is indeed bound to say that

Brahms is a composer; so he is, but put him in his proper place, so that our young composers and musicians will be better qualified to judge him from that particular standpoint. I can only say that I have never yet met with an opinion of Wagner's that did not seem to me to be a most remarkable critical opinion. [U]

A ROYAL COLLEGE ORFEO
The World, 14 December 1892

I have to complain strongly of the Royal College of Music for its neglect to exclude the parents and relatives of the students from its performance of Gluck's Orfeo on Saturday afternoon. The barbarous demonstrations of these Philistines, who treated the band just as they would have treated a quadrille player at one of their own dances, spoiled many a final strain in the score. Surely, if the students are to be nurtured as artists, the first and most obvious step is to cut off all communication between them and their families.

A member of an ordinary British household cannot become an artist: the thing is impossible. This was well understood in former ages with regard to the religious life, the devotees of which invariably began by cutting all their people dead, knowing full well that on no other terms was any unworldly life possible. Now the artistic life is the most unworldly of lives; and how can it be lived in any sort of association with people who, rather than wait for the band to finish *Che faro senza, Euridice?* break into uncouth noise the moment the singer's mouth is closed?

Giulia Ravogli came to the performance, presumably to see what Gluck's Orfeo looked like. The unfamiliar spectacle must have made her envy those obscure students the artistic framework which she, one of the greatest Orfeos in the world, cannot get in the richest capital in Europe. The work was admirably put on the stage. One scene, in which a soul newly released from earth came groping into the Elysian fields, bewildered and lonely, and was discovered and welcomed by two child-shades, was a most pathetic piece of pantomime. That shade one believed to be the lost Euridice, until Euridice appeared later on in the person of quite another young lady—no great pantomimist. Very pretty, too, was the array of spirits stretching their hands after the departing Orpheus as he started on his return to earth.

The Elysian fields were situated on the uplands between Frensham and Selborne: I know the place, and thought it well chosen for the purpose. The furies and spectres were not quite up to the artistic level of the blesseder shades; and they gave no adequate sign of the shock given to them by the first note of Orpheus's lute in that dreadful region. I think, too, that the orchestral piece in D minor, since it was not danced to by the spectres, should have been played with the tableau curtain down, instead of as a storm symphony to a lightning and thunder cloth which became ridiculous after its levin bolts had remained for a couple of minutes without getting along. But the fact that these two matters exhaust my fault-finding speaks for the general excellence and artistic integrity of the staging.

The principal performer, Miss Clara Butt, a comparatively raw recruit from Bristol, far surpassed the utmost expectations that could have been reasonably entertained. She has a good voice, and went at her work without the least conceit, though with plenty of courage and originality, shewing an honesty of artistic character which is perhaps the most promising quality a novice can display. She has a rich measure of dramatic sympathy; and, considering that the management of the costume and deportment proper to the part would tax the powers of our most experienced actresses, her impersonation suffered surprisingly little from awkwardness. If Miss Butt has sufficient strength of mind to keep her eyes, ears, and mind open in the artistic atmosphere of the Royal College, without for a moment allowing herself to be taught (a process which instantly stops the alternative process of learning), she may make a considerable career for herself.

Euridice (Miss Maggie Purvis) sang like a pupil of the Royal Academy. She had apparently been taught to practise all over her voice on the vowel *a,* because that is the most beautiful vowel. The way in which a soprano produces the G or A flat above the stave had been taken as a model for the production of every sound within her compass. To make a *crescendo* she simply breathed harder; and she attacked her notes with the *coup de glotte.* I have heard basses—actually basses—who had been taught to do exactly the same thing; and the difference between their voices and that of Edouard de Reszke was very striking.

Imagine that genial giant with his voice trained like the top register of a soprano, bleating a few genteel notes between his upper B and D with the feather-edge of his vocal cords (the E natural and F not to be practised too much lest they should fatigue the larynx), and with all the middle of his voice worn to the sound of a cracked Pandean pipe. I do not know the names of the teaching staff at the Royal College, nor of Euridice's preceptor, whose instructions she may, of course, have been systematically violating, as the wont of pupils is when they get before the public.

But I am bound to say that though she sang prettily, and is not at all deficient in capacity, the sort of voice she produces would never stand the knocking about of real dramatic work, nor has it the least force or variety of color. It is impossible for me to go at length into the system of teaching singing which has prevailed for so long in our own Royal Academy and many of the foreign Conservatoires, and which has been maintained so ably by that clever and dramatically gifted family, the Garcias. Suffice it to say that I have heard a good many pupils of the Garcias in my time, and a good many pupils of other masters, too, from Santley to Melba and our modern American *prima donnas*; and I must frankly say that though I do not doubt that all the great Garcias were masterful people and powerful actors, I am a confirmed skeptic as to the practical value of their system of vocal instruction. And I was sorry to infer, from Euridice's singing, and from my recollection of the previous annual operatic performances, that the Garcia method is in the ascendant at Kensington as well as in Tenterden-street.

My observation has led me to believe that if you take an ordinary English girl and try to make her sing, your business is not to elicit from her sounds as fine as G above the stave on the vowel *a* (Italian) as Patti would sing it, but to work her voice on *aw* (without rolling her tongue up into a ball, *bien entendu*) below the stave, on *oo* and *ee* in the middle, and on *a* at the top only, shewing her how to manage her breathing and so forth meanwhile, and keeping her at that until she has learnt the physical act of singing, and is in possession of a fully developed voice well under her control, which she can use as vigorously as she wants to without any damage. Then, and not until then, is the time to awaken her artistic conscience, to purify her pronunciation, refine her tone, and, in short, turn your mere singer into an artist.

Try to make her into an artist before she can sing by worrying her at the very first lesson to produce the ideal tone aimed at by Garcia, and unless her physical endowment is so rich and her vocation so strong that she stumbles into the right path in spite of you, you will arrive at that melancholy result, the ordinary Academy pupil who, after a brief trial of her thin and colorless perfections on the public, takes to helping herself out by brute force, and presently grinds away her voice and takes to teaching the art in which she has failed. Of course she has been repeatedly warned that she must not force her voice; but when she finds that she can produce no effect in any other way, all these excellent negative precepts are thrown to the winds. No method that is merely negative is of any use to a dramatic singer, or indeed to any artist whatever.

Unless singers have a positive method, into which they can throw their utmost energy and temper at moments when they are about as much interested in the quality of the vowel *a* as a tiger is in the quality of his roar as he springs on a sheep, they *must* resort to brute force on the stage, or else fail through an obvious gingerly preoccupation with their negative instructions. The first demand of the dramatic instinct is for a safe and powerful *fortissimo*. To tell students of dramatic singing that there is no need for vehemence in singing is only an evasion, like telling the student who wants to paint a white cat that "in the grand school, all cats are grey." Shouting is not necessary in political oratory; but I should like to see the political speaker who would put up with a teacher unable to put him in the way of thundering a little occasionally.

It so happened on Saturday that Miss Purvis did not particularly want to be vehement. But if she had been playing Elvira or Valentine or Fidelio, I wonder how much use her academic method in its negative purity would have been to her. Much less, I venture to affirm, than no method at all. She would simply have had to scream through all the formidable passages.

I turn with relief to the subject of the band. Here the performers, having all been taught their instruments by men who earn their living by playing them, knew their business, and were no worse than their instructors in respect of not always sustaining the tone for the full duration of the notes. The execution was smart, and the quality of sound remarkably bright and fine.

The conductor, Professor Stanford, guided, as I judged, by a genuine love of the work and an intimate knowledge of it, only went astray once—in the immensely grand chorus *Che mai dell' Erebo*, which he took, like a true Irishman, as he would have taken the first movement of the Eroica, and not in the *tempo* of God Save the Queen, which would have been much nearer the mark, reserving the quick *tempo* for the later repetitions. For the performance as a whole there can be nothing but praise. It could only be possible in an institution where there was a well-spring of genuine enthusiasm for art. The credit of stimulating and centring that enthusiasm belongs, I imagine, to Sir George Grove, whose life-work has been of more value than that of all the Prime Ministers of the century.

Let me add, by the way, that the Royal College has selected its opera much better this year and last than it used to. Tales like those of The Barber of Bagdad, and classic legends like Orpheus, are understood by young students far better than silly intrigues like Così fan tutte, or—with all due respect to Shakespear—explosions of what I may call sex-Podsnappery* like that atrocious play The Taming of the Shrew.

* A Dickensian term meaning smug self-satisfaction, as exemplified by Mr John Podsnap in Our Mutual Friend.

A MISCELLANEOUS CONCERT

The World, 21 December 1892

The nursing homes of St Mary's, Plaistow, succeeded in making up a program at St James's Hall on Thursday, which induced me to go, for once in a way, to a miscellaneous concert. I there heard Mrs Katharine Fisk, the American contralto, who seems to have made a considerable impression on her first appearance (at which I was unable to assist) some weeks ago. She selected a song called Calm as the Night, by Bohm, and, by dint of grinding and driving her voice hard down on every note, produced a certain effect which may have appealed to some of the audience as one of brooding intensity. To me it seemed a mechanical device which any contralto could acquire at the risk of being left presently with a hollow and unsympathetic voice, almost useless for what I, according to my particular prejudice on the subject, consider legitimate singing. However, Mrs Fisk obtained her share of applause; and, as it is her business to please the public and not to conform to my notions of voice production, I have nothing more to say.

Giulia Ravogli sang a *scena* from Vaccai's Giulietta e Romeo, chosen for the sake of one of those long recitatives beginning with *In questo loco* (In this neighborhood), and proceeding with the usual observations. I like to hear Signorina Giulia singing *In questo loco,* just as I should have liked to hear Mrs Siddons asking the linen-draper "Will it wash?" But let there be no mistake about the fact that *In questo loco* is as dead as My name is Norval. No doubt if Mr Irving suddenly took a fancy to Norval and began reciting about the Grampian Hills, and his father feeding his flock, a frugal swain, whose constant care was to increase his store,★ we should listen to him with high enjoyment, much as we listen to Miss Ellen Terry bringing Monk Lewis back to life with her pet recitation of Stay, gaoler, stay: I am not mad. But we should not regard the entertainment as up to date. And that is my objection to Vaccai. Like Monk Lewis and Home, he was a man for an age, but most emphatically not for all time.

Sofia Ravogli joined her sister in a duet from [Massenet's] Le Roi de Lahore, which they sang with a distinction and quiet perfection of style which shewed that they have found out the good side of the London artistic atmosphere, and profited by it. Their former touch of provinciality, which one did not care to mention, so trivial a drawback was it to their genuine musical and dramatic force, has vanished without taking any of their intensity away with it; and we may now esteem ourselves rarely fortunate in having, apparently, attached them to England. No doubt we shall shew our sense of that by offering them the chance of some half a dozen appearances on the stage every year in the height of the season, with a turn at the Philharmonic and Crystal Palace, a liberal allowance of charity concerts, and plenty of private engagements. Nothing is sadder than the way in which London attracts dramatic genius to itself and then helplessly wastes it.

The concert, I should explain, was varied by the appearance from time to time of a cheerful clergyman, who made the most sinister announcements without blenching, and retired each time smiling blandly at the horror-stricken audience. Thus he would say, after waiting for dead silence with a reassuring beam in his eye, "Ladies and gentlemen: Miss Esther Palliser will

★ The reference is to Act III of Douglas (1756), a play by the Scottish dramatist John Home.

not be able to sing for you this afternoon, as she is all but asphyxiated"; or "Ladies and gentlemen: we must omit the next item, as one of the ladies in the quartet has suddenly lost her voice"; or, "Ladies and gentlemen: if Mr Wyndham and Miss Mary Moore give us their duologue, they will fall into the hands of the law, as this hall is not licensed by the County Council for dramatic entertainments; but they will do the best they can separately under the circumstances." He might have thrown in an apology for the excruciating discrepancy between the pitch of the pianoforte and that of Miss Eldina Bligh's fiddle.

I had rather have drunk a tumbler of vinegar than listen to those Brahms-Joachim Hungarian dances with the violin virtually in one key and the piano in another. It was a pity; for the young lady would have pleased the audience very well if there had been no accompaniment. When she reappeared later on with Miss Macintyre, to play the *obbligato* to the inevitable intermezzo from Cavalleria, the audience received her with the liveliest apprehensions. This time, however, the pitch was adjusted; and she played the *obbligato* much better, I must say, than Miss Macintyre sang the Ave Maria.

Miss Macintyre's style is not prayerful, nor her execution smooth; and when she finished her self-assertive orison with a vigorous *forte* on the last note, we thought of the saintlike Calvé and her touching *pianissimo*, and blessed the singer for resisting the *encore* which the intermezzo-maniacs promptly tried to force upon her. I rather admired her for singing the piece in her own way instead of imitating Calvé; but I cannot say that I thought her own way particularly appropriate; though far be it from me to make a serious matter of the treatment of what is, at best, an arrant piece of claptrap.

An interesting point in the program was Mr Henschel's singing of Schumann's setting of Heine's Two

Grenadiers, followed by Mr Bispham with Wagner's setting of a French version—one of the *pièces de salon* which he produced in his early Parisian days. Mr Henschel sat down comfortably to the piano and murdered Schumann in cold blood. He played the mournful, weary-footed, quasi-military dead march accompaniment anyhow, flicking off the semiquaver turn in semidemisemiquavers, and beginning the Marseillaise at the top of his voice, which is the surest way I know to make the song fail. And it did fail, in spite of Mr Henschel's popularity, his staleness in it being obvious.

Mr Bispham, thoroughly on the alert, took his turn like the intelligent and cultivated artist he is; and though Wagner's setting taxed his voice fully twenty shillings in the pound, he came off solvent. I then fled from the miscellaneous scene, and so cannot say how the last quarter of the program was done, or whether it was done at all.

On the previous Tuesday I went to the Royal Academy of Music to hear Mr Ashton Ellis confront the Musical Association on the subject of Wagner's prose. There was a time when Mr Ellis would have taken his life in his hand on such an errand; but he now holds the field unopposed. I looked round for the old gang (if I may use that convenient political term without offence), and looked in vain.

When Mr Ellis sat down, after a sufficiently provocative exposure of the garblings of Opera and Drama which used to appear in the Musical World in the old days of anti-Wagnerism, I asked myself was there no man left to get up and complain of the "false relations" in Tristan, to plead for "a full close in the key" at frequent intervals during Der Ring, to explain that Wagner's music shattered the human voice and overpowered it with deafening instrumentation, to deplore the total absence of melody in Lohengrin, to praise the Tannhäuser march as the sole endurable work of Wagner (because plagiarized from the great *scena* in Der Freischütz)—in short, to put himself totally out of the question, for ever and a day, with every musician whose ideas of art were wider than those of a provincial organist?

But the enemy was chapfallen and speechless—that is, if the enemy was present; but I think he had stayed away. At any rate, Mr Ellis's party had the discussion all to themselves.

CHRISTMAS AND AFTER
The World, 4 January 1893

These are not busy times for musical critics. In London everything serves as an excuse for having no music, from the death of a Royal personage to Christmas, just as in school everything serves as an excuse for a holiday. I have been in the country, in an old English manor house,* where we all agreed to try and forget the festive season. We were not altogether successful. On the very first evening we were invaded by "the mummers," who were not in the least like the husbands of Mr George Moore's Mummer's Wife. They were laborers, over-grown with strips of colored paper as a rock is overgrown with seaweed; and they went through an operatic performance which I did not quite follow, as they were quite equal to professional opera singers in point of unintelligibility, and, being simple country folk, were so unversed in the etiquet of first nights that they neglected to provide me with a libretto. I gathered that

* Kelmscott House, Shaw's host being William Morris.

one of them was King Alfred, and another St George. A third, equipped with a stale tall hat, was announced as "the doctor." He drew a tooth from the *prima donna*, whom I did not succeed in identifying; revived the other characters when they were slain in single combat; and sang a ballad expressive of his aspiration to live and die "a varmer's b'woy." This he delivered with such a concentrated lack of conviction that I at once concluded that he actually was a farmer's boy; and my subsequent inquiries as to the rate of wages in the district confirmed my surmise. We of the audience had to assume the character of good old English gentlemen and ladies keeping up a seasonable custom; and it would be difficult to say whether we or the performers were the most put out of countenance. I have seldom been so disconcerted; and my host, though he kept it up amazingly, confessed to sharing my feelings; whilst the eagerness of the artists to escape from our presence when their performance was concluded and suitably acknowledged, testified to the total failure of our efforts to make them feel at home. We were perfectly friendly at heart, and would have been delighted to sit round the fire with them and talk; but the conventions of the season forbad it. Since we had to be mock-baronial, they had to be mock-servile; and so we made an uneasy company of Christmas humbugs, and had nothing to cheer us except the consciousness of heartily forgiving oneanother and being forgiven. On Christmas Eve there was more music, performed by the school children, the carol singers, and finally by an orchestra consisting of a violin, a tambourine, a toy instrument with a compass of one wrong note, which it played steadily on the second and third beats in the bar, and anything else that would make a noise *ripieno, ad lib*. The singers sang traditional— *i.e.* inaccurate—versions of old airs and modern music hall songs, the latter strangely modified by transmission

[775]

from mouth to ear along the whole length of the Thames.

On my return to town I was casting about me in an unsettled state of mind for some pretext for keeping away for another evening from my work, when I found myself, as luck would have it, outside the Lyceum Theatre. Recollecting that I had not heard Mr Hamilton Clarke's incidental music to King Lear, I went inside, and found myself late for the overture, and only just in time for the march to which the Court enters. Mr Hamilton Clarke's music is graceful, and sensitive to the tenderer emotions of the drama. It is far too civilized for Lear; but it is, perhaps, unreasonable to expect a composer to aim at the powerful and barbaric when he well knows that the orchestral resources at his disposal will not be adequate to much more than sentimental *mélodrame*. I may add that I decidedly prefer Mr Ford Madox Brown as an illustrator of Shakespear to Mr Frank Dicksee; and as Mr Hamilton Clarke is in music exactly what Mr Frank Dicksee is in painting, his interludes do not altogether satisfy me. Which is nobody's fault, and my own misfortune.

Whilst I am on the subject of the Lyceum, I may as well extract the following from a letter in one of the musical papers: "Speaking of the letter O, Mr G. B. S. says that Mr Irving is the only living Englishman who makes it a pure vowel. What a marvelous being Mr G.B.S. must be! All the English, twentyseven millions in number, have passed in review before him, and only one has succeeded in properly pronouncing the vowel O!" Now I did not say that Mr Irving pronounces O *properly*; I said that he makes a pure vowel of it. The effect was so strange at first that for years his pronunciation of "gold," "bowl," "pole to pole" (in Vanderdecken), &c., was unsparingly ridiculed and mimicked. I should like to have it settled whether Mr Irving is right or wrong.

[776]

There can be no doubt that the usage is to make O a diphthong: one hears "goh-oold," "gowld," "gah-oold," in all directions, but never pure "gold," except from Mr Irving or his imitators. On the other hand, the pure vowel is, to my artistic sense, much pleasanter. Which, then, should be recommended to the young actor? This question is much better suited for discussion in a musical paper than the misapprehensions arising from my unfortunate habit of saying things I do not mean, such as "the barbarous thoroughbass of Handel and Mozart." My critic has deserved well of his country for nipping that thoughtless slander in the bud.

I also hasten to explain that when I called Sterndale Bennett a convinced Dayite, I did not mean that he agreed with Day's derivations of chords. The first symptom of inveterate Dayism used generally to be a violent attack on one of Day's imaginary "roots." My impression is that Bennett believed in "roots," and that certain "intellectual harmonies" of his are logical applications of the root theory. Also, that the change from the rule-of-thumb thoroughbass taught by Mozart to Sussmayer, to the pseudo-scientific systems of Day and Macfarren, was forwarded instead of opposed by Sterndale Bennett. My critic contradicts me; but as his style does not inspire me with unreserved confidence, I remain, pending further information, in the same mind still.

THE PROFESSIONAL MUSICIAN
The World, 11 January 1893

The Incorporated Society of Musicians has been holding its annual conference. Being rather short of subjects to confer about, it has taken to listening to music—even on the organ—to while away the time. It is a pity we have not an incorporated society of critics, so that the musicians and critics might confer together, with a strong police force present to maintain order. It would be more amusing, even to the provincials, than organs and schools for the musical training of the blind; and the eternal question of raising the status of the musician could perhaps be met by the previous question as to what is the matter with the musician's status that he should want it raised.

It seems to me that the social opportunities of the musician are greater, instead of less, than those of other craftsmen. The church organist may find, like the rest of us, that those who pay the piper insist on calling the tune; and if they happen to have no ear and no soul for music—nay, if, as may very easily be the case, they actually make a virtue of disparaging it—the unfortunate musician may be grievously oppressed; but he is not compelled to put up with oppression because he is a musician, but solely because he depends on his post for his bread-and-butter. He is at a disadvantage: not as artist, but as employee, just as he would be in any other trade or profession. He is certainly at no social disadvantage: on the contrary, it is always assumed that the professional player of a musical instrument is socially superior to the skilled mechanic or artisan, though there is no reason in the world why he should be.

An orchestral player may be a person of distinguished culture and address; but he may also be illiterate, coarse, drunken, not scrupulously honest, and in short, a person whom sensitive composers and conductors would not employ if his mechanical dexterity could be dispensed with. An organist may be in every respect the superior of the rector; but he is just as likely to be the inferior of the keeper of the village shop, who does not complain particularly about his status. Some of the more innocent of my readers may be shocked at this, and may demand of me whether a man whose occupation is to interpret Handel, Mozart, Beethoven, or even Jackson in B flat, is not likely to have a more elevated soul than a buyer and seller of pots and pans. I reply, not in the least. You might as well ask whether a navvy, constantly employed on vast engineering schemes, is not likely to be more large-minded than a watchmaker.

Take a man with a quick ear and quick fingers; teach him how to play an instrument and to read staff notation; give him some band practice; and there you have your "professional," able to do what Wagner could not have done for the life of him, but no more necessarily a musician in the wider sense than a regimental marksman or broadsword instructor is necessarily a general or a master of foreign policy. He need make no more distinction between Beethoven and Brahms than a compositor does between Shakespear and Tennyson: even when he has an exceptionally fine sense of the difference between good and bad execution, he may not have the ghost of an idea of the difference between good and bad music.

Orchestral players, good enough to find constant employment in the best European orchestras, and yet with the manners, ideas, and conversation of ordinary private soldiers, are less common than formerly; but they are still contemporary facts, and not at all anomalous ones, except to muddle-headed people who imagine that every man who can play a string of notes written down by Mozart or Bach must have the heart and mind of Mozart and Bach. No doubt I shall presently be told that I have slandered an honorable profession by declaring that the members of our London orchestras are all illiterate, drunken, private-soldierly rapscallions. That is quite as near what I have just said as some of my musician-critics ever get to the meaning of my most careful and discriminate statements, let alone my more epigrammatic ones.

But the fact remains as I have stated it, that the professional musician, as such, can have no special social status whatever, because he may be anything, from an ex-drummer boy to an artist and philosopher of world-wide reputation. It would be far more reasonable to demand a special status for the musical critic as such, since he is bound to be skilled in music, in literature, and in criticism, which no man can be without a far wider culture than an executive musician need possess. But I never have any trouble about my status, though I probably should have if I were asked to draw the line between myself and the country-town reporter who occasionally copies out a concert program and prefaces it with a few commonplaces. I am welcome among the people who like my ways and manners; and I believe musicians enjoy the same advantage.

When we are not welcome, probably the ways and manners are to blame, and not the profession.

With this soothing contribution to the ever-burning question of the conference, I pass on to the part of it which I personally attended: to wit, the lecture on the spinet, harpsichord, and clavichord by Mr Hipkins, and that on the lute and viols by Mr Arnold Dolmetsch. Mr Hipkins's proficiency as a player on the harpsichord and clavichord is an old story upon which I need not dwell. If any swaggering pianist is inclined to undervalue that proficiency, let him try his hand on a clavichord and see what he can make of an instrument which depends for its "action," not on the elaborate mechanism of Erard or any modification thereof, but on the dexterity of the player.

Not to mention, by the bye, that clavichord music is mostly of that sort in which every wrong note or rough touch betrays itself at once, unlike your modern thickly harmonized pieces, in which one fistful of notes is as good as another when a grandiose chord is wanted. The Rosencrantzes who know no touch of the old instruments, but who are not content to leave them alone, should go to Mr Hipkins, consider his ways, and be wise. For my own part, I hope Mr Hipkins will find many imitators. There is no sort of doubt that the pianoforte must succumb sooner or later to the overwhelming objection that you can hear it next door. In an age of general insensibility to music this does not matter: the ordinary citizen today, who regards pianoforte playing as a mere noise, may drop an oath or two when the young lady at the other side of the party-wall begins practising; but he soon gets used to it as he gets used to passing trains, factory hooters, fog signals, and wheel traffic. Make a musician of him, however, and his tolerance will vanish. I live, when I am at home, in a London square which is in a state of transition from the Russell Square private house stage to the Soho or Golden Square stage of letting for all sorts of purposes. There are a couple of clubs, with "bars" and social musical evenings, not unrelieved by occasional clog dances audible a quarter of a mile off. There is a residence for the staff of a monster emporium which employs several talented tenors behind its counters. There is a volunteer headquarters in which the band practises on the first floors whilst the combatants train themselves for the thousand yards range by shooting through Morris tubes in the area. Yet I have sat at work on a summer evening, with every window in the square open and all these resources in full blast, and found myself less disturbed than I have been by a single private pianoforte, of the sort that the British householder thinks "brilliant," played by a female with no music in her whole composition, simply getting up an "accomplishment" either to satisfy her own vanity or to obey the orders of her misguided mother. Now if such females had spinets to play on instead of pianos, I should probably not hear them. Again, take the fiddle. It is a good sign, no doubt, that it is so much more generally practised than it used to be. But it is a terribly powerful instrument in neighborhoods where only millionaires can afford to live in detached houses.

How much pleasanter it would be to live next to Mr Arnold Dolmetsch, with his lutes, love viols, and leg viols, than to an ordinary string quartet! You can study the difference at Covent Garden on a Huguenots night, when the leader of the violas, after playing the prelude to Raoul's air in the first act on a ravishingly harmonious *viole d'amour*, reverts to his modern viola when he begins the *obbligato* to the air itself, and is promptly execrated for a harsh and tuneless scraper. A mouthful of margarine after a mouthful of honey would be far less disappointing. But if we went back to the old viols with sympathetic strings and the old harpsichords, I suppose we should have to begin to make them again; and I wonder what would be the result of that.

To me the difference between the beautiful spinet which Mr Hipkins played the other day and a modern cottage pianoforte of the sort that sells best in England is as the difference between the coloring of Bellini or Carpaccio and that of the late Frank Holl. But hereupon comes the horrible reflection that most of us prefer Frank Holl's pictures to Bellini's. Is there the smallest reason to suppose that if we took to making harpsichords we would make good ones? Alas! the question is already answered. Mr Hipkins not only played on the beautiful spinet already mentioned, and on a comparatively middling harpsichord, but also on a new harpsichord manufactured by a very eminent Parisian firm of pianoforte makers; and not only did it prove itself a snarling abomination, with vices of tone that even a harmonium would have been ashamed of, but it had evidently been deliberately made so in order to meet the ordinary customer's notion of a powerful and brilliant instrument.

Mr Dolmetsch did not exhibit any modern lutes, perhaps because none have been made; but if our fiddle makers were to attempt to revive them they would probably aim at the sort of "power" of tone produced by those violins which ingenious street players make out of empty Australian mutton tins and odd legs of stools.

I must not omit to say that Mr Dolmetsch's viol concerts, apart from their historical interest, are highly enjoyable from the purely musical point of view, his own playing and that of his daughter (on the viol da gamba) being excellent.

A REPLY TO MR LUNN
The World, 18 January 1893

Lest I should seem to slight that deservedly esteemed champion of good singing, Mr Charles Lunn, by taking no notice of his criticism of my utterances on his pet subject, I shall answer it, in spite of the difficulty created by the fact that whilst Mr Lunn firmly believes himself a disciple of Garcia and an advocate of the *coup de glotte*, he has, as a matter of fact, spent his life in fighting against the practical results of Garcia's method of instruction, and is no more a *coup de glottist* than I am. It will be remembered that I recently mentioned Santley and Melba as examples of the long line of good singers who have had nothing of the Academy method about them.

Mr Lunn, in reply, claims Santley and Melba as virtual pupils of Garcia. He says "I have a letter before

[783]

me in which I am informed 'Santley told me he had learned more in twelve lessons from my father than in all the years he had studied with others.'" To which I answer (1) that there is no evidence that when Santley made that polite but ingeniously ambiguous speech to Garcia's son he was alluding to the subject of voice production; (2) that in Santley's history of himself lately noticed in this column I read of his having grown up as a choirboy to the profession of singer, and his obligations to his master Gaetano Nava of Milan, but not a solitary word of Garcia; and (3) that I have heard a Garcia sing, and that he did not sing like Santley. However, I must honestly add that the one lesson I ever had from a pupil of the Garcia school was prodigiously instructive, especially as to whether it was advisable to take another.

Mr Lunn proceeds: "Next, as to Melba. She was trained by Marchesi; and Marchesi was trained by Garcia and Viardot his sister." This proves exactly nothing. Marchesi may, for aught I know, have greatly modified, or even entirely abandoned, the method imparted to her by the Garcias. And Melba's method is not the method of the Academy pupils, nor of the young ladies whom I have heard as they came fresh from the tuition of Madame Viardot. If I knew Madame Melba's personal history, I might possibly be able to shew that it was her success as a singer in Australia that induced her to seek from Marchesi and others that criticism and advice as to style, habits, phrasing, pronunciation, stage business and tradition which makes our eminent professors of singing so useful to pupils who, like Santley, already know how to sing.

Mr Lunn defends the vowel *Ah* on the extremely cheerful ground that "with death the jaw drops, and the last exhalation is *ah!*" Therefore *ah*, says Mr Lunn, is not metaphysical, like the other vowels, but physical. It is nature revealing itself. But I did not say it was not: all

I contended for was that if, when the ordinary young Englishwoman is not dropping her jaw in death, but simply singing scales in life, she practises on *ah* instead of *oo* and *ee* in the middle, and *aw* in her lowest register, she will sing like an Academy pupil instead of developing the full vocal capacity, physical and metaphysical, needed by a public singer.

Sing on Garcia's method when you are dead by all means; but whilst you are alive you will find Edouard de Reszke's more useful: only dont abuse your power when you have gained it by wilful bawling for the mere fun of making a thundering noise, as he sometimes does. If you want to study nature freely expressing itself in vowels, and are averse to post-mortem examinations, you can pursue the following methods. To get the vowel *O*, with a marked *coup de glotte*, surprise a gentleman of full habit by a smart dig of your finger into his epigastrium at the moment when he has taken a full inspiration. For *oo*, with a B prefixed, simply write a play and appear before the curtain at the end. For *ah*, stick a pin into a lady. And so on.

The notion that *ah* is the best vowel and that no other should be used for practice is cognate to that of the gentlemen who tell you that D or F or B flat is the best note on their voice, though they do not go on to recommend you to practise exclusively on that note and to mistrust the others as "metaphysical." In Mr Lunn's own terminology, my contention is that the vowel which is physical at one pitch is metaphysical at another, and that nature does not freely express itself on a bass's low G in the same vowel as on the soprano's high A. Also that the dead-man, "no effort," unvolitional theory of singing, though it has arisen, naturally enough, in protest against the tight chin, rolled-up tongue, squeezed throat, and blowhard method, is just as impracticable, and consequently just as revolting to the student's commonsense, as the celebrated instruction in the old volunteer drillbook "Bring the rifle smartly to the shoulder without moving the hands."

Expert teachers and singers, knowing what the "no effort" precepts mean, approving of their drift, and careless of accuracy of statement, may declare their adhesion to it offhand; but I, as an expert writer, have to say what I mean as exactly as possible. And I mean, among other things, that dramatic singing is one of the most arduously volitional acts that man can perform; and whoever compares it in that respect to moribund collapse says (to quote a well-known controversialist) that which is not the truth, but so far from it, on the contrary, quite the reverse.*

Whilst I am on the subject of my critics (whom I pass over in dignified silence only when they happen to have the best of the argument), I may as well astonish the gentleman who gives me such a tremendous taking-down over the competition of the School Board children. He is evidently a professional musician; for in no other class could such innocence be found as he displays in his interpretation of my recent remarks about the extent to which systems of sight-reading get credited with feats that are really due to the pupils having the power of remembering the absolute pitch of sounds.

Long ago I compared Hullah's "fixed Do" system with the Chevé and Tonic Sol-fa systems, and drew the inevitable conclusion that Hullah's was impracticable, wheras the other two were reasonable enough, though Rousseau's objection that no notation is so graphic as the staff, as far as pitch is concerned, rather inclined me to recommend some method of applying the movable Do system to the ordinary notation. But when I came from theory to practice, and found that the Hullah system

* Samuel Weller in Dickens's Pickwick Papers.

seemed to produce much the same sort of result in classes as its more plausible rivals, I became skeptical.

My attention was presently drawn to a young lady who was exhibited as a marvelous example of the success of the Chevé system as a training for the staff notation. I was impressed at first; but eventually I discovered that she was an absolute pitcher, and could not only have read the staff notation just as well if she had never heard of Chevé or Galin,* but that she could get the hang of any sort of notation, numeral or syllabic, with amazing quickness, and translate it into absolute pitch. I was slow to find this out, because I cannot remember absolute pitch myself; and the faculty for doing so was at first as inexplicable to me as were the feats of the pupils of "Professors of Memory" until I read Mr Galton's work on Human Faculty, and learnt for the first time that there was such a faculty as "visualization."

Granted a faculty of "auralization," by which the auralizer can remember notes quite independently of oneanother, just as the visualizer remembers numbers; and the practicability of Hullah's system becomes quite intelligible. I soon came to the conclusions set forth in my previous article, which will probably be accepted by most disinterested musicians who have themselves the sense of absolute pitch, or have discovered its existence. For example, that excellent musician, Mr W. H. Cummings, whom I once heard inform an audience that when he was a boy his father struck a note on the piano and told him that it was A, and that he always remembered A from that, would be easily able to explain to my critic what has puzzled him so much.

* Pierre Galin (1786–1821), French mathematician, was the practical developer of a figure notation in music which led eventually to the Chevé method of teaching sight-reading and part-singing.

However, I rather object to being contemptuously informed that the Chevé and Tonic Sol-fa systems are relative pitch systems. If I am ignorant of these systems I may deserve to be snubbed; but I ought to be told the truth. The Tonic Sol-fa is not a relative pitch system; and that is just where it is superior to the movable Do system applied to the staff notation—I think they call it the Lancashire Sol-fa. The genuine Tonic Sol-faist remembers his note by its dramatic effect in the key. He feels Soh (Tonic Sol-faese for Sol) as Wagner felt it when he wrote the Flying Dutchman motive, and not by calculating a fifth above Doh. Some day I must write a supplement to Schumann's Advice to Young Musicians. The title will be Advice to Old Musicians; and the first precept will run, "Dont be in a hurry to contradict G. B. S., as he never commits himself on a musical subject until he knows at least six times as much about it as you do." But then I hate saying conceited things, however true they may be, even to people who seem to regard me as a mere Aunt Sally instead of a fellow creature.

A notable event of the week is the publication by Messrs Kegan Paul & Trübner of the first volume of Wagner's prose works, translated by Mr Ashton Ellis. It contains two works of the first importance, The Art Work of the Future (once well known to those who had not read it as The Music of the Future), and the Communication to My Friends, a unique artistic document, and one, by the bye, which every woman who admires Lohengrin should read, as it contains that remarkable account of his conversion to the view that Elsa, whom he at first conceived as having "failed" Lohengrin, was quite right in insisting on knowing all about him. In the later dramas, you will remember, the woman's part is as heroic as the man's.

The rest of the volume is taken up with Art and

[788]

Revolution, a classic example of brilliant pamphleteering; the Autobiographic Sketch, which will amuse those for whom the communication is too deep; the essay on Art and Climate, and the tolerably full design for the unfinished poem of Wieland the Smith. This instalment will suffice to open the eyes of English readers to the absurdity of the notions concerning Wagner and his views which were current here until quite lately, and which only began to collapse when the public, instead of reading about his music, got opportunities of listening to it, and lost all patience with the old nonsense about its dulness, harshness, lack of melody, and so on.

Mr Edward Dannreuthers's translation of On Conducting, too, revealed the supposed obscure and fantastic theorist as a very practical person, with simple and broad tastes in music, and with that saving salt of humor and commonsense which are so vital to the sanity of an art enthusiast. And his attacks were so sympathetically aimed at the very incompetencies and impostures from which we ourselves are suffering that those who read the essay at once concluded that the disparagement and ridicule which had been heaped on Wagner the writer were just as stupid as those which had been heaped on Wagner the composer. Besides, Wagner never stopped short at the merely negative "Thats not the way to do it": he always said "This is the way to do it," and did it forthwith.

There is something pleasant, too, in the thorough popularity of his likes and dislikes in music. His love of Beethoven and Mozart, and of the Mendelssohn of the Scotch symphony and the Hebrides overture, and his sovereign contempt for the efforts of Schumann and Brahms to be "profound," taken with the positive productive power of the man to realize his own ideas with his own hand, make up a personality as convincing and as genial as that of William Morris, who has a

[789]

prodigious appetite for Dickens and Dumas (need I say which Dumas?*), and his masterpieces in poetry, in prose, in printing, in picture-glass, in tapestry and household wares of all kinds.

In proof of my own sympathy with the practical and popular side of Wagner, I hasten to add that the volume in question costs 12s. 6d. net, and is well worth the money. The translation is so good that it deserves the praise that Wagner gave to Liszt's interpretation of Beethoven's sonatas.

Grateful acknowledgments to the member of the "the Rag" who sets me right as to the key of "Jackson." I said "Jackson in B flat": I should have said in F. "Only fancy the additional horror of the thing a fifth higher" exclaims my correspondent. I shake that warrior's hand. He, too, has suffered as I have.

MISS SMYTH'S DECORATIVE INSTINCT

The World, 25 January 1893

To Miss E. M. Smyth, the composer of the Mass performed for the first time at the Albert Hall last Wednesday, I owe at least one hearty acknowledgment. Her Mass was not a Requiem. True, it was carefully announced as "a Solemn Mass"; but when it came to the point it was not so very solemn: in fact, the Gloria, which was taken out of its proper place and sung at the end by way of a finish, began exactly like the opening

---

* Should the reader be unfamiliar with French literature, the Morris preference was for the novels of Dumas *père*, which included The Three Musketeers and The Count of Monte Cristo, rather than for dramas like Camille and novels on moral and social themes written by Dumas *fils*.

choruses which are now *de rigueur* in comic operas. Indeed, the whole work, though externally highly decorous, has an underlying profanity that makes the audience's work easy.

If you take an average mundane young lady, and ask her what service to religion she most enjoys rendering, she will probably, if she is a reasonably truthful person, instance the decoration of a church at Christmas. And, beyond question, a girl of taste in that direction will often set forth in a very attractive and becoming way texts of the deepest and most moving significance, which, nevertheless, mean no more to her than the Chinese alphabet. Now I will not go so far as to say that Miss Smyth's musical decoration of the Mass is an exactly analogous case; for there are several passages in which her sense of what is pretty and becoming deepens into sentimental fervor, just as it also slips back occasionally into a very unmistakable reminiscence of the enjoyment of the ballroom; but I must at least declare that the decorative instinct is decidedly in front of the religious instinct all through, and that the religion is not of the widest and most satisfying sort.

There are great passages in the Mass, such as "I look for the life of the world to come," which stir all men who have any faith or hope left in them, whether the life they look for is to be lived in London streets and squares, or in another world, and which stand out in adequate modern settings of religious services from among the outworn, dead matter with which creeds inevitably become clogged in the course of centuries. Every critic who goes to hear a setting of words written hundreds of years ago knows that some of them will have lost their sincerity, if not their very meaning, to the composer of today; and at such points he looks for a display of pure musicianship to fill the void; whilst he waits with intense interest and hope for the live bits.

Miss Smyth, however, makes no distinctions. She writes undiscriminatingly, with the faith of a child and the orthodoxy of a lady. She has not even those strong preferences which appear in the early religious works of Mozart and Raphael. Consequently, her Mass belongs to the light literature of Church music, though it is not frivolous and vulgar, as so much Church music unfortunately is. It repeatedly spurts ahead in the briskest fashion; so that one or two of the drum flourishes reminded me, not of anything so vulgar as the Salvation Army, but of a crack cavalry band.

There is, too, an oddly pagan but entirely pleasant association in Miss Smyth's mind of the heavenly with the pastoral: the curious trillings and pipings, with violin *obbligato*, which came into the Creed at the descent from heaven; the Et vitam venturi, on the model of the trio of the Ninth Symphony; and the multitudinous warblings, as of all the finches of the grove, at the end of the Gloria, conveyed to me just such an imagination of the plains of heaven as was painted by John Martin. Much of the orchestral decoration is very pretty, and shews a genuine feeling for the instruments. The passage in the Hosanna for the long trumpet which Mr Morrow mastered for the use of the Bach Choir, fairly brought down the house.

I have often tried to induce composers to avail themselves of this instrument; and now that Miss Smyth has set the example, with immediate results in the way of applause both for herself and the player, I do not see what there is to prevent a triumphant renovation of the treble section of the brass, especially now that Mr Wyatt's application of the double slide to the trumpet has at last made the slide-trumpet as practicable as the incurably vulgar but hitherto unavoidable cornet. Miss Smyth's powers of expression do not go beyond what the orchestra can do for her. None of the vocal solos in the

Mass have that peculiar variety and eloquence which are distinctively human: the contralto solo, in which the voice is treated merely as a pretty organ-stop, and the setting of the Agnus Dei for the tenor, which is frank violin music, conclusively prove her limitations, which, let us hope, are only due to want of experience of what can be done with really expressive singers.

The work, as a whole, is fragmentary, with too many pretentious *fugato* beginnings which presently come to nothing, and with some appallingly commonplace preparatory passages before the sections of the continuous numbers; but it is very far from being utterly tedious and mechanical like Dvořák's Requiem, or heavy, sententious, and mock-profound like—well, no matter. Above all, it is interesting as the beginning of what I have so often prophesied—the conquest of popular music by woman. Whenever I hear the dictum "Women cannot compose" uttered by some male musician whose whole endowment, intellectual and artistic, might be generously estimated as equivalent to that of the little finger of Miss Braddon or Miss Broughton,★ I always chuckle and say to myself "Wait a bit, my lad, until they find out how much easier it is than literature, and how little the public shares your objection to hidden consecutives, descending leading notes, ascending sevenths, false relations, and all the other items in your *index expurgatorius!*"

What musician that has ever read a novel of Ouida's has not exclaimed sometimes "If she would only lay on this sort of thing with an orchestra, how concerts would begin to pay!" Since women have succeeded conspicuously in Victor Hugo's profession, I cannot see why they should not succeed equally in Liszt's if they turned their attention to it.

★ Mary Elizabeth Braddon and Rhoda Broughton were prolific authors of best-selling romantic fiction.

The night before the Mass I went to a comic opera at the Shaftesbury; and the night after it I went to another at the Lyric. Miss Smyth could have written up both of them with considerable advantage to the *finales*. They resemble oneanother in shewing the composer to much greater advantage than the librettist. The book of La Rosière is by Mr Monkhouse, who has never shewn himself such a thorough actor as in the invention of this opera book. Such a hotch-potch of points, situations, *contretemps*, and Monkhousisms, unattached, unprovoked, uncaused, unrelated, and consequently unmeaning and unsuccessful, was never emptied out of any actor's budget. The utmost that can be said for it is that there are some passages which would be funny if the author himself were on the stage to take them in hand. Unfortunately, they do not suit the style of Messrs Robertson and Barrington Foote. The one advantage of Mr Monkhouse's dramatic method is that the opportunity for improvisation offered to the actors is only limited by the need for finishing in time for the last trains, since the characters and circumstances are nebulous enough to admit of any possible remark falling from the persons on the stage without incongruity. The who, the what, the when, the where, and the how of the play remain undecided to the last; and Mr Elton took full advantage of this on the night of my visit, when his colleagues were obviously wondering half the time what he was going to say next. He certainly did manage to dance and droll an impossible part into toleration, and even into popularity. But what saved the piece was the music, the czardas in the second act (a hint taken, possibly, from the vogue of Liszt's Hungarian Rhapsodies in the concert room), and, I hope, the scenery—I can only hope it, because it is not easy to guess how far audiences appreciate the fact that the finest art presented to them on the stage is often to be found, not in the music, or the singing, or the acting, but in the painting of the back-cloth. Such a scene as Mr Hann's Outside the Village is not only charming in itself, but critically interesting in a high degree to those who remember how Telbin would have handled the same subject; and yet it passes unnoticed, whilst yards of criticism are written every week about Bond-street exhibitions of watercolor sketches which are the merest trumpery compared to it or to Mr Hemsley's scene in the first act.* For my part, I am bound to say that these two scenes gave me greater pleasure than any other part of La Rosière; and since they have no chance of being "collected" and passed down to future generations, with an occasional airing at Christie's or the Winter Exhibition at the Academy, there is all the more reason why I should make my acknowledgments on the spot.

The music of La Rosière presents no new developments; but it is more generous and vigorous than the French work to which we are accustomed, the treatment of the orchestra in particular being as broad as the work will bear, and so escaping the reproach of timorous elegance and mean facetiousness which many recent comic opera scores have incurred. The orchestra, conducted by Mr Barter Johns, is remarkably good. Miss Marie Halton acts somewhat in the manner of Mrs Bancroft†, and sings somewhat in the manner of Miss St John, though, of course, chiefly in her own manner, which is vivacious and effective enough to keep her part from obeying the laws of Nature by falling flat. Miss Violet Cameron and Miss Lucille Saunders add to the interest of the cast, if not of the opera.

* Walter Hann, William Telbin, and W. T. Hemsley were contemporary scenic artists.

† Actress-manager, who with her husband Squire Bancroft had specialized in producing and acting in the "cup and saucer" plays of T. W. Robertson.

The Magic Opal, at the Lyric, is a copious example of that excessive fluency in composition of which Señor Albéniz has already given us sufficient proofs. His music is pretty, shapely, unstinted, lively, goodnatured, and far too romantic and refined for the stuff which Mr Arthur Law has given him to set. But Albéniz has the faults as well as the qualities of his happy and uncritical disposition; and the grace and spirit of his strains are of rather too obvious a kind to make a very deep impression. And he does not write well for the singers. It is not that the phrases are unvocal, or that the notes lie badly for the voice, but that he does not set the words from the comedian's point of view, his double disability as a pianist and a foreigner handicapping him in this department. The favorite performers of the company are not well fitted with parts. Poor Miss Aida Jenoure, whose forte is dancing, pantomime, and sprightly comedy with some brains in it, is a mere walking *prima donna* doomed to execute a florid vocal waltz. She could not sing it the least bit; but she dodged her way through it with a pluck and cleverness which earned her an *encore*. Mr Monkhouse, of whom it has been apparent any time these two years that he is potentially much more than a mere buffoon, has to buffoon away all the evening for want of anything better to do with his part. Mr Fred Kaye, too, is wasted. The only success of the first night was made by a Miss May Yohé, who, though she spoke the American language, actually had *not* ordered her florist to deliver half his stock to her across the footlights. She is personally attractive; her face, figure, and movements are lively and expressive; and her voice is extraordinarily telling: it sounds like a deep contralto; but the low notes beneath the stave, which are powerful in a normally trained contralto, are weak; and she has practically no high notes. But the middle of the voice, which she uses apparently by forcing her chest register, is penetrating and effective. In giving this account of her method I am describing what an ordinary singer would have to do to imitate her (with inevitably ruinous consequences), rather than what she does herself, as to which I am not quite assured. Probably she has one of those abnormal larynxes, examples of which may be found in Sir Morell Mackenzie's list of the singers whose registering he examined. Mr Wallace Brownlow was restless and off his balance, which is exactly what an artist ought not to be. Miss Susie Vaughan helped matters considerably as an amiable Azucena, her mock ballet with Mr Monkhouse being one of the funniest things in the piece. I must apologize to Mlle Candida for having missed her dance through running away for half an hour to the London Symphony Concert, where Mr Henschel, with an ingratitude that took me quite aback, celebrated my entrance by striking up Brahms in F.

THE PLOWITZ CONCERTS

A note in the column What the World Says, The World,
1 February 1893

[U] A series of concerts are being given at Prince's Hall by Professor Theodor Plowitz, who has brought us a string quartet of remarkable merit. At the first concert, on Monday last week, the performances of Brahms's pianoforte quartet in G minor (would that Johannes always composed thus!) and Mendelssohn's pianoforte trio in D minor were thoroughly enjoyable. With reference to the other items in the program, all I need say for the present is that Herr Plowitz has not quite taken the measure of central London yet, either in the selection of pieces or in the standard of delicacy of touch

[797]

and purity of intonation which we demand from soloists at concerts of chamber music; but his artists do not fall short, and they will, no doubt, soon be completely metropolitanized.[U]

THE PALACE THEATRE OF VARIETIES

The World, 8 February 1893

Mr Henschel is to be congratulated on his last Symphony Concert, not only for having brought a really practicable choir into the field, but for having shewn by an exceptionally good performance of the Pastoral Symphony that he had fully completed his first labor of forming a first-rate orchestra before attempting to add a choir to it. In the long intervals between the visits of Richter it is an unspeakable relief to hear a London band in St James's Hall that has spirit and purpose in its execution, and in its tone a firmness, and at need a depth and richness, which it can sustain for as many bars as you please in the broadest movements without flinching or trailing off.

When we last heard the Pastoral Symphony from the Philharmonic (potentially and by common consent of the profession—on strictly reciprocal terms—the finest band in the world, and actually the most futile), the conductor had to apologize for the performance beforehand. On Thursday last Mr Henschel had to return to the platform twice *after* the performance to be tremendously applauded. This is the second time that he has deliberately picked a specially remarkable orchestral work out of the Philharmonic program in order to shew us the difference between the Philharmonic accomplishment of reading band parts at sight and the true art of orchestral execution. In Raff's Lenore he achieved a comparatively easy and certain success. In Beethoven he has gone deeper and been more conclusively successful. The first two movements were presented in a masterly way: I have not yet heard Mr Henschel accomplish so convincing a reading of a classic. In the third movement he was a little hampered by individual shortcomings in the band, the oboe being painfully out of tune; and the climax to the storm was a trifle discounted by letting the band explode too freely before it was reached; but these blemishes were outweighed by the bringing out of many touches which usually go for nothing.

The only thing that was old-fashioned about the concert was the inevitable remark in the analytic program that Beethoven had "*descended* to positive imitation" (of the quail, cuckoo, and nightingale) in the *andante*. Now I appeal to Mr Bennett as a man and a brother whether we need keep waving this snippet of impertinent small talk over the Pastoral Symphony for ever. There is no more beautiful bar in the work than that which consists of the "imitations" in question. It is exquisitely constructed and infinitely poetic; and we all like it and wait for it expectantly, and shiver with agony whenever some confounded flautist who never appreciated the nightingale—perhaps never even heard one— dots half the quavers and turns the other half into semiquavers. And then we go and gravely reproach Beethoven for having "descended" to the low and inartistic device of imitating a vulgar bird that never had a proper singing lesson in its life.

I can only say that after many years of attentive observation, devoted to determining which of the two parties—Beethoven or the critic—cut the more foolish figure after each repetition of the rebuke, I have reluctantly come to the conclusion that we had better drop it. Our profession affords us so many suitable and unobtrusive opportunities for making donkeys of ourselves when we are so disposed, that there is no excuse for our clinging to the most conspicuous and unpopular of them all.

The work selected for the *début* of the choir was Mendelssohn's Hear my Prayer. I desire to skate over this part of the concert as lightly as possible; but I must just ask Mrs Henschel to hear *my* prayer and never again meddle with Mendelssohn. Mind, I do not asperse Mrs Henschel's professional competence. I do not find fault with her technical execution: she sang the notes in time and tune; pronounced the words duly; and longed for the wings of a dove and worked up to the shouting of the enemy very intelligently. Nothing could have been more thoroughly businesslike from beginning to end.

But that is not enough for Hear my Prayer. Unless you can sing those opening lines with the rarest nobility of tone and the most touching depth of expression, your one duty to them is to let them alone. They are like the opening phrase of the quartet in Don Giovanni, *Non ti fidar, O misera*: success in delivering them is only possible to singers who have the finest temperamental sympathy with their spirit; and anything short of success is utter failure. And that is what befell Mrs Henschel—failure, not apparent, as an ordinary breakdown would have been, to those who did not know the work—for they, indeed, applauded her plentifully—but deeply disappointing to us who have it in our hearts as a cherished early love. Perhaps it is strength of character rather than any artistic weakness that makes Mrs Henschel sing *Die Lorelei* charmingly, and *Kennst du das Land* or Hear my Prayer most disenchantingly; but in any case it is clear that it is the charm of romance and not the depths and heights of emotion and devotion that she was born to sing for us.

However, Hear my Prayer was soon over; and the Pastoral Symphony and the Meistersinger selection made amends for the disappointment. The choir is bright, vigorous, and spirited; and the volume of tone they produce is adequate to their numbers, instead of, as usual, every ten young women producing about as much voice as might be expected from a very little girl with a very bad cold. Their introduction was certainly most promising; and I begin to think I shall hear some decent choral work at St James's Hall before I die, after all.

Curiosity to see the New English Opera House in its latest character of "Palace Theatre of Varieties" led me the other evening to make another trial of music hall art. Previous attempts had taught me to be careful as to how far I should permit myself to criticize. I had learnt that writers of music hall songs attribute to their verses a moral elevation which David would have modestly hesitated to claim for the Psalms, and that a remark which would be taken by Broadwood or Steinway as a handsome compliment is resented as an actionable insult by makers of music hall instruments. Add to this that the Palace Theatre of Varieties is under highly sensitive management, and the perils of my position may be faintly realized. However, I ventured in, and found palatial provisions for smoking, lounging, and drinking. This was thrown away on me, as I do not smoke, do not drink, and feel like a pickpocket whenever circumstances compel me to lounge. So I hastened to the auditorium to see the performance, and found palatial provision for this also in a comfortable chair, to the elegance and luxury of which I can pay but a feeble tribute by calling it, on the suggestion of the bill, a *fauteuil*. Herein reclining, I contemplated the "new and novel act-drop by Mr J. Harker," representing a magnificent studio in which a model, undeniably a fine figure of a woman, stood posed before a number of infantine art students, certain portions of whose persons were colored up to the point of presenting an inflamed appearance, as if they had been unmercifully corrected for faults in their drawing. For in this studio the model was draped and the artists were naked, the model being the person on whom the suspicions of the iconoclastic section of the County Council were most likely to fall. The performance, apart from the usual "turns," shewed a determination on the part of the management to popularize ballet by mixing it with comic opera. Even if this were the right way to popularize ballet—and I shall presently explain why I think it the wrong way—the first ballet we had, The Sleeper Awakened, seemed to me an example of how not to do it. A couple of scenes of the usual pantomime-opening kind were tacked on to an ordinary ballet *finale*, the dancers having nothing to do with the dramatic section, nor the actors with the dancing section. The result was, of course, that the beginning, played by ordinary burlesque actors with none of the grace, the agility, the distinction of the pantomimic dancer, was common to a degree; and the ending, owing to the sudden withdrawal of all pretence of meaning from a piece which had begun as a good story, was even more vapid than ballet *finales* usually are.

Much more successful was From London to Paris, in which there is a genuine collaboration between the authors (Mr Cecil Raleigh and Sir Augustus Harris) and the composer (Mr J. M. Glover); whilst in the representation there is a genuine collaboration of the actors with the pantomimists. The result is a really amusing entertainment. Mr Glover has entered thoroughly into the spirit of the piece: his score grows naturally out of the action, and is consequently free from the stereo which makes most ballet music so worrying. The allusions to popular comic songs come in with a musical humor and a daintiness which makes them quite witty and pretty; and some of the points—for instance, the sea-sickly harmonies to Rule Britannia in the storm scene—are irresistibly funny. In short, Mr Glover's music has all the liveliness and adroitness of the ordinary imported French ballet music, without its staleness and without its foreignness. Mr Raleigh has made the Palace Theatre a present of a character from one of his comedies in the person of Velvet Sam, created, if I mistake not, by Mr Somerset some years ago at a *matinée*, and now brought back to life in a speechless condition by Mr Paul Martinetti, whose admirable and original pantomime strikes the highest note attained in the acting of the piece. The combination of spoken dialogue with pantomime leads to a scene between the low comedian and the high pantomimist in which the comedian, hopelessly misunderstanding all the exquisitely graphic gestures of the subtler artist, gives gratifying expression to the feelings which we have all shared when trying to follow the conventional Italian dumb-show.

The panoramic scene of the voyage from Dover to Calais ought to be prohibited: it carries the joke too far. The moment those two sponsons and the bridge began to rock I began to feel ill; and the flying clouds and general moving and pitching and rolling that went on so intensified my symptoms that if the Calais light (exactly like the real thing, and not less welcome) had not appeared much sooner than it usually does, I should have had to leave the auditorium precipitately. This sort of stage realism is all very well for good sailors; but as these gifted persons form considerably less than one per cent. of the population, I make bold to remind the managers that all the great composers have recognized that a Calm Sea is an indispensable condition of a Prosperous Voyage. The following scenes, like the preceding one at Charing Cross Station, are of the same topical sort; and the piece goes on vivaciously enough until it fades into pure *ballet divertissement,* relieved only by a funereal clog-dance and a *can-can* at the end. It left me more convinced than ever that what is wanted to make the ballet more popular is not its wholesale adulteration with comic opera, but its internal reform.

It should be recognized that the stock of movements out of which the principal dancers make up their solos is so limited that the frequent playgoer soon learns them off by heart, and comes to regard the solo as a dreary platitude, only to be endured when the dancer has extraordinary charm of person and brilliancy of execution. In order to get even a very conventional round of applause, and that, too, from people who obviously have no more sense of dancing than the oratorio audiences who applaud interpolated high notes have of music, a principal dancer must spoil her solo by a silly, flustering, ugly, teetotum spin, which no really fine dancer should condescend to. Then there is the *corps de ballet,* consisting of rows of commonplace dancers, individually uninteresting (from the artistic point of view), but useful for the production of lines and masses of color in rhythmic motion—for realizing, in short, the artistic conception which was in Mr Swiveller's imagination when he described the dance as "the mazy."*

Now in planning the evolutions of the *corps de ballet,* nothing is easier than to ring the changes on mere drill, or harder than to devize really artistic combinations and developments. The natural result is a tendency to give us an intolerable deal of drill with each halfpennyworth of poetic color and motion. The last scene of a ballet is generally a bore, to which some sort of non-artistic interest is occasionally imparted by such desperate devices as making successive squads of girls represent

* In Dickens's The Old Curiosity Shop.

different nations, or different uniforms in the services, or different periods of civilization, or what not, with the result, generally, of making the whole affair twice as stale and tedious. All such mechanical efforts to make lifeless entertainments attractive invariably lead to frightful expenditure, the last thousand pounds of which rarely produce sixpenn'orth of effect. Why not, then, call in the services of a dramatic storyteller, with the requisite sense of the poetry of motion and movement and spectacle, and make a clean sweep of all the merely habitual business that has no purpose and no meaning? The monotony and limitation of the dancer's art vanishes when it becomes dramatic. The detestable *bravura* solos which everybody hates, and which belong to the same obsolete phase of art as the XVIII century florid arias written for the singing *virtuosi* of the Italian stage by Hasse, Porpora, and Mozart in his boyhood, would soon fall into disuse and ridicule; and we could say to our *prima ballerina assolutissima,* when she attempted a "variation," "Spare us, dear lady. Dont do it. Our cherished Cavallazzi, a superb dancer, never does it. It was not that sort of thing that made the success of Yolande, of Asmodeus, of Excelsior, or of any of the ballets that are still borne in mind years after their withdrawal. Hundreds of forgotten *assolutissimas* have done it just as well as you are going to do it; and none of them are remembered save those who stamped themselves on our memories in their dramatic moments. Move us; act for us; make our favorite stories real to us; weave your grace and skill into the fabric of our life; but dont put us off for the thousandth time with those dreary pirouettes and *entrechats* and arabesques and whatd'yecallems." That is the cry of humanity to the *danseuse,* the ballet master, and the manager; and it is in response to it that we are getting Round the Town and From London to Paris.

But in The Sleeper Awakened and From London to Paris there are signs of a movement to substitute, not dramatic pantomime for mere step exhibition, but comic opera of the lowest type for ballet; and this false start must not be followed up. It is one thing to give us what Martinetti does instead of what Albertieri does: it is quite another to give us what any vulgar low comedian can do. I am very fond of dramatic pantomime and of the dancing that grows out of it; and I think it important to the stage in general that we should have a school of the art among us. But I have had more than enough of the sort of gorgeously spectacular, farcical, rather rowdy comic opera that flourished at the old Alhambra in the days of Stoyle, Paulton, Kitty Munroe, and Rose Bell. People of taste went to the Alhambra in those days only to see Pertoldi and Gillert dance; and in the end it proved that even from a commercial point of view the ballet paid well enough to be worth retaining when the comic opera was dropped. I therefore suggest that the true policy is to follow the line so successfully pursued at the Empire, of reforming and developing the ballet as ballet, without allowing a single spoken word to open the way for a relapse into decadent comic opera. And the Palace management can do it at this advantage, that they have in Mr Cecil Raleigh and Mr Glover just the dramatist and musician for their purpose. As to the people who have no sense of the art of theatrical dancing at all, they will be satisfied if the music hall turns are kept up to the mark, and if the ballet exhibits plenty of feminine beauty.

FINE STROKES OF COMEDY

The World, 15 February 1893

I do not know how far the matter is worth mentioning, but music is dying out in London. The Monday Popular and Ballad concerts go on from mere force of habit; the Crystal Palace concerts will begin again next Saturday, because they rashly promised to do so last year; oratorios are solemnized at the usual intervals in the Albert Hall; Sarasate goes and Joachim comes; and Mr Henschel's band is heard twice a month as usual. It is true that early February is not exactly the height of the musical season, and that this year the light opera houses produced their novelties much earlier in the year than is customary.

But when all allowances are made, it must be admitted that things for the moment are slack; and I have once or twice thought of raising an Unemployed Deadheads' agitation, and calling on the Government to at once set on foot a series of Relief Concerts, at which these unhappy people may pass their afternoons and evenings. The Abolition of Piecework for critics would be a prominent plank in the program of such an agitation; for even a critic must live, and if the agents will not give concerts and recitals, the critics will be driven to invent them; that is the long and short of it.

A man cannot go on repeating what he has said a thousand times about the way the Monday Popular quartet played Haydn in G, No. 12 of Opus 756, or about Santley as Elijah. I turn in desperation to the musical journals, and my hopes rise as I see the words "Ignorant Misstatement." But it is actually not G. B. S. this time; somebody else, I suppose, has made a remark sufficiently obvious to shake the foundation of make-believe on which "art" of the usual professional type is built. The tenants of that fashionable edifice are always protesting that I am an impudent pretender to musical authority, betraying my ignorance, in spite of my diabolical cunning, in every second sentence. And I do not mind confessing that I do not know half as much as you would suppose from my articles; but in the kingdom of the deaf the one-eared is king.

The other evening I was looking into a shop window in Oxford-street, when a gentleman accosted me modestly, and, after flattering me with great taste and modesty into an entire willingness to make his acquaintance, began with evident misgiving and hesitation, but with no less evident curiosity, to approach the subject of these columns. At last he came to his point with a rush by desperately risking the question "Excuse me, Mr G. B. S., but *do* you know anything about music? The fact is, I am not capable of forming an opinion myself; but Dr Blank says you dont, and—er—Dr Blank is such a great authority that one hardly knows what to think." Now this question put me into a difficulty, because I had already learnt by experience that the reason my writings on music and musicians are so highly appreciated is, that they are supposed by many of my greatest admirers to be a huge joke, the point of which lies in the fact that I am totally ignorant of music, and that my character of critic is an exquisitely ingenious piece of acting, undertaken to gratify my love of mystification and paradox.

From this point of view every one of my articles appears as a fine stroke of comedy, occasionally broadening into a harlequinade, in which I am the clown, and Dr Blank the policeman. At first I did not realize this, and could not understand the air of utter disillusion and loss of interest in me that would come over people in whose houses I incautiously betrayed some scrap of amateurish enlightenment. But the *naïve* exclamation "Oh! you *do* know something about it, then" at last became familiar to me; and I now take particular care not to expose my knowledge. When people hand me a sheet of instrumental music, and ask my opinion of it, I carefully hold it upside down, and pretend to study it in that position with the eye of an expert. When they invite me to try their new grand piano, I attempt to open it at the wrong end; and when a young lady of the house informs me that she is practising the cello, I innocently ask her whether the mouthpiece did not cut her lips dreadfully at first. This line of conduct gives enormous satisfaction, in which I share to a rather greater extent than is generally supposed. But, after all, the people whom I take in thus are only amateurs.

To place my impostorship beyond question I require to be certified as such by authorities like our Bachelors and Doctors of music—gentlemen who can write a Nunc Dimittis in five real parts, and know the difference between a tonal fugue and a real one, and can tell you how old Monteverdi was on his thirtieth birthday, and have views as to the true root of the discord of the seventh on the supertonic, and devoutly believe that *si contra fa diabolus est*. But I have only to present myself to them in the character of a man who has been through these dreary games without ever discovering the remotest vital connexion between them and the art of music— a state of mind so inconceivable by them—to make them exclaim:

Preposterous ass! that never read so far
To know the cause why music was ordained,*

and give me the desired testimonials at once. And so I manage to scrape along without falling under suspicion of being an honest man.

* Shakespear's The Taming of the Shrew, III, 1.

However, since mystification is not likely to advance us in the long run, may I suggest that there must be something wrong in the professional tests which have been successively applied to Handel, to Mozart, to Beethoven, to Wagner, and last, though not least, to me, with the result in every case of our condemnation as ignoramuses and charlatans. Why is it that when Dr Blank writes about music nobody but a professional musician can understand him; wheras the man-in-the-street, if fond of art and capable of music, can understand the writings of Mendelssohn, Wagner, Liszt, Berlioz, or any of the composers?

Why, again, is it that my colleague William Archer, for instance, in criticizing Mr Henry Arthur Jones's play the other day, did not *parse* all the leading sentences in it? I will not be so merciless as to answer these questions now, though I know the solution, and am capable of giving it if provoked beyond endurance. Let it suffice for the moment that writing is a very difficult art, criticism a very difficult process, and music not easily to be distinguished, without special critical training, from the scientific, technical, and professional conditions of its performance, composition, and teaching. And if the critic is to please the congregation, who want to read only about the music, it is plain that he must appear quite beside the point to the organ-blower, who wants to read about his bellows, which he can prove to be the true source of all the harmony.

Some weeks ago, in speaking of the lecture and viol concert given by Mr Arnold Dolmetsch before the conference of the Incorporated Society of Musicians, I seized the opportunity to put in a protest on behalf of opera-goers against the horrible custom of playing the prelude to the tenor air in the first act of Les Huguenots on the viole d'amour, and then returning to the ordinary viola, with detestable effect, for the *obbligato*. Mr

Dolmetsch, who is giving viol concerts on alternate Tuesdays at Barnard's Inn, Holborn, promises to bring a viole d'amour, tuned for playing this *obbligato*, to his next concert on the 14th, and to say something on the subject. I hope the upshot will be to get the *obbligato* played at the opera as Meyerbeer meant it to be played. The difference to the singer, who would be coaxed into the dulcet style, instead of having his teeth set on edge and his worst shouting propensities stirred up, would be considerable, and the difference to the audience incalculable.

I see that Mr Lunn is not quite convinced that he and I mean the same thing by the *coup de glotte*. But it is clear from his last utterance on the subject that we do. Marchesi's "sudden and energetic drawing together of the lips of the glottis an instant before expiration commences" is exactly what I mean, and what I object to. I never heard Titiens sing Hear ye, Israel; so I will take it on Mr Lunn's authority that she used to attack the *allegro* with a *coup de glotte* on the I, I am He that comforteth, although Titiens was certainly not a *coup de glottist* in her ordinary practice. I myself, in the very rare instances when I pronounce the word "I" in a self-assertive mood, may sometimes attack it with a *coup de glotte*; but I always regret it the moment the sound strikes my conscience, which, in my case, as in that of all musical critics, is situated in my ear.

But when Mr Lunn goes on to say that if Titiens had not used the *coup de glotte* she must "inevitably" have produced the sentence as "Hi! Hi! am He that comforteth," I can only assure him that he is wrong on the point of fact. If Titiens had been an Academy pupil, with no power of distending and bracing her pharynx, and helplessly dependent on a carefully cultivated method of bleating with the vocal cords alone, then undoubtedly she could not have produced any vowel whatsoever without a *coup de glotte,* except by fairly gasping it into existence by a strong aspirate.

Being what she was, a practical dramatic singer, she could have attacked any vowel with a perfectly open glottis and without an aspirate, exactly as an organ flue-pipe attacks its note, or as I can attack a note in whistling, without closing my lips, by simply putting them in the proper position first, and then directing a stream of air through them. Now a flue-pipe is just as "natural" an instrument as a reed-pipe; and I will by no means admit that a vocal method based on the analogy of the reed mechanism is any more "natural," or "normal," or "spontaneous" than a method based on the analogy of the flue construction. Infants may, as Mr Lunn says, yell with a *coup de glotte* (the method of the yelling infant being instinctively vicious); but children croon or "sing to themselves" on the other plan; so I claim the child's evidence as on my side, though I attach no importance to it.

Consequently we may get rid of all discussion as to whether the *coup de glotte* reed-pipe method or the open glottis flue-pipe method is Nature's method. The question is, which of the two sounds better and wears better. The first point is a matter of taste: the second, a matter of experience and observation; and I declare for the flue-pipe on both issues.

GOUNOD'S MUSIC
The World, 22 February 1893

Many who hear Gounod's Redemption cannot but feel somewhat scandalized by the identity in treatment and spirit of the death on the Cross with the death of Valentin in Faust. He has to remind himself at such moments that it is in the opera and not in the oratorio that the music is out of place. Goethe's Valentin is a blunt and rather ruffianly medieval soldier, with all the indignant insistence on the need for virtue in other people which a man would naturally have after studying human nature in the course of helping to sack a town or two. His last words are a quaint combination of a regret that he cannot get at old Martha to blacken her eyes, with a reminder to the Almighty that a brave soldier is about to exercise his right of going to heaven.

Gounod, who has no turn for this sort of realism, made Valentin a saint and a martyr; and the ideal actor for a true Gounod performance of the part is a dreamy and pathetically beautiful youth with a pure young voice. Jean de Reszke, when he sang baritone parts, and was eighteen years younger and some thirty odd pounds lighter than today, was far more moving and memorable as Valentin than Maurel is now, though Maurel acts with great power, and reconstitutes the medieval soldier in spite of Gounod's teeth, or than Lassalle, who, conscious of his merits as a singer, avoids invidious comparisons by the quick-witted expedient of not acting at all. The chief disadvantage of turning the death of Valentin into a Calvary was that when Gounod wrote Passion music he was told that it sounded operatic. To which he can only reply that if operatic means like a Gounod opera, the term is not one of reproach. This is a good answer; but Gounod should not have pressed us too hard on the point. When we have been led to associate a particular eight bars of music with the words in which the dying Valentin warns Margaret that she, too, must face her day of reckoning, it is rather disconcerting, to say the least, to hear the central figure in the Redemption transposing those very eight bars from D into B, and using them to declaim "If my deeds have been evil, bear witness against me," &c.

And those angelic progressions which lift the voice

from semitone to semitone on ineffable resolutions of diminished sevenths on to six-four chords, though beyond question most heavenly, are so welded in our minds to Gretchen's awakening from her miserable prison dreams to the consciousness of Faust's presence in her cell, that it is not easy to keep in the proper oratorio frame of mind when they begin. In fact a knowledge of Gounod's operas is a disadvantage at the Albert Hall on Redemption nights, even to the ordinary occasional opera-goer. What must it be then to the professional critic, who has to spend about ten years out of every twelve of his life listening to Faust? If Gounod's music were less seraphically soothing, it would have long ago produced an inflammatory disease—Faustitis—in my profession. Even as it is, I am far from sure that my eyesight has not been damaged by protracted contemplation of the scarlet coat and red limelight of Mephistopheles.

That is why I was so grateful to Maurel for changing the customary hue to an unexciting mouse color. However, I am wandering away from the Redemption, as to which I have no more to say generally than that if you will only take the precaution to go in long enough after it commences and to come out long enough before it is over you will not find it wearisome. Indeed some people do not find it wearisome even at full length, just as, I suppose, they would not mind going through five miles of pictures by Fra Angelico; but I am unfortunately so constituted that if I were actually in Heaven itself I should have to earn my enjoyment of it by turning out and doing a stroke of work of some sort, at the rate of at least a fortnight's hard labor for one celestial evening hour. There is nothing so insufferable as happiness, except perhaps unhappiness; and this is at the bottom of the inferiority of Gounod and Mendelssohn to Handel as oratorio writers.

Whilst I am on this part of the subject, let me deplore the childish incapacity which the people who run after happiness always shew for being satisfied with it when they get it. For instance, when Miss Palliser sang They who seek things eternal, with a beautiful high C which should have made any reasonable person ashamed to ask for anything more for a whole month, the audience, with odious ingratitude, insisted on having it again, with the result that Miss Palliser, thrown into competition with herself, and hindered from letting well alone, could only give a comparative scrape to the C the second time. The greatest offenders in this *encore* were the choristers. Your chorister is generally a person who is always watching for high C's from sopranos and tenors, or G sharps from baritones, or low D's from basses, having, poor wretch! no other notion of what is excellent in music.

Even if this were not so, choristers ought not to be allowed to applaud at all, as under the existing toleration every choral concert and Handel Festival provides itself automatically with a huge army of *claqueurs,* full to their scalps with spurious connoisseurship. However, the Albert Hall connoisseurs did not sing badly, the performance on the whole being a very good one. Miss Marie Brema sang While my watch I am keeping with a gentler vocal touch and a nearer approach to purely lyric style than I had heard from her before; and it now seems not unlikely that Miss Palliser and Miss Brema may in the course of time succeed Albani and Madame Belle Cole on the oratorio platform. All the gentlemen, especially Mr Watkin Mills, were very efficient.

At Mr Dolmetsch's viol concert in Barnard's Inn yesterday week I enjoyed the unexpected sensation of having one of my criticisms read aloud to the audience. "This" added Mr Dolmetsch with an air of conviction "is severe language; but it is true." Wherat the audience—

well, I had better say they smiled, but sniggered is the expression I should use in unrestrained private conversation. The precedent appears to me an excellent one. I am confident that the Philharmonic concerts and those of the Bach choir, nay, the very Opera itself, could be most agreeably enlivened by a judicious selection from my articles.

A legitimate development of the idea would be to engage me to mount the platform after each number in the program and deliver an impromptu five minutes' criticism. I shall be most happy to entertain any proposals of this nature; and I suggest that it might be possible to arrange for each of my appearances without adding to the expenses, as Mr Henschel would probably pay my Philharmonic fees, Signor Lago my Covent Garden fees, and againwards (which in modern English is *vice versa*).

I have a small criticism to offer on Mr Dolmetsch's method of explaining the construction of the old dances. Those who saw the Masque of Flowers in Gray's Inn Hall some years ago are probably the only amateurs in London who have any really artistic insight to the old dance forms. If you want to explain a dance form to me, there is only one way of doing it; and that is to shew me the dance for which the music was required. Until I see that, no information about sections and variations and ground basses can interest me in the least, because nothing that is arbitrary and unrelated to any artistic purpose can interest any human being unless he has taken a musical degree.

I know, of course, that Mr Dolmetsch cannot get up the dances for us, though that old hall of the Art Workers' Guild in Clifford's Inn would be the very place for a Masque if there were only a little more room in it; but I submit that if there is to be any oral description at all (and Mr Dolmetsch talks to his audience most discreetly and amusingly) the thing to describe is the suppressed part of the dance and not the performed part of it. If people hear a musical note or an harmonic progression, it does not add to their knowledge of it to tell them that its name is B flat or the plagal cadence. If it did we could teach music to the deaf. But if people hear B flat or the plagal cadence talked about, and they ask what these two terms mean, you can enlighten them completely by letting them hear the note and the progression.

Mr Dolmetsch's answer to the question "What is a pavan or a galliard?" should be to have it played and danced on the spot. This Mr Dolmetsch does, as regards the playing, to the entire satisfaction of his audience; and so he need say nothing about the music. What we are left in the dark about is the dance; and for the suggestion of this to the imagination, the chin music of the lecturer may legitimately be called in.

The Wagner program at the London Symphony Concert last Thursday drew a large audience. I never can quite reconcile myself to the entry of the gods into Valhalla across the rainbow bridge, as arranged for concert use without the voices and without the multitudinous harps of the original score; and matters were not improved on this occasion by the reeds giving us the lamentation of the Rhine daughters almost as flat as if they had been real German singers. But still, it is better to hear the Rhinegold music that way than not to hear it at all. The Meistersinger quintet soon degenerated into a mere bawling match, the tenor and soprano exciting general admiration by their stupendous and perfectly gratuitous exertions. I do not think their mistake arose from lack of artistic feeling, but partly from the fact of the music not being sufficiently easily within their powers, and partly from exaggerating the difficulty of making themselves heard in St James's Hall against the orchestra. When I last heard the London Symphony band attempt the Siegfried Idyll, the result was a second-rate performance: this time it was first-rate, another proof of the artistic maturity of Mr Henschel's enterprise. The Liebestod transcription from Tristan was well played, but it was taken much too fast, in my judgment. The Eroica also suffered for a few moments in the middle of the last movement by expressive whipping up: otherwise it went admirably, especially the funeral march, but always excepting the first movement, which we shall hear in its glory, I suppose, when we get an orchestra of heros to play it and a demigod to conduct it. Nothing will ever persuade me that Beethoven meant it to begin in a hurry, with the theme stumping along to catch the last train, and the syncopations for the violins in the fifth bar coming in like the gasps of a blown pedestrian. Imagine the effect of tackling Mozart's E flat symphony that way!

TOO LONG
The World, 1 March 1893

I presume I may congratulate Sir Charles Hallé this time on the result of his expedition to London. As I have lost no opportunity of opening the eyes of our London amateurs to the value of the Manchester orchestra as a real band with a mastered repertory, and not a mere muster of good executants who can be depended on for sight-reading, Sir Charles Hallé's agents, fearing that they might seem to be corruptly returning a compliment, have carefully abstained from offering me any of the customary civilities by which a critic is kept informed of what is going on at St James's Hall. Consequently it was quite by accident that I learnt, last Wednesday evening, that the Manchester band was performing there. I hastened to the spot half an hour late and proffered a modest half-crown for admission, but was told that there was only standing room, of which I decided not to deprive somebody else. I mention the incident partly to explain my having nothing to say about the performance, and partly to shew that the public has found out what a mistake it made last year in neglecting the Manchester band.

Let me, however, offer a criticism on the program. It was too long. Concert programs always are. The fact is, music is in much the same phase as that of the drama in "the palmy days." We have two farces, a Shakespearean tragedy, and a Christmas pantomime all in the same evening—a sort of thing only possible with audiences consisting of persons so callous that they are as triflingly affected by works of art as they are inconvenienced by bad ventilation. Now the completely sensitized listener is as intensely active in the theatre or concert room as a photographic plate is during exposure; and when the light is of Wagnerian or Beethovenian power it cannot be endured for two hours without exhaustion. When Mr Henschel started the London Symphony concerts this season, he promised that they should be over always at a quarter past ten; but he is a deceiver: the last concert left that hour far behind, and sent me home a shattered man. At the Crystal Palace the same inhumanity passes without protest. Mr Manns appears to me to subordinate all other considerations, artistic and humanitarian, to keeping me late for the four-fifty-four train, which, if this country were properly governed, would be a five o'clock express.

This may be all very well for the refreshment contractors, and for the victims of that most horrible form of dipsomania, the craving for afternoon tea; but to me it is only an aggravation of the trials of my profession. Besides, the tea-room is a mockery even to those who use it. Sometimes, when I have a dipsomaniac lady with me, she insists on being taken thither; and we enter at ten minutes past five, with twenty minutes to spare before the train starts. Five of these minutes are consumed in finding a place at the crowded tables, and five more in attracting the attention of the distracted waitress, a process which the crusty old gentlemen conduct by peremptory vociferation, the handsome young ones by what Darwin calls sexual selection, and mild and irresolute persons like myself by the silent pathos of infinite patience, which, however, is only practicable when the dipsomaniac is not of an impetuous disposition; for if she is, she nags, and declares aloud that the arrangements are scandalous. When the waitress is secured, she, if smart and willing, executes the order in five minutes more; and if you are wise you pay her on the nail lest you should have to find her all over again. Allowing two and a half minutes to catch the train, this leaves another two and a half to poison yourself in. And all this because there are seven—sometimes eight—numbers in a program which should contain five.

Let me come to the practical question, what would I cut out of the existing program scheme? Well, obviously not the symphony, nor the concerto, nor the overture. But what about the customary vocal pieces? Granted that a song forms a convenient interpolation between the concerto and symphony, is it worth while, when there is the cheap and simple alternative of a brief interval for reading Sir George Grove's inimitable programs, to secure the interpolation at the cost of having to give the vocalist another turn later on when nobody wants it? Besides, do the singers deserve any consideration? Have they done anything to make or maintain the reputation of the concerts? How many of

[820]

them ever fill the gaps left for them in the programs with the faintest sense of appropriateness?

How often, on the contrary, do they not strut in between the Schumann concerto and a Beethoven symphony, and strike up some *scena* by Massenet, well enough in its place on the stage perhaps, but appearing only an ill-bred intruder in such noble company. And these singers are so insufferably unconscious of their ineptitude! You will see a woman who professes to be an artist expressing in every toss of her head her conviction that a pretty face, a smart bonnet, and a ripping B flat are of more importance than all the concertos and symphonies in the world. And nothing will ever convince her that she is mistaken until Mr Manns summarily removes her from the program scheme of his concerts. Why in the name of commonsense should the singers have privileges which are denied to the instrumentalists?

Mr Manns would not for a moment dream of engaging a popular cornet player to treat the Saturday audience to The Lost Chord or The Staccato Polka, or a popular drawing-room pianist and miscellaneous concert "conductor" to rattle off a Grande Valse Brillante or Perles de l'Orient. Yet with the singers he is contemptuously indulgent. They may bring their ballads and *bravuras* straight from the miscellaneous and promenade concerts without any worse check than the discovery that the conductor does not take the smallest interest in them. Now I am for getting rid of these people, relics as they are of the savagery in which Sydenham was plunged when Mr Manns first arrived there—an heroic artist-missionary. Not that I would have vocal music altogether banned. On the contrary, I would elevate the singers to the level of the pianist and violinist by demanding an equally high class of work from them.

If anybody will sing for us some of these arrangements of Scotch songs by Beethoven, with string accompaniments—Treuer Johnnie, for instance—or the great concert arias of Mozart and Beethoven, let them by all means have the same importance and consideration in the making up of the program as Paderewski or Joachim. Provided we get rid of the promiscuous "vocal piece," the fragments of opera or oratorio, the sentimental trivialities in Norwegian and German which would not be tolerated if they were in familiar English; provided, above all, that I catch the four-fifty-four train, all will be well.

Before quitting this subject I may as well make my comment on the selection of choral works for the present season: that is, of Dvořák's new Mass in D on March 11th, and the Berlioz Faust on April 15th. I do not love these choral concerts: they bring down a horde of the oratorio public, which consists mostly of persons who mistake their curiosity to hear celebrated singers and celebrated compositions for a love of music. However, I admit—grudgingly—their right to live and enjoy themselves in their own miserable manner; and I recognize that they bring their money down and leave some of it behind for the better support of the concerts which please me; and so I put up with them for once in a way. But I do not see why they should not profit a little from the higher atmosphere of the Saturday concerts by being compelled to listen to their favorite singers in works that lie outside the ordinary Albert Hall repertory.

Of Dvořák's work I cannot of course speak, since the performance will be the first in England, though I should not greatly mind offering to eat the full score, covers and all, if it proves a serious contribution to Church music. Dvořák is a romantic composer; and the announcement of a Mass by him affects me much as if it were the announcement of a Divine Comedy in ever so many cantos by Mr R.L. Stevenson. His symphony in G, to which Mr Manns condescended last Saturday, is very nearly up to the level of a Rossini overture, and would make excellent promenade music at the summer *fêtes* out in the grounds. Berlioz's Faust seems to me to be altogether superfluous at the Crystal Palace, since it can now be heard often enough elsewhere.

Why not let us hear Schumann's Faust, with Mr Santley in the title part, or, if he does not care for it, Mr Bispham? Years ago I remember the Philharmonic producing the third section, and gravely informing the public that the first and second were not worth doing. As a matter of fact, the scene in which Faust is dazzled by the rising sun, with the trio of Want, Care, and Guilt, Faust's blindness, his orders to build the great dyke, the digging of the grave by the Lemures under the direction of Mephistopheles, Faust's quiet exultation at what he believes to be the progress of his great work, his declaration that life and freedom are for those alone who can fight every day for them, and his death in the moment of his fulfilled aspiration: all these are in the second part, which is the summit of Schumann's achievement in dramatic music, and is far superior to the rest of the work. I have often wondered that no baritone singer has succeeded in inducing one of our societies to undertake a performance; and it seems to me that at the Crystal Palace, where Schumann is especially beloved, and where the conductor is far more successful with him and more in sympathy with him than with Berlioz, Schumann's Faust would be heard to special advantage.

I may add that the Crystal Palace is rather on my mind for a reason altogether creditable to it. At the first concert of the spring season, on the 18th, the band, which is not usually at its best in the earlier concerts of the season, unexpectedly rose to the occasion with a performance of the [Beethoven] C minor symphony so fine that it must have somewhat astonished Mr Manns himself. I hope Mr Henschel was present; for, in spite of his recent successes, he may take a lesson from Mr Manns as to the possibility of combining a vigorous and eloquent interpretation with refinement of execution and beauty of tone in the wind band. Young Hegner played Beethoven's fourth concerto, and, bar one or two little callousnesses proper to his juvenility, played it intelligently and appreciatively, shewing that he quite understood that he was there to give us the concerto and not to display his own powers. Later on he gave an excellent little performance of Schumann's Des Abends. The concert finished with some charming dance music by Nicodé, prettily spiced by certain fanciful polyphonic *hardiesses* in the style of Bruneau; Dvořák would have worked it up heavily into a symphony, and spoiled it. Last Saturday we had Dvořák in G, as aforesaid; and a Miss Mary Cardew, a remarkable violinist of the Joachim school, who ventured on Bach's Chaconne in D minor, and got through it and through Bruch's first concerto with adequate ambidexterity, but without quite settling the question as to the extent of her original artistic gifts. Santley sang *L'orage s'est calmé,* from Bizet's Pearl Fishers; and I wish the French baritone who introduced that air to us at Covent Garden had been present to hear what an unspoiled human voice, skilfully produced, and guided by a tender and upright artistic conscience, can do in French opera. Many of the audience had evidently expected him to howl in the customary manner, for they seemed a little surprised, and were probably disappointed, poor wretches. He also gave us his own Ave Maria; and I desire to be as gentle as possible in breaking to Mr Lunn and Signor Garcia the news of his having attacked the repeated Aves and Oras without the very least *coup de glotte.*

THE NINTH SYMPHONY
The World, 8 March 1893

A performance of the Ninth Symphony always brings a special audience to St James's Hall; for it is known to be the masterpiece of modern tone-poetry, and the literary man comes to complete his culture by listening to it. I always pity him as he sits there, bothered and exhausted, wondering how soon the choir will begin to sing those verses which are the only part of the analytic program of which he can make head or tail, and hardly able to believe that the conductor can be serious in keeping the band moodling on for fortyfive mortal minutes before the singers get to business. Time was when the conductor himself was often still more astray than the literary man as to the intention of Beethoven, and when those who knew the work by heart sat snorting in contemptuous rage, or enduring with the habitual resignation of tamed despair, whilst the dreary ceremony of reading through the band parts was proceeding.

When I say "time *was*," I do not for a moment question the ability of London to reproduce the same discouraging results still: no doubt anyone who may be curious to know exactly what I mean will find sufficient opportunity before we have lost all the traditions of the time when the Ninth Symphony was treated exactly as if it were a quintet for pianoforte, flute, &c., by Hummel, re-scored for full orchestra by Beethoven. But it has now become a matter of tolerably common knowledge that this sort of handling stamps a conductor, not as a leading authority on Beethoven, but as a nincompoop. How far the work has become really popular it would be hard to determine, because, as I

[825]

have said, so many people come whenever it is in the bills, not to enjoy themselves, but to improve themselves. To them the culmination of its boredom in an Ode to Joy must seem a wanton mockery, since they always hear it for the first time; for a man does not sacrifice himself in that way twice, just as he does not read [George Eliot's] Daniel Deronda twice; and consequently, since it is pre-eminently true of the Ninth Symphony as of the hero of the music hall song, that it is all right when you know it but youve got to know it first, he never becomes sufficiently familiar with the work to delight in it.

On the other hand, there must be a growing number of persons who, like myself, would rather have the Ninth Symphony, even from the purely musical point of view, than all the other eight put together, and to whom, besides, it is religious music, and its performance a celebration rather than an entertainment. I am highly susceptible to the force of all truly religious music, no matter to what Church it belongs; but the music of my own Church—for which I may be allowed, like other people, to have a partiality—is to be found in the Die Zauberflöte and the Ninth Symphony. I was born into evil days, when Les Huguenots was considered a sublime creation, and Die Zauberflöte "a damned pantomime" (as they say nowadays of its legitimate successor, Das Rheingold), and when the Ninth Symphony was regarded as a too long and perversely ugly and difficult concert piece, much inferior to such august neo-classics as Spohr's Consecration of Sound and Mendelssohn's Italian Symphony; and if I had won all my knowledge of the great Singspiel and the great Symphony from their interpreters, instead of from Mozart and Beethoven themselves, small and darkened would that knowledge have been.

In bygone days I have often sat at performances, and

said, under my breath, to the conductor or the artist, "Ah! if I were only a musical critic, how I would pay you out for this, you impostor, you pedant, you miserable artistic deaf-mute, you bawling upstart, you conceited minx," &c. &c. &c. That was in the day of my hot youth. Fortunately, I never became a professed critic—to my own great surprise—until age and experience had softened me to my present indulgent mellowness; but I am by nature vindictive, and find myself not always proof against the temptation to pay off old scores against hardened sinners; so that sometimes, when a fellow-creature is catching it in this column ostensibly for some shortcoming in the previous week, he (or she) is really expiating some murderous art outrage perpetrated on a defenceless child a quarter of a century ago—perhaps even—and this, I admit, is the climax of injustice—by somebody else of whom the performance has too vividly reminded me.

Therefore I implore all young artists to do their best under all circumstances; for they can never know who is listening to them, or how soon some insignificant brat in the cheap seats in a provincial Town Hall or Atheneum may rise up, an avenging fury, armed with all the terrors of the London Press.

As to Mr Henschel and his performance of the Ninth Symphony last Thursday, when I say that he quite understood the nature of the work, and was not for a moment in danger of the old fundamental error of treating it as mere musical arabesque, I imply that the performance was a success; for, with a good band and a right understanding, the obscurities and difficulties of the Ninth Symphony vanish, and a child may lead it. The concert began with Schubert's unfinished symphony, which on this occasion ought to have been his uncommenced symphony. The Ninth Symphony is quite enough for one evening; and I purposely came late for the first movement of the Schubert part of the program, and did not listen to the second. When we got to Beethoven our minds were soon set at ease as to Mr Henschel's grasp of the situation by the vigor and decision with which we got the first subject, especially those two final bars with which Beethoven so powerfully clinches it. But though the main point was thus secured, the handling of the movement as it proceeded was not by any means above criticism.

Mr Henschel, like Ibsen's Master Builder, and like all good conductors, has a troll in him; and this troll occasionally takes to rampaging and filibustering, at which seasons Mr Henschel will not only tolerate, and even relish, rough and blatant attacks on imposing passages, but will overdrive his band in a manner recalling some of the most remarkable achievements of Bevignani. Now, Beethoven must have known well that this was one of the common faults of the qualities he required in a conductor; and it seems clear to me that it was his dread lest any vulgar urgency or excitement should mar the grandeur of his symphonic masterpiece that led him to give the *tempo* of the first movement not merely as *allegro,* but as "*allegro,* but not too much so— rather majestically." Mr Henschel certainly missed the full significance of this "*un poco maestoso.*" He made more than one undignified spurt; and at each of these incontinences the execution became blurred and confused, even to the point, if I mistake not, of notes being dropped and hasty recoveries made in the next bar by the woodwind.

In the *scherzo,* which lends itself to impetuous treatment, the *tempo* was perfect, varying between a normal hundred and seventeen bars per minute and an exceptional hundred and twenty. There were many admirable points in the execution of the slow movement, notably the *cantabile* of the second violins in the first of the *andante* sections; and the only matter on which I found myself at odds with the conductor was the concluding twelve-eight section, where the fact, hardly noticeable at first in the common time, that the pace was a shade too fast for a true Beethoven *adagio*, became quite obvious. Later on, Mr Henschel rather astonished some of us by the apparently very slow *tempo* he adopted for the *allegro assai*, in which the basses give out the theme of the Ode to Joy. We are so accustomed to hear this played exactly twice too fast, as if the minims and crotchets were quavers and semiquavers, and treated as a Haydn *allegro* instead of as an expressive melody, that some of the older listeners felt a little indignant with Mr Henschel for not taking the usual wrong course.

I will even confess that I myself think that the thirty-three bars per minute, increasing to thirtysix at the *forte*, might have been changed to thirtysix and forty respectively without any worse effect than the correction of a slight failing that leaned to virtue's side. The choral portion was perhaps as well done as was possible under the circumstances at English concert pitch; but the strain was inhuman; and the florid variation beat both the choir and the principals, since it required smooth vocal execution as well as mere pluck, which quality the choir shewed abundantly as they held on desperately to high A after high A. On the whole, if we cannot get the pitch down, I am prepared to face the transposition of the choral section a semitone rather than have it marred by tearing and straining at impossibilities. The best points in the vocal work were the charming *piano* on the lines Who can not, oh let him, weeping, Steal away and live alone; the great chorus, Oh! embrace now, all ye millions, and the martial tenor solo, which was sung with intelligence and spirit by Mr Henry McKinley.

May I suggest, on behalf of the choir, that if their voices are not to be relieved by the introduction of

French pitch, at least their lungs might be refreshed by the introduction of a little fresh air? My enjoyment of the symphony was considerably interfered with by the background of young women, beauteous in their virgin robes, but visibly stifling, and agitating fans and sheets of music in all sorts of contradictory rhythms. At last, just as the exquisite *coda* of the *adagio* was stealing on me, I happened to catch sight of a face which had gone perfectly white; and then, of course, I gave up the *adagio* with a sigh, and resigned myself to watch the progress of the struggle not to faint and disturb the performance, the conviction that fresh air was the only salvation, the dreadful sense of the impossibility of climbing to the door over those giddy seats with the lights whirling round and the ground reeling, the alarm spreading to the neighbors, the proffering of fans and smelling-bottles, the commotion among gallant tenors and basses at the back, and the final desperate rally of the patient, and her triumphant postponement of her collapse to the top of the steep ladder at the other side of the door. During all which the band might have been playing Pop Goes the Weasel with no more fear of detection than if we had all been a St John's Ambulance class.

At the Crystal Palace on Saturday we had a Concert Overture by Mr Marshall-Hall. It began as if it really were going to be a concert overture, and a good one; but when it got to the double bar it rambled off into dreams and visions, dropped into Siegfried (the forest music) for a moment, much as Mr Silas Wegg* used to drop into poetry, and finally lost all hold on my attention; so that I cannot say how it ended. Mr Marshall-Hall will know that this is not a hostile verdict—I am of his faction, and not of the academic one; but I would

* Character in Dickens's Our Mutual Friend.

sacrifice my own father if he wrote in sonata form and began to ramble in the fantasia section. Choose what form you please; but when you have chosen it, keep your grip of it like Beethoven, and dont wander and maunder like Schumann and Brahms. The aggravating part of the business in Mr Marshall-Hall's case is that there is no lack of beauty and imaginative handling in his opening section; and he is hardly to be forgiven for not knowing the value and sufficiency of these for the work he had in hand.

Slivinski was the pianist at this concert, and he was mightily applauded. He played one of those concertos of Chopin's which should never have been written by a man of genius after Beethoven's fourth and fifth concertos had been given to the world. The edition used was Tausig's; and I am now more than ever convinced that Tausig's early death was, like that of Ananias, the result of supernatural interposition for the extermination of a sacrilegious meddler. The concert, I beg to add, was much too long.

CARRYING ON WAGNER'S BUSINESS
The World, 15 March 1893

The notices of the production of Cyrill Kistler's Kunihild at Würzburg remind me that I have often intended, and as often omitted, to call attention to the one composer who, as far as I know, has definitely set to work to continue Wagner's business on what I suppose I must now call the old lines, although it seems but yesterday that they were being denounced all over Europe as unbearably new lines. This, of course, is not altogether a fair description of Kistler; but I know so little about him that nobody can reasonably expect me to be accurate on the subject. I hear that he is very poor, and highly unpopular in academic circles; both of which facts, if they be facts, naturally predispose me to believe that he must be a man of some character and originality, and that he can easily get them recognized, even to the extent of a public statue, by simply begging or borrowing enough to keep him alive until he has produced a few great works, and then dying and waiting quietly in his coffin until his countrymen find him out. It is by offering the citizen every possible inducement not to be a man of genius that we keep him to safe everyday work; and this system is so completely successful that we may confidently boast that we never waste a man on high art unless he is so obsessed with it as to be fit for nothing else.

Kistler appears to be the victim of this sort of diabolic possession, brought on him, apparently, by exposure at a tender age to performances of Wagner's Ring trilogy; for he cannot get Valhalla and Odin and Loki and the Valkyries and dwarfs out of his head, and his solemn trombonings are beginning to be heard and talked of in the Fatherland. The Wagner Societies are charmed with him; but I do not regard their approval as conclusive; for I have had occasion to observe that it is possible to cultivate a taste for Wagner without cultivating a taste for music; I suspect the Wagner Societies of including a considerable percentage of members who would rather have imitation Wagner than genuine Mozart, if, indeed, they do not positively dislike Mozart as their idol's rival before posterity. For in art, as in more personal matters, there is a love which means hating everybody else, and which ought to be capitally punished; as well as a love which spreads to everyone else, and which increases your regard for every man or woman, or piece of music, for the sake of one man or woman or piece of music.

Catholicity is the stamp of the higher love, as jealousy is of the lower; and I grievously mistrust the amateur who worships Wagner without sharing Wagner's delight in the works of other musicians, both great and small. Observe, catholicity is not Don Juanism. I much prefer Don Juan to the faithful French wife who throws vitriol in her rival's face, knowing that a French jury will let her off if she only dresses her part well enough; but still Don Juan did not love anybody: he was an Indifferentist. If I had been the petrified Commander, I should not have talked conventionally to him about repentance: I should have offered to let him off if he could rise for a moment to a preference for some woman above another, say for Elvira above her maid—though without in the least objecting to his appreciating the maid for what she was worth.

Nobody objects to Wagner's being delighted with La Sonnambula and Masaniello; but if they had served his turn as well as Die Zauberflöte and Fidelio, we should at once have seen that he had no more feeling for music than most bookbinders have for literature. Even the jealous lover is better worth consulting than the indifferent, who has no opinion at all, except that a book is a book, an opera an opera, and a petticoat a petticoat, and that books, operas, and petticoats are all enjoyable. But I prefer to consult the true catholic; and catholicism has not yet spoken on the merits of Kistler, except that he does not seem to be getting extinguished as the years go on—a fact which looks as if he were gaining ground with the final arbiter, Monsieur Tout-le-Monde. For my own part, I know nothing of his music, except what may be gathered from the vocal score of his Baldur's Tod, which does not contain his ripest work, and which, though it would certainly be a most remarkable and original music-drama if there had never been such a person as Richard Wagner—just as Rienzi would have astonished the world greatly if Spontini and Meyerbeer had been out of the question—hardly proves more than a true discipleship (as distinct from a mere gleanership or imitatorship) on the part of its composer.

Of Kunihild I have very favorable accounts from trustworthy intelligencers; but for the moment I content myself with informing my readers that Cyrill Kistler should be noted as one of the coming men in Germany. It will take him longer to come all the way than it has taken Mascagni; but there will certainly be more to shew at the end of the journey: Baldur's Tod setties at least that much.

The first Philharmonic concert took place last Thursday. It began at eight, and was actually not over at eleven. And as I am a living man, they played the overture to Marco Spada! Perhaps it is too much to ask the public to believe such a thing on my unsupported statement; but there are the papers, the printed program, the testimony of the audience to support me; and I repeat, they played Marco Spada—Auber's Marco Spada—at a Philharmonic Concert at the end of the XIX century, with the bust of Beethoven in its usual place before the orchestra! But that is just like the Philharmonic directors. They never could hear any qualitative difference between Rossini or Auber and Mozart or Beethoven. All four wrote overtures—William Tell, La Muette, Le Nozze di Figaro, Egmont; and an overture is an overture, as all the world knows—Don Juanism again, you see.

I may add that a band is a band, whether it is in St James's Hall or at a flower show: nevertheless, one does not draw up quite the same program for both places, except, apparently, at Philharmonic Concerts. I verily believe that if the composer of The Man that broke the Bank at Monte Carlo had only called his *chef-d'œuvre* an aria, and prefixed a recitative to it, we should have had

Mr Coborn* among the artists engaged during the Philharmonic season. One of the jokes of the present year is the reappearance in the programs of that history of the Society which figured in them all through last season. It will be remembered that this same last season ended somewhat scandalously for the Society through Mr Cowen, the conductor, publicly apologizing for the unrehearsed condition of the Pastoral Symphony, and being thereupon dislodged from his post by the indignant directors, who, having been exposed before all Europe and America by Wagner (whom they also dislodged after a year's trial in 1855) for offering monstrously long programs of scamped work to the public, were no doubt annoyed by being convicted by Mr Cowen of having persisted in their evil courses for nearly forty years.

However, before this happened they had, in the aforesaid historical sketch, made much of Mr Cowen in the following terms: "The Directors have ground for sincere congratulation for the choice [of a conductor] they have made for the present season." I quote the Philharmonic English verbatim, as the meaning may readily be guessed; and for the rest, why, as Rossini used to say when his serious style petered out too obviously into a galop, *"Excusez du peu."* "It would scarcely be possible to find a more efficient or more popular conductor than Mr F. Cowen." The congratulations have been turned into condolements and gnashings of teeth, and the efficient and popular one has bitten the bosom that cherished him; yet the passage is still offered magnanimously to the public for a shilling, without even a note to indicate that the present

* Charles Coborn, celebrated comic singer, had recently made an enormous music hall success of Fred. Gilbert's song The Man that broke the Bank at Monte Carlo.

conductor is Dr Mackenzie. He, in accepting the post, practically declared against Mr Cowen—a course which he has now to justify by producing better results than Mr Cowen, with no better preparation. When he appeared on the platform on Thursday there was an awful moment, caused by his coming somewhat pointedly to the front of the platform and facing the audience with a certain air of being about to make a speech; so that there began an awe-struck wondering whisper of "Is he also going to apologize?"

But he did not, happily; and next moment the band was shewing off in true Philharmonic style over the Euryanthe overture, as to which it is clear to me that either I know how Weber meant it to be played better than Dr Mackenzie does, or else Dr Mackenzie knows better than I do, which, as he is the Principal of the Royal Academy of Music, is no doubt the preferable view. Why, then, should I hesitate to express my opinion that the overture is thrown away on him—that he does not appreciate even the second subject, with that exquisite seventh bar which at its repetition in the last *fortissimo* becomes so gloriously transformed that no orchestra can ever saturate it with the flood of tone it requires? As it was, the band conveyed to me but one sentiment, which might have been expressed by the words "Aint we just makin' it spin, eh?" And they certainly did make it spin: it sounded almost as smart as Marco Spada; and the *pianissimo* in the largo was undeniably *pianissimo*, if it was nothing else.

The Eroica Symphony was a great improvement on this: I judge that Dr Mackenzie knows and likes the work; and though the performance was not nearly so thoroughly studied as that recently given by Mr Henschel, and was consequently much less interesting, yet the score was very respectfully and delicately read through. The funeral march, of course, collapsed at the more powerful passages, as the wind would not hold their notes, perhaps because it is the custom for a Philharmonic conductor to throw up his hands in agony and cry "Sh—sh—sh!" at rehearsal whenever the brass ventures beyond a timid little bark. And the last episode, numbered 14 in the program, was made ridiculous in the traditional way by giving the quavers, obviously meant to be played very *legato*, as detached semiquavers, an absurdity which Mr Henschel also tolerated. But on the whole, the symphony did not need an apology. Marco Spada was of course brilliant—no one can pretend that the Philharmonic band cannot do justice to Auber, and Mancinelli's Suite and Cowen's Language of Flowers, and all manner of pretty things. Decidedly Marco Spada was an excellent example of the best work the Philharmonic system can produce.

Slivinski played Schumann's concerto very brilliantly; but he made nothing of the slow movement, and did not throw any new light on the rest. He played Chopin's Nocturne in F sharp charmingly but inaccurately. *Tempo rubato* is all very well; but two semiquavers are two semiquavers all the world over, and not a dotted semiquaver and a demi-semiquaver. Excuse these barbarous expressions.

Dvořak's rather amusing Mass in D and Goring Thomas's rather serious comic opera, The Golden Web, must stand over until next week.

THE PROBLEMS OF TRANSLATION
The World, 22 March 1893

I wish we had a Minister of the Fine Arts in this country, with a well-equipped statistical department behind him, and absolutely autocratic powers over everybody except myself. Were I such a Minister, I would allow the managers to do as they pleased in the way of producing plays; but I would compel them to submit their accounts to me, so that I might issue Blue Books containing the exact truth as to the financial results of every play or opera produced in the kingdom. My object would be to shew that hundreds of thousands of pounds are wasted annually in producing obvious trash on the chance of its "catching on." Except actor-management and management to oblige a lady, management is mainly a department of sport into which artistic aims enter about as deeply as the improvement of national horsebreeding enters into the ambition of our gentlemen of the Turf. Consequently, we have an enormous proportion of failure to success; and we have the public going more and more to music halls because a music hall is the only place of entertainment where you can be quite sure of not having your evening and your money entirely wasted.

To avoid leveling these observations at any individual, I will now pass to the subject of Goring Thomas's Golden Web at the Lyric Theatre, since Goring Thomas attained a position as a dramatic composer which places the production of an opera of his beyond all suspicion as a legitimate artistic enterprise. Unfortunately, one of the effects of the experiment will be to confirm the association between the legitimate and the old-fashioned. In The Golden Web we have the composer utterly ignoring not only Wagner, but even Gilbert and Sullivan, by tacking so many numbers of what is practically "absolute music" to a book which, poor enough as a play, is quite wretched as a libretto, void as it is of a single passage which calls for musical expression: indeed, it is difficult to conceive how the work could have been made into an opera at all but for the stale interpolations of drinking-chorus, ballad, dance, and so forth, which have done duty in a hundred other operas before. Stuff of this kind apart, the music is essentially undramatic, and necessarily so, since the only truly dramatic music for such a play would be no music at all (I speak as an Irishman).

If Goring Thomas had been a dramatic composer instead of a mere musician ambitious to compose for the stage, he would have refused the book. There are degrees in the toleration of bad librettos: for instance, the late Francis Hueffer only pleaded for the reform of Now good red wine we will be drinking into Now let us drink some good red wine; wheras Sterndale Bennett insisted on total abstinence, and is said to have failed to leave us an opera only because he never could get a libretto in which some act did not begin with Soldiers discovered drinking. Bennett was quite right to object to the drinking-chorus altogether, not on account of its wording, but because no real dramatic poem could possibly contain such a thing. Goring Thomas, however, had no such scruples. He has provided music in The Golden Web for —

Let there be no more despair, boys;
Come along, tis share and share, boys,
Theres enough to drown all care, boys,
But remember, pray drink fair, boys.
A bottle—yes, a good old bottle,
Amazement and gratitude close up each throttle.
A glass of such medicine out of the bottle
Will stir up a blush our complexions to mottle.

It is quite unnecessary for me to state my opinion of these lines. I will do Mr Corder, one of the authors, the justice to assume that he entirely agrees with me; but Mr B. C. Stephenson, his collaborator, must remain under suspicion of being rather proud of them until he writes to the papers repudiating any such notion. Mr

Corder's excuse, no doubt, is that he has had to translate foreign opera texts into English versions capable of being sung to the original notes, a process in which all literary conscience and even common sanity vanishes, the job being in the nature of things an impossible one from the first. The public probably does not understand the difficulty; but it can easily do so by studying some of Schubert's settings of German translations of English poems by Sir Walter Scott. To the inconsiderate outsider, nothing would appear to have been simpler, when the time came to bring Schubert's settings to England, than to substitute the original text of Scott for the German translation. But the result would have been such an outrageous misfit, in consequence of the disparity in number of syllables and position of accent between many English words and their German equivalents, that it was necessary to contrive new English versions of the German translations, absurdly inferior to the original English.

Such English versions, which sometimes get re-translated into German and back again—for there is no logical end to the process—are makeshifts from beginning to end; and the difficulty of fitting them to the music is so great that the adapter soon grows desperate, and snatches at the most ludicrous and farfetched solutions, not merely with resignation, but with positive complacency. Mr Corder achieved a surprising degree of success in making an English version of Wagner's Nibelungen tetralogy; but the success did not go to the length of enabling him to avoid making one of the giants remark, in dunning Wotan for the agreed wage of building Valhalla, "Pay fails to appear"—a flash of dialogue which, whilst fully up to the highest libretto standard, has not the atmosphere of "god-home" about it. But I not only should not think of finding fault with it, but do hereby absolve Mr Corder, as Nibelungen

English versionist, from all literary responsibility for ever, in consideration of pre-eminent service and superhuman trials; and I shall not now say one unkind word about the following lyric, lest he, and not Mr Stephenson, should prove the author of it. Here it is:

> Oh dear! I am so frightened,
> My pulse is madly heightened,
> And every nerve is tightened—
>   Aunt Pamela is lost.
> I turned my head a moment,
> A lovely dress, for show meant,
> All lace and furbelowment,
> Had caught my eye a moment—
>   Aunt Pamela is lost.
> Geoffrey, say not our dream of love is oer.
> Aunt Pamela in vain I search,
> In vain I call.

How Goring Thomas set this sort of poetry can be imagined by anyone who knows the facility with which he turned out opera scores musically as advanced as Gounod's, yet dramatically not an inch in front of Balfe's. In fact, Balfe was the more original of the two, since he came first, although of course Goring Thomas never bungled his music as Balfe would bungle a whole opera from the first page to the last, the ballads only excepted. In The Golden Web, the music, considered as absolute music, is graceful, workmanlike, and occasionally vigorous enough; but it does not even pretend anywhere to novelty—the very overture begins at once with a thoroughly well-worn Gounodism, and has for its second subject The heart bowed down from The Bohemian Girl, not more altered than it would have been by Balfe himself if he had used it in an overture and been able to handle it as cleverly as Goring Thomas. The non-musical part of the play is a rococo comedy, with a crusty father, a runaway pair of lovers, an elderly beau and belle, a gentleman's gentleman, a Fleet parson with a comic drunken servant, and so on. It is not actually stupid, but it is a poor affair, neither the authors nor the composer having taken their work seriously. If it succeeds, its success will be due largely to Miss Alice Esty, a born musician and singer, with an invaluable quickness and good sense, and a certain fresh charm of manner and appearance which at once broke down a virtuous resolution against *encores* promulgated by a man of few words in the gallery, who simply said, "No *encores*, boys," and carried his point thereafter against everybody except Miss Esty. It must be added that part of Miss Esty's freshness is due to the fact that neither her acting nor her speaking has any definitely artistic character. She turns her hand willingly and intelligently to the business of her part; but it is through the natural charm of her unspoiled voice, which tells through the heaviest *ensembles* by its quality alone (it is perfectly light and delicate), and through the pleasure taken by the public in her musical facility and confidence of execution, that she succeeds, and not in the least by the sort of artistic purpose and skill which have enabled less gifted persons to conquer a place on the stage in spite of refractory voices, slow ears, and unattractive faces and figures. Mr Wallace Brownlow acted humorously in an amateur way as the Fleet parson. The music suits his voice so well that he is on good terms with the audience all through; but I advise Mr Brownlow, now that he holds a leading position at a West End London theatre, not, even in a comic part, to allow his diction to sink to the point at which "gimme" passes for "give me," or "virchew" and "disconcerchew" for "virtue" and "disconcert you."

The Mass by Dvořák which was performed for the first time in England at the Crystal Palace last Saturday week, contains a good deal of *fugato*, which is all the funnier because the composer evidently meant it to be ecclesiastical and impressive. The Credo, in his romantic style, is not bad as an example of that style, though it is not good as a Credo. Some of the words of the Mass are omitted from the setting; but though the omissions seem to have been deliberate, I failed to infer from them the exact limits to Dvořák's orthodoxy.

At the Palace concert last Saturday, Joachim, whose finest qualities seem to improve as the years make him serener, gave us Mozart's concerto in A, the last movement in which is an experiment in combining the minuet and *finale* into a single movement in rondo form. Also a capriccio by Niels Gade—a novelty. Miss Mary Harris, who has been harmlessly—that is, excellently—trained, and whose purely musical qualifications are considerable, saw no difficulty whatever either in Mozart's *Mi tradi* from Don Giovanni or in Schubert's Ave Maria. In fact, finding both compositions rather uninteresting as they stood, she touched up the first with a B flat at the end, and even lent Schubert an A flat which was so unexpected that gentlemen were seen doubling up in all directions in the part of the room more especially affected by the connoisseurs.

I hope Miss Harris will understand that she must not do that again if she wishes to be respected as an artist as well as admired as a young lady with a pretty voice; and also, I must add, that she is not yet within ten years of attaining the expression and eloquence which can alone give her the right to touch in public a masterpiece like *Mi tradi*. For the rest, Miss Harris is to be congratulated on being a nice singer, since she is now in a position to begin to teach herself to be an artist.

THE YOUNGER GENERATION

The World, 29 March 1893

I seldom go to a Monday Popular Concert without wondering how many of the people who sit out the quartets and sonatas feel the heavy responsibility which they incur as the dispensers of applause and success to young artists. Last Monday week I heard them give a tremendous ovation to Joachim, who had played Bach's Chaconne in D minor, and played it, certainly, with a fineness of tone and a perfect dignity of style and fitness of phrasing that can fairly be described as magnificent. If the intonation had only had the exquisite natural justice of Sarasate's, instead of the austerity of that peculiar scale which may be called the Joachim mode, and which is tempered according to Joachim's temperament and not according to that of the sunny South, I should have confidently said to my neighbor that this particular performance could never be surpassed by mortal violinist.

But the thought that the miracle of miracles might arrive in the shape of a violinist with Sarasate's intonation and Joachim's style made me forbear. This peculiar intonation of Joachim's for a long time greatly hindered my appreciation of his art: the Celtic troll in me rebelled against intervals that were not the same as my intervals. For I may as well make known, as a remarkable discovery in psychical physics, that the modes in which we express ourselves musically, that is, the major and minor scales, though in theory series of sounds bearing a fixed pitch relation to oneanother, are in practice tempered by every musician just as the proportions of the human figure are tempered by a sculptor. Some physicist should make a tonometer giving a theoretically perfect major scale, in order that Joachim, Sarasate, Ysaÿe, and Remenyi should have an opportunity of hearing how far the four different tone figures which they have made for themselves as major scales differ from the theoretic scale and from oneanother. Only the worst of it is that the tonometer would probably turn out to be inaccurate, as scientific instruments usually are.

Schumann's metronome led him a pretty dance; and Appun's tonometer bothered the late Alexander J. Ellis handsomely until it occurred to him that a box of reeds was much more likely to get out of condition than the organ of Corti inside the head of a musician. Still, the fact that a tonometer is quite as likely as a violinist to set up a scale peculiar to its individual self does not affect my contention that every artist modifies the scale to suit his own ear; that every nation does the same; and that the musical critic of the future, instead of crudely saying, as I do, that the Germans have every musical qualification except ear, will classify the national and individual modes, and dispassionately announce that the intonation of So-and-So, the new virtuoso, is German-lymphatic, or Spanish-bilious, or English-evangelical, or what not. And he will train himself to tolerate and appreciate all these different modes, just as I have come to such a perfect toleration of Joachim's that I no longer have the least feeling that he is playing out of tune except when he is false to his own scale.

I submit this enlightened attitude for the imitation of those rash persons who accuse Joachim of playing out of tune, and whose standard of intonation is often founded on the luscious strains of the accordion as made in Italy, or on keyed instruments like the common pianoforte, with its sharp thirds, flat fifths, and generally tinkered and compromised tuning. Even if Joachim played every note out of tune, the quality of his tone and the thoroughness of his intepretation would compel us to listen to him though we groaned with anguish at every stroke of the bow.

However, I am wandering, as usual; for all I specially want to point out about this concert is that the same audience which apparently revelled in the masterly playing of Bach's Chaconne by Joachim, shewed equal delight at Miss Ilona Eibenschütz's attack on Beethoven's pianoforte sonata in F minor, popularly nicknamed Appassionata. Now, at the risk of greatly astonishing Miss Eibenschütz, whose talent I quite appreciate and whose enthusiasm I should be sorry to damp, I must, on behalf of Beethoven, mention that the sonata could hardly have been worse played by an artist of Miss Eibenschütz's endowment. I am not now thinking of the last movement: a young player may be forgiven for trying to carry that by storm: and Miss Eibenschütz, who evidently enjoyed the excitement of the rush, at her age will be none the worse for it, though the music all but disappeared in the dust and hurry. But we have really had enough of hearing the first movement trifled with as if it were a mere *bravura*. No orator ever declaimed a sentence more gravely beautiful than that with which the sonata opens: words could add nothing to its feeling, though they could give it—quite superfluously—some specific relevancy. To seize such a poetic speech by main force and gallop it along as if it were a quickstep, and to follow it up in the same fashion, turning all its kindlings of heart into mere spurts of impetuosity, and retiring finally amid the sort of enthusiasm that follows a pluckily rowed boat race, is to fail as a Beethoven interpreter in the most obvious way.

Every student knows that it is difficult to play the Appassionata or the Moonlight or the Waldstein sonata accurately, and exciting to play them fast. But that is not what they are for; and when a great artist wishes to give the public some fun of that kind, there are plenty of Hungarian rhapsodies and toccatas of all sorts ready to hand for the purpose. To put a tone-poem to such a use is like using an ivory sceptre as a singlestick; and if Miss Eibenschütz were ten years older there would be no pardon for her having done this wrong to the F minor sonata, and that, too, with artists like Joachim and Piatti listening to her. Yet the audience, foolishly excited by the mere haste of the performance, encored her with enthusiasm, and thereby heavily discounted the value of the same compliment paid shortly afterwards to Joachim for the Chaconne. In the Eibenschütz furore, however, I think there was a passionate student element; for the young player, with her dark hair braided over her pale face and great eyes, her black dress emphasizing the slightness of her figure, and her quick, half-tamed movements, appealed with instinctive feminine art to the student imagination.

Fortunately, I have no imagination: I am proof against all illusions except illusions which flatter me; I am middle-aged in years and patriarchal in wisdom; and so before the end of the first bar I knew that the sonata was going to be a failure; and I hope Miss Eibenschütz will give due weight to that opinion from a critic whose first impression of her ability was highly favorable.

A very remarkable performance was that of Brahms's violin concerto by Miss Wietrowetz at the Philharmonic last Thursday. It was not by any means musically satisfactory; for Miss Wietrowetz is powerful, impatient, and, like all modern women, somewhat contemptuous of manly gentleness. I confess I am afraid of Miss Wietrowetz: she is so strong and wilful that even her playing gives me a humiliating sense of being ordered about—positively of being henpecked. Joachim is called by courtesy her master; but I suspect that what really happened was that Miss Wietrowetz bought a fiddle; took it to his house; and said "Here, shew me how to play this, if you please. Look sharp"; and that he meekly obeyed.

That is the way the younger generation comes knocking at the door nowadays. There is no longer any doubt about it: we of the nobler sex must give up the old assortment of "manly qualities"; for they are passing away from us to the young women, who beat all our records with triumphant ease. If the supremacy of man is to be maintained, we must develop a quite new set of qualities and hasten to the very heights; for I feel that nothing but a perfectly blinding moral splendor can protect me against the masterful will, the determined courage, the practicality, the executive skill of such a personality as Miss Wietrowetz's. Suppose she were to find out how easily I could be bullied into declaring her the greatest player that ever lived, where should I be?

But whilst I am still my own master I will maintain, even if I were to be taken by the collar and well shaken for it next day, that Joachim's patience, and his complete subjugation of his will to a purely artistic end, produce greater results in Brahms's concerto, or any other concerto, than the mettlesomeness of this formidable pupil of his, who, by the bye, has acquired his peculiar intonation as perfectly as Miss Nettie Carpenter has acquired Sarasate's. I repeat, they are wonderful, these young women: they do by sheer resolution what men are only able to do by extraordinary natural gifts.

Before I leave the subject of the Philharmonic concert, I must chronicle the performance of Mr Somervell's orchestral ballad Helen of Kirkconnel, a simple affair which disarmed criticism by its unpretentiousness. The band played the Brahms concerto in a rather ramshackle fashion (I think Miss Wietrowetz put them out of countenance); but in Sullivan's Macbeth overture they handled the wind parts with a firmness that quite took away my breath; and once or twice they positively approached a genuine *fortissimo*. My compliments, Dr Mackenzie! I begin to believe, for the first time in my life, that there is some use in criticism, and that the Philharmonic Society may earn its reputation yet, after all. I did not wait for Mr Cliffe's symphony, of which I have already expressed my opinion; but I have no doubt that, as the program promised, the first *allegro* gave "a general impression of the splendor of nature under the declining sun," and that the semiquaver figure duly "stood for the quivering beams of the great luminary."

The operetta called Mr Jericho, by "Harry Greenbank" (I take this to be an *alias*),* which now precedes Haddon Hall at the Savoy, is funnily absurd and wittily funny, a fact which dawned on a rather stupid audience on the night of my visit after a page of really laughable dialogue had been listened to in dead silence. It has been passably upholstered with requisite music by Mr Ernest Ford; and the acting and singing, though jolly enough to carry the piece through acceptably, are abysmally beneath notice from the point of view of the critic of skilled art.

The concerts of the Wind Instrument Chamber Music Society are now in progress at St James's Banqueting Hall. I can do no more than mention the fact, as the night fixed for the concerts (Friday) is one on which I am seldom able to attend.

* Shaw was mistaken about the pseudonym. Henry H. (Harry) Greenbank was a young dramatist who died, in 1899, at the age of 33.

VERDI'S FALSTAFF

The World, 12 April 1893

Easter has afforded me an opportunity for a look through the vocal score of Verdi's Falstaff, now to be had at Ricordi's for sixteen shillings, a price which must obviously be reduced before the opera can get into the hands of the amateur at large. I did not go to Milan to hear the first performance for several reasons, the chief being that I am not enough of a first-nighter to face the huge tedium and probable sickness of the journey from Holborn to Basle (the rest I do not mind) in order merely to knock at the tradesman's door of Italy, so to speak, and turn back after hearing an opera half murdered by La Scala *prima donnas* with shattering *tremolos,* and witnessing a Grand Old Man demonstration conducted for the most part by people who know about as much of music as the average worshiper of Mr Gladstone does of statesmanship. In short, being lazy and heavily preoccupied, I cried sour grapes and stayed at home, knowing that the mountain would come to Mahomet soon enough.

Let it be understood, then, that since I have not been present at a complete performance of Falstaff I do not know the work: I only know some things about it. And of these I need not repeat what has already been sufficiently told: as, for instance, that Falstaff is a music-drama, not an opera, and that consequently it is by Shakespear, Boïto, and Verdi, and not by Verdi alone. The fact that it is a music-drama explains the whole mystery of its composition by a man eighty years old. If there were another *Il balen* or *La donna è mobile* in it, I should have been greatly astonished; but there is nothing of the sort: the fire and heroism of his earlier works blaze up now only on strong provocation.

Falstaff is lighted and warmed only by the afterglow of the fierce noonday sun of Ernani; but the gain in beauty conceals the loss in heat—if, indeed, it be a loss to replace intensity of passion and spontaneity of song by fulness of insight and perfect mastery of workmanship. Verdi has exchanged the excess of his qualities for the wisdom to supply his deficiencies; his weaknesses have disappeared with his superfluous force; and he is now, in his dignified competence, the greatest of living dramatic composers. It is not often that a man's strength is so immense that he can remain an athlete after bartering half of it to old age for experience; but the thing happens occasionally, and need not so greatly surprise us in Verdi's case, especially those of us who, long ago, when Von Bülow and others were contemptuously repudiating him, were able to discern in him a man possessing more power than he knew how to use, or indeed was permitted to use by the old operatic forms imposed on him by circumstances.

I have noticed one or two exclamations of surprise at the supposed revelation in Falstaff of a "hitherto unsuspected" humorous force in the veteran tragic composer. This must be the result of the enormous popularity which Il Trovatore first and Aïda afterwards attained in this country. I grant that these operas are quite guiltless of comic relief; but what about Un Ballo, with its exquisitely lighthearted *E scherzo od e follia*, and the *finale* to the third act, where Renato is sarcastically complimented on his domestic virtue by the conspirators who have just shewn him that the Duke's veiled mistress, whom he is defending from them after devotedly saving the Duke's life, is his own wife. Stupidly as that tragicomic quartet and chorus has always been mishandled on our wretched operatic stage, I cannot understand anyone who knows it denying Verdi's gift of dramatic humor.

In the first act of Otello, the *stretto* made in the drinking song by Cassio when he gets drunk is very funny without being in the least unmusical. The grim humor of Sparafucile, the terrible ironic humor of Iago, the agonized humor of Rigoletto: these surely settled the question as to Verdi's capacity for Falstaff none the less because the works in which they occur are tragedies and not comedies. All that could be said on the other side was that Verdi was no Mozart, which was as idle as saying that Victor Hugo was no Molière. Verdi's vein of humor is all the more Shakespearean on that account.

Verdi's worst sins as a composer have been sins against the human voice. His habit of taking the upper fifth of the compass of an exceptionally high voice, and treating that fifth as the normal range, has a great deal to do with the fact that the Italian singer is now the worst singer in the world, just as Wagner's return to Handel's way of using the voice all over its compass and obtaining physical relief for the singer and artistic relief for the audience by the contrast of the upper and lower registers has made the Wagnerian singer now the best singer in the world. Verdi applied his system with special severity to baritones.

If you look at the score of Don Giovanni, you will find three different male voices written for on the bass clef, and so treated as to leave no doubt that Mozart, as he wrote the music, had a particular sort of voice for each part constantly in his head, and that one (Masetto's) was a rough peasant's bass, another (Leporello's) a ready, fluent, copious *basso cantante*; and the third a light fine baritone, the voice of a gentleman. I have heard public meetings addressed successively by an agricultural laborer's delegate, a representative of the skilled artisans, and a university man; and they have taught me what all the treatises on singing in the world could not about the Mozartian differentiation between Masetto, Leporello, and Don Giovanni.

But now please remark that there is no difference of range between the three parts. Any man who can sing the notes of one of them can sing the notes of the others. Let Masetto and the Don exchange characters, and though the Don will be utterly ineffective in the concerted music on Masetto's lower G's and B flats, whilst Masetto will rob the serenade of all its delicacy, yet neither singer will encounter any more impossibility, or even inconvenience, in singing the notes than Mr Toole would have in reading the part of Hamlet. The same thing is true of the parts of Bartolo, Figaro, and Almaviva in Le Nozze; of San Bris and Nevers in Les Huguenots; of Wotan and Alberich in The Niblung's Ring; and of Amfortas and Klingsor in Parsifal. The dramatic distinction between these parts is so strong that only an artist of remarkable versatility could play one as well as the other; but there is practically no distinction of vocal range any more than there is a distinction of physical stature or strength.

But if we turn to Il Trovatore, we find two vocal parts written in the bass clef, of which the lower, Ferrando, is not a *basso profundo* like Osmin or Marcel, but a *basso cantante* like San Bris or Leporello; yet the baritone part (Di Luna) is beyond the reach of any normal *basso cantante*, and treats a baritone voice as consisting of about one effective octave, from G on the fourth space of the bass stave to the G above. In *Il balen* there are from two hundred and ten to two hundred and twenty notes, including the *cadenza*, &c. Barring five notes in the *cadenza*, which is never sung as written, only three are below F on the fourth line, whilst nearly one hundred and forty lie above the stave between B flat and the high G. The singing is practically continuous from end to end; and the strain on a normal baritone voice is frightful, even when the song is transposed half a tone as it usually is to bring it within the bare limits of possibility. Di Luna is in this respect a typical Verdi baritone; and the result has been that only singers with abnormally high voices have been able to sing it without effort.

As to the normal baritones who have made a speciality of bawling fiercely up to G sharp, they have so lost the power of producing an endurable tone in their lower octave, or of pitching its notes with even approximate accuracy, that they have all but destroyed the popularity of Mozart's operas by their occasional appearances as Don Giovanni, Figaro, &c. I have often wished that the law would permit me to destroy these unhappy wretches, whose lives must be a burden to them. It is easy to go into raptures over the superiority of the Italian master in vocal writing because his phrases are melodious, easily learned, symmetrical, and often grandiose; but when you have to sing the melodious well-turned phrases, and find that they lie a tone higher than you can comfortably manage them, and a third higher than you can keep on managing them for five minutes at a stretch (for music that *lies* rather high is much more trying than music that *ventures* very high occasionally), you begin to appreciate the sort of knowledge of and consideration for the voice shewn by Purcell, Handel, and Wagner, and to very decidedly resent Verdi's mere partiality for the top end of it.

Now comes the question, what sort of voice is needed for the part of Falstaff? Well, Ferrando and the Count di Luna rolled into one—Amonasro, in short. A rich *basso cantante*, who can knock out a vigorous high G and play with F sharp as Melba plays with B flat. Polyphemus in Handel's Acis and Valentin in Gounod's Faust might do it justice between them. Barely reasonable this, even at French pitch, and monstrous at Philharmonic pitch. And yet it is the fashion to say that Verdi is a master of the art of writing singable music.

The score is necessarily occupied to a great extent by the discourses of Falstaff, which are set with the most expert ingenuity and subtlety, the advance in this respect from the declamation of Charles V. in Ernani to that of Falstaff being as great as from Tannhäuser's to Parsifal's, or from Vanderdecken's to Hans Sachs's. One capital effect—the negative answers in the manner of Mr Chadband to the repeated questions as to what honor is—is, musically, a happy adaptation from Boïto's Mefistofele, and is, as far as I have discovered, the only direct Boïtoism in the work, though I imagine that Verdi has profited generally by having so fine an artist and critic as Boïto at his elbow when composing Otello and Falstaff. There are some amusing passages of instrumental music: for instance, a highly expressive accompaniment to a colossal drink taken by Falstaff.

During the abundant action and stage bustle of the piece we get a symphonic treatment, which belongs exclusively to Verdi's latest manner. Some tripping figuration, which creates perpetual motion by its ceaseless repetition in all sorts of ingenious sequences, as in Mendelssohn's *scherzos* or the *finales* to his concertos, is taken as the musical groundwork upon which the vocal parts are put in, the whole fabric being wrought with the most skilful elegance. This is a matter for some of our musical pundits to consider rather anxiously. For, if I had said ten years ago that Ernani was a much greater musical composition than Mendelssohn's Scotch symphony or any of his concertos, words could not have conveyed the scorn with which so gross an opinion would have been received. But here, today, is the scorned one, whom even Browning thought it safe to represent as an empty blusterer shrinking amid a torrent of vulgar applause from the grave eye of—of—of—well, of ROSSINI! (poor Browning!) falling back in his old age on the Mendelssohnian method, and employing it with ease and brilliancy.

Perhaps, when Verdi turns a hundred and feels too old for opera composition, he will take to concerto writing, and cut out Mendelssohn and Schumann in the pretty pattern work which the pundits love them for. Which will shew how very easy it is for a good musician, when he happens to be a bad critic, to admire a great composer for the wrong thing.

A GOOD CONCERT
The World, 19 April 1893

Last week an unexpected event occurred—nothing less than a concert. I had been for a long time wishing to hear a little music; so I went off to Prince's Hall and found Miss Dora Bright wasting a very good program on a very bad audience, with the help of Messrs Willy Hess, Kreuz, and Whitehouse. They began with Mozart's pianoforte quartet in G minor, to my delight, as all my musical self-respect is based on my keen appreciation of Mozart's works. It is still as true as it was before the Eroica symphony existed, that there is nothing better in art than Mozart's best. We have had Beethoven, Schubert, Mendelssohn, Schumann, Goetz, and Brahms since his time: we have even had Dr Parry, Professor Stanford, Mr Cowen, Dr Mackenzie, and Sir Arthur Sullivan; but the more they have left the Mozart quartet or quintet behind, the further it comes out ahead in its perfection of temper and refinement of consciousness.

In the ardent regions where all the rest are excited

and vehement, Mozart alone is completely self-possessed: where they are clutching their bars with a grip
of iron and forging them with Cyclopean blows, his
gentleness of touch never deserts him: he is considerate,
economical, practical under the same pressure of
inspiration that throws your Titan into convulsions.
This is the secret of his unpopularity with Titan fanciers.
We all in our native barbarism have a relish for the
strenuous: your tenor whose B flat is like the bursting of
a boiler always brings down the house, even when the
note brutally effaces the song; and the composer who
can artistically express in music a transport of vigor and
passion of the more muscular kind, such as the *finale* to
the seventh symphony, the Walkürenritt, or the Hail-
stone chorus,* not to mention the orgies of Raff, Liszt,
and Berlioz, is always a hero with the intemperate in
music, who are so numerous nowadays that we may
confidently expect to see some day a British Minister of
the Fine Arts introducing a local Option Bill applied to
concert rooms.

With Mozart you are safe from inebriety. Hurry,
excitement, eagerness, loss of consideration, are to him
purely comic or vicious states of mind: he gives us
Monostatos and the Queen of Night on the stage, but
not in his chamber music. Now it happens that I have,
deep in my nature, which is quite as deep as the average
rainfall in England, a frightful contempt for your
Queens of Night and Titans and their like. The true
Parnassian air acts on these people like oxygen on a
mouse: it first excites them, and then kills them. Give
me the artist who breathes it like a native, and goes
about his work in it as quietly as a common man goes
about his ordinary business. Mozart did so; and that is
why I like him. Even if I did not, I should pretend to;

* In Handel's oratorio Israel in Egypt.

[857]

for a taste for his music is a mark of caste among musicians, and should be worn, like a tall hat, by the amateur who wishes to pass for a true Brahmin.

Miss Dora Bright's concert left me with a huge opinion of Mr Willy Hess, who gave a remarkable performance of Brahms's violin sonata in G, in spite of the parching, freezing northeast wind which was making even me conscious of having a liver. Mr Hess, always an exceptionally dexterous manipulator of the violin, used to lack artistic grip and earnestness; but he has matured, and is now a distinguished player, though an occasional careless phrase, or a final note petering out rather than being finished, still from time to time, reminds one of the old superficiality. His performance of the sonata, one of those compositions of Brahms which I can enjoy because, whilst they are rich in music, they are undisturbed by those intellectual pretensions which in Brahms (as in Tennyson) are so desperately common-place, would, at a Monday Popular Concert, have roused a good deal of enthusiasm. Unluckily for him, Miss Dora Bright's enterprise being a new one, the genuine audience at this first concert was not very large, and was reinforced by a contingent of inferior miscellaneous concert deadheads; so that the success of the sonata remained a secret between Mr Hess and the critics, who had come chiefly to witness the first public appearance in England of Miss Atalja Van Niessen, who speedily made her mark as a sort of Scandinavian Giulia Ravogli. In personal appearance and artistic temperament she is as emphatically northern as Giulia is emphatically southern; but the corresponding difference in the quality of the two voices is not so great as might be expected: all the superficial differences which repudiate the comparison are overcome by the identity of the underlying dramatic force. Miss Van Niessen will make her way on to the stage without difficulty in any country where the opera is under intelligent artistic management. On the whole, Miss Bright is to be congratulated on her concert; and if the three which she is giving on successive Tuesdays do not succeed well enough to induce her to repeat and extend her enterprise next season, so much the worse for the public. Her own playing is satisfactory in Prince's Hall, where the absence of the athletic qualities which distinguish the pianist proper, as trained by Rubinstein or Leschetitzky, from the musician who plays the piano is not felt as a defect. Even if it were, the musicianly qualities of Miss Bright's playing would go far to make amends, her faults being those of an excess of musical facility. If her powers had cost her a harder wrestle she would probably have used them to enter more deeply into the poetic basis of modern music.

An attempt has been made to rescue Señor Albéniz's score of The Magic Opal from sinking under the weight of its libretto. It is now being played under the composer's *bâton* at the Prince of Wales' Theatre as The Magic Ring, with considerable alterations and extensions. As far as these afford larger opportunities for the drollery of Mr Monkhouse and the appalling cleverness of Miss Susie Vaughan, they improve the chances of the opera. As far as they are meant to heighten the musical interest, they are failures, not in the least because Señor Albéniz has not risen to the occasion—on the contrary, the revised version of the opera leaves him easily ahead of the best of his rivals—but because they depend for their effect on having the tenor and soprano parts filled by singers of the same musical class as Mr Norman Salmond, who now takes Mr Wallace Brownlow's old part of Trabucos with excellent effect. Unfortunately the management has here put round pegs into square holes; and Señor Albéniz's labor has been consequently wasted. Mr Wareham is ineffective from beginning to end; and the part of Lolika is such a complete misfit for Miss Marie Halton that she appears to be playing as a superfluous second comedian to Miss Vaughan, and leaving the opera without a *prima donna*. I rather doubt whether The Magic Ring can survive on these terms, although, adequately cast on the musical side, the charm and vivacity of the score ought to secure it a handsome run.

Grieg has made a second orchestral suite out of his incidental music to Ibsen's Peer Gynt, concerning which I must really address a friendly remonstrance to Mr C. A. Barry, the author of the analytic program. On whose authority does he make Solveig "a gypsy woman" who had loved Peer "from a child," and in whose arms he dies as she sings a dream song over him? I admit the dream song; but the gypsy is really too much; and if Mr Barry thinks that Peer was the man to die in anybody's arms he little knows Mr Gynt's number, which was always number one. Nor do I recognize in Anitra "the very type of a hero-hunting woman,"unless that means a woman who listens to an amorous hero without understanding a word he says, and then decamps with all his portable property. And why is Peer the bride-robber to be allowed the extenuating circumstance of "entertaining a secret passion for Ingrid," when it was plainly that lady's by no means secret passion for Peer that suggested his idea of shewing off before Solveig and the rest by abducting her.

I submit to Mr Barry that he has mixed Anitra with Hedda Gabler, and Solveig with the gypsy mother in Brand; and as his program will be stereotyped for use in the Crystal Palace programs to all eternity if he does not alter it now, I implore him to read Peer Gynt two or three times (an inevitable result of reading it once) and then revise his narrative. It would be well, perhaps, to amplify the bald statement that Peer's friends "treacherously run off with his vessel and are blown up for their pains," which only suggests that he remonstrated vigorously with them, wheras they were actually and literally blown to smithereens. The suite will not be so popular as the first one, which naturally contained the pick of the music for suite purposes. It consists of the wedding prelude, the Arabian dance, the storm, and a transcription of Solveig's by this time rather hackneyed song from the fourth act. The first performance in England took place at the Crystal Palace on the 8th, when we also had a fine performance of Raff's Im Walde symphony (why dont they cut away all that repetition of the ghostly hunt stuff in the *finale?*), and a triumph for Miss Fanny Davies in Chopin's F minor concerto— the most successful feat of interpretation and execution I have ever heard her achieve.

THE AMATEUR ORCHESTRA
The World, 26 April 1893

In the eye of an inconsiderate public, concerts given by amateur orchestral societies hardly seem worth the serious attention of a critic who is busy watching the symptoms of the Philharmonic, the Crystal Palace, the London Symphony, the Richter, and the Hallé orchestras. Yet to me the amateur orchestra is all-important; for out of every ten people who support music in England, at least nine and three-quarters must have acquired their knowledge of it as amateurs and from amateurs. The musician of professional antecedents is an incorrigible deadhead: whether he performs or listens, music has to support him, instead of being supported by him.

It is clear that a man cannot cultivate a taste for

orchestral music by listening once a week to a church service accompanied by the combination of pan-pipes and accordion which has replaced the old-fashioned village church band, or even by occasionally patronizing a traveling dramatic company in the town hall, and studying the efforts of a pianist, backed by three fiddles and a cornet, to give a satisfactory account of the overture to William Tell, Mascagni's intermezzo, and a twenty-year-old waltz by Waldteufel. The moment you step outside the circle of London, Birmingham, Manchester, Bristol, Glasgow, and towns of their calibre, you have to choose between amateur music and no music at all; whilst even in these big towns music is really kept alive by professional musicians who as teachers discover amateur talent, and as conductors and concert givers organize it for the performance of the masterpieces of modern music.

The professional orchestral conductor who is a conductor and nothing else, and who conducts professional singers and players exclusively, only exists in great capitals. It takes London and Vienna combined to keep Richter in this position, and Glasgow and the Crystal Palace combined to keep Manns in it; and both these eminent conductors have to depend on amateurs for the performance of choral works. Had Destiny buried them in a small provincial town, they would, whilst they remained there, have had to put up with an amateur band, and amateur principal singers into the bargain. And there are suburbs of London which are in darkness more deplorable than any country town.

Under these circumstances, it seems to me that the critic who considers an amateur orchestra beneath his notice stamps himself as a hopeless Cockney—that is, a man who does not know the country because he has never lived there, and does not know London because he has never lived anywhere else. Last week Mr James

Brown, the conductor of the Richmond Orchestral Society, had the gumption to surmise that a stroll out to Richmond Hill to hear what his Society can do might seem to me at least as tempting a way of spending an evening as a visit to Steinway or Prince's Hall to hear the annual concert of Miss Smith or Miss Brown, aided by more or less distinguished artists singing exactly what they have sung on similar occasions for a whole generation of miscellaneous concerts. I accepted his invitation, and arrived at sundown on the terrace, where I mused over the site of that Wagner Theatre which yet remains unbuilt, until it was time to go into the "Star and Garter" and to get to business.

The program was of the usual amateur kind: that is to say, it would have taxed the finest qualities of the best band in the world. Mozart's G Minor symphony, the Lohengrin prelude, Mendelssohn's Athalie overture and his violin concerto: only such works as these can inspire the mighty craving and dogged perseverance which carry a man through that forlorn hope, the making of an orchestra out of nothing. When you start you are received with enthusiasm by men who can play the posthorn, the banjo, the concertina, and every other instrument not used in the orchestra. You enlist trombone players only to find that though they can "vamp" they cannot read, and propose to assist you by improvizing a bass continuously to whatever may be going on. You can choose the two least execrable out of twenty cornet players at the cost of making eighteen bitter enemies in the neighborhood; but you are lucky if you find one horn player, although you require four. Flutes, too, are comparatively plentiful; whilst clarinets are scarce, oboes all but unknown, and bassoons quite out of the question (although there is a lady bassoonist at Richmond).

In the string department the same difficulty arises.

Young ladies who can play much better than the average professional "leader" of twenty years ago are discoverable with a little research in sufficient abundance nowadays (chiefly because Madame Neruda proved at that time that the violin shews off a good figure); and the violoncello, for some less obvious reason, fascinates tiny women sufficiently to keep itself fairly alive in amateur circles. But nobody will touch the doublebass; and the viola comes to grief almost as signally as it used to do in the professional band in the old days, when only worn-out violinists scraped the tenor, and when such viola parts as those in Tristan or Harold, and such players as Hollander condescending to the instrument, were unknown.

When trying to get an orchestra together the conductor stops at nothing, except at houses whence come sounds of practising on an orchestral instrument. I have known a man, on catching this doleful noise at midnight on his way from rehearsal, listen at the area-railings, take a note of the address, and call next day to kidnap the practiser by reckless flatteries. I have known valuable appointments, involving the transfer of learned professors from the Metropolis to provincial towns, decided by the frantic efforts of a local conductor to secure the election of a candidate who was said to be a proficient player on one of the scarcer instruments. But it is when the orchestra is actually formed and set to work that its creator tastes the full bitterness of his position.

The unredeemed villainy of the amateur nature is not easy to describe adequately. Its outrageous frivolity, to which no engagement is sacred, and its incredible vanity, to which art is nothing and the lower self everything, baffle my powers of description, and make me for once regret that I do not wield one of those bitter, biting pens which were made to lash offenders on whom mercy is thrown away—for instance, those two amateur extremes, the man who never attends a rehearsal but always turns up at the concert, and the man who attends all the rehearsals and blenches from the concert. Even your leader will miss a rehearsal to go to a dance, or will coolly tell you on the morning of the concert that he cannot play because his father is dead, or some such frivolous excuse. Then there is the incompetent wind player who has a bit of solo which he cannot execute, and who at the last moment must have his part doubled by a professional to save public disgrace and breakdown.

On such occasions the professional, regarding all amateurs as blacklegs, is offensive; objects to having his part doubled; says "Look here! Who's going to play this—me or you?" &c. &c. The amateur sulks, broods over his injuries, leaves the orchestra, and probably tries to establish a rival society for the performance of wind-instrument chamber music. The difficulties are endless, and the artistic results agonizing, since the progress made by the people who stick to the rehearsals is always spoiled at the last moment by the backwardness of those who dont.

I will not pretend that the concert at Richmond did not bear the marks of these hard conditions. It began short-handed, especially in the horn department. At the end of the overture a gentleman in irreproachable evening dress, smiling, and carrying a black bag presenting the general outline of a French horn, appeared and climbed up on the platform with a sort of "Here I am, you see, safe and sound—never say die" air about him. As he mounted there was a crash of breaking wood, from which I gathered that he had succeeded in completing the sensation by shattering the platform. The conductor received him with grim patience, concealing all signs of the murderous thoughts that must have raged within him. Just imagine Mr Borsdorf, for instance, playing that trick on Richter! I wonder did it occur to the gentleman that money had been obtained from the public, with his consent, on the strength of his being in his place to play one of the horn parts in the overture. If it is too much to expect an ordinary English gentleman to be artistically conscientious, surely we may at least call on him to be commercially honest. However, justice forbids me to urge too harshly the offence of the man who came in after the overture, since I must perforce say nothing of the worse offenders who did not come at all. Almost immediately after the beginning of the Lohengrin prelude the band divided itself into two resolute factions, one maintaining that the bar in hand was the sixth bar, and the other equally convinced that it was the seventh. So they agreed to differ; and I listened with a drunken sensation of hearing the prelude double until the wind instruments rushed into the fray, and, mostly taking the side which the conductor had supported from the first, made the opposition waver and finally come over one by one, the *fortissimo* being played with almost entire unanimity. In the accompaniment to O star of eve! (Tannhäuser) the *tremolando* to the words *Da scheinest du*, &c., was ruined by the shirking of some lady violinists, who, with faces expressive of the most shameful irresolution, and fear of being heard, rested their bows helplessly on the strings and sat quivering—an exceedingly amateur way of *tremolando*ing. But in spite of these and similar mishaps, I felt throughout that the thing was well worth doing. The conductor was always right in what he was driving at; and in some instances he had used that enormous advantage of the amateur—the unlimited rehearsal which is commercially impossible to the professional— to obtain graces of artistic treatment which were fresh and convincing: in fact, he snatched from that atmos- phere of inevitable nervousness, blundering, and inept- itude (concerning much of which, however *tout com-*

prendre, c'est tout pardonner) successful moments which I have too often missed from the performances of conductors with the best players in the world at their disposal. The leader, Mr J. S. Liddle, stood up to Mendelssohn's violin concerto, and dealt faithfully to the height of his powers. Mr Charles Phillips, a robust baritone, manfully shouted a most patriotically orchestrated ballad of Agincourt; but the first bar and a half led us to expect that what was coming was The Old Kent Road; and the disappointment was rather severe. Miss Florence Hudson got a tremendous *encore* for a harp solo; and Miss Emily Squire received a similar compliment for the Mignon gavotte, which she sang with a spirited facility which was none the less pleasant because of her thorough belief in the universality of the British vowel—"Say mwaw: Zjay too breezay, &c."

A comparatively unimportant matter was the Philharmonic concert of last Thursday, half an hour too long, and crowded to the doors. Sapellnikoff played Chopin's E minor concerto. He has turned his back on the thundering animal style, and has cultivated the purely musical and tactile quality of his playing to an extraordinary pitch, his left hand being now a marvel even among right hands for delicacy of touch and independence and swiftness of action. This time, it is to be hoped, he will not go away without giving recitals, or at least a technical demonstration at some of our musical schools. Miss Palliser was too ill to sing, and was replaced by Miss Marie Brema, who, happening to be tremendously in the dramatic vein, positively rampaged through a Schiller-Joachim *scena* and through Beethoven's Creation's Hymn, scandalizing the Philharmonic, but carrying away the multitude.

The band distinguished itself in Mendelssohn's Italian symphony, though I must again put it to Dr Mackenzie whether in his opinion a long note written for the brass, and marked *fortissimo*, should be played as a bark lasting one quaver, followed by a *mezzo forte* of depraved quality lasting a few more quavers, and tailing off finally into premature silence. I submit that Mendelssohn meant it to be sustained with full tone to the bitter end; and I take the liberty to add that a band that cannot hold up a powerful *fortissimo* in this way is only fit for quiet and select private parties and *tableaux vivants*, however genteelly it may pick its way through the Pilgrims' March. Imagine having a splendid band like that, and being afraid to let its full voice be heard. When a band is weak in the artillery department, its refinement becomes mere effeminacy and cowardice.

Two concerts at St James's Hall on Saturday afternoons (clashing, of course, with the Crystal Palace concerts) have been given—one by Sauret, and the other by Miss Agnes Janson. Sauret still remembers the days when he was famous for having mastered the difficulties of the concertos of Vieuxtemps; and now that his artistic interest in them is so utterly worn out that he rasps through them without one gentle touch or one moment of concern as to whether he is playing in tune or not, he still goes through the old display, and still finds a few old moustaches to cry Bravo because they know how horribly difficult the passages are. As for me, it tortures and exasperates me. Vieuxtemps's real name now is Vieuxjeu; and I appeal to Sauret to let him rest, with Alfred Mellon and other relics of the sixties. Otherwise the concert was enjoyable enough, Miss Muriel Elliot, Ernest Gillet, and Miss Dews reinforcing Sauret for the occasion. Miss Elliot, by the bye, requires a more thorough physical training to make her musical gifts fully effective in large rooms like St James's Hall. Miss Agnes Janson's concert, an excellent one of its kind, shewed, among other things, that Miss Janson knows how to make the most of her voice by a perfectly sound method, a good ear, and a nice sense of vocal touch. With this invaluable equipment, however, she takes things rather too easily, singing cheap operatic and quasi-operatic music frankly and genially, but without originality or conviction—in short, without having troubled herself seriously about its poetic or dramatic content. Mr Henschel's five vocal quartets *à la Russe* succeeded to admiration; and Sauret, again, won over the audience by a Beethoven sonata, only to disillusion them subsequently by a superannuated monstrosity of Ernst's—that wretched old fantasia on airs from Rossini's Otello. When Sauret's memory begins to fail he will become one of our most popular violinists.

THE MOST UTTER FAILURE EVER ACHIEVED
The World, 3 May 1893

For some time past I have been carefully dodging Dr Hubert Parry's Job. I had presentiments about it from the first. I foresaw that all the other critics would cleverly imply that they thought it the greatest oratorio of ancient or modern times—that Handel is rebuked, Mendelssohn eclipsed, and the rest nowhere. And I was right: they did. The future historian of music, studying the English papers of 1892-3, will learn that these years produced two entire and perfect chrysolites, Job and Falstaff, especially Job. I was so afraid of being unable to concur unreservedly in the verdict that I lay low and stopped my ears. The first step was to avoid the Gloucester Festival. That gave me no trouble: nothing is easier than not to go to Gloucester.

I am, to tell the truth, not very fond of Festivals. It is

not that the oratorios bore me, or even the new works "composed expressly," the word "expressly" here indicating the extra-special dulness supposed to be proper to such solemn occasions. These things are the inevitable hardships of my profession: I face them as the soldier faces fire, feeling that it is the heroic endurance of them that raises criticism from a mere trade to a profession or calling. But a man is expected to have the courage of his own profession only. The soldier must face cold steel; but he may without derogation be afraid of ghosts. The doctor who braves fever may blench from shipwreck; and the clergyman who wars daily against the Prince of Darkness is permitted to quit a field in which he unexpectedly meets a mad bull. The musical critic is ready at duty's call to stand up fearlessly to oratorios, miscellaneous concerts, requiems, and comic operas; but it is no part of his bargain to put up with the stewards at a provincial festival. It is not that these gentlemen intend to be uncivil, or are by nature more evilly dispositioned than their fellow creatures; but they have no manners, no *savoir vivre*: they are unsocially afraid of the public, snobbishly afraid of being mistaken for professional attendants, unaccustomed to their work (which requires either experience or tact and self-possession), and inflated with a sense of their importance instead of sobered by a sense of their responsibility.

Consequently they are fussy, suspicious, rude or nervous, as the case may be, constantly referring helplessly to the one or two of their number who have their wits about them, and not unfrequently blundering unintentionally to within a perilous distance of the point at which the more choleric and muscular sort of visitor will threaten violence and execute profanity, and the more subtly malicious will patronizingly offer the blunderer a tip. By good luck, I have never myself been outraged by a festival steward; but the mere flavor of irresponsible and incompetent officialism poisons the artistic atmosphere for me.

It brings before me the appalling centralization of English intellectual and artistic life, and therefore of social grace, with the consequent boorification of the provinces. It will never be merrie England until every man who goes down from London to a festival or other provincial function will frankly say to his host "My friend: your house is uncommonly comfortable, and your grub of the best. You are hospitable; and you gratify my vanity by treating me, who am a Nobody at home, as a Somebody from London. You are not bad company when you go out into the fields to kill something. But owing to the fact that you have been brought up in a town where the theatre, the picture gallery, and the orchestra count for nothing, and the exchanges count for everything, you are, saving your presence, a hopelessly dull dog; and your son is growing up as dull a dog as you." Not a polite speech, maybe; but you cannot make revolutions with rosewater; and what is wanted in English provincial life is nothing short of a revolution.

Such being my sentiments, it will be understood that I forewent Gloucester and Job last autumn without regret. I have explained the matter at some length, not because I have not said all the above before, but solely to put off for awhile the moment when I must at last say what I think of Dr Parry's masterpiece. For I unluckily went last Wednesday to the concert of the Middlesex Choral Union, where the first thing that happened was the appearance of Dr Parry amid the burst of affectionate applause which always greets him. That made me uneasy; and I was not reassured when he mounted the conductor's rostrum, and led the band into a prelude which struck me as being a serious set of footnotes to the bridal march from Lohengrin. Presently up got Mr

Bantock Pierpoint, and sang, without a word of warning,
There was a man in the land of Uz whose name was Job.
Then I knew I was in for it; and now I must do my duty.

I take Job to be, on the whole, the most utter failure
ever achieved by a thoroughly respectworthy musician.
There is not one bar in it that comes within fifty
thousand miles of the tamest line in the poem. This is
the naked, unexaggerated truth. Is anybody surprised
at it? Here, on the one hand, is an ancient poem which
has lived from civilization to civilization, and has been
translated into an English version of haunting beauty
and nobility of style, offering to the musician a subject
which would have taxed to the utmost the highest
powers of Bach, Handel, Mozart, Beethoven, or Wagner. Here on the other is, not Bach nor Handel nor
Mozart nor Beethoven nor Wagner, not even Mendelssohn or Schumann, but Dr Parry, an enthusiastic and
popular professor, fortyfive years old, and therefore of
ascertained powers.

Now, will any reasonable person pretend that it lies
within the limits of those powers to let us hear the
morning stars singing together and the sons of God
shouting for joy? True, it is impossible to say what a
man can do until he tries. I may before the end of this
year write a tragedy on the subject of King Lear that
will efface Shakespear's; but if I do it will be a surprise,
not perhaps to myself, but to the public. It is certain that
if I took the work in hand I should be able to turn out
five acts about King Lear that would be, at least,
grammatical, superficially coherent, and arranged in
lines that would scan. And I doubt not at all that some
friendly and ingenuous critic would say of it "Lear is,
from beginning to end, a remarkable work, and one
which nobody but an English author could have written.
Every page bears the stamp of G. B. S.'s genius; and no
higher praise can be awarded to it than to say that it is

fully worthy of his reputation." What critic would need to be so unfriendly as to face the plain question "Has the author been able for his subject?"

I might easily shirk that question in the case of Job: there are no end of nice little things I could point out about the workmanship shewn in the score, its fine feeling, its scrupulous moderation, its entire freedom from any base element of art or character, and so on through a whole epitaph of pleasant and perfectly true irrelevancies. I might even say that Dr Parry's setting of Job placed him infinitely above the gentleman who set to music The Man that broke the Bank. But would that alter the fact that Dr Parry has left his subject practically untouched, whilst his music hall rival has most exhaustively succeeded in covering his? It is the great glory of Job that he shamed the devil. Let me imitate him by telling the truth about the work as it appeared to me. Of course I may be wrong: even I am not infallible, at least not always.

And it must be remembered that I am violently prejudiced against the professorial school of which Dr Parry is a distinguished member. I always said, and say still, that his much-admired oratorio Judith has absolutely no merit whatever. I allowed a certain vigor and geniality in his L'Allegro ed il Penseroso, and a certain youthful inspiration in his Prometheus. But even these admissions I regarded as concessions to the academic faction which he leans to; and I was so afraid of being further disarmed that I lived in fear of meeting him and making his acquaintance; for I had noticed that the critics to whom this happens become hopelessly corrupt, and say anything to please him without the least regard to public duty. Let Job then have the benefit of whatever suspicion may be cast on my verdict by my prepossessions against the composer's school.

The first conspicuous failure in the work is Satan,

who, after a feeble attempt to give himself an infernal air by getting the bassoon to announce him with a few frog-like croaks, gives up the pretence, and, though a tenor and a fiend, models himself on Mendelssohn's St Paul. He has no tact as an orator. For example, when he says "Put forth thine hand now and touch all that he hath, and he will curse thee to thy face," there is not a shade of skepticism or irony in him; and he ineptly tries to drive his point home by a melodramatic shriek on the word "curse." When one thinks—I will not say of Loki or Klingsor, but of Verdi's Iago and Boïto's Mefistofele, and even of Gounod's stage devil, it is impossible to accept this pale shadow of an excitable curate as one of the poles of the great world magnet.

As to Job, there is no sort of grit in him: he is abject from first to last, and is only genuinely touching when he longs to lie still and be quiet where the wicked cease from troubling and the weary are at rest. That is the one tolerable moment in the work; and Job passes from it to relapse into dulness, not to rise into greater strength of spirit. He is much distracted by fragments of themes from the best composers coming into his head from time to time, and sometimes cutting off the thread of his discourse altogether. When he talks of mountains being removed, he flourishes on the flute in an absurdly inadequate manner; and his challenge to God, Shew me wherefore Thou contendest with me, is too poor to be described.

Not until he has given in completely, and is saying his last word, does it suddenly occur to him to make a hit; and then, in announcing that he repents in dust and ashes, he explodes in the most unlooked-for way on the final word "ashes," which produces the effect of a sneeze. The expostulation of God with Job is given to the chorus: the voice that sometimes speaks through the mouths of babes and sucklings here speaks through the mouths of Brixton and Bayswater, and the effect is precisely what might have been expected. It is hard to come down thus from the "heil'gen Hallen" of Sarastro to the suburbs.

There is one stroke of humor in the work. When Job says, The Lord gave, and the Lord taketh away: blessed be the name of the Lord, a long and rueful interval after the words "taketh away" elapses before poor Job can resign himself to utter the last clause. That is the sole trace of real dramatic treatment in this dreary ramble of Dr Parry's through the wastes of artistic error. It is the old academic story—an attempt to bedizen a dramatic poem with scraps of sonata music.

Dr Parry reads, The wall are broken down: destroyed are the pleasant places; and it sounds beautifully to him. So it associates itself with something else that sounds beautifully—Mendelssohn's violin concerto, as it happens in this case—and straightway he rambles off into a rhythm suggested by the first movement of the concerto, and produces a tedious combination which has none of the charm or propriety of either poem or concerto. For the sake of relief he drags in by the ears a piece of martial tumult—See! upon the distant plain, a white cloud of dust, the ravagers come—compounded from the same academic prescription as the business of the dragon's teeth coming up armed men in Mackenzie's Jason; and the two pieces of music are consequently indistinguishable in my memory—in fact, I do not remember a note of either of them.

I have no wish to linger over a barbarous task. In time I may forgive Dr Parry, especially if he will write a few more essays on the great composers, and confine himself to the composition of "absolute music," with not more than three pedal points to the page. But at this moment I feel sore. He might have let Job alone, and let me alone; for, patient as we both are, there are limits to human endurance. I hope he will burn the score, and throw Judith in when the blaze begins to flag.

As to the performance, it did not greatly matter. On the whole, it was somewhat tame, even relatively to the music. Mr Piercy's treatment of the high notes in his part offended all my notions of artistic singing. Mr Newman did what he could with the part of Job; and his performance was entirely creditable to him. Mr Bantock Pierpoint, as the Narrator, gave more pleasure than any of his colleagues. Miss Palliser was the shepherd boy. The chorus was not very vigorous or majestic; but it made the most of itself.

GOING FANTEE
The World, 10 May 1893

The success of Professor Stanford's Irish Symphony last Thursday was, from the Philharmonic point of view, somewhat scandalous. The spectacle of a university professor "going Fantee" is indecorous, though to me personally it is delightful. When Professor Stanford is genteel, cultured, classic, pious, and experimentally mixolydian, he is dull beyond belief. His dulness is all the harder to bear because it is the restless, ingenious, trifling, flippant dulness of the Irishman, instead of the stupid, bovine, sleepable-through dulness of the Englishman, or even the aggressive, ambitious, sentimental dulness of the Scot. But Mr Villiers Stanford cannot be dismissed as merely the Irish variety of the professorial species.

Take any of the British oratorios and cantatas which have been produced recently for the Festivals, and your single comment on any of them will be—if you know anything about music—"Oh! anybody with a bachelor's degree could have written that." But you cannot say this of Stanford's Eden. It is as insufferable a composition as any Festival committee could desire; but it is ingenious and peculiar; and although in it you see the Irish professor trifling in a world of ideas, in marked contrast to the English professor conscientiously wrestling in a vacuum, yet over and above this national difference, which would assert itself equally in the case of any other Irishman, you find certain traces of a talent for composition, which is precisely what the ordinary professor, with all his grammatical and historical accomplishments, utterly lacks. But the conditions of making this talent serviceable are not supplied by Festival commissions. Far from being a respectable oratorio-manufacturing talent, it is, when it gets loose, eccentric, violent, romantic, patriotic, and held in check only by a mortal fear of being found deficient in what are called "the manners and tone of good society."* This fear, too, is Irish: it is, possibly, the racial consciousness of having missed that four hundred years of Roman civilization which gave England a sort of university education when Ireland was in the hedge school.†

In those periods when nobody questions the superiority of the university to the hedge school, the Irishman, lamed by a sense of inferiority, blusters most intolerably, and not unfrequently goes the length of alleging that Balfe was a great composer. Then the fashion changes; Ruskin leads young Oxford out into the hedge school to dig roads; there is general disparagement in advanced

* Manners and Tone of Good Society, or, Solecisms to be Avoided, by "A Member of the Aristocracy," was, Shaw later told Frank Harris, the first book he had ever consulted in the British Museum, in 1880.

† In earlier days Irish classes were held out of doors. The term carries the imputation of "low class."

circles of civilization, the university, respectability, law and order; and a heroic renunciation of worldly and artificial things is insisted upon by those who, having had their fling, are tired of them, a demand powerfully reinforced by the multitude, who want to have their fling but cannot get it under existing circumstances, and are driven to console themselves by crying sour grapes.

This reaction is the opportunity of the Irishman in England to rehabilitate his self-respect, since it gives him a standpoint from which he can value himself as a hedge-school man, patronize the university product, and escape from the dreary and abortive task of branding himself all over as an Irish snob under the impression that he is hallmarking himself as an English gentleman. If he seizes the opportunity, he may end in founding a race of cultivated Irishmen whose mission in England will be to teach Englishmen to play with their brains as well as with their bodies; for it is all work and no play in the brain department that makes John Bull such an uncommonly dull boy.

The beginning of this "return to nature" in music has been effected, not by a sudden repudiation of the whole academic system, but by the smuggling into academic music of ancient folk music under various pretences as to its archeological importance; its real recommendation, of course, being that the musicians like the tunes, and the critics and programists find it much easier to write about "national characteristics" and "the interval of the augmented second" than to write to the point. First we had Mendelssohn's "Scotch" Symphony, and then came a deluge of pseudo-Hungarian, gypsy, and other folk music—Liszt, Bruch, Dvořák, and Brahms all trying their hands—with, in due course, "pibrochs" by Dr Mackenzie, Land of the Mountain and the Flood overture from Mr Hamish MacCunn, and Villiers

Stanford's Irish Symphony. No general criticism of the works produced in this movement is possible.

The poorer composers, unable to invent interesting themes for their works in sonata form, gladly availed themselves of the license to steal popular airs, with results that left them as far as ever behind the geniuses who assimilated what served their turn in folk music as in every other store of music. But, at all events, the new fashion produced music quite different in kind from the Turkish music devized by the German Mozart for Il Seraglio, the Arabian music copied by his countryman Weber for Oberon, or the African and Scotch music invented by Mendelssohn and Meyerbeer (both Jews) for L'Africaine and the Scotch Symphony. This sort of "national" music takes the artificial operatic or sonata forms quite easily, submitting to be soaped and washed and toileted for its visit to Covent Garden or St James's Hall without the least awkwardness.

But in the recent cases where the so-called folk music is written by a composer born of the folk himself, and especially of the Celtic folk, with its intense national sentiment, there is the most violent repugnance between the popular music and the sonata form. The Irish Symphony, composed by an Irishman, is a record of fearful conflict between the aboriginal Celt and the Professor. The *scherzo* is not a *scherzo* at all, but a shindy, expending its force in riotous dancing. However hopelessly an English orchestra may fail to catch the wild nuances of the Irish fiddler, it cannot altogether drown the "hurroosh" with which Stanford the Celt drags Stanford the Professor into the orgy. Again, in the slow movement the emotional development is such as would not be possible in an English or German symphony. At first it is slow, plaintive, passionately sad about nothing.

According to all classic precedent, it should end in

[879]

hopeless gloom, in healing resignation, or in pathetic sentiment. What it does end in is blue murder, the Professor this time aiding and abetting the transition with all his contrapuntal might. In the last movement the rival Stanfords agree to a compromise which does not work. The essence of the sonata form is the development of themes; and even in a rondo a theme that will not develop will not fit the form. Now the greatest folk songs are final developments themselves: they cannot be carried any further. You cannot develop God Save the Queen, though you may, like Beethoven, write some interesting but retrograde variations on it. Neither can you develop Let Erin remember. You might, of course, develop it inversely, debasing it touch by touch until you had the Marseillaise in all its vulgarity; and the doing of this might be instructive, though it would not be symphony writing. But no forward development is possible.

Yet in the last movement of the Irish Symphony, Stanford the Celt, wishing to rejoice in Molly Macalpine (Remember the glories) and The Red Fox (Let Erin remember),* insisted that if Stanford the Professor wanted to develop themes, he should develop these two. The Professor succumbed to the shillelagh of his double, but, finding development impossible, got out of the difficulty by breaking Molly up into fragments, exhibiting these fantastically, and then putting them together again. This process is not in the least like the true sonata development. It would not work at all with The Red Fox, which comes in as a flagrant patch upon the rondo—for the perfect tune that is one moment a war song, and the next, without the alteration of a single

* Thomas Moore's lyric Let Erin Remember (which Shaw slightly misquotes ten lines later) is set to a tune which is a variant of the folk air The Little Red Fox.

note, the saddest of patriotic reveries "on Lough Neagh's bank where the fisherman strays in the clear cold eve's declining," flatly refuses to merge itself into any sonata movement, and loftily asserts itself in right of ancient descent as entitled to walk before any symphony that ever professor penned.

It is only in the second subject of this movement, an original theme of the composer's own minting, that the form and the material really combine chemically into sonata. And this satisfactory result is presently upset by the digression to the utterly incompatible aim of the composer to display the charms of his native folk music. In the first movement the sonata writer keeps to his point better: there are no national airs lifted bodily into it. Nevertheless the first movement does not convince me that Professor Stanford's talent is a symphonic talent any more than Meyerbeer's was. In mentioning Meyerbeer I know I run the risk of having the implied comparison interpreted in the light of the Wagnerian criticism—that is, as a deliberate disparagement. I do not mean it so. The Wagnerian criticism of Meyerbeer is valid only as a page in the history of the development of opera into Wagnerian music-drama. Taken out of this connexion it will not stand verification for a moment.

If you try to form a critical scheme of the development of English poetry from Pope to Walt Whitman, you cannot by any stretch of ingenuity make a place in it for Thomas Moore, who is accordingly either ignored in such schemes or else contemptuously dismissed as a flowery trifler. In the same way you cannot get Meyerbeer into the Wagnerian scheme except as the Autolycus* of the piece. But this proves nothing except

* Autolycus, the peddler in Shakespear's The Winter's Tale, is "a snapper-up of unconsidered trifles" (IV, 2).

that criticism cannot give an absolutely true and just account of any artist: it can at best explain its point of view and then describe the artist from that point of view. You have only to shift yourself an inch to the right or left of my own point of view to find this column full of grotesque exaggerations and distortions; and if you read the musical papers you will sometimes find some *naïf* doing this, and verdantly assuming that *his* point of view commands the absolute truth and that I am the father of lies.

Let me therefore make it clear that I am not likening Stanford to Meyerbeer from the Wagnerian point of view. I am thinking of Meyerbeer's individual characteristics as a composer: for instance, the singularity which is not always originality, the inventiveness which is not always fecundity, the love of the curious and piquant, the fastidious industry and cleverness, the intense and jealous individualism with its resultant treatment of the executants as mere instruments and not as artistic comrades and cooperators, the retreating from any effect that cannot be exactly and mechanically planned by himself as from an impossibility, the love of the fantastic, legendary, non-human element in folk music (compare Stanford's settings of Irish songs with Dinorah), and the almost selfishly concentrated feeling, the fire, the distinction, the passion that flash out occasionally through much artifice and much trifling.

The parallel is of course not exact; and the temperament indicated by it does not disqualify Stanford from writing symphonies any more than it disqualified Raff; but it suggests my view of the composer of the Irish Symphony as compendiously as is possible within present limits. With the right sort of book, and the right sort of opportunity in other respects, Stanford might produce a powerful and brilliant opera without creating any of the amazement which would certainly be caused by any such feat on the part of his academic rivals.

The performance of the Irish Symphony was decisively successful. Except to briefly and gratefully note a marked improvement on the part of the Philharmonic band, I can say nothing more at present. Dozens of pianists and other concert givers are hereby begged to excuse me until next week.

CONCERTS AND RECITALS
The World, 17 May 1893

I have never heard an orchestra more completely thrown away than the one conducted by Sir Arthur Sullivan at the opening of the Imperial Institute. When I was outside, making my way to the hall, I heard it pretty well: when I got inside I heard it only now and then. In the march from Le Prophète, played as the Court withdrew, not a note of the section where the theme is taken up by the trumpet and bass clarinet reached me at the dais end of the hall. The overture to Euryanthe was fitfully audible, the *pianissimo* for muted strings coming off rather better than the more powerful passages. Under these circumstances, the effect produced by the conductor's new Imperial March was very like a stage wait in the proceedings. I reserve my opinion until I get an opportunity of really hearing it, only certifying for the present that it contains a long flowing theme which shews off the strings very cleverly. In the evening, at the Albert Hall, we had Stanford's setting of Swinburne's Exhibition ode entitled East to West— Putney to Chicago.* As a rule, exhibition art is not high

* Composed for the World's Columbian Exposition, held in Chicago, 1893, and dedicated by Stanford to the President and the people of the United States of America.

[883]

art. Doubtless it would be an exaggeration to say that the average exhibition gallery picture or choral ode, or grand march, is something that no self-respecting hangman would condescend to burn; but there is no harm in recalling the fact that even Wagner, when he replenished his exchequer by the Centennial March, came rather nearer disgracing himself than Beethoven did in The Battle of Vittoria; and that is saying a good deal. The amateur who knows good art from bad may pick up treasures in exhibitions just as he may pick them up in pawnshops and boxes of secondhand books: for example, it was at the Italian Exhibition at Earl's Court that the painter Segantini was introduced to English connoisseurs. But the treasures are never among the works commissioned and advertized by the promoters of the show.

Consequently Professor Stanford, if he had composed a particularly bad ode, might have pleaded that this is just what a great composer invariably does on such occasions. However, as it happens, the apology is not needed. The two qualities needed for a good Chicago ode are tunefulness and bounce; and there is an allowance of both in East to West, though it is certainly stinted by the professorism which is Stanford's bane. I cry "Professor!" whenever I hear the natural flow of music checked by some crude and wooden progression, inscrutable in its motive—perhaps an idle experiment in the introduction and resolution of a discord, perhaps an austere compliance with some imaginary obligation of the sham grammar which is called scientific harmony, perhaps—and of this I often very grievously suspect Stanford—a forced avoidance of the vernacular in music under the impression that it is vulgar.

The result of this last notion as a principle of composition may be illustrated by imagining an author not only searching the dictionary for out-of-the-way

[884]

words so as to avoid using any that might drop from the man in the street, but distorting the more obvious ideas as well with the same motive. Professors of literature have tried to do this before now, and produced the tedious pedant's jargon that we all know and dread in books. Your men who really can write, your Dickenses, Ruskins, Carlyles, and their like, are vernacular above all things: they cling to the locutions which everyday use has made a part of our common life. The professors may ask me whether I seriously invite them to make their music out of the commonplaces of the comic song writer? I reply, unabashed, that I do.

That arrant commonplace, the opening strain of *Dove sono*, made out of the most hackneyed cadence in modern music, pleases me better than all their Tenter-den-street specialities. When I wrote last week of Stanford's talent for composition, I was not thinking of the mixolydian nonsense in his Eden—the angels' choruses written in no mode at all, because, as I take it, he conceives angels as too "genteel" to sing in anything so vulgar as the major and minor modes used at the music halls. I was thinking, on the contrary, of his straightforward rum-tum setting of Browning's Cavalier Romances, as fiery and original as they are vernacular from beginning to end, and of that charming Bower of Roses song with its simple tonic and subdominant Irish harmonies, which is the only number I know from his opera The Veiled Prophet.

Well, East to West is not as good as either of these compositions, because it is too frequently turned aside from its natural course for the purpose, apparently, of taking it out of the common run, at which moments I find it dry, perverse, and unaffected. But the native audacity of the composer asserts itself more freely than in any of his recent compositions; and the entire welcomeness of the change was proved by a tremendous ovation at the conclusion of the performance, very different in spirit from that which greeted the mixolydian angels at Birmingham.

Pianism has prevailed very fearfully for the last few weeks. Essipoff has given three recitals. No technical difficulties give her trouble enough to rouse her: sometimes she is interested and interesting, sometimes cold and absent, always amazing. The cobbler's wife may be the worst shod woman in the parish; but Leschetitzky's wife is undeniably one of the greatest exponents of his technique in Europe. If it were possible to believe that she cares two straws about what she plays, she would be also one of the greatest executive musicians in Europe. But she has discovered that all this also is vanity; and so, with her indifference cloaked by a superb habit of style, and by the activity of her unerring mechanism, she gets through a recital as a queen might through a drawing room, and sets one thinking about Arabella Goddard, who was a player of the same sort, and then wandering off into all manner of idle afternoon reveries. In addition to the usual classics she introduces Leschetitzky, Moszkowski, and Schytte, apparently finding them a relief.

Mr Lennart Lundberg would have been more fortunate in his first recital if it had not happened on an Essipoff afternoon. He is a Dane, trained in Paris, which is the very last place in the world to train a Dane in, or indeed anybody else as far as music is concerned. Beethoven sonata being *de rigueur* in London, he rattled off the Waldstein sonata, throwing in a French grace here and there to keep up our spirits. I have no patience with Paris: provincialism I do not mind, but a metropolitanism that is fifty years behind the time is insufferable. Why could not Mr Lundberg, with his northern temperament, have gone to Vienna, Brussels, Moscow—anywhither except to the city where, musically speaking, you still find 1850 fighting in its last ditch? Fortunately, the neatness and brilliancy which seem so artificial, and after a time become so wearisome, in players who are Frenchified without being genuinely French, are charming in their best native form as combined with the freshness and simplicity of the "adorable" variety of Parisienne. We had this type exemplified by Mlle Simonnet, who sang in Bruneau's La Rêve and in Gounod's Philémon at Covent Garden; and we have it also in Clotilde Kleeberg, who revived a barren but clever and elegant pianoforte concerto of Ferdinand Hiller's at the last Philharmonic concert with great success, and who was even petted at the Crystal Palace, where she ran her hands daintily up and down Beethoven's fourth concerto without once awakening it. For there are limits to the realm of adorability; and Beethovenland is some distance outside that frontier.

Talking of Parisian freshness and adorability reminds me of German freshness and adorability, personified in a Mädchen named Margarethe Eussert, who made her first appearance at Prince's Hall on the 5th. She dressed the part, smiled it, curtsied it, and coifed it so consummately that her artistic instincts were proved before she struck a note. Her playing is still girlish; but it is vigorous and promising; and her master and discoverer, Klindworth, has laid the foundations of her technique with tolerable solidity. Another young lady, also in the stage in which the human female is called in America "a bud," and also most effectively got up for the part, is Miss Nellie Kauffmann. She is goodlooking, confident, and not without some natural talent and dexterity; so she will be able without much trouble to persuade some first-rate teacher to take her in hand and shew her how to begin her apprenticeship. She seems to have had but little artistic guidance hitherto: otherwise she could hardly believe that gabbling thoughtlessly over the notes of a Bach fugue and a Beethoven allegro at breakneck speed is pianoforte playing in the St James's Hall sense. Besides, she does not even gabble accurately. Young as she is, we have players who are hardly more than children—Ethel Barnes and Elsie Hall, for instance—who are enormously superior to her as artists; and nothing could be more cruel than to applaud her mere musical handiness and engaging appearance at the risk of persuading her that she has finished the training that she has hardly yet begun, and that would possibly make her a very worthy artist.

Herr Isidor Cohn has also given a recital in St James's Hall. To him it is not necessary to offer paternal advice, as he is an artist who has unquestionably made the most of his natural talent. He is not by temperament a Beethoven player; but in pieces by Hiller, Moszkowski, Dvořák, and Liszt he reaps the full reward of his skill and industry. Madame Grimaldi, another pianist, who has given an evening recital at Prince's Hall, is not very easy to criticize. As a rule I do not hazard guesses about artists until I have privately ascertained that my guesses are correct, which in this case I have had no opportunity of doing. Nevertheless I will venture to make public my surmise that Madame Grimaldi has played a great deal before fashionable audiences in drawing rooms, depending a good deal on her memory, and that she has not submitted her readings of Chopin to any very severe criticism for some years past. I find her exclusive, private, tastefully superficial, altogether wanting in that deep need for the sympathy, or at least the attention, of the farthest away and humblest person in the shilling gallery, which marks the great public artist. Further, I find the pieces she plays most extraordinarily mannered and transmogrified, apparently by a long course of repetition without occasional careful verification by the score. As Madame Grimaldi's powers are of no mean order, I think she might produce interesting results by becoming as a little child again for a few months and spending them under the tuition of, say, Leschetitzky.

Of violin playing I have heard comparatively little; but violin recitals are never so plentiful as pianoforte recitals, for the prosaic reason that they do not advertize the instruments of any living maker, and are therefore not given unless they pay directly, which many of the pianoforte recitals of course do not. In the fiddle department, then, I have only to record that Mr Willy Hess played Beethoven's concerto at the Philharmonic. What with his habit, gained as leader of the Manchester band, of driving fast movements along without much reference to their poetic content, and his weakness for exhibitions of his skill in trick fiddling, which led him to substitute a very flagrant display of it for a *cadenza*, he rather threw away his chance in the first movement, the only part of the work that really tries a player. Mr Arnold Dolmetsch, whose unique viol concerts in the hall of Clifford's Inn, Holborn, are gems of musical entertainment in their way, gave an Italian concert last Tuesday week, to be followed by a French concert on June 6th, and a Bach concert on July 4th. I heard the last half of the Italian one, and was delighted by a sonata for the viol da gamba by Marcello, with a peculiar effect made by an interrupted cadence which sounds as fresh now as it did when first written. It was beautifully played by Miss Hélène Dolmetsch. Mr Fuller Maitland, who was to have played the harpsichord, was unwell; and his place was taken at short notice by Mr C. H. Kempling, organist of St John's, Kennington, who rose to the occasion with an aptitude which was very remarkable considering that he had no great experience of the instrument. The two big "concertos" by Vivaldi and Corelli were interesting; but as they required eight or nine players they would have been the better for a conductor, failing more exhaustive rehearsal than they are worth nowadays. Among the miscellaneous concerts of which I have had somewhat precarious glimpses, I may mention those of Miss Elsie Mackenzie, who is sure to be at least a favorite ballad singer by the time she is personally as mature as her talent already seems to be; of Miss Kathleen Walton, a contralto whose powers I could not fully judge in the only song I was fortunate enough to hear during my brief visit to her concert; and of Mr Charles Phillips, who, with the cooperation of Mrs Trust, Miss Damian, and Mr Braxton Smith, introduced a set of five "Spanish" songs for four voices with pianoforte duet accompaniment, by Mr William Wallace. They were very pretty and fluent, and did not sound hackneyed, though I cannot say that they contained anything unfamiliar.

A BARRIE AND CONAN DOYLE
COMIC OPERA
The World, 24 May 1893

The new Savoy opera would not occupy me very long here if the comic opera stage were in a reasonably presentable condition. If I ask Messrs Barrie and Conan Doyle whether I am to regard their reputations as founded on Jane Annie, or Jane Annie on their reputations, I have no doubt they will hastily declare for the second alternative. And, indeed, it would ill become me, as a brother of the literary craft, to pretend to congratulate them seriously upon the most unblushing outburst of tomfoolery that two responsible citizens could conceivably indulge in publicly. Still less can I, as a musical critic, encourage them in their want of respect for opera as an artistic entertainment. I do not mean that a comic opera writer would be tolerable if he bore himself reverently; but there is a conscientious irreverence which aims at comic perfection, and a reckless irreverence which ridicules its own work and throws away the efforts of the composer and the artists; and I must say that there is a good deal of this sort of irreverence in Jane Annie.

After all, nothing requires so much gravity as joking; and when the authors of Jane Annie begin by admitting that they are not in earnest, they literally give the show away. They no doubt secure from the public a certain indulgence by openly confessing that their work will not bear being taken soberly; but this confession is a throwing up of the sponge: after it, it is idle to talk of success. A retreat may be executed with great tact and humor, but cannot thereby be turned into a victory. The question then arises, Is victory possible on purely humorous lines? Well, who is the great fountainhead of the modern humorous school, from Artemus Ward down to Messrs Barrie and Doyle themselves? Clearly Dickens, who has saturated the whole English-speaking world with his humor. We have whole squadrons of humorous writers who, if they had never read him, would have produced nothing but sectarian tracts, or, worse still, magazine articles. His ascendancy is greater now than ever, because, like Beethoven, he had "a third manner," in which he produced works which influenced his contemporaries as little as the Ninth Symphony influenced Spohr or Weber, but which are influencing the present generation of writers as much as the Ninth Symphony influenced Schumann and Wagner. When I first read Great Expectations I was not much older than Pip was when the convict turned him upside down in the churchyard: in fact, I was so young that I was astonished beyond measure when it came out that the convict was the author of Pip's mysterious fortune, although Dickens took care to make that fact obvious all along to every reader of adult capacity. My first acquaintance with the French Revolution was acquired at the same age, from A Tale of Two Cities; and I also struggled with Little Dorrit at this time. I say struggled; for the books oppressed my imagination most fearfully, so real were they to me. It was not until I became a cynical *blasé* person of twelve or thirteen that I read Pickwick, Bleak House, and the intervening works. Now it is pretty clear that Dickens, having caught me young when he was working with his deepest intensity of conviction, must have left his mark on me far more deeply than on his own contemporaries, who read Pickwick when they were twenty, and Our Mutual Friend when they were fifty, if indeed they kept up with him at all. Every successive generation of his readers had a greater advantage. The generation twenty years younger than his was the first that knew his value; and it is probable that the generation which will be born as the copyrights of his latest works expire, and leave the market open to sixpenny editions of them, will be the most extensively Dickensized of any.

Now I do not see why the disciples should not be expected to keep up to the master's standard of hard work, as far as that can be done by elbow grease, which is a more important factor in good art work than lazy artists like to admit. The fun of Dickens without his knowledge and capacity for taking pains can only end in what I have called Jane Annie—mere tomfoolery. The pains without the humor, or, indeed, any other artistic quality, as we get it occasionally from an industrious "naturalist" when he is not also an artist, is far more respectable. There are a fair number of humorists who can throw off conceits as laughable as Mr Silas Wegg's comments on the decline and fall of the Roman Empire, or his version of Oh, weep for the hour! But Wegg himself is not to be had so cheaply: all the "photographic realism" in the world is distanced by the power and labor which gave us this study of a rascal, so complete inside and out, body and soul, that the most fantastic playing with it cannot destroy the illusion it creates.

You have only to compare Dickens's pictures of people as they really are with the best contemporary pictures of people as they imagine each other to be (Trollope's, for instance) to understand how Dickens, taking life with intense interest, and observing, analyzing, remembering with amazing scientific power, got more hard work crammed into a thumbnail sketch than ordinary men do into colossal statues. The high privilege of joking in public should never be granted except to people who know thoroughly what they are joking about—that is, to exceptionally serious and laborious people. Now, in Jane Annie the authors do not impress me as having taken their work seriously or labored honestly over it. I make no allowances for their performances in ordinary fiction: anybody can write a novel. A play—especially a music-play—is a different matter—different, too, in the sense of being weightier, not lighter.

Messrs Doyle and Barrie have not thought so: they have, with a Philistinism as to music of which only literary men are capable, regarded their commission as an opportunity for a lark, and nothing more. Fortunately, they have larked better than they knew. Flimsy as their work is compared to the fiction of the founder of their school, they have made something like a revolution in comic opera by bringing that school on to the comic opera stage. For years past managers have allowed themselves to be persuaded that in comic opera books they must choose between Mr Gilbert's librettos and a style of writing which would have disgraced the Cities of the Plain.

In all populous places there is a currency of slang phrases, catch words, scraps from comic songs, and petty verbal indecencies which get into circulation among bar loafers and, after being accepted by them as facetious, get a certain vogue in that fringe of the sporting and dramatic worlds which cannot be accurately described without an appearance of Puritanism which I wish to avoid. An operatic style based on this currency, and requiring for its complete enjoyment nothing else except an exhaustive knowledge of the names and prices of drinks of all kinds, and an almost inconceivable callousness to, and impatience of, every other subject on the face of the earth, does not seem possible; but it certainly exists, and has, in fact, prevailed to the extent of keeping the comic opera stage in a distinctly blackguardly condition for some time past.

Now the fun in Jane Annie, senseless as some of it is, is not in the least of this order. If anyone had offered at the end of the performance to introduce me to the authors, I should not have hastily declined; and this is saying a good deal. Further, the characters, always excepting the pageboy, whose point lies in his impossibility, and who is a most degenerate descendant of Bailey junior,* are so sketched as to make it not only possible but necessary for the performers to act, thereby departing from tradition of the "good acting play," the goodness of which consists in the skill with which it is constructed so as to require no acting for its successful performance.

Miss Dorothy Vane acted, and acted cleverly, as Jane Annie. I never knew before that she could act, though I had seen her in other comic operas. Mr Kenningham, whose want of skill as a comedian has not hitherto been any great disadvantage to him, was very decidedly

* Character in Dickens's Martin Chuzzlewit.

hampered by it this time. The thinness of Miss Decima Moore's dramatic accomplishments were also more apparent than usual; and her efforts to make her part go by mere restlessness did not altogether help her out. The honors of *prima donna* fell virtually to Miss Rosina Brandram, who, like Mr Rutland Barrington and Messrs Gridley and Passmore, profited by the change in style.

A remarkable success was scored by a surpassingly beautiful young gentleman named Scott Fishe, with plenty of musical aptitude and a penetrating but agreeable bass voice, who looked the part of the handsome Lancer to perfection, and was received with shouts of laughter and an *encore* on the extravagantly silly occasion of his first entry. Mr Scott Fishe must, however, excuse me if, whilst admitting that he is a pleasant and amusing person, I dare not add anything as to his general ability on the strength of his success in the character of a consummate ass.

As to the music, a few numbers, notably the prelude, which sounds suspiciously like some old attempt at a concerto utilized for the occasion, and the love duet in the first act, have the effect of patches on the score; but the rest is often as adroit, lively, and humorous as Sir Arthur Sullivan's work. There is one plagiarism, curious because it is obvious enough to convince everyone of its unconsciousness. It is the "I dont know why" refrain to the proctor's song, treated exactly like the "I cant think why" in the king's song in Princess Ida. I may add generally that the effect of Jane Annie was so novel that I have no idea whether it was a success or not; but it certainly amused me more than most comic operas do.

I have to record the production by the Philharmonic Society of a Scotch ballad for soprano solo, chorus, and orchestra, entitled Annie of Lochroyan, by Erskine Allon. When Mr Hamish MacCunn hit on this form of composition with his spirited Lord Ullin's Daughter, I solemnly warned all whom it might concern that the feat, once invented, was an extremely easy one, and was likely to be extensively imitated if it were made too much of. And now in due course comes Mr Allon, tackling another ballad as solemnly as if it were the Mass, and spinning it out with wearisome interludes and repetitions beyond all patience. If Mr Allon will revise his score, and make a point of going straight through as quickly, concisely, and imaginatively as Mr MacCunn went through the better half of Lord Ullin's Daughter, I am prepared to deliver judgment on it; but as it stands I should only waste my time in attempting to pick the raisins out of the suet. Why Miss Liza Lehmann, with her very German intonation, should have been chosen to sing a Celtic ballad remains to be explained. With the utmost stretch of the high consideration which all musicians owe her, I cannot pretend that the effect was agreeable. At the same concert young Otto Hegner played a sort of glockenspiel *obbligato* to a bustling orchestral piece by Huber, the last movement of which was a rather barefaced attempt to make a *finale* by spinning a few barren figures out into sequences and rosalias. The work was announced as a pianoforte concerto. I did not hear the rest of the concert, a retouch of influenza having crippled my powers of endurance last week. It prevented me from hearing more than a portion of the last item in the concert of the Laistner Choir, the said last item being Schumann's Pilgrimage of the Rose, a work full of that original and expressive harmony which is so charming in Schumann when he is using it poetically instead of pedantically. What I heard of the performance gave me a highly favorable opinion of Herr Laistner's capacity as a choirmaster and conductor.

The most notable pianoforte recital has been that of

Louis Diémer, a remarkably clever, self-reliant, and brilliant pianist, artistically rather stale, and quite breath-bereavingly unscrupulous in using the works of the great composers as stalking horses for his own powers. The mere recollection of his version of the Zauberflöte overture causes the pen to drop from my hand.

FORM AND DESIGN IN MUSIC
The World, 31 May 1893

Whitsuntide brought me a week's ticket-of-leave from St James's Hall. By way of setting me a holiday task, Messrs Chapman & Hall sent me Mr H. Heathcote Statham's Form and Design in Music to study. I always enjoy Mr Statham's essays on Music, because, as he is a thorough architect, and writes about music like one, I get the benefit of a sidelight on the art. This particular essay is only a chapter from his Thoughts on Music and Musicians. It contains his five famous examples of melody, taken from Bach, Mozart, and Beethoven, followed by a sixth example of which he says: "As an instructive contrast the reader may take this cacophonous string of notes, which is put forth as a melody, but has no analogy in structure with those quoted above except in the mere fact that it consists of a succession of notes; these, however, have neither a common law of rhythm nor of tonal relation, nor any definite form or balance as a whole; the passage has, so to speak, neither beginning, middle, nor ending, in any organic sense, and there seems no reason why it should not wriggle on in the same fashion indefinitely: it is a formless thing."

After this, what do you suppose the "cacophonous string of notes" is? Obviously (to those who know Mr

Statham) something out of Wagner. And in fact it is the mother motive from Parsifal, that haunting theme that gives you *Herzeleide* merely to think of it. Mr Statham, having thus squarely confronted you with the dilemma that either Wagner was a cacophonous humbug or he himself hopelessly out of the question as an authority on form or design or any other artistic element in music, takes it for granted that you will throw over Wagner at once, and proceeds to kill time by making an "analysis" of Mozart's G minor symphony, which he parses in the most edifying academic manner.

Here is the sort of thing: "The principal subject, hitherto only heard in the treble, is transferred to the bass (Ex. 28), the violins playing a new counterpoint to it instead of the original mere accompaniment figure of the first part. Then the parts are reversed, the violins taking the subject and the basses the counterpoint figure, and so on till we come to a close on the dominant of D minor, a nearly related key (commencement of Ex. 29), and then comes the passage by which we return to the first subject in its original form and key."

How succulent this is; and how full of Mesopotamian words* like "the dominant of D minor"! I will now, ladies and gentlemen, give you my celebrated "analysis" of Hamlet's soliloquy on suicide, in the same scientific style. "Shakespear, dispensing with the customary exordium, announces his subject at once in the infinitive, in which mood it is presently repeated after a short connecting passage in which, brief as it is, we recognize the alternative and negative forms on which so much of the significance of repetition depends. Here we reach a colon; and a pointed pository phrase, in which the accent falls decisively on the relative pronoun, brings us to the first full stop."

* See I, 483n.

I break off here, because, to confess the truth, my grammar is giving out. But I want to know whether it is just that a literary critic should be forbidden to make his living in this way on pain of being interviewed by two doctors and a magistrate, and haled off to Bedlam forthwith; whilst the more a musical critic does it, the deeper the veneration he inspires. By systematically neglecting it I have lost caste as a critic even in the eyes of those who hail my abstinence with the greatest relief; and I should be tempted to eke out these columns in the Mesopotamian manner if I were not the slave of a commercial necessity and a vulgar ambition to have my articles read, this being indeed the main reason why I write them, and the secret of the constant "straining after effect" observable in my style.

I remember once in bygone years accepting a commission as musical critic from a distinguished editor [T. P. O'Connor] who had been described by Atlas★ as a Chinese gentleman, he being a native of that part of Cathay which lies on the west coast of Ireland. He placed himself in my hands with one reservation only. "Say what you like" he said; "but for—[here I omit a pathetic Oriental adjuration]—dont tell us anything about Bach in B minor." It was a bold speech, considering the superstitious terror in which the man who has the abracadabra of musical technology at his fingers' ends holds the uninitiated editor; but it conveyed a golden rule. The truth is that "Bach in B minor" is not criticism, not good sense, not interesting to the general reader, not useful to the student—very much the reverse, in fact, and consequently exceedingly out of place in "a brief outline of the esthetic conditions of the art," as Mr Statham calls his essay, which would be quite unreadable by ordinary mortals if it were not for the fact that the

★ Pseudonym of Edmund Yates, editor of The World.

author is a clever man, who knows and likes a great deal of good music (notably organ music, on which I always read him with pleasure), and therefore cannot help occasionally writing about it in an interesting way.

If Mr Statham will study the work of a modern experienced practical critic, and compare it with the work of an amateur like, let us say, the late Edmund Gurney, he will be struck by the fact that the expert carefully avoids "Bach in B minor," whilst the amateur is full of it; and the amateur, when he dislikes a piece of music, invariably enters into an elaborate demonstration that the composer's proceedings are "wrong," his melody not being "true melody," nor his harmony "scientific harmony," wheras the expert gives you his personal opinion for what it is worth. Mr Statham evidently thinks that it would not be criticism to say that he finds Wagner an offensive charlatan and his themes cacophonous strings of notes. He feels bound to *prove* him so by laying down the first principles of character and composition, and shewing that Wagner's conduct and his works are incompatible with these principles.

I wonder what Mr Statham would think of me if I objected to Brahms's Requiem, not on the ground that it bores me to distraction, but as a violation of the laws of nature.

Miss Martha Möller, who gave a concert at Prince's Hall last week, was clever enough to appear in a national costume, the most notable feature of which was a white tablecloth spread above her head by some ingenious contrivance. One gets so desperately tired of fashionable modes and materials that a stroke of this kind tells effectively at the height of the season. It gives Miss Möller a a Swedish Nightingale air, raising expectations which are heightened by her intelligent face and interesting demeanor. But when the singing begins it becomes apparent that though Miss Möller has the

[900]

strong natural feeling and quietly fervid expression which belong to the national costume and the silver ornaments, and can give an exceptionally able reading of anything from a folk song to an aria by Meyerbeer, she has not been altogether successful in teaching herself to sing. Her voice is naturally a clear free soprano of normal quality; but she has been fascinated by the richer, stronger, more sympathetic tone natural to some contraltos, and has imitated it, much as if Madame Melba had taught herself to sing by imitating Miss Alice Gomez. The imitation has unfortunately involved a constrained action of the lower jaw and retraction of the tongue which are fatal to good singing. Her tone is dry and artificial, and her execution forced and uneasy; so the verdict for the present must be that though Miss Möller imitates good singing with remarkable talent she does not sing well. She was assisted by Miss Yrrac, who plays the violin with a trenchant, well-resined bow, and knocks a good deal of exhilarating noise out of it; also by a young pianist [Jules Hollander] who gave a presentable performance of Chopin's Berceuse, but made only a poor business of Rubinstein's Valse Caprice, which requires a degree of power admitting of immense abandonment on the part of the player.

We have had a casual orchestral concert at St James's Hall from Hans Wessely, one of the professors of the R.A.M. There was certainly no lack of masterpieces for our souls to adventure among. The overture (Le Nozze) was followed by Brahms's and Mendelssohn's violin concertos, with Beethoven's pianoforte concerto in E flat between them. Wessely was not altogether successful with Mendelssohn. There is a certain quality in the style of that fastidious and carefully reared composer which can only be described as his gentility; and Wessely, who is a sincere, unreserved, original player, made rather short work of some of Mendelssohn's more decorous measures. Even with Brahms he once or twice sounded a little brusque; but the fault is a refreshing one at St James's Hall, and it weighed very lightly against the qualities he revealed, chief among them being a considerable degree of that prime requisite of the concerto player, a sympathetic comprehension of the whole score, instead of a mere readiness to give a verbatim report, so to speak, of the solo part. This stood him in good stead in the first movement of the Brahms concerto. Thanks to it and to his smart execution, his excellent intonation, and a *cantabile* which proclaimed the natural musician, he won ovations which were by no means confined to the Academy students in the gallery. The pianist, Mr Isidor Cohn, did not venture to approach the first movement of the great Beethoven concerto in the spirit of a masterplayer—indeed, he made less than nothing of the exordium; and he missed (in my judgment) the indicated treatment of the accompaniment in the second half of the slow movement. Still, his performance was conscientiously thought out and not uninteresting, which is more than could be said for some older and more eminent pianists than Mr Cohn. The band, a Philharmonic contingent under Dr Mackenzie, who is beginning to take advantage of his great opportunities as an orchestral conductor, played the Figaro overture in a little under four and a half minutes, a great improvement on the silly tradition of scampering through it in three and a half. I should add, by the way, that some songs were sung with exceptional skill and delicacy by Miss Schidrowitz, who, though her light agile soprano voice was the worse for a cold, shewed herself an accomplished vocalist and a clever interpreter. She has only one habit which I dislike; and that is the preparation of a minor trill by a slow alteration of the notes of the major trill. The effect of the change is not pleasant to my ear.

A CONCERT OF NEARLY
REASONABLE LENGTH

The World, 7 June 1893

I have to congratulate the Philharmonic Society on having at last made a resolute and fairly successful effort to give a concert of nearly reasonable length. Instead of the usual two or three concertos, five or six symphonies, selection of overtures, suite from the latest "incidental music" composed for the theatres by one of our professors, and a march or so, besides the vocal pieces, we had only about two hours' music; and though that is a good half-hour too much, still, it is better than two hours and forty or fifty minutes. We also had the orchestra under the command of conductors who, as their own works were in hand, were strongly interested in making the most of the occasion; and the result was instructive.

Saint-Saëns' Rouet d'Omphale is trivial enough to satisfy even the weariest of the unhappy persons who go to the Philharmonic for the sake of culture, under compulsion of fashion or their parents, and who invariably betray themselves by the rapture with which they greet any of those bogus concertos or symphonies which are really only very slightly developed *suites de ballet*, with episodical barcarolles disguised as "second subjects." But it afforded the relief of contemplating a broad expanse of finely graded sound between the *fortissimo* of the band as Saint-Saëns handled it and its *pianissimo*. There were ten degrees of color and force in the gradation where there is usually only one; and even these did not exhaust the possible range of effect, for the orchestra is capable of a much more powerful *fortissimo* than Saint-Saëns required from it.

Again, in the *scherzo* of Tchaikovsky's symphony, a movement of purely orchestral display, the quality of tone in the *pizzicato* for the strings and in the section for the brass was wonderful. Probably Tchaikovsky could not have achieved such a result anywhere else in the world at equally short notice. But why is it that but for the occasional visits of strangers like Grieg, Tchaikovsky, and Saint-Saëns, we should never know what our best London band can do? Solely, I take it, because the visitors are virtually independent of that impossible body of hardened malversators of our English funds of musical skill, the Philharmonic directors. For their displeasure the distinguished foreign composer does not care a brass farthing: he comes and instals himself at the rehearsals, making their insufficiency suffice for his own work by prolonging and monopolizing them.

On the other hand, the official conductor is the slave of the directors: if he complains to them they take no notice of his complaints: if he complains to the public, as Mr Cowen did in desperation, they dismiss him, knowing, unfortunately, that there will be no difficulty in finding someone else to take his place, which, except artistically, is a highly desirable one.

This season, thanks to the scandal of Mr Cowen's complaint and dismissal, and to such tweaking of the Philharmonic nose, and tripping up of its heels, and unexpected hurling of sharp-cornered bricks at its third waistcoat button as those critics who have the Society's interests really at heart can find time for, there has been an improvement, of which I, for one, have given rather exaggerated accounts for the better encouragement of the directors in the right path; but, after all, here I am face to face with a concert in which the band did admirable work under the *bâtons* of Russian and French strangers, whilst, under the official conductor, it played the accompaniment to Isolde's Liebestod in a way that would have fully justified poor Miss Macintyre in sending for the police.

To make that song produce no effect whatever may seem hardly feasible; but the Philharmonic band—this very same band that distinguished itself so remarkably in Tchaikovsky's symphony a few minutes later—did it quite easily. I need not describe the familiar process— the parts read off with businesslike insensibility at a steady *mezzo forte*, and with just enough artistic habit to make the result presentable to those who were unac- quainted with the work. That is the sort of thing that turns me from a reasonable and indulgent critic into a mere musical dynamitard.

Of Tchaikovsky's symphony [No. 4 in F minor] apart from its performance I need only say that it is highly characteristic of him. In the first movement, the only one with a distinctly poetic basis, he is, as ever, "le Byron de nos jours"; and in the later ones, where he is confessedly the orchestral voluptuary, he is Byronic in that too. The notablest merit of the symphony is its freedom from the frightful effeminacy of most modern works of the romantic school. It is worth remarking, too, considering the general prevalence in recent music of restless modulation for modulation's sake, that Tchaikovsky often sticks to the same key rather longer than the freshness of his melodic resources warrants. He also insists upon some of his conceits—for example, that Kentish Fire interlude in the slow movement—more than they sound worth to me; but perhaps fresh young listeners with healthy appetites would not agree with me. The symphony, brilliantly performed, was hand- somely received; and neither Saint-Saëns nor Tchai- kovsky can complain that they were not made as much of as they deserved, especially Saint-Saëns, who was recalled again and again after playing his G minor concerto in the hope that he would throw in a solo. This,

[905]

however, he evidently did not understand; and the audience had at last to give over the attempt.

On Saturday afternoon the Albert Hall was filled by the attraction of our still adored Patti, now the most accomplished of mezzo-sopranos. It always amuses me to see that vast audience from the squares and villas listening with moist eyes whilst the opulent lady from the celebrated Welsh castle fervently sings Oh give me my lowly thatched cottage again. The concert was a huge success: there were bouquets, raptures, effusions, kissings of children, graceful sharings of the applause with *obbligato* players—in short, the usual exhibition of the British bourgeoisie in the part of Bottom and the *prima donna* in the part of Titania.

Patti hazarded none of her old exploits as a florid soprano with an exceptional range: her most arduous achievement was *Ah, fors' è lui*, so liberally transposed that the highest notes in the rapid traits were almost all sharp, the artist having been accustomed for so many years to sing them at a higher pitch. Time has transposed Patti a minor third down; but the middle of her voice is still even and beautiful; and this, with her unsurpassed phrasing and that delicate touch and expressive *nuance* which make her cantabile singing so captivating, enables her to maintain what was, to my mind, always the best part of her old supremacy. She was assisted by Mr Santley; by Mr Ben Davies, who distinguished himself in an excellent delivery of Deeper and deeper still; by Madame de Pachmann, whose talent was thrown away in the Albert Hall, where a pianoforte is worse than useless; by Miss Clara and Miss Marianne Eissler with harp and violin; and by Mr Lemare, who revelled among the stops of the organ, which are mighty ones and millions, but who does not understand—what organist does?—how very disagreeable are those sudden *pianos* which are produced by stifling the organ with the swell shutters. Lastly, there was Miss Alice Gomez, now become a ravishing singer, with high notes of delicious quality and an exquisite delicacy of artistic treatment, not to mention all her old feeling and her rich contralto tones.

An orchestral concert was given by Herr Benno Schönberger last week. Instead of the Mozartean band for concerto accompaniments usual on such occasions, we had Mr Henschel with an orchestra on the scale of the London Symphony Concerts; and very pleasant it was, I must say, to hear the power and breadth produced by the firmly sustained wind playing upon which Mr Henschel insists, after months of the Philhar-monic band, with its inveterate habit of pecking at the chords instead of holding them. He turned the oppor-tunity to account by introducing a new symphony by Emmanuel Moor, which was, on the whole, well worth the trouble.

I do not know the composer's nationality; but he seems to me to have that warmblooded racial disquali-fication for orthodox symphony-writing which consists in having no musical impulses except passionate ones. A perfectly tranquil *andante*, a purely humorous *scherzo*, a continent or reflective first movement, seem out of the question with Mr Moor. He is clever and self-possessed enough; but he is always more or less vehement and ardent, and would, I should imagine, succeed better at a Lisztian "symphonic poem" than in sonata form. Herr Schönberger played Beethoven's fourth concerto and Saint-Saëns' Concerto in G minor with the dexterity which he has so resolutely cultivated. His passion for the mechanical part of his art seems to have filled him with an ambition to play like clockwork; and all I can say is that if he is not very careful he will succeed. I did not hear the Beethoven concerto, as I was detained at the *matinée* of Captain Thérèse given by Miss Emmott-

Herbert at the Criterion as a specimen of the work she has been doing in the provinces. The company consisted of performers not less capable and comely by nature than those who, under fair artistic influences, achieve success in metropolitan centres. They had, however, habituated themselves to the influence of the provincial gallery; and the London critic, fresh from the Savoy, woke up grinning from his jaded apathy and enjoyed what was to him something of a novelty.

The concert given by Miss Edith Blyth and Miss Mabel Wood at Steinway Hall introduced an able and brilliant Italian violoncellist, Ronchini, who played the inevitable Chopin nocturne and the equally inevitable Popper *morçeau*, but played them *à l'Italienne*, impetuously and originally, with Southern accuracy of intonation and richness of tone, besides delicate and swift execution. Miss Edith Blyth was very nervous; but she may take courage: her performance of so difficult a piece as the cavatina from La Gazza Ladra was highly creditable; and she need no longer fear that great booby, the public, which, in its helplessness, will always respond warmly to honest service in such pleasant and easily intelligible forms as Miss Blyth's singing. Miss Mabel Wood, keeping on the smoother ground of sympathetic ballad singing, acquitted herself with good sense and feeling, and, helped by a pleasant voice and good musical endowment, made an excellent beginning. Miss Ada Wright, the pianist, played Schumann's Faschingsschwank with adequate manual skill and truly English coolness—that coolness which, in people who feel deeply, is really shyness. Miss Wright must give herself away to her audience more freely if she wishes to change their respect into enthusiasm.

Mr Ernest Kiver gave his annual concert last week at Prince's Hall, and, with his usual enterprise, introduced two new trios for pianoforte and strings, by G. J. Bennett and Eduard Schütt. More I cannot say, as I was, unfortunately, unable to be present.

A CAGED CRITIC
The World, 14 June 1893

If many concerts make a good season, the present must be of the best. There are not only concerts, but audiences; and these audiences include a certain proportion of persons who conceivably pay for their tickets. One of the novelties of the year is a new concert room in the depths of the Grafton Gallery, very pleasant in this weather, whatever it may prove in winter, and offering to the critic an opportunity of sneaking away from the music to look at the pictures. A caged bird, with no change of air except as between two perches and a ring, must feel much the same as I do when caged in London in June hopping restlessly from St James's to Prince's Hall, and from that again to Steinway Hall. The Grafton Gallery is an extra perch for me; and I offer my blessing to Mr Farley Sinkins, the enterprising concert agent who has discovered it. I visited it for the first time last week to hear Madame Swiatlowsky's concert, where I found Madame Haas and Max Reichel playing a sonata presentably, but with no extraordinary solicitude, Herr Reichel giving himself no more trouble than a good first violin in the orchestra would take over a rather difficult score. Madame Swiatlowsky sang a florid air of Handel's in an original and very un-English fashion. Instead of making it as like a foot rule as possible, with the minims, crotchets, quavers, and semiquavers all mechanically marked off, she managed to strike out a purely musical treatment in which the hard outlines vanished and the aria, though somewhat jellified (if I may so express myself), came to life as a song instead of remaining a mere "*étude de la vélocité.*" She also sang a serenade from Saint-Saëns' Ascanio, greatly to my surprise; for, though I well remember conscientiously sitting out that solemnly manufactured grand opera in Paris, I can recall no such alleviation of my prodigious boredom on that occasion as this serenade would certainly have been had Madame Swiatlowsky sung it. She has the merit of inventing her own way of singing a song, and realizing it how she can, without preoccupying herself with academic considerations: for example, the quaint contrast between her lowest and highest register is a quality which she exploits instead of a defect which she tries to conceal. After the serenade I went to look at the pictures, as I seldom lose an opportunity of deserting my post at a miscellaneous concert.

If one may judge by their success in filling St James's Hall, the combination of Eugène Oudin and Tivadar Nachéz has been a fortunate one. I must frankly say that I should not care to listen to Oudin for more than, say, twentynine or thirty songs in succession; for he now specializes himself remorselessly for melancholy ditties, sung very slowly so as to admit of the most minute examination by the ear of the quality of one particular stop on his voice. No doubt it is a luscious stop; but its charms are not inexhaustible: after a while it becomes rather monotonous, later on decidedly monotonous, then very monotonous, and at last exasperatingly monotonous. It sets up an itching to hear him sing The Vicar of Bray, or *Non più andrai*, or Hans Sachs's cobbling song. If he has no turn for the humorous, and prefers his refined vein of lovesickness, *siècle de Louis Quatorze*, I make bold to remind him that there is plenty of English music in that vein and of that period, and that no concert singer ever reaches the very front rank in England—the Sims Reeves, Santley, Patti rank—by persistently singing in a foreign language. Tivadar Nachéz paid homage to the great by playing a good deal of Bach—the chaconne in D minor, &c.—but he was not in a classical humor, and, I thought, trotted his *chevaux de bataille* round with a certain forcing of his inclination. The Beethoven romance was the first piece which he played as if for its own sake. The Beethoven concerto I was unable to wait for, and indeed unwilling, in view of the fact that there was no orchestra. What with the way in which concerts are jostling oneanother at present, and the circumstance that the influenza fiend has left me in a condition quite incompatible with prolonged doses of concert-room air, my appearances just now are unusually fragmentary. From the point of view of ventilation my most terrific recent experience has been the concert of the Handel Society, a hospitable body which takes St James's Hall once a year, and invites an overwhelming audience, without reservation of seats. When I entered, the temperature was about two hundred and fifty in the draught; and I deemed myself fortunate in securing an angle of the wall to lean against whilst August Manns, in the centre of a sort of Mahometan paradise of lady violinists, with a trusty professional lurking here and there, mostly in the wind department, was bringing off a very creditable performance of the overture to [Cherubini's] Lodoïska. After this we had an admirable little cantata for band and chorus called The Storm, by Father Haydn, who, if he gave it to his children the public indulgently as a piece of claptrap, certainly took good care that it should do them no harm. The instrumentation and the vocal harmony sounded much fresher than they would have done half a century ago; and I waited for the last note before I fled, gasping for air, into Regent-street. Had I come earlier I should have heard the only Beethoven symphony I never yet heard an orchestral performance of: to wit, number one. I was prevented by Miss Dora Barrington's concert at Prince's Hall, where I heard, besides various songs from Miss Barrington, Mr Reginald Groome, Mr Ben Grove, and Mr Brockbank, a fine performance of Franz Abt's *Schlaf wohl* from Madame Belle Cole, who was in one of her finer artistic moods, and a rather impatient handling of Svendsen's Romance and Wieniawski's Scherzo Tarantelle, by Henry Seiffert, a violinist of remarkable talent, who nevertheless generally plays either as if he were heavily preoccupied with something else, or at best as if he had not quite made up his mind whether he cared for the violin or not.

Miss Marie Roberts, who gave a concert at Steinway Hall last Thursday, is one of those artists who sit down at the piano and play their own accompaniments at their ease. In this way they offer me, not an orthodox feat of concert singing to be measured by the regulation standards, but an entertainment to be judged on its own merits as a method of pleasing an audience. All I can say of Miss Roberts is that she does this successfully. She can sing a bit, and play a bit, and compose a bit, and eke out these little gifts by acting a bit in the character of a fully accomplished musician; so that everyone finds her very clever and agreeable. It is not "legitimate"; but then, why should it be? Only I would say this to all singers who accompany themselves in public, from Mr Henschel and Mr Shakespeare downwards. It is undoubtedly better to be accompanied well by oneself than accompanied badly by somebody else. But nobody can do two difficult things at a time as well as they can do one. If an accompaniment is so simple that the singer can play it and yet have more than enough attention to spare for the song, well and good; but this means that both song and accompaniment must be very easy relatively to the singer's capacity; and this consideration must limit the repertory of the self-accompanying singer, who is likely to sing The Lass of Richmond Hill rather more successfully than Adelaide.

Mr Edgar Hulland's recital at Prince's Hall began about ten minutes past three with a violin sonata by Rubinstein. Sauret played it very well; but after about twenty minutes or so it struck me that the first movement was rather diffuse. However, I sat there patiently, noting that Mr Hulland, though not an exquisitely delicate or sentimental pianist, was an intelligent and ready one, and wondering whether Sauret was completely reformed, or whether he would relapse into Vieuxtemps or Ernst before the end of the concert. Then I thought over my past life exhaustively, and elaborated several plans for the future. Finally I had a long and delicious sleep, from which I woke to find by the change in the light that the afternoon was now far advanced. But the Rubinstein sonata was still in a comparatively early stage of performance. I respectfully suggest that it be treated henceforth as a tetralogy, like Der Ring des Nibelungen, and spread over four concerts, one movement to each. When it at last came to an end, Miss Evangeline Florence, whose style has been considerably smartened by her stay in London, sang an air from Handel's Alessandro, which takes a good deal of singing, to which Miss Florence proved equal. She was followed by Mr Hulland with the fifteen variations and fugue on the Prometheus-Eroica theme, played with the impetuosity and inconsiderateness of youth, the general effect being to make them appear insufferably long. When he retired Sauret appeared, and cast, I thought, a dark look in my direction. I glanced at the program; saw the name Ernst there; realized Sauret's fell design; and fled from the hall.

I do not know whom I have to thank for the invitation

to hear Mr T. A. Wallworth's lecture at Trinity College on Wagner's compositions and their influence on vocal art as compared with those of earlier composers; nor do I exactly know what I am expected to say about it. The lecture had already been delivered to the Guildhall students; so that the Trinity College authorities must have known precisely what it was going to be like. Besides, Dr Turpin took the chair in his academic gown, and wound up with a benediction on Mr Wallworth which was meant, I presume, as an official sanction of the lecture on behalf of the College.

Mr Wallworth informed us that the peculiarity which differentiates Wagnerian music-drama from opera as composed by the great masters consists in the fact that Wagner attempted to express all the incidents and emotions of the drama by means of the orchestra alone, reducing the singers to mere lay-figures. This method led him to so overwhelm the voice with unsuitable instrumentation that his singers speedily lost their voices in their attempts to shout down the band; and the real reason why the Bayreuth performances have been suspended this year is that all the singers are disabled permanently, and an interval is necessary in order that a new supply of artists may be grown, to pass in turn to their doom. (Continental papers, please copy.)

These deplorable results were brought about by Wagner's conceited contempt for all the great composers who preceded him. He was totally indifferent to the setting of words to music (like Beckmesser), and whenever in his works the musical accent follows the verbal accent, the agreement is to be regarded as a fortuitous coincidence, unintended by the composer. Mr Wallworth then sang, as an example of perfect setting of words to music, the recitative to The trumpet shall sound from the Messiah, and gave the phrase "in the twinkling of an eye" exactly as Handel wrote it: that is, with the accent on the "of." Altogether it was a very remarkable lecture, well worthy the consideration of those who may have an interest in estimating the value of Trinity College as an educational institution.

A SENTIMENTAL VOLUPTUARY
The World, 21 June 1893

A concert of chamber music selected exclusively from the works of Johannes Brahms is not supposed to be the sort of entertainment to put me into the highest good humor. Herein, however, I am wronged. Such a reputation as that of Brahms is not to be won without great talent. Unfortunately, music is still so much of a mystery in this country that people get bewildered if they are told that the same man has produced an execrable requiem and an excellent sonata. There seems to them to be no sense in going on in this inconsistent way; for clearly a requiem is a musical composition, and if a man composes it badly he is a bad composer; and a bad composer cannot compose a good sonata, since that also is a musical composition. Yet these very people can often see plainly enough that in pictorial art the same man may be an admirable decorative designer, colorist, or landscape painter, and an atrocious figure draughtsman; or, in literature, that good stories and bad plays, charming poems and fatuous criticisms, may come from the same hand.

The departments of music are not less various than those of the other arts; and Brahms is no more disposed of by the condemnation as tedious, commonplace, and incoherent, of those works of his which profess an intellectual or poetic basis than—well, the comparisons which offer themselves are numerous and tempting; but perhaps I had better leave them alone. Suffice it to say that whilst Brahms is successful neither as an intellectual nor a poetic composer, but only as a purely sensuous musician, his musical sense is so much more developed than that of the average audience that many of the harmonies and rhythms which are to him simply voluptuous and impetuous, sound puzzling and imposing to the public, and are therefore surmised to be profoundly intellectual.

To me it seems quite obvious that the real Brahms is nothing more than a sentimental voluptuary with a wonderful ear. For respectability's sake he adopts the forms academically supposed to be proper to great composers, since it gives him no trouble to pile up *points d'orgue*, as in the Requiem, or to call a childishly sensuous reverie on a few simple chords, arranged into the simplest of strains for chaconne purposes by Handel, a set of variations on a theme by that master, or to adapt a ramble in search of fresh delights more or less to sonata form; but you have only to compare his symphonies and quintets with those of Beethoven or Mozart to become conscious that he is the most wanton of composers, that he is only ingenious in his wantonness, and that when his ambition leads him to turn his industry in any other direction his charm does not turn with it, and he becomes the most superficial and irrelevant of formalists.

Only, his wantonness is not vicious: it is that of a great baby, gifted enough to play with harmonies that would baffle most grown-up men, but still a baby, never more happy than when he has a crooning song to play with, always ready for the rocking-horse and the sugar-stick, and rather tiresomely addicted to dressing himself up as Handel or Beethoven and making a prolonged and intolerable noise. That this masquerade of his has taken in a considerable number of persons in Berlin and London is easily explicable on the hypothesis that they see no more in Handel or Beethoven than Brahms can imitate; but again you have only to compare the agonies of lassitude undergone by a Requiem audience with the general purring over his violin concerto, or the *encores* Miss Lehmann gets for his cradle songs, to see that Monsieur Tout-le-Monde is not in the least taken in, though he does not venture to say so in the teeth of eminent counsel's opinion to the effect that he ought to be.

These being my views, I accepted Mr Ernest Fowles's invitation to his Brahms recital without misgiving, especially as the program did not include any of Brahms's enormities. It is true that I did not arrive in time for the first piece, nor wait for the whole of the last, as I should certainly have done had they been by Mozart; but that was because, being a more farsighted voluptuary than Brahms, I know that the pleasures of sense should be tasted with a fresh palate, and not wallowed in. So I left the audience wallowing the moment the sweetness began to pall; and they may be there still for all I know.

What I heard was the twentyfive variations and fugue (save the mark!) on that theme which Handel has already furnished with quite enough variations to supply the world for some centuries to come. Brahms's variations might, however, just as well be called variations on the key of B flat as on Handel's air. Mr Ernest Fowles played with much devotion and enjoyment; and though his technique and style are not of the calibre by which huge assemblies can be seized and carried away, being distinctly a chamber technique rather than a concert-room technique, yet, on that very account, the concert being one of chamber music, he gave the right feeling to several passages which would certainly have been knocked on the head by a fully equipped Rubinsteiner or Leschetitzkeian, especially in the violin sonata in G, which he played with Joseph Ludwig, who handled the violin part with discretion and sympathy, if not with a very ardent appetite for its luxuries.

There was a tremendous crush at the Philharmonic to hear, or possibly to see, Paderewski. Gangways were abolished and narrow benches substituted for wide ones to make the most of the available space. Paderewski took advantage of the occasion to bring forward for the second time his own concerto, which is a very bad one. No doubt it was "frightfully thrilling" to Paderewski himself to fly up and down the keyboard, playing the piccolo and the cymbals and the big drum and every instrument except the pianoforte on it, and driving the band along, in spite of Dr Mackenzie, as if it were a coach-and-seventy thundering down a steep mountain road; but to me it was simply a waste of the talent I wanted to hear applied to some true masterpiece of pianoforte music.

I could see that he felt like a Titan when he was threshing out those *fortissimos* with the full band; but he had the advantage of me, for he could hear what he was doing, wheras he might just as well have been addressing postcards for all that reached me through the din of the orchestra. I do not want ever to hear that concerto again. It is riotous, strenuous, bold, vigorous, abounding in ready-made themes and figures, scored without one touch of sympathetic feeling for any instrument—least of all for the pianoforte, pardonable on the plea of youth and stimulating wilfulness in the first movement, clever and pleasing in the *andante*, and vulgar and cheap in the *finale*, which repeatedly made me rub my eyes and ask myself whether I was not really in the Empire Music Hall listening to a rattling ballet scene.

Perhaps the most exasperating feature of the work is that, with all its obstreperousness, the form is timidly conventional. Besides, Paderewski did not play it at all as well as Sapellnikoff, for instance, would have done.

His almost insolent masterfulness of execution and his anxiety to get the last inch of effect out of the work destroyed his artistic integrity as pianist. At the end there came a contest of obstinacy between him and the audience. He, very naturally, only valued the torrent of applause as an acknowledgment of the merits of his concerto, wheras many of the applauders plainly meant "We have sat out your confounded concerto like angels; now give us a nice little solo."

Over and over again he came up the steps only to retire again after that curious bow of his which is so like the action of a critic who, falling asleep at a concert, nods forward until he overbalances himself and recovers himself just in time to avoid falling with a crash on his nose. At last he relented and gave us a commonplace of his own which at least shewed that his power of treating a melody is unimpaired—though this had already appeared in the slow movement of the concerto. His recital this week, however, must settle what America has done or undone for him in other respects. It will also enable us to turn from his immature and second-hand achievements as an orchestral composer to his really creative achievements as the greatest of living pianists.

As for the rest of the concert, it was, of course, most horribly long, a second concerto (Max Bruch in G minor, conducted by the composer and played by Górski) having been wantonly thrust into it in order that the audience might enjoy their Turkish bath as long over two hours as possible. I therefore take a malign pleasure in recording the fact that the extra concerto had very poor luck, Górski being bothered from the first by the high pitch. When he found that he was agonizingly out of tune in the first solo, he took advantage of every *tutti* to screw up; but as the wind got sharper and sharper in the heat, whilst he, standing amid the strings, could not quite realize how flat he was, he never completely remedied matters; and the warm applause he received was a recognition that he was not to blame, and had heroically made the best of a bad job, rather than an expression of any very exquisite pleasure experienced during the performance. Bruch's Achilleus spectacle music was brilliantly fired off by the band; but it contained nothing fresh. The Haydn symphony (E flat, with the drum roll) was so mechanically and unaffectionately played that it was hardly possible to pay any attention to it. The strings lumbered over the *andante* like a traction engine; and the one moment of relief was when the flattened-out major subject breathed for just a moment in the hands of the oboe. Madame Melba did not appear: her place was taken by Miss Palliser, who sang *Divinités du Styx*, a great air, too little known here, like all Gluck's music; also Grétry's *Plus de dépits*, which ought to have been sung more neatly or else not at all.

The concert ended with Sir Arthur Sullivan's new Imperial March, which will undoubtedly have a considerable vogue in the suburbs as a pianoforte duet. This finished the Philharmonic season, which has been, on the whole, one of improvement in the value and prospects of the Society. All that is wanted to accelerate the improvement is a rigid restriction of the duration of the concerts to a hundred and ten minutes at the outside, and the compulsory retirement of all directors at the age of ninetyfive, into a lethal chamber if possible.

I remember wandering into a theatre one oppressively warm evening in Munich, and seeing a comic opera, which presented the novel feature of a chorus in ordinary evening dress. It was a rollicking, Bohemian, *naïve* affair enough, good fun for a willing audience admitted on a modest scale of charges, but hardly suited for a London house with half-guinea stalls and a half-crown pit. There was a comic man whose sallies were immensely laughed at; and as I could not understand one of them I fell into a deep melancholy, and at last went out and sentimentally gazed on Iser rolling rapidly by moonlight for the rest of the evening. This coat-and-waistcoat comic opera has turned up again, much glorified, at the Prince of Wales' Theatre as Millöcker's Poor Jonathan, himself none other than the comic man, now become intelligible to me and very funny into the bargain, in the person of Mr Harry Monkhouse. The additions made by Señor Albéniz and Mr Brookfield have made the work more pretentious; but they have also, I am afraid, weakened it by making it far too long. It contains much talk about music halls and opera companies which might pass if it were satire, but which, being in fact nothing else than theatrical "shop," ought not to have survived the first rehearsal. Mr Monkhouse is a coster who obtains a place as *chef* to a millionaire by writing himself a flattering testimonial, having learnt the necessary accomplishment in a reformatory. The millionaire first discharges him for making an ice pudding with mottled soap, and then, finding him about to commit suicide rather than face destitution, hands him over all his property. What is wanted to give the piece a chance of success is a vigorous blue pencil, to be wielded with a frank recognition of two facts: first, that Millöcker wrote quite as much vocal music as the piece will bear; and, second, that the parts on which Messrs Denny and Kaye waste their ability are worthless, and should, with the contingent parts for their pupils and *prima donnas*, be cut down to the barest cues for Miss Schuberth's songs and for such of the dances as the public shew any interest in. It will be a pity if Señor Albéniz's enterprise should suffer for want of a little energetic revision; for his management is an example to London in point of artistic aim and liberal spirit.

KARL LOEWE'S BALLADS

The World, 28 June 1893

Mr Albert Bach's Loewe recital at Steinway Hall was rather a propagandist demonstration than a concert. Just as the late Walter Bache preached Liszt, so does Mr Bach preach Loewe. I have every sympathy with him in his work; but this is just why I submit that such a recital as that of Thursday last may do Loewe harm as well as good. Mr Bach is a powerful German *basso cantante*, with much more dramatic force than lyric charm, and with a robust German conscience in the matter of intonation. Loewe was a tenor singer, probably of exceptional compass, as he often wrote with a wicked disregard for the normal limits of the human voice.

In nearly all the ballads of his which are known to me there are smooth lyric passages of intense expression (as in Archibald Douglas), and stirring excursions into the high, clear, ringing vocal regions where the least mixture of the earthy roughness of the heavy bass is not to be tolerated. Some songs lie in this region altogether, notably that charming ballad *Des Glockenthürmers Töchterlein*, the notes of which should soar like those of a carillon in a Flemish tower two hundred and fifty feet above the plain. I agree with Mr Bach that this happiest of songs should be made known to the benighted British public; but I ask him whether he really achieved that end the other evening by transposing it into a subterranean key and almost growling it at us. The audience may have been previously unconscious of the existence of the ballad; but surely that state was more blessed than their present one of believing it to be a dull, clumsy, unmanageable tune in the wrong place.

The fact is, Mr Bach, by undertaking the whole program himself, was placed in this dilemma, that he had either to make his presentation to Loewe one-sided, or else to vary it by introducing songs not suited to his voice and style. It seems clear to me that he would have done better to have secured the cooperation of other singers, if only to relieve the monotony of his own voice. A concert on the fourth string makes one long for the *chanterelle*; and I confess that after hearing Mr Bach sing twelve times in succession, I would willingly have exchanged the thirteenth item, though it was no less a ballad than the famous setting of Uhland's *Die drei Lieder*, for Miss Palliser's song from The Gondoliers or any other frivolity that would have brought me a breath of clear soprano air.

I do not believe the most versatile bass singer in the world, however perfect his intonation and great his lyric gift, could carry off a Loewe concert singlehanded; and Mr Bach's overwhelming dramatic bent deprives him of versatility, whilst, as I have already said, he is comparatively careless as to his intonation, and sometimes shews so little lyric feeling that his tone, instead of being sustained, breaks out and lapses from syllable to syllable almost as much as it would if he were making a vehement political speech. It is with some reluctance that I press Mr Bach thus hardly on the shortcomings of an enterprise which engages my entire respect; for he carries the banner of Loewe with ability and enthusiasm, and in interpreting some of the most striking and difficult of the ballads—the *Hochzeitlied*, the Three Songs, and Henry the Fowler, for instance—attains a remarkable degree of success, which would, I think, be heightened if he accustomed himself to study the peculiar fastidiousness of London audiences whilst taking care to preserve his force and freshness.

But the fact remains that his recital, interesting as it

was, did not altogether do justice either to Loewe or to himself. I should shew myself even more ignorant of Loewe than I actually am if I passed over the important share taken in the recital by Mrs Bach at the piano. Playing, as she does, with a most un-Lisztianly stiff wrist, she rather failed to maintain the swing of such galloping accompaniments as that to The Erl King; but in the sparkling, tinkling, busy merriment of the *Hochzeitlied*, and indeed in almost all the daintier traits, she distinguished herself highly.

Before leaving the subject, it may be as well to mention, for the benefit of the uninitiated, that Loewe was a Westphalian, born 1796, deceased 1869. The ballad poetry beloved of Sir Walter Scott, with its witches, warlocks, and freebooters, was in vogue in his young days; and Loewe, by saturating himself with it and seeking musical expression for it, produced a store of perfectly original and very clever and imaginative settings of the ballads of Goethe, Uhland, Herder, &c.

Schubert, saturated with the music of Haydn, Mozart, and Beethoven, and using all the songs and ballads he came across as excuses for his music (thus reversing Loewe's process), never, even in The Erl King, succeeded in growing his music from the ballad stem as Loewe did, although Loewe was, as far as I can judge, less gifted as a musician. Intellectually and dramatically, however, he had powers of the Gluck-Wagner order, and might possibly have done something for the stage if his vocation for it had been stronger and his opportunities wider than those of a provincial organist. I speak, however, without first-hand knowledge of his operas; and my opinion is, therefore, worth exactly nothing.

Mrs Henschel, giving a recital the night after Mr Bach, was assuredly not, like him, hampered by an unpopular and neglected cause. She took St James's Hall, brought her husband (an incomparable accompanist), brought his choir, brought her audience, and took her success without effort or anxiety. She certainly sang admirably, some of the Irish and Scotch folk songs being quite irresistibly given, not in point of national color or dialect, for neither of which has Mrs Henschel any genius, but solely in pure feeling for the melody— the only feeling, by the bye, she ever condescends to display, and one which she possesses in a degree that would make the fortune of a violinist, especially if his touch were as delicate and sure as hers.

With her complete and self-contained individuality, her cool superiority to sentimental or devotional moods, and her susceptibility to absolute music, she presents a fascinating subject to the critic, and one which I will not pretend to have mastered. If the gentlemen who talk about "analytic criticism" will make me a complete psychology of Mrs Henschel, explaining why she will sing a folk song or a Schubert or Liszt melody with exquisite feeling, and then go through a prayer by Mendelssohn or an elegiac tone-poem by Beethoven quite hardheartedly, then I will give them credit for knowing something more of a critic's business than can be gathered from their ready grasp of Professor So-and-so's view as to the root of the seventh on the supertonic.

Paderewski's recital was so crowded that the fall of the thermometer the night before must be regarded as a special providence. In spite of the crowd, the final degrees of excellence in his playing remain a secret between himself and those of us who would very willingly have let him off those brilliant but shallow numbers in his program which plenty of other players can play as well as they need or can be played, but which are applauded at his recitals more noisily than those greater compositions in which he applies all his insight, judgment, and skill most intensely to every phrase and progression.

[925]

I did not hear the whole recital; but what I did hear was, humanly speaking, faultless; by which I do not mean that I liked all his mannerisms, and would have played the pieces exactly as he did if I had the skill, still less that his way is the only right way, and every other way consequently wrong. I simply mean that all the work he did was exhaustively studied, and that the reading founded on the study was successfully executed, and was in no case trivial, cheap, or unworthy of a great artist. And I would recommend all singers and players, no matter what their instruments may be, to hear Paderewski, and carefully consider the secret of his pre-eminence.

Infant phenomena have been rife lately; but I managed to avoid them until last week, when, at Mr Strelitski's concert at Portman Rooms, a bright, nimble, sure-fingered boy pupil of his, in the usual black velvet tunic and antimacassar, rattled off Mendelssohn's violin concerto. He evidently did not think much of it, and, no doubt, deemed us fools for wanting to listen to it—in which he had my hearty agreement.

I strongly object to the practice of using works of this class as stalking-horses for children. It is possible to teach a small boy the sword-exercise; but that would not justify his immediately taking part in a cavalry charge; and, cleverly as this youngster had picked up all the difficult passages in the concerto, he should not have been allowed to play it at a concert. Mr Strelitski himself, though announced as flautist and violinist, only played the flute, on which he executed the usual feats, labial and digital, without, however, displaying that exceptional lip-power of correcting the machine into something like perfect tune which, combined with excellence of style, alone justifies a flautist in taking so imperfect an instrument out of the orchestra.

Still, Mr Strelitski shewed a good deal of the right

artistic spirit in the pains he took to make his concert a success. He had engaged a band which did not give itself too much trouble on his account, but which enlivened a very hot afternoon with some new and pretty pieces by Mr Silas, and by the overture to William Tell, which I did not wait for, as it is not such a novelty to me as it is to the generation born when I was twenty. Miss Duma, by the way, sang Mascheroni's Ave Maria with a vigor and grandiosity which would not have overcharged Rossini's Inflammatus.

Sir Arthur Sullivan's Golden Legend was done at the Crystal Palace on Saturday afternoon on the Handel festival scale, with Albani, Miss Marian McKenzie, Messrs Ben Davies, Henschel, and Grice. I look with indulgence on The Golden Legend, because I know that the composer really loves "those evening bells" and all that sincerely sentimental prettiness, with a dash of piety here and a dash of fun there (as in Lucifer's comic song with the Kneller Hall accompaniment), not to mention the liberal allowance of blissful but indeterminate meandering for mere love of musical sound.

I am not that sort of person myself; but I must not therefore churlishly withhold my blessing. The chorus was good, especially the men; but the dainty orchestration was for the most part wasted on the huge scattered band, always the weak point in these monster performances.

Miss Elsie Hall, still in comparatively short frocks, but tamer than of yore, gave a concert at Lady Stanley of Alderley's, with the assistance of Mr Stanley Blagrove. It was, to tell the truth, a somewhat jejune affair; and the sooner Miss Elsie takes her undeniable talent and intelligence off to Leschetitzky to be seriously trained, the better.

IMPERVIOUS TO COUNTERPOINT
The World, 5 July 1893

The utilization for concerts of the very convenient room of the extinct Meistersingers' Club, at 63 St James's-street, reminds me to ask what has become of the mushroom-crop of clubs which sprang up a year or two ago, and were nothing more than cooperative concert-giving societies. The Meistersingers alone, though described as "the late," have escaped dismantling; for their concert room is still available; and very glad I was to take refuge in it from the rain at Mr Hirwen Jones's concert, where I found Mr Shortis* playing the banjo with a delicacy and conscientiousness that ought to have been devoted to some musical instrument. Also there played a Mr Squire, who gave us a couple of tunes of the more obvious sort, with some trick effects, prettily executed, on the violoncello. The concert giver sang a couple of songs by Mr Cowen, who accompanied in person; Mrs Mary Davies sang one good song and one trumpery one, both by Sullivan, with her fine natural artistic faculty; Miss Rosa Leo chaminaded as well as a lady can who has the wrong temperament for that *genre*; and, the rain having intermitted, I made off.

The Begum Ahmadee's concert at the Grosvenor Club must have puzzled some of the audience a good deal. It was undeniably a novel experience; and I am afraid that some of us thought that the Begum sang a good deal out of tune. She certainly gave a very Oriental version of the intervals of our scale, the keynote itself

* C.P. Shortis, an American banjo virtuoso, performed in minstrel shows and variety.

being so modified when it was approached in certain ways as to suggest doubts whether it had the character of a keynote for her at all. But there is a great difference between a young Englishwoman trying to sing our major or minor scale and doing it inaccurately through defect of ear, and a young Oriental with a good ear tempering our scale with the intervals to which she is accustomed. I found the effect interesting and by no means disagreeable.

Still my toleration for foreign intervals must not be abused. I bar duets between the Begum tempering the scale in her Indian manner, and Mr Joseph O'Mara tempering it in our native manner. *Una notte a Venezia*, sung under these conditions, inflicted such exquisite anguish on the more sensitive persons present that they had to set their teeth and hold firmly on to their chairs to endure it with outward calm. I think this was partly due to a gallant attempt on Mr O'Mara's part not to sing obtrusively in tune from the European point of view, and to attenuate his tone as much as possible so as not to drown the Begum, who was suffering from the effects of an attack of influenza; but the result, however well meant, was disastrous.

It was in a solo that the Oriental peculiarity first asserted itself as a charm. The influenza had produced an inharmonious pallor which deprived the Begum of the great personal advantage of "the shadow'd livery of the burnish'd sun"*; but when this passes away she will be powerfully aided by her appearance. Her voice is a mezzo-soprano of agreeable quality.

Among the artists I heard during the few minutes I was able to spend at the Grosvenor Club was Mr Charles Copland, who treated Stradella's *Pietà, Signore,* so as to exhibit a good voice and some skill in using it, without

*Shakespear's The Merchant of Venice, Act II, Scene 1.

the slightest regard for appropriate expression. If I were an Olympian deity, and a mere mortal were to demand *"pietà"* from me with the peremptory incisiveness of Mr Copland, I should certainly reply with the heaviest thunderbolt I could lay my hand on.

I also heard a couple of violin solos from Johannes Wolff, who has carried his spontaneity, his initiative, his freedom of expression, and some (though by no means all) of his neatness of execution unimpaired through a thousand drawing rooms. But the enervating atmosphere of these artistically noxious places, the confined space, the stifling carpets and curtains, the crosscurrents of wandering attention and contrary squalls of whispering, have left their mark on his tone. His bow is nothing like so patient and sensitive as it used to be; and he plays his *pièces de salon* as if he had worn out every sensation they could give him except that of astonishing private audiences with his execution of them. He was quite another man in the evening at Steinway Hall, where he led a Beethoven pianoforte trio with some real artistic enjoyment, and instinctively got back some of his old fineness of tone. This was at a concert given by Alfred Gallrein, a competent executant on the violoncello, but not an extraordinary musician, as I judged by his rather commonplace treatment of a suite by Corelli. Miss Liza Lehmann sang *Vieni, Dorina bella*, known to this generation, as far as it is known at all, by Weber's pianoforte variations.* The disappointment caused by the absence of Mr Bispham was relieved by the appearance of Hugo Heinz, a cultivated, intelligent, and sympathic German singer, whom I occasionally hear at concerts, never without pleasure.

An excellent concert was that given by Mr Maud

* Seven Pianoforte Variations on Francesco Bianchi's *Vien quà, Dorina bella*, Op. 7 (1807).

Crament at the Town Hall, Kensington. This I may say with a clear conscience; though I am, I confess, strongly biassed in Mr Crament's favor by an act of extraordinary and benevolent intrepidity performed by him years ago. This was nothing less than an entirely disinterested attempt to teach me counterpoint, an art to which I am constitutionally impervious. Lest this statement, now published for the first time, should ruin him professionally, I hasten to add that he is in no way responsible for my present attitude towards the academic training in music. When I think of the appalling facility with which he could write canons at all sorts of intervals, and choruses in an unlimited number of real parts, so that even the piously contrapuntal Friedrich Kiel could teach him no more, and an Oxford musical degree cost him nothing but the fees and a hasty look at the date of Monteverdi's birth or the like, I cannot help admiring him from my soul for all the oratorios and festival cantatas he has *not* written. For if he had chosen to abuse his powers, "analytic criticism" would certainly have pronounced him another Handel. Unfortunately for the analysts, he was not only a contrapuntist; but a musician and a man of sense, and so lost his chance of a nine days' immortality. At this concert he did not put a single composition of his own in the program; and there was, unluckily, no organ in the building: else I should certainly have got up and moved that the concert giver play a Bach fugue. It is odd, by the bye, that even in St James's Hall nobody ever seems to think of varying a concert with an organ piece.

Saint-Saëns, for instance, is an excellent organist: I heard him play Bach's Fugue in A minor at a concert in St James's Hall more than a dozen years ago; and he might most opportunely have repeated the experiment at the Philharmonic the other night; but nobody dreamt of suggesting it. The stock objection "They [the audience] get enough of it on Sunday" does not appear to me to be conclusive as against the value of a great mass of organ music which is quite unknown to the public, and, I may add, to myself. I am thinking, not only of the fugues and passacailles of Bach and Handel, but of works by Sweelinck and other brilliant composers of the old Netherlands school, of which I have heard just enough to make me believe that a specimen or two would be more refreshing, even to a miscellaneous concert audience, than the forty-thousandth repetition of Popper's Papillons.

Two singers who had the advantage of Popper in respect of novelty appeared at Mr Crament's concert. One, Miss Minnie Tracy, a soprano from the Opéra at Nice, did due credit to that establishment, being a very capable young lady. The other, Mr Fawcett, is a tenor with two strong points in his favor—a distinguished presence, and an unmistakable devotion to his art. In aiming at a style much above that of the ordinary rough-and-ready robust tenor or the pretty drawing room *tenorino*, he is still a little preoccupied by his method, which has not yet become automatic with him; and for the moment he is put at some disadvantage as compared with less scrupulous singers by his altogether dignified and artistic determination to fall short in trying to sing finely rather than succeed by shouting his way out of every difficulty.

His voice, though its quality is uncommon and expressive, is at present a little careworn, so to speak, by study: he lacks freshness of tone, complete certainty of execution, vigor of attack—in short, mastery, which, however, is slow and difficult of attainment on the plane on which he is striving for it. In a year or two more Mr Fawcett will be able to challenge a final criticism; meanwhile, he can make himself acceptable to an audience, and so can afford to wait.

I heard also a few pieces from Tivadar Nachéz, who was in the vein and played very well; a renewed success of Norman Salmond's with that charming old song, My love is like the red, red rose; and an admirable delivery of Grieg's remarkable little tone landscape called Autumnal Gale by Miss Agnes Janson, one of the best examples of this particular kind of concert singing I have heard this season.

To Jan Mulder, the Dutch cellist, who introduced a string quartet by A. Borodin at his concert at the Meistersingers' on Saturday, I can offer only my old excuse for absence—that I cannot be in more than four places at most at the same time. The Patti concert also escaped me, though I got as near it as Palace Gate, where Mrs Charles Yates, who might very well have ventured upon a pianoforte recital, was led into a concert by the assistance of such a stupendous array of artists— Carlotta Elliot, Clara Samuell, Agnes Janson, Madame Valda, Nachéz, Oudin, Norman Salmond, Lawrence Kellie, Claus, Thorndike, Brandon Thomas, and a score or so more—that I can only express a hope that they all sang and played and recited excellently; for the program so far exceeded my ideas of a reasonable day's work for a critic that I fled after hearing Mrs Charles Yates play Grieg's rococo suite, Op. 40,* which she handled to the greater advantage as her school of pianism, which is that of Theodor Kullak and Madame Schumann rather than that of Liszt, Leschetitzky, or Rubinstein, is also that of Grieg himself, his countrywoman Agathe Backer-Gröndahl being, as far as I know, the greatest living exponent of it.

Miss Estrella Belinfante, who gave a concert at St James's Hall on Friday, and who is built on the lines of

* Fra Holbergs Tid (Holberg Suite), for solo piano (1884). Grieg arranged it for string orchestra a year later.

Signora Duse, is not, as well as I could judge from hearing her sing one song, which she appeared to be reading at sight, a concert singer, but rather a stage singer who has had to resort to the concert platform as a means of introducing herself to the London public. I should not be surprised to find her, on the stage, a dramatic artist of exceptional force and charm. Hollmann, with the air of a man introducing a striking novelty to an awestruck nation, played Popper's Papillons. Hollmann is, on the whole, and without any exception, the greatest violoncellist I have ever heard; but I wish he would learn a new piece. He clings to those Papillons as Sims Reeves does to Come into the garden, Maud, or Patti to Home, Sweet Home.

On Saturday evening the Lord Mayor of London invited me to the Mansion House to meet about three hundred and forty representatives of Art and Literature. Music, the art for which England was once famous throughout Europe, was represented by the police band, Mr Ganz, Mr Kuhe, Sir Joseph Barnby, and myself. I fully expected that one of our names would have been coupled with the toast of Art; but no: the City, which should before this have built that Wagner theatre on Richmond Hill for me, has not yet discovered that music is an art. I could not eat: my feelings as a musician and vegetarian were too much for me; and save for some two or three pounds of ice pudding I came away empty, unless I take account of the great feast of chin music afterwards, which I cannot criticize without unpardonable breaches of politeness to the most distinguished of my fellow guests. Our host apologized for the absence of Sir Frederick Leighton. It never occurred to him to allude to the absence of Dr Mackenzie or Sir George Grove. Poor Music!

PLAYING FAVORITE
The World, 12 July 1893

Last week was one of almost complete immunity from concerts, every musical person being engaged in playing the Wedding March in one form or another. Madame Inverni, however, ventured on a concert on Monday afternoon, with a rather strong program, which attracted a comparatively large audience. Slivinski played Mendelssohn's Variations Sérieuses, and some other pieces which I did not hear. He has resolved to join the ranks of the bearded so recently that he presents, for the moment, an alarmingly neglected appearance. Somehow, Slivinski has not, so far, been very handsomely treated here. When he first appeared he shewed technical powers of an altogether extraordinary kind: his mere displays of execution—in some of Liszt's operatic fantasias, for example—were intensely interesting and brilliant. His style and force were essentially of the order needed for large audiences and large halls; and one felt that the strain of these was essential to his continued development as an artist. He came, too, at a moment when what was wanted above all things, from a business point of view, was a rival to Paderewski. Slivinski, on the whole, might have played that part better than anyone else had he been vigorously seconded. But we have no great captains in the concert industry nowadays: our agents wait, dreaming Alnaschar dreams,* until some single mighty artist makes a success, and then content themselves with running that artist for all he has made himself worth.

* Arabian Nights equivalent of Esop's fable about not counting one's chickens until they are hatched.

This is very well as far as it goes; but it leaves to the artists and the public the work that should be done by the *entrepreneur*—the work, that is, of making them acquainted with oneanother. And when the public is very full of an established favorite, and is convinced that when it has heard him play it has heard everything it ought to hear, and may now go home and have done with the classics, any later arrival, however remarkable, cannot get adequately recognized without some determined, skilful, and longsighted business handling—unless, indeed, he is a supreme genius, and can oust the favorite. Now, a player good enough to oust Sarasate or Joachim, for instance, is not reasonably possible. When a player like Ysaÿe comes to London, he finds that Sarasate and Joachim are supposed to represent all the first-rate violin-playing there is in the world; and when he suggests that he too can fiddle a little, he finds only two sorts of agents: the one who says "But I have got Sarasate, and I shall be ruined if the British public discovers that there is any other violinist extant"; and the one who sighs, and says "Ah, if only I could get hold of Sarasate, what could I not make him!" The net result being, of course, that Ysaÿe, unaccustomed to be treated as a second-rater, and tired of agents who throw away the king of trumps because they cannot have the ace, gives up London as a bad job, to our infinite artistic loss. Slivinski has hitherto, it seems to me, been in much the same predicament. The business of making a reputation for him, as far as that is a business matter, has not attracted British enterprise, either because he is not Paderewski, or because he would be a dangerous rival to Paderewski. Of course this may be a sound business policy for anything I know to the contrary; but from the point of view of the interest of the public, which is the one I am bound to take, whether the public understands its interest or not, it is altogether unsatisfactory, since it ends in a little pianoforte-playing by Paderewski at doubled prices, and a great deal by third-rate players at practically no prices at all; whilst artists like Sapellnikoff, Stavenhagen, De Greef, Sophie Menter, and Agathe Backer-Gröndhal (to mention only those whose names occur to me hastily) seem, after a trial or two, to prefer every other musical centre in Europe to London.

Instead of getting our reasonable annual share of the best European art in all departments, we find the business of organizing the supply monstrously overdone one year, not done at all for the two years following, timidly underdone the fourth year, profusely but cheaply done the next year if the underdoing has proved encouraging, and finally overdone again the following year out of mere business jealousy—with, of course, a recurring cycle of depression following as before. All this, by the bye, is somewhat wide of Madame Inverni's concert. Besides Slivinski, there was a composer who announced herself as Guy d'Hardelot, a name in which I confess I do not altogether believe. She accompanied Madame Inverni and Mr Isidor de Lara in a cycle of her love songs—fluent and pretty outpourings of a harmless Muse with an unsuspiciously retentive memory. The two singers were quite equal to them, Mr de Lara, in fact, being considerably underweighted. Madame Inverni, who has a voice of nice quality and a good ear and method, has been a little too severely trained. Although English is evidently her native language, she has acquired a diction so artificial that I have no doubt that many of her hearers took her for a foreigner who had made a very close and conscientious study of English for artistic purposes. Whatever her natural delivery may be, she has thrown away its qualities as well as its faults. It is greatly to her credit that she has studied singing and diction so resolutely; but she must now study music and her own self with equal determination, in order to get

[937]

rid of some of those over-refined vowels, and to recover her own artistic individuality, which she seems to have been taught, in the usual professorial fashion, to regard as a department of original sin.

MEMO TO CONCERT GIVERS
The World, 19 July 1893

An autumnal delight will be the Norwich Musical Festival, which will rage with unabated fury from the 3rd to the 6th of October. The most splendid feature in the announcements is the engagement of both Paderewski and Sarasate, Paderewski to play a new Polish fantasia of his own composition for pianoforte and orchestra, and Sarasate the well-worn rondo by Saint-Saëns, and Mackenzie's Pibroch. Everybody except Santley will sing—Albani, Helen Trust, and Anna Williams; Lloyd and Ben Davies; Marian McKenzie and Belle Cole; Norman Salmond, Bantock Pierpont, and Henschel.

The choral diversions will be of the most festive kind. Judith will have a whole evening to herself, the East Anglians being curious to hear whether so famous a work can possibly be as bad as I think it; and three cantatas will be performed for the first time under the *bâtons* of the composers themselves, though only one of them hallmarks his opus as "composed expressly for the festival." Mr Cowen and Mr Barnett have not claimed that speciality for The Water Lily and The Wishing Bell. There will be a new symphony, "composed expressly" by Mr Edward German; and the dizziest heights will be scaled in The Golden Legend and St Paul. Handel's Messiah is also in the bill, with a clear day between it and Judith, so that the older work may not be hopelessly put out of countenance by a too close comparison with the new.

Mr Randegger will conduct; and it will unquestionably be "all werry capital," and well worth six guineas for a patron's stall or three for a seat among the patronized in the gallery. I note that the committee includes twentyfive peers or sons of peers, nineteen baronets, sixteen members of Parliament, four knights, three mayors, a high sheriff and an ordinary sheriff, two judges (of law), a dean, an esquire, a colonel, and not a solitary musician or artist of any degree—not even a critic to see fair. There will therefore be no danger of having the festival spoiled by the interference of specialists.

The proceeds will be handed over to the principal charities in Norfolk and Norwich instead of being used, as they ought to be, for the endowment of art in the county. If the inhabitants wish, for instance, to celebrate the first performance of Judith in their midst by giving some rising local sculptor a commission for a public statue in honor of Holofernes, they will have to do so by subscription. Art, being a beggar in England, is to be robbed of her casual earnings to save rich East Anglians from supporting their local charities. I never heard a meaner proposal.

I must offer my apologies to Mrs Lynedoch Moncrieff, of whose songs, as far as I know them, I am an admirer, and to Bentayoux for having missed their concerts last Thursday, the invitations not having reached me until the performances were over. I may as well take this opportunity of repeating my periodic plea for at least a few days' notice of concerts. The notion that I live on the premises, and that my attendance can be instantly secured at any hour by ringing the night bell, is one which a reflective mind ought to reject without any prompting from me; and yet it must prevail very largely in the musical profession, if I may judge from the fact that when invitations do not reach me through a regular agent, in which case I get them a fortnight or so beforehand, they are as likely as not to reach me the day after the fair. Another precaution which I recommend to concert givers is the sending of a program. All experienced critics assume, in the absence of evidence to the contrary, that a miscellaneous concert is not worth going to—or, to put it more gracefully, that it will contain nothing new. Besides, when it happens, as it often does at the height of the season, that the utmost time that can be spared to any one concert in an afternoon is fifteen minutes, a critic duly supplied with programs can arrange his engagements so as to avoid happening upon Popper's Papillons and On the Ling ho four times over by the same artists, and not hearing a single note from any one of the concert givers. And, be it noted, what is convenient for the critic is convenient for everybody else too. If it is good for me to know a fortnight beforehand that I have to be at such and such a place at such and such a quarter of an hour on such and such a day, it is no less good for the artists and for the hostess—I say the hostess, because it is in the case of concerts at private houses that the tendency to leave everything to the last moment is strongest, the public halls being only obtainable on condition of being booked for a long time beforehand. I have no doubt that often, when I have been invited to a rather good concert and not accepted the invitation, whilst in the same week I have paid some attention to a rather bad one, the neglected giver of the better concert has wondered whether the opposition management enclosed me a ten-pound note along with the ticket. But the ten-pound note, though I should like it extremely, would make no difference, wheras a week's notice accompanied by a program would make all the difference in the world;

[940]

and I ask those concert givers who have misinterpreted my partialities to consider whether they have not deprived themselves of the solace of my criticisms by indulgence in business habits of the same pattern as my own. I have enough to do to struggle with the effects of my incorrigible procrastinativeness without being hampered by that of others as well.

The most considerate artist I have yet met is Mrs Aylmer Jones, who gave a concert last week in Stanhope Gardens. She not only gave me timely warning, but when I arrived she immediately sang all the items set down for her in the first part of the concert, one after the other. I do not suggest that this was done on my account; but it made me acquainted in the shortest possible space of time with Mrs Aylmer Jones's merits as a singer, which are, a soprano voice of nice quality, a sensitive ear, a refined style, and an intelligent delivery. I do not recommend Mrs Aylmer Jones to go on the stage and play Carmen: she is too ladylike for that sort of success; but at this concert she was quite equal to the occasion.

MADAME ANGOT RETURNS
The World, 26 July 1893

The musical season took advantage of the nuptial festivities at Court* to fall down in a swoon; and it may now, I suppose, be regarded as stone-dead. It ended piously with a cantata at the Crystal Palace, on the Handel Festival scale, at popular prices, relieved by a mild fling at the Criterion in the evening, where Mr Wyndham has revived La Fille de Madame Angot for the benefit of the autumnal visitor. Whether it has been

*The marriage on 6 July of the Duke of York (later King George V.) to the Princess Victoria Mary of Teck.

a good season or not I cannot say: the usual number of assurances that it has been "the worst ever known" are to hand; but it has been quite busy enough for me, even though my labors have been lightened by the retirement of some of our *entrepreneurs* from an unequal combat with my criticism. On looking back over it I recall, with a certain hopeful satisfaction, the failure of innumerable comic operas. They were not worse than the comic operas which used to succeed—quite the contrary. On the musical side, both as to composition and execution, there has been a steady improvement. The comic opera stage now exchanges artists with the grand opera stage and the oratorio platform; and the orchestras, compared to their predecessors, are exquisite and imperial.

The difficulty lies on the dramatic side. I have often expressed my opinion of the average comic opera librettist with pointed frankness; and I have not changed my mind in the least. Mr D'Oyly Carte's attempt to keep the Savoy stage up to the Gilbertian level by calling in Messrs Grundy, Barrie, and Conan Doyle is part of a sound policy, however this or that particular application of it may fail. But for the moment the effect on our younger comic opera artists of having been trained so extensively at bad dramatic work is that the rank and file of them cannot act; and when good work is put into their hands, they are unable to execute it effectively. On the ordinary stage the incapacity of the actors is got over by the ingenuity of the authors, who, by adroitly contriving a constant supply of effective lines, situations, and passages of pure stage management, reduce the function of the actor to the display of fairly good stage manners; but the ordinary opera librettist has not the skill thus to substitute good parts for good acting, nor the imagination to write drama of the order which stimulates actors to genuine feats of impersonation, and eventually teaches them their business.

And so a comic opera, on its dramatic side, has come to mean mostly an inane and occasionally indecorous play, performed by self-satisfied bunglers who have all the amateur's ineptitude without his disinterestedness, one or two experienced and popular comedians being thrown in to help the rest out by such fun as they can improvize.

The effect on the public of the long degeneration from La Grande Duchesse, with its witty book and effervescent score, down to the last dregs of that school (tainted as it was from its birth, one must admit, with a certain dissoluteness which we soon turned into graceless rowdyness) seems now to be nearly complete. In the days when La Grande Duchesse was shuddered at as something frightfully wicked, when improper stories about Schneider formed the staple of polite conversation, and young persons were withheld from the interpolated can-can in the second act as from a spectacle that must deprave them for ever, the many-headed received a rapturous impression of opéra bouffe as a delightful and complete initiation into life—the very next thing, in fact, to a visit to the Paris of Napoleon III., represented in the British imagination chiefly by the Mabille Gardens.

Now the theatre-going public may be divided roughly into three classes. First, a very small class of experts who know the exact value of the entertainment, and who do not give it a second trial if it does not please them. Second, a much larger class, which can be persuaded by puffs or by the general curiosity about a novelty which "catches on," to accept it at twice or thrice its real value. Third, a mob of persons who, when their imaginations are excited, will accept everything at from ten times to a million times its real value, and who will, in this condition, make a hero of everybody who comes within their ken—manager, composer, author, comedian, and even critic. When a form of art, originally good enough to "catch on," begins to go down hill as *opéra bouffe* did, the first class drops off at once; and the second, after some years, begins to follow suit gradually.

But the third class still worships its own illusion, and enjoys itself rather more or less as the stuff becomes more and more familiar, obvious, and vulgar; and in this folly the managers keep speculating until that generation passes away, and its idols are too degraded to attract fresh worshipers. Managers are still trying to pick profits out of the dregs of the Offenbach movement; and the question of the day for Mr D'Oyly Carte is, how to keep the Gilbert-Sullivan movement from following the Offenbach movement into the abyss.

This being the situation, up comes an interesting question. Why not go back and begin over again? Generations of play-goers are happily shorter than generations of men; for most men only begin to go to the theatre when they arrive at the stage of having a latchkey and pocket money, but no family; and they leave off when they arrive at the stage of a family and (consequently) no pocket money. As for myself, I can be proved by figures to have completely outgrown that boyish shyness which still compels me to regard myself as a young man; but I am not so very old—nothing like what you would suppose from the wisdom and serenity of my writing. Yet I have the flight of time brought home to me at every theatrical "revival" by the number of men, to all appearance my contemporaries, for whom the operas and plays and artists which seem to me those of yesterday are as Edmund Kean's Richard or Pasta's Medea. I have hardly yet lost the habit of considering myself a child because I never saw Charles Kean, Macready, or even Grisi; yet I am confronted already with a generation which is in the same predicament with regard to Titiens and Costa, Julia Mathews and

Stoyle. Twenty years of playgoing makes you a veteran, an oldest inhabitant, an authority to your face and an old fogey behind your back—all before you are forty—long before you begin to be spoken of outside as a callow young man. Under these circumstances La Grande Duchesse and La Fille de Madame Angot may surely be produced today as absolute novelties. La Grand Duchesse and La Belle Hélène belong to the sixties, Madame Angot to the early seventies. Compared to them Madame Favart, Le Voyage dans la Lune, and La Fille du Tambour Major are quite recent works, although these last three are also ripe for revival—that is, if revival proves a practicable expedient. Somehow the Zeitgeist, as it stalks along, brushes the sparkling bloom off operas just as it does off pastel drawings; and even an *opera buffa* like Mozart's Don Juan, which turns out to be not of an age but for all time (meaning a few hundred years or so), survives as a repertory opera, to be heard once a year or so, instead of being boomed into a furorious run of five hundred nights.

And Don Juan is a very different affair from Madame Angot. I wish I had some music type at my disposal to shew exactly what Lecocq would have made out of *Là ci darem la mano*. To begin with, he would have simply composed the first line and the fourth, and then repeated them without altering a note. In the sixties and seventies nobody minded this: Offenbach is full of it; and Sir Arthur Sullivan was not ashamed to give us a most flagrant example of it in the sailors' chorus which opens H.M.S. Pinafore. It not only saved the composer the trouble of composing: it was positively popular; for it made the tunes easier to learn. Besides, I need hardly say that there are all sorts of precedents, from The Vicar of Bray to the *finale* of Beethoven's choral symphony, to countenance it. Still, there is a difference between the repetition of a phrase which is worth repeating and one which is not; and the song in which the market-woman describes the career of Madame Angot in the first act of Lecocq's opera may be taken as a convincing sample of a series of repetitions of phrases which are not worth hearing once, much less twice. They delighted 1873; but I am happy to say that on last Saturday 1893 saw through their flimsiness at once, and would have damned the whole opera as *vieux jeu* if the rest of it had been no better.

Probably Wagner has a good deal to do with this advance; for even our comic opera composers have become so accustomed by him to associate unprecedented persistence in repetition with apparently inexhaustible variation and development, that they are now too sensible of the absurd woodenness of the repetitions of Offenbach and Lecocq to resort to them so impudently. Anyhow, it was clear on Saturday night that the old quadrille padding, in spite of its mechanical vivacity, will no longer pass muster, even in an *opéra bouffe*, as lyric or dramatic music. As to the conspirators' chorus, its original success seems to have vaccinated the English nation against a recurrence of the epidemic; for it was not even encored.

And we nourish our orchestral accompaniments so much better nowadays that the score sounded a little thin; although that was partly due to the fact that Mr Wyndham, who, as frequenters of his theatre know, is not a judge of a band, has made no such orchestral provision as would be a matter of course at the Lyric or Savoy. Still, the band did well enough to shew that we now expect more substance and color in accompaniments, and will not be put off with mere movement and froth.

In other respects the opera stood the test of revival very well. The mounting was, for a West End theatre, decidedly modest, the whimsicalities of the *incroyable* period being cheaply and uninventively represented. The choristers sang but little: they for the most part bawled, screamed, and shouted in a manner that would have been trying in a large theatre, and was intolerable in the Criterion. The men were especially objectionable; and I implore Mr Wyndham to send them all for a week to a respectable cathedral, to learn how to make some passably civilized sort of noise. The success of the performance was due altogether to the principals. Everything depends in Madame Angot on Clairette and Lange; and Miss Decima Moore took unsparing trouble with Clairette, and brought off the first act triumphantly, though in the third her attempt at the gay vulgarity and braggart combativeness of the daughter of the market was rather forced, and, as far as it was successful, hopelessly British.

Miss Amy Augarde, as Lange, was the only one who seemed to breathe the national and historical atmosphere burlesqued in the piece. She took her part in thorough artistic earnest, and brought down the curtain at the end of the second act amid the most solid applause of the evening; although the famous waltz *finale* was robbed of much of its illusion, not only by want of imaginative inscenation, but by the execrably rough singing of Augereau's hussars behind the scenes, and the ridiculous effect of their trumpet being sounded in the orchestra instead of in its proper place. Miss Augarde was perhaps more tragic and dignified than Lange is meant to be; but she was quite successful in imposing her reading on the part.

Mr Courtice Pounds was a neutral sort of Ange Pitou, bringing out neither the humor nor the *naïveté* of the part; but he was at least inoffensive; and his singing, thanks to a liberal mixture of head voice, was rather pretty. Mr Blakely amused himself and us by a sufficiently outrageous Louchard; and Mr Sydney

Valentine made a courageous operatic essay as Larivau-dière. Pomponnet was impersonated by an eminent composer,* who is too much of a musician to be surprised at my confessing that I thought him the very worst Pomponnet I ever heard. The last act was liberally cut, and diversified by a grotesque quadrille and a skirt dance which, like most skirt dances, was not a dance at all.

SHALL SIR AUGUSTUS HAVE A TESTIMONIAL?

The World, 2 August 1893

I have received a circular letter, which I give here in full, although some of my readers will have already seen it elsewhere. Its reappearance in this column may be the means of adding a few more donations to the one which it announces.

PROPOSED TESTIMONIAL TO SIR AUGUSTUS HARRIS

To the Editor

Sir,—As a very old musician, and one that admires talent, energy, and perseverance, I have watched with keen interest the extraordinary success which has attended the efforts of Sir Augustus Harris to establish in this country an opera worthy of the name, and in accordance with the best traditions of its history. This, in my own opinion, deserves some sort of public recognition, and I have therefore ventured to suggest that all lovers of high-class music, and all admirers of

*Charles Davenport, pianist and composer of numerous popular songs.

managerial enterprise, should be invited to subscribe towards an appropriate souvenir which shall serve as a testimonial to the Impresario of our Royal Opera House, who, for the reasons just stated, I cannot but regard as a benefactor to his country.

Except for the unceasing exertions of Sir Augustus Harris, and his persistent determination to revive our Covent Garden Opera at any personal cost or sacrifice, that time-honored institution would have long since died a natural death. Indeed, at one period it gave sufficient promise of becoming for ever extinct, in spite of the repeated attempts of La Porte, Lumley, E. T. Smith, Gye, and Mapleson to save it from this doom. At last people began to believe that the failures were due not so much to want of managerial enterprise as to want of operatic attractions, and it was said that the "palmy days" of opera—which I myself so well remember—were completely over, never to be revived again. This was, however, by no means the view taken by the present Manager of Covent Garden. In his own estimation, there were as many good fish in the operatic sea as were ever produced out of it. So Sir Augustus Harris betook himself to the Continent, and ransacked every leading opera house there, with the result that he returned triumphant with a company which, regarded as a whole, I have no hesitation in pronouncing the completest and most brilliant that has ever yet appeared upon the boards of Covent Garden during her Majesty's reign.

It is in view of these circumstances that I have proposed to open the fund for the souvenir already referred to, under the title of "The Operatic Testimonial Fund," and I shall be pleased to head the list of subscribers to it by a donation of ten guineas. Should the readers of this letter be disposed to follow my example in any way, their contributions, whether in the form of cheques or otherwise, will be received by the National

Bank, Oxford-street branch, if sent on behalf of "The Operatic Testimonial Fund."—I am, Sir, yours, &c.

(Signed) HENRY RUSSELL.

18 Howley Place, Maida Vale, July 26th, 1893.

Now I have no objection on general grounds to a testimonial to Sir Augustus, though I would not, if I were Mr Russell, call it an "operatic" testimonial. Let it by all means be a genuine, enthusiastic, munificently subscribed and influentially patronized tribute; and since Sir Augustus knows what is due to himself, let us not insult him with anything meaner than a life-size statue of solid gold, with suitable quotations from the opera criticisms in the Sunday Times on the four sides of the pedestal. And let Mr Henry Russell, as the leader of the enterprise, inaugurate the monument by once more singing I am not mad; by heavens! I am not mad.

But it would be a mistake, as well as a very left-handed compliment, to attribute to our illustrious *impresario* any design to revive the palmy days. Mr Russell was born more than forty years before I was, and so belongs to a younger period of the world's history. I am therefore to all intents and purposes his senior; and I can assure him, as one who remembers the end of the palmy days, and whose youth was blighted by their accursed traditions, that they deserved their fate, and are not only dead, but—I use the word in the profoundest serious sense—damned. If you discuss them with one of their veteran admirers, you will find that all the triumphs which his memory fondles are not feats of management, but strokes of genius by individual artists. Indeed, so far is he from being able to conceive an operatic performance as an artistic whole, that he will describe the most absurd *contretemps* and the most disastrous shortcomings in the stage management, the band, chorus, dresses and scenery, as excellent jokes.

My readers will remember the examples of this which I was able to give from Santley's Student and Singer, culminating in his playing Don Giovanni for the first time after one rehearsal, at which the tenor (Mario) did not turn up until it was half over. As to the mutilations, the spurious scorings, the "additional accompaniments," and the dozen other violations of artistic good faith which were played off on palmy nights as a matter of course, you will find the average veteran either unconscious of them or utterly unconcerned about them. He is content to remember Ambrogetti as "the Don" (an almost centenarian reminiscence), Piccolomini as Zerlina, Taglioni as La Sylphide, Malibran as Amina, Grisi and Rubini, Tamburini and Lablache in the Puritani quartet; and so on up to Titiens and Giuglini, and those post-Giuglinian days when "the mantle of Mario" was tried on every trooper, porter, or ice-barrow man who could bawl a high C, until at last the jeremiads of Berlioz and Wagner were fulfilled, and palmy Italian opera, which had been corrupt even in its prime, openly putrified and had to be embalmed, in which condition its mummy still draws audiences in the United States and other back-eddies of civilization.

Mr Russell, under the impression that he is paying Sir Augustus a compliment, accuses him of having tried to play the resurrection-man. I believe this to be unjust. I admit that there are certain scattered materials for Mr Russell's case—tentative Favoritas, Lucias, and Trovatores (palmy style, with Signor Rawner as Manrico), which had a somewhat retrograde air; but they cannot outweigh the broad fact that the Italian operas which were the staple of the old repertory are the mere stopgaps and makeshifts of the new. If the testimonial is to be given for palminess, then let it be transferred to Colonel

Mapleson, whose gallant attempt to revive the old repertory in competition with Sir Augustus a few years ago utterly failed. And the failure was so certain from the first, that for the sake of old times, I refrained from attending a single performance, although I have no doubt that I could have had three or four rows of stalls any night for the asking. No, Covent Garden has its defects, as I have had occasionally to remark; but such as it is, it has been created by Sir Augustus, and is no mere revival of the palmy imposture which still takes in Mr Russell.

Is Sir Augustus then, as Mr Russell says, "a benefactor to his country"? The standard definition of a national benefactor is "the man who causes two blades of grass to grow where one grew before." Now Sir Augustus, on the contrary, has caused one opera house to keep open where two kept open before. But I do not think he ought to be disqualified on so highly technical a point. He established an opera where, for the moment, there was no opera at all; and if this was not a benefaction I do not know what is.

Therefore, instead of churlishly asking why he should have a testimonial, let us rather ask why he should not have one, and why Mr D'Oyly Carte should not have one, and why Signor Lago should not have one, and why, above all, I should not have one? Signor Lago discovered Giulia Ravogli and Ancona, Orfeo and Cavalleria; and although Sir Augustus is no doubt right in preferring to take his own discoveries ready-made, still, the original discoverer is useful in his little way too, and should not be overlooked. Mr D'Oyly Carte founded a new school of English comic opera; raised operatic inscenation to the rank of a fine art; and finally built a new English Opera House, and made a magnificent effort to do for English grand opera what he had done for comic opera, with the result that Sir Augustus is now conducting a music hall on the ruins of the enterprise.

As to my own claims, modesty forbids me to ask whose pen has done more to revive public interest in dramatic music during the past five or six years than mine. It is true that I have done it because I have been paid to do it; but even Sir Augustus does not play the public benefactor for nothing. A man must live. Take the case of August Manns, whose enormous services to music in England do not need the penetrating eye of an octogenarian to discover them: even he does not scorn to accept his bread-and-butter. If there is any spare cash left in the country when the Harris testimonial is fully subscribed, some little token—say a cheap conducting stick—might be offered to the untitled Augustus of Sydenham.

But now that I think of it, such a proceeding might be construed as a slight to the conducting staff at Covent Garden. And we must not thoughtlessly appear to undervalue what Sir Augustus has done for us in placing his orchestra in the hands of three such *chefs* as Mancinelli, Bevignani, and Randegger. Although they are so devoted to the traditions of the house that Sir Augustus has to send to Germany for help whenever the Nibelungen dramas are performed, yet Mancinelli can conduct Die Meistersinger and Bevignani Tannhäuser in a way that I am sure I for one can never forget. Why not give them testimonials? The stage manager, too— he who staged Gluck's Orfeo and Das Rheingold—that "damned pantomime," as somebody* is said to have called it—why should not something be done for him? But I am opening up too vast a field. There are so many public benefactors about.

I should be less than candid on the subject, however, if I were to take the proposal quite uncritically. I do not

*Sir Augustus Harris.

[953]

see how it is possible for an *impresario* to maintain Covent Garden in such a fashion as to deserve a testimonial as a public benefactor. As I have often pointed out, fashionable grand opera does not pay its own expenses in London any more than it does in Paris or Berlin. A subvention is necessary; and if the State does not provide it, a body of private guarantors must. In England there are so many irrational people who think the National Gallery and the British Museum virtuous and Opera vicious (because it takes place in a theatre), that the State leaves Covent Garden to a knot of rich people for whom Opera is not a form of art but simply an item of fashion. These people pay the piper; and they naturally expect to call the tune.

Now suppose an artist or a clique of artists get at the guarantors behind the *impresario's* back, they can make it very difficult for him to do anything that they disapprove of, whether it be in the public interest or not. To such means of resistance to the manager must be added the already enormous powers possessed by leading artists in virtue of their personal monopoly of voice and talent. The *impresario's* one defence is his own monopoly of the power of making London reputations. To preserve this monopoly, and at the same time to provide for the danger always latent in the fact that London will support one guaranteed Opera handsomely, but not two, must strain all his commercial genius to suppress competition; and this means not only taking every theatre large enough to be used as a rival house, but engaging several superfluous artists for the sole purpose of forestalling their possible engagement by someone else, the result being, of course, to waste their talents most frightfully.

Finally, he must by hook or crook, by conciliation or intimidation, gag independent criticism, because his greatest need is prestige, and this the press can mar if it chooses. His prestige is his life-blood: it convinces meddling guarantors and mutinous artists that he is the only possible man to run the Italian Opera; and it paralyzes his competitors, making their attempts to raise a rival guarantee unavailing, and stamping them from the outset as second-rate. And this prestige, which is at once his sword and shield, propagates itself by all the operations which he undertakes for its sake. The theatres leased and kept closed, or sublet on conditions which bar opera; the magnificent list of artists engaged apparently out of an insatiable artistic enthusiasm which takes no account of salaries; even the running of two sets of performances to prevent the superfluous artists from eating their heads off: all these master moves, with the huge turnover of money they involve, heap prestige on prestige, until at last the public gets dazzled, and ancient men call for testimonials to the national benefactor.

Then there is only one enemy left; and that is the unhypnotizable critic who, having his own prestige to look after, persists in explaining the situation to the public and criticizing the performances for just what they are worth, and no more. And such critics are scarce, not because of their Roman virtue, but because they must have an eye for the economics of the situation; and a musical critic who is a bit of an economist as well is a very rare bird.

Under these circumstances I do not see how the public services of Sir Augustus as *impresario* can run to a testimonial. However high-mindedly and ably he may have struggled to do his best within the limits of his very narrow freedom of action, or however Napoleonically he may have faced and fought the opposing economic forces, the fact remains that Covent Garden, with all its boasted resources, could not put the four Nibelung dramas on the stage last year except by the pure showman's expedient of sending for a German company, orchestra, conductor and all.

I do not blame Sir Augustus for this: I pointed out again and again (before the event as well as after) that the real difficulty was the incorrigible *fainéantise* of the De Reszkes, with their perpetual schoolboy Faust and Mephistopheles, Roméo and Frère Laurent, and their determination to make Covent Garden a mere special edition of the Paris Grand Opéra. Sir Augustus did contrive to get one triumph out of Jean de Reszke and Lassalle—Die Meistersinger. But from the moment when Jean allowed Alvary to take Siegfried from him, and Edouard left Wotan to Grengg (I hope I have the name correctly), there was an end of all possibility of a testimonial for Covent Garden.

Give me one performance of Die Walküre or Siegfried by the De Reszkes, Calvé, and Giulia Ravogli, with the orchestral work done by the regular band of the house, and a competent conductor of the calibre of Richter or Faccio in permanent command, and then Mr Russell may apply again. At present I am not at home.

Let me point out, however, that there may be an opening on the dramatic side, as to which I, of course, cannot speak. Sir Augustus is famous for his pantomimes and popular dramas, in producing which he is unhampered by guarantors or tenors, and can face competition without misgiving. My duties as musical critic make me a stranger to his work in this department. There, where his qualities have fuller scope, no doubt they take effect in the high artistic temper and wholesome moral atmosphere of his productions. If so, perhaps my friend William Archer will give Mr Russell's project his blessing and his subscription.

CULTURE FOR THE PROVINCES

The World, 9 August 1893

A letter which is quite a masterpiece of inconsiderateness has come to me on the subject of the Norwich Festival and my late remarks thereon. Those remarks were precisely accurate; were based on the prospectus issued to the public by the committee along with the usual forms of application for seats; and were, in my opinion, of first-rate importance. I therefore jump at the opportunity of rubbing them in. My correspondent, on the strength of certain irrelevant facts of which I was perfectly well aware and which I never contradicted, offers me grievous incivilities, such as that I am an idle babbler, steeped in manifest ignorance and entire and absurd error, and that I have "little in common" with the charities of Norwich.

Now if this gentleman were a hospital governor to whom a concert is nothing but a dodge for raising the wind of charity, I should pass his assault over indulgently. But he is a musical critic, and a young one—exactly, that is, the sort of person whose vigorous support I should have for my efforts to knock into the provincial mind the idea that Music is worth cultivating for its own sake, and that the man who is brought up in a town where there are exchanges and chambers of commerce, but no orchestra and no opera, will never be a cultivated citizen of the world, though he were rich as Crœsus. I believe the provincials feel this themselves; for they buy innumerable books about Art, and pore reverentially over my articles, heedless of the fact that you may read all the writers on Art from Ruskin and Wagner downwards until you know their opinions by heart and are aglow (as you imagine) with their enthusiasms, yet at the end you will not be able to distinguish a Teniers from a Burne-Jones without looking at your catalog, or a Beethoven symphony from a selection from the Mikado without looking at your program.

How then can a movement for the culture of the provinces best be opened on the side of Music? Obviously, to my mind, by beginning with the Festival, which is our leading musical institution, and making a vigorous protest against its present footing of a mere pretext for sending round the hat for the local hospitals under cover of my correspondent's eloquent flummeries about "an innocent cause," "splendid usefulness," "a city famous for its charity," and so forth. Let me make the issue clear. Norwich has to provide for a certain number of accidents and illnesses occurring to people who are too poor to pay for proper treatment for themselves, but whose labor Norwich is not in a position to do without. This provision, which is now regarded by sensible people as part of the working expenses of our civilization, can be met either by the private subscriptions of those who have money to spare, or by hospitals' rate, or, of course, by a combination of the two. The Norwich people can settle the method among themselves: all I need insist on here is that the expense has to be met somehow, willy-nilly, whether the inhabitants are the most generous or the stingiest in England.

Now any adventitious aid will relieve the people who pay for the hospitals, whether they are subscribers or ratepayers. Accordingly, such adventitious aid is always welcome. For instance, there is the bazaar, where the moral law is suspended for a day in the name of charity, and gambling, overcharging, and sale of innocent favors by the ladies are tolerated and encouraged. You have also the sermon on Hospital Sunday, and the street collection on Hospital Saturday. Now it happens that in some cathedrals the simple, old-fashioned charity sermon, in which the plate started its round with a few decoy banknotes and sovereigns on it, developed in the course of time into an annual oratorio performance, which later on developed into the Festival as we know it. The charitable institution thus became a musical institution; and yet charity, as represented by subscribers and ratepayers on the alert for a grant in aid of hospital expenses, continued to pocket the proceeds as a matter of course.

I now, as a musical critic, raise a protest against this, on the plain ground that as Music has earned the money it should go to her own support, and that a good orchestra is every whit as important to a town as a good hospital. Even a Philistine will admit that the absence of high-class recreation means a resort to low-class recreation, which runs up a heavy police bill and hospitals bill. I therefore denounced, and do here again denounce, the proposal to devote the proceeds of the surplus from the Norwich Festival to the Norwich hospitals, as a device on the part of the general committee to lighten the burden of their charities at the expense of the starving Art of Music and of the culture of the townsfolk.

If I, or anyone with the interests of Music at heart, had been upon that general committee, an attempt would have been made to have the surplus (if any) devoted to the bringing down to Norwich of Richter and his band for a few concerts, or of Jean de Reszke, Lassalle, and the rest, for a performance of Die Meistersinger, or for such other demonstration of the best that can be done in music as the money might run to. But no: the musicians are relegated to the managing committee, which has to look after all the work connected with the performance, but has no voice in the disposition of the proceeds—a vital distinction which my irate correspondent has overlooked to the extent of actually abusing me heartily for not overlooking it.

If a vigorous agitation on these lines were made by the critics and musicians at every Festival, it would very soon produce practical results; and in the end it is not inconceivable that all the Festivals might be rescued from the clutches of the hospital governors, and begin mightily to nourish and propagate artistic life in this, at present, barren and boorish country. I am well pleased to find that my sally has elicited a vehement protest on the ground that "since The World is perhaps the most widely-read newspaper in the Eastern Counties, a great deal of harm may be inflicted upon an innocent cause." When that sort of thing begins, I feel that I am making way.

Besides, the "innocent cause"—the hospitals—may surely be left to those charitable instincts which the author of the protest so enthusiastically extols; wheras the cause of music, which appears to me quite as innocent as the other, must depend on what it can earn. Why it should be saddled with more than its share of the cost of the hospitals does not appear in the letter of my correspondent, who on thinking the matter over a little further will, I hope, see the advisability of backing his own side in this matter, and leaving the hospital governors to take care of their pockets for themselves.

ANALYTIC CRITICISM
The World, 16 August 1893

[U] I have just been reading Mr Charles Willeby's Masters of Contemporary Music, containing accounts of Sir Arthur Sullivan, Dr Mackenzie, Mr Cowen, Dr Parry and Professor Stanford—accounts which have the fulness and detail of good biographical notices with the freshness and vividness of good interviews. There is a

strange and sad side to the book too; for who could have
supposed that Dr Mackenzie, Dr Parry, and Professor
Stanford were in their boyhood really fond of music? I
think of their Jasons and Jubals, their Jobs and Judiths,
their mixolydian angels and experiments in "the Eolian
mode transposed," and I ask myself where has that love
gone to? The answer is to be found between the lines on
Mr Willeby's pages. There I discover that these
gentlemen, having been born with a natural power of
composition, mistrusted themselves too much to cultivate it, and went to the schools to learn some other
musical occupation, which was duly imparted to them
by learned professors who, being notoriously incapable
of even a respectable improvisation on the accordion,
had kindly undertaken to instruct all and sundry in the
ways of Beethoven and Bach. I wonder what sort of
critic I should have been had I spent my apprenticeship
in "analyzing" the grammar of Burney, Lord Mount
Edgcumbe, and Chorley* and writing all my essays in
the subjunctive mood transposed.

This unhappy country would be as prolific of musical
as of literary composers if it were not for our schools of
music, where they seize the young musician, turn his
attention forcibly away from the artistic element in his
art, and make him morbidly conscious of its mechanical
conditions, especially the obsolete ones, until he at last
becomes, not a composer, but an adept in a horribly dull
sort of chess played with lines and dots, each player
having different notions of what the right rules are, and
playing his game so as to flourish his views under the
noses of those who differ from him. Then he offers his

*Charles Burney (1726–1814) was a musician and author of
a History of Music (1776–89). Henry Fothergill Chorley (1808–
72) was musical critic of The Athenaeum from 1830 to 1868.
He published several volumes of musical memoirs, 1841–62.

insufferable gambits to the public as music, and is outraged because I criticize it as music and not as chess. Only the other day somebody proposed a great national protest against my criticism of Job because it was "not analytic." I do not object to the national protest: an advertisement is always welcome. But I will at once admit, in justice to Dr Parry, that Job will be found, on analysis, to consist of notes, chords, suspensions, cadences, &c., just as the works of the great masters do. *Ergo*, Dr Parry is a great master. Let nobody say, after this, that I am not capable of "analytic criticism."

The reason I avoid it as a rule is simply that it is too brutal for me. It takes for granted that a composer cannot compose, and proceeds politely to make the best of him on that heartless hypothesis. I cannot bring myself to despair of a fellow creature like that. It seems to me that if the world sturdily refused to analyze the academic oratorio or cantata, if the stalls yawned in its face and the gallery threw brickbats at it, if it could once be borne in on the composer's mind that nobody cares two straws for its irrelevant ingenuities, then he might creep off disillusioned to the top of the nearest hill, and there, after solemnly devoting Albrechtsberger and Marpurg and Cherubini and all the other pedants to dusty oblivion, write a tune like *Bei Männern, welche Liebe fühlen*,* or the theme of the Choral Fantasia,† and come back a real composer, albeit unanalyzable. Mr Willeby does not share my weakness. He takes one of our champion academic composers remorselessly at his own word, and lets him have it in the following inhuman fashion:

"It is by his scholarship that he achieves most. Double

*In Mozart's Die Zauberflöte.
†Beethoven's Fantasia in C minor for piano, chorus and orchestra, Op. 80.

counterpoint and fugue are to him but child's play. There is no trace of effort about those gigantic twelve-part choruses of the De Profundis. His mind is as much that of the mathematician as of the musician. It is impossible to get away from his tremendous learning; and it is no exaggeration to say that there are times when the process of analysis does more to reveal the value of his work than mere performance. And he is seldom, if ever, to be caught tripping. Admire his work as one will and must, admiration does not do it full justice. It is essentially music to be *esteemed*—that is the only word that expresses what I mean. One cannot help feeling that the correct thing to do with his scores is to have them bound in morocco and placed in one's library in some such position and in some such company as one would place Buckle's History of Civilization or Hallam's Middle Ages."

There is something Satanic about all this. Most of the phrases—"mind of the mathematician," "impossible to get away from his learning," "mere performance" (a bitter word), "music to be *esteemed*," "Hallam and Buckle" (not Shelley and Goethe, observe)—are ferocious; but they shew how these scores, which are so interesting in the library—that is, the room in which *silence* is the first rule of conduct—provoke, even from keen amateurs at the academic game, criticisms which, when they also are analyzed, are far more damning than the mild remonstrances which I occasionally venture upon as an avowed enemy of the whole academic system. The only composers mentioned in Mr Willeby's book who have escaped the pit of professordom are Sir Arthur Sullivan and Mr Cowen, both of whom, as popular composers of drawing room ballads, were forced early to draw a sharp distinction between sounds that human beings may conceivably want to hear and transpositions of the Eolian mode. Mr Willeby has much more to say about them than about the others, obviously because they had a much richer artistic experience to communicate to him, and much more freedom of self-expression in communicating it. One consequence of which is that Mr Willeby has come to know them so well that they will find it hard to live up to the handsomest things he has said of them. However, no reasonable person will be displeased by this; and I will now slip away from the subject by mentioning that Mr Cowen is engaged by Mr Farley Sinkins to conduct the season of Promenade Concerts at Covent Garden, a function once discharged by Sir Arthur Sullivan. These concerts, as far as my experience of them goes, can do very important musical work, and are never more popular than when they are doing it. The engagement of Mr Cowen is a sort of guarantee that they will be turned to the best account this year; and I wish them all possible success accordingly.[U]

BEETHOVEN AND POPPING CORKS
The World, 23 August 1893

Passing through town from Switzerland to some deserted corner of England in which to lie down and recover from a holiday,* I find promenade concerts in full swing at Covent Garden. It is the custom to disparage promenade concerts as involving "Beethoven to an accompaniment of popping corks." That is the epigrammatic formula which crops up autumn after autumn. No doubt in weather like this the whole life of London

---

* Shaw had attended the International Socialist Conference at Zurich in early August. Shortly after his return he joined Beatrice and Sidney Webb in Monmouth.

may be said to proceed to an accompaniment of cork popping; but one should not, in dealing with the effect of this small artillery on particular incidents, quite overlook the question of how far off the corks are. As a matter of fact a great artist can obtain as complete a silence at Covent Garden on a "classical night" as in St James's Hall; and the shilling public can watch the performance much more closely, since it can get right up to the platform instead of having to observe the pianist's fingers or "the marvelous fiddle bow" from afar across a vast space of half-guinea and five-shilling stalls.

The facility with which you can change your place, stroll about, hold a conversation, avoid a tedious item in the program, have a cork popped on your own account, or go to a corridor window for a draught of such fresh air as may be available in Bow-street, are points of superiority secured to the promenader by that great advantage, a uniform price. For though you can get any sort of privilege of place, from a two-guinea box to an eighteenpenny amphitheatre stall, still, the general freedom of circulation round the orchestra and from the gallery to the floor practically gives the shilling the run of the house. Further, the arrangements admit of two concerts every evening. From a quarter to eight til about half-past nine you get an overture, a concerto, a symphony, and a couple of songs, just as at any first-rate orchestral concert. For the rest of the time you have your "grand selections" and vocal waltzes and ballads, and so on—in short, the promenade concert in the ordinary sense.

The orchestra, except perhaps whilst a provincial festival is in progress, is always potentially as good as any in the world. Consequently it only needs the engagement of a conductor of high standing and *virtuosos* of the first rank to make the promenade season as important artistically as that of the Philharmonic, the

Richter, the London Symphony, or the Crystal Palace Saturday concerts. It is, of course, equally easy, by engaging a seaside bandmaster whose highest flight is a comfortable jaunt through "the world-renowned masterpiece, Mozart's Jupiter Symphony," to reduce promenade concerts to the artistic insignificance of an entertainment at a Hall-by-the-Sea.

There have been seasons when I have never dreamt of the promenade concerts as concerning me more closely than the street pianos (on which, nevertheless, as on everything else that is a part of our musical life, I keep an observant ear). And there have been seasons which have marked important stages in the development of popular taste, on the one hand, and of the conquest of London by notable artists on the other.

I am sorry to say that I do not know which of these two policies pays the *entrepreneur* best. The high art policy is never persevered in, and yet never finally abandoned. After one or two first-rate years, the rule appears to be three or four second-rate years, after which rapid decay sets in until another first-rate year or so is administered by way of tonic. This year, fortunately, there can be no doubt that the turn of the tonic has come round. Mr Farley Sinkins has done the very handsomest thing in his power by engaging Ysaÿe, who divides with Sarasate the position of greatest living violinist, and Slivinski, who, among pianists of the Leschetitzky school, is second only to Paderewski, and who, within a certain range of very brilliant and popular qualities, is second to none.

The other day, glancing through the last number of The Meister, I came across the following passage from one of the articles written by Wagner from Paris in 1841, about a concert given by Liszt, under the conductorship of Berlioz, to raise funds for a memorial to Beethoven:

"The Parisian public demands from Liszt at all costs wonders and foolish tricks: he gives it what it wants, lets himself be carried away at its hands—actually plays, in a concert for Beethoven's memorial, a fantasia on Robert the Devil! This happened, however, against his will. The program consisted solely of Beethoven's compositions. Nevertheless, the fatal public demanded with a voice of thunder Liszt's *tour de force par excellence*, that Fantaisie. For the gifted man there was no help. With words hastily extorted from his chagrin, '*Je suis le serviteur du public: cela va sans dire*,' he sat down to the piano, and played with crashing brilliancy the favored piece. Thus avenges itself each crime on earth. One day in heaven, before the assembled angel public, will Liszt have to perform that fantasia on the devil."

Now, as it happens, I never heard that fantasia performed until, not very long ago, Slivinski revived it as a sample of his extraordinary powers in that sort of "transcendent" execution. And nobody seemed particularly amazed by it, although not long before Paderewski had thrown his audience into ecstasies by a performance of Liszt's transcription of Schubert's Erl King, of which, as it happened, he made a laughable mess through a slip of his hand or memory at a critical moment. As far as this shews that everybody knows and delights in The Erl King, wheras only a few obsolete survivors from the Meyerbeerian age know Robert the Devil by heart, or care two straws about its *valse infernale*, it is an incident to rejoice in; but it bore hardly on Slivinski, who should try his hand on the Don Juan fantasia, and find whether he cannot get the same intoxicating effect as Paderewski did out of its final apotheosis of *Finch' han dal vino*.

I heard Slivinski, on Tuesday last week, play Tchaikovsky's concerto, which was last heard here at the Crystal Palace, where Mr Lamond played it with a rough Cyclopean force and somewhat smoky fire, which by no means anticipated the version given by the refined strength and feathery swiftness of Slivinski. He had some trouble in the last movement to avoid being baulked by Mr Cowen, who is seldom equal to the occasion when a movement has to be saved by pure *entrain,* and who was himself probably baulked by his consciousness of the artificiality with which the concerto is pieced together from independent and discontinuous conceits.

On Wednesday Ysaÿe played Bruch's Scotch Fantasia, a work so easily within his power that he played it better than one would have supposed it capable of being played, and set a rather diffident audience cheering at the end. Decidedly, if Ysaÿe only perseveres in playing splendidly to us for twentyfive years more or so, it will dawn on us at last that he is one of the greatest of living artists; and then he may play how he pleases until he turns ninety without the risk of ever hearing a word of disparagement or faint praise.

The orchestra is on its good behavior with Mr Cowen. It reflects his qualities, and, with the help of an occasional spur from Slivinski and Ysaÿe, covers some of his faults. To me it sounded wonderfully distinguished; but after a fortnight of Swiss art, musical and pictorial, anything would have produced that impression on me; so I had better reserve my opinion until I have recovered my critical balance. By the bye, since I have mentioned pictorial and musical art together, may I appeal to Madame Belle Cole not to sing that old-fashioned piece of secondhand Rossini about Judith (not Dr Parry's, but Concone's) in a dress evidently designed—very successfully—by the colorists of the Glasgow school? The anachronism is too violent.

If anyone is curious about the poem (by Count Sporck) of Cyrill Kistler's Wagnerian music-drama Kunihild, which we shall hear some of these days, I suppose, he can now procure for eighteenpence an English metrical translation by Mr Ashton Ellis. I may also remind Wagnerians that by making a dash for Munich at once on seeing this, they may arrive in time for some of the Wagner performances there, though some of the Ring nights will have already passed before the day of publication.

SAMSON ET DALILA
The World, 4 October 1893

I cannot imagine why the Paris Grand Opéra should fascinate English *impresarios* as it does. Here is Mr Farley Sinkins putting himself out of his way and charging double prices to produce a concert recital of Samson et Dalila. Who wants to hear Samson et Dalila? I respectfully suggest, Nobody. In Paris that is not a reason for not producing it, because Saint-Saëns is an illustrious French composer, and the Opéra a national institution; consequently, Saint-Saëns must occasionally compose an opera, and the director produce it, for the satisfaction of the taxpayers. In the same way, we produce specially composed oratorios at our English festivals. We cannot sit them out without wishing we had never been born; but we do sit them out for all that; and though the English school does not immediately become famous over the earth, at least Messrs Novello sell a great many copies of the new work to provincial choral societies.

Now I am strongly of opinion that each nation should bear its own burden in this department of life. We do not ask the Parisians to share the weight of Job with us; then let them not foist on to us the load of Samson. However, on reflection, this is hardly reasonable; for it is our English Mr Sinkins who has insisted on our listening to Samson; whilst the composer and the tenor, representing the French nation, have done their best to save us by bolting at the last moment. The story of their flight; of Mr Sinkins's diplomatic masterstroke of sending the soprano to win them back; and of the fugitives rising to the height of the occasion by capturing the soprano, has already been told, though not explained. The sequel, shewing how Mr Bernard Lane came to the rescue by taking the part of Samson, is, I suppose, for me to tell; but I propose to shirk that duty, out of regard for Mr Lane's feelings.

Samson with the part of Samson read at sight is perhaps better than Samson with the part of Samson left out: anyhow Mr Lane thought so; and no doubt in acting on that opinion he did his best under the circumstances. Miss Edith Miller, who undertook Dalila at equally short notice, was less at a disadvantage. Lyrical expression, to a musician, is much more obvious at first than dramatic expression, which can be planned only by careful study; and as Dalila's music is much more lyrical than Samson's, not to mention the fact that the most important number in it is already hackneyed by concert use, Miss Miller was able to make the most of her opportunity and to come off handsomely, all things considered.

The other parts, in the hands of Messrs Oudin, Barlow, Magrath, and Gawthrop, would no doubt have been well done if they had possessed any artistic substance for these gentlemen to bite on, so to speak. But the impossible Meyerbeerian Abimelech, with his brusque measures and his grim orchestral clinkings and whistlings, could have come from no place in the world but Paris, where they still regard Meyerbeer as a sort of musical Michael Angelo, and gravely offer to the wondering world commonplace imitations of the petty monstrosities and abortions of Le Prophète as sublime *hardiesses*, and pages of history read by flashes of lightning. No doubt Saint-Saëns had to copy Meyerbeer, just as poor Meyerbeer had to copy himself from the day when he made a speciality of religious fanaticism in Les Huguenots.

After the Huguenots and Catholics came the Anabaptists; and now, the Philistines and the Israelites being in question, we have Abimelech clinking and whistling as aforesaid; Samson calling his sect to arms to a trumpet motive in the best style of Raoul de Nangis at the ball given by Marguerite de Valois; stage rushes of the two factions at each other's throats, with every eye, aflame with bigotry, flashing on the conductor; and the inevitable love duet, in which the tenor is torn by the conflicting calls of passion and party in a key with several flats in it. I did not wait for the third act of Samson; but I assume that the hero attempted to bring the house down by a drinking song before resorting to the pillars.

If Saint-Saëns were to be commissioned to write a new "historical opera" entitled Ulster, we should have the zealous Protestants of that region devoting the Pope to perdition in a Rataplan chorus, and confining themselves to ascetic accompaniments of double bass and piccolo; whilst their opponents would pay the same compliment to King William of glorious, pious, and immortal memory, in crisp waltzes and galops, whipped along into movements of popular fury by flicks on the side-drum, *strettos*, sham *fugatos*, and *pas redoublés*, with a grand climax of all the national airs of Ireland worked in double counterpoint with suitable extracts from the Church music of the rivals' creeds, played simultaneously on several military bands and a pair of organs. This is the sort of thing a French composer dreams of as the summit of operatic achievement. I feel that my own view of it cuts off my artistic sympathy with Paris at the musical main. But I cannot help that. It is not good sense to expect me to sacrifice my reputation as a serious critic for the sake of such tinpot stage history. Besides, I long ago gave up Paris as impossible from the artistic point of view. London I do not so much mind.

Your average Londoner is, no doubt, as void of feeling for the fine arts as a man can be without collapsing bodily; but then he is not ashamed of his condition. On the contrary, he is rather proud of it, and never feels obliged to pretend that he is an artist to the tips of his fingers. His pretences are confined to piety and politics, in both of which he is an unspeakable impostor. It is your Parisian who concentrates his ignorance and hypocrisy, not on politics and religion, but on art. He believes that Europe expects him to be, before every-thing, artistic. In this unwholesome state of self-con-ciousness he demands statues and pictures and operas in all directions, long before any appetite for beauty has set his eyes or ears aching; so that he at once becomes the prey of pedants who undertake to supply him with classical works, and swaggerers who set up in the romantic department. Hence, as the Parisian, like other people, likes to enjoy himself, and as pure pedantry is tedious and pure swaggering tiresome, what Paris chiefly loves is a genius who can make the classic voluptuous and the romantic amusing.

And so, though you cannot walk through Paris without coming at every corner upon some fountain or trophy or monument for which the only possible remedy is dynamite, you can always count upon the design including a female figure free from the defect known to photographers as under-exposure; and if you go to the Opéra—which is, happily, an easily avoidable fate—you may wonder at the expensive trifling that passes as musical poetry and drama, but you will be compelled to admit that the composer has moments, carried as far as academic propriety permits, in which he rises from sham history and tragedy to genuine polka and barcarolle; whilst there is, to boot, always one happy halfhour when the opera singers vanish, and capable, thoroughly trained, hardworking, technically skilled executants entertain you with a ballet. Of course the ballet, like everything else in Paris, is a provincial survival, fifty years behind English time, but still it is generally complete, and well done by people who understand ballet, wheras the opera is generally mutilated, and ill-done by people who dont understand opera.

Such being my prejudices against Paris, it is vain to expect enthusiasm from me on the subject of Samson et Dalila. Saint-Saëns would feel sufficiently flattered, perhaps, if I were to pronounce it as good as Les Huguenots; but I cannot do that, for a variety of reasons, among which I may mention that if Saint-Saëns had successfully imitated Meyerbeer's masterpiece, the effect would have been, not to establish the merit of the imitation, but rather to destroy one of the chief merits of the original—its uniqueness. Besides, Les Huguenots made the Paris Opéra what it is; wheras the Paris Opéra has made Samson what *it* is, unluckily for Saint-Saëns.

Some of the improvements on Meyerbeer are questionable: for instance, in the instrumental prelude to Les Huguenots Meyerbeer borrowed the tune and invented only the accompaniment; but Saint-Saëns, scorning to borrow, has written a prelude consisting of an accompaniment without any tune at all, and not a very original accompaniment at that. I own I like Meyerbeer's plan better. I have already confessed to a preference for Raoul over Samson; and I defy anyone to blame me for thinking Valentine and Marcel in the Pré-aux-Clercs worth a dozen of Dalila and the High Priest of Dagon in a place described by the program, in the manner of a postal address, as "The Valley of Soreck, Palestine."

As to the orchestral part of the performance, those who heard Saint-Saëns' Rouet d'Omphale conducted by himself at the Philharmonic last season may possibly have been able to judge how the score of Samson would have come out under the composer's *bâton*. Mr Cowen is quite a hopeless conductor for this sort of music. It requires a continual *entrain*, even at its quietest; and from this normal activity it has to be repeatedly worked up to the utmost vivacity and impetuosity. Mr Cowen's worst enemies have never accused him of impetuosity or vivacity in conducting; and as to *entrain*, he has cultivated to perfection a habit entirely fatal to it: that is to say, he checks the band in every bar between the first and second beat. I do not say that the interval is long enough to eat a sandwich in; but sometimes, when I am in my best critical condition, with my rhythmical sensitiveness highly exalted, it seems to me, even during a *presto*, that Mr Cowen always allows time somewhere in the bar for all ordinary exigencies of turning over, using one's handkerchief, nodding to an acquaintance, or the like.

If Mr Cowen were to equip Saint-Saëns with a long pair of spurs, and carry him pick-a-back during the performance, he might possibly get through Samson with some effect, albeit with much loss of blood; but I doubt if any less heroic measure would meet the occasion; and even then it would be easier to let Saint-Saëns conduct himself. All sorts of excellent qualities in Mr Cowen are thrown away when it comes to dealing with French operatic music, for want of the vulgar little gift—contemptible enough by itself—called "go."

In conclusion, lest anything that I have said about the

Parisians should unduly strain international relations, let me add that we already have in this country a class— and a growing class—of amateurs who have totally discarded our national hobbies of politics and piety, and taken on the Parisian hobby of Art. As like causes produce like effects in both countries, will these ladies and gentlemen kindly apply to themselves everything that I have said about their neighbors across the water.

UTOPIAN GILBERT AND SULLIVAN
The World, 11 October 1893

Pleasant it is to see Mr Gilbert and Sir Arthur Sullivan working together again full brotherly. They should be on the best of terms; for henceforth Sir Arthur can always say "Any other librettist would do just as well: look at Haddon Hall"; whilst Mr Gilbert can retort "Any other musician would do just as well: look at The Mountebanks." Thus have the years of divorce cemented the happy reunion at which we all assisted last Saturday. The twain still excite the expectations of the public as much as ever. How Trial by Jury and The Sorcerer surprised the public, and how Pinafore, The Pirates, and Patience kept the sensation fresh, can be guessed by the youngest man from the fact that the announcement of a new Savoy opera always throws the middle-aged playgoer into the attitude of expecting a surprise. As for me, I avoid this attitude, if only because it is a middle-aged one. Still, I expect a good deal that I could not have hoped for when I first made the acquaintance of comic opera.

Those who are old enough to compare the Savoy performances with those of the dark ages, taking into account the pictorial treatment of the fabrics and colors on the stage, the cultivation and intelligence of the choristers, the quality of the orchestra, and the degree of artistic good breeding, so to speak, expected from the principals, best know how great an advance has been made by Mr D'Oyly Carte in organizing and harmonizing that complex cooperation of artists of all kinds which goes to make up a satisfactory operatic performance. Long before the run of a successful Savoy opera is over Sir Arthur's melodies are dinned into our ears by every promenade band and street piano, and Mr Gilbert's sallies are quoted threadbare by conversationalists and journalists; but the whole work as presented to eye and ear on the Savoy stage remains unhackneyed.

Further, no theatre in London is more independent of those executants whose personal popularity enables them to demand ruinous salaries; and this is not the least advantageous of the differences between opera as the work of a combination of manager, poet, and musician, all three making the most of oneanother in their concerted striving for the common object of a completely successful representation, and opera as the result of a speculator picking up a libretto, getting somebody with a name to set it to music, ordering a few tradesmen to "mount" it, and then, with a stage manager hired here, an acting manager hired there, and a popular *prima donna*, comedian, and serpentine dancer stuck in at reckless salaries like almonds into an underdone dumpling, engaging some empty theatre on the chance of the affair "catching on."

If any capitalist wants to succeed with comic opera, I can assure him that he can do so with tolerable security if he only possesses the requisite managerial ability. There is no lack of artistic material for him to set to work on: London is overstocked with artistic talent ready to the hand of anyone who can recognize it and select from it. The difficulty is to find the man with this power of recognition and selection. The effect of the finer artistic temperaments and talents on the ordinary speculator is not merely nil (for in that case he might give them an engagement by accident), but antipathetic. People sometimes complain of the indifference of the public and the managers to the highest elements in fine art. There never was a greater mistake. The Philistine is not indifferent to fine art: he *hates* it.

The relevance of these observations will be apparent when I say that, though I enjoyed the score of Utopia more than that of any of the previous Savoy operas, I am quite prepared to hear that it is not as palatable to the majority of the human race—otherwise the mob—as it was to me. It is written with an artistic absorption and enjoyment of which Sir Arthur Sullivan always had moments, but which seem to have become constant with him only since he was knighted, though I do not suggest that the two things stand in the relation of cause and effect. The orchestral work is charmingly humorous; and as I happen to mean by this only what I say, perhaps I had better warn my readers not to infer that Utopia is full of buffooneries with the bassoon and piccolo, or of patter and tum-tum.

Whoever can listen to such caressing wind parts— zephyr parts, in fact—as those in the *trio* for the King and the two Judges in the first act, without being coaxed to feel pleased and amused, is not fit even for treasons, stratagems, and spoils; whilst anyone whose ears are capable of taking in more than one thing at a time must be tickled by the sudden busyness of the orchestra as the city man takes up the parable. I also confidently recommend those who go into solemn academic raptures over themes "in diminution" to go and hear how prettily the chorus of the Christy Minstrel song (borrowed from the plantation dance Johnnie, get a gun) is used, very much in diminution, to make an exquisite mock-banjo accompaniment. In these examples we are on the plane, not of the bones and tambourine, but of Mozart's accompaniments to *Soave sia il vento* in Così fan tutte and the entry of the gardener in Le Nozze di Figaro. Of course these things are as much thrown away on people who are not musicians as a copy of Fliegende Blätter on people who do not read German, wheras anyone can understand mere horseplay with the instruments.

But people who are not musicians should not intrude into opera houses: indeed, it is to me an open question whether they ought to be allowed to exist at all. As to the score generally, I have only one fault to find with Sir Arthur's luxurious ingenuity in finding pretty timbres of all sorts, and that is that it still leads him to abuse the human voice most unmercifully. I will say nothing about the part he has written for the unfortunate soprano, who might as well leave her lower octave at home for all the relief she gets from the use of her upper one. But take the case of Mr Scott Fishe, one of Mr Carte's most promising discoveries, who did so much to make the ill-fated Jane Annie endurable.

What made Mr Fishe's voice so welcome was that it was neither the eternal callow baritone nor the growling bass: it rang like a genuine "singing bass"; and one felt that here at last was a chance of an English dramatic *basso cantante*, able to "sing both high and low," and to contrast his high D with an equally fine one an octave below. Unfortunately, the upper fifth of Mr Fishe's voice, being flexible and of excellent quality, gives him easy command (on occasion) of high passages; and Sir Arthur has ruthlessly seized on this to write for him an excessively specialized baritone part, in which we get not one of those deep, ringing tones which relieved the Jane Annie music so attractively. I have in my time heard so many singers reduced by parts of this sort, in the operas of Verdi and Gounod, to a condition in which they could bawl F sharps *ad lib.* at high pressure, but could neither place a note accurately nor produce any tolerable tone from B flat downwards, that I always protest against vocal parts, no matter what voice they are written for, if they do not employ the voice all over its range, though lying mainly where the singer can sing continuously without fatigue.

A composer who uses up young voices by harping on the prettiest notes in them is an ogreish voluptuary; and if Sir Arthur does not wish posterity either to see the stage whitened with the bones of his victims or else to hear his music transposed wholesale, as Lassalle transposes Rigoletto, he should make up his mind whether he means to write for a tenor or a baritone, and place the part accordingly. Considering that since Santley retired from the stage and Jean de Reszke turned tenor all the big reputations have been made by *bassi cantanti* like Edouard de Reszke and Lassalle, and that all the great Wagner parts in which reputations of the same calibre will be made for some time to come are impossible to completely specialized baritones, I venture, as a critic who greatly enjoys Mr Fishe's performance, to recommend him to ask the composer politely not to treat him worse than Mozart treated Don Giovanni, than Wagner treated Wolfram, or than Sir Arthur himself would treat a clarinet. Miss Nancy McIntosh, who was introduced to us, it will be remembered, by Mr Henschel at the London Symphony Concerts, where she sang in a selection from Die Meistersinger and in the Choral Symphony, came through the trials of a most inconsiderate vocal part very cleverly, evading the worst of the strain by a treatment which, if a little flimsy, was always pretty. She spoke her part admirably, and, by dint of natural tact, managed to make a positive advantage of her stage inexperience, so that she won over the audience in no time. As to Miss Brandram, Mr Barrington (who by means of a remarkable pair of eyebrows transformed himself into a surprising compound of Mr Goschen and the late Sir William Cusins), Messrs Denny, Kenningham, Le Hay, Gridley, and the rest, everybody knows what they can do; and I need only particularize as to Miss Owen and Miss Florence Perry, who gave us some excellent pantomime in the very amusing lecture scene, contrived by Mr Gilbert, and set to perfection by Sir Arthur, in the first act.

The book has Mr Gilbert's lighter qualities without his faults. Its main idea, the Anglicization of Utopia by the people boundlessly credulous as to the superiority of the English race, is as certain of popularity as that reference to England by the Gravedigger in Hamlet, which never yet failed to make the house laugh. There is, happily, no plot; and the stage business is fresh and well invented—for instance, the lecture already alluded to, the adoration of the troopers by the female Utopians, the Cabinet Council "as held at the Court of St James's Hall," and the quadrille, are capital strokes. As to the "Drawing Room," with *débutantes*, cards, trains, and presentations all complete, and the little innovation of a cup of tea and a plate of cheap biscuits, I cannot vouch for its verisimilitude, as I have never, strange as it may appear, been present at a Drawing Room; but that is exactly why I enjoyed it, and why the majority of the Savoyards will share my appreciation of it.

A BODILESS SPOOK

The World, 18 October 1893

The historian Robertson, in his history of Mary Queen of Scots, approaches the delicate subject of Rizzio with an elaborate apology for mentioning a person so entirely beneath the dignity of history as a professional musician,

and an Italian one at that. For obvious reasons, I am
compelled in this column to be more tolerant than
Robertson; but there are moments when I, too, feel that
the art I profess has no concern with some of the
entertainments upon which I am invited to exercise it.
This superior mood came strongly upon me at the first
performance of Little Christopher Columbus at the
Lyric Theatre. I thought it utterly beneath serious
criticism; and on thinking it over since, my sense of
indignity has grown rather than abated. As far as I could
understand the situation, Mr Sedger had made expensive provision for the production of an opera. He had
engaged Mr Caryll to furnish the score, Miss Yohé and
Mr Lonnen to draw the audience, Messrs Sims and
Raleigh to provide Miss Yohé and Mr. Lonnen with
something to say, Mr D'Auban to invent dances, and
various other artists to provide costumes, scenery,
limelight, and so forth.

The only thing omitted was the opera itself. There
was no opera; and nobody pretended that there was—
not even the author of the playbill, in which the *genre* of
Little Christopher was left carefully unspecified. Most
of the lines spoken by the two principals were frankly
written for them in what would ordinarily be called
their private capacities. They had no parts, only
dialogue; and when this dialogue ran into puns on the
name Yohé, or references to Mr Lonnen's old Gaiety
success, The Bogie Man, the effect was not incongruous,
as it would have been in a real opera, but simply tedious,
as if the two artists were neglecting their business to
indulge in some private chaff between themselves. The
other characters, having neither parts nor personalities,
attained to perfect nothingness.

The cardinal flaw in the planning of Little Christopher
was a mistaken estimate of Miss Yohé's talent. If she had
comic genius, if her high spirits and love of fun had any

artistic character whatever, she might have turned this bodiless spook of a comic opera into a passable burlesque by the style of play which made Miss Farren famous at the Gaiety. As it was, Miss Yohé caught nothing of the trick of burlesque except some of its vulgarity; and vulgarity, racy as it may be in the true street-Arab breed, is not enjoyable in a pathetically pretty young woman who, though touched with something of the rudeness as well as the *naïveté* of—let us say a wilder civilization, only requires a little refining and softening to be a charming artist.

Miss Yohé had only two really successful moments on Tuesday in Little Christopher: to wit, the siesta song, Lazily, lazily; drowsily, drowsily, and the plantation melody, Listen to the music far away, both of which took her completely out of her forced *rôle* of burlesque actress, and gave her an opportunity of appealing to the audience on the imaginative and sentimental side. For the rest, she had to rely on the general indulgent disposition to spoil her for the sake of her prettiness and the fascination of the few effective notes of that extraordinary *chalumeau* register to which she confines herself, and which is, perhaps, the whole of her voice. Mr Lonnen, less gifted with personal beauty than Miss Yohé, had much the same class of task to perform; but he, being a born droll, was at no very great loss, though even he could do no more for me than help to make my heavy boredom just bearable.

However, let it be remembered that I am a superior person, and that what seemed incoherent and wearisome fooling to me may have seemed an exhilarating pastime to others. My heart knows only its own bitterness; and I do not desire to intermeddle with the joys of those among whom I am a stranger. I assert my intellectual superiority to those who enjoyed Little Christopher Columbus—that is all.

The composer, Mr Caryll, comes off with a certain consideration, because he has taken his work seriously and done his utmost to put at least some bounce, if not some life and substance, into the—I was about to call it the opera, but, as I have said, Mr Sedger did not commit himself to that description of the entertainment. But the harder Mr Caryll works, the more it becomes apparent that he is not naturally frolicsome. He has energy and determination, which he puts into his composition in an intelligent, mechanical way; but even the most impetuous pages in his score have not a smile in them. His orchestration is clever, active, full of traits and points, but certainly not normally smooth and beautiful, and often uneasy, self-conscious, and obtrusive. There is no pretence of novelty in the melodies and rhythms. I should imagine that Mr Caryll would find romantic opera of the tragic cast more congenial to him than the buffooneries of Little Christopher, which I may now dismiss with a word of remonstrance against the feeble *pas de quatre* in which four ladies, attired in what I really must denounce as stupidly ugly costumes, make a bid for the most worthless sort of applause by turning cartwheels. After this Miss St Cyr's plastic display in the second act is at least artistically respectable. It is difficult, original, and could not have been invented without some imagination and forethought, qualities which give it eminence in an entertainment otherwise rather stinted in them.

But Miss St Cyr is still a fascinating woman who dances, rather than a fascinating dancer. If she had no more beauty than the dance has grace, its ingenuity would hardly save it. The art of being a handsome woman is not the same thing as the art of dancing; and many passages in Miss St Cyr's feats are curious exhibitions of success in the one discounted by comparative failure in the other.

The serious business of the winter season began with the Crystal Palace Saturday Concerts last week. It will be remembered that last year a considerable advance was made in the accommodation of regular attendants from London, by issuing in a single batch for twentyone shillings the twenty first-class railway tickets which used to cost two pounds. This year the occasional visitor, who did not benefit by the railway arrangement, has his expenses reduced eighteenpence per concert by the abolition of the special charge for admission to the Palace on Saturdays, which is now a shilling day like the rest. At the same time, the numbered stalls, which were formerly half-a-crown, are now divided into two sets at four shillings and two shillings, the usual shilling admission to an unnumbered seat remaining as before; and the ordinary two-guinea serial stall-ticket is supplemented by a three-guinea one, which includes admission to the Palace on concert days only—though, as the same money will buy a two-guinea serial stall-ticket and a season ticket admitting to the Palace every day, no commercially sane human being will take a three-guinea ticket unless he wishes his admission, like his stall, to be transferable. It is now at last possible for the third-class traveler, by contenting himself with an unnumbered seat (no great disadvantage if he knows how to select it) and dispensing with an analytic program, to come from the City or West End and hear a Saturday concert for half-a-crown, whilst a regular attendant can travel first-class, sit in a reserved stall, buy a program, and indulge in two-penn'orth of refreshment for double that sum. These matters are worth noting; for the cost of attending the Crystal Palace concerts has hitherto greatly diminished their social utility. It now appears that the directors are sufficiently doubtful as to its having increased the total profit on each Saturday to make the reductions I have described. The immediate reason given is that

"Saturday afternoon has now become a general holiday in London"; but this, though new in comparison with the death of Queen Anne, must surely have come to the notice of the directors before the present year. However, better late than never. I hope the public, however scarce its half-crowns may be, will bear in mind that it is a poor heart that never rejoices, and that except when there is something specially dismal on in the way of an oratorio, or specially attractive to star-gazers in the way of a soloist, there is generally plenty of room in the huge concert hall for a few hundred more unreserved shillings.

The opening concert last Saturday, which was, as usual, too long, brought forward a new work by a young English composer. Similar items are set down for most of the other concerts. It cannot be said that Mr Manns does not give young England its chance. Young England, I am sorry to say, does not always make much of it, being for the most part able to do nothing but take some ballad for a program, and orchestrate away to its young heart's content upon a couple of well-worn themes, a climax or two, and a sentimental *pianissimo* to finish with. Still, these compositions are genuine as far as they go: they are not regulation exercises in sonata form: they represent the best the composer is able to do. Mr Godfrey Pringle's Ballad for Orchestra, supposed to illustrate Uhland's Durand, is in no way a specially remarkable example of its kind. It shews the influence of young Italy—that is to say, of Cavalleria—here and there. The scoring needs some revision; for the wood-wind parts in the serenade are ineffective, and an attempt to bring out a melody by reinforcing it with two trombones in unison is as disagreeable as Mr Pringle, one would think, might have expected. Slivinski threw away an opportunity by playing Saint-Saëns' concerto in G minor, of which we have had more than enough lately. He made an attempt to treat it seriously, with the result that it became very dull, wheras in the hands of the composer it is at least gay. The only really good bit in it is borrowed from the prelude to Bach's organ fugue in A minor, a favorite of Saint-Saëns, as I guess from having heard him play it. The overture was Sullivan's Macbeth, with its funny lapses from drama into drawingroom decoration. It was played with perfect neatness, and with great spirit, which latter compliment I cannot extend to what I heard of Beethoven's fourth symphony, though I will not undertake to say whether it was I, or the band, or both of us who were demoralized and bored by the long interval of Saint-Saëns, &c., that came between it and a transcription of the Apostrophe to Night from the second act of Tristan, in which the two vocal parts were given to a cornet and a tenor trombone. These were obviously the right instruments to use for the purpose, since they alone were able to maintain the necessary distinction and power against the accompaniment; and the display by Mr Hadfield and his colleague of what can be done in the way of expressive execution and sensitive vocal touch with the brass was interesting; but the makeshift produced an effect of solemn burlesque which forced one to smile in spite of the fascination of a wonderful page of music. If a couple of singers had been substituted for the cornet and trombone, and the solos and pianoforte concerto omitted from the program, we should have had a thoroughly enjoyable concert of just the right length.